Organization Theory

Organization Theory: An Integrated Approach

Richard N. Osborn
James G. Hunt
Lawrence R. Jauch
Southern Illinois University at Carbondale

JOHN WILEY & SONS
New York • Chichester • Brisbane • Toronto

Library of Congress Cataloging in Publication Data:

Osborn, Richard.
    Organization theory: an integrated approach.

    (Wiley series in management)
    Includes index.
    1. Organization. 2. Management. I. Hunt,
James G., 1932–   joint author. II. Jauch, Lawrence
R., joint author. III. Title.
HD31.0788   658.4   79-19533
ISBN 0-471-02173-3

Printed in the United States of America

10 9 8 7 6 5 4 3 2 1

To Judy, Donna, and Cathy

About the Authors

Richard N. Osborn is Professor of Organization Theory in the Administrative Sciences Department, Southern Illinois University at Carbondale. A graduate of Kent State University's D.B.A. program, Professor Osborn has conducted courses and seminars for students and managers interested in business, public administration, and voluntary organizations. He is the author of more than fifty articles and papers on organizations, organizational environments, and leadership. Professor Osborn is active in the Academy of Management (serving as the current secretary–treasurer of the Midwest Division and soon to be its president). In his work, he is extending organization theory to include the arena of leadership, by empirically examining environmental and organizational factors associated with leadership effectiveness in the military.

James G. (Jerry) Hunt is Professor of Administrative Sciences, Southern Illinois University at Carbondale. He received a doctorate degree in business from the University of Illinois and has also taught at West Virginia Tech, Millikin, University of Illinois, and University of Texas. He is the editor of five books on leadership and is the author of more than sixty articles and papers on leadership and organizations. He is a fellow of the Academy of Management and on its Board of Governors. He is currently chairman of the Academy's Organizational Behavior Division and a past president of its Midwest Division. Professor Hunt is on the editorial review board of the *Academy of Management Review* and the *Journal of Business Research*.

Lawrence R. Jauch is Associate Professor in the Administrative Sciences Department, Southern Illinois University at Carbondale. He received his Ph.D. from the University of Missouri-Columbia. Before coming to SIU-C, Professor Jauch taught at Kansas State University and the University of Missouri at Columbia. He has authored or coauthored numerous articles on organization behavior, theory, and policy in such journals as *Management Science, Academy of Management Journal, Journal of Higher Education,* and others. He is also the coauthor of *The Managerial Experience: Cases, Exercises and Readings.* Professor Jauch is currently the secretary for the Business Policy and Planning Division of the Academy of Management.

Note to the Instructor

This is a book on organization theory or what many have recently come to call the *macro* aspects of organizations. It is designed for graduate students and advanced undergraduates and will probably be most widely used in business schools. However, its use of research evidence from outside business and its inclusion of a wide range of organizations make it also suitable for areas such as sociology, public administration, and the like.

We take the term "integrated" in the subtitle quite seriously. Indeed, it might well be expanded to "integrated contingency." As the term "systems" was used in the 1960s, the term "contingency" has been used (some might say overused) in the 1970s in many textbooks on organizations. A typical pattern of approach discusses contingency thoroughly in the introductory chapter, but then presents the rest of the book in much the way it would have been in the absence of contingency notions. Another approach builds on the introductory contingency chapter by using a schematic throughout the text to show where different variables fit. Here, the contingency or integration theme is carried much further than in the first pattern; however, even these books may fall short of what a comprehensive contingency or integrative approach should do. While these books use a systematic model, they still tend to treat each variable in isolation from the others.

This book tackles the challenge in three ways. First, it uses a systematic top-down organization of the chapters, so that one moves from the environment and total organization down into the organization, ending at the work unit level. Second, it consistently uses these variables to predict and explain various aspects of organization and subunit "success." We concentrate on a wide range of measures of success. Third, there is a contingency chapter concluding each of the first four parts of the book. Each of these four contingency chapters builds on the material included in the individual chapters in the part. Later contingency chapters also build on the material included in earlier contingency chapters. Thus each tends to become more and more comprehensive.

Our focus is pictorially illustrated in the top-down cone model, shown in Figure 1-1. This model is used throughout the book, first at the beginning of each part introduction and then at the beginning of each chapter. In addition to an emphasis on organization structure and context typically found in organization theory books, two chapters are devoted to the environment, and its various components are treated as operationally as possible. Because we find a discussion of organizational outputs or measures of success central to organization theory, we devote Part I to that topic. Chapter 2 covers macro measures and Chapter 3 covers subsystems and work unit measures. Along with these, a whole host of employee maintenance (satisfaction, etc.) variables are covered, culminating in the so-called "quality of working life" variables now so common in the literature.

In addition to its emphasis on contingencies, measures of success, environment, and context-structure, Figure 1-1, our cone model, also highlights other major topics of this book: subsystems, work units, and leadership. These topics are often only cursorily treated in books on organization theory. We believe that they must receive heavy emphasis if a book on organizations is to give more than lip service to the "integrative contingency" approach. In this sense, then, the book, though clearly macro in nature, integrates some topics treated at length in books on organizational behavior.

We have indicated that this book is geared to advanced undergraduate students and graduate students; therefore, we assume a general knowledge of management and organizations such as would be gained from one or two previous management courses. We rely heavily on the available research literature to minimize armchair speculation, except in the contingency chapters where we have often moved beyond the current state of knowledge. We have tried to introduce the student to this way of thinking in Chapter 1. As we mentioned earlier, the evidence that we use comes from a wide variety of disciplines and organizations, so you are just as likely to find a university treated as you are a large industrial organization.

To reinforce the rigor with which we treat the topics and to reduce the abstractness typically found in organization theory books, we include a "Measurement Module" in each chapter. Here we discuss ways of measuring many of the concepts treated earlier in the chapter. We have found that the use of these modules helps nail down many of the abstract notions floating around in the organization theory literature. Furthermore, these reinforce our emphasis on rigor and evidence.

At the same time, Part V includes a number of cases and some exercises for those who wish to combine application with the theoretical orientation of the book. These have been carefully prepared to cover the wide range of issues treated in the text. In many cases these can be used in conjunction with material in the Measurement Modules to emphasize both measurement and application.

As we have tried to show, the book has been designed with a number of different pedagogical features to enhance its flexibility. It may not be possible to use all of these features in one semester. However, they could all be used in a two-semester course. There are also other alternative approaches that can be used in the one-semester course.

In one approach, all of the noncontingency chapters, plus case and exercise material selected from Part V, could be covered. The Measurement Modules can be optional. Thus the instructor could provide a balance between theory and application.

In a second approach, all of the chapters, including the theoretical and relatively abstract contingency ones, could be covered in a semester. Measurement Modules would also be used. This approach might be used with advanced graduate students interested in theory and research.

Other approaches could compress or expand these two plans, depending on the time available, the level and orientation of students, and so forth. There is an ongoing exercise in Part V that may be of interest to many instructors as a way of illustrating application even if the cases are not used. The book, less cases and exercises, can be supplemented with readings that could well serve as a nucleus for a doctoral course.

It's our feeling that there are many keys to the organization theory kingdom. A book should help each to find his or her own. Thus, many detailed plans, including possible use in combined masters and doctoral courses, are provided in our instructor's manual. The instructor's manual also provides additional teaching aids to help bring this important area of research alive to the student.

Finally, we should note that, in addition to serving the educational needs of students, we wrote this book to help advance the field of organization theory. Although the emphasis is more macro than micro, we hope that our efforts at integration have moved us a bit closer to a unified view of the two areas and that this book will provide another building block toward a complete theory of organizations.

Richard N. Osborn
James G. Hunt
Lawrence R. Jauch

Note to the Student

There are several types of information and skills you will need to become a successful manager. Your future organization will provide you with some valuable information and hone your skills in a particular area. Courses in management can also provide valuable information concerning how different functions should be performed and how to deal with people. But you will also need in-depth information about organizations. That is what this book is all about. How and why organizations function as they do is described in a framework designed to help improve organizational success.

Knowledge of the bigger picture of organizations is important. As a manager you need to understand how and why some organizations are more effective than others. You need to understand what organizations want to do, and how they are likely to respond to different pressures. You also need answers to questions such as: Why are there so many different ways organizations are put together? Are there ways of designing organizations, departments, and groups so that they will be more successful? How can I as a lower-level manager successfully adjust my work unit to the opportunities and demands facing my organization? While we cannot answer all these questions completely, the text does provide some of the information needed to understand organizations and to operate in them more effectively. This information exists in a systematic framework that you can use to diagnose and evaluate how and why organizations and subunits may differ. This can help you choose the type of firm that is the best suited to you, solve problems you may face as a manager, or use your capacity to develop analytical and conceptual skills.

After some introductory material, we start with the bottom line: What do various individuals want from the organization? We will pay particular attention to success from the vantage point of the chief executive officer (CEO). The way in which CEOs evaluate success reflects the expectations of others and sets the tone for those at lower levels in the organization. Since management is fast becoming a profession, we take care to outline expectations of society and also how those inside the organization can judge the performance of their units. We will spend considerable time discussing the linkages among subunit performance (where you are likely to be operating) and that of the organization higher up. If you think just a bit about where you are likely to be working, the importance of an understanding of that linkage and the way in which performance is evaluated at various levels should be quite obvious.

In the remainder of the book we consider a model that progressively moves from organizational environments through size, technology, top management philosophy, and structure to an examination of various subsystems and work units within them. We finally culminate with a discussion of leadership.

In making this journey you will learn not only how organizational environments affect top management, but how these effects filter down to affect those at the work unit level as well. You will learn how environment influences organization and work unit success. And you will learn how size, technology, top management philosophy, and organizational structure influence what happens at various levels in an organization. Along with this, you will find out why various subsystems in organizations behave as they do, and you will see what impact size, technology, and other variables have on the subsystems. Finally, you will discover the impact of all of these variables on the kinds of work units in which many of you are likely to be starting your careers. As part of your study, you will also find out how leadership fits into the "big picture" of the organization.

In dealing with this material, you will learn to make careful analyses of the effects that different combinations of these variables have on organization and work unit success. This analysis will enable you to predict the most likely consequences of various "fits" and "misfits" among these variables. These are exactly the kinds of skills needed whether you are involved in: (1) designing more successful organizations or (2) understanding what is likely to occur in your work unit because these variables are the way they are.

In keeping with this theme, you will find the book to be quite eclectic. It uses examples from many different kinds of organizations and many different organizational environments. It uses a mix of public and private, large and small organizations. It also draws on the literature from many disciplines and can be useful to students from different curricula, including business administration, sociology, public administration, and others.

All of this can be very challenging. And it can be taught in different ways. If your instructor wants to emphasize rigorous and intricate analysis to aid in integration, he or she can use the four "contingency" chapters, which are designed for integration. If the instructor wants to provide a more "action-oriented" emphasis, exercises and cases have been provided in Part V of the book. In either case, a thorough review of what we know and don't know is provided in each chapter. And that review is supplemented with end-of-chapter references for a more in-depth exploration.

But we have detained you long enough. Let's move into Chapter 1 and add some meat to the skeleton we have outlined in this note.

R. N. O.
J. G. H.
L. R. J.

Acknowledgments

This book is the product of more people than we can ever hope to thank. But we must acknowledge those most directly involved.

First, we thank our wives Judy, Donna, and Cathy. Not only did they put up with our orneriness, which only authors-to-be can exhibit, but they helped with the typing. Thus, they deserve not only the dedication, but to be acknowledged here as well.

The departmental secretaries at SIU-C, Sharon Pinkerton, Carol Shirley, Kim Stover, Bobbi Garrett, and Sharon Hamilton, as well as student workers, also helped in typing the manuscript. Golda King and Irene Kobey provided typing help at University of Texas at Arlington while one of us was a visiting professor. We wish to thank Bob Bussom and John Sutherland, our two former chairmen, for making these as well as other resources available.

We would also like to acknowledge the assistance of our colleagues who reviewed the manuscript at various stages: Wilmar F. Bernthal (University of Colorado, Boulder), Elwood S. Buffa (UCLA), Patrick E. Connor (Oregon State University), Martin Gannon (University of Maryland), Manuel London (University of Illinois, Urbana-Champaign), Bernard C. Reimann (Cleveland State University), John P. Wanous (Michigan State University), and David A. Whetten (University of Illinois, Urbana-Champaign).

Without the help of all these people, and the investigators on whose shoulders we stand, this effort would not have come to fruition. Of course, any error, omissions, or inadequate interpretations are our responsibility. Lastly, we want to thank those scholars who have shown us where not to tread. While their work may not always be cited, it too forms an important aspect of our knowledge about organizations.

R. N. O.
J. G. H.
L. R. J.

Contents

chapter **1** **FIRST THINGS FIRST**

I. **Perspective of the Book**

II. **Theoretical Bases**

    A. **Systems and Contingency Theory**
        1. **Contingency and Situational Approaches**

    B. **Key Systems Notions**
        1. **Open Systems**
        2. **System as a Whole**
        3. **Boundaries**
        4. **Equifinality and Fit**

    C. **Perception**
        1. **Selectivity**
        2. **Interpretation**
        3. **Closure**
        4. **Perception Formation and Behavior**

III. **Using the Literature**

    A. **Science Versus Common Sense**
    B. **The Scientific Approach**
    C. **Deductive and Inductive Approaches**
    D. **Research Methodologies**
    E. **Evaluating the Evidence**
        1. **Sources of Organizational Information**
        2. **How to Evaluate What You Read**

IV. **Appendix 1. Selected Periodicals for Organization Theory**

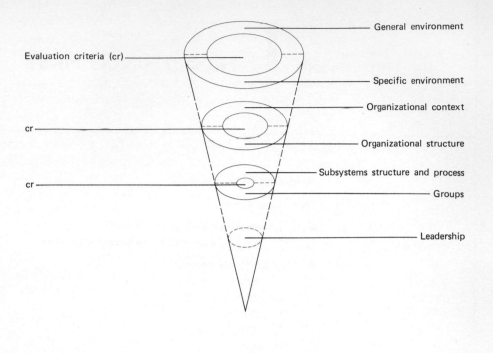

General environment

Evaluation criteria (cr)

Specific environment

Organizational context

cr

Organizational structure

Subsystems structure and process

cr

Groups

Leadership

What would you find if you went to your library and spent a few minutes looking at the card catalog under the subject of organizations? We suspect that even a casual search would reveal many books on the topics of organization theory, organizational behavior, organization design, managing organizations, and so on. You might ask, then, is this book different enough to justify its existence? We think it is. Let's see why.

First, if you looked more closely at the books concerned with organizations, you would find that they primarily explore topics such as motivation, communication, and leadership from the point of view of *individuals*. They explain how and why people behave as they do in organizations. These organizational behavior books rely heavily on psychological theory, and they are important. But psychological views often ignore the influence of the organization itself on behavior. Other books tend to focus on the design of an organization from a structural point of view. Topics such as size and technology, and internal features such as departmentation, are explained in detail to prescribe how the organization should be specialized and coordinated. The foundations of knowledge rely more on sociological theory. These are important too. Yet many of these texts ignore environmental factors or fail to carefully integrate the topics to explain the processes needed for organizational success. The emphasis is on prescribing a structure. Other texts explore and explain the kinds of activities performed by managers of organizations. The emphasis tends to be on "principles" of planning, organizing, controlling, and so forth. Again, these are important. But we think many of these books ignore various "contingencies" that suggest that managers should alter how they function under different conditions.

This book incorporates aspects of each of these outlooks. We look at some of the activities managers perform. As the table of contents reveals, the activities we focus on include: analyzing the general and specific environment to assess its impact on the organization's mission, structure, and functioning; examining contextual variables such as size, technology, and administrative philosophy; establishing a structure to coordinate and control the organization; determining the structure and process of subsystems and groups; and providing influence and leadership necessary to integrate and carry out these functions. The perspective is from the top down, with a view toward various organizational success criteria. We also explore how the organization itself influences behavior. But the focus is on groups of people in an organization more than individual members.

Perhaps the major distinguishing feature of this book is the integrative contingency approach. Contingency approaches move us away from so-called organizational "principles." Principles are supposed to hold regardless of the situation. Instead, contingency approaches talk about relationships that hold for clearly specified conditions. If the conditions change, the relationships change. The contingency notion itself is not profound. It has been intuitively utilized by insightful people for many years. However, we have only recently learned enough about organizations so we can begin to zero in more precisely on the nature of these contingencies. And you will find we still have a long way to go.

The relationships we are concerned about are those that help us explain organizational success. The first part of this book carefully describes the various views of what criteria can be used to evaluate organizations. The remainder of the book defines some of the critical contingencies affecting these criteria, and integrates them into a whole. This has been termed a "systems" approach. These terms are explained in more detail later in this chapter.

You should realize that this book still does not explore the entire picture of why organizations are successful, or the entire range of managerial functions. As we will explain in detail later, organization theory concentrates on the outcomes and actions of organizations as well as the behavior of individuals and groups within an organizational setting. Remember, however, that managers also have many technical duties. We are looking primarily at the setting within which these duties are performed.

Another feature of this book is that, unlike many other texts covering organization theory, we are concerned with action implications implied by the theory. We define a theory as a set of interrelated concepts that present a systematic view of something for the purpose of explaining and predicting. Thus, as some have argued, "there is nothing more practical than a good theory." It provides the base upon which to take intelligent action. The often heard lament, "it is good in theory but not in practice," only indicates the theory is poor or is not being properly applied.

We provide some cases and exercises that you can use to see the action implications of the theory, and predict what action needs to be taken to achieve defined success criteria. We also provide, in Measurement Modules, examples of how the theory can be made operational. Too often, abstract terms and variables are used in texts, and there is uncertainty about what they mean. We try to remedy this by providing examples of how researchers define and measure the variables of interest. We also provide these because our book relies on the research evidence available. We want you to see what the research is based on, and how to evaluate it.

That brings us to another feature of this book that is a little different. We are concerned about its readability and usability. To aid you in your study we provide alphabetical and numbered references at the end of each chapter by major subheading. The use of names of authors will be held to a minimum in the text, but we provide the numbers of the references in the text where appropriate to provide support and documentation for statements made. Thus, by topic area, you can trace the contributions of the researchers and writers who have aided in the development of the body of knowledge and theory we rely on. Those interested in pursuing a topic in greater depth can easily find sources for initiating a thorough literature review. We have also sequentially numbered all illustrative material (tables, figures, and exhibits) within each chapter. (For example, Table 1-2 might follow Figure 1-1; there will be no Table 1-1.)

PERSPECTIVE OF THE BOOK

With the foregoing purposes in mind, let's look more specifically at the design of the book, and what you can expect in later chapters. Look at Figure 1-1. This is our top-down cone model.

For simplicity, we've split the various aspects of this model into separate

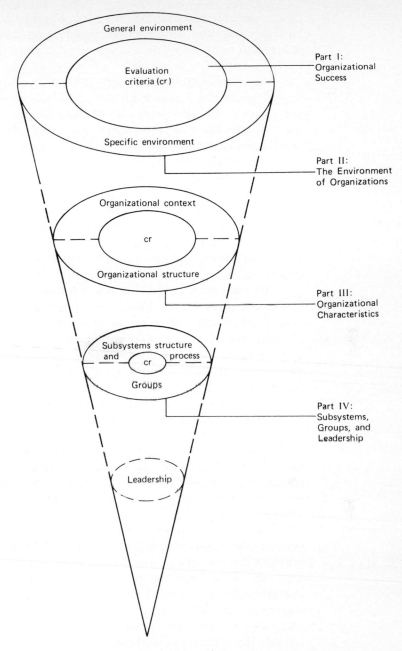

Figure 1-1 A cone model for organizational analysis.

parts corresponding to those in the book. In actuality, we expect that there will be interrelationships among these variables. We develop these in contingency chapters to be described in a moment. For now, let's look at each part of the book.

After reading this first chapter, which deals with introductory notions, the book consists of five parts. Each part contains several chapters. Part I discusses ways of evaluating the "success" of organizations. This includes questions of survival, effectiveness, performance, and employee maintenance criteria and how to measure them. This is the core of the cone as viewed from outside and inside the organization.

Part II then treats the external environment of organizations. We move into the top part of the cone. Major emphasis is placed on what are termed the "general environment" and the "specific environment." The general environment is concerned with those forces that influence all organizations operating within a given geographical area. The specific environment contains those conditions unique to one organization or a small number of organizations.

We then move in Part III to the internal characteristics of organizations. These are contextual variables such as size and technology as well as a whole host of structural variables reflecting the degree of bureaucratization.

Consistent with our top-down approach, Part IV then looks at subsystems characteristics and some determinants of intergroup relationships. That is followed by consideration of group characteristics and influence, power, and leadership.

The last part (V), provides some cases and exercises that allow you to try to apply many of the notions discussed in the chapters.

In each part we first devote chapters to what is known about each of these areas. Then we attempt to combine the findings into an integrated contingency chapter at the end of each part. Since we use a top-down approach, the book successively narrows the unit of analysis as we move down the cone. Consistent with this, the contingency chapters progressively use each of the major concepts introduced.

Thus, early in the book, effects of different environmental components on organizational survival and goal attainment are discussed. Each has a separate impact on these criteria. But they also have a combined (interactive) effect with other variables in the model. As more concepts are introduced they are systematically incorporated into our contingency approach. It becomes more and more comprehensive as you move through the book. However, major categories of contingency variables are systematically combined and collapsed. This is done so that the approach, though broader, is still manageable. We should warn you that these chapters require some serious study and thought. These are more abstract than a literature review or measuring instruments. Relational and integrative concepts are harder to conceptualize. You will need a command of the theory discussion, aided by measurement illustrations. We did a readability analysis on this. You will find the contingency chapters harder to get through, so plan on spending a bit more time with them. We should also point out, though, that these chapters rely much more on our own viewpoints and speculations about the theory. As we said before, there's still a great deal to learn. Contingency theory is in its infancy. You may find that your instructor disagrees with our viewpoints. Your instructor may not even require you to use these chapters. Such is the state of the art in this field.

In addition to using our contingency chapters to tie things together, we use a consistent layout in the other chapters in each part. We first indicate why the topic is important. Then we review the literature on the subject. Wherever possible we draw on carefully conducted empirical work. You will find, however, disputes in the literature. In many cases we will try to provide a creative resolution. Again, be aware that others may disagree with our interpretations.

Next we have the Measurement Module. As explained earlier, the instruments illustrate important concepts; we hope they will make the theoretical discussions a bit clearer. However, the state of our discipline and copyright laws are such that we sometimes can only provide samples of items rather than an entire instrument. Please note that in many of the instruments exhibited in the Measurement Modules copyright laws require us to continue to use the impersonal *he, him,* or *his,* or illustrations of males. Be assured that managers and organization theorists can be either male or female. In our own text material we have deliberately avoided use of the generic "he" for sex-indefinite antecedents. However, for some terms, (e.g., mankind) common usage is followed and the words should be considered as universal terms, denoting all human beings.

In all cases we provide references at the end of each chapter. You can refer to these sources for more details if you need them.

So, after you complete each part, you should be familiar with the theory and literature on the topic. You should also be able to see how some important variables are measured. And you should be able to see how the area relates to others.

It is probably worth mentioning at this point that the book is very eclectic in the organizations considered. Some books have a bias toward industrial organizations. We use all kinds, including a number of examples from college and university settings. This broad treatment of organizations is in keeping with the spirit of organization theory. It is not just organization theory for industrial organizations. It applies to organizations in whatever the context.

The remainder of this chapter explores in more detail the theoretical bases we are relying upon and the scientific attitudes we hope to impart.

THEORETICAL BASES

We first describe the notions of systems and contingency theory. Then we explore perception. These are important foundations that underly organization theory and the evidence used to support the theory.

Systems and Contingency Theory

Systems thinking goes back to ancient times. The genesis of modern general systems theory (GST) was developed nearly fifty years ago by von Bertalanffy.[2] However, GST has only recently been applied in the study of organizations. GST was originally embraced enthusiastically as a way of bringing order out of the increasingly diverse approaches to organization theory. It seemed to offer a potential framework for tidying up what to many was becoming a highly chaotic field.

Stated simply, the systems approach means that all parts are interrelated and interdependent to form a whole. That is, a system is composed of components or subsystems that are related or dependent upon one another. When these subsystems interact with one another, they form a unitary whole. Hence, it follows that virtually any phenomenon can be analyzed within a systems framework.

This generality is the major strength of a systems approach. But it is so vague and abstract that it has been hard to utilize it in practical operational terms. Kast and Rosenzweig's[1] excellent review of GST discusses a number of its problems. They conclude that it's better to try to deal with the problems than to revert back to presystems approaches. Specifically, they suggest moving down a level of abstraction to consider what they term "second-order systems studies or midrange concepts." They go on to say, "These will be based on general systems theory but will be more concrete and will emphasize more specific characteristics and relationships in social organizations" (p. 458). In other words, they will be consistent with a general systems approach but at a less abstract level. Organization theory is developing as a discipline from such a "midrange approach."

Kast and Rosenzweig call this midrange level of analysis a "contingency approach" and summarize it as follows:

> The contingency view of organizations and their management suggest that an organization is a system composed of subsystems and delineated by identifiable boundaries from its environmental supra-system. The contingency view seeks to understand the interrelationships within and among subsystems as well as between the organization and its environment and to define patterns of relationships or

configurations of variables. It emphasizes the multivariate nature of organizations and attempts to understand how organizations operate under varying conditions and in specific circumstances. Contingency views are ultimately directed toward suggesting organizational designs and managerial systems most appropriate for specific situations [p. 460].

The approach used in this book is consistent with this contingency view.

Now let's look at some of these contingency and systems notions in more detail. This will set the stage for our contingency model discussed later in this chapter.

Contingency and Situational Approaches. The words "contingency," "situational," and "it all depends" have often been used interchangeably. Luthans[2] argues that there is a difference between contingency and the latter two approaches. A contingency approach implies a functional relationship of the *if* A *then* B variety. This is opposed to the situational approach, which generally means diagnosing a given situation and adapting to it without seeking to find functional relationships among variables. In other words, a contingency approach is based on a *systematic* organizational framework or theory. A situational or it all depends approach is less specific.

What do we mean by an *if-then* functional relationship? Let's use an example with technology and organizational structure. Evidence might suggest, *if* the structure is bureaucratic *then* a routine technology will lead to higher organizational performance. It is also possible to reverse the relationship here. If the technology is routine, *then* a bureaucratic structure will lead to higher organizational performance. You would need some theoretical rationale here to tell you which of these formulations is the correct one. Simply utilizing an *if-then* approach will not answer that for you. We will use contingency theory in this book. This will allow you to analyze the nature of important functional relationships and, we hope, will result in improved organizational "success."

Key Systems Notions

GST provides a number of systems notions useful for the analysis of organizations. Of these, four are especially important in the development of our contingency approach.

Open Systems. First, we use an open systems approach. That is, we treat the organization as being "open" to the influence of the external environment.

Many of the earlier management and organizational books treated organizations as if they were ''closed systems'' or not open to environmental influences. As open systems, organizations receive inputs from the environment, transform them, and send these outputs back to the environment.

System as a Whole. Second, we are interested not only in each of the separate organizational components (structure variables, technology, etc.) but in the system as a whole.

Boundaries. Third, we are concerned with the importance of boundaries in defining our units of analysis. For example, we clearly differentiate between total organizational, subsystem, and group performance. Boundary definition is also important in separating external environment components from organizational components or in determining what is in and outside the system for analysis purposes. For example, for one kind of analysis the supply firm for General Motors would be defined as part of the organizational system. For another analysis the firm would be considered part of the external environment.

Equifinality and Fit. Fourth, the concept of equifinality or functional equivalency is very important.[3] This means that a system can reach the same final state through different paths of development. It's possible, for example, that a particular organization structure variable and a given technological variable will each have a similar influence on performance or for a given *if-then* relationship. In other words, one might be substituted for the other with the same general effect on other variables.

Related to this equifinality notion is that of congruence or fit among variables. For example, you might ask, ''*if* a complex environment is faced, *then* should organization structure be complex or simple to ensure an appropriate 'fit' for optimum performance?'' Let's say the evidence indicated that for a complex environment there should be a complex structure. Then we would prescribe complexity in the structure to achieve consistency. Evans[1] discusses other types of 'fits.' We will be using the idea of *fit* primarily in contingency chapters.

In summary, then, we consider a contingency approach as a less abstract approach than general systems theory. However, it is subsumed within GST and utilizes a number of systems concepts. It's also important to point out that GST makes another important contribution only hinted at previously. That contribution is a way of thinking that gets us out of what Seiler[2] calls ''the single cause fallacy.'' Many people tend to think in single cause terms (e.g., Chris' production is poor due to laziness). People who think this way tend to jump to unwarranted conclusions. The systems philosophy forces us to consider whether Chris' performance is due to laziness, or whether a host of factors might be operating (such as poor co-workers, poor supervision, inadequate machinery, etc.). While general systems theory adds complexity, it at least keeps us out of single cause thinking. It allows us to trace possible multiple *if-then* relationships.

Perception

In addition to systems concepts, another key notion is that of perception. You will find it mentioned throughout the book. The reason for this is that those in organizations act on the basis of perception. And perceptions may differ from "objective" reality. This is important for organization theory. For example, we referred to environmental complexity above. In Part II this is developed further. You will find that you can get "hard" data about various aspects of complexity. You can also get perceptual measures of it. In many cases, what you predict the organization might do in response to complexity will vary depending on how you have measured it. So let's look at this in more detail.

Perception is an internal process. It serves as a filter and a method for organizing the many complex stimuli that bombard us every day. The perceptual process is the mechanism through which stimuli are selected and grouped meaningfully. Without that process we would be swamped by the numerous stimuli.[2] We would literally not be able to function. At the heart of the perceptual process are three key mechanisms that provide for perception formation. Litterer notes these as: selectivity, interpretation, and closure.[3]

Selectivity. Here, certain pieces of information are separated for further consideration by thresholds. Thresholds serve as barriers regulating which stimuli from the outside world reach our consciousness. These barriers can be quite high, shutting out stimuli. Or they can be quite low, encouraging as many stimuli as possible to reach our consciousness. What stimuli do you react to when you walk through a manufacturing plant? You shut out many and concentrate on a few. A friend walking with you might shut out some of the ones to which you react. Others, ignored by you, enter the friend's consciousness. For example, if you are an engineer, you might be particularly intrigued by the machinery. Your companion with no interest in machinery might ignore that stimulus and concentrate on how people are behaving. However, thresholds are not constant. Assume an employee has an accident on one of the machines. It is likely that the employee involved will enter your consciousness quite quickly. And your friend's threshold regarding machine safety design might be raised for some time.

Interpretation. Here you evaluate the stimuli that you have let enter your consciousness via selectivity. Consider the previous example. You might interpret the cause of the accident as poor safety engineering. But your friend might interpret the accident as resulting from poor employee training or supervision. Though the stimulus is the same, the interpretation differs.

Differing interpretations of the same data are most common where the stimulus is ambiguous. A famous series of experiments by Asch[1] illustrates the point. Subjects were found to perceive the lengths of lines differently. Their interpretation of line length depended on reinforcement by others. The stimulus of two employees pushing each other might be interpreted differently depending on whether you thought the employees were friends or not.

Closure. Here, stimuli are formed into a meaningful whole. For example, what kind of picture is shown in Figure 1-2?

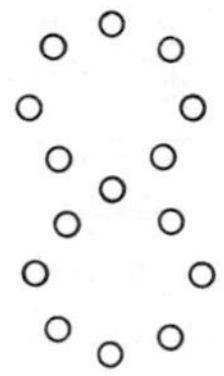

Figure 1-2 An illustration of closure.

Actually it's just an unconnected group of dots. Your closure process, though, reveals a figure eight. (If you are lying down, maybe you see infinity). It should be apparent that closure and interpretation are closely related. Now, ask a person who is not familiar with the Arabic numbering system to interpret that figure. Even if closure were made, it might be uninterpretable. Or it would be interpreted as something different from a figure eight (or infinity). It might "look like" a race track.

Perception Formation and Behavior. We have treated these three mechanisms sequentially and separately. But they operate simultaneously. They interact to affect perception formation. And this has a major impact on behavior. As noted above, people act on the basis of what they see, not on what is "really out there." If I see my boss as inconsiderate, I'll react to that. It makes no difference whether he is "really" inconsiderate or not. To *me*, the perception *is* the reality. Thus, perception has a substantial influence on behavior in organizations and the measurement of organization variables. It is one of the important contingency concepts that influences systematic organization theory.

USING THE LITERATURE

So far we have outlined the theoretical groundings. We have one more task before moving to Part I. We want to develop a critical attitude for evaluating the theory. The attitude is one of relying on science to support your thinking, as well as to support action based on theory. Of course, science is applied in more than one way. So let's look at why you should use science, the approaches used, and the kind of evidence you should seek to support your positions.

Science Versus Common Sense

Let's assume that you are in the section of your local library that contains books on business administration. You just picked up a book entitled *How to be a Successful Manager*. You discover that it was written by a retired president of a prominent company. After reminiscing about early childhood and various experiences with the company, a number of chapters are devoted to "traits of a successful manager." As you read this material you discover that these traits are based on one person's experience. While it doesn't say it in so many words, it appears as if the writer is suggesting that these traits should be generalizable to all managers. The traits appear reasonable to you. They jibe with common sense. In short, you are impressed with the book. It seems eminently reasonable for example, that successful managers should be extroverts. After all, who is in a better position than a highly successful executive to indicate those traits that lead to managerial success? The question is, should you be impressed? Just how good is a book like this?

First, let's examine the source of the data. It is entirely anecdotal, based on the experience of a single individual. The data seem logical in that they appear consistent with common sense. Is it appropriate to draw conclusions simply on the basis of common sense? To many, an appeal to common sense is probably good enough. It is frequently done. However, it fails on several counts to be acceptable to the modern-day behavioral scientist or sophisticated student of organizations. They would insist that a more scientific approach be used.

Kerlinger[1] specifies a number of ways in which a scientific approach and a common sense approach differ. All of these differences are built around the emphasis on "systematic" and "controlled." First, the uses of conceptual schemes and theoretical structures differ. Most of us are ordinarily quite loose in our use of these. We often accept explanations with little real evidence. Furthermore, there is a strong tendency to fall heir to the single cause fallacy.

A single variable is assumed to explain a given phenomenon. On the other hand, if we followed the scientific approach we would make sure explanations are internally consistent and that, wherever possible, they could be empirically tested.

Second, and related to the first point, the scientist attempts to systematically and empirically test his or her tentative explanations. Many of us will often use "selected" evidence in support of our tentative explanations. If, for example, we think redheads are hot tempered, we are likely to consider that statement to be proved if we see one redhead express anger. We don't look at other redheads to see if they express anger. Nor do we ask whether expressing anger necessarily indicates a hot temper. The scientist, on the other hand, would insist on systematic, controlled study before drawing any conclusions about color of hair and temperament.

Third, the scientist is concerned with trying to rule out possible competing explanations for a phenomenon in question. The scientist tries to examine relations between the variables of interest, with other variables controlled. However, most of us are normally not so particular. Again, the tendency to rely on a single cause and to selectively use evidence to support preconceptions are likely to cut short a search for alternate explanations.

Finally, the scientist is unwilling to use metaphysical explanations for observed phenomena. A metaphysical explanation is one that can't be subjected to scientific proof. "My child is sick because God wills it," is one example. A special case is the so-called normative or prescriptive statement. This is based mainly on an individual's value structure. "It is wrong to be an authoritarian supervisor." "All work and no play makes Jack a dull boy." It is conceivable that these statements can be tested. They are not testable in their present form. They are too vague and value laden. It is not uncommon, however, to see people describing phenomena in just such metaphysical or value-laden terms. The scientist would be quick to separate statements that are testable from those that are not. Nonauthoritarian supervisors might be personally favored by the scientist. But a nonauthoritarian leadership style would not be recommended unless systematically controlled empirical evidence could be provided that such leadership was indeed superior to authoritarian leadership in some measurable way.

What does the scientist do if no data are available? They, like you, must rely on common sense and extensions of the thinking of other scientists. Since organization theory is a comparatively new discipline, we must often speculate. However we stress the use of research support where possible and label our speculations as such. Furthermore, where some information is available, we apply it to areas where no data exist. This is an underlying tenet of the deductive approach to be discussed below. Of course, not all data generated carry equal weight. Many studies have not been treated in the book simply because the research was poorly done. Let's take a closer look at the scientific approach so that when you must weigh evidence, you can separate the wheat from the chaff.

The Scientific Approach

The first step in the scientific approach is that of recognizing a problem. Kerlinger[1] suggests that the problem be stated in question form. Let's return to our mythical book by the company president. "Are there identifiable traits that separate the successful from the unsuccessful manager?"

The next step is to formulate one or more hypotheses. These are statements that speculate about the relation between two or more variables. *If* A *then* B. "More extroverted managers will be more successful." In formulating hypotheses you can draw on any number of sources. You may use previous experience, logic, authoritative statements of others, and so on. However, these are not used to provide the answer. They only provide information for the statement of a tentative proposition to be tested (the hypothesis).

An hypothesis must be testable. It must be stated so that the variables included in it can be made operational. Does our previously stated hypothesis, "more extroverted managers will be more successful," meet this key requirement? It does when we can: (1) define what we mean by manager so that we can separate managers from others; (2) measure extroversion; and (3) measure managerial success.

It appears as if (1) could be met by starting with those people classified as managers in the organization in question. You could then check to see if any of them might be ruled out because of more restrictive criteria that might be set for the definition. The degree of extroversion might be determined by means of a personality test. Finally, managerial success might be measured by a performance evaluation or some kind of measure of the performance of the group(s) under a given manager, and so on. In short, it appears as if our hypothesis is stated specifically enough to be capable of verification or nonverification.

A test for acceptance or rejection of an hypothesis is the third step of the scientific approach. This verification phase involves testing of the hypothesis in question, and attempting to eliminate competing explanations as well. If the hypothesis is verified, it may become part of a theory or model.* If it is not verified, then you go back to the original problem statement and reformulate the hypothesis.

*See Kelley[3] for some distinctions between models and theories.

Deductive and Inductive Approaches

In the development of theories or models, there are two basic approaches. In the deductive approach there is a flow of logic from abstraction to data. In the inductive approach just the opposite occurs. You start with data and work back to abstraction.[2]

In the deductive approach you would start with a series of definitions and assumptions. Then you logically build up to a theory that expresses relationships between two or more variables. If there is logical internal consistency among all of the components making up the theory, then it passes one major test. The other major test is one of empirical verification either as a part of your theoretical development or later. Deductively derived theories are sometimes accepted without empirical verification if they meet the internal consistency test. Obviously, though, we would put more faith in the theory if it met both tests.

In the inductive approach to theory derivation you would start with observations or data. You then work back to a set of hypotheses that would explain the relationships revealed by the data. These hypotheses should then be empirically tested in subsequent research to investigate the validity of your deductive conclusions.

You start from a different place in deductive and inductive analysis. But you need logic and empirical verification for both.[1] Our book uses both these approaches.

Research Methodologies*

Here we highlight some of the basic research methods that are used to generate and/or test hypotheses used in building models and theories, whether inductively or deductively. Filley, House, and Kerr[2] have a discussion of three different types of scientific study that is useful to look at. It is important to heed their warning that the types do not necessarily vary in quality. Any of these studies can be poorly done, regardless of type. The types are important, though. They help to determine the use to be made of the data and the extent to which generalizations may be drawn.

Type I studies consist of authoritative opinions, case studies, or narrative histories. These treat data qualitatively rather than quantitatively, with a minimum of classification or enumeration of variables. They are more useful for generating than for testing hypotheses.

*For more detail concerning these approaches study research methods books such as Emory[1] or Kerlinger.[3] We have only skimmed the surface here.

The clinical or case study approach is akin to the anecdotes that our hypothetical company president used to come up with traits of a successful manager. However, we would expect the observations to be much more systematic than those based on the company president's experience. Experienced observers can use the clinical approach to provide great depth of knowledge about a given phenomenon. However, it's hard to generalize very much.

The narrative history is a retrospective analysis of events that have been reported or taken place in the past. Its chief limitations are that, because events took place in the past, much opinion, interpretation, and judgment concerning the validity of the data are required. Thus, much subjectivity is involved.

Type II methodologies consist essentially of field studies. The field study is an on-site technique. It may be conducted in one or many organizations using a variety of techniques ranging from interviews to sample surveys. All organizational members may be utilized. Or some sort of sampling technique may be employed. A field study, unlike the clinical approach, will normally utilize data, which may be quantified in some way, and enough subjects, so that some type of statistical analysis may be employed. Breadth is typically emphasized at the expense of depth. Field studies may be used for either hypothesis generation or hypothesis testing.

Included here are longitudinal (time-series) field studies where observations are obtained at more than one point in time. These come closer to getting at causality than cross-sectional (data gathered at one point in time) field studies. They allow you to argue that a given variable precedes another one. In cross-sectional studies the most that can be said is that the two variables vary together. None of these kinds of field studies, though, allows for the control of extraneous variables, the hallmark of the type III studies. Without such control you can never be certain about causality.

Type III studies refer to field experiments, laboratory studies, and experimental simulation. The field experiment is another on-site method. It attempts to combine the advantages of the field study with the more controlled but less realistic laboratory study to be discussed below. Here a change or "treatment" is instituted in one or more units (organizations, subsystems, etc.) in order to determine its impact on the variable you are trying to predict (criterion). Ideally we would also like to have at least one comparable unit to serve as a control. This would help rule out alternative explanations for findings. However, it is difficult to gain entry into organizations to make changes unless the changes were going to be made by the organization anyway. Thus, reports of field experiments with control groups are relatively rare in the literature.

Unlike the on-site techniques, laboratory studies are conducted in some kind of artificial setting. Generally, one or more variables are experimentally manipulated. Before and after measures are also obtained. There are a number of experimental designs that may be used. Many of these are quite sophisticated in terms of providing control and allowing you to get at causality—the bain of the cross-sectional field study. The laboratory study is strong on control and causality. But many argue that it lacks relevance.* Indeed, much of psychology has been criticized as being based on data obtained from college sophomores in introductory psychology classes.

Experimental simulations attempt to study continuous organizational processes rather than effects of separate interventions or discrete changes made by experimenters. Those of you familiar with economics will recognize this as a dynamic as compared to a comparative statics approach. In the first case it is as if you compared two snapshots at a different point in time. In the latter case it is as if there were a moving picture. Here, an attempt is made to create a relatively realistic representation of a real world organization.

The major virtue of well-done type III studies is that they allow careful control of extraneous variables. This allows cause-effect relationships to be determined with a great deal of certainty. Studies of the other two types no matter how well done, simply will not allow you to be really certain about causality.

Evaluating the Evidence

Up to now we have proceeded as if you will be spending most of your time conducting empirical studies of organizational phenomena. In point of fact you need to be familiar with how one goes about obtaining scientific data about organizations. However, we don't expect that you will actually be gathering much of the scientific data yourself. (Although a number of the cases and exercises will get you involved to some extent.) We do expect, however, that you will be an intelligent "consumer" of organizational knowledge. Hence you need to know how information about organizations is obtained, where to find it, and how to evaluate its quality after you've found it.

We have covered how it is obtained—by the methods of science. Now, let's look at organizational information. How to evaluate it after you've found it is covered in the last section.

Sources of Organizational Information. A textbook such as this is often used as a major source for information about organizations. It can serve as a framework on which to hang more current and specific information. However, it is often so old and general that it's not very suitable if you need up-to-date information on a hot issue.

For that you will need to rely on journals and professional papers. Jour-

*Weick[4] however makes a convincing argument that laboratory studies can be designed to provide relevance to real world problems to a much greater extent than is generally believed.

nals, in turn, may be placed into two broad categories—trade and scholarly. Trade journals are those designed to appeal primarily to practitioners. Thus, they tend to be written so that they're easy and quick to read. Frequently, however, readability is gained at the expense of rigor. In other words, you are likely to find a relatively large amount of type I material in many of them. So long as you recognize the limitations of type I material, this is not necessarily bad.

We have indicated and briefly characterized a number of relevant trade journals in Appendix 1 of this chapter. We haven't attempted to rate the quality of their contents. You will be in a position to do that for yourself after you complete the next section.

Scholarly journals are those designed primarily for academicians or highly educated specialists in given areas. They are usually in the forefront, providing thorough and up-to-date knowledge, although even here such knowledge may be a year or more old. It typically takes that long or longer for potential articles to be reviewed, revised, and appear in print.

Unfortunately, most of these journals tend to be tough going. As specialized knowledge increases, more jargon and statistical sophistication become inevitable. A good bit of the additional difficulty, though, seems to be due to the turgid writing style of many academicians.

At any rate, a number of these journals are also summarized in Appendix 1. You will need to check them for level II and III type studies. Though they're likely to be tougher going than other material, they provide the current and in-depth research on organizational topics.

A third section of Appendix 1 summarizes some key abstracting services for organization theory material. You should start with these to find out which journals to check for material concerning a topic of interest. They are periodically updated and can save you much time. A reasonable strategy in obtaining organizational material is to start with the abstracting services. Then, for additional material, check bibliographies of articles initially located.

Finally, we should note that the most up-to-date material of all is available from papers presented at professional meetings. Unfortunately, this material generally is not as widely available as that in texts and journals. Your first step in trying to obtain it is to check proceedings such as those listed in Appendix 1. Those are available in many libraries and are published at least once a year. From them you can get up-to-date material. You can also contact the authors for additional material cited and for material so current it hasn't yet appeared in proceedings.

How to Evaluate What You Read. A reasonably good list of evaluation steps is that provided by Fox.[2] A similar but somewhat longer list is provided by Nemmers and Myers.[4]

Here are Fox's requirements.

1. The purpose of the research, or the problem involved, should be clearly defined and sharply delineated in terms as unambiguous as possible.

The statement of the research problem should include analysis into its simplest elements, its scope and limitations, and precise specifications of the meanings of all words significant to the research. Failure of the researcher to do this adequately may raise legitimate doubts in the minds of readers as to whether the researcher has sufficient understanding of the problem to make a sound attack upon it.

2. The research procedures used should be described in sufficient detail to permit another researcher to repeat the research.

Excepting when secrecy is imposed in the national interest, research reports should reveal with candor the sources of data and the means by which they were obtained. Omission of significant procedural details makes it difficult or impossible to estimate the validity and reliability of the data and justifiably weakens the confidence of the reader in research.

3. The procedural design of the research should be carefully planned to yield results that are as objective as possible.

When a sampling of a population in involved, the report should include evidence concerning the degree of representativeness of the sample. A questionnaire ought not to be used when more reliable evidence is available from documentary sources or by direct observation. Bibliographic searches should be as thorough and complete as possible. Experiments should have satisfactory controls. Direct observations should be recorded in writing as soon as possible after the event. Efforts should be made to minimize the influence of personal bias in selecting and recording data.

4. The researcher should report, with complete frankness, flaws in procedural design and estimate their effect upon the findings.

There are very few perfect research designs. Some of the imperfections may have little effect upon the validity and reliability of the data; others may invalidate them entirely. A competent researcher should be sensitive to the effects of imperfect design and his experience in analyzing the data should give him a basis for estimating their influence.

5. Analysis of the data should be sufficiently adequate to reveal its significance; and the methods of analysis used should be appropriate.

The extent to which this criterion is met is frequently a good measure of the competence of the researcher. Twenty years of experience in guiding the research of graduate students leads the writer to conclude that adequate analysis of the data is the most difficult phase of research for the novice.

The validity and reliability of data should be checked carefully. The data should be classified in ways that assist the researcher to reach pertinent conclusions. When statistical methods are used, the probability of error should be estimated and the criteria of statistical significance applied.

6. Conclusions should be confined to those justified by the data of the research and limited to those for which the data provide an adequate basis.

Researchers are often tempted to broaden the basis of inductions by including personal experiences not subject to the controls under which the research data were gathered. This tends to decrease the objectivity of the research and weakens confidence in the findings.

Equally undesirable is the all-too-frequent practice of drawing conclusions from study of a limited population and applying them universally. Good researchers specify the conditions under which their conclusions seem to be valid. Failure to do so justifiably weakens confidence in the research.

7. Greater confidence in the research is warranted if the researcher is experienced, has a good reputation in research, and is a person of integrity.

Were it possible for the reader of a research report to obtain sufficient information about the researcher, this criterion perhaps would be one of the best bases for judging the degree of confidence a piece of research warrants. For this reason, the research report should be accompanied by more information about the qualification of the researcher than is the usual practice.

Some evidence pertinent to estimates of the competence and integrity of the researcher may be found in the report itself. Language that is restrained, clear, and precise; assertions that are carefully drawn and hedged with appropriate reservations; and an apparent effort to achieve maximum objectivity tend to leave a favorable impression of the researcher. On the other hand, generalizations that outrun the evidence upon which they are based, exaggerations, and unnecessary verbiage tend to leave an unfavorable impression.

Utilization of this list and the scientific criteria outlined earlier should help make you a better consumer of organizational research.* If you do in-depth study on a topic using references we provide as well as other sources, these criteria should help you decide whether the evidence supports the theory. If it does, then the theory should be more useful to you, and you can be more confident in applying it.

*Those unfamiliar with terms like sampling, validity, reliability, and other technical aspects of research design and data analysis may want to refer to References 1 and 3.

REFERENCES

II. Theoretical Bases
A. Systems and Contingency Theory
  [1]Kast, F. E., and Rosenzweig, J. E. "General Systems Theory: Applications for Organization and Management," *Academy of Management Journal*, 15 (1972), 447–465.

[2]Luthans, F. *Introduction to Management: A Contingency Approach*. New York: McGraw-Hill, 1976.
B. Key Systems Notions
  [1]Evans, M. G. "Discussant's Comments," In E. A. Fleishman and J. G. Hunt (eds.), *Current Developments in the Study of Leader-*

Appendix 1 SELECTED PERIODICALS FOR ORGANIZATION THEORY*

I. Trade Journals. These are oriented primarily toward practitioners.

1. *Advanced Management Journal*. Society for Advancement of Management, 135 West 50th Street, New York, N.Y. 10020. Formerly the *S.A.M. Advanced Management Journal*. Quarterly. Replaces *Advanced Management*. Has a good mix of management and organizational articles.

2. *American Management Association Research Reports*. American Management Association, 135 West 50th Street, New York, N.Y. 10020. Irregular, since 1942. Reports of company philosophy, policy, and practice in all phases of management and organization.

3. *Business Horizons*. Graduate School of Business, Indiana University, Bloomington, Ind. 47401. Bimonthly, since 1958. Covers business and organizational topics.

4. *Business Week*. McGraw-Hill, Inc., 1221 Avenue of the Americas, New York, N.Y. 10020. Weekly, since 1929. Contains a journalistic review in the broad field of business with some coverage of organization theory.

5. *California Management Review*. Graduate School of Business Administration, University of Calif., Berkeley, Calif. 94720. Quarterly, since 1958. Covers management and organizational topics.

6. *Harvard Business Review*. Harvard Graduate School of Business Administration, Boston, Mass. 02163. Bimonthly, since 1922. Covers business and organizational topics.

7. *Journal of Contemporary Business*. University of Washington, Graduate School of Business Administration, Seattle, Wash. 98195. Quarterly, since 1972. Formerly was the *University of Washington Business Review*. Each issue covers a special topic in a business or organizational area.

8. *Management Record*. National Industrial Conference Board, 247 Park Avenue, New York, N.Y. 10022. Monthly, since 1916. Numerous reports of both experience and research surveys conducted by the

*This listing makes no pretense at being complete, but it should be comprehensive enough for most purposes.

N.I.C.B. staff, digests of symposia.

9. *Management Review*. American Management Association, 135 West 50th Street, New York, N.Y. 10020. Monthly, since 1923. Has general coverage of all phases of management and organization.

10. *MSU Business Topics*. Division of Research, Graduate School of Business Administration, Michigan State University, East Lansing, Mich. 48824. Quarterly, since 1953. Covers business and organizational topics.

11. *Organizational Dynamics*. American Management Association, 135 West 50th Street, New York, N.Y. 10020. Quarterly, since 1973. Covers organization theory topics.

12. *Personnel*. America Management Association, 135 West 50th Street, New York, N.Y. 10020. Bimonthly, since 1919. Has broad personnel and employee-focused management topics as well as organization theory coverage.

13. *Personnel Journal*. 100 Park Avenue, Swarthmore, Penn. 19081. Monthly. Has a primary emphasis on personnel and industrial relations with some coverage of organization theory topics.

14. *Personnel Series*. American Management Association, 330 West 42nd Street, New York, N.Y. Irregularly (several per year), since 1930. Reports of papers and discussions at A.M.A. personnel conferences. Broad coverage of the personnel and organization theory fields.

15. *Public Personnel Management*. Room 240, 1313 East 60th Street, Chicago, Ill. 60637. Bimonthly, since 1973. This journal is a merger of *Personnel Administration* and *Public Personnel Review*. Covers personnel and organization theory topics with an emphasis on the public sector.

16. *Social Science Reporter*. Rex F. Harlow, editor and publisher, 365 Guinda Street, Palo Alto, Calif. Semimonthly, since 1952. Current reports for executives on social science research—covering industrial relations, psychology, sociology, and co-disciplinary studies.

17. *Supervision*. Supervision, Editorial offices, 424 North Third Street, Burlington, Iowa 52601. Monthly. Emphasizes managerial topics with some coverage of organization theory.

18. *Training and Development Journal*. American Society of Training Directors, ASTD, P.O. Box 5307, Madison, Wis. 53705. Monthly. Primarily emphasizes training and development and human resource development, but often includes topics relevant to organization theory.

II. Scholarly Journals. These are oriented primarily toward the academician or specialist.

1. *Academy of Management Journal*. Academy of Management, Graduate School of Business, Southern Methodist

University, Dallas, Tex. 75221. Quarterly, since 1958. Provides empirical coverage of management and organization theory topics.

2. *Academy of Management Review.* Academy of Management, Graduate School of Business Administration, University of Washington, Seattle, Wash. 98195. Quarterly, since 1976. Covers theoretical aspects of management and organization theory.

3. *Administrative Science Quarterly.* Graduate School of Business and Public Administration, Cornell University, Ithaca, N.Y. 14850. Quarterly. Has a heavy emphasis on organization theory.

4. *American Journal of Sociology.* University of Chicago Press, 5801 Ellis Avenue, Chicago, Ill. 60637. Bimonthly, since 1895. Covers the general area of sociology with increasing emphasis on the organization theory area.

5. *American Political Science Review.* American Political Science Assn., 1527 New Hampshire Avenue, N. W., Washington, D.C. 20036. Quarterly, since 1906. Covers the general field of political science with some organization theory material.

6. *American Sociological Review.* American Sociological Assn., 1722 N Street, N. W., Washington, D.C. 20036. Bimonthly, since 1936. Contains theoretical empirical work on sociology with some consideration of organization theory.

7. *Behavioral Science.* University of Louisville, P.O. Box 1055, Louisville, Ky. 40401. Bimonthly. Emphasizes theoretical and empirical aspects of systems with some coverage of organization theory.

8. *Decision Sciences.* American Institute for Decision Sciences, 33 Gilmer Street, Atlanta, Ga. 30303. Quarterly. Stresses quantitative and behavioral approaches to problems of administration and organization.

9. *Human Organization.* Society for Applied Anthropology, 1703 New Hampshire Avenue, N. W., Washington, D.C. 20009. Quarterly. Intercultural approach to human behavior including some coverage of the organization theory area.

10. *Human Relations.* The Tavistock Institute, London, England. Monthly. Theoretical developments and reports of empirical research in the organizational area.

11. *Industrial Relations.* Institute of Industrial Relations, University of California, Berkeley, Calif. 94720. Published three times per year. Contains articles and symposia on all aspects of employment and organizational relationship.

12. *Journal of Applied Behavioral Sciences.* Box 9155, Rosslyn Station, Arlington, Va. 22209. Quarterly. Emphasizes interdisciplinary work in the behavioral sciences including some coverage of organization theory.

13. *Journal of Applied Psychology.*

American Psychological Assn., 1220 17th Street, N. W., Washington, D.C. 20036. Bimonthly. Stresses empirical investigations of psychological and organizational topics.

14. *Journal of Applied Social Psychology.* V. H. Winston & Sons, Inc., 1511 K Street, N. W., Washington, D.C. 20005. Quarterly, since 1971. Stresses empirical investigations utilizing the behavioral sciences to problems of current interest to society.

15. *Journal of Business.* Editor, Rosenwald 331, University of Chicago, Chicago, Ill. 60637. Quarterly. Covers a wide range of business and organizational topics.

16. *Journal of Business Research* (Formerly the *Southern Journal of Business*). Elsevier North-Holland, 52 Vanderbilt Avenue, New York, N.Y. 10017. Empirical research is emphasized, but not to the exclusion of theoretical and conceptual contributions in the areas of business and organizations.

17. *Journal of Conflict Resolution.* Department of Political Science, Yale University, 124 Prospect Street, New Haven, Conn. 06520. Quarterly. Emphasizes all aspects of conflict.

18. *Journal of Management Studies.* Manchester Business School, Booth Street West, Manchester, England. Published three times per year. Covers research in management and organization.

19. *International Studies of Management and Organization.* Baruch College, CUNY, 17 Lexington Avenue, New York, N.Y. 10010. Quarterly. Has translations of management and organizational material that have appeared originally in scholarly journals and books throughout the world.

20. *Management Science.* The Institute of Management Science, Room 405, 146 Westminster Street, Providence, R.I. 02903. Monthly, since 1954. Covers management and organizational topics with special emphasis on organizational design.

21. *Occupational Psychology.* British Psychological Society, 18–19 Albermarie Street, London, W1X 4DN, England. Quarterly. Covers psychological and organization theory material.

22. *Organization and Administrative Sciences.* Kent State University, Comparative Administration, Research Institute, Kent, Ohio 44242. Quarterly, since 1970. Formerly *Quarterly Journal of Management Development*. Has a heavy emphasis on cross-cultural and organization theory topics.

23. *Organizational Behavior and Human Performance.* Department of Psychological Sciences, Purdue University, West Lafayette, Ind. 47907. Bimonthly. Contains empirical research and theoretical developments in all areas of human performance theory and organizational psychology.

24. *Personnel Management.* Mercury House Publications, Ltd., Waterloo Road, London, SE1 8UL, England. Monthly. Covers empirical and theoretical work in personnel and organization theory.

25. *Personnel Psychology.* Personnel Psychology, Inc., Box 6965 College Station, Durham, N.C. 27708. Quarterly, since 1948. Covers research in industrial and organizational psychology and organization theory.

26. *Psychological Bulletin.* American Psychological Assn., Inc., 1200 17th Street, N. W. Washington, D.C. 20036. Bimonthly, since 1904. Covers theoretical reviews in psychology with some work in organization theory.

27. *Public Administration Review.* American Society for Public Administration, 1225 Connecticut Avenue, N. W., Washington, D.C. 20036. Bimonthly, since 1940. Covers management and organization theory in the public sector.

28. *Sociology.* British Sociological Assn., Oxford University Press, Press Road, Nessden, London, N.W. 10, England. Three issues per year, since 1967. Covers sociological topics, but with a heavy emphasis on organization theory.

29. *Sociometry.* American Sociological Assn., 1722 N Street, N. W., Washington, D.C. 20036. Quarterly, since 1937. Covers work in the behavioral sciences with some coverage of organization theory topics.

III. Abstracting Services. These are useful for finding relevant organization theory material in journals and books.

1. *Business Periodicals Index.* H. W. Wilson Co., 950 University Avenue, Bronx, N.Y. 10452. Monthly, except August, since 1958. Cumulative index to the functional areas of business with some coverage of management and organizational literature.

2. *Employment Relations Abstracts.* Information Service, Inc., 10 West Warren Street, Detroit, Mich. 48201. Semi-monthly, looseleaf service, since 1950. The title from 1950 through 1959 was *Labor-Personnel Index.* Abstracts current books and approximately 120 journals in the industrial relations and organizational areas.

3. *Management Abstracts.* All India Management Assn., 29 Nizamuddin East, New Delhi, 110013, India. Quarterly, since 1972. Abstracts materials throughout the management and organizational areas.

4. *Management Research.* School of Business Administration, University of Massachusetts, Amherst, Mass. 01002. Bimonthly. Abstracts over 100 journal articles and many books in the management and organization areas.

5. *Personnel Management Abstracts.* University of Michigan, Graduate School of Business Administration, Ann Arbor, Mich. 43104. Quart-

erly, since 1955. Abstracts journals and books in the management and organizational areas.

6. *Psychological Abstracts.* American Psychological Assn., Inc., 1200 17th Street, N. W., Washington, D.C. 20036. Monthly, since 1927. Contains a bibliographic listing of new books and articles in psychology grouped by subject, with an abstract of each item.

7. *Sociological Abstracts.* Sociological Abstracts, Inc., Box 22206, San Diego, Calif. 92122. Cosponsored by the Eastern Sociological Society and the Mid-west Sociological Society. Nine issues a year with varying frequency. Abstracts sociological publications by subject and author.

IV. Proceedings from Professional Associations. These present more current material than journals.

1. *Academy of Management Proceedings.* Academy of Management. College of Business Administration. Cleveland State University, Cleveland, Ohio, 44115. Published at different institutions, yearly. Contains some complete papers and abstracts of others.

2. *American Psychological Association Proceedings.* American Psychological Association, Inc., 1200 17th Street, N. W., Washington, D.C. 20036. Yearly. These contain abstracts of papers presented at the APA annual convention.

3. *American Sociological Association Proceedings.* These are contained in *The Management Sociologist,* Brown University, Box 1836, Providence, R.I. 02912. Quarterly.

4. *Industrial Relations Research Association Proceedings.* Industrial Relations Research Association, Social Science Building, University of Wisconsin, Madison, Wis. 53706. Proceedings published after spring and winter meetings.

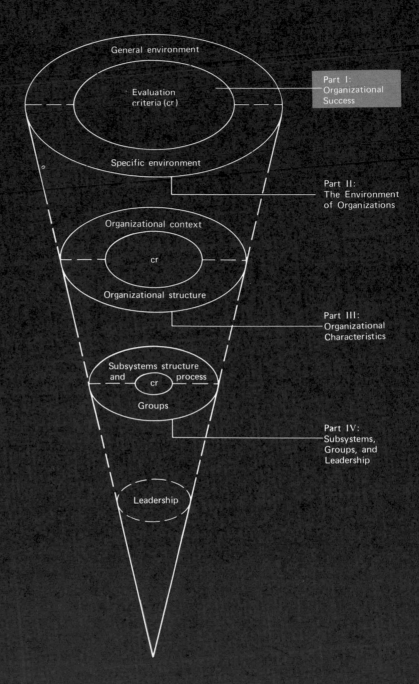

Figure I-1 A cone model for organizational analysis.

part

I

criteria for evaluating organizational success

Dimly, through the haze, a bright golden glow spreads beauty, truth, light, salvation, prosperity, harmony, world peace, and the quality of life. No one can see it clearly and some even doubt it exists. It's doing everything for everybody. The mathematician provides a series of proofs showing it is not rational. But he didn't think it was rational in the first place. It passes the litmus test of the psychologists in improving the quality of life regardless of the definition of the quality of life. The skeptical sociologists can't believe it. It contributes to society without detracting from it. The economist finds it is optimal. Students feel that at last the "Force" is with them. In unison, business leaders, politicians, administrators, consultants, and students clamor—I want to talk with whoever is running that thing. Finally, a small child tugs at an adult, "What is it; I don't see anything." In hushed tones of reverence the adults softly purr—It's the successful organization.

Farfetched as our tale may sound, an organization must meet all the tests in our fable and perhaps even more if all are to agree it is successful. Organization theory is a strange mixture of theories and practice. Virtually everyone is willing to evaluate an organization, cite some deficiency, and plunge into an expensive program to cure its ills. Without tests few physicians would diagnose a patient and perform surgery. But without a moment's thought, one might call an organization unsuccessful and reorganize its entire operations.

CONTRASTING VIEWS OF SUCCESS

For scholars the definition of success of organizations often intertwines with their academic specialty. Different schools of administrative theory tend to view organizational success differently. To an economist the question of success is theoretically quite simple. The more efficient (greater ratio of output to input) the organization the more successful it is. In the everyday operations of organizations, this view can be found in industrial engineering and operations research. It's implicitly assumed that if a worker or a unit can be made more efficient, then the organization and ultimately society will benefit.

Psychologists seem to be a quite different breed. They accept notions of efficiency from economists and industrial engineers. Global ratios of inputs to outputs and worker productivity are considered measures of performance. Yet, effectiveness often includes the psychological well-being of workers and managers. Unfortunately for the study of organizations, early writings in "human relations" implied that happy workers were more productive. As we note later, satisfaction and productivity may or may not be associated.

Many psychologists appear to accept the goals organizations give them as aspects of performance. Most sociologists do not. To them the organization is merely an instrument of society that can be used or misused. The success of an organization, then, depends upon its contribution to society, which in turn depends upon the vision of society the sociologist favors. For instance, a staunch Marxist would never call *ITT* successful.

In recent years there has been a mingling of economic, psychological, and sociological thought concerning organizations. Yet the emphasis on either individuals and their role in the organization or the role of the organization in society still persists. These are characterized in Table I-2.

The differences represented by this continuum reflect a concern with different units of analysis. The total systems group analyzes organizations as a

Table I-2 Typical Systems Versus Subsystems Views of Successfulness

	Systems Views	*Subsystems Views*
1. Closest discipline in behavioral science	Sociology	Psychology
2. Focus	Goals, outputs, and operations of the organization related to survival	Individual needs and attitudes and management's desires
3. Methodology	Derivations from ideals and comparative case studies	Surveys, direct observation, one-case studies
4. Criteria emphasized	Outputs to outsiders or measures reflecting outputs	Internal operations and individual contribution
5. Underlying perspective stresses	Conflict, competition	Harmony, status quo, and equity
6. Orientation of key authors	Abstract theorists who stress why and have few commitments to any one organization. The search is for a contingency model.	Practical consultants and scholars who stress techniques, a la MBO, and have close ties with businesses. The search is often for the "one best way" or at least a better way.

Source: Adapted from Kassem, S. "Organization Theory: American and European Styles," *Management International Review,* 17 (1977), 11–18.

whole and relates organizational goals to a broader outlook, frequently external to the organization. The subsystems group primarily focuses on subunits and individuals within an organization.

You will note that in the cone model for this part (repeated from Figure 1-1) the core of the cone refers to criteria of success. We devote the next three chapters to this core. Chapter 2 focuses on the systems group's approach at the top of the cone. The emphasis is on survival, goal attainment, and mission accomplishment. Chapter 3 moves you down into the subsystems views of the organization. The emphasis shifts to performance and employee maintenance. Chapter 4 integrates these views and suggests our views on the importance of these criteria for different units of analysis. Later chapters deal with the variables surrounding the criteria core (abbreviated "cr").

Before moving to the chapters in Part I a bit more overview may help you to put this in perspective.

Systems Views—Chapter 2

The systems group, centering on the organization's role, is often concerned with organizational goals and survival. Organizations accomplishing their goals and mission are termed "effective." Yet even here there is a continuum reflecting the extent to which goals of top management are accepted by the "analyst." At one extreme are consultants who accept the stated goals of top management as given. The consultant's role is to help the organization reach these goals (e.g., by suggesting ways to get better profit, market share, more revenue, etc.). They are not concerned about the theory of why the organization is effective. At the other extreme is a group of individuals using more traditional sociological analysis. They try to establish standards to judge the organization in terms of its stated contribution to society. Yet their performance measures often reflect their own values of how the organization *should* contribute. For instance, a mental health facility's goal may be to cure the mentally ill. Instead of measuring *whether* this is achieved, this group judges *how* a sick person was transformed into a healthy one. Given high standards often set by this group, considerable effort is spent trying to understand why many of these organizations are ineffective (by their definition).

Between these extremes is the systems group you find in Table I-2. This group considers the survival of organizations and the conditions related to the longer-term existence of complex systems. A mixture of goals from the top brass, from their estimate of conditions enhancing survival, and from their view of society is used to evaluate the organization. Evaluation may be used to improve it. But the major thrust is to understand why an organization acts as it does.

Chapter 2 explores aspects of two of these three outlooks. First we discuss the societal contributions of organizations using different classification systems. The highlight is on the outputs they provide. Two key questions are— What outputs should be rated? Who should do the rating? Then we move to the middle position of the systems continuum to look at organizational goals. By distinguishing among types of goals, you should get a feel for expectations established for various institutions. As you will see, managers often take a more restricted view of goals than do sociologists. They often establish a series of limited objectives and try to meet "satisfactory" targets. This is conceived as the "goals as constraints" argument.

We don't treat the consultants' viewpoint. It fails to provide an explanation of why or how goals operate as they do. As in later chapters, our Measurement Module outlines approaches to measuring criteria—in this case, organizational effectiveness.

Subsystems Views—Chapter 3

In the second chapter of Part I, we move down the core of the cone to the subsystems perspective reflected in Table I-2. We note how targets management sets for organizational units relate to organizational goals. The discussion of unit and individual performance measures mirrors the treatment of societal contribution and organizational goals. We ask, as outside observers, how the efforts of the individual contribute to the unit and the unit to the organization. We show how managerial expectations are used for setting standards and evaluating performance. We also explore dimensions of employee maintenance—withdrawal and attachment—and quality of working life.

The Measurement Module provides selected measures of subsystems performance as well as some of the major instruments used to assess selected aspects of employee maintenance. Unlike effectiveness analyses for the total organization, the scholar-consultant combination has yielded a number of relatively well-developed instruments at the subsystems level of analysis.

Contingency Views—Chapter 4

In the contingency chapter we discuss some problems regarding criteria, and how the systems and subsystems views can be linked. For instance, we'll note that different standards of desirability can be established, and that there are links between organizational actions and desired outputs. Essentially, we argue that more precise estimates of goal attainment are possible when we know what is socially desired of the organization and how it can produce these desired outcomes. We also note problems of measuring performance when standards are vague. Here, management may not be able to clearly link individual performance to unit accomplishment, and unit outputs to organizational success. Finally, we attempt to derive an overall view of organizational success by linking societal contribution, organizational goals, and employee maintenance considerations. We don't expect complete agreement with our view. But we raise the issue of integrating multiple views of successfulness.

chapter 2 SOCIETAL CONTRIBUTION AND ORGANIZATIONAL GOALS

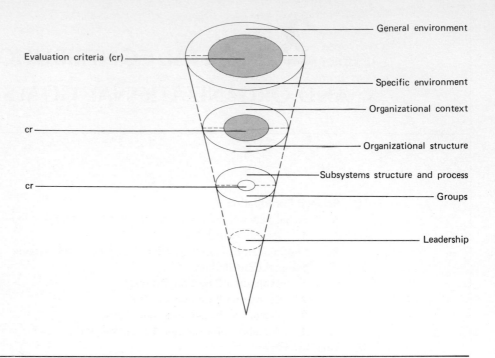

Evaluation criteria (cr)

General environment

Specific environment

Organizational context

Organizational structure

cr

Subsystems structure and process

cr

Groups

Leadership

Just how well are General Motors, The Environmental Protection Agency, the Mafia, and St. John's Hospital doing? The profits of GM are substantially up as of this writing. The EPA seems to be facing substantial funding problems in addition to a reassessment by Congress and by the President. Latest estimates for the Mafia show continued growth. And St. John's Hospital just purchased a heart-lung machine after completing a successful funding drive. Such are the comments you're likely to get if you ask about the success or failure of an organization. Unstated is a general feeling that GM, EPA, the Mafia, and St. John's Hospital should not be judged on the same basis.

But why use profits as success criteria for business organizations and quality care as success criteria for hospitals? Shouldn't business organizations be judged by more than dollar return? What if a hospital restricts quality care to the rich? Is this similar to GM producing cars exclusively for the middle and upper classes? Is there any way of comparing the relative success of a business firm and hospital? These are the types of questions we address in this chapter.

As noted in the overview, we will explore two major systems perspectives on success criteria. The chapter looks at societal contribution and goal attainment. That is, one way of judging the success of an organization is to ask how "effective" it is in making a contribution to the society in which it functions. A second viewpoint is goal attainment. Here, success is viewed in terms of how effective an organization is in achieving specified goals. As you will see, there are a variety of perspectives about both societal contribution and which goals are most important. Note that the emphasis in both, though, is on "effectiveness." After discussing these viewpoints, we show ways of measuring various aspects of them in the Measurement Module.

SOCIETAL CONTRIBUTION

Analyses of effectiveness from a societal view help us to understand the broad cultural forces surrounding organizations. And they show some of the specific pressures organizations may face from important and powerful groups in their environment.[3]

Organizations are but parts of society. So they may be judged on their contribution to the overall welfare of it. The more contributions an organization makes, the more *effective* it is. There are several variations on this general theme. Some variations ask the rater to decide what the organization should contribute to society—what should it do? Some suggest that the evaluator can rely upon the judgments of others and outline who should be asked to evaluate the organization. Each is based on a typology of organizations—a classification that provides the basis for judging the organization.

Social Function as a Basis for Judging Societal Contribution

By far the most comprehensive and abstract view of societal contribution is provided by Parsons.*,[8,9,10,11] Essentially, he argues that an organization is more effective to the extent that it performs the vital activities needed by society. In our society organizations are the major institutions for performing the activities needed to keep a complex society viable. Based on their primary contribution, organizations can be placed in one of four categories—economic, political, integrative, and pattern maintenance. Let's examine the categories in more detail to see how they can be used to evaluate organizations.

You can easily recognize the first two groups. Economic institutions produce the goods and services used in society. The primary contribution of political organizations, according to Parsons, lies in generating and allocating

*Our terminology is not identical to Parson's but is intended to convey the major aspects of his view. Other theorists with similar views are noted in the References at the end of the chapter.

power. Under his model, in addition to the common political groups, institutions like banks and insurance companies are "political" since their primary function is to generate and allocate economic power. The primary function of integrative organizations is to settle conflicts, direct motivations toward societal goals, and provide a framework that ties together dissimilar societal interests. For instance, both the police and the court system may be expected to resolve conflict and provide motivation (either positive or negative) to help individuals realize the expectations of society. The institutions that deal with the cultural, educational, health, and expressive activities of society are placed in the pattern maintenance category. Churches, universities, and private foundations are examples. Hospitals can be placed in this category in that they provide physical maintenance.

Parsons compares corporations and universities to highlight factors often used in evaluating these organizations.[10,11] Since corporations operate in a free-market economy, they should be judged by economic yardsticks, with an emphasis on maximum production at minimal cost. Thus, efficiency becomes crucial and evaluation is performed by market forces. But universities are different. They socialize students. They create and modify cultural tradition through research. They should be judged on these outputs, even though these are difficult to measure. Universities are to be held accountable to the law of social values, recognizing that their services are "good in themselves."

To a greater or lesser extent, the bias of the evaluator may be reflected in an evaluation based on Parson's social functions.[12] If we agree with the often unstated values of the rater, the evaluation may appear reasonable. If there is an apparent difference in values, we often dismiss the judgment as biased. This has been well stated by Milton Friedman, a critic of the business world's "social" responsibility. To him the function of business is clear—maximize long-run monetary returns. Societal desires for political, integrative, and pattern maintenance contributions by corporations are illegitimate. These are to be done by other institutions. Unfortunately, few state their assumptions as clearly as Friedman.[4]

Problems with Parsons. In trying to use this framework for evaluating organizations, we can run into several problems. For instance, in the process of meeting one social function, the organization may end up harming the society in other areas, or prevent other organizations from performing their social function. Some critics of regulatory agencies point out how they inhibit competition by setting prices, excluding competitors from the marketplace, and protecting favored business.[6] And critics of business are quick to show that in the process of producing economic goods (their social function), they may inadvertently detract from other societal objectives such as clean air.[5] So how do you evaluate their net effectiveness from a societal viewpoint? If they get high marks for contributing to their major social function, do you subtract the undesirable consequences in other areas? Parsons' analysis does not provide an easy answer to this complex question.

If an organization is placed in a particular category, it should attempt to seek goals consistent with its social function. But, some organizations fall into two of Parsons' categories. AMTRAK and TVA are, by design, partially economic and partially pattern maintenance. By which are they evaluated?[3] Similarly, you may evaluate any one organization on more than one social function. For example, university administrators should be no more surprised to find that efficiency (cost per student hour, etc.) is used to rate their organizations than are business executives who feel pressures for pollution control.[1] Of course, the balance among different functions and the requirements that should be placed on a particular organization is hotly contested.

Another dilemma is that the Parsons' framework assumes that organizations that perform their functions will *survive*. Those that do not are assumed to die. For instance, if mental health facilities are placed in the pattern maintenance category, they should attempt to cure the mentally ill. But some are little more than warehouses to keep the deviants away from "normal people." It's possible that an organization may not contribute much in its primary social function for several years after being developed. And a number of authors suggest that social contribution may only be vaguely related to organizational survival.[2,7] For instance, it would be difficult to argue that the Mafia is a net contributor to the viability of society.

Our last example highlights both the basic strength and weakness of Parsons' approach. To follow Parsons you must have a clear vision of an ideal society and deduce how each type of organization should contribute to societal functioning.[13] Few have this vision. Fewer can develop practical measures for their ideals. Still fewer have enough data to clearly assess the positive and negative contributions an organization makes across functions. There are, of course, attempts to provide indicators to evaluate an ideal society. Table 2-1 presents one approach to this.[15] Yet differing assumptions about socially desirable conditions lead to different visions of how to evaluate organizations. Look at the positions of two influential economists to illustrate this.

John Kenneth Galbraith called for substantially more governmental action based on his view of an ideal society.[5] Essentially, he argued that business was so successful that it had deprived society of more balanced development. As allocator of power, he argued, the government should step in to substantially increase the level of social services. The social programs of the Kennedy and Johnson era found intellectual support in Galbraith's analysis. In stark contrast to that of Galbraith, we find Schumacher's influential *Small is Beautiful*.[14] Schumacher states a preference for economic institutions that promote methods that are cheap enough to be accessible to virtually everyone, suitable for

Table 2-1 Selected Measures of Social Conditions Organized by Parsons' Function Perspective

Economic (Production)
    Personal income per capita
    Association between father and son occupational status
Integrative
    Public Order and Security—FBI Uniform Crime Reports Index of Crimes
    Value of property involved in theft per $1000
Pattern Maintenance
    Expectancy of healthy life (free of bed disability and institutionalization)
    Performance on selected (academic) achievement tests
    Technological balance of payments
    Attendance at theaters, operas, ballets
Political
    Ratio of actual level of pollution to an acceptable standard
    Number in poverty
    Proportion of housing that is substandard

Source: Toward a Social Report. U.S. Department of Health, Education and Welfare, 1969.

small scale production, and compatible with man's need for creativity (p. 32). Galbraith felt growth would rid society of private affluence and public squalor. Schumacher opts for smaller public as well as private organizations. Thus, various operational definitions of organizational functions in ideal societies lead to conflicting views about how to judge organizational contributions to society.

Output, Control, and Beneficiaries as Bases for Judging Societal Contribution

As we have seen, the Parsons' model attempts to judge organizational effectiveness according to the degree to which it accomplishes its societal function. Unfortunately, there are difficulties due to disagreements about how to measure this, and who should be the judge.

In this section, we provide three other classification systems that reflect more traditional views of organizations. Each assumes some degree of organizational rationality—organizations act in a particular fashion because they are seeking goals. However, the three schemes suggest other ways in which overall estimates of effectiveness can be evaluated (in contrast to the social functions approach). Each also helps show the types of pressures found in a complex society. All place organizations in one of four categories and recognize that any particular organization may be a mix of two or more types.

Evaluation Based on Output. Katz and Kahn offer a scheme that places considerable emphasis on the outputs of an organization.[13] Economic organizations produce goods and services. This is further subdivided into primary (farming and mining), secondary (manufacturing), and tertiary (services such as communications and banking) systems. A managerial-political category includes government agencies, the courts and other units that provide social services. Also included here are interest groups, professional associations, and unions since all are concerned with "adjudication, coordination, and control of resources, people and subsystems" (p. 112).[13] Much like Parsons, there is a sociocultural group of maintenance institutions. These are devoted to socialization and physical care. Elementary schools, churches and the like are placed here for their socialization. Hospitals and mental health facilities are also considered part of this group for their restorative outputs. A fourth group is somewhat unique. Katz and Kahn single out organizations that create knowledge and develop and test theories. These are called adaptive organizations.

The Katz and Kahn framework provides a somewhat more common format than Parsons' for grouping organizations by output. But it still does not suggest who should benefit most from organizations in a particular category and who should be asked to rate a particular type of system.[25] Evaluation rests with deciding whether an organization is creating appropriate outputs.[22]

Evaluation Based on Control. A scheme by Farmer and Richman attempts to answer both questions: What outputs should be rated and who should judge them?[8] Economic organizations produce goods and services and should be controlled by market forces. Thus, economic efficiency should loom large in rating businesses. Legal-political organizations provide social control and social services. They're to be controlled by the public at large via political representation. Sociocultural systems serve maintenance needs. They should be controlled both by members and the societal elite (the elite being the rich and powerful, the top 1 percent of the community).[17] The last group consists of educational institutions that provide information (both securing and disseminating). These are controlled by a mix of members and elites. Following Farmer and Richman's scheme, to evaluate a high school you would first ascertain from members of the elite the information that students should learn. Then educators are asked for measures of achievement. If reading, writing, and math were deemed important, then the evaluator would ask educators to provide student achievement test scores. You might not be particularly interested in student ratings unless members of the elite indicated this was an important output of the educational system.

Evaluation Based on Beneficiaries. Blau and Scott develop the notion of primary beneficiary to evaluate organization effectiveness.[4] The primary beneficiary is the group that receives, or at least should receive, the most benefits from the organization. In economic organizations the primary beneficiary is the owners. If clients or customers are the primary beneficiary the system is called a service organization. If members receive the most, the organization is called a mutual benefit association. Those that appear to serve the public in general are called commonwealth organizations. According to Blau and Scott this view helps explain how organizational members participate in the system and what are some of the major problems faced by the organization.[4] For instance, economic institutions find it more difficult to use ideology in stimulating membership effort than the service, mutual benefit, or commonwealth organizations. Maximizing profits for owners just doesn't have the same appeal as curing the sick.

For evaluation of organizations, this view highlights the different groups that often judge them. Members may expect their organization to act as if it were a mutual benefit association. But outsiders may want it to act as if it were a commonwealth system. For instance, professors cherish academic freedom and expect the university to protect this valuable right via support of tenure and protection from those funding the institution. But as a commonwealth organization, the general public may not be particularly interested in the academic freedom of a radical professor.[22]

A simple extension alerts us to power differences within units. Some members of a system are in a good position to direct organizational resources toward their own benefit.[26] Top-level administrators may have such clout.[20] Thus, some may treat their organization as a mutual benefit system even though the primary beneficiary ought to be, say, owners.[18] Several critics of big business, big labor, and big government suggest that these organizations often act as if the prime beneficiaries were top management.[3,9] Thus, they seek goals, such as growth, which may not be clearly related to objective assessments based on function, output, control, or primary beneficiary.[18]

Societal Contribution: A Common View. You may have noted the substantial disagreement across these three approaches. For instance, the "control" viewpoint would ask us to rate a corporation on market efficiency. The "beneficiary" approach might concentrate on profits. Thus, OPEC, the oil cartel, following Farmer and Richman, would be criticized. The market really doesn't influence OPEC's output as much as it should. Blau and Scott's approach gives OPEC high marks. The owners, primarily Mideast countries, are accumulating wealth rapidly.

The problem in studying organizations is that none of these views dominates organizational evaluation.[24,25] As of now, these divergent viewpoints often tell us more about the assumptions behind a person's analysis than the success of the system.[21]

We have given very little attention to employee maintenance criteria.[1,15,16] Yet, as we will show here and in the next chapter, some believe that to be successful all organizations must provide satisfaction or psychological growth to members (an aspect of employee maintenance).[2,5] Interestingly, authors stressing employee maintenance rarely place much emphasis on what the organization is providing owners, customers, or society. Or, they implicitly assume that employee satisfaction will eventually lead to more desirable outputs for all.[14]

We think a choice of a classification scheme and an evaluation based on any of them reflects cultural values.[7] When you are analyzing organizational success, you implicitly state a value system. You can do this by selecting the outputs that you consider to be important and by selecting those who will provide evaluative information. If the evaluators and the outputs are consistent with dominant cultural values, then evaluations of societal contribution are useful in showing the fit between the outputs of the organization and the desires of the larger environment.* Thus, such evaluations help provide an estimate of long-run *survival*. If these ratings also conform to the desires of powerful groups in society, then you may have a fair estimate of survival in the intermediate run. However, short-run survival may not rest on societal contribution.

The various views also help us understand that there are several organizational contributions and many desirable conditions that organizations might seek.[10,27] Some global estimate of success is likely to hide substantial variation in the contributions an organization makes to different individuals in different areas of society.[11,21] However, the societal contribution viewpoint clearly shows that factors outside the organization are likely to have considerable influence on its operations and output.[4,6,8,19,23] Whether we recognize it or not, the way in which we look at organizations and the manner in which they are evaluated depends in large part on value systems and the power of outsiders.[22]

In Chapter 4 we attempt to make this abstract view of organizational effectiveness more concrete. This need for clarity has lead many to stress the more concrete achievements of organizations. Many emphasize the goal attainment of a system as an indicator of effectiveness. Let's take a look at this viewpoint.

*Cultural values are discussed in Chapter 5.

GOAL ATTAINMENT

By far the most popular view of organizational effectiveness rests on the "goal paradigm."[1,4,6] Etzioni states, "Effectiveness is the degree to which an organization realizes its goals."[2] For instance, if the Mafia wants to get a thousand New York City children addicted to heroin and it does so, then it may be called as effective as a church that saves a thousand souls. Embodied in this view of effectiveness is the attempt to avoid making value statements about what the organization *should* do.[4] This view is also used to help explain the activities of an organization,[6] justify choices among alternatives,[3] and provide a rationale for the organization's existence.[5]

Etzioni's simple definition of effectiveness really hides more than we realize. Do we "know" what the goals of the organization really are? Typically we assume we do in some vague sense. Yet how many people can list the major goals of a university, a business, or a church if we go beyond educating students, making profits, or saving souls? What are the goals of an organization? We think it is useful to look at four types of goals: the mission of the system, output (product and service) goals, systems goals, and derived goals.

The Mission of the System

We often talk of an organization as if it had but one overriding goal.[5] Organizations often support this notion by publicly stating their purposes and objectives.[2] For incorporation in most states businesses must provide a statement of purpose. An early goal for Henry Ford was to produce a car for the common person. Governmental agencies are given objectives in the laws that create them. The Equal Employment Opportunity Commission (EEOC) has the objective of promoting what its title conveys. Table 2-2 provides one such statement for a university.

We call these pronouncements *mission statements*. They are the publicly stated objectives. These are most often phrased in terms of some ideal. Mission statements usually outline the major societal contribution and often mention the types of outputs outsiders should expect.* If rated solely on the basis of mission accomplishment, we know of no organization that would be called effective. All fail to reach the ideal state.

Mission statements can provide a link between social function and the more specific targets expected from an organization.[4] The mission statement leads to criteria for evaluating an organization in much the same manner

---

*Mission statements are given other names by different authors. For instance, Perrow calls these output goals. Etzioni would cite mission statements as one type of official goal.

described for rating societal contribution. It may also be used by the organization to reject socially desirable but expensive projects. For instance, some corporate executives, such as Henry Ford II, sincerely want a revitalization of our urban areas.[6] But they note that it is not within the mission of their corporation. Universities may be interested in developing economic growth plans for their regions. However, most universities carry mission statements that place such activities at the fringe of their stated contribution.[1] Thus, the mission statement may not accurately reflect the *operative goals* that are the "real" goals of the organization.[3]

Table 2-2   What's Above the Library Water Fountain: The Mission Statement of a University.

To Exalt Beauty
  In God
    In Nature
      and In Art
Teaching how to love the best but to keep the human touch

To Advance Learning
  In all lines of truth wherever they may lead
  Showing how to think
    Rather than what to think
  Assisting the powers of the mind in their self-development

To Forward Ideas and Ideals
  In our democracy, inspiring respect for others
  as for ourselves
  Ever promoting freedom with responsibility

To become a center of order and light
  That knowledge may lead to understanding
  and understanding to wisdom

Output Goals

Individuals are probably most familiar with an organization's products and services (outputs).[5] Output goals are the technical aspects of the goods and services offered to customers and clients. Some of these may appear frivolous. For example, through advertising you might think that Procter and Gamble is only interested in "new" detergent formulas. They will make whites even whiter and colors even more colorful. But output goals are better known for other reasons. You can clearly see and understand physical changes in products. Product developments are a part of our competitive system. We expect them as a matter of course. The services offered by public agencies are the most visible aspect of their operations.[2] Discussions concerning funding rarely focus on missions.[1] They typically emphasize the specific service package (outputs) an agency should or should not offer.[4] For example, who should get welfare funds, what programs should be offered to help the poor, and how should payments be made—in cash or services?

Products and services may be deceptively easy to link to the mission of an organization since they are often mentioned in these pronouncements. You might assume that if an organization is meeting its output goals, it must be effective. But accomplishing product or service objectives does not mean other types of goals are also being met.[3] The firm that produces the highest quality auto may not be the most profitable.[5] Nor is the hospital offering the largest range of services, with the best physical equipment, necessarily contributing the most to society.

Using only output goals to measure effectiveness can lead to problems. Take the case in which organizations are dominated by professionals (such as engineering firms, universities, the courts, hospitals). There is a tendency for product and service criteria to drive out other potentially important aspects of organizational effectiveness or success.[1] Professionals are frequently considered the only group technically qualified to judge the operations of an organization.[2] So evaluators may rely almost exclusively upon their estimates of effectiveness.[7] Who but a physician, for instance, can rate the effectiveness of a hospital? But professional criteria are centered on products and services—not necessarily systems goals or societal contribution. Each professional group, professors included, probably overrates the importance of its profession to society. Such groups may understate aspects of effectiveness important to other groups.[6] Based solely on technical grounds, professionals may demand more resources for their units than is in the long-term best interests of society or even the organization itself.

Survival and Systems Goals

Throughout our discussion we have implicitly assumed that the organization that contributes to society and produces "better" outputs will have a greater chance of survival. However, others argue that societal contribution and organizational outputs are important only because they contribute to the primary goal of survival.[4,5,12] Taking this tack, they then attempt to outline the conditions that enhance the probability of survival over the long term.[9] Societal contribution and organizational outputs are two conditions.[2] But most are conditions that describe the organization as a system—thus the tag, "systems goals." So, what conditions should the organization focus on to survive?

For most organizations, growth, productivity, stability, harmony, flexibility, and prestige are considered important systems goals.*,[10,11] To apply the notions of productivity to a particular organization, you can use one or some combination of the societal views outlined earlier. Thus, productivity for a business firm is frequently measured by profitablity.[4] Changes in sales, market share, or assets may be considered relevant aspects of growth.[9] (Note that these are also potential measures of effectiveness from a societal viewpoint, depending on the basis of evaluation you choose.) The specific items selected to measure various systems goals most often reflect the interests of top management, the expectations of powerful outside groups, and the background of the evaluator.[8]

A key problem with systems goals is that the appropriate balance among various systems goals is unknown.[1] There are few studies that specify the conditions needed for long-term survival. This is particularly vexing since some systems goals appear to be contradictory. Table 2-3 provides some examples. For instance, organizations are admonished to be both stable and flexible.† Or they're encouraged to promote both cooperation and competition.

Table 2-3 Five Conflicting Sets of Systems Goals

---

1. The organization should promote cooperation and competition.
2. The organization should be highly diversified with extensive coordination mechanisms.
3. The organization should be hierarchically structured, with those at the top being in control, and organically structured to facilitate employee participation.
4. The organization should plan extensively yet not waste time on inappropriate planning in uncertain situations.
5. The organization should be efficient and flexible with a reserve of underutilized resources.

Source: Adapted from Anderson, J., and Duncan, W. "The Scientific Significance of the Paradox in Administration Theory," *Management International Review*, 17 (1977), 99–106.

*See the end-of-chapter References for a partial list of those using systems goals to evaluate organizations.

†Recently this contradiction has been partially resolved by stressing control over the environment to ensure stability in the production units of the organization. Flexibility is obtained through the financial, marketing, research and development, and personnel units. The idea is that the chances of survival are better if the organization can maintain stability in short-term demands placed on it by others while developing internal flexibility to meet long-term changes beyond its control.

Yet the balance among systems goals is important. Chandler notes that this is a critical problem for top administrators and often guides the strategies and structures they develop for the organization.[3] For example—to what extent should stability be stressed over growth and its accompanying risk? Should the organization forego exploiting new markets or innovations that may threaten its prestige? Answers to these questions partly involve managerial philosophy, which we'll discuss in Chapter 8.

For now you should recognize that systems goals can be used to judge the overall survival potential even if not all the goals are compatible.[6] Furthermore, systems goals are the major basis for evaluating some organizations.[11] Perhaps the best example is the role of profits in rating businesses. Even if a business firm is contributing to society, moving toward mission accomplishment, and producing quality products (i.e., effective), it is rarely called successful unless it is also profitable.[7] If systems goals are not met, the organization may not be viable from a survival point of view.

Derived Goals

Perrow refers to derived goals as uses of power not apparently directed toward accomplishing systems goals or output goals that are consistent with the major societal contribution of an organization.[2] Derived goals stem from an organization's attempt to cope with internal and external pressures.[6] For example, business firms often embrace social responsibility. Top-level executives may or may not personally believe their corporations should do this. But government agencies, public interest groups, and the press are powerful enough to require it.[3] Organizations seeking support from outside units may thus accept goals in return for money, personnel, clients, or legitimization.[5] (Of course, organizations also attempt to influence or manipulate outside groups.)

Similarly, employees may force an organization to favor their goals. For example, the organization may be asked to accept high wages and stable employment as goals. Some go so far as to propose that organizational goals are, or should be, the result of interpersonal interactions within the system that incorporate the goals of the organizational members.[1] In any event, organizations do assume responsibility for actions that appear unrelated to effectiveness or survival.[4] These become derived goals.

Goals and Organizational Rationality—Problems with Goals as Measures of Effectiveness

If you consider organizations to have multiple goals, it is deceptively easy to assume that all organizational activities are rational (goal directed). Philanthropic contributions by business firms can be attributed to the pursuit of some derived goal. Expenditures by a hospital for expensive but rarely used equipment may be related to the desire of the system to be a technical leader in its field. Thus, organizations, like individuals, may try to "keep up with the Joneses." The dominance of one systems goal over another might explain profit restriction in favor of stable growth. Can you explain why a university may be more interested in how decisions are made than in the decisions themselves? You might argue that faculty participation in decision making is an important derived goal. In each case, you might conclude that the action was rational. But, the actions of an organization do not automatically show its intentions.[2,7]

Evaluators outside an organization may be forced to assume rationality to come up with a meaningful set of standards to judge it. But these may not be the goals the organization has set for itself. Etzioni argues that effectiveness studies clearly show that the goals derived from mission statements and official pronouncements are not a meaningful way of assessing organizational intentions.[4] That is, goals *should* rationally tell us what the organization will do and how it intends to organize itself. But they do not provide a very clear picture.[1,11] Operative goals may differ from official goals. Georgiou has gone so far as to suggest that the goal approach has actually limited our understanding of organizations and their operations.[5] There is evidence that large business organizations, for instance, do not "act as if" profits are their primary goal. Instead the desires of powerful administrators and the stability of important external units may be more important in predicting at least one critical concern to managers—whether they keep their jobs. Thus, the question is raised—whose intentions reflect those of the organization?

Even within organizations there appears to be some question as to the relevance of organizational goals in explaining and predicting the actions of the system. Mahoney and Wetcel found striking differences in goal priorities within a sample of corporations.[8] Executives stressed systems goals such as overall productivity. Research and development managers felt these were secondary. They stressed cooperative behavior, staff development, and reliable performance.

To get a more short-term view of an organization's goals, Etzioni, among others, asks the evaluator to look at year-to-year targets.[4] For instance, the *Wall Street Journal* reports that after the 1976 election the Republican Party made a commitment to substantially increase the number of minority Republicans. Some ninety percent of the black vote went Democratic, at the national level. So this seems to be a reasonable way of increasing the chances of electing a Republican president. In 1980 we can see whether or not the Republican party did, indeed, receive substantially more of the black vote.

Accepting the short-run expectations of top managers as organizational goals may provide very useful yardsticks for judging an organization.[10,12] Did

General Motors, for example, maintain its share of the market and get a better return on investment than last year? Yet the precision of these narrow measures comes at the substantial cost of a more accurate picture of organizational outputs.[3] Further, the short-term objectives of top management may merely reflect a strategy for reaching systems, output or derived goals.[6]

Goal-Related Views of Effectiveness

Given the problems of the goal paradigm, you might expect to find a number of alternative approaches in the literature. We outline two related views of effectiveness—systems resource and efficiency—and look at the "goals as constraints" viewpoint.[12]

The Systems Resource Approach. The goal paradigm downplays the importance of environmental factors in evaluating organizations. For instance, one university or corporation may be more successful in reaching its goals merely because it is in a better environment. The systems resource approach starts with the idea that an organization is a transformation system that draws inputs from the environment, transforms these inputs, and then offers its outputs to the environment.[15] Thus, an organization is a giant transformation machine. Several important organizational characteristics are apparent from this view. First, organizations import more resources than they export—they are not perpetual-motion systems. Some resources are "lost" in converting inputs to outputs and in maintaining an organization as a viable entity. The natural tendency of the system is to disintegrate (i.e., it is subject to entropy).[5] Second, the less resources an organization uses to produce a given output the more efficient it is. Third, organizations operate in different environments. Some environments are more fertile than others. Taken as a whole, the organization that efficiently exploits its environment is seen as more effective than one that is efficient but does not take full advantage of external resources.[16]

The concept of effectiveness partially stems from biology.[15] Thus, corn and soybeans are two alternative food sources. When planted in the same field (environment) soybeans yield more protein than corn. The soybean is not necessarily more efficient at transforming soil nutrients into protein, but it better utilizes resources from the air to produce protein than does corn. Hence, soybeans are more "effective" plants. If more effective, why don't we have soybean "toasties" or "soybeans—the breakfast of champions"? The answer is simple and demonstrates the organizational or internal bias of the systems resource approach. Soybeans have a very distinctive flavor that many people do not like. Consumers prefer cornflakes. Similarly, consumers may prefer the products of less exploitive organizations even though these organizations may be less efficient.

There is a second problem with the systems resource approach. Exploitation is a two-way street that may involve a sacrifice in social integration. That is, the exploiting organizations may appear to be more effective by making other parts of the society less effective.[2] For instance, a firm that pollutes the air and water is exploiting natural resources. It could be rated more effective than an organization that institutes expensive pollution controls (but loses efficiency in the process). An organization may be rated more effective because it exploits low-paid female workers or because it appeals to the short-term interests of consumers. As before, the organization rated effective using a systems resource approach might not fare as well when considering social contribution criteria.

Efficiency. Efficiency, in terms of some ratio of inputs to outputs has often been proposed as an indicator of effectiveness.[3,6,8] Any economist can graphically or mathematically "prove" that the more efficient the firm, the greater its profitability (effectiveness).[11] But like other social sciences, economic analysis is built upon stated and unstated assumptions. Three of these are important in analyzing the differences between efficiency and effectiveness: (1) firms are profit-seeking systems; (2) decision makers in firms are rational; and (3) firms operate in a condition of perfect knowledge. But as we have seen, business organizations have multiple goals.[9] Their contributions to society are not just profits but include goods and services. The economic retort is that business firms *act as if* profit were their only goal. Expenditures for pollution control or philanthropy are really consistent with maximizing profit *in the long run*. We could accept such an argument if we were confident that executives reported some positive relationship between philanthropy and future profits. Instead they talk of responsibility to society (a derived goal).[4]

Katz and Kahn see efficiency as one necessity of systems effectiveness (p. 170).[5] Efficiency is, by definition, a ratio of inputs to outputs. Thus, the more efficient unit should be able to get more accomplished with the same resources. Measures of efficiency are concrete and quantifiable, such as units produced in relation to raw materials purchased or the dollar costs of labor. We recognize that the inputs will be greater than the outputs due to loss of energy in the transformation process. But where does all this lost energy go? Does it all just disappear? Some goes for administration, planning, research and development, and the like. There are also organizational outputs that are not easily measured in dollar amounts or not measured at all. Not all of these outputs, if counted, would increase efficiency ratios. External factors such as dirty air, polluted water, and our shrinking wilderness are not included in efficiency ratios.

When efficiency is equated with effectiveness we make two related but subtle assumptions. One, the environmental demands placed on the firm will not change. Two, environmental conditions have an identical impact on the monetary values of inputs and outputs. If the environment changes, the firm must alter its inputs, transformation system, and outputs. Systems designed exclusively to maximize efficiency are rarely flexible. (Human beings, for example, can survive in many physical environments because they are adaptable creatures.) Changes in the quality of inputs or outputs used to compute the ratio may not be reflected in their monetary values. Alterations in the nature and design of products also limit our ability to compare different organizations in the same industry or to plot historically the efficiency of any one organization.

In summary, effectiveness refers to the internal states and outputs of a system compared to other systems or ideals. Efficiency, on the other hand, is a ratio of selected inputs and selected outputs. We propose that efficiency measures may reflect effectiveness when: (1) the objectives of the unit are limited, (2) the environment of the unit is stable, (3) all the inputs and outputs of the unit, both intended and unintended, can be measured in monetary terms. Thus, individual productivity of a machine operator is more appropriate than the number of graduates per full-time faculty member. While overall input-output ratios are often employed to evaluate organizations, they should be used with extreme caution.

Organizational Goals as Constraints. The analyses of societal contribution, organizational goals, and even the systems resource approach all implicitly assume an organization will attempt to maximize its accomplishments. However, several people argue that it is useful to view organization goals as contraints.[10] March and Simon argue there are limits to rationality.[7] Managers do not attempt to maximize goal attainment. Instead, they search for solutions to problems that yield satisfactory outcomes (i.e., "satisficing").[11] Furthermore, it is argued that managers rarely take a global view of effectiveness that would call for optimal balancing among societal contribution, organizational goals, or exploitation of the environment. Managers deal with problems in a piecemeal fashion and search until an acceptable alternative is found.[1]

This view makes practical sense given our ignorance about the interrelationships among various types of goals and our inability to definitively chart the impact of decisions on goal attainment. For instance, profitability for business organizations is not always a desired end but often a constraint. When the profitability constraint is met, the organization may move on to meet the next obstacle.[12] Some of these obstacles are created by those outside the organization. That is, an organization interacts with suppliers, distributors, customers or clients, regulatory agencies, owners, unions, and so on. These groups or individuals want the organization to give them something in exchange for the resources they provide. In this process, depending on the value of the resource and the power to withhold it, these "outsiders" may influence, or even require, an organization to pursue specific goals. For example, a bank may require that a particular financial structure (say a ratio of debt to equity) be maintained by a firm as a condition for a loan. Or the EEOC may require affirmative action programs before a university is eligible for government funding. In this sense, conflicting goals will serve as constraints on an organization. The decision makers may need to consider the trade-offs of accepting these goals at the expense of others. Those who view goals as constraints suggest that the decision makers will find a goal set that satisfies these demands.[11] We will have more to say about the influence of other organizations in the specific environment in Chapter 6. For now, recognize that because of many competing pressures, it is not hard to understand why managers rarely use the more idealized viewpoints that we have stressed. They do not get disturbed when their organizations do not reach toward the ideal.

CONTRASTING THE VIEWS OF ORGANIZATIONAL EFFECTIVENESS—A SUMMARY

In this chapter we've outlined a number of different approaches you can use to evaluate the effectiveness of organizations. Our discussion has stressed the possible inconsistency among evaluations based on societal contribution and different organizational goals.

We first argued that the societal contribution of an organization may be viewed in at least two ways. First is the extent to which the system contributes to society in its major functional area. This view is based on an analysis of societal functions, and partially indicates the values of both the rater and society. A series of views that attempts to minimize the values of the rater are based on the major outputs of the system and the groups that control the organization and benefit from it. Although each system is implicitly or explicitly judged on its major outputs to society, its contribution in other areas is also stressed. If you look at part I of Table 2-4, you can see some illustrations of this perspective.

While the long-term survival of a system may rest on its contribution to society, a more specific series of criteria must be used. We assume that organizations are goal-seeking and can be evaluated on their degree of goal-attainment. Mission, output, systems, and derived goals are major types of objectives. The mission statement helps tie an organization to its societal function. Systems, output, and derived goals are important to an organization and

Table 2-4 Example Effectiveness Criteria For Selected Organizations

	Example Organizations and Expectations			
View of Effectiveness	GM	St. Johns Hospital	EPA	Mafia
I. SOCIETAL CONTRIBUTION				
a. Primary social function	Contribute to economic development	Prolong useful life of individuals	Improve and preserve physical environment	Generate greater power for societal deviants
b. Evaluation of main outputs	Manufacture as many autos as market desires	Provide treatment to the ill	Organize and coordinate efforts to improve environment	Organize and control criminal element in society
c. Evaluation based on control	Increase economic efficiency (profits)	Develop and maintain prestigious staff	More public awareness of EPA role	Develop broader public acceptance of victimless crime
d. Evaluation based on prime beneficiary	Maintain high profits and dividends	Return as many patients to useful lives as possible	Higher air and water quality in major metro areas	More financial returns and power to Dons
II. GOAL ATTAINMENT				
a. Mission	Produce desired products at a profit	Cure the sick	Higher air and water quality	Maximize long-term profits

demonstrate the goal multiplicity found in most units. Of course, goals can also be viewed as constraints. The degree to which the system exploits the environment and systems efficiency has also been used to define effectiveness. Again, Table 2-4 (parts II and III) illustrates these perspectives.

While the goals of an organization can provide a rationale for decision making, it is quite obvious that many different rationales are present in larger organizations. An organization may be evaluated by many individuals on just one aspect of societal contribution or just one type of goal. Yet the astute manager realizes that individuals from different segments of society are likely to judge an organization in a variety of ways. Overemphasis on one goal may

Table 2-4 Example Effectiveness Criteria For Selected Organizations (*Continued*)

	Example Organizations and Expectations			
View of Effectiveness	*GM*	*St. Johns Hospital*	*EPA*	*Mafia*
b. Output goals	Produce best engineered autos in the industry	Have the most technically qualified staff and best equipment	Develop toughest standards possible	Distribution of only highest quality drugs
c. Survival and systems goals	Increase sales and be aware of market conditions	Enhance prestige	Increase congressional support	Minimize public awareness of the Mafia
d. Derived goals	Average 25 MPG for all cars produced	Increase wages for maintenance personnel	Provide clearly written standards	Promote ethnic solidarity
III. GOAL-RELATED VIEWS				
a. Systems resource	Require dealers to repair manufacturer defects	Support preventive health care programs of the government	Get business and critics to develop and enforce codes	Help elect lenient judges
b. Efficiency	Increase output per labor hour	Cut administrative costs	Minimize revisions of codes	Increase revenue per "soldier"

hide deficiencies in other areas. Thus, management must carefully consider a wide range of goals in establishing its own priorities.

Furthermore, as you may note in Table 2-4, some measures are used in more than one category. Profits are the best example. Where one measure reflects more than one type of success, we argue it will become a primary method for evaluating a type of organization. Profits, then, are important not just because they reflect potential returns to stockholders (primary beneficiary view), but because profits have been used as an indicator of systems goal attainment *and* in the systems resource approach to effectiveness. For many corporations' profits are the "bottom line" from several different points of view.

As we mentioned in the overview to this part of the book, societal contribution and goal attainment are broad ways of looking at organizational effectiveness. They provide different perspectives about the success of a system. But our discussion of societal contribution and the different referents for judging goal attainment introduced the idea that environmental, technical, or managerial factors may alter both the goals established for the organization as well as its success. Later in the book we will provide an analysis for predicting various criteria based on other variables in our cone model. Recognize, then, that goals influence and are influenced by a great number of factors.

Lastly, societal contributions and organizational goals do not exhaust the ways of looking at success. Other criteria are important to managers and organization theorists. We will turn to some of these in the next chapter.

MEASUREMENT
MODULE

Here we present some measures of organizational effectiveness that are consistent with the views presented earlier. Obviously, we can't provide *the* measure of effectiveness nor a complete set of measures for any one organization. However, we can provide some examples. We hope these will make the concepts of societal contribution and goal attainment more concrete. First, we'll consider societal contribution. Then we move into some example measures for goal attainment. The presentation of the measures follows the same order as in the literature review.

Our View of Parsons

To us the societal contribution of an organization rests mainly upon its traditional social function. The stress on secondary impacts tends to ignore the basic strength of collective action: the concentration of efforts on limited objectives. For example, business organizations have been criticized because they have not led society in rebuilding our urban centers.[1] We think this type of criticism is misdirected. Instead, you might ask which institutions society asks to maintain our urban centers. Then call these systems to account. If our cities are a mess, and they appear to become more unlivable every day, then our legal-political institutions should be criticized, not businesses or universities.

We would hold organizations accountable in secondary areas of contribution if either of the following conditions is met: (1) the societal impact can be directly linked to the organization; and (2) there are few, if any, organizations in the secondary area to protect the interests of society. For instance, we would hold business firms accountable for pollution based on their production processes.

Analyses of societal contribution are difficult to compare and tend to show deficiencies in the outputs of groups of systems. So let's look at a description of how you might approach the societal contribution of an organization.

Following Parsons, first, you specify some "realistic" assumptions concerning the goals of society.[3] Next, focus on the functional category of the organization to be evaluated. For analyses of economic systems, Johnson considers these societal goals:[2] (1) high and growing Gross National Product (GNP); (2) economic stability; (3) economic efficiency; (4) economic justice;

(5) economic freedom; (6) economic security; and (7) development of honest, hard-working individuals. Organizational outputs and characteristics that appear to increase gross national product, efficiency, and the like are called functional. Similarly, you would list the negative outputs in the major functional areas of the system. This process is difficult and controversial. But it can be supported through the opinions of the general public, industry officials, or others familiar with the role of the organization and its outputs.

You have now estimated the primary contributions of the system in its functional area. You should next attempt to estimate outputs that influence other functions. To continue the example of economic systems, what is the influence of the organization's operations and outputs on the legal-political, sociocultural, and educational aspects of society? Do business firms violate the law in their attempts to promote economic growth and stability, for instance? The end result is likely to be an estimate of accomplishments and deficiencies. These may or may not be summarized into some gross rating of overall effectiveness.

Using Outputs, Control, and Beneficiaries to Estimate Societal Contribution

Friedlander and Pickle provide a format for small business organizations using outputs to selected members of society.[1] They don't try to estimate the contribution of an individual organization against some value structure. Instead, they rely upon the judgments of executives and outsiders familiar with the system. Further, they talk of "fulfillment" rather than contribution. Specifically, they contend that an organization contributes more to society as different members of the firm's environment are more "fulfilled." They concentrate on the community, government, customers, suppliers, and creditors. Exhibit 2-5 shows their criteria. Note that they did not find a very high correspondence among the measures of "fulfillment." Thus, an overall judgement would depend on whom the rater felt was most important. If you are a decision maker following the "goals as constraints" approach, this is very crucial.[2]

Judging Mission Accomplishment

Let's use Community Action Agencies to illustrate the measurement of mission accomplishment. From their outset there were various interpretations of what these agencies really should do. Among the objectives attributed to the Community Action Agencies were: (1) to create political organizations for the poor; (2) to mobilize all the resources of the community to wage an effective "war

Exhibit 2-5   Estimating Societal Contribution for Small Business Firms

Community fulfillment—interviews with executives to estimate their involvement in community affairs including participation in community organizations and fund-raising dinners.

Government fulfillment—interviews with executives concerning income tax penalties, reprimands by tax officials, and compliance with other government regulations.

Suppliers fulfillment—questionnaires mailed to suppliers stressing promptness of payment, fairness of transaction, and the like.

Customer fulfillment—interviews with customers relating to quality of goods or services, neatness, dependability, and overall performance.

Creditor fulfillment—interviews of financial institutions to obtain a series of financial measures of organizational health.

Source: Summarized from Friedlander, F., and Pickle, H. "Components of Effectiveness in Small Organizations," *Administrative Science Quarterly,* 13 (1968), 289–304.

on poverty;" (3) to maintain "maximum feasible participation" of the poor in social welfare programs; (4) to give employment to minorities; (5) to improve the ability of educated minorities to become top-level managers and decision makers.[1] It was some five years and many millions of dollars after the first Community Action Agency opened before there were systematic attempts to decide what they had done! Prior to that, most Agency efforts were expended on developing proper procedures for problem definition.

Exhibit 2-6 shows an attempt at evaluating these agencies based on their mission as outlined in the legislation establishing the units. The list of characteristics of effective and ineffective units includes a number of implicit assumptions. For instance, a clear statement of purpose and actual programs consistent with such statements are assumed desirable. It is also assumed that participation by the poor and greater cooperation are ways in which the agency can alter the conditions of the poor. We should note that the opposite case could be built. Lack of clarity of stated purpose could hide the threat of the agency to powerful community leaders and be considered desirable. Given the complex nature of poverty, perhaps diverse efforts along a broad front are needed. Some might even desire apathy by the poor. Defeat through controversy over an internal power struggle might be rated as an indication that while the agency lost a battle, it started winning the war on poverty. However, Clark[1] has attempted to outline his view so that these issues can be more clearly discussed. He has attempted to measure characteristics either stated or implied in the formal mission.

Exhibit 2-6 Selected Characteristics of Effective and Ineffective Community Action Agencies in Terms of Mission Accomplishment

Effective agencies had:

1. A clear statement of purpose.[a]
2. Actual programs consistent with that purpose.[a]
3. Strong, effective, and articulate leadership—staff and board—of courage, integrity, empathy, and intelligence; a board with some basis of realistic power, tight fiscal controls, and a system for determining quality, relevance, and accountability of programs.
4. Some form of involvement or representation of the poor on the staff at policy-making level.[a]
5. The development of dependable allies in an early confrontation with the local political or other leadership; and the working out of the program either with minimum political interference and with integrity or with the political apparatus as an ally actively protecting the integrity and effectiveness of the community action, anti-poverty program.
6. Some early observable evidence of actual positive changes in the conditions of the poor.[a]

Ineffective agencies had:

1. Lack of clarity of stated purpose.
2. Ambiguity of program in spite of clarity of verbal goals.
3. Weak, and competent, or politically dominated board and staff.
4. Diversion of energies to preoccupation with the form rather than the substance of programs as, for example, preoccupation with the problem of indigenous representation on boards; or the mobilizing of vast energy toward too modest goals, deluding with the appearance of activity; or the tendency to increase the cynicism or apathy of the poor.
5. Inadequate communication between those in the community poverty and the more privileged members of the staff and board; ineffective alliances with persons and groups with power.
6. Defeat through controversy over internal struggle for power; or retreat from community action programs in the face of direct confrontation and conflict with vested interests.
7. Failure to achieve genuine social change.

Source: Clark, K. *A Relevant War Against Poverty* (New York: Metropolitan Applied Research Center, 1966). Reprinted by permission of the author.

[a]Mentioned in the mission statement for Community Action Agencies.

Measuring Output Goals

Output goals may remain fairly constant for a long time. You may need to be technically qualified to evaluate the products and services of an organization. In 1970 the Office of Economic Opportunity attempted to develop an overall estimate of performance for all Community Action Agencies in a selected state.[3] First, there was an attempt to estimate whether programs offered actually provided the services outlined in planning and funding documents. This was accomplished by a series of on-site visits to the local agencies and analyses of reports required for refunding of projects. Next, personnel familiar with the agencies were asked to rate them on outputs using a 27-item questionnaire. While, the questionnaire is considered "confidential," 4 questions have been published and are listed in Exhibit 2-7. Evaluators ranked the agencies they were familiar with on these 4 questions as well as the 23 others. A series of meetings was also conducted in an attempt to derive one overall ranking of the agencies. There was, as you would expect, quite a bit of controversy. But the evaluators finally agreed upon one overall "effectiveness ranking." Agencies were ranked highest to lowest and grouped into 4 categories ranging from superior to ineffective.

Exhibit 2-7   Sample Items Used in an Overall Evaluation of Community Action Agencies

Concerning program performance—how well does the agency achieve the program objectives taking into account qualitative factors and timetables set forth in work programs?

In regard to relations with other social agencies—how well has the agency promoted an understanding of the problems of poverty, strengthened the capacity of other community agencies, stimulated and improved community-wide planning and coordination of programs affecting the poor?

Concerning mobilizing resources—to what extent has the agency, outside its program (a) increased the total flow of resources into the community, and (b) stimulated the redirection of available community resources? How effective are the delivery services of the agency?

Source: Adapted from Osborn, R. N., and Hunt, J. G. "Environment and Organizational Effectiveness," *Administrative Science Quarterly,* 19 (1974).

We should also note that these evaluations of effectiveness were not related to the funding given the agencies either in the year of the evaluation or in subsequent years.[3] Nor did the agencies automatically meet the criteria outlined by Clark.[1] Regardless of how a particular unit was evaluated, it continued to receive about the same amount of federal funds.

Measuring Systems Goals

Perhaps the most detailed and widespread measures of systems goals are used for business organizations. Many people generally assume the short-term financial health of a corporation is crucial to its longer term survival. Let's briefly look at some of the measures used to assess the systems goal attainment of corporations.

The profits of a corporation in the current year and changes from previous profit levels are the simplest and most common measures. However, neither figure is particularly valuable for evaluation in and of itself. We expect large corporations to have huge absolute profits just as we expect the individual who has a large savings account to receive a large interest payment. Thus, the crucial question is relative profits.

Return on investment (ROI) is one of the most popular measures of profitability. It shows the absolute profits in relation to the assets employed to generate revenues. It is simply profits/total assets.

ROI is often broken down into two other ratios that help explain the rate of return. Gross margin is profits/sales; it is a measure of the profits made on each dollar of revenue. Capital turnover is sales/total assets. This indicates a firm's efficiency in using its physical assets. These indicators of relative profitability are often accompanied with other measures of financial health of a firm.

Industry ratios are published regularly in a variety of sources; *Dun's Review and Modern Industry* and Robert Morris Associates' *Statement Studies* are two of the more accessible. Many trade associations, such as the National Hardwood Association, provide balance sheet and income statement analyses for their members. The *Barometer of Small Business* published by the Accounting Corporation of America provides aggregate balance sheet figures and rather extensive income statement data for different regions by sales volume. Also, government agencies such as the Small Business Administration, the U.S. Department of Commerce, the Federal Trade Commission, and the Securities and Exchange Commission publish studies of small businesses, which often include standard financial ratios.

The derivation of systems goals for nonprofit systems is quite difficult. The Iowa State Studies described by Etzioni provide a way of measuring systems goal attainment.[1] It is consistent with our treatment of Parsons' social functions. They focus on four systems goals—adaptation, integration, latency, and goal attainment in the short run. Adaptation was measured in one study of civil defense units by the increase in office space, increases in the personnel budget, the fiscal autonomy of the unit (did it have a separate budget), and whether it was complying with federal paper-shuffling requirements (e.g., relevant forms were filed in Washington). Integration was defined in terms of cooperation with other local units. Specifically, how many formal contacts had been made with local government units, voluntary associations, and the like?* Latency, (pattern maintenance) as defined by Etzioni refers to the human side of the organization. For the civil defense units it was measured by manager satisfaction (in related studies employee commitment and participation were measured). Goal attainment was measured by a mix of subjective judgments of managers and comparison of actual outputs to plans. Interestingly, if an organization was given high marks on meeting short-term objectives, it also rated highly on the other three systems goals. Later analyses also show that managers feel the pressure to meet these systems goals even if their ratings of importance differ.

Measuring Derived Goals

Derived goals are those uses of power not apparently or directly related to specific products or services of the system in its major area of societal contribution. Thus, they're specific to an organization. They often chart the environmental influences the organization deems most important. For business organizations these standards of conduct are tagged "social responsibility."[3] One list of the policies an organization might adopt if it considers itself socially responsible is shown in Exhibit 2-8.

Steiner's list is not the only view of social responsibility. And Friedman and others might criticize organizations that followed Steiner's recommended policies. There can be no question, though, that government standards for pollution, equal opportunity, and employee health and safety become derived goals. Other derived goals are often reflected in a "social audit," which attempts to enumerate the uses of power the business organization deems legitimate.[1] The insurance industry, for instance, lists voluntarism, equality in employment, environmental protection, charitable contributions, community development, and investments for social development (e.g., investments in hospitals where the return is below the market rate).[2]

*In a later study of trade associations the incorporation of member desires by decision makers was used to measure integration.

Exhibit 2-8   Some Policies for Corporate Social Responsibility

"It is the policy of this company . . ."

1. To think carefully about its social responsibility.
2. To make full use of tax deductibility laws through contributions, when profit margins permit.
3. To bear the social costs attendant upon its operations when it is possible to do so without jeopardizing its competitive or financial position.
4. To concentrate action programs on limited objectives.
5. To concentrate action programs on areas strategically related to the present and prospective functions of the business, to begin action programs close to home before acting in far distant regions, and to deal first with what appears to be the most urgent areas of concern to the company.
6. To facilitate employee actions which can be taken as individuals rather than as representatives of the company.
7. To search for product and service opportunities to permit our company and others to make profits while at the same time advancing the social interest; but not all social actions should be taken solely for profit.
8. To take actions in the name of social responsibilities but not at the expense of the required level of rising profits needed to maintain the economic strength and dynamism desired by top management.
9. To take socially responsive actions on a continuous basis, rather than ad hoc, one at a time, or for a short duration.
10. To examine carefully, before proceeding, the socially responsive needs which the company wishes to address, the contributions which the company can make, the risks involved for the company, and the potential benefits to both the company and the society.

Source: Abstracted from Steiner, G. (ed.). *Changing Business Society Interrelationships* (Los Angeles: Graduate School of Management, UCLA, 1975) 145–148. Reprinted by permission of the author.

REFERENCES

I. Societal Contribution

A. Social Function as a Basis for Judging Societal Contribution

[1]Cameron, K. "Measuring Organizational Effectiveness in Institutions of Higher Education," *Administrative Science Quarterly,* 23, 4 (1978), 604–634.

[2]Drucker, P. *Technology, Management, and Society.* New York: Harper & Row, 1970.

[3]Etzioni, A. "The Third Sector in Domestic Missions," *Public Administration Review,* 33, 4 (1973), 311–323.

[4]Friedman, M. "The Social Responsibility of Business is to Increase Profits," *The New Times Magazine.* September 13, 1970, 33, 122–126.

[5]Galbraith, J. K. *The Affluent Society.* Boston: Houghton Mifflin, 1958.

[6]Green, M. J. (ed.). *The Monopoly Makers.* New York: Grossman Publishers, 1973.

[7]Jackson, J. H., and Morgan, C. *Organization Theory: A Macro Perspective for Management.* Englewood Cliffs, N.J.: Prentice-Hall, 1978.

[8]Parsons, H. T., and Kroeber, A. "The Concepts of Culture and of Social System," *American Sociological Review,* 23 (1958), 582–583.

[9]Parsons, H. T., and Smelser, N. *Economy and Society: A Study in the Integration of Economic and Social Theory.* New York: The Free Press, 1956.

[10]Parsons, H. T. *The Social System.* New York: The Free Press, 1951.

[11]Parsons, H. T. *Structure and Processes in Modern Societies.* New York: The Free Press, 1960.

[12]Perrow, C. *Organizational Analysis: A Sociological View.* Belmont, Calif.: Brooks-Cole, 1970.

[13]Pfeffer, J., and Salancik, G. *The External Control of Organizations: A Resource Dependence Approach.* New York: Harper & Row, 1978.

[14]Schumacher, E. F. *Small is Beautiful.* New York: Harper & Row, 1973.

[15]U.S. Department of Health, Education, and Welfare. *Towards a Social Report.* Washington, D.C.: U.S. Government Printing Office, 1969.

B. Output, Control, and Beneficiaries as Bases for Judging Societal Contribution

[1]Argyris, C. *Interpersonal Competence and Organizational Effectiveness.* Homewood, Ill.: Irwin, 1962.

[2]Bass, B. M. "Ultimate Criteria of Organizational Worth," *Personnel Psychology,* 5 (1952), 157–173.

[3]Bender, M. "The Executives' Tax-Free Perk," *The New York Times,* November 30, 1975, Sec. 3, 1–14.

[4]Blau, P., and Scott, W. *Formal Organizations.* San Francisco: Chandler, 1962.

[5]Cyert, R. M., and March, J. G. *A Behavioral Theory of the Firm.* Englewood Cliffs, N.J.: Prentice-Hall, 1963.

[6]Dubin, Robert "Organizational Effectiveness: Some Dilemmas of Perspective," *Organization and Administrative Sciences,* 7 (1976), 7–14.

[7]Etzioni, A. *A Comparative Analysis of Complex Organizations* (revised edition). New York: Free Press, 1975.

[8]Farmer, R., and Richman, B. *Comparative Management and Economic Progress.* Homewood, Ill.: Irwin, 1965.

[9]Green, 1973.

[10]Gross, E. "The Definition of Organizational Goals," *British Journal of Sociology,* 20 (1969), 277–294.

[11]Hall, R. P. "Conceptual, Methodological, and Moral Issues in the Study of Organizational Effectiveness." Working paper, State University of New York, Albany, 1978.

[12]Helmich, D. "Executive Succession in the Corporate Organization: A Current Integration," *Academy of Management Review,* 2 (1977), 252–266.

[13]Katz, D., and Kahn, R. *The Social Psychology of Organizations.* New York: Wiley, 1978.

[14]Keeley, M. "A Social-Justice Approach to Organizational Evalu-

ation," *Administrative Science Quarterly,* 23, 2 (1978), 272–293.

[15]Lawler, E., Hall, D., and Oldham, G. "Organizational Climate: Relationship to Organizational Structure, Process, and Performance," *Organizational Behavior and Human Performance,* 11 (1974), 139–145.

[16]Likert, R. "Some Empirical Tests of System 4." Paper presented at the Annual Meeting of the Academy of Management, Orlando, Florida, August 1977.

[17]Mills, C. *The Power Elite.* New York: Oxford University Press, 1959.

[18]Osborn, R., Jauch, L., and Martin, T. "CEO Succession, Performance and Environmental Conditions." Working paper, Southern Illinois University, Carbondale, 1978.

[19]Parsons, 1960.

[20]Pennings, J. M., and Goodman, P. S. "Toward a Workable Framework." In Paul S. Goodman and Johannes M. Pennings (eds.), *New Perspectives on Organizational Effectiveness.* San Francisco: Jossey-Bass, 1977, 146–184.

[21]Perrow, C. *Organizational Analysis: A Sociological View.* Belmont, Calif.: Brooks-Cole, 1970.

[22]Pfeffer and Salancik, 1978.

[23]Scott, W. "Effectiveness of Organizational Effectiveness Studies." In P. S. Goodman and J. Pennings (eds.), *New Perspectives on Organizational Effectiveness.* San Francisco: Jossey-Bass, 1977, 63–95.

[24]Steers, R. M. "Problems in Measurement of Organizational Effectiveness," *Administrative Science Quarterly,* 20 (1975), 546–558.

[25]Steers, R. *Organizational Effectiveness: A Behavioral View.* Santa Monica, Calif.: Goodyear, 1977.

[26]Thompson, J. D. *Organizations in Action.* New York: McGraw-Hill, 1967.

[27]Webb, R. "Organizational Effectiveness and the Voluntary Organization," *Academy of Management Journal,* 17 (1974), 663–677.

II. Goal Attainment

[1]Cameron, 1978.

[2]Etzioni, A. *A Comparative Analysis of Complex Organizations.* New York: The Free Press, 1961.

[3]Hall, R. H. *Organizations: Structure and Process.* Englewood Cliffs, N.J.: Prentice-Hall, 1972.

[4]Keeley, 1978.

[5]Perrow, C. "Goals in Complex Organizations," *American Sociological Review,* 6 (1961), 854–865.

[6]Steers, 1977.

A. The Mission of the System

[1]Cameron, 1978.

[2]Etzioni, 1973.

[3]Etzioni, 1975.

[4]Khandwalla, P. *The Design of Organizations.* New York: Harcourt, Brace, 1977.

[5]Perrow, 1970.

[6]Steiner, G. *Business and Society.* New York: Random House, 1975.

B. Output Goals

[1]Cameron, 1978.

[2]Clark, K. *A Relevant War Against Poverty.* New York: Metropolitan Applied Research Center, 1966.

[3]Hall, R. *Organizations: Structures and Process.* Englewood Cliffs, N.J.: Prentice-Hall, 1972.

[4]Katz, D., and Kahn, R. *The Social Psychology of Organizations.* New York: Wiley, 1978.

[5]Khandwalla, 1977.

[6]Mott, P. E. *The Characteristics of Effective Organizations.* New York: Harper & Row, 1972.

[7]Osborn, R. N., and Hunt, J. G. "Environment and Organizational Ef-

fectiveness," *Administrative Science Quarterly,* 19 (1974).

[8]Perrow, 1970.

[9]Steiner, G. *Business and Society.* New York: Random House, 1975.

C. Survival and Systems Goals

[1]Anderson, J., and Duncan, W. "The Scientific Significance of the Paradox in Administration Theory," *Management International Review,* 17 (1977), 99–106.

[2]Caplow, T. *Principles of Organization.* New York: Harcourt, Brace and World, 1964.

[3]Chandler, A. *Strategy and Structure.* Cambridge, Mass.: The MIT Press, 1962.

[4]Gibson, J. L., Ivancevich, J. M., and Donnelly, J. H. *Organizations: Structure, Process, and Behavior.* Dallas: Business Publications, Inc., 1973.

[5]Hall, 1978.

[6]Mahoney, T., and Wetcel, W. "Managerial Models of Organizational Effectiveness," *Administrative Science Quarterly,* 14, 3 (1969), 357–365.

[7]Negandhi, A., and Reimann, B. "Task Environment, Decentralization, and Organizational Effectiveness," *Human Relations,* 26 (1973), 203–214.

[8]Pfeffer and Salancik, 1978.

[9]Price, J. L. *Organizational Effectiveness: An Inventory of Propositions.* Homewood, Ill.: Richard D. Irwin, Inc., 1968.

[10]Schein, E. *Organizational Psychology.* Englewood Cliffs, N.J.: Prentice-Hall, 1965.

[11]Steers, 1975.

[12]Thompson, 1967.

D. Derived Goals

[1]Georgiou, P. "The Goal Paradigm," *Administrative Science Quarterly,* 18 (1973), 291–310.

[2]Perrow, 1970.

[3]Pfeffer and Salancik, 1978.

[4]Sebring, R. H. "The Five Million Dollar Misunderstanding: A Perspective on State Government—University Interorganizational Conflicts," *Administrative Science Quarterly,* 22 (1977), 505–523.

[5]Selznick, P. *TVA and the Grass Roots.* Berkeley, Calif.: University of California Press, 1949.

[6]Thompson, J. D., and McEwen, W. "Organizational Goals and Environment," *American Sociological Review,* 23 (1958), 23–30.

E. Goals and Organizational Rationality

[1]Cyert and March, 1963.

[2]Dent, J. "Organizational Correlates of the Goals of Business Managers," *Personnel Management,* 12 (1959), 365–393.

[3]Dubin, 1976.

[4]Etzioni, 1975.

[5]Georgiou, 1973.

[6]Katz and Kahn, 1978.

[7]Keeley, 1978.

[8]Mahoney and Weitzel, 1969.

[9]Osborn et al., 1978.

[10]Pennings, J. M. "The Relevance of the Structural-Contingency Model for Organizational Effectiveness," *Administrative Science Quarterly,* 20 (1975), 393–410.

[11]Simon, H. "On the Concept of Organizational Goal," *Administrative Science Quarterly,* 9 (1964), 1–22.

[12]Steers, 1975.

F. Goal-Related Views of Effectiveness

[1]Behling, O., and Schriesheim, C. *Organizational Behavior: Theory Research and Application.* Boston: Allyn and Bacon, 1976.

[2]Hirsch, Paul M. "Organizational Effectiveness and the Institutional Environment," *Administrative*

Science Quarterly, 20 (1975), 327–344.

[3]Holzer, M. (ed.). *Productivity in Public Organizations.* Port Washington, N.Y.: Kennikut Press, 1966.

[4]Johnson, H. L. *Business in Contemporary Society: Framework and Issues.* Belmont, Calif.: Wadsworth Publishing Co., 1971.

[5]Katz and Kahn, 1978.

[6]Kinckman, R. "Conceptual and Technical Considerations in Cost Benefit Analysis." In J. Sutherland (ed.), *Management Handbook for Public Administrators.* New York: Van Nostrand Reinhold, 1978.

[7]March, J. G., and Simon, G. *Organizations.* New York: Wiley, 1958.

[8]McLaughlin, C. P. "Productivity and Effectiveness in Government." In J. Sutherland (ed.), *Management Handbook for Public Administrators.* New York: Van Nostrand Reinhold, 1978.

[9]Parsons, 1956.

[10]Pfeffer and Salancik, 1978.

[11]Samuelson, P. A. *Economics.* New York: McGraw-Hill, 1973.

[12]Seashore, S. E., and Yuchtman, E. "Factorial Analysis of Organizational Performance," *Administrative Science Quarterly,* 12 (1967), 337–395.

[13]Simon, H. A. *Administrative Behavior* (2nd edition). New York: The Free Press, 1957.

[14]Steiner, 1975.

[15]Von Bertalanffy, L. *General Systems Theory.* New York: George Braziller, 1968.

[16]Yuchtman, E. and Seashore, S. E. "A System Resource Approach to Organizational Effectiveness," *American Sociological Review,* 32 (1967), 891–903.

IV. Measurement Module
A. Our View Of Parsons

[1]Edmunds, S., and Letey, J. *Environmental Administration.* New York: McGraw-Hill, 1973.

[2]Johnson, 1971.

[3]Parsons, 1956.

B. Using Outputs, Control, and Beneficiaries To Estimate Societal Contribution

[1]Friedlander, F., and Pickle, H. "Components of Effectiveness in Small Organizations," *Administrative Science Quarterly,* 13 (1968), 289–304.

[2]Steers, 1975.

C. Judging Mission Accomplishment

[1]Clark, 1966.

[2]Friedlander and Pickle, 1968.

D. Measuring Output Goals

[1]Clark, 1966.

[2]Osborn, R. "Environment and Organizational Effectiveness." Unpublished dissertation, Kent State University, 1971.

[3]Osborn and Hunt, 1974.

E. Measuring Systems Goals

[1]Etzioni, 1975.

[2]Kroncke, C. O., Nemmers, E. E., and Grunewald, A. E. *Managerial Finance Essentials.* St. Paul: West, 1976.

[3]Sprecher, C. R. *Introduction to Investment Management.* Boston: Houghton Mifflin, 1975.

[4]Van Horne, J. C. *Financial Management and Policy.* Englewood Cliffs, N.J.: Prentice-Hall, 1977.

F. Measuring Derived Goals

[1]Bauer, R. A., and Fenn, D., Jr. *The Corporate Social Audit.* New York: Russell Sage Foundation, 1972.

[2]Preston, L. E., and Post, J. *Private Management and Public Policy.* Englewood Cliffs, N.J.: Prentice-Hall, 1975.

[3]Steiner, 1975.

chapter **3** PERFORMANCE AND
EMPLOYEE MAINTENANCE

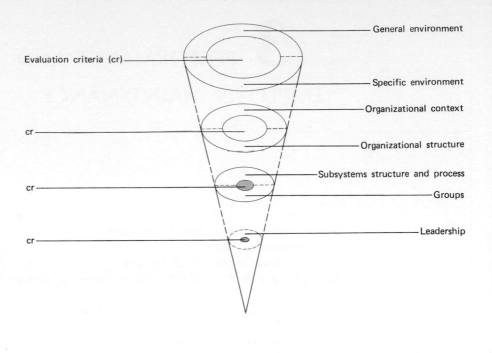

The previous chapter explored evaluation of the organization on the basis of its effectiveness. As a manager, you may never be asked to systematically evaluate the effectiveness of an organization. But you probably will have to evaluate the performance of units and individuals. Thus, this chapter explores another class of success criteria for evaluating organizations.

As a manager you are likely to be judged on the performance of your unit, even though it may be virtually impossible to identify the outputs of that unit. Furthermore, if present trends continue, you will probably judge and be judged on a whole set of employee-based criteria. We call these employee maintenance criteria because they center on factors necessary to attract and maintain an adequate work force. Included here are variables such as satisfaction, morale, involvement, commitment, turnover, and absenteeism. At the same time, organizations and their managers are beginning to be evaluated on a new series of standards. While these are presently an inconsistent collection of questions and yardsticks, they carry an impressive banner. They are called "quality of working life."

Our discussion of performance centers most on the pragmatic develop-ment of standards for evaluation. Thus, we begin the discussion with an anal-ysis of organizational means-ends chains. Then we show how evaluations of subsystems can be related to evaluation of organizational effectiveness. As we show, there are a number of issues involved in moving from one to the other. The treatment of employee maintenance criteria is more academic, mainly because of a common misconception. Many managers believe that all main-tenance criteria are about the same and that they're good predictors of per-formance. As we will see, not all employee maintenance criteria are highly interrelated. Moreover, satisfaction is not a good predictor of performance.

SYSTEMS GOALS AND SUBSYSTEMS PERFORMANCE

To understand the types of goals faced by most managers, it is important to grasp the link between the actions of units and the goals of an organization. It is convenient to look at the process used to translate organizational goals into action. This process can be called the organization's means-ends chain. Although many organizations may not systematically develop means-ends chains, it appears that most can be studied as if they had.

Means-Ends Chains

As a way of translating organizational goals into action, we can start with the operative goals of an organization. Operative goals can be divided and as-signed to administrative units. The subdivision and assignment yields a series of specific objectives that are the means toward accomplishing an organiza-tion's broader operative goals. For the administrative units, however, these specific objectives become their goals. In turn, the "goals" of each adminis-trative unit are further elaborated and subdivided. They are assigned to lower level units as goals. This process of dividing and elaborating means, which become goals for lower-level units, can continue down to the individual worker.

This division of goals into more specific subcomponents and the alloca-tion of individuals, money, and materials to accomplish specific tasks yields a division of labor. Of course, the means-ends chain and its accompanying division of labor don't just automatically occur in an organization. They are influenced by environmental, technological, organizational, and personnel factors. All of this is discussed at greater length in later chapters. For now it's important to understand that means-ends chains exist. They provide a basis for measuring the contribution of subunits and individuals to the goal accomplishment of an organization, and they are specific to it.

Let's look at means-ends chains more closely. We consider how a portion of such a chain might look for a small, electronic components manufacturer. The owner and president has established three important operative goals for the coming year: (1) growth in sales; (2) adequate return on investment; and (3) perfection of a new component. The president and key department heads covering production, marketing, finance, product development, and personnel decide on the general activities (means) necessary in each of these areas to accomplish these three goals. The means to accomplish the president's operative goals then become the goals for each of the areas. These are then broken down further within each area until we get to the worker level. In production this means-ends chain might culminate in a set of numerical production standards for such things as output, scrap rate, and rework time for each production employee.

Our example means-ends chain culminates in a set of numerical performance standards. It is appropriate where standards of performance desirability can clearly be established. However, in many cases (e.g. research and development) it's difficult if not impossible to set such standards, at least in the short run. Here, if you have a good idea about cause and effect relationships,[3] a means-ends chain might emphasize *activities* rather than end results. The activities are believed to lead to desired end results even though it is impossible to set standards for them. In this case, job descriptions may serve as the basis for performance evaluation.

Miner and Miner define a job description as a written statement of the tasks, duties, and behaviors required in a given job (p. 151).[1] Here these things would be considered the means for accomplishing higher level goals. The performance measures would be based on how well these things were carried out. A less direct variation of this would move one step further to define the means in terms of qualifications that individuals are thought to need to perform job activities. Often these characteristics are formally specified in a written job specification, which may elaborate on the job description.*

A widely discussed management technique that has been designed to facilitate the all-important means-ends analysis is that of management by objectives (MBO). There are a number of variations of the procedure. In essence it requires individuals and supervisors to work out specific statements of performance objectives and action plans in a number of areas. Each of these objectives has a specific time period for its accomplishment. At the end of that

---

*In addition to their possible use for performance evaluation, job descriptions and specifications are used for a number of other organizational activities (see Reference 1 for a good discussion).

time, performance is compared against objectives. The nature of the objectives can vary from activities to specific performance standards. A well-developed MBO system simply makes sure action plans and "goals" are clearly articulated and measured. While easiest to apply where performance standards are clearly measurable, MBO systems have also been used where such standards are not possible.*

Issues in Means-Ends Analysis. In the process of developing means-to-ends, we often see global goals split into tasks that are assigned to individuals and subunits. In this process, three key issues emerge. Let's highlight these with our previous example of the electronic components producer.

First, even though the production workers met their assigned performance standards, the plant could be closed for failure to meet pollution standards. Organizational effectiveness may depend on external factors beyond the control of subunits in the system.

The second issue is that aggregating individual measures may fail to represent organizational effectiveness due to suboptimization. The division of goals results in gaps and contradictory assignments to different subunits. For example, the marketing department may be assigned a sales target. The financial unit may be charged with minimizing credit losses. If the finance unit minimized credit losses, sales would be hurt. If sales were made to risky customers, credit losses would increase. Thus, to maximize one at the expense of the other would result in lower effectiveness for the organization as a whole even though each unit would be meeting its assigned goals. Suboptimization is also seen when organizations attempt to meet multiple goals. Too much emphasis on one goal forces the sacrifice of achieving another. Short-term profitability and efficiency may be emphasized at the expense of long-term goals such as prestige or flexibility. In the case of the electronics firm, the president would want to be careful not to suboptimize by increasing short-term output at the expense of long-term adaptability.

A third important concern involves positive synergy. The total performance of an organization can be greater than the sum performance of its subsystems. Thus, a measure of effectiveness based on aggregating individual data can understate the effectiveness of the system. If this understatement were a constant across units, the concept of synergy would not be important in judging unit performance. But such is not the case. It is influenced by how well the coordination or integration function is handled. This function is discussed in Chapter 9. For now you should recognize that synergy, like suboptimization and factors beyond the control of subunits, suggests that aggregating the lower-level goals to make statements about overall effectiveness may be

*Tosi and Carroll[4] and Odiorne[3] discuss MBO systems in considerable detail.

a misleading procedure. Aggregated measures may overstate (due to suboptimization), understate (due to synergy), or well represent the global measure.

Changing the Focus of Criteria from Systems to Subsystems Levels

So far we have assumed that at the subsystems level you are only concerned with output goals. Indeed, these are important as the means-ends chain analysis suggests. But there are other parallels between criteria at the systems level (discussed in Chapter 2) and those at subsystems levels.

Just as at the systems level, heads of subsystems are concerned with survival and "systems goals." Here, however, it's not the total organization, but flexibility and growth of the *subunit itself* that becomes prime. This may help you to see why suboptimization can occur—more emphasis may be placed on survival of the unit than on how it contributes to the organization.

Yet another basis for evaluating subsystems is whether they are accomplishing their mission and contributing to the organization (a parallel to societal contribution and mission accomplishment at the systems level). The subsystem could be performing well with respect to its mission from an output point of view, yet its relative contribution to the system may be minimal. Let's look at a couple of examples.

The Civil Defense (CD) agency of the Department of Defense might be judged superior on output goals. Development of survival plans and early warning capabilities might be accomplished given its budget (efficient). Yet, compared to the Army or Navy as a subunit, you might not consider CD as particularly important. Similarly, the registrar's office at your university may be very efficient. But relative to other academic subunits, its mission may be judged to be much less important, even though it was successful in its accomplishment.

From the standpoint of a subsystems manager, you are likely to face a whole series of means-ends chains developed for different types of organizational success criteria. Just as at the organizational level, the contribution of your unit may be judged on the quality of its goods and/or services, its adaptability and flexibility, and probably a whole host of derived goals. And again, as in evaluating organizational effectiveness, judging a subsystem on different criteria is likely to yield different ratings of performance. We will analyze the organizational function of different types of subsystems in Chapter 11. For now you should recognize that many subsystems are primarily evaluated on the basis of an implicit or explicit means-ends chain related to its organizational function and on a series of derived goals.

Problems in Evaluating Subsystems Performance

Since you will probably be asked to evaluate units, let's look at potential problems in evaluating subsystems performance. We will address employee maintenance in more detail shortly. We think evaluators should be particularly sensitive to the purpose of the rating, the dangers of measuring irrelevant outputs, relative contribution, and bias.

Purpose. For some purposes, raw performance data will be used to compare one unit with another, or a unit to its mission. In others, various factors that may have caused the performance will be taken into account. For instance, you may judge the performance of a marketing unit based on whether total sales volume reached its target. You may or may not be concerned with *why* the sales volume failed to reach the target (e.g., did production produce enough goods to satisfy demand generated?). This can create a problem for determining whether the performance of a unit was in or out of control of those responsible for its performance. Thus, some prefer to adjust performance criteria for critical contingencies.

Our primary concern in this book is with the absolute level of subunit performance (and organizational effectiveness) without adjusting for contingencies. We will be interested later in how well various conditions help us in predicting or explaining performance differences.

For purposes of allocating rewards or instituting corrective action for substandard performance (performance appraisal) on the other hand, you would want to use adjusted performance figures that did reflect various contingencies. Let's look at a couple of examples to clarify this.

Suppose that you are interested in evaluating several academic departments at a university. As one indicator, you might use the number of articles published by the professors in each department. To do that you would simply need to come up with a total count of articles and use that as a performance measure—the higher the total, the better the performance. Similarly, you might evaluate the performance of sales personnel in terms of total sales less returns. Conditions such as computer facilities or graduate assistance in the case of professors, or territorial potential or advertising in the case of sales personnel, would not be reflected in the performance measure as such. Instead, they would be used as contingency variables for analysis purposes. However, if you are interested in deciding on how large a raise to give to the professors or salespeople, or whether to allocate resources to one department rather than another, you would want to adjust their performance to take into account their "opportunities to perform." Of course, efficiency measures and those based on a systems resource approach already incorporate one or a number of contingencies. This is because they are input/output measures, whereas contingencies are a part of the input component of the measure.

Regardless of the purpose of the evaluation, you should be aware of three additional potential problems—irrelevant criteria, relative contribution, and measurement bias.

Measuring Irrelevant Outputs. Each performance measure should be directly related to the objectives established for the subsystem.[4] Thus, estimates of personality characteristics, education, or experience of members of the subsystem are not always relevant when performance evaluation of the unit is seen strictly under a goals approach to systems effectiveness. Unfortunately, the outputs of a subsystem may be difficult to measure, aren't apparent in the short-run, or can't be specified, as for some research and development groups. Thus, indirect and sometimes apparently irrelevant characteristics must be used to estimate outputs. Further, one measure won't tap all the performance dimensions desired by top-level management. You're often forced into a trade-off between global measures, which tend to cover up important differences, and specific detailed measures that by themselves may be irrelevant or not inclusive enough.

Relative Contribution. We previously examined one aspect of relative contribution (the performance of the subunit relative to its own mission and that of other subunits). Another aspect of relative contribution centers on the difficulty in separating subsystems from individual performance. In evaluating managers it's not unusual to cite the performance of the units they supervise. The manager of a profitable regional outlet of a large conglomerate might be called successful. However, management is only one component of unit performance. It's reasonable to expect that there may be high-performing managers in charge of low-performing units, and vice versa. While there's no decent solution, evaluation of managers may be based on those individual actions and attitudes higher level managers or the evaluator thinks are related to high unit output (i.e., measures of potential contribution). A related aspect of separating subsystems and individual performance is isolating the unique contribution of any one group member. We discuss this problem at greater length in the chapter on groups.

The heart of these relevancy- and relative-contribution problems is summarized by Campbell et al.[2] in terms of a "deficiency-excessiveness continuum" (pp. 107–108). This means that measures that are too narrow or irrelevant are *deficient* in terms of what they should be measuring. Measures that are so broad that they include aspects beyond the control of the unit in question are termed *excessive*.

Bias. Bias in evaluating a unit or individual manager is always a problem. Many bias problems are more evident when using rating scales. Ratings are subject to halo, constant error, recency error and central tendency error, among other problems.[1,3] Halo refers to the tendency to use only one aspect of performance in judging a unit or its members. For example, a high-sales producer could also be called dynamic, easy to get along with, and a self-starter solely on the basis of sales volume. An academic department may be rated as excellent based on the prestige of one or a few professors (much as a university can be rated based on its football team's record).

Constant error refers to different raters using different standards when judging the performance of employees with similar jobs. Their standards are not "constant." An "A" may be harder to get from one instructor than another. Even though they teach the same course, some raters are tougher than others. Recency error is the tendency for recent actions to drive out a balanced evaluation of a unit or individual over time. Central tendency error occurs when groups or individuals are rated as quite similar when in fact there are differences among them. We don't discuss these problems nor some of the possible solutions in detail. But you should be aware that developing a rating scale for judging unit or individual performance isn't a simple task.* In the Measurement Module, you will see some measures and instruments that illustrate the approaches and problems of lower-echelon performance assessment.

EMPLOYEE MAINTENANCE

Employee maintenance is a term used to describe a whole series of criteria centering on the attachment (or withdrawal) of employees to an organization, their satisfaction, morale and esprit de corps. In many organizations employee maintenance is an important derived goal. Many managers appear to believe that employee maintenance factors predict performance and/or reflect the degree of goal attainment. As we will see, maintenance is not a consistent predictor of performance. But it is likely you'll be expected to develop satisfied, committed subordinates, and that your unit will be expected to have low absenteeism and turnover.

Satisfaction, Morale, and Esprit de Corps

Perhaps the most frequently mentioned aspects of employee maintenance are satisfaction and morale. Since these terms can have different meanings, let's examine each in detail.

*See References 1, 2, and 3.

Job satisfaction is "a pleasurable or positive emotional state resulting from the appraisal of one's job or job experiences." Morale is often used as a synonym for satisfaction.*,[1]

Morale also has another meaning. It can be defined as "an attitude of satisfaction with, a desire to continue in, and a willingness to strive for the goals of a particular group or organization."[1,4]Note that this definition is more future oriented than the definition of satisfaction and that it is based on a sense of common purpose. Moreover, it presumes that individual and unit goals are compatible. We prefer the term esprit de corps. Is the difference between satisfaction and esprit de corps important? Yes. An individual's appraisal of a specific job situation may not share a common purpose with others in an organization. While an individual who achieves his or her job goals may feel more confident about the future, the reverse may not hold.[1] Furthermore, satisfaction and esprit de corps may not be related to the same conditions. Lastly, the notion of esprit de corps assumes that satisfaction and a willingness to strive toward group or organizational goals are highly interrelated. They may or may not be. Here, we will concentrate on satisfaction.

While we can talk of job satisfaction as a global factor, it is also useful to break it down into components. Table 3-1 shows nine such components. The first six deal with events or conditions. The last three ask individuals about organizational agents. We should note that satisfaction with different events or agents may vary. You may be satisfied with the work but not the pay. You may be satisfied with co-workers but not with the company and management. Note also that an attitude toward an agent (e.g., supervision) may be influenced by events (e.g., pay or promotion). Or the attitude toward agents (co-workers) could alter satisfaction with events (e.g., recognition).[1]

Involvement and Commitment

With a clearer division of esprit de corps and satisfaction, we find criteria centering on involvement and commitment. Job involvement is the extent to which an individual is preoccupied or fully absorbed with his or her job. Locke[1] suggests that a person involved in a job would take it seriously, be preoccupied with it, and would have important values at stake in the job. That person's moods and feelings would also be significantly affected. Such a person would be more likely, according to Locke, to feel extremely satisfied or *extremely dissatisfied* with a job depending upon accomplishments. On the other hand, an uninvolved person would have less extreme emotional responses.*

*See References 2 and 3.
*Additional ways of looking at job involvement are treated in Rabinowitz and Hall.[3]

Table 3-1 Some Popular Dimensions of Job Satisfaction

1. Work: Intrinsic interest, variety, opportunity for learning, difficulty, amount, chances for success, control over pace and methods.
2. Pay: Amount, fairness or equity, payment method.
3. Promotion: Opportunities, fairness.
4. Recognition: Praise for accomplishment, credit for work done, criticism.
5. Benefits: Pension, medical, annual leave, vacation.
6. Working conditions: Hours, rest pauses, equipment, temperature, ventilation, humidity, location, physical layout.
7. Supervision: Supervisory style and influence, technical, human relations, administrative skill.
8. Co-workers: Competence, helpfulness, friendliness.
9. Company and management: Concern for workers, pay and benefit policies.

Source: Summarized from Locke, E. A. "The Nature and Causes of Job Satisfaction." In Dunnette, M. D. (ed.), *Handbook of Industrial and Organizational Psychology* (Chicago: Rand McNally, 1976).

While involvement and commitment may sometimes be used interchangeably, they are also differentiated from each other. Commitment is a broader term, centering on attitudes toward an organization. Porter and Smith define it as "the nature of an individual's relationship to an organization, such that a highly committed person will indicate: (1) a strong desire to remain a member of the particular organization, (2) a willingness to exert high levels of effort on behalf of the organization, and (3) a definite belief in and acceptance of the values and goals of the organization" (p. 2).[2]

As with esprit de corps, commitment is more management oriented than involvement. You can be involved in your work but not committed to the organization.

Withdrawal

The flip side of attachment, measures such as satisfaction, involvement and commitment, is withdrawal. Turnover (job separation) is one key measure of withdrawal. Absenteeism is another. Less direct indicators would also include injuries or accidents, and dispensary visits, among other things.[1,2,3] It has been argued that those upset at work are more susceptible to injury and/or illness. There is also evidence that some employees will use dispensary visits to get away from an unpleasant work setting. Frequent "sick call visits" in the army are often interpreted as just such an indicator.

Turnover and absenteeism have often been treated as being similar. Yet they differ in at least three important ways.[5] First, the negative consequences to employees are generally less severe for absenteeism than for turnover. This is especially true when there is a sick leave or other excused absence policy through which employees may be paid even when absent. It might not be true, of course, where an organization evoked strict disciplinary measures (e.g., docked pay, threat of firing) for absenteeism. Second, absenteeism is more likely than termination to be a spur-of-the-moment reaction. Finally, absenteeism may sometimes be a substitute for turnover, especially if there aren't many alternative job opportunities. Here, there is temporary avoidance of an unpleasant situation without the loss of benefits, and so on, that would occur with separation.[4]

Empirical Relationships among Maintenance Criteria

We have compared and contrasted various maintenance criteria, conceptually. Now let's go a bit further and examine empirical relationships among the measures. While there is some inconsistency in the literature, the following patterns have received empirical support. Satisfaction, commitment, and involvement all seem to tap slightly different aspects of attachment to the organization.[11] That is, attachment could arise from several different sources including colleagues, professional opportunities, and/or rewards offered by the organization. These various bases for attachment may be partial substitutes for one another. You might feel a strong attachment to the organization because it provides ties to your profession even though the rewards the organization provides may not interest you very much.[3,4]

A number of studies suggest that job satisfaction and involvement are moderately related.[5,11] Thus, it is possible for an individual to find several sources of attachment to an organization.

What relationship do withdrawal measures have with attachment? Turnover and absenteeism have received the most research interest. Thus, we focus on these.

Early reviews suggested that low satisfaction would lead to high turnover. Porter and Steers[9] reviewed 15 recent studies of which 14 support this negative relationship for overall satisfaction and its components. One causal study demonstrated that raising satisfaction (through changes in company policies) reduced later turnover.[2]

As for absenteeism, early reviews suggested that high satisfaction would lead to less absenteeism. Porter and Steers[9] found limited support for this. Recent reviews suggest that there is no *necessary* relationship between the two. A possible explanation for this is that contingency variables may operate between satisfaction and absenteeism.[13] Another possibility is that absenteeism will only be related to satisfaction when such behavior is under the control of the employee. Here the argument is that, in many cases, absenteeism is subject to extraneous forces such that satisfaction has little or no impact on it.[1,12]

A number of studies have found turnover to be related to job involvement and organizational commitment. Interestingly, there was evidence in these studies indicating that the relationship between turnover and these variables was stronger than between turnover and satisfaction.[5,8,10] There was also mixed evidence for absenteeism and job involvement. In one case there was no relationship, while in another case the hypothesized negative relationship was found.

What can we conclude from the studies? When evaluating individuals, it may be important to examine elements such as job satisfaction, involvement, commitment, absenteeism, and turnover separately. It's apparent that each of these has slightly different causes and implications for an organization. To link these criteria more closely, one or a number of contingency variables needs to be included. Also, more causal research needs to be conducted before we can assert a pattern of relationships that will lead from commitment to involvement to satisfaction to withdrawal.

Organizational Implications

These relationships, though complex, have important organizational implications. Managers want committed individuals who are involved in their jobs, and they often believe that less-satisfied individuals are more likely to be absent and more likely to leave the organization. Thus, we treat all of these variables in one category: employee maintenance. Furthermore, satisfaction, involvement, commitment, and withdrawal, separately and together, are often viewed as important derived goals.

As we explained in Chapter 2, derived goals may not be directly related to mission accomplishment. Yet they are goals toward which an organization will strive. Managers of subunits may be evaluated on the basis of whether unit-member attachment is high, or withdrawal is low. For instance, the organization may be genuinely concerned with employee satisfaction as an end in itself. There is evidence that job satisfaction is related to family attitudes and relationships, a person's self-concept, physical and mental health, and even mortality.[6] The research is not always clear as to causality. But some employers with true concern for employees will attempt to provide high job satisfaction. Further, to the extent that factors like satisfaction do cause turnover, important cost savings can result if it can be controlled.[7]

The final reason why these maintenance criteria are important is because there is a *belief* that there is a relationship between these and performance criteria (e.g., many managers argue that happy workers are more productive). Thus, you should recognize that when managers of subsystems are evaluated, these criteria are likely to be included as part of the means-ends chain *assumed* to be important for accomplishing the unit's goals. (Remember, earlier in the chapter we suggested that sometimes critical contingencies were used to analyze causes for performance.)

Unfortunately, these assumptions are not very valid, which brings us to a related question. One, so important, that we devote a separate section to the relationship between performance and employee maintenance. The major question seems to be, is employee maintenance a criterion, or is it a variable used to predict other phenomena like performance?

Performance and Employee Maintenance

Attachment. As noted above, many treat attachment as important, under the assumption that this "causes" better performance. However, no consistent relationship has been found between performance and job involvement or commitment.[10] The bulk of research here, though, has focused on satisfaction.

Is there justification for the intuitive feeling that greater satisfaction leads to higher performance? Over a half a century ago there was evidence that productivity could improve or remain constant while satisfaction was *declining*.[7,12] Numerous studies and reviews suggest that satisfaction is a poor predictor of performance.[3,5,11]

A more fruitful direction seems to assume that previous performance causes later satisfaction. That may appear strange to you at first. But think about the last time you won a competitive event. Didn't that lead to a feeling of satisfaction? Probably the best known advocates of the performance causes satisfaction notion are Porter and Lawler.[9] They present some evidence indicating that differential performance determines rewards, which then produce variance in satisfaction. The rewards can either be intrinsic (self-reward) or extrinsic (given by someone else). In either case, satisfaction is considered to be a result of performance-related rewards. This position has received some recent research support using methodologies allowing causal tests.[1,2,3]

Locke[5] and Triandis, among others, suggest that satisfaction and performance may be linked indirectly.[13] Let's summarize Triandis' approach, which uses pressure for production as a variable influencing the satisfaction-performance relationship. Figure 3-2 highlights the key points. Point 1 is the condition of minimum pressure and maximum satisfaction (found in utopia); a worker gets out much and puts in little. A small amount of performance would be observed based on a person's activity drive. Pressure increases through point 4. There, satisfaction is still high and performance is very high. From point 4 to 5 the increase in pressure increases dissatisfaction so performance drops. Point 5 is the "just get by" position of indifference. From here on performance may be driven up by pressure while satisfaction drops sharply to point 7. Only a small amount of pressure beyond point 7 moves the worker to point 8 ("shoot me, I don't care").

While Triandis reports no direct evidence bearing on this explanation, the literature concerning standards is consistent with the general notion.[6]

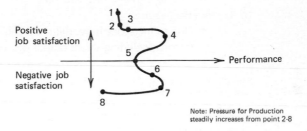

Figure 3-2 Job satisfaction—productivity relationships conditioned by pressure for production.

Turnover from a Different Perspective. We have treated turnover as a form of organizational withdrawal. Indeed, that is one way of looking at it. However, if we consider turnover in general and not just involuntary turnover (which is what withdrawal implies), then turnover can be looked at as something more than a simple withdrawal measure. Price[9] describes turnover "as the degree of movement across the membership boundary of an organization" (p. 61). Included here are persons either *coming into or leaving* an organization. Excluded are those who are promoted and transferred from within. Given this notion of turnover as not just involuntary separation but the flow of people in and out of an organization or subunit, Price sets forth a number of propositions, which have varying amounts of support in the literature. The essence of these is summarized in Table 3-3.

Perhaps, the key point to note about the items in the table is that Price treats turnover as a *causal* variable. In traditional discussions it tends to be treated as a resultant rather than as a cause of dissatisfaction and the like.

Turnover in top management (succession) has received special attention

Table 3-3 The Essence of a Number of Turnover Propositions by Price

Increasing turnover *causes:*

1. Increased bureaucratization,[a] via:

   Increasing administrative staff ratio, increased formalization, less participation
   - Due to more training and development and the disruption of informal processes

2. Lower satisfaction[b]
   - Due to increased conflict and difficulty reaching consensus

3. Higher innovation[b]
   - Due to reduced previous obligations, disruption of previous communication process, expectation of changes by power holders

4. Lower subordinate conformity[b]
   - Due to turnover of a superior

5. Lower effectiveness[c]
   - Due to increases in recruitment, selection and placement, on-the-job factors (including direct output decreases), and separation

Source: Summarized from Price, J. L., "The Effects of Turnover on the Organization, *Organization and Administrative Sciences,* 7 (1976), 61–88.

[a]Medium amount of research support.

[b]Lower amount of research support.

[c]Large amount of research support.

in the literature.[4] Studies of large corporations suggest that low profitability may not be the most important predictor of who remains in the executive suite. Top management appears to be held accountable for developing a stable and favorable organizational environment. Succession studies have also been used to estimate which goals large corporations give the highest priority. Some analyses suggest that growth may be given more weight than short-term profitability. Further succession studies suggest that a chief executive brought in from the outside is more likely to reshuffle the executive suite. However, just replacing top management may not be the key to improving short-term corporate performance. Who runs the organization does make a difference; but it is only one factor among many. Lastly, some scholars suggest that succession in the boardroom may be a way an organization develops closer ties with related ones. That is, succession is a mechanism for coping with environmental pressure.

Again, we see how a criterion may be viewed as both an end in itself and a contingency that influences other criteria such as effectiveness. Since we aren't absolutely certain about various causal relationships, we'll continue to use employee maintenance as criteria. Once again, these are often viewed this way in organizations. Evaluation of your performance as a unit manager may be based on aggregate data, which reflect the state of withdrawal and attachment to the organization, in your unit.

THE QUALITY OF WORKING LIFE

There are several individuals who argue that providing employee maintenance is not enough.[2,3] Organizations should shoulder a broad set of responsibilities to ensure that they promote employee growth and development. There are several different views of how and why organizations should promote the "quality of working life." However, most authors in the area are deeply concerned about how organizations treat individuals. Some are concerned just with employees while some are more concerned with how organizations relate to all individuals in the society.

Table 3-4 provides a range of views held by people active in this area.[1,4,5,0,7,8] As you study the table keep the following information in mind.

First, these quality of working-life conceptions differ substantially in terms of breadth and/or depth. The narrowest is perhaps Chernes. He essentially defines quality of working life in terms of job characteristics.

Walton utilizes an approach that concentrates in considerable depth on a broad range of organizational variables. Sheppard, in contrast, emphasizes a classification scheme that allows systematic comparison of working-life indicators across regions, industries, and so on.

Taking a still different tack, Seashore argues that you need to look at the quality of working life from the standpoint of different audiences. The indicators will not necessarily be the same for each.

Finally, Dyer and Hoffenberg, and Goodale, Hall, Burke, and Joyner look at quality of working life as encompassing societal as well as job indicators. Goodale et al. attempt to integrate quality of working-life concerns with the broader concept of overall quality of life.

Second, these views vary in terms of how operational the criteria are. Some, such as Lupton's, can be used with measures currently available. Others, such as that by Dyer and Hoffenberg, appear to require a considerable amount of work to measure.

Third, it is interesting that many of the indicators do not ask for a direct evaluation on the part of the respondent. Instead, they ask for descriptions of certain characteristics. From these descriptions quality of working life is inferred. For instance, jobs with low autonomy, variety, challenge, and so on, may be seen as indicators of low quality working life.

Table 3-4 Factors Used to Evaluate the Quality of Working Life

CHERNES[a]

1. Reasonably demanding job content in terms other than sheer endurance and some minimum level of variety.
2. A job that allows a worker to learn and go on learning (neither too much nor too little).
3. Some minimal area of decision making in which workers can truly feel that they have participated.
4. Some minimal degree of social support and recognition in the work place.
5. A job that allows employees to relate what they do and what they produce to their social life.
6. A job that lends promise of some sort of desirable future (not necessarily a promotion).

WALTON[b]

1. Adequate and fair compensation
   a. Adequate income. Does full-time work income meet socially determined standards of sufficiency or the subjective standard of the recipient?
   b. Fair compensation. Does the pay received for certain work bear an appropriate relationship to that for other work?
2. Safe and healthy working conditions
   a. Reasonable hours beyond which premium pay required.
   b. Physical conditions that minimize illness and injury risk.
   c. Age limits imposed when work potentially destructive to welfare of persons above or below a certain age.
3. Opportunity to use and develop human capacities
   a. Autonomy. Allowed by job relative to external controls.
   b. Multiple skills. Learning a wide range rather than repetitive application of narrow skills.
   c. Information and perspective. Worker able to obtain information about total work process and consequences of own actions as basis for self-regulation.
   d. Whole tasks. Job involves whole task or some fragment of a task.
   c. Planning. Planning as well as implementation activities.
4. Opportunity for continued growth and security
   A. Development. Extent to which current assignments maintain and expand one's capabilities.
   b. Prospective application. Expectation to use newly acquired knowledge and skills in future.
   c. Advancement opportunities. Opportunities to advance careerwise recognized by

peers, associates, family members. Employment or income security from job.

5. Social integration in the work organization
   a. Freedom from prejudice. Recognized for job performance rather than irrelevant characteristics.
   b. Equalitarianism. Absence of stratification in terms of status symbols and/or steep hierarchies.
   c. Mobility. Existence of upward mobility.
   d. Supportive primary groups. Friendly and helpful face-to-face work groups.
   e. Community. Sense of community in work organization going beyond face-to-face work groups.
   f. Interpersonal openness. The way organization members relate to one another about ideas and feelings.

6. Constitutionalism in the work organization
   a. Privacy. Right to withhold personal information from employer.
   b. Free speech. Right to openly disagree with views of superiors.
   c. Equity. Right to equitable treatment (e.g., compensation, symbolic rewards, job security).
   d. Due process. Governance by rule of law rather than rule of persons.

7. Work and the total life space Balanced role of work. Work requirements do not regularly disrupt family life

8. Social relevance of work life Social responsibility. Organization is seen as socially responsible (e.g., products, waste disposal, etc.).

SEASHORE[c]

Examples of indicators from three perspectives:

1. From the perspective of a worker
   a. Job satisfaction assessed both generally and with regard to specific aspects of job and job environment.
   b. Job-related feelings of excessive strain or tension.
   c. Self-esteem.
   d. Affective states, such as anxiety, depression, resentment, hopelessness, and so on.
   e. Physiological states, such as fatigue, work-related illnesses or injuries, coronary heart disease risk symptoms, drug dependency if work-related.
   f. Satisfaction with work-role potential for personal development, adaptability, career-long value realization, and so forth.

2. From the perspective of an employer
   a. Productivity, including quantity and quality of output, innovative behavior, initiation of new techniques or procedures that increase productivity.
   b. Adaptability to changing work procedures, skill acquisition.
   c. Turnover, absenteeism, lateness.
   d. Counterproductive behaviors, such as theft, sabotage, work stoppage, and so on.
   e. Alienation from work.
   f. Identification with work organization.

3. From the perspective of society
   a. Gross national product.
   b. Increasing value of manpower pool.
   c. Cost of welfare protection for workers and their dependents.
   d. Political behaviors and attitudes.
   e. Consumer behaviors and attitudes.
   f. Societal adaptability.
   g. Life satisfaction rates in society.
   h. Alienation.
   i. Quality of life with regard to nonwork roles and situations.

DYER AND HOFFENBERG[d]

Assume quality of working life defined in terms of the organization's contributions to economic and sociopsychological needs of individuals actively engaged in furthering its goals. These contributions accrue to individuals either directly on the job or indirectly through influences of the organization on society. The authors reviewed the job-organization design literature and derived 40 quality-of-working-life concerns. A representative sampling of these is summarized here:

1. Technology. Eight items concerned with specialization, uncertainty, control, flexibility, and so on.

2. Organization
   a. Formal structure. Seven items concerned with role identification and differentiation, clarity of assignments, incentives for participation, structural adaptability.
   b. Decision making and control system. Five items concerned with mutually reinforcing goals, generating new goals, providing basis for appropriate decision making, implementing decisions and getting them accepted.
   c. Information system. Four items concerned with information and decision level, employee feedback, consumer and society feedback, and communication channels.

3. Personal needs. Five items concerned with satisfaction of

material needs, social interaction, self esteem, self actualization and differences in personalities and values.

4. Needs of society and physical environment. Seven items concerned with off-job social interaction, more effective home

life, product with high social value, nonworkplace learning, and personal growth.

5. Job design. Four items concerned with job variety, community respect, contribution to product utility, and job rotation.

GOODALE, HALL, BURKE, AND JOYNER[e]

Have developed 17 quality-of-life indicators and are in the process of determining the impact of each of these indicators in the contexts of: work, home, community, and recreation. Thus, an attempt is made at integrating quality of life and quality of working life and getting at the relative impact of given job situations on overall quality of life as opposed to quality of work life.

The 17 indicators are grouped into four categories as follows:

1. Personal characteristics
   a. Self-control
   b. Self-esteem
   c. Self-identity
2. Activities
   a. Work activity
   b. Social activity and participation
   c. Self-development activity

3. Objective outcomes
   a. Task success
   b. Physical health
   c. Physical and economic security
4. Perceived outcomes
   a. Task involvement
   b. Task satisfaction
   c. Social involvement and relatedness feelings
   d. Self-reported health
   e. Perceived security, fears, anxieties
   f. Perceived growth and mastery
   g. Global evaluative feelings
   h. Fulfillment in context X value of control

SHEPPARD[f]

Sheppard uses a 16-cell matrix as shown below. Here, "frequency of job satisfaction" is measured by asking, "How much of the time are you satisfied with your job?" It is treated as

an indicator of the quality of working life, along with the other variables in the matrix. Note that cell I would have the highest quality and cell XVI the lowest.

Measures of Work Satisfaction		Measure of Economic Concern			
		Steady Employment		*Unsteady Employment*	
		Wages or Salaries		*Wages or Salaries*	
		High	*Low*	*High*	*Low*
		(*u*)	(x)	(y)	(z)
Frequency of Job Satisfaction (JSF)					
High (JSF)	(a) In standard or above-standard physical work environment (PWE)	I			
	(*b*) Below standard PWE.				
Low (JSF)	(*a*) In standard or above standard PWE.				
	(*b*) Below standard PWE.				XVI

Note: Each of the attributes or variables in this typology is, of course, not operationally or quantitatively defined here, for example, "high" versus "low" wage, "standard," PWE, and so on, but they would and could be.

Sheppard suggests that this typology could be used to obtain valuable information: First to determine the proportion of a nation's (or an enterprise's) work force in each of the categories, from (I) the presumably "ideal" type with good physical work environment, high job security, high wages, and high job satisfaction, to (XVI), the presumably "least ideal" type with low job security and wages, low job satisfaction, and so on. The remaining categories could be compressed into an intermediate classification (or type), but other combinations or aggregations are possible too.

Second, changes over time in each of these categories could be monitored within an industry's, a region's, or a country's labor force, examining shifts in the proportion that is in the most or least ideal category.

Third, at any time the distribution of each of the types can be determined according to other socioeconomic criteria of a country's work force, such as occupation, industry, age, sex, religion, and so on, as a basis of the need for, and choice of, "intervention strategies."

Sources:

[a]Chernes, A. B. "Can Behavioral Science Help Design Organizations?" *Organizational Dynamics*, 5 (1977), 44–64.

[b]Walton, R. E. "Criteria for Quality of Working Life." In Davis, L. E., and Cherns, A. B. (eds.), *The Quality of Working Life* (New York: The Free Press, 1975).

[c]Seashore, S. E. "Defining and Measuring the Quality of Working Life." In Davis and Cherns, 1975.

[d]Dyer, J. S., and Hoffenberg, M. "Evaluating The Quality of Working Life—Some Reflections on Production and Costs and A Method Problem Definition." In Davis and Cherns, 1975.

[e]Goodale, J. G., Hall, D. T., Burke, R. J., and Joyner, R. C. "Some Significant Contexts and Components of Individual Quality of Life." In Davis and Cherns, 1975.

[f]Sheppard, H. L. "Some Indicators of the Quality of Working Life: A Simplified Approach." In Davis and Cherns, 1975. Sheppard's matrix is reprinted with permission of Macmillan Publishing Co., Inc., from *The Quality of Working Life, Volume 1,* by Davis., L. E., and Cherns, A. B. Copyright © 1975, Louis E. Davis and Albert B. Cherns.

Fourth, regardless of their breadth or depth, all the views of working life quality go beyond just considering satisfaction. Typical "morale surveys" that measure satisfaction pick up some quality of working-life aspects. But they do not go as far as these authors would like.

Finally, an article by Lawler[6] goes beyond simply discussing quality of working life. He talks about the role of government in not only monitoring such quality but regulating it as well. Such a view is implicit in some of the works in the table, but is most explicit in Lawler's article. Thus, not only may we see government safety and pollution regulations and standards, but perhaps quality of working-life standards as well.

To conclude, quality of working life is still in its infancy as a research topic. Similar to what we found in conceiving of organizational effectiveness, there are many different ways of looking at quality of working life. As we noted in the overview to Part I, it is difficult for organizations to be all things to all people. Chapter 4 looks at some of the trade-offs among criteria in more detail. But quality of working life, like survival, effectiveness, performance, and employee maintenance, may become an important criterion for judging the success of an organization.

MEASUREMENT
MODULE

Here we include measures of various kinds of performance ratings and indicators of employee maintenance criteria.

PERFORMANCE RATING SCALES

We start with a rating form developed in cooperation with top-level management of resident institutions for the mentally ill and mentally retarded.[3] It was designed to measure the performance of mental health patient-care teams on various aspects of patient care. Top management felt that three specific dimensions plus an overall performance measure were important in evaluating work-team patient-care performance. The specific dimensions were: (1) physical care—physical care of the patient, such as feeding, clothing, and medical attention; (2) psychological and emotional care—developing and maintaining goals and skills in patients so that they may better cope with their environment; and (3) group operation—ability of the work team to handle administrative matters, such as paperwork and housekeeping. All of these used the same seven-point format (1 = poor through 7 = outstanding) as the overall performance measure shown in Exhibit 3-5. These rating forms were completed by managerial personnel in three organizations. They were familiar enough with the work teams to evaluate their performance.

Exhibit 3-5 Overall Group Performance Measure Used in Mental Health Organizations

Rate each group's performance on:[a]

Overall Performance:

Taking everything into consideration that you believe to be important to the goals of this work group and how successful they are in accomplishing these goals.

Explanation		*Rating Box*
7. The performance of this group on the characteristic above *could not be improved upon; as a group their performance deserves the highest praise and reward.*	7. Outstanding	

6. The performance of this group on the characteristic above is *equal to that of 9 out of 10 groups* that I know well. There are *only one or two minor details* that could possibly improve it. They deserve considerable praise and reward for their performance.

6. Excellent ☐

5. The performance of this group on the characteristic above is *equal to that of 8 out of 10 groups* that I know well. There are *only three or four details* that could improve it. They deserve more than occasional praise and reward for their performance.

5. Very Good ☐

4. The performance of this group on the characteristic above is *equal to 7 out of 10 groups* that I know well. There is *only one, major fault* that could be corrected. They deserve occasional praise and reward for their performance.

4. Good ☐

3. The performance of this group on the characteristic above is *equal to about 5 out of 10 groups* that I know well. They have *about as many faults to improve as most groups do.* They deserve about as much praise and reward as most groups do for their performance.

3. Fair ☐

2. The performance of this group on the characteristic above *is worse than many groups* that I know well. They have *more faults than the average* that should be corrected. They require more correction than praise for their performance.

2. Rather Poor ☐

1. The performance of this group on the characteristic above is *among the worst of any groups* that I know well. They do very little that is proper and *require constant correction* and no praise or reward to speak of.

1. Poor ☐

Source: Hunt, J. G., Osborn, R. N., and Larson, L. L. *Leadership Effectiveness in Mental Institutions* (Final Technical Report to Health Services Branch of the National Institute of Mental Health, 1973).

[a]The same format was used for the dimensions of: physical care, psychological and emotional care, and group operations. The higher the score the better the performance.

Note the following. First, these are ratings of desired end results or goals (e.g., patient care) and very general activities believed necessary to achieve the goals (e.g., feeding and clothing). Second, the scales were designed to discriminate more at the favorable than at the unfavorable end. This is to help compensate for the tendency among raters to bias their ratings toward the favorable end of the scale. Third, it was felt that the dimensions identified here should be relatively independent of one another. In practice they were found

Exhibit 3-6   A Rating Scale of Managerial Performance

Superiors are asked to evaluate the present job performance of their subordinates on the following activities using the seven-point scale at the bottom of the page:

1. *Planning:* Determining goals, policies, and course of action. __

2. *Investigating:* Collecting and preparing of information, usually in the form of records, reports, and accounts. __

3. *Coordinating:* Exchanging information with people in the organization other than his subordinates in order to relate and adjust programs. __

4. *Evaluting:* Assessment and appraisal of proposals or of reported or observed performance. __

5. *Supervising:* Directing, leading, and developing subordinates. __

6. *Staffing:* Maintaining the workforce of his unit or of several units. __

7. *Negotiating:* Purchasing, selling, or contracting for goods or services. __

8. *Representing:* Advancing the general interests of his organization through speeches, consultation, and contracts with individuals or groups outside the organization. __

Performance on Present Job

Scale for use with above ratings

   1   2   3   4   5   6   7

Low   Average   High

Source: Based on Heneman, H. G., "Comparisons of Self and Superior Ratings of Managerial Performance," *Journal of Applied Psychology,* 59 (1974), 638–642. Adapted with permission of the author.

to be highly related to each other. Thus, the scale was not successful in eliminating the halo effect. Finally, the scales were found to be reasonably reliable (i.e., there was reasonable agreement) across the different evaluators.

Let's now look at a different kind of performance rating used to evaluate managerial performance (Exhibit 3-6). This is based on earlier studies of functional activities performed by managers. Heneman[2] used these eight managerial activities as performance dimensions. The evaluator rates each activity on a seven-point scale as shown. These dimensions, unlike those discussed earlier, concentrate exclusively on activities or behaviors believed to influence end results. They would be especially useful where measures of end results or standards of desirability were hard to obtain. The strengths and weaknesses of this instrument as well as more details on its development are discussed by Heneman.

An instrument tapping a different set of activities and using some "behavioral anchors" is summarized in Exhibit 3-7.[1] Note that the different positions on the seven-point scale have been defined in terms of behavioral anchors in an attempt to make the ratings more meaningful.* Again, the activities were chosen in terms of their believed cause and effect relations with desired end results. They appear to be generalizable to a wide range of organizations.

The measures discussed above convey the flavor of performance-rating forms. Other references at the end of the chapter provide a more complete discussion.

EMPLOYEE MAINTENANCE

Included here are measures of *withdrawal* and *attachment*.

Withdrawal Measures

There are several specific measures of withdrawal, including turnover, absenteeism, and so forth. There are various ways of calculating turnover indexes. A common one is[7]:

$$\text{Turnover (for each unit)} = \frac{\text{number of separations} \times 100}{\text{midmonth employment}}$$

*See Reference 4.

Exhibit 3-7 An Individual Performance Measure

I. A. *Dependability*—maintains high standards of work and performs all needed work.

   7. Can be counted on not only to perform assigned jobs without being watched, but to perform without being told, other jobs that should be done.

   6. More like 7 than like 4.

   5. More like 4 than like 7.

   4. Can be counted on to perform assigned jobs without being watched.

   3. More like 4 than like 1.

   2. More like 1 than like 4.

   1. Cuts corners; must be watched closely to make sure work is done right.

   B. How confident do you feel about the above ratings?

a	b	c	d
Not Confident at All	Somewhat Confident	Very Confident	Certain

II. *Skill in Dealing with People*—does and says the right things at the right time.

   7. Even in "hot" situations with other people does and says the right things to cool people down.

   4. In "hot" situations with other people, does and says things that do not make the problems worse.

   1. In "hot" situations with other people, does and says things that make the problems worse. (The other scale positions here and later are exactly as in IA. The rating in IB is also asked for here.)

III. *Alertness*—sees action and changes that might affect his work.

   7. Sees the little as well as the big changes in his work and surroundings.

   4. Sees only the big changes in his work and surroundings.

   1. Fails to see even the big changes in his work and surroundings until they are almost out of control.

IV. *Planning*—makes good use of time, equipment, and people.

   7. Even when overloaded with work, can pick out the most important job to do first, and makes the best use of time, material and people to get the job done.

4. Usually can pick out most important job to do first, and make good use of time, material and people to get the job done.

1. Even on daily routine work, does not pick out most important job to do first, and makes poor use of time, material, and people to get the job done.

V. *Know-how and Judgment*—needed to do the job right.

7. Work shows he has know-how and judgment needed not only to do the basic job, but to foresee and handle unusual job problems as well.

4. Work shows he has know-how and judgment needed to do the basic job.

1. Work shows he has not enough know-how and judgment needed to do the basic job.

VI. *Present Level of Performance*—in meeting work standards.

9. I am very certain he is an outstanding performer.

8. I am quite certain he is an outstanding performer.

7. I am rather certain he is a good performer.

6. I think he probably is a satisfactory performer.

5. I am completely uncertain about whether he is a good or poor performer.

4. I think he is a poor performer.

3. I am rather certain he is a poor performer.

2. I am quite certain he is an unsatisfactory performer.

1. I am *very certain* he is an unsatisfactory performer.

Source: Adapted from Danserau, F. "Some Correlates of Supervisory Behavior." Unpublished Masters thesis, University of Illinois, August 1970. Adapted with permission of the author.

Turnover indexes should be corrected for obvious involuntary separations such as death, illness, and mandatory retirement. Details of such corrected turnover indexes are included in Mirvis and Macy.[8] Some advocate making further adjustments based on exit interview information, asking why an individual left. Others argue that this information is likely to be distorted and one is better off without it.[6] You would also be interested in turnover figures over a long enough period of time to eliminate seasonal and other possibly temporary fluctuations.

Like turnover, absenteeism can be measured by various kinds of indexes. A representative one is[7]:

$$\text{Absenteeism} = \frac{\text{number of man-days lost through job absence during period}}{\text{average number of employees} \times \text{number of work days}} \times 100$$

As with turnover, there are questions concerning adjustments to this index. Should absences be divided into excused versus unexcused, or left "unadjusted?" Mirvis and Macy[8] discuss an index that is adjusted for a number of different absenteeism categories. Those arguing against adjustment maintain that it is difficult to get the true reason for absences. It may not be worth the effort, at least beyond those instances where you are virtually certain of the reason for the absence. Latham[4] goes a step further and argues that because of these kinds of problems we should be measuring the number of people who come to work, rather than the number absent. He presents some data in support of his argument, though it's controversial.[2]

Other less common withdrawal indicators include an index of employee grievances within a given time period, indexes of accident rates, and such things as tardiness, strikes, slowdowns, and so forth. We will not go into these here, but they are treated in personnel texts.[1,7]

Attachment Measures

The most thoroughly developed instrument in this Module is the one dealing with job satisfaction. Exhibit 3-8 presents sample items for an instrument known as the Job Descriptive Index (JDI). It considers five aspects of the work situation.[10] We've also included a separate measure of overall satisfaction called the Job in General scale (Exhibit 3-9).[3] The overall measure, while related to a total score based on summing JDI scores for each individual aspect, is nevertheless different both theoretically and empirically. It's probably a more valid measure of overall satisfaction than is the sum score. Early work on the JDI instrument resulted in a book. Later data concerning the instrument are available as indicated in Exhibit 3-8. A large number of studies have used the JDI as an indicator of job satisfaction.

Job involvement and organizational commitment scales have a smaller amount of developmental data available. A widely used job involvement measure is shown in Exhibit 3-10.[5] A recently developed organizational commitment measure is presented in Exhibit 3-11.[9]

These and other scales measuring these general notions and quality of working life are receiving increasing attention in the literature. Yet, as we showed earlier, there is still some question about what is being measured, not to mention how to measure the concepts.

Exhibit 3-8 Sample Items from the Job Descriptive Index (Each scale is presented on a separate page.)

Think of your present work. What is it like most of the time? In the blank beside each word given below, write

__Y__ for "Yes" if it describes your work

__N__ for "No" if it does NOT describe it

__?__ if you cannot decide

Work on Present Job

_____Routine

_____Satisfying

_____Good

_____On your feet

Think of the pay you get now. How well does each of the following words describe your present pay? In the blank beside each work, put

__Y__ if it describes your pay

__N__ if it does NOT describe it

__?__ if you cannot decide

Present Pay

_____income adequate for normal expenses

_____insecure

_____less than I deserve

_____highly paid

Think of the opportunities for promotion that you have now. How well does each of the following words describe these? In the blank beside each word put

__Y__ for "Yes" if it describes your opportunities for promotion

__N__ for "No" if it does NOT describe them

__?__ if you cannot decide

Opportunities for Promotion

_____promotion on ability

_____dead-end job

_____unfair promotion policy

_____regular promotions

Think of the kind of supervision that you get on your job. How well does each of the following words describe this supervision? In the blank beside each word below, put

__Y__ if it describes the supervision you get on your job

__N__ if it does NOT describe it

__?__ if you cannot decide

Supervision on Present Job

_____impolite

_____praises good work

_____influential

_____doesn't supervise enough

Think of the majority of the people that you work with now or the people you meet in connection with your work. How well does each of the following words describe these people? In the blank beside each word below, put

__Y__ if it describes the people you work with

__N__ if it does NOT describe them

__?__ if you cannot decide

People on Your Present Job

_____boring

_____responsible

_____intelligent

_____talk too much

Source: The Job Descriptive Index is copyrighted by Bowling Green State University. The complete forms, scoring key, instructions, and norms can be obtained from Dr. Patricia C. Smith, Department of Psychology, Bowling Green State University, Bowling Green, Ohio 43403.

Exhibit 3-9 "Faces" Scale for Job in General (JIG)

Put a check under the face that expresses how you feel about your job in general, including the work, the pay, the supervision, the opportunities for promotion, and the people you work with.

Scoring:

6 (big smile) to 1 (big frown).

Source: Kunin, T. "The Construction of a New Type of Attitude Measure," *Personnel Psychology,* 8 (1955), 65–75. Reprinted by permission of Theodore Kunin and Personnel Psychology.

Exhibit 3-10 A Job Involvement Scale

1. The major satisfactions in my life come from my work.
2. The most important things that happen to me involve my work.
3. I'm really a perfectionist about my work.
4. I live, eat, and breathe my job.
5. I am very much involved personally in my work.
6. Most things in life are more important than work.

Responses and Scoring

A four-point response format is used for each item, as follows: Strongly agree; agree; disagree; and strongly disagree. For the first five questions, the strongly agree category is scored "1," with strongly disagree scored "4," and the other categories scored in-between. Item 6 is scored in the reverse direction. The involvement score is the sum of the six items; the *lower* the score, the *more* the involvement.

Source: Lodahl, T. M., and Kejner, M. "The Definition and Measurement of Job Involvement," *Journal of Applied Psychology,* 49 (1965), 24–33. Copyright © 1965 by the American Psychological Association. Reprinted by permission.

Exhibit 3-11 Organizational Commitment Scale

Instructions

Listed below are a series of statements that represent possible feelings that individuals might have about the company or organization for which they work. With respect to your own feelings about the particular organization for which you are now working, please indicate the degree of your agreement or disagreement with each statement by checking one of the seven alternatives below each statement:

1. I am willing to put in a great deal of effort beyond that normally expected in order to help this organization be successful.

Strongly Disagree	Moderately Disagree	Slightly Disagree	Neither Disagree nor Agree	Slightly Agree	Moderately Agree	Strongly Agree

2. I talk up this organization to my friends as a great organization to work for.
3. I feel very little loyalty to this organization.
4. I would accept almost any type job assignment in order to keep working for this organization.
5. I find that my values and the organization's values are very similar.
6. I am proud to tell others that I am part of this organization.
7. I could just as well be working for a different organization as long as the type of work were similar.
8. This organization really inspires the very best in me in the way of job performance.
9. It would take very little change in my present circumstances to cause me to leave this organization.
10. I am extremely glad that I chose this organization to work for, over others I was considering at the time I joined.
11. There's not too much to be gained by sticking with this organization indefinitely.
12. Often, I find it difficult to agree with this organization's policies on important matters relating to its employees.
13. I really care about the fate of this organization.
14. For me this is the best of all possible organizations for which to work.
15. Deciding to work for this organization was a definite mistake on my part.

Scoring

For items 1, 2, 4, 5, 6, 8, 10, 13, 14 strongly agree = 7, moderately agree = 6, and so forth, to strongly disagree = 1. Items 3, 7, 9, 11, 12, 15 are scored in the opposite direction so that strongly agree = 1, and so forth. The higher the score, the higher the commitment.

Source: Porter, L. W., Steers, R. M., Mowday, R. T., and Boulian, P. W. "Organizational Commitment, Job Satisfaction and Turnover Among Psychiatric Technicians," *Journal of Applied Psychology,* 59 (1974), 603–609. Reprinted by permission of Lyman Porter.

REFERENCES

I. Systems Goals and Subsystems Performance

A. Means-Ends Chains

[1]Miner, J. B., and Miner, M. G. *Personnel and Industrial Relations* (3rd edition). New York: Macmillan, 1977.

[2]Odiorne, G. S. *Management by Objectives* New York: Putman, 1965.

[3]Thompson, J. D. *Organizations in Action*. New York:McGraw-Hill, 1967.

[4]Tosi, H. L., and Carroll, S. J. *Management Contingencies, Structure and Process*. Chicago: St. Clair Press, 1976.

C. Problems in Evaluating Subsystems Performance

[1]Beach, D. S. *Personnel: The Management of People at Work* (3rd edition). New York: Macmillan, 1975.

[2]Campbell, J. P., Dunnette, M. D., Lawler, E. E., and Weick, K. E. *Managerial Behavior, Performance, and Effectiveness*. New York: McGraw-Hill, 1970.

[3]Miner and Miner, 1977.

[4]Odiorne, 1965.

II. Employee Maintenance

A. Satisfaction, Morale, Esprit de Corps

[1]Locke, E. A. "The Nature and Causes of Job Satisfaction." In M. D. Dunnette (ed.), *Handbook of Industrial and Organizational Psychology*. Chicago: Rand McNally, 1976.

[2]Schwab, D. P., and Cummings, L. L. "Theories of Performance and Satisfaction: A Review," *Industrial Relations*, 9 (1970) 408–430.

[3]Smith, P. C. "The Development of a Method of Measuring Job Satisfaction: The Cornell Studies." In E. A. Fleishman (ed.), *Studies in Personnel and Industrial Psychology*. Homewood, Ill.: Dorsey Press, 1967.

[4]Vitales, M. S. *Motivation and Morale in Industry*. New York: W. W. Norton, 1953.

B. Involvement And Commitment

[1]Locke, 1976.

[2]Porter, L. W., and Smith, F. J. "The Etiology of Organizational Commitment." Unpublished paper, University of California, Irvine, 1970.

[3]Rabinowitz, S., and Hall, D. T. "Organizational Research on Job Involvement," *Psychological Bulletin*, 84 (1977), 265–288.

C. Withdrawal

[1]Glueck, W. F. *Personnel: A Diagnostic Approach* (2nd edition). Dallas: Business Publications, Inc., 1978.

[2]Locke, 1976.

[3]Miner and Miner, 1977.

[4]Porter, L. W., and Steers, R. M. "Organizational, Work, and Personal Factors in Employee Turnover and Absenteeism," *Psychological Bulletin*, 80 (1973), 151–176.

[5]Steers, R. M., and Porter, L. W. *Motivation and Work Behavior*. New York: McGraw-Hill, 1977.

D. Empirical Relationships among Maintenance Criteria

[1]Herman, J. B. "Are Situational Contingencies Limiting Job Attitude—Job Performance Relationships?," *Organizational Behavior and Human Performance*, 10 (1973), 208–224.

[2]Hulin, C. L. "Effects of Changes in Job-Satisfaction Levels on Employee Turnover," *Journal of Applied Psychology*, 52 (1968), 122–128.

[3]Jauch, L. R., Glueck, W. F., and Osborn, R. N. "Organizational Loyalty, Professional Commitment,

and Academic Research Productivity," *Academy of Management Journal,* 21 (1978), 84–92.

⁴Kidron, A. G. "Individual Differences, Job Characteristics, and Commitment to the Organization." Doctoral dissertation, The Ohio State University, 1976.

⁵Koch, J. L., and Steers, R. M. "Job Attachment, Satisfaction and Turnover Among Public Sector Employees." Paper presented at the annual meeting of the Academy of Management, Kissimmee, Florida, August 1977.

⁶Locke, 1976.

⁷Mirvis, P. H., and Lawler, E. E., III "Measuring the Financial Impact of Employee Attitudes," *Journal of Applied Pscyhology,* 62 (1977), 1–8.

⁸Mobley, W. H., Griffeth, R. W., Hand, H. H., and Meglino, B. M. "Review and Conceptual Analysis of the Employee Turnover Process," *Psychological Bulletin,* in press.

⁹Porter and Steers, 1973.

¹⁰Porter, L. W., Steers, R. M., Mowday, R. T., and Boulian, P. V. "Organizational Commitment, Job Satisfaction, and Turnover Among Psychiatric Technicians," *Journal of Applied Psychology,* 59 (1974), 603–609.

¹¹Rabinowitz and Hall, 1977.

¹²Smith, F. J. "Work Attitudes as Predictors of Attendance on a Specific Day," *Journal of Applied Psychology,* 62 (1977), 16–19.

¹³Steers, R. M., and Rhodes, S. P. "Major Influences on Employee Attendance: A Process Model," *Journal of Applied Psychology,* 63 (1978), 391–407.

F. Performance And Employee Maintenance

¹Bowen, D., and Siegel, J. P. "The Relationship Between Satisfaction and Performance: The Question of Causality." Paper presented at the annual meeting of the American Psychological Association, Miami Beach, September 1970.

²Cherrington, J. J., Reitz, H. J., and Scott, W. E., Jr. "Effects of Contingent and Non-contingent Reward on the Relationship Between Satisfaction and Task Performance," *Journal of Applied Psychology,* 55 (1971), 531–536.

³Greene, C. N. "A Causal Interpretation of Relationship Among Pay, Performance, and Satisfaction." Paper presented at the annual meeting of the Midwest Psychological Association, Cleveland, Ohio, May 1972.

⁴Jauch, L. R., Osborn, R. N., and Martin, T. N. "The Role of Strategy Performance and Environment in Managerial Succession," National Academy of Management Meetings, San Francisco, Calif. 1978.

⁵Locke, 1976.

⁶Melcher, A. J. *Structure and Process of Organizations: A Systems Approach.* Englewood Cliffs, N.J.: Prentice-Hall, 1976.

⁷Poffenberger, A. T. "The Effects of Continuous Work Output and Feelings," *Journal of Applied Psychology,* 12 (1928), 459–467.

⁸Porter, L. W., and Lawler, E. E., III. *Managerial Attitudes and Behavior.* Homewood, Ill.: Richard D. Irwin, Inc., 1968.

⁹Price, J. L. "The Effects of Turnover on the Organization," *Organization and Administrative Sciences,* 7 (1976), 61–88.

¹⁰Rabinowitz and Hall, 1977.

¹¹Schwab and Cummings, 1970.

[12]Thorndike, E. L. "The Curve of Work and the Curve of Satisfyingness," *Journal of Applied Psychology*, 1 (1917), 265–267.

[13]Triandis, H. C. "Notes on the Design of Organizations." In J. D. Thompson (ed.), *Approaches to Organizational Design*. Pittsburgh: University of Pittsburgh Press, 1966.

III. The Quality Of Working Life

[1]Cherns, A. B. "Can Behavioral Science Help Design Organizations?," *Organizational Dynamics*, 5 (1977), 44–64.

[2]Davis, L. E, and Cherns, A. B. (eds.). *The Quality of Working Life, Volume One: Problems, Prospects, and the State of the Art*. New York: The Free Press, 1975.

[3]Davis, L. E., and Cherns, A. B. (eds.). *The Quality of Working Life, Volume Two: Cases and Commentary*. New York: The Free Press, 1975.

[4]Dyer, J. S., and Hoffenberg, M. "Evaluating the Quality of Working Life—Some Reflections on Production and Costs and a Method Problem Definition." In L. E. Davis and A. B. Cherns (eds.), *The Quality of Working Life, Volume One*. New York: The Free Press, 1975.

[5]Goodale, J. G., Hall, D. T., Burke, R. J., and Joyner, R. C. "Some Significant Contexts and Components of Individual Quality of Life." In L. E. Davis and A. B. Cherns (eds.), *The Quality of Working Life, Volume One*. New York: The Free Press, 1975.

[6]Lawler, E. E., III. "Measuring the Psychological Quality of Working Life: The Why and How of It." In L. E. Davis and A. B. Cherns (eds.), *The Quality of Working Life, Volume One*. New York: The Free Press, 1975.

[7]Seashore, S. E. "Defining and Measuring the Quality of Working Life." In L. E. Davis and A. B. Cherns (eds.), *The Quality of Working Life Volume One*. New York: The Free Press, 1975.

[8]Walton, R. E. "Criteria for Quality of Working Life." In L. E. Davis and A. B. Cherns (eds.), *The Quality of Working Life, Volume One*. New York: The Free Press, 1975.

IV. Measurement Module

A. Performance Rating Scales

[1]Dansereau, F., Jr. "Some Correlates of Supervisory Behavior." Unpublished masters thesis, University of Illinois, 1970.

[2]Heneman, H. G., III "Comparisons of Self- and Superior Ratings of Managerial Performance," *Journal of Applied Psychology*, 59 (1974), 638–642.

[3]Hunt, J. G., Osborn, R. N., and Larson, L. L. "Leadership Effectiveness in Mental Institutions." Final technical report to Health Services Development Branch of the National Institute of Mental Health, 1973.

[4]Schwab, D. P., Heneman, H. G., III, and DeCotiis, T. A. "Behaviorally Anchored Rating Scales: A Review of the Literature," *Personnel Psychology*, 28 (1975), 549–562.

B. Employee Maintenance

[1]Glueck, 1978.

[2]Ilgen, D. R. "Attendance Behavior: A Reevaluation of Latham and Pursell's Conclusions," *Journal of Applied Psychology*, 62 (1977), 230–233.

[3]Kunin, T. "The Construction of A New Type of Attitude Measure,"

Personnel Psychology, 8 (1955), 65–75.

[4]Latham, G. P., and Pursell, E. D. "Measuring Absenteeism from the Opposite Side of the Coin," *Journal of Applied Psychology,* 60 (1975), 369–371.

[5]Lodahl, T. M., and Kejner, M. "The Definition and Measurement of Job Involvement," *Journal of Applied Psychology,* 49 (1965), 24–33.

[6]Lopez, F. M. *Personnel Interviewing—Theory and Practice.* New York: McGraw-Hill, 1965.

[7]Miner and Miner, 1977.

[8]Mirvis, P. H., and Macy, B. A. "Behavioral-Economic Measurement System." In Michigan Organizational Assessment Package, Progress Report II. Ann Arbor: Institute for Social Research, University of Michigan, 1975.

[9]Porter, Steers, Mowday, and Bouliars, 1974.

[10]Smith, P. C., Kendall, L., and Hulin, C. L. *The Measurement of Satisfaction in Work and Retirement: A Strategy for the Study of Attitudes.* Chicago: Rand McNally, 1969.

chapter 4 ORGANIZATIONAL AND SUBSYSTEMS CRITERIA: SOME EXTENSIONS AND CONTINGENCIES

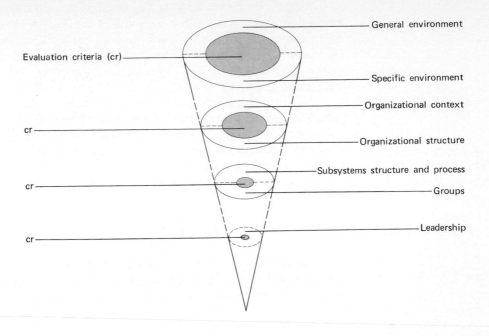

Evaluation criteria (cr)

General environment

Specific environment

Organizational context

cr

Organizational structure

Subsystems structure and process

cr

Groups

Leadership

cr

This is the first contingency chapter. These chapters extend current research findings. They also contain our speculations and reflect our own bias and opinions much more than other portions of the text. Thus, they're likely to be controversial and your instructor may take issue with some of our contentions. If so, so much the better. Lively discussion can be a useful learning device.

Even more than eliciting controversy, the chapters are designed to integrate material in previous chapters. They do this by discussing the if-then conditions under which various environmental, organizational, and subsystems characteristics will be related to criteria. In this chapter, since we haven't yet considered these characteristics, the major emphasis is on the criteria themselves.

Our review of the literature has left some knotty issues where there is considerable degree of controversy. How detailed should the measurement of organizational success be? Should the manager or the evaluator always attempt to secure quantitative estimates? When might specific measures be inappropriate?

Another important issue is the linkages among different organizational and subsystems criteria. What are some of the linkages among organizational effectiveness and subsystems performance? For instance, there is considerable controversy over the association between performance and the quality of working life. Some would sacrifice one for the other. Some do not see that a trade-off is required.

We also think it is important to concentrate on the major predictors of a particular aspect of organizational success. For instance, changes in the law may alter an individual's satisfaction. But most research suggests that factors closer to a person's organizational role are probably more important. We'll provide our viewpoint in the last section of this chapter. Now let's return to the first series of questions. How detailed should measures of success be?

EVALUATING ORGANIZATIONAL SUCCESS

In discussing the various ways of evaluating an organization and its subsystems we have provided some vague ways of estimating success along with some very specific measuring instruments. The measures of performance and satisfaction are very detailed. In contrast, estimates of societal contribution can be quite vague. Is it possible or desirable to develop very specific measures for all criteria? Thompson, among others, argues that the answer depends upon two factors: (1) do the organization and the evaluator know what is desired? (2) do the organization and the evaluator know how the actions of the organization lead to success?[3] Let's take a look at these two separately. Then we'll combine them.

To develop specific measures of organizational or subsystems success Thompson argues that "standards of desirability" should be clear-cut. There may be general agreement on what an organization is expected to do. Conversely, standards of desirability may be ambiguous. Some individuals may not know what they want the organization to do. Or there may be considerable controversy over what the organization should be contributing and to whom. We suggested in our analysis of societal contribution that there were several different viewpoints. Some of these were quite vague as in the case of Parsons. As we moved into the evaluations based on output, control, and prime beneficiary, the standards of desirability appeared somewhat clearer. At least the number of individuals and interest groups considered important in estimating societal contribution was known.

In estimating the degree of goal attainment we again can see that different types of goals are more or less clear-cut. Mission accomplishment yields a vague series of standards. In contrast, some organizations can precisely measure the quality of their outputs.

In our discussion of systems goals we noted that many were inconsistent.

The organization could not maximize both flexibility and efficiency, for instance. In a similar manner what we called derived goals represent the diverse and often conflicting desires of powerful groups both inside and outside the organization. Clearly, some aspects of success rest on ambiguous standards of desirability. Yet, some aspects of success, such as economic efficiency may be clear. We caution against relying entirely upon quantitative measures. Just because you can't find agreement on societal contribution doesn't mean it is irrelevant.

In the analysis of employee maintenance, different standards are established by workers, managers, and social scientists. Satisfaction, for instance, can be considered a clearly articulated standard of desirability when talking to many organization theorists. The quality of working life is yet to be clearly defined even though most would prefer to see it improved.

We suggested that survival may be the ultimate goal for most organizations, yet it could only be measured historically. We also suggested that the extent to which an organization met its systems goals might be used to estimate its chances of survival. This brings us to Thompson's second question. To what extent do managers and evaluators see clear-cut cause-effect relationships? That is, what are the beliefs about cause and effect. The more complete the cause-effect beliefs, the more likely specific measures will be used. If you assume greater flexibility and efficiency increase the chances of survival then beliefs about cause and effect are more complete than if you are unwilling to make such an argument. If you assume cause-effect relationships are complete, then you may use internal organizational characteristics to estimate success. This is like a doctor who sees a runny nose as symptomatic of a cold. It has long been assumed, for instance, that higher profits suggest greater societal contribution for those business firms operating in a competitive market; that is, profits are a symptom of societal contribution.[2] We are not so sure, but several scholars and managers do believe this cause-effect linkage.

To estimate what types of measures should be used to assess the organization, Thompson combines his two questions. The combination yields Thompson's assessment cells as shown in Figure 4-1. Different cells call for different types of measures.

		Beliefs about Cause and Effect Relationships	
		Complete	Incomplete
Standards of desirability	Crystallized	I	II
	Ambiguous	III	IV

Figure 4-1 Thompson's Assessment Cells

Where possible most managers attempt to move into Cell I where standards are clear and cause-effect relationships are complete. Here you can use efficiency ratios. For instance if comparative financial ratios are used to evaluate a corporation it is assumed that higher short-term profitability increases survival potential and that financial standards are widely accepted. As we suggested in Chapter 3, many measures of unit and individual performance presume the conditions of Cell I. We'll take a look at this in the next section of the chapter.

In Cell II we find a well-accepted set of standards but knowledge of cause-effect relationships is incomplete. Here Thompson suggests the use of "instrumental tests." Instrumental tests attempt to suggest whether a desired state was reached. For instance, are employees generally satisfied with their jobs? Instrumental tests are not as precise as efficiency ratings. But the executive or evaluator may ask whether the system reaches acceptable levels of profit, flexibility, and the like. The result may be a series of subjective ratings in several different areas.

In Cell I, management may have a well-developed notion of how to reach several different goals. For instance, managers may know how to improve product quality, increase production efficiency, and individually tailor products or services to particular clients. Yet there may be considerable controversy over which of these standards is most important and what trade-offs among them should be made. In Cell III you are likely to find a case of competing value systems. Within an organization the administrative philosophy of top management may provide a mechanism for clarifying standards of desirability when evaluating various subsystems. We will discuss this at length in Chapters 8 and 10. When evaluating an organization the interests of powerful units in its environment may clarify the priority among different aspects of success. Of course, organizations do operate within a larger setting that provides a whole series of expectations. As we noted in our discussion of societal contribution, different types of organizations are often expected to concentrate their efforts on one type of contribution. These expectations clarify some standards of desirability. A more detailed discussion of the association between conditions in the general environment and organizational success is provided in Chapters 5 and 7. For now it is sufficient to realize that several external and internal forces often work to clarify standards of desirability. Organizations do have choices, but conflicting standards are often established outside the organization. The best a person can hope for in estimating organizational success is to develop a series of instrumental tests that reflect the dominant views of powerful individuals inside and outside the organization. One overall estimate of success will rarely be seen as appropriate by all interested parties even where the organization knows how to reach several different types of goals.

In Cell IV standards of desirability are ambiguous and cause-effect relationships are incomplete. Here, Thompson argues that measures of fitness in "satisficing" terms may be employed. Here, you attempt to assess the extent to which the organization is viable. We think this calls for an analysis of systems goals including growth, stability, flexibility, and the like. But how should these be judged? We agree with Thompson that the most appropriate standards for acceptability are likely to be based on historical comparisons. How does the organization match up with last year's standards or those of five years ago? We don't think it's appropriate to call an organization unsuccessful because standards of desirability are ambiguous or because managers report that cause-effect linkages are incomplete.

Since the standards of desirability and the cause and effect relationships are usually vague, much of organization theory deals with such characteristics as flexibility and the like or overall descriptions of the system's capability for survival. We will focus on several criteria. The last portion of the chapter highlights which criteria tend to be most relevant, depending on what is being analyzed. But remember that ambiguity about standards and cause-effect relationships should influence how precisely you evaluate organizations and their subsystems.

We should note one interesting misconception held by many neophyte managers. They often assume that only those aspects of performance that are precisely measured are used to evaluate their units and their performance. Such is not the case. Bishop, for instance, has suggested that a number of instrumental and "satisficing" estimates are made in deciding who will be promoted.[1] Even in organizations with a well-developed series of quantitative measures of performance, the manager with the highest scores may not be the one promoted or the individual considered by superiors to be the best manager. Further, as suggested in Chapter 3, the overall assessment of the individual might be heavily weighted toward a stated or unstated criterion. The astute manager carefully analyzes both the stated and unstated criteria used for managerial and unit evaluation.

RELATIONSHIPS AMONG CRITERIA

Links between Organizational Effectiveness and Subunit Performance

We discussed some of the problems in linking effectiveness and performance in Chapter 3. We showed that managers attempted to link effectiveness with lower-level performance via means-ends chains. Yet when managers establish means-ends chains they don't always know what they're doing. In Thompson's terms, standards of desirability would be ambiguous and cause-effect relationships would be incomplete. Managers' beliefs are used to crystallize standards and complete cause-effect relationships. But managers would probably rarely admit this to subordinates. Instead, the uninitiated are told that superiors do know what they're doing. New strategies, programs, and products are launched with considerable publicity. The plans are correct; only appropriate implementation is needed. If problems occur few managers publicly suggest that an inappropriate path (means-ends chain) was established. Managers blame poor performance on external forces, poor communication, and the like. The reverse is less true. Managers often congratulate themselves if performance is high. Many of you realize that individuals often attribute success to their efforts and blame outside forces for failures. But there may be something more deep-seated.

Some argue that the hierarchy of most organizations doesn't rest on as firm a ground as is often believed. Failures by those at lower levels reflect poorly on those higher in the organization. Managers are expected to develop a strong cadre of subordinates willing to do or die for the organization. Further, the authority of managers to some extent rests on the shared belief that they at least know more than most individuals. This knowledge need not be technical. The lore of administration suggests that it is something quite different. Mystical terms such as judgment, insight, wisdom, and diplomacy are used to describe those at the top. Who would ever describe the head of a large organization as an obese old man with dirty fingernails? Instead, a distinguished elder statesman heads the organization. Thus, it may be very important for the governance of an organization to keep various myths alive.

One myth Ritti and Funkhouser[3] suggest organizations keep alive is the close relationship between executive performance and organizational success. But these authors also hint that the association may be one-sided. That is, the link will be made when the organization is successful. But when performance is poor, executives are unlikely to blame themselves.

There are several possible explanations for this. Bishop[1] suggests that selective perception and a strong recognition of negative external factors are incorporated into public evaluations. Administrative lore clearly indicates executives should share the glory while protecting subordinates in defeat. Thus, executives can blame themselves for uncontrollable events. Those who violate the code and blame subordinates place themselves in jeopardy. Executives are expected to select good subordinate managers and develop their subordinates into good managers. When subordinates fail, then the manager may be cited for poor selection and/or inadequate training. Lastly, we often assume managers know the reasons for success or failure. They may not. For instance, would John Kennedy attribute his Presidential election to the ability of Chicago mayor Richard Daley to stuff more ballot boxes than downstate Republicans? We doubt it. Yet this is alleged to be a factor in his election. Cynics also expect the most publicly acceptable reasons for success or failure to be given the most attention. What corporation executive would claim the high profits of the corporation were due to monopoly power or a favorable governmental ruling?

A less cynical view of organizations should also be considered. Since various aspects of unit performance may not be highly interrelated, we think you should ask exactly which aspects of organizational and unit performance are being linked, and for which units. Some linkages make more sense than others. If we talk about the surgical teams of a hospital and the quality of patient care, then the linkage is obvious. It may be dubious, however, to link patient care and janitorial services. A direct cause-effect relationship between the hospital's community services unit and patient care may also be difficult to see. We would caution you against a common mistake, however. Just because a direct link can't be made, don't assume the performance of the unit is irrelevant. The performance of staff units such as janitorial services or community services may only be obvious when they're doing a poor job. Wouldn't you notice a dirty hospital?

Let's also note that previous success may provide organizations with more resources for increasing unit and individual performance.[2] Assume for instance, your unit wants to improve its efficiency in processing insurance claims. It might be particularly helpful to use a computer. Whether you get a computer may, in large part, rest on the previous success of the organization. Just as the rich get richer, high-performing organizations often spawn high-performing units via investments.

Thus, the success of the organization and the performance of units within the system may be linked indirectly. Some of the linkages exist only in the minds of managers and evaluators. But these are real to them and potentially quite useful to the organization. Some linkages are easier to see than others.

Links between Organizational Effectiveness and Employee Maintenance

We discussed possible links between subsystems performance and employee maintenance in Chapter 3. Here we consider the same question with a focus on evaluation of the entire organization.

To some organization theorists, selected aspects of organizational maintenance partially characterize the system's contribution to society. They suggest that if all employees of organizations were unhappy, then it would be difficult to have a satisfied society. Thus each organization should be rated on its ability to satisfy employees.[3,4] Of course this position assumes that organizations are and should be the dominant set of institutions in the society. As we will see in the next chapter, this is an important cultural value shared in many developed nations.

As we pointed out in Chapter 3, employee maintenance is considered a derived goal. There's no reason to believe it will automatically be associated with other derived goals, mission accomplishment, systems goal attainment, or the achievement of output goals anymore than there are automatic associations for any other derived goals. Often, employee maintenance may be given a lower priority than systems and output goals. Then only after satisfying these goals might the system concentrate on employee maintenance. In such an organization, the linkage among maintenance and other goals would be tenuous at best.

A more compelling argument for the association between organizational effectiveness and employee maintenance involves the notion of organizational slack. More effective organizations (in terms of reaching systems and output goals), are likely to have more uncommitted resources.[5] This slack can be used to relax standards, increase rewards to productive employees, and even keep marginal workers on the payroll. We should note, though, that employees may take additional resources in the form of absenteeism instead of higher pay or more challenging jobs. Thus, slack allows the organization to "give" all employees more freedom to select the jobs, rewards, and activities they want. However, they may or may not want more involvement in organizational affairs. We should also note that positive ratings of organizational effectiveness may have a direct bearing on satisfaction, particularly in organizations dominated by professionals. When professional organizations are rated highly, employees may believe, and are often told, it is because of their efforts. Good individuals work for good (highly effective) organizations.

Still others argue that higher satisfaction leads to higher organizational effectiveness. To some this is just a simple extension of the happy worker-productive worker argument discussed in the previous chapter. For others, the linkage is via one or a number of contingency factors. Several authors suggest that high maintenance provides a reservoir of employee goodwill.[1,2] It is suggested that the organization may draw upon this goodwill where there is a peak demand and/or a crisis. We think the extent to which an organization can store goodwill and use it in a crisis may have substantial limitations. Employees may not have the technical capability to meet the crisis. Rolls Royce found this to be the case. Employees were dedicated and hard working but not up to the job.[6] Employees may not remember the good deeds of the organization. Employees may expect continual investment as a matter of course. Once given, benefits to employees are difficult to rescind.

Possible Relationships between Quality of Working Life and Performance

In the last few years there has been a growing movement to link the quality of working life with performance or productivity of workers. Typically these arguments go beyond the simple happy worker-productive worker notion. Instead, the discussion has centered on possible areas of congruence and trade-off between productivity and the quality of working life.[2] Walton describes a number of possibilities concerning the nature of these trade-offs.

Lupton[1] looks at this question a little differently by identifying four possible positions concerning the relationships between performance and the quality of working life. First, is what he terms position A, the "conventional position." Here, primacy is given to markets and profits. A worker exchanges services for money and that's it. In other words, he or she gives "a fair day's work for a fair day's pay."

Second, is position B. Here it is assumed that the greatest good for the greatest number comes about automatically as the sum total of the competition between equally selfish people motivated by the pleasure-seeking principle. According to Lupton, this position assumes: (a) that all people have the same job expectations; and (b) that management recognizes employee expectations and structures the requirements of most jobs in a way to satisfy them. In turn, satisfaction following from fulfillment of these expectations motivates workers to work toward managerially assigned goals. While there is a germ of truth in the position, the assumptions are oversimplified.

Third is position C. Termed the "radical orientation" by Lupton, this position places quality of working life above all else. Quality of working life should be pursued for its own sake whether performance is enhanced or not. Though this position can be defended philosophically, it neglects the performance and effectiveness consideration so crucial in most organizations.

The final position is D, termed the "new logic" by Lupton. Here it is maintained that quality of working life, together with performance/effectiveness, are equally important concerns for organizations. This orientation comes closest to our own position. It's probably the easiest to defend, at least given our present state of knowledge.

Furthermore, position D considers a point made not only by Lupton but by a number of other people writing on quality of working life. Namely, that what workers believe and think and how they define quality of working life can only be discovered by systematic investigation. In other words, one worker may require a great deal of job autonomy to have a high-quality working life. Another may not. One worker may be so deprived that a high-quality working life is the removal of one or more unpleasant conditions. Another worker may place more weight on some factors than others (e.g., pay rather than promotion, an interesting job rather than promotion, etc.).

Some workers, when given the chance, have been known to trade off all the quality of working-life factors for high pay and short hours. They then compensate by living it up off the job. For them, quality of working life appears to translate into more general quality of life. Work is only one small part. For those who want such things as responsibility, involvement, and the like, we think these things should be available. Those who don't want these things should not be forced to have them. Such a position is, of course, entirely consistent with the logic underlying the contingency thrust of this book.

Beliefs about Links among Various Organizational Criteria

You shouldn't expect executives to agree with our analysis of linkages among various organizational criteria. We suggested earlier that some linkages will be made by executives merely because it is in their own best interest. In other cases we expect managers simply to be wrong. Regardless of the evidence, they may link survival, effectiveness, performance, maintenance, or other criteria using some commonsense notions. For instance, happy workers will be seen as more productive because they work harder. More productive workers will be seen as making organizations more effective.

We suspect that as standards of desirability become ambiguous and beliefs about cause and effect are more incomplete (Cell 4 of Thompson's matrix), you will find more executives linking performance and satisfaction. Why? It is possible to get an informal handle on satisfaction even if output is difficult to assess. Furthermore, it's beguilingly simple to link satisfaction to systems stability, flexibility, and potential. Without contradictory evidence provided by widely accepted standards of performance or organizational effectiveness, such linkages cannot be refuted. Where standards of desirability are more crystallized, there are more likely to be separate measures of performance, satisfaction, and organizational effectiveness. With better measurement, we believe that most executives will recognize the uncertain relationship among various measures of success at different levels of analysis.

EMPHASIS ON DIFFERENT CRITERIA

In this part of the book we have focused on the crucial criteria used to evaluate "success" of organizations and their subunits. In the remainder of the book we look at how different environmental, organizational, and subsystems characteristics affect these criteria. A key point to keep in mind as you consider each of these characteristics is that the emphasis on different kinds of "success" measures will be different. This is summarized in Table 4-2.

Table 4-2 shows, for example, that in Part II of the text, where environmental factors are treated, survival is the primary success measure. Goal attainment/mission accomplishment (effectiveness) is secondary and performance and employee maintenance are tertiary in importance. Note that the emphasis

Table 4-2 Criterion Emphasis as a Function of Environmental, Organizational, or Subsystems Characteristics

Characteristics	Portion of Text Where Characteristics Emphasized	Criterion	Time Frame	Emphasis
Environmental	Part II	Survival	Long term	Primary
		Goal attainment/ mission accomplishment	Intermediate term	Secondary
		Performance and employee maintenance	Short term	Tertiary
Organizational	Part III	Goal attainment/ mission accomplishment	Intermediate term	Primary
		Survival	Long term	Secondary
		Performance and employee maintenance	Short term	Tertiary
Subsystems and leadership influence	Part IV	Performance and employee maintenance	Short term	Primary
		Goal attainment/ mission accomplishment	Intermediate term	Secondary
		Survival	Long term	Tertiary

is primarily a function of time frame. Environmental characteristics tend to have a long-run emphasis. Hence, they tend to have their greatest impact on survival, a long-term criterion.

On the other hand, when you move down to the subsystems level (Part IV) there is a short-term emphasis. Thus, performance and employee maintenance become primary and subsystems impact on long-term survival is tertiary. Note, however, that subsystems managers may still be concerned about the survival and effectiveness of their units.

In summary, success means different things depending on whether you are concentrating on environmental, organizational, or subsystems characteristics. And the structure of the book reflects this.

REFERENCES

I. Evaluating Organizational Success

[1]Bishop, R. "The Relationship Between Objective Criteria and Subjective Judgments in Performance Appraisal," *Academy of Management Journal,* 17 (1974), 558–563.

[2]Samuelson, P. A. *Economics.* New York: McGraw-Hill, 1973.

[3]Thompson, J. *Organizations in Action.* New York: McGraw-Hill, 1967.

II. Relationships among Criteria

A. Links between Organizational Effectiveness and Subunit Performance

[1]Bishop, 1974.

[2]Osborn, R. N., Jauch, L. R., and Martin, T. "CEO Succession, Performance and Environmental Conditions." Working paper, Southern Illinois University, 1978.

[3]Ritti, R., and Funkhouser, G. *The Ropes to Skip and the Ropes to Know.* Columbus, Ohio: Grid, 1977.

B. Links between Organizational Effectiveness and Employee Maintenance

[1]Davis, L. E., and Cherns, A. B. (eds.) *The Quality of Working Life, Volume One: Problems, Prospects, and the State of the Art.* New York: The Free Press, 1975.

[2]Davis, L. E., and Cherns, A. B. (eds.). *The Quality of Working Life, Volume Two: Cases and Commentary.* New York: The Free Press, 1975.

[3]Likert, R. *New Patterns of Management.* New York: McGraw-Hill, 1961.

[4]Likert, R. *The Human Organization: Its Management and Value.* New York: McGraw-Hill, 1967.

[5]March, J. G., and Simon, H. A. *Organizations.* New York: Wiley, 1958.

[6]"Rolls Seeks New RB.211 Contract," *Aviation Week,* 94, 7 (1971), 32–34.

C. Possible Relationships between Quality of Working Life and Performance

[1]Lupton, T. "Efficiency and the Quality of Worklife: The Technology of Reconciliation," *Organizational Dynamics,* 3(4) (Autumn 1975), 68–80.

[2]Walton, R. E. "Criteria for Quality of Working Life," In L. E. Davis and A. B. Cherns (eds.), *The Quality of Working Life, Volume One.* New York: The Free Press, 1975.

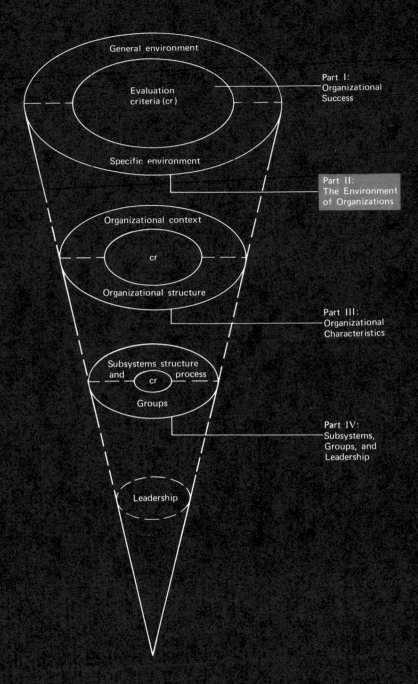

Figure II-1 A cone model for organizational analysis.

part

the environment
of organizations

We indicated in Chapter 1 that the organization may be viewed as an input-transformation-output system. If an organization cannot draw inputs from the environment or export its output, it will die. Many early administrative scholars appeared to believe that as long as the system had the outputs the system would survive. Thus, studying the transformation of resources formed a major aspect of organization theory in its early beginnings. The impact of external forces was generally ignored. Since the environment was assumed constant, or changing very slowly, management strategies devised in one time period were proposed as generally applicable. The manager who adequately planned, organized, staffed, directed, and controlled would automatically anticipate and adjust to any environmental variation. It was assumed that these managerial functions, found successful in the United States, would be equally successful throughout the world.

But doubts were raised about the universality of management principles when American management scholars began to travel to other countries. Firms found unexpected problems with their overseas operations. Foreign workers, managers, markets, suppliers, and governments were different. The whole culture seemed to permeate the system. Now there is quite a controversy over the transferability of American management theory and practice. The environment in which the organization operates seems to have the potential to influence the success of various patterns and practices, while others seem to be universal.

How managers and their organizations are evaluated is substantially influenced by cultural values. Organizations operating in different cultures performing the same societal function are often quite different. Yet the precise influence of external factors on organizations and managerial practices is unknown. Recent cross-cultural and comparative management studies are beginning to show the nature of some important environmental influences. But most of the evidence is quite speculative. Most studies that focus on external variables are case analyses. As a whole they seem to show both cultural differences and management universals.

In the next three chapters we look at the external setting of organizations. We attempt to answer some apparently simple questions: What is the environment? What factors outside the boundaries of the organization are important? How do these factors influence organizational goals, goal attainment, internal operations, and structure? We incorporate research findings and concepts from a broad range of disciplines—sociology, anthropology, political science, and economics.

Differences between organizations may or may not be due to external factors. For instance, few argue that the differences between GM and Ford are due to environmental variables. Variations across organizations in different environments may be explained by "functional equivalence" and equifinality. Two organizations operating in exactly the same environment may select quite different ways of accomplishing the same goal and be equally successful. In the same fashion, organizations operating in two different settings may select identical paths to quite dissimilar goals. What does all this mean for the analysis of organizational environments?

Given equifinality and functional equivalence, organization analysts must define the environment in specific, measurable ways and identify the factors that influence organizations.

Traditionally, the environment of an organization has been defined as everything outside the boundaries of the system. This definition is too vague. This kind of "residual" analysis is not enough. All differences between organizations operating in different settings are not due to external factors. However, defining the environment is difficult.

We divide the environment into two partially overlapping parts: the general environment and the specific environment.* The general environment contains those forces that influence all organizations operating within a given geographic area. The specific environment contains those conditions unique to one organization or a small number of organizations. As our knowledge of external forces advances, more precise divisions among various parts of the environment should emerge. But at this time, the general and specific categories are about as far as the field has progressed.

The general environment consists of all those forces (economic, educational, political, and cultural) that influence all the organizations operating within a given geographical area.† Governmental units are often used to form the outer perimeter of the general environment. Economic, educational, or cultural criteria could be used. But for most purposes, we think political boundaries help us the most.

Why use political boundaries? There are several important practical and theoretical reasons. First, economic, educational, and political data are readily available for political units. For example, detailed information concerning per capita income by state, county, and city is routinely published by the U.S. Bureau of the Census. Second, most organizations (with the obvious exception

---

*A third "miscellaneous" category would include other factors not included in these two. We won't confuse the issue further, however.

†Definition of the specific environment is reserved for Chapter 6. The definition is detailed and dependent on how you define an organization.

of the Mafia and some political parties) exist under governmental sanction. United States corporations are chartered; the domains of government agencies usually correspond to city, county, state, or national boundaries.

Third, the increased emphasis on nationalism has helped forge more consistent economic, educational, political, and cultural patterns within national political units. Finally, large-scale organizations are characteristic of more developed and stable societies where national boundaries signify changes in legal, political, educational, and economic systems.

But what then is the appropriate governmental unit? Is it the city, county, state, nation, or empire? A detailed theoretical rule for drawing the boundaries of the general environment is beyond the scope of this book. However, you can usually draw the boundaries by a quick analysis of the physical location of a system and its major area of operations. That is, where does the system draw its employees, money and resources, and where is it geographically located?

Even with this criterion you should recognize that most organizations cross the boundaries of the general environment through contact with other systems. Multinational corporations are an example. They import resources or export finished products or services to systems operating in other nations. Many of their problems stem from operating across several political, cultural, and social boundaries.

Chapters 5, 6, and 7

Chapter 5 deals with the general environment. In keeping with our approach to moving from the general to the specific, we start with the general environment in its broadest dimensions. Chapter 5 uses both national and regional boundaries as its unit of analysis. If you're concerned with organizations operating in international arenas, the cultural, educational, economic, and political forces at work in different regions of the world become crucial. We distinguish between developed and underdeveloped nations and their impact on organizations. Chapter 5 also focuses on these forces that appear to influence organizations within primarily developed nations. Even here, however, there are differences in the patterns of development among regions.

The second chapter in this part deals with the specific environment of organizations. Here there are a few empirical studies mostly concerning nonprofit organizations. But as with the analysis of the general environment, we must speculate quite often. The contingency chapter rounds out Part II by drawing together analyses of the general and specific environments into one integrated framework. This part, then, begins our analysis of the top parts of the contingency cone (see Figure II-1).

chapter 5 THE GENERAL ENVIRONMENT

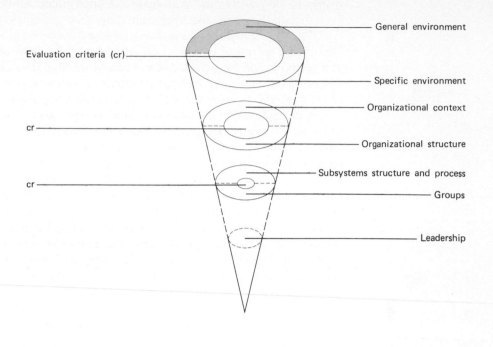

General environment

Evaluation criteria (cr)

Specific environment

Organizational context

cr

Organizational structure

Subsystems structure and process

cr

Groups

Leadership

In late 1969 Leslie Landrover was transferred to South America and charged with heading the construction of a new plant. At first everyone in the country appeared to be friendly and willing to help. But quickly Leslie ran into problems with suppliers. Critical material could not get through customs. After six months of frustration Leslie discussed these problems with one of the "locals." He appeared to have little trouble getting supplies. The native asked a few questions. How much money had been transferred to the customs agents? Did Leslie contribute to the President's welfare fund and to the union charities? Had Leslie taken Juan Corlata, the minister for development, to dinner and offered the good services of the corporation? The local knew, for example, that the development minister was interested in getting his son Jose on the staff of a multinational corporation.

Leslie was shocked. Bribes and political payoffs are illegal in the United States. Nepotism was unethical. Leslie wrote the national headquarters for instructions. Should officials be bribed, relatives hired, political contributions made? The response was: "It's part of your job, Leslie, to adjust to local business conditions in the appropriate fashion. You're in charge." In other words, Leslie was told to "Watergate it." Appropriate adjustments were made. Even though the plant cost 20 percent more than anticipated, construction was completed on schedule. Leslie was promoted to the New York Headquarters. There is no record of whether Leslie transferred funds to political parties. But in a memo to the New York office, Leslie notes that Jose Corlata would make a good plant manager. The organization's "commitment to the social welfare of the country" was clearly indicated to Leslie's successor.

In the example of the unnamed South American country, taxes on business firms were comparatively small. But corporations were expected to support customs officials and charities. Thus, instead of paying taxes to the government, which were then disbursed to customs officials and charities, there was an informal system of support. Payments to customs officials, for example, were a fixed percentage of the cash value of the imported items. Gifts to charities were expected only if the firm was profitable. Nepotism was maintained to ensure that contracts would be honored with a minimum of legal complications. Business deals were both contracts between systems and arrangements between individuals. If the individual was a member of a prominent family, the entire family was also committed to the contract. Thus, some questionable practices might be seen as merely alternate cultural patterns for supporting specific government agencies, maintaining a form of social responsibility and ensuring an organization's commitment to a transaction.

This example illustrates how some key concepts in this chapter will be used. Culture is treated as the set of forces that establishes the game in which organizations develop their goals and operate. Economic conditions reveal the physical and service resources potentially available to players of the game. Educational institutions provide the skilled players available to organizations. The rules of the game and the basic allocations of power to different players are established in the legal-political sector. This chapter explores each of these four areas across nations and within the United States. For each sector, we explain the organizational implications and responses.

Now let's move to an analysis of the first major component of the general environment. Since cultural forces establish the name of the game, we start with this sector of the general environment.

CULTURE

Culture's traditional definition dates to the nineteenth century. Taylor defined culture as, "that complex whole which includes knowledge, belief, art, morals, law, custom and any other capabilities and habits acquired by man as a member of society. . ."[3] We need to be more specific and limited. First, we will look for consistency among knowledge, beliefs, art, morals, and customs of individuals living in an *identifiable geographic area.*[1] Second, we are interested in concepts and analyses that appear applicable to a variety of cultures.[2] What then is important in the culture for the analysis of organizational environments? The literature suggests that cultural values may be the key aspect of culture for such an analysis.[4]

Cultural Values

It is popular to center on one overriding value that explains the collective action of a society. For example, some might say Americans are materialistic, Germans are authoritarian, South Americans are emotional. But as Service warns, "environments are so diverse, the problems so numerous, and the solutions potentially so various that no single determinant can be equally powerful for all cases" (p. 25).[27]

Much of the literature concerning the general environment of organizations assumes that differences in values lead to different organizational goals, internal structures, and internal operations. Crozier argues that, "organizational systems are cultural answers to the problems encountered by human beings in achieving their collective ends."[3] But if cultural values underlie organizations, which values are important? What do we mean by cultural values?

Important Cultural Values. Cultural values are those desirable conditions that form an individual's view of the universe and man's role in it. Redfield argues that every culture provides its people with concepts of: (1) generalized others, (2) the distinctions between members of the culture and outsiders, (3) the differences between males and females, (4) temporal orientation, (5) abstractions including beings, forces, and principles, (6) animals and nature, and (7) groups of people.[*,25] Together these form a pattern of cultural values which influences every individual and institution in the nation. While each culture is unique, these key concepts can be combined into a profile for analyzing the cultural demands placed on organizations. Table 5-1 shows our estimate of how these concepts combine to form prescientific, scientific, and postscientific patterns of values.[10,11,13]

The prescientific value system does not provide a favorable climate for complex organizations. Just compare the characteristics of this pattern with the common characteristics of organizations.[31] Organizations have a set of

*Other categories are discussed by Redfield, but we focus only on those enumerated.

Table 5-1. Prescientific, Scientific, and Postscientific Value Patterns

Value Dimension	Value Pattern		
	Prescientific	Scientific	Postscientific
View of Generalized others	Distrust—Theory *X* assumes that people dislike work, must be coerced, controlled, and disciplined	Trust if people are educated, Theory *X* assumptions if they are not	Trust—Theory *Y* assumes that people exert self-direction and self-control and can be committed to work and the organization
Distinctions between members of the culture and others			
a. Who are in the culture	Those in the family and the tribe	Those in the nation	Those in developed nations
b. View of outsiders	Alien and inferior	Inferior	Disadvantaged but still inferior
Differences between males and females	Males superior in all areas	Males superior in scientific and administrative activities	Except for some biological differences, they are equal
Temporal orientation	Time unimportant, follows nature's rhythm	Time is money, efficient use is important	Time is important, effective use is stressed
Abstractions	Few, based on dominant religion or political philosophy	Several, most based on scientific rationalism	Many, inconsistent mix of religious, political, and scientific abstractions
View of animals and nature	People must adjust but may use symbols and rituals to induce miracles to partially control nature	Animals and nature are to be conquered and controlled	Animals and nature are to be protected and restored
Groups of people	Family and tribe are the only important groups and dominate determined positions in organizations	Family and occupational groups are important and set guidelines for behavior	Family and social groups are important, occupational groups are a necessary evil

Source: Based on analyses by Hay and Grey,[11] Honegmann,[13] and Havilland,[10] among others

abstract rules for reaching a limited set of goals. Predictability and uniformity are prized. Expertise is the base for selecting, promoting, and firing members. The system runs on a set of "scientifically rational," formal relationships. Under a prescientific culture many of these hallmarks of organizations are foreign. Kinship, not expertise, is used for selection. Members outside the extended family and the tribe cannot be trusted. Scientific rationalism must be explained in terms of the dominant religion or philosophy.

A simple example here illustrates the point. In Malaysia, women employees who said they had been molested by a headless, 10-foot ghost, led a stampede of workers out of an electrical equipment factory. The factory was closed for three days until arrangements were made to satisfy the angry spirit. The witch doctor sprinkled rice and water around the factory and sacrificed a goat. A feast for the workers followed.[1] Thus, organizations, as we know them, are not consistent with these prescientific values.

The cultural demands placed on organizations by the scientific and postscientific value patterns is a little more difficult to assess.[4,9,20,22] We think it is important to recognize a confounding factor in cultural analyses. Namely, dominant values are accompanied by contradictory ones.[17] A partial list of these is provided in Table 5-2. Interestingly, many of the dominant values are consistent with the postscientific values listed in Table 5-1. Many of the "contradictory values" are the distinguishing characteristics of large organizations and consistent with the scientific pattern. For instance, collectivism, leadership, equal opportunity, manipulation, and the like, are popular terms in organization analysis. They reflect underlying values consistent with behavior in complex systems.[15] Is there a fundamental difference between scientific and postscientific cultural values?

Values and Goals. Yes, there is an important difference for organizations! Namely, the goal structure stemming from postscientific values deemphasizes output and systems goals. There is a broader social concern and an emphasis on individualism.[12] Hay and Grey, for instance, argue that we have passed away from a phase that held profits and economic efficiency as the sole criterion for business actions.[11] We are now in a phase between scientific and postscientific value systems where organizations are responsible to customers, employees, suppliers, creditors, and stockholders collectively. But these authors envision a phase they call the "quality of life" orientation. It is consistent with our postscientific category. Here management would consider the impact of all its actions on society and take an active hand in solving major societal problems. For example, under a scientific value system, General Motors would argue: What's good for GM is good for the nation. Under a postscientific culture GM might argue: We're a leader in pollution control, minority hiring, and the development of mass transit and still provide a return to stockholders.

Table 5-2   Selected Dominant and Contradictory American Values

Dominant Value	Contradictory Value
Individualism: the secret of American greatness	*Collectivism:* people should stand together and work for common purposes
Initiative: people can be trusted if let alone to guide their conduct wisely	*Leadership:* you cannot simply afford to sit and wait for people to make up their minds
Democracy: the ultimate form of living together	*Authoritarianism:* nothing would get done if everything were left to a popular vote
Goal Attainment: everyone should attempt to be successful	*Method:* what kind of person you are is more important than success
Family Orientation: the family is the basic institution of the society	*Economic Orientation:* other institutions must conform to the needs of economic organizations since the national welfare depends on them
Equality of Opportunity: America is the land of opportunity and all people should get a fair chance	*Unequal Opportunity:* not everybody is equal and the best should be put in charge
Academic Achievement: education is important in itself	*Practical Achievement:* it is practical people who get things done
Scientific Orientation: science is good and the road to development	*Ascientific Orientations:* science has no right to upset fundamental institutions
Justice: the American judicial system ensures equal treatment	*Manipulation:* persons are fools if they don't hire the best lawyer they can afford

Source: Adapted from Lynd, R. *Knowledge for What? The Place of Science in American Culture* (Princeton: Princeton University Press, 1939).

You may think this is a very subtle difference. It isn't to the practicing executive. Pollution control, research and development for mass transit, and minority hiring all cut short-run profits.

Values and Internal Operations. Myers and Myers also expect that while becoming more socially responsive, internal operations will change as organizations begin to confront a postscientific value system.[21] Employees won't accept conformity and manipulation. Organizations will be forced into becoming more internally oriented and participative. Individualism will be prized and replace the emphasis on higher status. If new policies and procedures are developed, they must be "sold" to employees. Universities have witnessed some of this already. For example, it was less than ten years ago that most universities enforced women's hours. Students were threatened with serious penalties for violation of even the most minor rules such as driving an unregistered car on campus. Now these rules sound a little ridiculous. Tannenbaum and Davis also argue that organizations will be forced to view employees as individuals, not mere role-holders.[30] For instance, what impact will a transfer have on the individual's family life? Perhaps it is oversimplistic, but the thrust of these predictions is that organizations will be asked to serve their members rather than have the members serve organizations.[34]

Terminal and Instrumental Values. So far we have treated cultural values as a homogeneous set of interrelated concepts. But most of us recognize that organizations appear to violate important cultural values and still grow and prosper.[26,33] For example, illegal political contributions, bribery, patronage jobs, et cetera, may violate cultural norms.[19] But the organization may benefit from these activities. While some organizations can temporarily escape value constraints, there appears to be a more complex and accurate explanation for cultural differences.[23] Individuals rank the relative importance of values differently.[9,28] Moreover, various institutions are likely to place different priorities on values.[2] Thus, dominant and contradictory values are scheduled into the society according to the function of the organization.[18] The Army is hardly democratic or vitally concerned with individualism. But it may attempt to develop equality of opportunity.

To understand this scheduling process it is useful to distinguish between terminal and instrumental values.[28] Terminal values center on the desirability of end-states. Instrumental values deal with the attractiveness of the means toward an end. Terminal values set boundaries on systems and output goals. Terminal values are also reflected in the derived goals of organizations.[6] Many business organizations in the United States now accept pollution control and equal opportunity as derived goals. But it is comparatively easy for an organization to hide its systems goals with a carefully worded and well-publicized mission statement.[8] It can legitimize output goals by selectively stressing the contribution of the most socially desirable products. For instance, during the Vietnamese War, Dow Chemical rarely mentioned that it produced napalm. Instead, it talked about the other more socially desirable chemicals it produced.

More important and less obvious is the subtle influence of instrumental values. For instance, job enrichment—the code word for taking routine, boring jobs and making them more difficult, exciting and challenging—may not increase employee performance.[29] But it may be used and accepted anyway because providing an interesting and challenging job is an important instrumental value itself.[14] If performance is not hurt, it will probably be accepted.

The most important terminal values for an organization are those associated with its social function. Economic systems stress a comfortable, prosperous life and the economic accomplishments its members can make. Religious institutions, of course, emphasize salvation and often justify the importance of this terminal value by linking it with the related terminal values of happiness, inner harmony, self-respect, and wisdom. With rare exceptions, it is comparatively easy for an organization to justify its intentions and actions by claiming it is pursuing one or more dominant terminal values. As we will see in the next chapter, the pursuit of terminal values helps the organization secure needed resources. Essentially organizations implicitly argue they should receive support because they are the instruments needed to accomplish desired terminal values.

The development of means-ends linkages helps the organization to cement terminal and instrumental values. For instance, executives should be ambitious, capable, helpful, polite, and self-controlled (instrumental values), so that they and the organization can provide a comfortable and prosperous society (terminal values). Yet in larger organizations with extensive specialization, means and ends are often so tightly linked that means become ends. Instrumental values replace and supplement terminal values. The linkage between the jobs of individuals and the terminal values that the organization supports is just too indirect. Thus, the day-to-day operations of large organizations rest primarily on instrumental values.

Perhaps the best-known and most important set of instrumental values is the "work ethic."[16] Work is its own reward, summarizes this set of values. Those subscribing to the work ethic need not see the linkage between the assigned duties and terminal values. Work is the path. While some have questioned the strength and persistence of the work ethic, it still appears to be a dominant instrumental value in industrialized nations.[6,24,33] Of course, there are other important instrumental values many organizations support. Farmer and Richman list a number of important value "constraints" that might be placed on economic systems.[7] To the extent these values are dominant, they constrain organizations (see Table 5-3).

If values are important and differ across nations, then we should see a different set of terminal and instrumental values for managers operating in different cultures. England and his associates have attempted to chart the values of administrators in different cultures.[5] They have found both similarities and differences in analyses of the United States, Japan, South Korea, and India. For instance, U.S. managers were more goal oriented than those in the other cultures. They placed more emphasis on efficiency. Yet, managers in the United States, Japan, South Korea, and India all emphasize competition. These

Table 5-3 Important Cultural Values That May Constrain Organizations

1. Managers and management should not be trusted.
2. Superiors should not be followed unless their requests match the desires of followers.
3. Career development and task accomplishment are not very important.
4. Birthright should be more important than accomplishment in determining social standing.
5. A son should follow in his father's footsteps.
6. A son should not be expected to do better than his father.
7. Organizations serving different societal functions should compete with one another.
8. Wealth and income should not be used to judge others and are not particularly desirable.
9. Feelings and emotions should be used to make decisions rather than cost-benefit analysis.
10. Attempting to predict the future is not very useful.
11. Stability is preferred to change.

Source: Adapted from Farmer, R., and Richman, B. *Comparative Management and Economic Progress.* (Homewood, Ill.: Richard D. Irwin, 1965). Copyright © 1971 by Cedarwood Press. All Rights Reserved.

data suggest that the social function of the organization and the culture are two important factors in predicting the dominant values held by managers.

Subcultural Values

So far we have looked at the culture of a nation as if it were identical throughout. But cultures are not homogeneous. There are substantial subcultural differences. How important are these? What aspects of subcultural differences are important for organizations? These are addressed here.

There are several reports concerning the impact of subcultural values on organizational goals and processes within the United States. Freeman argues that when the community thinks the organization is supporting dominant values, personnel, money, and legitimacy are comparatively easy to get.[1] Conversely, with little information about the system, or the view that the organization is not in tune with dominant values, the organization will find it difficult to obtain local support. Some organizations assume that if the community is aware of its goals and operations, help will come automatically. Support will only be forthcoming if key individuals and institutions believe the organization contributes to the terminal values they deem important and follow the instrumental values they cherish.

Several authors argue that organizations are likely to change their operative goals to mesh with the dominant terminal and instrumental values of the community.[3,2,4] But in the process of adapting to the community, Selznick shows that organizations may alter the terminal and instrumental values of important local institutions as well.[3]

States as Subcultures

These general notions fit common sense. But they are of comparatively little value unless you know the dominant local value system. Elazar has made an elaborate attempt to categorize state subcultures. He notes three dominant subcultural patterns.[2] No one state completely matches any one of the three patterns. But each can be placed in one of the following three categories: (1) traditionalistic, (2) moralistic, and (3) individualistic (see Table 5-4).

As the name implies, the traditionalistic subculture still contains a preindustrial flavor—an emphasis on paternalism and elitism with strong ties to the history of the area. In traditionalistic states, Elazar would expect that institutions promoting paternalism, elitism, and conservative administrative practices would receive support. He notes that state government agencies use federal funds in this manner.

The major characteristic of the moralistic subculture is the search for societal good. Here, government control over individuals is more likely. The emphasis in the individualistic states is on the mutual obligations of individuals and organizations. Ironically, though, you are likely to find the greatest degree of government intervention in the individualistic states.[4] An attempt will be made to equalize exchange relationships among all groups in the subculture. Unlike the moralistic subculture, individuals are encouraged to seek their own view of important terminal values. No one set of terminal values is considered the most appropriate in an individualistic subculture.

As a close examination of Table 5-4 suggests, richer and more densely populated states are usually in the individualistic category. The moralistic group is a mix of rich and poor states with varying degrees of population density. Traditionalistic states are in or immediately adjacent to the Old South.

Table 5-4 1974 Per Capita Income and Population Density for Traditionalistic, Moralistic, and Individualistic States

	Traditionalistic[a]			Moralistic			Individualistic	
	Per Capita Income[b]	Population Density[c]		Per Capita Income	Population Density		Per Capita Income	Population Density
Alabama	2800	68	California	4500	128	Connecticut	4800	623
Arizona	3500	16	Colorado	3800	21	Delaware	4200	276
Arkansas	2700	37	Idaho	3200	9	Illinois	4500	199
Florida	3500	126	Iowa	3100	51	Indiana	3800	143
Georgia	3300	79	Kansas	3800	28	Massachusetts	4300	727
Kentucky	3000	81	Maine	3200	32	Maryland	4200	397
Louisiana	3000	81	Michigan	4000	136	Missouri	3700	68
Mississippi	2500	47	Minnesota	3800	48	Nebraska	3700	19
New Mexico	3000	8	Montana	3400	5	Nevada	4500	4
North Carolina	3200	104	New Hampshire	3600	82	New Jersey	4500	953
Oklahoma	3300	37	North Dakota	3000	9	New York	4800	381
South Carolina	2900	86	Oregon	3700	21	Ohio	4000	260
Tennessee	3000	94	South Dakota	3200	9	Pennsylvania	3900	262
Texas	3500	43	Utah	3200	13	Rhode Island	3900	905
West Virginia	2900	73	Vermont	3500	48	Wyoming	3400	4
Virginia	3600	116	Washington	4000	51			
			Wisconsin	3700	81			

Sources:

[a]Based on Elazar, D. J. American Federalism: A View from the States (New York: Thomas Y. Crowell, 1966).

[b]U.S. per capita income in 1974 = $3900. From Survey of Current Business (1975).

[c]U.S. population density in 1974 = 57.5 per square mile. From World Almanac & Book of Facts (1975).

There are, of course, some substantial variations within states. For instance, California is a mix of individualistic urban centers and moralistic rural areas. Illinois, Indiana, and Ohio are categorized overall as individualistic states. But the southern regions of each of these are traditionalistic. In the same fashion Florida is traditionalistic. But the urban complex surrounding Miami would probably be tagged individualistic.

The contributions organizations are expected to make, therefore, are likely to vary between and within states. For small organizations operating within a very small geographic area, this is not a problem. They can adjust to the subculture. But what of the larger systems that span several subcultures? The disparity in subcultures can be a problem. For example, there is a large university located in an isolated, traditionalistic area of a predominately individualistic state. It draws students from both urban and rural areas. Students continually ask the university to intervene in the community to make housing contracts, installment purchases, and legal enforcement more "even handed." Community leaders, on the other hand, want the university to exercise more control over students and keep them from disrupting the community. Historically, the university bent to the wishes of the community. There may have been a number of reasons, but one important one seems to stick out. Funds for the university were allocated by a state legislature, which overrepresented traditionalistic areas. Recently, however, the trend has shifted in favor of the students. The state legislature has been reapportioned. A state coordinating unit allocates funds in large part on the basis of enrollment. And the university is recovering from a decline in student population. In essence, when a system operates in more than one subculture, it is likely to subscribe to the values that increase its chances for growth and survival.

Urban-Rural Differences. Cultural value patterns may not be identical in both urban and rural areas. The urban-rural differences noted by Elazar in the United States parallel those in many European, South American, and Asian nations. Rural areas tend to be more traditionalistic than urban areas. There are fewer large, complex organizations. Family and kinship patterns appear much more important. Social position is often more important in estimating compliance to a contract than the legality of an agreement. We should note, however, some substantial variations in this basic proposition. Urban areas in underdeveloped countries may indeed be less traditionalistic than the rural areas.[7] But this doesn't automatically indicate a more favorable climate for organizations. People with skill and money are needed for organizational survival.[3] Unskilled, illiterate, and starving peasants in urban areas may be only slightly less traditionalistic than their rural counterparts.[6] But neither group is particularly useful for complex organizations. Within the United States there is a slightly different phenomenon. Large urban areas consist of several rings or areas.[8] The urban areas as a whole may be individualistic. But the inner city may be an entirely different subculture.[5] The urban poor may or may not share the same dominant cultural values as their richer suburban counterparts. The social structure of the two areas may be dramatically different.[1,9]

At the very least, these cultural differences require organizations to alter personnel practices, and can influence derived goals. A trivial but relevant example might be that of holidays granted by business firms. In certain regions on the first day of the hunting season an organization might just as well close its doors. In urban areas, the birthday of Martin Luther King, Jr., might be a day off. With respect to goals, the firm located in urban areas may be pressed to invest in urban renewal. Pressures in small towns can also exist. Here, anecdotal evidence suggests that there has traditionally been a more paternalistic attitude taken by managers regarding the role of the firm vis-à-vis the community.

Socialization: An Organizational Response to Subcultural Differences

It might appear that the pressure only flows toward the organization to adapt and adjust to the values of its environment. But this is not the case. The organization also pressures the environment. Equally important are organizational attempts to alter the values its members bring to it. These occur through a process known as *socialization*.

As Schein notes, socialization involves learning and internalizing:

1. The basic goals of the organization.
2. The preferred means by which the goals should be attained.
3. The basic responsibility of the member and the role that is being granted that member by the organization.
4. The behavior patterns that are required for effective performance in the role.
5. A set of rules or principles that pertain to the maintenance of the identity and integrity of the organization (p. 3).[15]

In summary, the organization attempts to condition the behavior of its members by getting them to accept the organization's ideology and goals. Organizational values may or may not conflict with the dominant subcultural values.[2] If there's little or no conflict, individuals have few problems accommodating themselves to the organization.[4,11]. However, if dominant subcultural values conflict with the organization, then it is faced with a more difficult socialization process. Members may be uncomfortable. They may resist or reject the values and goals of the organization. Litterer suggests there may be a third mode between acceptance and rejection.[13] That is, some values will be accommodated while others are ignored or rejected. Some will be more responsive than others to socialization attempts.[5] But even journalists, trained to hold a value of objectivity, have been found to be socialized such that they accept the values of their publishers and editors.[16]

Individual responses to socialization attempts may vary by level in the organization.[17] At lower levels, socialization may be more concerned with responsibilities and roles and performance standards.[8] Thus, typically, organizations rely on work groups to secure adherence to work values, rules, and expectations for getting the job done.[9,14] At higher levels, though, the emphasis may be on goals, ideology, and identity and integrity of the organization.[1] For higher level personnel, the organization may assume that it is the primary force in the individual's life.[9]

We don't wish to get deeply involved with how the socialization process works here.[6] Suffice it to say that this process can and does lead to alterations in the subcultural values members bring to the organization. Evidence for this has been provided for managers by England.[3] He studied the importance of different groups of people to 1072 managers. The most important reference group was "my company." This reference group was rated as more important than my boss, owners, government, employees, and even "me."

Apparently, socialization is a powerful force in combating cultural values that may run counter to those of the organization.[7,12,18]

Clearly, cultural and subcultural values influence the organization. The organization also influences the values of its members. Organizations are not just reactive. The values of their members are not just accepted as given. Through socialization, organizations seek to gain commitment of their members to their goals and ideology.

THE ECONOMIC CLIMATE

Organizations may be solutions to cultural problems; but solutions require resources. Economists have long realized that land, labor, and capital are the basic building blocks of organized activity.[1] Without all three, organizations cannot exist. Organizations are built upon and generate surpluses. This means energy must be diverted from current consumption toward investment if organizations are to survive. All nations have some surpluses that can be invested in organizations.

With larger surpluses, more organizations get the resources they need to produce products or services. As the economy becomes more economically developed, organizations can increase specialization and build upon each other's strengths.[2] More developed economies mean more people with more money and, therefore, larger markets. Organizations can expand to meet demand and reap internal economies of scale.[3] One organization doesn't perform all the steps necessary to produce a product or service. Instead, it can purchase semicompleted parts and services from other more specialized systems. Economic development is also accompanied by more social overhead such as roads, bridges, financial institutions, and information systems.

Greater surpluses also translate into more available resources for nonprofit systems. Just as individuals and organizations invest, the society as a whole reaps returns from social programs. Economic development means that more money can be put into defense, health care, education, rehabilitation programs for the physically and mentally handicapped, legal services, churches, fraternal groups, and entertainment. All organizations can benefit from economic growth.

Sources of Surplus

As you might expect, economic output is derived from various sources in different nations. Agriculture and nonmanufacturing are dominant in the less developed nations.[3] A large percent of the population and an enormous percent of the economic effort is used for food production. The land is poor, farms are small, and agricultural overhead (dams, irrigation, facilities, and storage elevators) is scarce. Yet population growth in these nations is high.[1] More and more food must be produced just to prevent mass starvation. Underdeveloped nations also rely heavily on one source of surplus (e.g., one major crop, or one major mineral or trade).[5] In the developed nations, agriculture is not so dominant.[4] Industrial activity in general, and manufacturing in particular, contributes a substantial percentage of the output.[2] And for the noncommunist nations, finance, insurance, real estate, and business services as well as local and national government contributions add substantially to the output. In other words, the more developed nations have better balanced economies. A natural disaster affecting agriculture does not destroy the economy. World price fluctuations in basic materials may hurt or help some organizations but don't usually upset the entire economic picture.[5]

Factors Associated with Overall Economic Development

There are other factors affecting economic development. In developing nations roads are often little more than donkey paths. Port facilities often appear straight out of the Middle Ages.[2] Electric power, a frequently used measure of development, may not be available outside major urban centers.[2] Insurance, finance, and real estate services may be difficult if not impossible to obtain. Even if local organizations want to import machinery, the country may not have the currency to pay for it.

Income of most citizens in poor nations is, of course, low. But distribution of income is another element affecting organizations. In all nations, incomes are unevenly distributed. But in poor nations the gap between the wealthy and the starving is even more pronounced.[2] This typically means starvation, high population growth, illiteracy, crowded urban centers cluttered with shanties, short life expectancies, and rampant disease. All the worst the world can offer. Thus, the markets for organizational output are quite different from what many of us are used to.

The human side of poverty is reflected in the goal structures of foreign organizations.[4] The concepts of human growth and development, self-actualization, clean and healthful working conditions, and job monotony are almost unknown. The basic problem is survival. You can hardly worry about destroying an animal species from industrial pollution when millions of people are starving. Increased efficiency in organizations is not just a socially desirable goal that means more luxury and leisure. It can be the difference between life and death. As Farmer and Richman point out, organizational efficiency is the key to economic growth and development for most, if not all, underdeveloped nations.[1]

There are a number of other factors associated with economic development. McClelland and Winter argue that inadequate motivation to achieve is both a cause of poverty and one of its most devastating outcomes.[3] Higgins, among others, notes the association between foreign domination and lack of development.[2] He argues very persuasively that "colonialism" not only exploited the economic resources of a nation, but severely undercut local entrepreneurs. His historical analysis seems to reveal that foreign domination served to inhibit the values associated with economic development.

Powelson's analysis of underdeveloped nations is another substantial departure from the explanations of traditional economic theory.[5] He suggests that investment may not be made in the most profitable ventures and organizations. Instead, those systems that embody the dominant values of powerful groups receive most favored treatment. Thus, even in the poorest nations, organizations that appear to support the dominant ideology get the resources they need to survive. Note that this is a radical departure from the idea prevalent in the

United States that organizations should receive inputs only to the extent that they help some outside group.

The Economic Climate within Regions of a Nation

Economic development is not spread equally across all regions in any nation. The largest urban center of a developing nation may provide an adequate resource base for large organizations. Conversely, there may be regions where the economic base will only support small, local retail, wholesale, and agricultural concerns. Political systems, educational units, and sociocultural systems may receive much of their financial support from the richer areas of the nation.[3]

Gross National Product (GNP) per capita is adequate for comparing nations.* For a more detailed picture, it can easily be supplemented for the analysis of regions within developed nations. As you might expect, there is a close correspondence among the measure of GNP per capita, unemployment, and the percent of individuals and families below the poverty line. As shown earlier in Table 5-4, there is a rough correspondence between economic conditions and whether the state is considered traditionalistic, moralistic, or individualistic.[2]

The Economic Climate of Urban Areas in the United States. To a large extent organizations in developed nations draw their resources from urban areas. This is more dramatic for systems that produce services since they are not tied to physical resources. As you might expect, different urban areas attract and specialize in slightly different economic functions.[3] Detroit is the auto center. Washington, D.C., is the political capital. Table 5-5 attempts to combine information concerning economic activity, size, and drawing power to estimate the breadth, depth, and stability of the economic environment of 50 important U.S. urban centers. The analysis uses *Standard Metropolitan Statistical Areas (SMSA)* rather than political boundaries. An SMSA is an identifiable urban area including a city and its major suburban areas. In some cases several smaller cities form one SMSA, for example, Tampa-St. Petersburg. Outlying suburban areas such as Arlington, Texas, are subsumed into a larger city such as Dallas.

Based on population and sphere of influence, three classes of cities can be identified: (a) national, (b) regional, and (c) local. As the title suggests, national cities are the largest urban centers with the greatest sphere of influence.

*See the Measurement Module for a discussion of GNP.

Table 5-5 The Economic Climate of 50 Important U.S. Urban Areas

Stability and Primary Economic Activity	Population and Sphere of Influence		
	National: Huge with National Sphere of Influence	Regional: Very Large or Large with Some National, but Predominantly Regional, Sphere of Influence	Local: Large or Moderate Size with Predominantly Local Sphere of Influence
Stable	1	2	3
a. Manufacturing and trade	New York, Boston, Chicago	Pittsburgh, St. Louis, Cleveland	Buffalo, Cincinnati
b. Diversified manufacturing	Los Angeles, Philadelphia	Baltimore, Milwaukee	Albany-Schenectady-Troy, Syracuse, Hartford
Somewhat stable	4	5	6
a. Trade	San Francisco	Minneapolis-St. Paul, Kansas City, Seattle, Portland, Atlanta, Dallas, Fort Worth, Denver, Houston, New Orleans	Louisville, Birmingham, Indianapolis, Columbus, Memphis, Omaha, Richmond, Jacksonville, Oklahoma City
b. Services	Washington, D.C.	San Diego, San Antonio, Miami	Tampa-St. Petersburg, Phoenix
Unstable	7	8	9
Specialized manufacturing	Detroit		Providence, Youngstown, Rochester, Dayton, Allentown-Bethlehem-Easton, Akron, Springfield-Holyoke, Wheeling-Stubenville, Charleston (W. Va.)

Source: Adapted from Duncan, O. D., et al. *Metropolis and Region* (Baltimore: The Johns Hopkins Press, 1960), 271; and Norse, H. O. *Regional Economics* (New York: McGraw-Hill, 1968).

These huge metropolitan areas are the centers of the emerging megalopolis.[1] Some of these national cities may not be growing as rapidly as the general economy. But they draw both resources and organizations from throughout the United States.

Regional cities are large but with a predominantly regional sphere of influence. They draw resources and organizations from a more limited area often bounded by national cities. For instance, Cleveland draws primarily from northern Ohio, northern Indiana, and eastern Pennsylvania. It is bounded by Chicago, Detroit, and the eastern megalopolis. Local cities are smaller and may dominate a state if it does not contain a regional or national city. For instance, Indianapolis dominates Indiana, while Buffalo does not dominate New York.

The stability and breadth of resources available is also considered in Table 5-5. When the primary economic activity is manufacturing and trade or diversified manufacturing, organizations enjoy both a broad spectrum of resources and a comparatively stable economic climate. Cities relying on trade or services provide a more limited range of resources and a somewhat stable economic climate. Finally, where specialized manufacturing is dominant, the range of resources is likely to be quite limited. The overall economic climate depends on the output of one major product.

If we combine all these factors, nine separate combinations can be devised. Generally as we move from category 1 to 9 the overall resource base for all organizations deteriorates. The drawing power of the city is smaller. Fewer and more limited resources are available to organizations. And the stability of the entire economic climate declines. Thus, we might assume that organizations would prefer national cities where the primary economic activity is manufacturing and trade or diversified manufacturing. This squares with common sense if we look at the home office of major corporations and foundations. But availability of resources and economic stability are not free. New York, Boston, Chicago, and Philadelphia are extremely expensive urban areas for both individuals and organizations. Furthermore, it is argued that as you move toward category 1 the overall environment becomes more complex and difficult to cope with. As a group, the category 5 cities are experiencing the most growth. They may provide a more munificent environment for most organizations.

In summary, major urban areas within the United States can be easily classified into similar groups on the basis of their size, scope of influence, stability, and primary economic activity. Such a classification suggests that if a broad range of resources is needed a move toward national cities would benefit an organization. If, however, a more limited range of resources is needed and the system can tolerate some instability, a movement toward category 5 might be beneficial.

THE EDUCATIONAL ENVIRONMENT

Organizations need economic resources for growth and development. They also must have educated individuals to survive. With educated populations, Japan, East Germany, and West Germany rebuilt their nations. Israel's highly educated population has literally created a nation out of the desert. People with knowledge and skills are the heart of any organization and a key to its survival.

Education and economic development are closely associated.[3] Improved education brings forth more development via higher productivity. Greater economic development stimulates the demand for education. Individuals with greater income tend to spend more on education. But expenditures on education in developing nations don't always pay off.[3] Even if developing nations are able to educate an elite, three problems often occur.

Table 5-6   Percentages of Individuals in Selected Occupational Categories

	1970[a]	1980[b]	Urban[c] (1970)	Rural (1970)
WHITE COLLAR				
Professional and technical	14	16	16	11
Managers and proprietors	11	10	9	7
Clerical	17	18	20	12
Sales	6	6	8	5
Total	48	50	53	35
BLUE COLLAR				
Skilled workers	13	13	13	16
Semiskilled workers	18	16	16	21
Unskilled workers	5	4	4	5
Total	36	33	33	42
OTHER				
Service workers	12	14	13	12
Farm workers	4	3	1	11
Total	16	17	14	23
Total	100	100	100	100

Sources:

[a]U.S. Department of Labor, Bureau of Manpower Administration, *Manpower Report of the President, 1972* (Washington, D.C.: U.S. Government Printing Office, 1972), 259.

[b]U.S. Department of Labor, Bureau of Labor Statistics, *The U.S. Economy in 1980* (Washington, D.C.: U.S. Government Printing Office, 1970), Bulletin 1673.

[c]U.S. Department of Commerce, Bureau of the Census, *General Social and Economic Characteristics: United States Summary* (Washington, D.C.: U.S. Government Printing Office, 1972), 408

First, there is a "brain drain."[1] Most students must be sent abroad for advanced training. Some of the best stay in the developed nations.[8] Second, there may be a poor match between the education and training given to individuals and the requirements of organizations.[2] The economies of developing nations are not built upon diversified manufacturing or services. Outside of government and a few multinational organizations, developing nations do not really need highly trained specialists, particularly if their advanced training is more theoretical than practical.[5] Organizations in these nations need lower and middle managers with technical skills.

Three, developing nations often find that the educational elite forms one half of a dual economy.[4] They work for a national monopoly or a multinational that can use their skills. But this separates them from the rest of society. Ripped from their cultural heritage, the educated elite may become less nationalistic and more oriented toward the demands of their profession or organization.[7] Thus, the group that developing nations must rely upon for growth and development may not subscribe to the dominant cultural values.[10]

Within developed nations we can clearly see the combined influence of economic and educational development in the occupational mix available to organizations.[6] Table 5-6 shows the proportion of working individuals in nine broad occupational groups for the United States. Note that in 1970 just under half of the labor force was in "white-collar" occupations. The larger the proportion of more highly trained individuals (e.g., professionals, small-business owners, executives, foremen, and minor executives) the more favorable the human resource base for organizations. Where semiskilled and unskilled workers dominate, larger organizations find it more difficult to obtain the specialized human resources they need.[9] We should note that the relationship between occupational mix and needed human resources may not hold for small organizations that operate in developing nations. Skilled and semi-skilled workers may be in considerable demand and short supply.[8]

The Occupational Environment of Urban Centers

Professionals are not evenly spread throughout a nation. They tend to concentrate in urban areas[5] (see Table 5-6). The opportunities for practicing their specialty are greater. National cities draw proportionately more professional groups than regional centers, and regional centers more than local cities. But national centers also draw the uneducated.[3] Historically, the drawing power of national cities for both professionals and the uneducated provided an adequate mix of human skills for organizations.[1] But now this picture has changed. Organizations no longer need the vast numbers of unskilled and semiskilled workers that once brought them success. The marginally educated can no longer expect to find jobs and move up the social and economic ladder.[2] They fill urban centers as unemployables who stifle growth and development.

Traditionally, organizations have had very little concern with those individuals unable to compete. But the number of unskilled workers in urban centers has grown.[1] So there is increasing pressure on both public and private organizations to somehow bring this group into the mainstream. Since a disproportionate number of the uneducated are in minority groups, much of this pressure has come through enforcement of the 1964 Civil Rights Act.[4] The long-term impact on organizations is difficult to assess. But as organizations are forced to accept less-qualified individuals we think there will be a trend toward centralization of decision making, less emphasis on participation, and a wider separation between managers and nonmanagers.

THE LEGAL-POLITICAL ENVIRONMENT

Here, we will chart the impact of the legal-political system on organizations. We will continue to show the interrelations among the cultural, economic, educational, and legal-political segments of the general environment.

In very simple terms, the legal-political system allocates power among various groups in the society.[1] It develops, administers, and enforces laws. As the allocator of power, the government may divert surpluses and/or grant unusual favors to a few organizations. For instance, when Lockheed Aircraft Corporation was unable to secure additional debt financing, the government guaranteed repayment of $250 million in loans. We are in an era where the legal-political system has chosen and been allowed to take a more dominant role.

The legal-political system can dominate all other societal institutions because of the nature of its social function and the power needed to successfully perform its overall mission. As Ranney shows, each nation asks the legal-political system to protect it from external threat, provide and enforce a rational and consistent set of rules based on dominant instrumental and terminal values, promote economic development, and foster an enduring collective identity.[2] To accomplish such a broad mission, legal-political units possess two unusual characteristics. One, they directly control or influence all societal members.[1] You may or may not choose to affiliate with a church, buy food from a particular grocer, or attend a state university. But you rarely select your legal-political system. Two, legal-political units hold overwhelming physical force and a legal monopoly over coercion.[1] Thus, in any direct confrontation between the legal-political system and an organization, the legal-political system holds the ultimate power to enforce its desires. But even with these unusual powers, the legal-political system is bounded by the will and capacity of society. It is subject to dominant cultural values, constrained by economic development, and substantially influenced by the degree of educational progress in the nation. And in many cases, other institutions place pressure on the legal-political system.

What does this mean for organizations? To chart the impact of the legal-political system on organizations you might ask three questions. First, to what extent is the legal-political system organized to perform its vital functions? Second, what is the existing domain of government action? Third, how stable is the legal-political system?

Legal-Political Development

The first question deals with the degree of political development in the nation. Political development has been used in a number of different ways.[1] Early analyses equated development and democracy.[7] But our view is based on more recent investigations. As political units become larger, more specialized and more bureaucratized, we call the legal-political system more developed.[5] As development increases, we argue, the climate for organizations becomes more favorable. There are many reasons, but three stand out. First, with larger and more sophisticated units, the potential for successfully performing their functions increases.[4] More information can be gathered; more elaborate and well-conceived alternatives can be generated; more consistent and precise legislation can be generated, backed up by more thorough enforcement and quicker adjudication. Second, greater political development allows other organizations to increase specialization.[3] It allows the legal-political system to take on more of the functions it should perform. Third, all organizations indirectly benefit from legal-political overhead just as they do from social capital. For instance, U.S. corporations routinely receive detailed estimates and reports on the economy.

The Domain of Government

Before we consider the second question, it is important to stress that political development is distinct from political ideology.[2] The United States, China, and the U.S.S.R. would all be considered politically developed. However, the question about the government's domain is directly involved with political ideology.

Berry envisions five types of legal-political systems on the basis of the domain of government actions.[1] At one end of the spectrum he sees the domain of government as balanced but limited. That is, the government is involved in the economy, educational systems, and sociocultural institutions. But its role is basically supportive. Here we might find the United States and Canada. At the other extreme, government would dominate all other institutions. Here we find the communist nations. Between these two extremes are several other combinations. Two are important. When government is heavily involved in the economy but not sociocultural or educational systems, the nation can be put in a social welfare category. Most Western European nations fall in this category. If the major thrust of government intervention is in the sociocultural area, the country can be tagged nationalistic. Many of the emerging nations of Africa and many South American countries seem to fit here.

We propose that the scope of governmental concern is negatively associated with nongovernmental organizational outcomes. We cannot cite supporting data. Instead, we merely argue that as governmental interference and control over an organization increase, autonomy and freedom of action decreases, thus blocking alternatives for growth and development. We should also note that an increased role of government does not automatically mean that societal development or development in the economic, educational, or sociocultural sectors of the society is hurt. Some developmental economists, for instance, argue that only with substantial government help will the economic systems in developing nations begin to grow substantially.[3] Furthermore, we should note that increased governmental interference may be beneficial for particular organizations. If the government, with all of its potential power, supports an organization and protects it, the net effect on the system may be beneficial. This is why organizations try to influence governmental practices. Again, organizations may not just be passive or reactive. They can be proactive.

Stability

Our third question deals with stability. For a number of years, political scientists have made detailed investigations into the stability of governments.[2,3] One of the most interesting was performed by Sorokin.[6] He studied conflict and stability in Europe from the ancient Greek civilization to 1925. He found it to be independent of political ideology, economic development, and basically the same across all European nations. His study and others seem to suggest one critical factor in minimizing instability. That is the degree to which the sociocultural network of values and interrelationships is strong and integrated. Thus, we argue stability is independent of the degree of political development (as defined earlier) and the domain of government. To us it's intuitively obvious that political instability is highly detrimental to organizations.[1,4,5]

Development, Domain, and Stability

Table 5-7 combines the information concerning political development, domain of government, and stability. Various combinations are given popular tags and sample countries are listed. In essence, the legal-political environment is more favorable as development increases, the domain is more balanced and limited, and stability increases. At the present time not all of the combinations exist. But it seems possible that as some nations develop, each category might be represented.

Table 5-7 attempts to classify these various countries on their overall favorability to organizations in general. We realize that this classification does not fit the dominant opinion found in many political science texts and is not the same as ratings of political democracy. Our point is quite simple. Individuals may prefer an unstable political democracy or unstable social welfare state to a stable communist state. But organizations may find a more favorable legal-political climate under the latter.[1]

The Legal-Political Climate within Regions of a Nation

The legal-political climate within a nation may be stable, developed, and have a comparatively narrow domain. But various regions may be considerably less developed and less stable. Earlier we presented Elazar's classification of state political subcultures[1] (see Table 5-4). If we add stability and governmental domain considerations to the existing criteria the classification of states changes very little.[2] For the traditional states, the domain of government is comparatively narrow. A single party has captured most of the political posts for the last twenty-five years. The moralistic states reveal a somewhat broader domain for government. But there is considerable stability in terms of voting patterns and state government policy. The individualistic states are perhaps the most politically liberal. And they tend to lead other states in terms of governmental intervention. Political stability is a hallmark of the United States.

Table 5-7 Favorability of the Legal-Political Environment for Organizations (Typical Political Titles and Sample Nations)

	Balanced and Comparatively Narrow Domain		Specialized Domain		Balanced and Comparatively Broad Domain	
	Liberal Democracies		Social Welfare State		Communist Nations	
	Stable	Unstable	Stable	Unstable	Stable	Unstable
Comparatively high political development	U.S.		Great Britain	India	U.S.S.R.	China
	Canada		Israel	Italy		
	a		a	b	a	b
	Laissez-Faire Capitalism		Nationalistic		Totalitarian	
	Stable	Unstable	Stable	Unstable	Stable	Unstable
Comparatively low political development			Nationalist China	Argentina	Saudi Arabia	Chile
			Zambia			Ethiopia
			Panama			
	a			c	b	c

[a]Favorable—liberal democracies, stable social welfare states, stable communist nations.

[b]Moderately favorable—unstable social welfare states, unstable communist nations, stable nationalistic states, stable totalitarian nations.

[c]Unfavorable—unstable nationalistic states, unstable totalitarian nations.

Yet there have been several party shifts in many of these states over the last twenty-five years. To the extent these shifts continue, those analyzing organizations will need to recognize how it will influence governmental domain and development.

THE INFLUENCE OF THE GENERAL ENVIRONMENT ON ORGANIZATIONS

In earlier sections we have tried to suggest how each sector of the general environment can influence an organization and how organizations might respond to these factors. To illustrate the argument that organizations respond to "Favorability" of these factors in the general environment, consider the trends occurring in the United States recently. Changes in population and per capita income have been accompanied by political and cultural shifts among regions of the country. And organizations are responding by locating in regions where the "climate" is more conducive to their operations. The old northeast industrial states are losing population and are not growing as fast as many states in the south and far west. The midwest is also beginning to stagnate. For instance, Texas has passed Illinois and Pennsylvania to become the third most populous state behind California and New York. Texas also enjoys a substantially higher change in per capita income than most of the industrialized east. These data confirm commonsense notions. The old industrialized sections of the east and to some extent the midwest are yielding to the west and south. The economic base of these more rapidly advancing regions is built upon services and light manufacturing. As the United States enters the postindustrial age, where services are more important in generating GNP than agriculture and manufacturing, the shift toward the south and west is likely to increase. Furthermore, were you to look at voting patterns (a measure of development) and the number of political party changes (a measure of stability) within Elazar's subculture classifications, the conclusion can be drawn that the regions where population and income growth are occurring are more favorable to organizations at the present. That is, political stability—coupled with demographic, economic, and cultural patterns—exerts influence on organizations, and they respond to these pressures. Moreover, as has been mentioned, organizations seek to influence their environments. This will be addressed in more detail in subsequent chapters.

MEASUREMENT
MODULE

In this module we consider measures of culture, subculture, economic development, educational climate, legal-political factors, and an overall summary measure of general environment favorability.

MEASURING CULTURE

Unfortunately, there hasn't been much empirical work we know of that measures the cultural impact on organizations.* Some of the literature tells what dimensions should be examined, as we have noted before. Anthropologists have some estimates of cultural values. But they haven't been particularly useful for organization theory. Conversely, management scholars often attribute organizational differences to culture without measuring culture.

One approach we wish to highlight has the potential for use by the analyst. The index by Schnaiberg measures what he calls "modernism."[5] As the society is more modern, in our terms it moves from prescientific to scientific values. Some of the scales and items used are shown in Exhibit 5-8. You could, for instance, ask experts for their estimates of the proportion of the culture's members who behave in ways investigated by this instrument. Note that this still falls short of measuring the dominant values of the culture, as such. But it does give you an idea of a way to formulate some statements about cultural differences.

While we have pointed out the potential importance of values in organizational research, there are few instruments available to measure values. A recent one developed by Rokeach appears to be particularly promising for organizational use.[4] So far, there are relatively few organizational data based on it. The instrument consists of a set of 18 terminal values (those measuring an end state of existence) and 18 instrumental values (those measuring a mode of conduct). The respondent is asked to independently rank-order the values within each set (these are shown in Exhibit 5-9).†

*We don't consider the comparative management literature since rarely is there a direct measure of cultural values. If firms in two countries differ it may be due to economic, legal-political factor differences in the specific environment.

†A number of psychologically based measures of values have also emerged. The work of England and his associates is one approach, while recent work by those at the University of Wisconsin uses a slightly different instrument.[1,2]

Exhibit 5-8 Selected Items from the Modernism Index

A. Mass-media index
   1. Attends movie at least once or twice a month
   2. Reads a newspaper daily
   3. Listens to the radio daily
B. Extended-family-ties index
   1. Not living with parents or in-laws now
   2. Have had a love marriage other than an arranged one
   3. No expectation of old-age support from children
C. Nuclear-family-role-structure index
   1. Disapproves or only mildly approves that males should make decisions
   2. Husband permits wearing of short dresses
   3. Wife has some leisure activities outside the home
D. Religiosity Index
   1. Couple has had a civil marriage only
   2. Wife prays less than five times per day
E. Environmental-orientation index
   1. Believes daughters need the same education as sons
   2. Believes success is based on hard work more than luck
   3. Desired occupational sphere in corporation or profession
F. Production consumption index
   1. Owns a radio
   2. Owns a sewing machine
   3. Does not produce home preserves very frequently

Scoring:

Respondents answer yes or no to each item. Add the number of "yes" responses. The more "yes" responses, the more "modern" the respondent is considered.

Source: Adapted from Schnaiberg, A. "Measuring Modernism: Theoretical and Empirical Explorations," *American Journal of Sociology,* (1970), 399–425. Adapted by permission of the author and the University of Chicago. Copyright © 1970 by the University of Chicago. All rights reserved.

Subcultural Measures

As suggested earlier, a basic indicator of rural-urban differentiation is population density. This represents the number of people in the region (or state or county, etc.) per square mile. Of course, higher densities represent urban areas. Other indicators might include the number and types of housing available, or the percent of the labor force in a union, or percent of the labor force in

Exhibit 5-9 Terminal and Instrumental Values in the Rokeach Value Survey

Terminal Values	Instrumental Values
A comfortable life (a prosperous life)	Ambitious (hard-working, aspiring)
An exciting life (a stimulating, active life)	Broadminded (open-minded)
A sense of accomplishment (lasting contribution)	Capable (competent, effective)
A world of peace (free of war and conflict	Cheerful (lighthearted, joyful)
A world of beauty (beauty of nature and the arts)	Clean (neat, tidy)
Equality (brotherhood, equal opportunity for all)	Courageous (standing up for your beliefs)
Family security (taking care of loved ones)	Helpful (working for the welfare of others)
Freedom (independence, free choice)	Honest (sincere, truthful)
Happiness (contentedness)	Imaginative (daring, creative)
Inner harmony (freedom from inner conflict)	Independent (self-reliant, self-sufficient)
Mature love (sexual and spiritual intimacy)	Intellectual (intelligent, reflective)
National security (protection from attack)	Logical (consistent, rational)
Pleasure (an enjoyable, leisurely life)	Loving (affectionate, tender)
Salvation (saved, eternal life)	Obedient (dutiful, respectful)
Self-respect (self-esteem)	Polite (courteous, well-mannered)
Social recognition (respect, admiration)	Responsible (dependable, reliable)
True friendship (close companionship)	Self-controlled (restrained, self-disciplined)
Wisdom (a mature understanding of life)	

Scoring

The instrumental and terminal values are independently rank ordered within each set. This rank ordering may be used in a number of ways. Two are suggested here. Individuals may be compared with each other on individual value rankings and on the correlation of their entire set of instrumental and terminal rankings with each other. For comparison of one culture with another, individual ranks or sets of ranks may be aggregated across individuals within cultures and the mean ranks for each culture compared with each other.

"white-collar" vs. "blue-collar" occupations. In a sense, though, these are surrogates for actual measurement of belief patterns or values of the population. If you closely examine the measures used by Elazar in his categorization of state subcultures, they rely heavily on indicators of the other three factors in the general environment.[3] These are, of course, related; so let's turn to these other areas.

MEASURING ECONOMIC DEVELOPMENT

As we indicated, the most common measure of overall economic development is Gross National Product (GNP) per capita. GNP is the monetary value of all goods and services produced in an area for one year.[1] It is usually divided by the total population for comparisons across nations or regions, and time.[2] Here the idea is simple. If population growth outpaces increases in GNP, the economic climate is worse.

We should note some of the measurement problems of GNP. One, GNP includes only those goods and services where there is a monetary transfer. In developing nations the economic activity of many individuals may not be fully measured.[2] They may be "outside" the economy. For instance, if a farmer grows enough grain to sell to a local miller, the monetary value of the miller's flour is counted in GNP. The grain milled and eaten by the farmer would not be included. Thus, we argue GNP per capita may be a better measure of economic conditions for organizations than for individuals.

Two, GNP data, particularly for developing countries, are only estimates.[2] There are substantial variations in reporting procedures across nations. Developing nations cannot afford to divert precious surpluses to derive exact measures of their own poverty. Three, centrally planned economies (communist nations) use a related measure of economic activity called gross material product.[1] Gross material product is roughly equal to GNP if we add business and government services as well as defense expenditures.[2]

Four, GNP data must be converted to a common currency for comparison of nations.[2] Unfortunately, the value of foreign currencies in dollar terms varies from day to day and may change substantially from one year to the next. Finally, comparisons over time call for adjustments for variations in price levels. Thus, data are often adjusted to some standard year (such as 1968) or put in index form.[2]

While per capita GNP is the most commonly used measure, a variety of indicators can be used to measure the economic health of a region.[3,5] The unemployment rate, though subject to measurement problems, is one measure of economic munificence.[4] Median income for families, and for persons, provides other information, as does the percent of families in the poverty range. This gives some clues about the distribution of wealth. This can be important. For instance, from a business firm's marketing viewpoint, buying power that is dispersed may be more favorable than that which is concentrated. Further, one year's data point should not be totally relied upon. Population shifts, per capita income changes, and the like are dynamic. These need to be projected and forecasted for an assessment of their impact on an organization.

As we mentioned before, another indicator of economic health is the breadth of economic activity. Those familiar with macroeconomics might recall data from National Accounts.[1] These break down the sources of GNP. If you were to look at these data, you would see low GNP and heavy dependence on agriculture for underdeveloped nations.

Again a word of caution is in order. The data can be misleading unless you are familiar with the exact calculations.

If the primary activity is one type of manufacturing in a region, this may be less favorable than if there is a spread of manufacturing, trade, service, and/or agricultural activity. In the United States this spread can be measured quite accurately by consulting statistical data published for each SMSA (from U.S. Commerce Department publications). *Sales Management* magazine publishes an annual "Survey of Buying Power," which also lists a wealth of data. Once again, as affluence increases, high-quality, high-priced organizations are likely to be attracted to these areas. If activity is specialized, this is not as attractive. An example is the impact on economic conditions in Seattle, Washington, when the aerospace industry lost ground.

MEASURING EDUCATIONAL CLIMATE

General educational levels are usually associated with per capita GNP. But the association across all indicators of educational characteristics and GNP per capita is not perfect. Higgins did a detailed analysis of the relationship between education and economic development.[1] He argues that balanced expenditures for education across primary, secondary, and tertiary levels in a number of subject areas are the key to growth. For our purposes we should note that such a balance signifies a broad range of human skills potentially available to organizations.[2]

Within regions or states, general educational levels can vary substantially. One indicator is the educational expenditure a state might make as a percent of total public outlays.[2] Of course, the literacy rate in developed countries tends to be high.[3] But some disparity across regions or states exists. Some of this can be measured by the median number of school years completed by the populace of the area examined. (Most state census compilations include such information.) Finally, you can gather data about the occupational distribution of individuals. This can be done by state or by SMSA, for example.

LEGAL-POLITICAL MEASURES

Political scientists' measures of legal-political factors often require "judgment" calls. We prefer less judgmental and ideological approaches to measuring favorability of this segment of the general environment. We suggest some ways to measure the legal-political situation even though we are not aware of these measures being used.*

As indicators of stability, you might look at the number of violent overthrows of heads of states, number of political disruptions, or how long the current form of government has been in existence. Longer periods of time, or less frequent changes in the head of state, should indicate greater stability.

With respect to domain, you might examine the proportion of gross national product contributed by government. You might also try to assess the relative degree of legal control of the national government over economic, education, and sociocultural institutions (e.g., federal chartering and types of laws affecting organizations). This might be done by looking at degrees of involvement and domination within and across the systems, *relative to* that of other countries. Finally, the degree of development of the legal-political system might be measured by the degree of size, specialization, and bureaucratization of governmental entities. Measures of these for any type of organization are provided in Chapter 9. They can be applied to government bodies. Total votes cast in an election as a percent of voting population is also a measure of legal-political development of an area. This information can be gathered by state, county, or other political subunit where available. The major political party in

---

*Measures of legal-political stability are being used to measure risk in investment decisions.[1,2]

a state may or may not be important. but the pattern of voting over time for one party or another is an indicator of political stability. These data are readily available from government publications.

A SUMMARY FOR MEASURING FAVORABILITY OF THE GENERAL ENVIRONMENT

We haven't begun to exhaust the multitude of data that are available for many of these variables, at least within the United States. These measures and sources of information can be used to assess the general environment. The key is to pinpoint the kinds of information in these four areas that indicate the favorability or unfavorability of this environment for the organization you are analyzing. We have provided a checklist in Exhibit 5-10 that indicates the kinds of factors you may want to measure.[1] This summarizes many of the indicators of favorability in the general environment. From these it is a matter of tracing the impact on that organization. But that is easier said than done. In Part I, we noted disagreements about means-ends relationships. Here, also, there appears to be no general consensus about how to measure the general environment. We have offered our suggestions and a few illustrations. But the state of the art is not well developed. There remains an element of subjectivity in assessing the degree of development and its favorability for organizations.

Exhibit 5-10 Summary of Indicators for Detailed Analysis of the General Environment

I. Educational characteristics (underdeveloped to developed)
  a. Literacy level (low to high)
  b. Expenditures per pupil (low to high)
     1. Grades 1–8
     2. Grades 9–12
     3. Grades 12–20 and higher
  c. Percentage enrollment (low to high)
     1. By age
     2. By race
     3. By sex
  d. Average number of school years completed (low to high)
  e. Educational expenditures (low to high)
     1. Per capita total population
     2. Per pupil in average daily attendance
     3. Per capita total school age population

    f. Teacher qualifications (low to high)
       1. Percent of teachers with substandard credentials
       2. Percent of teachers with advanced degrees
       3. Average number of teaching years
    g. Educational output measures (low to high)
       1. Average achievement test scores per age bracket
       2. School retention rate
       3. Percent of graduates enrolling in higher education
       4. Percent of student population under special programs
    h. Other indications of educational quality (low to high)
       1. Pupil-teacher ratio
       2. Vocational program expenditures per capita total population

II. Political and legal characteristics (underdeveloped to developed)
    a. Crime and crime rates (high to low)
       1. Crime rate per 1000
          a. Offenses against persons
          b. Offenses against property
       2. Law enforcement expenditures per capita total population
       3. Number of court cases per judge
          a. Criminal
          b. Civil
    b. Political participation (low to high)
       1. Voter participation in last election
       2. Percent of potential population registered to vote
    c. Legal system efficiency (low to high)
       1. Average delay in hearing cases
          a. Criminal
          b. Civil
       2. Average case load per judge (high to low)
    d. Political stability
       1. Number of political party changes in the last five elections (high to low)
       2. Number of civil disturbances in the last five years (high to low)

III. Economic characteristics
    a. Economic aid (low to high)
       1. Federal aid per person
       2. Transfer payments per person
          a. Welfare
          b. General assistance
    b. Asset values (low to high)
       1. Assessed value of property subject to local taxation per person
       2. Principal assets of commercial banks

    c. Asset construction (low to high)
       1. Value of construction per capita
       2. Residential expenditures per capita
       3. New housing starts per capita
    d. Employment (low to high)
       1. Unemployment rate (high to low)
       2. Percent of population employed
    e. Income (low to high)
       1. GNP per capita
       2. Income per capita
       3. Average income
       4. Individuals considered poor per capita total population
    f. Other economic activity indicators (low to high)
       1. Retail sales per capita
       2. Welfare participants per capita
       3. Home ownership rate
IV. Sociocultural characteristics
    a. Health conditions (low to high)
       1. Infant mortality rate
       2. Morbidity rate
       3. Expected life span
       4. Physicians per capita
       5. Hospital beds per capita
    b. Family conditions (low to high)
       1. Divorce rate
       2. Average number of children per family
       3. Percent of female heads of household
    c. Ethnic and religious domination (extensive to little)
       1. Population percent belonging to largest sect or denomination
       2. Per capita asset value of largest denomination or sect
       3. Unemployment rate for largest minority versus majority
       4. Infant mortality rate for largest minority versus majority
    d. Recreational facilities (little to extensive)
       1. Public parks and recreational facilities, square miles per capita
       2. Participation per capita in outdoor activities

Scoring

To compare favorability of several systems, scale each system on each indicator within each sector. For example for, say, county welfare agencies in the United States, rank the county on each item. Then rank the sum of the ranks for a comparative estimate.

If you want to measure the relative degree of favorability within each of the four sectors across systems, find the sum of the ranks for the components of each sector.

Source: Osborn, R. N. "Environment and Organization Effectiveness" (unpublished dissertation, Kent State University, Kent, Ohio, 1971). Published by permission of the author.

REFERENCES

I. Culture

[1]Ajiferuke, M., and Boddewyn, J. "Culture and Other Explanatory Variables in Comparative Management Studies," *Academy of Management Journal,* 13 (1970), 153–163.

[2]Roberts, K. H. "On Looking at an Elephant: An Evaluation of Cross-Cultural Research Related to Organizations," *Psychological Bulletin,* 74 (1970), 327–350.

[3]Taylor, E. B. *Primitive Culture.* London: Murray, 1871, 71.

[4]Triandis, H. C., Malpass, R. S., and Davidson, A. R. "Psychology and Culture," *Annual Review of Psychology,* 24 (1973), 205–378.

A. Cultural Values

[1]Associated Press, "Shrieking Women Lead Stampede of Workers," *Saint Louis Post Dispatch,* June 3 (1977), 26.

[2]Blau, P. M. *Inequality and Heterogeneity.* New York: The Free Press, 1977.

[3]Crozier, M. "The Relationship between Micro and Macro Sociology," *Human Relations,* 25 (1972), 239–251.

[4]Eells, R. "Multinational Corporations under Fire," *Management Review,* 64 (1975), 43–45.

[5]England, G. W., Dhingva, O. P., and Agarwal, N. C. "The Manager and the Man: A Cross-Cultural Study of Personal Values," *Organization and Administrative Sciences,* 5 (1974), 17–33.

[6]England, G. W., Agarwal, N. C., and Dhingva, O. P. *Personal Value Systems of Indian Managers.* Minneapolis: University of Minnesota Press, 1974.

[7]Farmer, R., and Richman, B. *Comparative Management and Economic Progress.* (Homewood, Ill.: Richard D. Irwin, 1963.

[8]Farmer, R. M., and Richman, B. N. *Management and Organizations.* New York: Random House, 1975.

[9]Haire, M., Ghiselli, E. and Porter, L. *Managerial Thinking: An International Study.* New York: Wiley, 1966.

[10]Haviland, W. A. *Anthropology.* New York: Holt, Rinehart and Winston, 1974.

[11]Hay, R., and Gray, E. "Social Responsibility of Business Managers," *Academy of Management Journal,* 17 (1974), 135–143.

[12]Hellriegel, D., and Slocum, J. W. *Organizational Behavior: Contingency Views.* St. Paul: West, 1976.

[13]Honigmann, J. J. *Culture and Personality.* New York: Harper & Row, 1954.

[14]Hulin, C. L., and Blood, M. R. "Job Enlargement, Individual Differences, and Worker Responses," *Psychological Bulletin,* 69 (1968), 41–55.

[15]Kraut, A. L. "Some Recent Advances in Cross-National Management Research," *Academy of Management Journal,* 18 (1975) 538–549.

[16]Long, J. D. "The Protestant Ethic Reexamined," *Business Horizons,* 15 (1972).

[17]Lynd, R. *Knowledge for What? The Place of Science in American Culture.* Princeton: Princeton University Press, 1939.

[18]Marsh, R. M. *Comparative Sociology.* New York: Harcourt, Brace and World, 1967.

[19]Massonrouge, J. C. "The Mythology of Multinationalism, Myth #4, MNCs and Nation-states are on a Collision Course," *Columbia*

Journal of World Business, 18 (1974), 10–12.

[20]Milne, R. S. "Mechanistic and Organic Models of Public Administration in Developing Countries," *Administrative Science Quarterly,* 15 (1970), 54–68.

[21]Myers, M. S., and Myers, S. S "Toward Understanding the Changing Work Ethic," *California Management Review,* 16 (1974), 7–14.

[22]Negandhi, A. R., and Estafen, B. D. "A Research Model to Determine the Applicability of American Management Know-How in Differing Cultures and/or Environments," *Academy of Management Journal,* 8 (1965), 309–318.

[23]Nord, W. R. "Culture and Organizational Behavior." In W. R. Nord (ed.), *Concepts and Controversy in Organizational Behavior.* Santa Monica, Calif.: Goodyear, 1976, 197–211.

[24]Ondrack, D. A. "Emerging Occupational Values: A Review and Some Findings," *Academy of Management Journal,* 16 (1973), 423–432.

[25]Redfield, R. *The Folk Culture of Yucatan.* Chicago: University of Chicago Press, 1941.

[26]Rogoff, N. "Social Stratification in France and in The United States," *American Journal of Sociology,* 58 (1953), 347–357.

[27]Service, E. R. *A Profile of Primitive Culture.* New York: Harper & Row, 1958.

[28]Spradley, J. P., and McCurdy, D. W. *Anthropology: The Cultural Perspective.* New York: Wiley, 1975.

[29]Susman, G. I. "Job Enlargement: Effects of Culture on Worker Responses," *Industrial Relations,* 12 (1973), 1–15.

[30]Tannenbaum, R., and Davis, S. A. "Values, Man and Organizations," *Industrial Management Review,* 10 (1964), 69–85.

[31]Weber, M. "Die Protestantische Ethik und der Geist des Kapitalismus," *Archiv fur Sozialwissenschaft und Sozial politik,* 20 (1904).

[32]Whyte, M. K. "Bureaucracy and Modernization in China: The Maoist Critique," *American Sociological Review,* 38 (1973), 149–163.

[33]Whyte, W. H., Jr. *The Organization Man.* New York: Doubleday, 1957.

[34]Williams, L. K., Whyte, W. F., and Green, C. S. "Do Cultural Differences Affect Workers' Attitudes?" *Industrial Relations,* 5 (1966).

B. Subcultural Values

[1]Freeman, L. C., Fararco, T. J., Bloomburg, W., and Sunshire, M. A. "Locating Leaders in Local Communities," *American Sociological Review,* 28 (1963), 791–798.

[2]Schaupp, D. L., and Kraut, A. "A Study of the Communality of Industrial Values Across Cultures," *Academy of Management Proceedings,* 1975, (1975), 291–293.

[3]Selznick, P. *TVA and the Grass Roots.* Berkeley: University of California Press, 1949.

[4]Simmonetti, J. L. "Management Policy toward Task Environment Agents: A Cross-cultural Study." Paper presented at the National Academy of Management meeting, Boston, 1973.

C. States as Subcultures

[1]Castellano, J. J. "Rural and Urban Differences: One More Time," *Academy of Management Journal,* 19 (1976), 495–502.

[2]Elazar, D. J. *American Federalism: A View from the States.* New York: Thomas Y. Crowell, 1966.

[3]Farmer, R., and Richman, B. *Comparative Management and Economic Progress.* Homewood, Ill.: Richard D. Irwin, 1965.

[4]Johnson, C. A. "Political Culture in American States: Elazar's Formulation Examined," *American Journal of Political Science,* 20 (1976), 491–509.

[5]Lewis, O. "The Culture of Poverty." In M. Pilisuk and P. Pilisuk (eds.), *Poor Americans: How the White Poor Live.* New York: Transaction, 1971.

[6]Marsh, R. M. *Comparative Sociology.* New York: Harcourt, Brace and World, 1967.

[7]Massonrouge, 1974.

[8]Pilisuk, M. and Pilisuk, P. "How the White Poor Live," *Poor Americans: How the White Poor Live.* New York: Transaction, 1971.

[9]Turner, A. N., and Lawrence, P. R. "The Town-City Difference: Possible Explanations." In J. G. Maurer (ed.), *Readings in Organizational Theory: Open System Approaches.* New York: Random House, 1971, 258–269.

D. Socialization: An Organizational Response to Subcultural Differences

[1]Baldridge, J. V. *Power and Conflict in the University.* New York: Wiley, 1971.

[2]Dubin, R., Champoux, J. E., and Porter, L. W. "Central Life Interests and Organizational Commitment of Blue Collar and Clerical Workers," *Administrative Science Quarterly,* 20 (1976), 411–421.

[3]England, G. W. "Personal Values of American Managers," *Academy of Management Journal,* 10, (1967), 53–68.

[4]Freid, M. *The World of the Urban Working Class.* Cambridge, Mass.: Harvard University Press, 1973.

[5]Gouldner, A. W. "Cosmopolitans and Locals: Toward an Analysis of Latent Social roles," *Administrative Science Quarterly* 1 & 2 (1957/1958), 281–306, 444–480.

[6]Hall, R. H. *Organizations: Structure and Process.* Englewood Cliffs, N. J. Prentice-Hall, 1977.

[7]Haug, M., and Sussman, M. B. "Professionalism and Unionism," *American Behavioral Scientist,* 14 (1971), 538–540.

[8]Kelman, H. C. "Compliance, Identification and Internalization: Three Processes of Attitude Change," *Journal of Conflict Resolution, 2 (1958),* 51–60.

[9]Kidron, A. "Work Values and Organizational Commitment," Academy of Management Journal, 20 (1978), 239–247.

[10]Kidron, A., and Osborn, R. N. "Managers and Non-Managers: A Look at Some Old Questions." Working paper, Department of Administrative Sciences, Southern Illinois University, 1975.

[11]Korblum, W. *Blue Collar Community.* Chicago: The University of Chicago Press, 1974.

[12]Lewis, L. S. "The University and the Professional Model," *American Behavioral Scientist,* 14 (1971), 541–562.

[13]Litterer, J. A. *An Introduction to*

Management. New York: Wiley, 1978.

[14]Meara, H. "Honor in Dirty Work: The Case of American Meat Cutters and Turkish Butchers," *Sociology of Work and Occupations,* 1 (1974), 259–283.

[15]Schein, E. H. *Organizational Psychology.* Englewood Cliffs, N. J.: Prentice-Hall, 1965.

[16]Sigelman, L. "An Organizational Analysis of News Reporting," *American Journal of Sociology,* 79 (1973), 132–151.

[17]Stincombe, A. L. "Bureaucratic and Craft Administration of Production: A Comparative Study." *Administrative Science Quarterly,* 4 (1969), 168–187.

[18]Steward, P. L., and Cantor, M. G. (eds.). *Varieties of Work Experience.* Cambridge, Mass.: Schenkman, 1974.

II. The Economic Climate

[1]Clifford, J., and Osmond, G. *World Development Handbook.* London: Charles Knight, 1971.

[2]Galbraith, J. K. *The Affluent Society.* Boston: Houghton Mifflin, 1958.

[3]Samuelson, P. A. *Economics.* New York: McGraw-Hill, 1973.

A. Sources of Surplus

[1]Clifford and Osmond, 1971.

[2]Florence, P. S. *Economics and Sociology of Industry.* Baltimore, Md.: Johns Hopkins Press, 1969.

[3]Hailstones, T. J. *Basic Economics.* Cincinnati, Ohio: Western Publishing, 1972.

[4]Lipsey, R. G., and Steiner, P. O. *Economics.* New York: Harper & Row, 1966.

[5]Morgan, T. *Economic Development, Concept and Strategy.* New York: Harper & Row, 1975.

B. Factors Associated with Overall Economic Development

[1]Farmer, R., and Richman, B. *Comparative Management and Economic Progress.* Homewood, Ill.: Richard D. Irwin, 1965.

[2]Higgins, B. *Economic Development: Problems, Principles and Policies.* New York: W. W. Norton, 1968.

[3]McClelland, D. C., and Winter, D. G. *Motivating Economic Achievement.* New York: The Free Press, 1969.

[4]Owens, E., and Shaw, R. *Development Reconsidered.* Lexington, Mass.: D. C. Heath, 1972.

[5]Powelson, J. P. *Institutions of Economic Growth: A Theory of Conflict in Developing Countries.* Princeton: Princeton University Press, 1972.

C. The Economic Climate within Regions of a Nation

[1]Duncan, O. D. *Metropolis and Region.* Baltimore: The Johns Hopkins Press, 1960.

[2]Elazar, 1966.

[3]Nourse, H. O. *Regional Economics.* New York: McGraw-Hill, 1968.

III. The Educational Environment

[1]Farmer and Richman, 1975.

[2]Higgins, B. *Economic Development* New York: W. W. Norton & Company, 1968.

[3]Holsinger, D. B., and Theisen, G. L. "Education, Individual Modernity and National Development: A Critical Appraisal," *The Journal of Developing Areas,* 3 (1977), 315–334.

[4]Hyman, H. H. "The Value System of Different Classes." In R. Bendix and S. M. Lipset (eds.), *Class, Status and Power.* New York: The Free Press, 1966.

[5]Johnson, H. G. *On Economics and Society.* Chicago: University of Chicago Press, 1975.

[6]Krause, E. A. *The Sociology of Occupations.* Boston: Little, Brown, 1971.

[7]Massonrouge, 1974.

[8]Montagna, P. D. *Occupations and Society.* New York: Wiley, 1977.

[9]Osborn, R. N. "The Search for Environmental Complexity," *Human Relations,* 29 (1976).

[10]Owens and Shaw, 1972.

A. The Occupational Environment of Urban Centers

[1]Fischer, C. S. *The Urban Experience.* New York: Harcourt Brace, Jovanovich, 1976.

[2]Liazos, A. "The Poverty of the Sociology of Deviance: Nuts, Sluts, and Perverts," *Social Problems,* 20 (1972), 107–118.

[3]Montagna, 1977.

[4]Purcell, T. V., and Cavanagh, G. F. *Blacks in the Industrial World,* New York: The Free Press, 1972.

[5]Zald, M. N. *Occupations and Organizations in American Society.* Chicago: Markham, 1971.

IV. Legal-Political Environment

[1]Conway, M. M., and Feigert, F. B. *Political Analysis: An Introduction.* Boston, Mass.: Allyn and Bacon, 1972.

[2]Ranney, A. *The Governing of Men.* New York: Holt, Rinehart and Winston, 1971.

A. Legal-Political Development

[1]Coleman, S. *Measurement and Analysis of Political Systems.* New York: Wiley, 1975.

[2]Connally, J. B. "The Case for the L-1011 Lockheed Transport Loan Guarantee." In G. A. Steiner (ed.), *Issues in Business and Society.* New York: Random House, 1972, 345–355.

[3]Dahl, R. A. *Modern Political Analysis.* Englewood Cliffs, N.J.: Prentice-Hall, 1970.

[4]Hill, R. "Which Countries are Best for Investment," *International Management,* (1974), 12–16.

[5]Nehrt, L. C. "The Political Climate for Private Investment," *Business Horizons,* 15 (1972), 51–58.

[6]Proxmire, W. "The Lockheed Bailout: A Threat to Free Enterprise." In G. A. Steiner (ed.), *Issues in Business & Society.* New York: Random House, 1972, 355–362.

[7]Smith, A. R., Jr. "Socioeconomic Development and Political Democracy: A Causal Analysis," *Midwest Journal of Political Science,* 12 (1969), 102–119.

B. The Domain of Government

[1]Berry, N. *Political Configurations.* Pacific Palisades, Calif.: Goodyear Publishing, 1972.

[2]Huntington, S. P. *Political Social Order in Changing Societies.* New Haven: Yale University Press, 1969.

[3]Rostow, W. W. *The Stages of Economic Growth.* Cambridge: Cambridge University Press, 1960.

C. Stability

[1]Antunes, G. E. "Socioeconomic, Political, and Violence Variables as Predictors of Government Expenditures in Nations: 1955, 1960, 1965." Unpublished doctoral dissertation, Northwestern University, Evanston, Ill., 1972.

[2]Apter, D. E. *Political Change:* Portland, Oregon: Frank Cass and Co., 1973.

[3]Dahl, 1970.

[4]Hill, 1974.

[5]Rummel, R. J., and Heenan, D. A. "How Multinationals Analyze Political Risks," *Harvard Business Review,* 1 (1978), 67–76.

[6]Sorokin, P. A. *Social and Cultural Dynamics.* Boston: Proter Sargent, 1957.

D. Development, Domain, and Stability

[1]Green, R. I., and Smith, C. "Multinational Profitability as a Function of Political Instability," *Management International Review,* 12 (1972), 23–29.

E. The Legal-Political Climate within Regions of a Nation

[1]Elazar, 1966.

[2]Johnson, 1976.

VI. Measurement Module

A. Measuring Culture

[1]Cummings, L. L., Hamet, D. L., and Schmidt, S. M. "International Cross-Language Factor Stability of Personality: An Analysis of the Share-Meeker Personality-Attitude Schedule," *The Journal of Psychology,* 82 (1972), 67–84.

[2]Cummings, L. L., Schmikl, E., and Blackburn, R. "The Attitudes of White South African Executives: Is South Africa Really that Different," *Academy of Management Proceedings,* 1976, (1976), 332–335.

[3]Elazar, 1966.

[4]Rokeach, M. *The Nature of Human Values.* New York: The Free Press, 1973.

[5]Schnaiberg, A. "Measuring Modernism: Theoretical and Empirical Explorations," *American Journal of Sociology,* 70 (1970), 399–425.

B. Measuring Economic Development

[1]Hailstones, 1972.

[2]Morgan, 1975.

[3]*1976 Statistical Yearbook of the United Nations.* New York: United Nations, 1974.

[4]*Readers' Digest Almanac and Yearbook.* New York: Readers Digest, 1976.

[5]*World Almanac, 1976.* New York: Newspaper Enterprise Association, 1977.

C. Measuring Educational Climate

[1]Higgins, 1968.

[2]Osborn, R. "Environment and Organizational Effectiveness." Unpublished dissertation, Kent State University, 1971.

[3]*United Nations Demographic Yearbook.* New York: United Nations, 1974.

D. Legal-Political Measures

[1]Bunn, D. W. and Mustafaoglu, M. M., "Forecasting Political Risk." *Management Science,* 24 (1978), 1557-1567.

[2]Haner, F. T., "Rating Investment Risks Abroad," *Business Horizons,* 22 (1979), 18-23.

E. A Summary for Measuring Favorability of the General Environment

[1]Osborn, 1971.

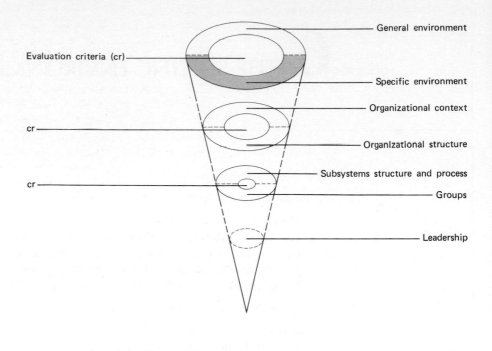

General environment

Evaluation criteria (cr)

Specific environment

Organizational context

cr

Organizational structure

Subsystems structure and process

cr

Groups

Leadership

What happens to General Motors when the United Rubber Workers go on strike? What happens to the expansion plans of St. John's Hospital if the prime interest rate of its main funding source rises? What happens to the Mafia when Miami joins New Jersey to legalize casino gambling? What happens to the Environmental Protection Agency if the courts rule that the snail darter can be destroyed in favor of a new dam?

In this chapter we focus on the aspects of the environment unique to each organization. All organizations in the same geographic area face common constraints from the general environment. But each organization also develops its own niche. As a member of a larger system (society) an organization builds upon many others. It gathers money, personnel, and raw materials from some organizations and sends its output to others. In its attempts to grow and survive, the organization confronts other organizations with partially similar and partially conflicting desires. Some of these are competitors with similar products and services. Others come from different segments of society. Organizations appear to compete for resources in the broader societal framework of cooperation and integration.

The interplay among organizations is important. Strikes, an inability to secure a bank loan, or financial cancellations of raw material orders can result in the death of an organization. A large contract, on the other hand, can all but assure survival. The arrival of a new organization into the specific environment of another can result in dramatic shifts in internal operations and effectiveness. A change in the balance of power among related systems can have much the same result. Thus, analysis of an organization's specific environment is an important component of organization theory.

Before we can discuss the specific environment of organizations we must first get a picture of what an organization is. Then we will develop the concept of organizational domain to help identify the components of the specific environment.

WHAT IS AN ORGANIZATION?

Organizations are often defined as collections of individuals seeking common goals.[1,3] We then attempt to ascertain the common goal being sought and look at the elements in the environment needed for goal attainment. This is useful in underdeveloped nations characterized by small, comparatively simple units. But in complex societies where organizations are huge and highly specialized, this approach breaks down.[7] For instance, can you state *the* goal for General Motors that is shared by all of its members? Let's take another tack.

A key feature of organizations is their ability to act as a collectivity.[6] Recognizing this we define an organization as any collection of individuals that can enter into a legally binding contract. The legal capacity to make contracts is used because it requires: (1) that the entity be recognized by others; and (2) that it can act as a collectivity.

This definition helps resolve a sticky problem in organization theory. Complex systems are typically broken down into major components. These components are treated as if they were organizations.[2] If the unit can act as a collectivity (possesses legal contractual capacity) we think this treatment is appropriate. State universities typically have this legal capacity even though they are only part of the state government. Likewise, wholly owned subsidiaries have contractual capacity and are frequently treated as organizations.[4]

Organizations can be classified as complex or simple. We may call an organization complex when it contains more than one unit with contractual capacity. If none of its components possesses this legal capacity, separate from the whole, the organization may be called simple. Thus, ITT, Xerox, and Exxon are complex organizations. So are the departments of Health Education and Welfare (HEW), Housing and Urban Development (HUD), Defense (DOD), and Interior. Most local churches are simple organizations as are local government agencies.

If a unit is part of an organization but does not possess legal contractual capacity it may be called a subsystem, department, or group. For instance, a state university has an auditing department that reports directly to a board of trustees. It's not an organization but a subsystem of the university. Units that are recognized externally as collections of individuals but which lack legal contractual capacity are referred to as aggregations or special interest groups.

Some units are formed by one or more individuals and/or organizations to accomplish a specific, limited, and short-range objective. Thompson calls these complex configurations.[5] They may have some ability to act as a collectivity. But that ability is frequently limited by sponsoring organizations. Examples of complex configurations include joint ventures or cooperative projects among government agencies. In the construction industry such cooperative ventures are the rule, not the exception. They are also common in oil exploration and basic research.

THE ORGANIZATION AND ITS SPECIFIC ENVIRONMENT

Our definition of an organization would apparently lead to a straightforward rule for separating it from its environment. What is inside an organization is that legally controlled by the system. However, this simple rule quickly leads to problems. Individuals, for instance, are typically members of many organizations. Let's use our legalistic approach after developing the notion of domain. Then we will modify the simple rule to include the complexity of defining the boundaries of an organization.

The Domain of an Organization

The domain of an organization is the set of claims it makes over societal resources.[21] To explain the notion it is necessary to briefly outline the elements organizations often attempt to control and how they may support their claims.

What can an organization attempt to lay claim upon? The literature concerning organizational characteristics suggests the following: goals, outputs (goods and services), property, technology, structure and members.[3,8,12] Earlier we introduced the notion of means-ends chains. We argued it was possible for an organization to take the overall social function of the system and devise a mission statement. From the mission statement more specific goals could be developed and from this point a strategy for goal attainment could be derived. The strategy would indicate the mix of property, technology, structure, and members needed to create and/or distribute specific outputs. We suggested that organizations that limit their social contribution and develop clear-cut means-ends chains have a better chance for survival. Our arguments centered on the benefits from economies of scale and the synergy received from using related resources. Now we are going to expand the arguments without relying upon the mission of the system as the driving force behind the strategy of an organization.

It is comparatively easy for an organization to claim control over goals, outputs, property, technology, structure, and individuals.[1] Although it's quite another matter for an organization to actually control any of the elements.[17] For an organization to use any one of the elements, it must exercise some degree of control over it.[7] For instance, members must be willing to work toward organization effectiveness and goals, follow the structure, and produce the desired outcomes.[5] To gain some degree of control an organization must back up its claims.[4] It can secure some control with an exchange of resources.[9] For instance, a business hires labor. Organizations can also back up their claims with ideology or a combination of ideology and resources.[20] Let's say the Cub Scouts of America ask parents to volunteer to help all boys in a pack to learn important skills and values. Ideology is preferred since it costs less than tangible resources. The closer the claim to the mission of the organization, the larger the ideological component can become. In no case does the organization obtain complete control.[6] The more control desired, the larger the cost in terms of resources and ideology.[13,18]

The concept of domain highlights several important notions about organizations. One, organizations often claim more territory than they are willing to back up with resources and ideology.[2] Two, outsiders may give an organization more "control" than it wants.[11] For instance, many critics of business argue that pollution control, decaying cities, and the development of equality in employment should be organizational goals. Parents may assume that public schools know how to educate children. Thus, the domain is at the same time larger and smaller than desired by the organization. Three, a claim over a particular element only continues as long as it is backed up with resources and/or ideology.[14] Once a claim is made it must be continually supported, since the value of resource exchanges and ideology decay over time.[10] We should note this also holds for goals. For instance, government may claim jurisdiction over police protection. If ineffective, however, vigilante groups may contest this aspect of the government's domain and claim it as part of their domain. Claims over goals establish expectations on the part of subgroups in society. Even organizations given exclusive jurisdiction over goals must provide some valuable output or face competition. Let's take a closer look at competing claims over key organizational elements.

The Boundary of an Organization. The outer limit of an organization's domain is often called its boundary.[21] At the boundary, control over internal elements is often contested.[16] It may be difficult to clearly separate one organization from another or delineate control from mere influence. Starbuck has recognized this by likening the organization to a cloud.[19] At times one cloud is clearly visible and distinct, even though its shape continually changes as it moves across the sky. Two clouds may partially overlap and even merge. It may be impossible to say a particular water droplet belongs to one cloud or another. With organizations, the problem is even more difficult. You are dealing with a large number of elements and potentially different areas of control.

Let's return to our decision rule and modify it. Originally, we stated that an element is inside an organization if it's legally controlled by the system. Let's refine that. An element is inside the system to the extent that it is legally controlled by an organization and to the extent that these claims are accepted by other individuals and institutions in society. Obviously, this is not a precise definition. But it appears to be a workable approach to drawing boundaries.

Defining the Specific Environment of an Organization

Let's restate the basic theme. To maintain control over internal elements an organization must continually replenish its resources and maintain its ideological legitimacy. The specific environment is the set of *external* organizations, individuals, and institutions that a given organization interacts with.[8,12] An organization does not exert legal control over these entities, though it may enter into legal contracts with them. These external units are contacted to enhance the probability of growth and survival as a result of an organization's domain choice.

The primary units in the specific environment of an organization are its input suppliers and output distributors.[12] Without their support it would be unable to function. Organizations need assured sources of labor, money, raw materials, and equipment.[16] They need distributors and customers to keep the system operating. This is done either directly via exchange of resources for products and services or indirectly via exchange with a supplier for service to a particular client group.[7]

The organization also interfaces with competitors. We most frequently think of competitors as those offering similar products and services.[15] But organizations face competitors in other areas as well. There is competition for inputs and outputs.

Less well recognized are a number of institutions that develop as a result of organizations attempting to claim jurisdiction over a particular element. As organizations lay claim to labor, unions and professional organizations are likely to develop to offset organizational control.[9] Slowly, large complex organizations are beginning to realize that their claims for control help span special interest groups. Who protects a "free good," such as air, if organizations claim they can use it as they see fit? First came the development of special interest groups. Now the U.S. government claims jurisdiction and limits the manner in which air can be used. Who ensures individual consumers will receive fair treatment from huge corporations? Currently, there are several interest groups pressuring the government to establish a new agency to work toward this end.

Thus, the government is a potential member of every organization's specific environment.[13] As the allocator of power it can establish organizations or eliminate them. However, the U.S. government is not a single organization. It is a complex configuration composed of a number of organizations. They compete with one another in a manner not dissimilar to businesses. However, the focal point of the competition often rests with goals and values, not products and services.

So far we have identified suppliers, distributors, customers, special interest groups, and the government as members of an organization's specific environment. Each of these has been related to the attempts of an organization to gain control over its internal elements. There is another group of institutions in the specific environment that most organizations tend to dismiss. These are organizations operating in areas not directly related to their mission or domain.[6] Many of these organizations have a different social function. They become a part of an organization's specific environment because each is part of the larger society.[4] For example, business organizations support charities and universities. Universities, in turn, lend technical assistance to business and government agencies. Churches may provide public schools with meeting rooms. The list is almost endless.

Immediate payoff is not automatically expected in many contacts between institutions with different social functions.[12] Many of these contacts appear to be made to improve the image and legitimize the organization. A few, however, may have direct payoff. For instance, large corporations are most likely to give money to a prestigious private university where their top executives hope their children might attend and from which they hope to obtain new employees. Such "gifts" are often publicized as evidence of the corporation's social responsibility. Universities often lend assistance to local governments as part of their "service obligation to the community." The fact that such help enhances the probability of greater state funding by local legislators is rarely mentioned.

For a large corporation the number of external individuals, organizations, and institutions composing its specific environment can run into the thousands. Even simple organizations may have a specific environment with hundreds of units. But only a comparatively few units in the specific environment receive very much attention by top management. Those external units that do receive attention from the organization appear to have an impact on its internal operations and decision-making structure. Let's take a look at these systems.

The Enacted Portion of the Specific Environment. Weick argues that organizations only respond to those external forces that are enacted.[19] That is, the system responds to those elements that demand its attention. Not all the institutions just described demand attention. And most managers in complex organizations face only a few portions of the specific environment. The literature on organizational environments splits on this key issue. Is the entire set of units comprising the specific environment important, or just those recognized by the system? While there is no clear-cut answer the following seems reasonable.

Some portions of the specific environment are more important than others.[13] Different portions of the specific environment are relevant to different managers.[1] The system cannot respond to environmental pressures that remain undetected.[19] Thus, we expect alterations in the domain of the organization to be partially explained by managerial perceptions. That is, the organization responds directly to the enacted part of the specific environment.

Conditions in the specific environment of the system probably have a direct impact on organizational outcomes whether they are perceived by managers or not. For instance, even if an organization does not see consumer resistance to a product, sales may suffer. Thus, the objective aspects of the specific environment are important when predicting organizational success.

Managerial perceptions of the specific environment do not automatically correspond to more objective descriptions.[17] However, it appears more likely that managerial perceptions and objective descriptions of the major units in the specific environment will become increasingly similar as you move higher into the managerial ranks.[12]

The definition of an organization as a legal entity should be carefully noted. Assume you are attempting to describe the specific environment of a simple organization, Sasquash Division, of a complex organization, Diversified Creatures. The perceptions of the important units in the specific environment of the head of Sasquash Division are likely to be very similar to objective measures for the division. It's unlikely, however, that the division head of

Sasquash knows very much about the specific environment of Diversified Creatures.

There may be a large overlap between the "enacted" environment and the actual environment when top-level decision makers are asked to describe important outside forces. Lower-echelon managers, however, probably have more difficulty in accurately assessing external pressures. They have a difficult time seeing the "big picture." But regardless of whose perceptions are used, we need to answer a critical question: Which are the most important units in the specific environment?

Important Units in the Specific Environment. We have asserted that suppliers, distributors, competitors, and government agencies are particularly important.[5] They have a direct bearing on the short-run survival of the organization.[12] Let's go a little farther.

If you accept the notion that exchange is the basis for interaction among organizations, it is quite obvious that most individuals or special interest groups have comparatively little to offer organizations.[18] In the case of individuals an organization can readily substitute one person for another.[4] Special interest groups have difficulty mounting the sustained effort needed to alter existing conditions.[10] Their claims over internal elements may be heavily weighted toward ideology. At the first sign of progress, members of special interests are likely to switch their affiliation to other groups. Unlike organizations, success may spell the death of a special interest group. For example, in the mid 1970s, a loose coalition of housewives boycotted meat to protest dramatically rising costs of beef. The boycott was successful in cutting demand and stemming price increases for a short time. With this success, however, the interest group dissolved. It did not reform when meat prices again jumped some six months later.

In contrast to individuals and special interest groups, the organization relies upon a mix of resources and ideologies. As a legal entity it can make and enforce contracts. Via specialization it can control resources needed by other organizations. It need not be concerned about complete consensus on every issue.[2] Resources can be substituted for ideology to maintain control over individuals. Success does not threaten survival but adds resources for growth and development.[12] Thus, organizations are the most important units in the specific environment of other organizations.

To a large extent, then, the important units in the specific environment of an organization consist of organizations it must rely upon for growth and development.[18] Suppliers of raw materials, financial institutions, unions, government agencies, and competitors are important for most organizations. Occasionally, individuals and special interest groups are important enough to become a part of the enacted environment (e.g., Ralph Nader and his raiders). Most, however, have used a strategy of operating through government agencies, which then become the relevant units of the enacted environment.

ASSESSING THE SPECIFIC ENVIRONMENT OF ORGANIZATIONS

Three variables appear to be particularly important in analyzing the impact of the specific environment on organizations. These are: (1) the degree of interdependence; (2) the extent of uncertainty; and (3) the opportunities for growth and development (or what we call development). Here, we look at each of these.

Interdependence, Power, and Reliance

When an organization establishes its domain it automatically becomes more reliant upon some organizations than others.[15] Via exchange, organizations attempt to grow, develop, and, in Thompson's words, manage their domains.[29] The degree of interdependence of one organization upon another not only defines the outer boundaries of the specific environment,[19] it also charts the relative importance of various organizations.[6]

We have chosen the term interdependence to highlight the reciprocal nature of exchanges among organizations.[30] If A and B are interdependent, both have some degree of clout over the other.[7] The pattern of dependence in the specific environment appears to have two dimensions. First, to what extent is the focal organization more dependent upon others than they are upon it?[23] That is, what is the relative power of the organization? Two, how interdependent are the members of the specific environment upon one another?[8] Even a powerful system may be forced to adapt if all the weaker units demand it.[26] Perhaps a variation of an Aesop fable will illustrate interdependence.

The lion and the fox agreed to cooperate in the hunt. The fox would chase the game and the lion would come in for an easy kill. Together they killed in one day what each could do alone in a week. When dividing the spoils the fox wisely asked the lion for a fair share. The lion gave the fox more than the fox could have killed alone, but still a very small share. The analogy to organizations is clear. The benefits from exchange need not be equivalent. If both parties benefit from the exchange, it is likely the relationship will be voluntarily maintained.[11]

The Relative Power of an Organization. We said the relative power of an organization vis-à-vis its specific environment is the first aspect of interdependence. But what is the overall pattern of reciprocation? Is the organization the fox or the lion? The greater the reliance of the organization upon others (the less it gains from exchanges compared to others), the more responsive the organization must be to environmental alterations.[14] Why? The organization receives comparatively less return for its efforts.[27] Thus, it has comparatively little margin for error. Slight changes can eliminate the benefits from exchanges. The organization has comparatively fewer internal resources to initiate new exchange relationships. Note, however, it's still better off with the exchanges than without them.

The pattern of dependence is rarely the same for goals, output, property, technology, structure, and members.[3] Some of these internal elements must be obtained from a single source. As economic theory clearly shows, the monopolist has a more favorable exchange condition.[5] For instance, if a union controls the labor supply, it can bargain for higher wages, fringe benefits, and worker prerogatives than would be found in a free labor market. It tilts the exchange in favor of the union.

However, unfavorable exchange situations can be eased or altered. To continue our example of the union, assume the organization has developed a favorable exchange relationship with distributors. To some extent higher wages can be passed on to these units which in turn are likely to pass them on to individual consumers. This directly eliminates the unfavorable exchange relationship.

An indirect way to reduce dependence might be through the use of other external forces.[5] Assume a business corporation faces the same union as before, but may be unable to pass on extra costs. In previous negotiations the corporation has already bargained away the right to promote employees on the basis of performance. Seniority determines progression. The business might ask the Equal Employment Opportunity Commission to rule that seniority was inherently discriminatory. Seniority reflects previous patterns of discrimination against females and minorities. Given such a ruling, the business has some additional leverage over the union. The seniority system is now a bargaining issue.

As these examples show, dependence is not static. Several entities may be involved to determine the degree of dependence on outside groups.

Domain Protection and Interdependence. We think organizations will seek areas where favorable exchange relationships are more likely and tend to expand their domain into areas they can dominate. They may even help develop new organizations that will offset the power of an important unit in the specific environment. Thompson argues that such efforts stem from the organization's desire to protect its "technical core."[29] This means that the organization will attempt to protect the major processes it uses to produce its products and services. Following Thompson's general notion we expect that an organization will be particularly vehement in protecting its fixed investment. Protection of an organization's fixed investment is needed to ensure long-term survival.

To produce the outputs needed, an organization must often invest in capital equipment, long-term employment contracts, and the like. For instance, producing automobiles requires a huge long-run commitment of resources in machinery and equipment. Only minor shifts from the existing technology are possible in the short run. Major alterations would threaten the existence of the system.[17] This rigidity results primarily from specialization. Specialization is both the organization's major strength and weakness. It's a basis for exchanges with members in the specific environment. But the rigidity inherent in specialization means an organization must protect its long-term investments. Conversely, if control over less critical elements is challenged, its survival may not be directly threatened.[12] It can move out of one area and seek favorable exchange relationships in others.

These arguments again reveal the critical importance of suppliers, distributors, and government agencies.[28] Suppliers and distributors are needed to protect internal operations. Government agencies can preempt the jurisdiction of an organization over elements needed to maintain its central technology. A complementary argument is that competitors are a critical feature of the specific environment. They also compete for suppliers and distributors and seek to protect their investments. It's no wonder, then, that organizations attempt to dilute the impact of these important members of the specific environment.[10] This is done by securing several sources of supply, developing numerous distributors, pitting one governmental agency against another wherever possible, and in some cases, trying to expand their domain.[12]

Interdependence within the Specific Environment. Let's return to the story of the lion and the fox to illustrate another aspect of interdependence. The arrangement between the fox and the lion was so successful that the fox convinced the lion to expand and make the same arrangement with twelve foxes. The kill rate was amazing. The arrangement was so efficient that game started to disappear. After a particularly poor day's hunt the foxes demanded and got a larger share of the spoils.

Collective action is not always needed to alter the policies or internal operations of a more powerful and autonomous organization. If each demanded a larger share separately, the lion might still have trouble. While busy with one fox, another could take more. In much the same fashion, when an organization faces an interdependent set of organizations in the specific environment, it must often succumb to the desires of less powerful and less autonomous units.[19] Thus, organizations seek a specific environment where the members are not interdependent. It is expected that interdependence among members of the specific environment has much the same impact on an organization as the degree of reliance upon one external unit.[4] The greater the interdependence, the greater the probability that the organization will: (a) seek to alter its domain; (b) become more responsive to pressures from members in the specific environment;[12] (c) derive less from exchanges with other organizations;[18] and (d) spend more effort on monitoring external conditions.[1]

The Impact of Interdependence on Organizations. We have already covered some kinds of organizational response to interdependence. Here, as in the Measurement Module, we will distinguish between objective and perceptual measures of interdependence. Let's look at a few studies that have been done about the effect of this on organizational operations and outcomes.

In a well-known and often criticized study, Aiken and Hage studied interdependence among health and welfare agencies, as measured by the number of joint programs.[2] Interdependence was positively associated with the degree of professional activity by members, the degree of specialization, the number of new innovative programs, as well as the amount of coordinative activities such as committee meetings.

In another sample of health-related organizations, Paulson found much the same as Aiken and Hage.[22] But his data raise an interesting question of causality. Most researchers assume that environmental conditions lead to alterations in the internal structure and operations of organizations. Paulson's data, however, suggested that this pattern of causation might be quite the opposite. Namely, a more sophisticated structure leads to greater interdependence (number of joint programs). This shouldn't be too surprising if we assume that organizations seek a favorable domain and establish mechanisms to accomplish control. It may very well be that the structure needed to interface with other organizations is established before detailed arrangements, like joint programs, are perfected. There may be a process of mutual adjustment over time (what some refer to as reciprocal causation). That is, environmental interdependence is altered by and alters organizational structure. We will continue to treat the major causation chain as moving from environmental conditions to organizational structure and operations. This is the most popular view. But you should be aware of the conflicting evidence. At any rate, interdependence has some influence on an organization and its members, when measured "objectively."

Studies relying upon executive perceptions of interdependence also show it is an important factor for organizations.[25,31] Even though top managers may not accurately perceive the degree of interdependence, they act on their perceptions.[14] When top managers see more interdependence (less autonomy), they tend to centralize decision making.[13] Specialized units may be formed to meet dependence on powerful units in the specific environment.[16] Greater reliance on outsiders has also been associated with an ideological shift toward the dominant values of more powerful external systems.[23] Freeman shows that reliance upon other units is associated with greater leadership activity on the part of unit heads, particularly in regard to developing more external contacts.[9,20,21]

Thus, results for both objective and perceptual measures seem to be consistent. Interdependence is related to organizational structure and operations as well as short-term effectiveness.* However, most of the empirical investigations are with small nonprofit organizations and center on "cooperation" as desirable among organizations. To include larger scale organizations and profit-seeking systems we must move to indirect measures of specific environment interdependence (such as measures of industry concentration ratios, and input-output analysis). Here the data are somewhat less clear. But they support the general notion that interdependence increases the complexity of an organization's structure, reduces the perceived autonomy of managers, and is positively related to short-term profitability. The overall impact on long-term survival and growth still awaits empirical investigation.

In sum, interdependence is an important variable in assessing the specific environment of an organization. Yet it is not the only important factor. Uncertainty in the specific environment has also been related to internal operations and effectiveness. So let's look at this variable.

Uncertainty in the Specific Environment

While there are many different views of environmental uncertainty, it is easiest to see in terms of interrelated dimensions: disparity and volatility. We will discuss each of these factors and their association with effectiveness and internal operations.

Disparity. The first aspect of uncertainty in the specific environment of an organization is called disparity. We have shown that an organization deals with several other organizations. These outside organizations constitute the core of the specific environment. As the number of types of these external

---

*As noted earlier, the degree of cooperation among government agencies and among nonprofit systems has often been used as a surrogate measure of effectiveness (see page 64 under the systems resource approach to organizational effectiveness).

organizations increases (become more heterogeneous), disparity increases.[1] These organizations may be different in many ways. An analysis of key organizational characteristics and of interdependence suggests that differences in goals, outputs, technology, structure, size, and employees are important.[19]

Disparity increases the risk for an organization. It does this in several different ways. The more varied the members, the greater the conflict potential.[1] As the membership of the specific environment becomes more varied, the probability of instability also increases.[19] Organizations face similar pressures from the general environment. When membership becomes more varied, however, the chances of unified pressures from the general environment decline rapidly. The ability of an organization to influence the specific environment also appears to decline as disparity of the environment increases.[1] Furthermore, greater disparity also reduces the ability of decision makers to accurately predict the actions of outside units.[8] Estimates for one outside organization do not apply to others.[14]

We should note that such disparity is a two-way street. While it increases risk, it also increases the autonomy executives see in their jobs.[6] At the same time the organization has less influence over outsiders, outsiders also have less control over the organization.

There are comparatively few empirical studies showing the association of disparity and organizational processes or outcomes.[19,8] Yet systems analysts have given disparity a key role in their analyses of organizations. Ashby among others, argues that greater disparity in external factors should be matched with greater variability internal to the organization.[2] Organizations that follow this "law of requisite variety" are expected to have higher survival potential. At least one empirical analysis suggests that organizations that follow this "law" are more likely to reach their output goals.[20]

Volatility. Many organizations find it particularly difficult to cope with changes in trends.[23] Figure 6-1 outlines three different types of trend changes. In panel A, we find little volatility even though there is considerable change. Here there is little uncertainty. The trend is relatively constant. In panel B there is fluctuation and directional instability; but we can still predict the cycle of change. Here, the organization faces some uncertainty. This is due to the lack of directional stability. Yet a trend is still present. In panel C the velocity, acceleration, and directional stability all appear random. Here the organization faces considerable uncertainty. There appears to be no trend. In our terms the specific environment would be volatile.

Volatility is the enemy of all organizations. It can upset established patterns of control and interdependence. It reduces the value of the organization's resources and signals a potential shift in the value of its ideology. Existing patterns of specialization and current outputs may no longer be appropriate.

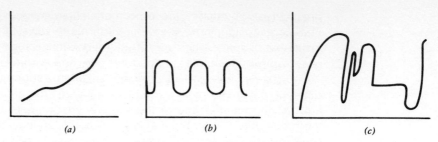

Figure 6-1 A graphic view of volatility.

Organizational and Managerial Responses to Uncertainty. Organizations appear to anticipate the value of future outcomes from current inputs, and discount for risk.[5] Many develop specialized units to cope with uncertainty, which can be linked to specific external units.[4,11] Environmental uncertainty appears to paralyze some decision makers.[8] When it appears that an organization no longer controls its fate, decision makers often attempt to build slack to buffer dysfunctional changes.[8] Let's look at an example to highlight these points.

When first formed, the Equal Employment Opportunity Commission (EEOC) frequently changed guidelines for minority hiring procedures. Many firms responded with centralized affirmative action units. You can imagine what happened. The EEOC issued new regulations for minority hiring that were to be implemented immediately. Regulations were filled with bureaucratic jargon that few could understand, and the EEOC kept reinterpreting the standards. The solution: put someone in charge of the minority relations program. That person can figure out what the EEOC really wants. The head of the new Minority Relations Office obviously needed a staff (the bigger the better) to cope with the ever changing demands of the EEOC. The Minority Relations Office also needed the support of the top brass for this important effort. Thus, the unit was placed near the top of the organizational hierarchy.

But was this typical response successful? It might be for the derived goal of hiring minority workers. But it might not be in regard to other goals. Several studies have found that firms that resisted the temptation to develop specialized units in the face of greater volatility had higher performance ratings on outputs, which could be directly linked with the mission of the system.[4,11] In slightly different terms, firms that desire greater overall success must, we think, resist the temptation of overstructuring in the face of environmental volatility. They should not develop specialized bureaus, departments, and agencies with a later increase in the number of rules, policies, and procedures.[3] Instead, the organization should rely more upon the informal organization.

Part of the reason for this suggestion is that managers operate in the face of perceptual as well as objective uncertainty. These presumptions influence how they operate. Specifically, fewer good decisions are made by individuals as uncertainty increases.[7] Managers move to a form of decision making where they consult more with each other.[8] They abandon rigid decision rules and circumvent the formal relationships dictated by the bureaucracy. Under high risk, then, the individual who has the relevant information becomes important and a key in the decision-making process. Organizations become more flexible and less bureaucratic as managers increase their lateral contacts.[18] Note that the creation of a specialized unit runs counter to managers' attempts to cope with uncertainty. It forces managers to interact when they don't want to.[15]

The amount of perceived uncertainty may also alter the success of a particular leadership style and particular leader behaviors. Nebecker shows that how a leader perceives environmental uncertainty will alter his other views of opportunities for influence.[17] This, in turn, may alter the impact of leadership style. For example, Hunt and Osborn suggest that since uncertainty cuts the discretion or clout of a leader, managers may withdraw from leadership roles.[12] Several other studies show the same disturbing negative effects of perceived environmental uncertainty on individual behavior and group conditions.[10] As a group the studies combining perceptual and objective uncertainty suggest the following: (1) some volatility seen by managers is not directly traceable to the specific environment; it appears to stem from a combination of personality factors, job experience, and internal organizational conditions;[14] (2) perceived uncertainty appears to foster more informal relations among managers; but such relations may be virtually eliminated if the organization becomes more bureaucratic; (3) the tendency of the organization to bureaucratize in response to uncertainty appears to lower effectiveness (even though it may reduce the anxiety and tension of managers); and (4) uncertainty appears to have a small negative impact on effectiveness of the organization but a larger and more profound negative impact on decision makers. In summary, environmental uncertainty appears quite harmful for bureaucracies that rely heavily on centralized decision making and rigidly adhere to rules.

Interdependence and Uncertainty. We argued earlier that interdependence has a favorable association with organizational performance. We also noted that uncertainty was generally unfavorable. A logical question is what happens when the specific environment is both highly interdependent and uncertain? The combination of high interdependence and high uncertainty is particularly damaging to the organization.[9,22] Put a different way, interdependence can be a double-edged sword. Greater dependence is favorable only when the specific environment has low uncertainty. Some analyses suggest that volatility is the chief culprit. The organization facing a volatile and highly interdependent specific environment can lose control. It can become a tool of outside interests and be unable to change operations to produce viable outputs. How can an organization cope with the high interdependence, high variability setting?

When two organizations attempt to control the same resources, there appear to be several techniques that can be used to resolve the conflict. The dispute may be resolved by custom, dominant values, or law. The legal technique is the most expensive and restrictive. We argue it is more likely to be used as the disparity of the specific environment increases. Organizations may also exchange resources, trade existing resources for contested ones, or develop a new ideology that minimizes the conflict. As organizations in the specific setting become more diverse, it is more difficult for any organization to develop an appropriate medium for exchange or forge a new ideology.

Contesting organizations may agree to disagree, with each claiming a different area of control. For instance, a medical association may share partial control over physicians with hospitals. The association will claim control over how physicians should practice medicine by instructing them in the latest techniques. The hospital will attempt to control physicians by deciding which types of illness it will treat. (Note how this decision is indirectly made in the purchase of equipment.) Since the associations and hospitals share similar domains, conflict is not typically extensive.

But now add a quite divergent group to the specific environment of the hospital. Assume it is owned by a religious order. Now the hospital must systematically consider how spiritual concerns will or will not constrain physicians. Again, greater disparity increases the difficulty in resolving conflict with this technique.

Another technique is merger.[21] Here one organization merely incorporates another. Again as disparity increases it becomes more difficult to use this technique. The benefits of merger are less the more diverse the merging organizations.

Two other possibilities are virtually eliminated by high interdependence. Remember, high interdependence means the organization must find some way of resolving domain conflict. One, they cannot withdraw without losing power.[16] Two, they can't eliminate the other organization without suffering the consequences. Thus, where there is considerable disparity among organizations in a specific environment, resolving domain disputes among highly interrelated organizations becomes more difficult and costly. Yet the organization can still have some control over its fate.

Development in the Specific Environment

Almost unrecognized in the current literature is the resource base of organizations comprising the specific environment. The composition of the specific environment changes slowly over time. An organization is typically committed to an ideology and a whole series of long-term investments. Thus, an organization is stuck with many units in the specific environment. It may be associated with a series of powerful organizations that are growing and contain large reserves of resources. Conversely, an organization may be interacting with a series of weak, declining organizations. Does it make a difference? Some data and several theoretical discussions suggest it makes a substantial difference on the outreach activity of the organization,[10] its internal operations[1] and its annual effectiveness.[13] First, let's briefly look at some different aspects of development. Then we can review the evidence suggesting the importance of development in predicting organizational success.

Development in the specific environment appears to have two dimensions. First, what is the pattern of growth in the specific environment of the organization?[13] Are the members growing in terms of power, size, technical sophistication, and the like? Or are they on the decline? When an organization interacts with growing systems there are greater opportunities for domain expansion.[9] Favorable exchange relationships are also more plentiful. Members of the specific environment are less concerned with getting the best exchange than in assuring needed inputs for continued growth.[14] With growth, outsiders are more willing to defer "payment" and accept future assurances. That is, they "bank" some of their excess in other organizations and "invest" resources in new exchange relationships with long-term payoffs.

Quite the opposite seems true for systems experiencing a decline. They cut "investment" in other organizations.[10] They become very concerned with immediate returns. They may attempt to "borrow" from members of the specific environment, placing a strain on existing exchange relationships. For instance, outsiders with excess labor are less likely to let an organization perform specialized services. They will attempt to use their excess labor even though outsiders could do a better and more efficient job. At the very time outsiders may need cooperative relationships to conserve resources and more efficiently use existing capacity, such efforts are not undertaken. Why? Cooperation among organizations primarily involves long-term payoffs after a period of expensive "investment."[19]

The second aspect of development is somewhat more complex since it involves the notion of the interorganizational set. An interorganizational set is a collection of organizations interrelated either directly via exchange relationships or via the production and distribution of a given product or service.[4] The notion of industry is very similar to that of the interorganizational set. It is an example of a set based on the production and distribution of a given product or service. Those familiar with market channels will note that a channel of distribution is another type of interorganizational set.

What is the relative power of the members of the organizational set(s) that an organization is a part of? If the set is large and powerful, members of the set are likely to face a more favorable environment.[16] Large organizations facing less competition are more likely to have excess resources they can divert toward their long-term growth and survival.[3] They are likely to be more specialized and maintain a cadre of technical experts. Since organizations rely upon other organizations, some of these excess resources can be diverted to outsiders.[7] For instance, major soda-extract companies (e.g., Coca Cola, Pepsi) have helped local bottlers fight restrictions on disposable containers. They work with bottlers on technical matters and, most of all, supplement local advertising. They will help perform market studies, lobby for the industry, and the like.[5] Similarly, some critics of the auto industry have argued that the major manufacturers are more interested in the dealers than in consumers.[20]

Organizational and Managerial Responses to Development. The power of the set does not come without a price. Evan argues that it comes at the expense of autonomy.[4] Each organization must anticipate the impact of its decisions on a whole series of external units. For instance, how do you price a product in an oligopolistic industry? You must consider the pricing strategy of competitors and the impact of the pricing strategy on the channel of distribution.[17] The organizational set and its members are less likely to innovate and anticipate broader social changes as the control and power of the set increases.[3] As Selznick noted, the major units of the set appear to exchange and modify their goals and ideology over time until there is a high degree of domain consensus.[18] Critics of federal regulatory agencies have noted a similar process. Major corporations and government agencies have become an interorganizational set with a common set of goals and compatible ideologies.[2]

Development may have its greatest direct impact on the performance of an organization and its managers. Just as powerful organizations may tip the balance of exchange in their favor, so can powerful organizational sets. They are in a position to lobby for favorable governmental action including protectionist legislation, direct subsidies, and price controls. By controlling the output of an important good or service they may increase its price to the society much as the Organization of Petroleum Exporting Countries has done with crude oil. For governmental units, development also has some very subtle overtones. Via cooperative action, government agencies can legitimize each other so that more funds flow into a given problem area.[11] For instance, state universities operating together can help promote the importance of a college degree regardless of which institution grants the diploma. But one university does not publicly criticize another much as one physician does not testify against a colleague.[8] It's bad for the set. Thus, both resources and performance distortion can occur when the set is growing. However, as a member of the set both the organization and its managers benefit.

To the extent that resources flow into an organization as a result of membership in a strong interorganizational set, managers have more resources to work with. Mistakes can be covered with abundant resources. Managers can take credit for growth. They can attract more qualified personnel, reward even marginal performers, and more easily maintain both high satisfaction and performance. However, when the efficiency crunch comes, as it did in education and aerospace, the opposite occurs. Organizations are not given credit for their outputs. Managers can't get the resources they need to maintain high performance and satisfaction. The brightest and the best move on to other areas; the set has problems attracting new blood. And successful administrators are deemed inadequate.

This second aspect of development is the least researched and most controversial. It can be supported by a number of theoretical articles.[1,12] But we are not aware of any empirical studies relating the power of the interorganizational set to the internal operations or effectiveness of organizations. Thus, you should view this aspect of development with caution.

Summary

To summarize, interdependence, uncertainty, and development are three important variables in the specific environment of an organization. Interdependence fosters growth and survival. Yet it may be detrimental if combined with high uncertainty. Uncertainty appears quite negative on managerial personnel and it is potentially damaging to an organization as a whole. Overall, organizations facing uncertain settings are expected to have more difficulty. Development is the least studied aspect of the variables in the specific environment. But it appears as important, if not more important, than the others for explaining and predicting organizational outcomes. A more favorable setting for the organization appears quite beneficial for managers. It allows them greater latitude for mistakes. With greater resources, organizations are more likely to form exchange relationships that enhance future growth and survival. Implicit in the discussion of each of these variables has been the combined impact of interdependency, uncertainty, and development. We have reserved this for the contingency chapter. Now, let's take a closer look at each of the variables in the Measurement Module.

MEASUREMENT
MODULE

We start here with a treatment of the enacted environment. Then we consider interdependence, uncertainty, and development within the specific environment.

The measurement of the specific environment is difficult due to the "perceptual" versus "objective" view of what is important for the organization. Estimates of environmental conditions by top-level executives and objective measures of the organizations in the specific environment may be quite similar. However, estimates of environmental conditions by lower-echelon managers may be substantially different. For instance, marketing managers in business organizations may view the competition as most relevant. Purchasing agents may see supply sources as most important. Thus, it is important to know who is analyzing the environment.

DEFINING THE ENACTED ENVIRONMENT

Which aspects of the environment are most important can be asked directly. For example, the first part of Exhibit 6-2 has been used by Osborn and Hunt to assess whether suppliers, financial institutions, unions, government agencies, and so on, are most important for the organization.[9]

Once again, it's important to analyze who is responding to these items. The same can be said for measures of interdependence, uncertainty, and development, to which we now turn.

MEASURING INTERDEPENDENCE

Power and reliance is not exclusively a function of size (note the lion and fox fable). But monopolists or larger entities tend to have an edge here. Thus, is the organization larger or smaller or about the same size as others with similar domains? Size can be measured in many ways. But number of employees is a common estimator. For business organizations, relative sales or market share, or dollar value of assets is also common. Interorganizational sets, as in "industries," can be gleaned from the standard industrial classification (SIC) system or by reference to membership and support of trade associations. And you can look at industry concentration ratios, as economists do, for the number of

Exhibit 6-2 Measures of the Enacted Environment, Interdependence, Uncertainty, and Development

To Be Completed by Unit Head + Unit Head's Superior

Defining the Enacted Environment

Here we are interested in the units with which your unit (name of unit) deals most frequently. Your unit may interact with a number of others in attempting to accomplish its mission. Please list at least five units that you think are important to your operations and goal attainment.

1.   6.

2.   7.

3.   8.

4.   9.

5.   10.

Approximately how many *other* outside units are you in contact with that are not listed above?____

The units you listed are the "important units." Now please describe these "important units" as well as the other outside units you interact with. The items are matched so that first you describe the important units and next the others, then both combined. (Please circle the best answer for each question)

Interdependence Items	No Extent	Little Extent	Some Extent	Great Extent	Very Great Extent
1. To what extent do the actions of the following units affect the operations of your unit?					
a. The important units	NE	LE	SE	GE	VGE
b. The other units	NE	LE	SE	GE	VGE
c. Both the important and other units	NE	LE	SE	GE	VGE
2. The action of any one unit may or may not affect the activities of others; to what extent do the actions of the following affect one another?					
a. The important units affect one another	NE	LE	SE	GE	VGE
b. The other units affect one another	NE	LE	SE	GE	VGE
c. Both the important and the other units affect one another	NE	LE	SE	GE	VGE

3. To what extent must the following units support a new project to ensure successful planning and implementation?

a. The important units	NE	LE	SE	GE	VGE
b. The other units	NE	LE	SE	GE	VGE
c. Both the important and other units	NE	LE	SE	GE	VGE

4. To what extent do the following units restrict the activities of your unit?

a. The important units	NE	LE	SE	GE	VGE
b. The other units	NE	LE	SE	GE	VGE
c. Both the important and the other units	NE	LE	SE	GE	VGE

Uncertainty Items	0–20%	21–40%	41–60%	61–80%	81–100%
5.* What percent of the time can you predict the actions of:					
a. The important units	A	B	C	D	E
b. The other units	A	B	C	D	E
c. Both the important and other units	A	B	C	D	E
6.* What percent of the time can you predict the expectations of:					
a. The important units	A	B	C	D	E
b. The other units	A	B	C	D	E
c. Both the important and other units	A	B	C	D	E
7. What percentage of time are you certain about how to respond to meet the actions or expectations of:					
a. The important units	A	B	C	D	E
b. The other units	A	B	C	D	E
c. Both the important and other units	A	B	C	D	E

8. What percent of the time do you receive information too

late to capitalize on or offset changes in actions or expectations of:

a. The important units	A	B	C	D	E
b. The other units	A	B	C	D	E
c. Both the important and other units	A	B	C	D	E

9.* What percent of the time can you determine whether a response to the actions or expectations of a unit was effective?

a. For the important units	A	B	C	D	E
b. For the other units	A	B	C	D	E
c. For both the important and other units	A	B	C	D	E

Development	No Extent	Little Extent	Some Extent	Great Extent	Very Great Extent
10. To what extent have the following been *growing* (e.g., in terms of budgets, personnel, projects) in the last three years?					
a. The important units	NE	LE	SE	GE	VGE
b. The other units	NE	LE	SE	GE	VGE
c. Both the important and other units	NE	LE	SE	GE	VGE
11. To what extent have the following received *new sources of support* in the last three years?					
a. The important units	NE	LE	SE	GE	VGE
b The other units	NE	LE	SE	GE	VGE
c. Both the important and other units	NE	LE	SE	GE	VGE
12.* To what extent are the *policies* of the following toward your unit *unfavorable*?					
a. The important units	NE	LE	SE	GE	VGE

		NE	LE	SE	GE	VGE
b.	The other units	NE	LE	SE	GE	VGE
c.	Both the important and other units	NE	LE	SE	GE	VGE

13. To what extent are the *policies* of the following toward your unit *consistent* over time?

		NE	LE	SE	GE	VGE
a.	The important units	NE	LE	SE	GE	VGE
b.	The other units	NE	LE	SE	GE	VGE
c.	Both the important and other units	NE	LE	SE	GE	VGE

14. To what extent do the following have *slack* or *reserves* in resources?

		NE	LE	SE	GE	VGE
a.	The important units	NE	LE	SE	GE	VGE
b.	The other units	NE	LE	SE	GE	VGE
c.	Both the important and other units	NE	LE	SE	GE	VGE

15. To what extent are the following units powerful?

		NE	LE	SE	GE	VGE
a.	The important units	NE	LE	SE	GE	VGE
b.	The other units	NE	LE	SE	GE	VGE
c.	Both the important and other units	NE	LE	SE	GE	VGE

16. To what extent are the following units able to adapt to change?

		NE	LE	SE	GE	VGE
a.	The important units	NE	LE	SE	GE	VGE
b.	The other units	NE	LE	SE	GE	VGE
c.	Both the important and other units	NE	LE	SE	GE	VGE

Scoring

All items are scored on a 1–5 basis with a 1 given to NE or 0–20%, except where there is an *. The items marked with an * are reverse scored. Each of the three dimensions is defined by the sum of the a, b, and c scores for all the items in its set.

Source: Modified from Hunt, J. G., & Osborn, R. N., *A Multiple Influence Model of Leadership.* Proposal funded by the U.S. Army Research Institute for the Behavioral and Social Sciences, May 1978. By permission of the authors.

firms with control over output. For example, some economists suggest that if one firm has over 60 percent of sales an effective monopoly exists. Four or five firms with 50 percent of sales may be an oligopoly.*

These kinds of objective measures of interdependence give you some clues about the relative power of the focal organization. But perceptual measures may be more important. Perceptual interdependence has been operationalized by Kochran, Freeman, and Osborn and Hunt, among others.[7,5,9] Exhibit 6-2 indicates the types of questions that can be used for interdependence.

MEASURING UNCERTAINTY

As noted before, there are a variety of ways in which uncertainty has been conceived and measured.[2,3] If you subscribe to our approach, you can get objective measures of disparity, velocity, acceleration, and directional change in the specific environment. For example, what is the nature of entry and exit of "suppliers?" How many different entities does the organization deal with? Consider personnel: is the organization facing a renegotiation of its labor contracts? What about competitors? Are their advertising expenditures predictable? Are government tax policies likely to proceed in the same direction as they have? For each area of the specific environment, you can find some objective indicators of the patterns of disparity associated with that sector.

Tosi et al. argue that for businesses: sales, research and development, and income volatility are particularly damaging.[12] These strike at the heart of corporations. A similar measure of market risk is available for most large corporations. Called beta, it is the market sensitivity of a firm's stock to market changes.[13] Those stocks that move with the market are considered less risky and have lower betas. The same concept can be applied for other suppliers as well as distributors. Universities, for instance, might calculate beta for per student funding changes or enrollment of one university compared to all others. Universities with higher betas would be more likely to have larger swings in funding than lower and less risky universities. By calculating betas for key inputs and outputs you could spot the most sensitive areas for a given organization. Is the organization hurt more by alterations (volatility) in the labor market, financial conditions, or research and development expenditures compared to similar organizations; that is what is the relative risk, area by area?

*There are, of course, economists who dispute the exact figures and how they are calculated. But the merger guidelines of the Antitrust Division in the Justice Department suggest that mergers would be challenged if the top four firms have 75 percent of the market, among other criteria.

We have indicated that perceived environmental uncertainty is very important. Yet there are different approaches here and quite a controversy over measurement. The research efforts of Duncan, Downey and his associates, and Lawrence and Lorsch alert us to the following.[3,2,8] The environment must be carefully defined if uncertainty is to be accurately assessed. The individual describing the environment must be knowledgeable. Internal uncertainty stemming from such factors as technology, formal structure, and individual personality must be controlled as much as possible in estimates of environmental uncertainty.[8] Finally, to some extent, all the measures of environmental uncertainty will be made through one or a number of perceptual screens. Different individuals will see the same environment in somewhat different ways.[2]

It is important to realize that several large-scale empirical investigations have raised a number of questions concerning the reliability and validity of some popular instruments used to measure perceived uncertainty. For instance, Downey et al. suggests that very simple- and very complex-minded individuals may see less uncertainty than the "typical" person.[2] When asked to estimate (a) the lack of information concerning external conditions, (b) the ability to predict the consequences of decisions, and (c) the impact of outside forces on the success of the organization, they found the following: the very simple minded do not appear to ask these questions while the very complex minded may need less information to cope.

A number of authors have attempted to integrate perceived and objective measures of uncertainty in the specific environment.[1,4,11] Exhibit 6-2 indicates one approach that has been used. While perceptual in nature, it is structured to ascertain the important elements of uncertainty.

Researchers are still trying to demonstrate the direct and indirect impacts of risk stemming from the specific environment.[10] But whether the uncertainty is "real" or merely due to perceptual bias, managers appear to alter the way in which they operate as perceived uncertainty changes.

MEASURING DEVELOPMENT

Measuring development objectively is, in a way, a combination of measures of interdependence and uncertainty. As noted above for interdependence, you can measure whether an organization in the environment is growing in size or power. Of course, you would also want to look at trends here, similar to those for uncertainty. But a whole series of indicators of the size and direction of the resource base (human, physical, and financial assets) should be used to ascertain whether important units of the specific environment are growing or declining.

Perceptually, Exhibit 6-2 again provides several items that ask decision makers to indicate how they view the development of these important units.[9] This includes a global estimate for all important units and other units. It can be used for comparing a number of organizations. We think that for analyzing a particular organization, these could be expanded to a series of items for each of the important units identified at the beginning of Exhibit 6-2. Of course, our earlier cautions concerning perceived environmental uncertainty also apply to perceptions of development in the specific environment.

REFERENCES

I. What is an Organization?

[1] Etzioni, A. *Modern Organizations.* Englewood Cliffs, N. J.: Prentice-Hall, 1964.

[2] Hall, R. *Organizations: Structure and Process.* Englewood Cliffs, N. J.: Prentice-Hall, 1977.

[3] Hicks, H. G., and Gullet, C. R. *Organizations: Theory and Behavior.* New York: McGraw-Hill, 1975.

[4] Pfeffer, J., and Salancik, G. *The External Control of Organizations: A Resource Dependence Approach.* New York: Harper & Row, 1978.

[5] Thompson, J. *Organizations in Action.* New York: McGraw-Hill, 1967.

[6] Thompson, J. "Society's Frontiers for Organizing Activities," *Public Administration Review,* 33 (1973), 327–335.

[7] Weick, K. E. *The Social Psychology of Organizing.* Reading, Mass.: Addison-Wesley, 1969.

II. The Organization and Its Specific Environment

A. The Domain of an Organization

[1] Akinbode, I. A., and Clark, R. "A Framework for Analyzing Interorganizational Relationships," *Human Relations,* 29 (1976), 101–114.

[2] Aldrich, H. "Organizational Boundaries and Interorganizational Conflict," *Human Relations,* 24 (1971), 279–293.

[3] Caplow, T. *Principles of Organization.* New York: Harcourt, Brace and World, 1964.

[4] Coser, L. A. *Continuities in the Study of Social Conflict.* New York: The Free Press, 1967.

[5] Drucker, P. F. *The Practice of Management.* New York: Harper & Brothers, 1954.

[6] Friesma, H. P. "Interjurisdictional Agreements in Metropolitan Areas," *Administrative Science Quarterly,* 15 (1970), 242–252.

[7] Haas, J. E., and Drabek, T. E. *Complex Organizations: A Sociological Perspective.* New York: Macmillian Publishing Co., 1973.

[8] Hostiuck, K. T. *Contemporary Organizations: An Introductory Approach.* Morristown, N. J.: General Learning Press, 1974.

[9] Jacobs, D. "Dependency and Vulnerability: An Exchange Approach to the Control of Organizations," *Administrative Science Quarterly,* 4 (1974), 45–60.

[10]Kast, F., and Rosenzweig, J. E. *Organization and Management: A Systems Approach.* New York: McGraw-Hill, 1970.

[11]Keller, R., Szilagyi, A., and Holland, W. "Boundary-Spanning Activity and Employee Reactions: An Empirical Study," *Human Relations,* 29 (1976), 699–710.

[12]Kelly, J. *Organizational Behavior.* Homewood, Ill.: Richard Irwin, 1974.

[13]Litwak, E. "Models of Bureaucracy Which Permit Conflict," *American Journal of Sociology,* 67 (1961), 177–184.

[14]Merton, R. K. *Social Theory and Social Structure.* New York: The Free Press, 1957.

[15]Meyer, M. "Organization Domains," *American Sociological Review,* 40 (1975), 599–615.

[16]Osborn, R., and Hunt, J. G. "The Environment and Organizational Effectiveness," *Administrative Science Quarterly,* 19 (1974), 231–246.

[17]Pfeffer and Salancik, 1978.

[18]Rogers, D. L. "Sociometric Analysis of Interorganizational Relations: Application of Theory and Measurement," *Rural Sociology,* 39 (1974), 487–503.

[19]Starbuck, W. H. "Organizations and Their Environment." In M. D. Dunnette, (ed.), *Handbook of Industrial and Organizational Psychology.* Chicago: Rand McNally, 1976.

[20]Terreberry, S. "The Evolution of Organizational Environments," *Administrative Science Quarterly,* 13 (1968), 590–613.

[21]Thompson, J. D. *Organizations in Action.* New York: McGraw-Hill, 1967.

B. Defining the Specific Environment of an Organization

[1]Adams, T. J. *The Business of Business.* San Francisco: Canfield Press, 1976.

[2]Aldrich, 1971.

[3]Coleman, J. "A Loss of Power," *American Sociological Review,* 38 (1973), 1–17.

[4]Coleman, S. *Measurement and Analysis of Political Systems.* New York: Wiley, 1975.

[5]Emery, W. E., and Trist, E. L. "The Causal Texture of Organizational Environments," *Human Relations,* 18 (1965), 21–31.

[6]Etzioni, 1964.

[7]Jacobs, 1974.

[8]Jurkovic, N. R. "A Core Typology of Organizational Environments," *Administrative Science Quarterly,* 19 (1974), 380–394.

[9]Katz, D., and Kahn, R. L. *The Social Psychology of Organizations.* New York: Wiley, 1966.

[10]Kronus, C. "Mobilizing Voluntary Associations into a Social Movement: The Case of Environmental Quality," *Sociological Quarterly,* 18 (1977), 267–283.

[11]Osborn, R. "The Search for Environmental Complexity," *Human Relations,* 29 (1976), 179–191.

[12]Osborn and Hunt, 1974.

[13]Schein, E. *Organizational Psychology.* Englewood Cliffs, N. J.: Prentice-Hall, 1965.

[14]Selznick, P. *TVA and the Grassroots.* Berkeley: University of California, 1949.

[15]Terreberry, 1968.

[16]Thompson, 1967.

[17]Tosi, H., Aldag, R., and Storey, R. "On the Measurement of the Environment: An Assessment of the Lawrence-Lorsch Environmental

Uncertainty Questionnaires," *Administrative Science Quarterly*, 18 (1973), 27–37.

[18]Warren, R. L. "The Interorganization Field as a Focus of Investigation," *Administrative Science Quarterly*, 12 (1967), 396–418.

[19]Weick, 1969.

III. Assessing the Specific Environment of Organizations

A. Interdependence, Power, and Reliance

[1]Adams, 1967.

[2]Aiken, M., and Hage, J. Organizational Interdependence and Infrastructure," *American Sociological Review*, 38 (1972), 912–929.

[3]Aldrich, 1971.

[4]Benson, J. K. "The Interorganizational Network as a Political Economy," *Administrative Science Quarterly*, 20 (1975), 165–176.

[5]Blumberg, P. *The Mega Corporation in American Society: The Scope of Corporate Power.* Englewood Cliffs, N. J.: Prentice-Hall, 1975.

[6]Dill, W. R. "Environment as an Influence on Managerial Autonomy," *Administrative Science Quarterly*, 2 (1958), 409–443.

[7]Emerson, R. M. "Power-Dependence Relations," *American Sociological Review*, 27 (1962), 31–41.

[8]Evan, W. E., "The Organizational Set: Toward a Theory of Interorganizational Relations." In J. Thompson, (ed.), *Approaches to Organizational Design.* Pittsburgh: University of Pittsburgh Press, 1966, 175.

[9]Freeman, J. H. "Environment, Technology, and the Administrative Intensity of Manufacturing Organizations," *American Sociological Review*, 38 (1972), 750–763.

[10]Ford, J. D., and Slocum, J. W. "Size, Technology, Environment and the Structure of Organizations," *Academy of Management Review*, 2 (1977), 561–575.

[11]Gouldner, A. "The Norm of Reciprocity: A Preliminary Examination," *American Sociological Review*, 25 (1960), 161–178.

[12]Jacobs, 1974.

[13]Kochran, T. A. "Determinants of the Power of Boundary Units: An Interorganizational Bargaining Relation," *Administrative Science Quarterly*, 20 (1975), 10–23.

[14]Lawrence, P. R., and Lorsch, J. W. *Organization and Environment: Managing Differentiation and Integration.* Homewood, Ill.: Richard D. Irwin, 1967.

[15]Levine, S., and White, P. "Exchanges as a Conceptual Framework for the Study of Interorganizational Relationships," *Administrative Science Quarterly*, 5 (1961), 583–601.

[16]Litwak, E., and Hylton, L. F. "Interorganizational Analysis: An Hypothesis on Co-ordinating Agencies," *Administrative Science Quarterly*, 6 (1962), 395–420.

[17]Miles, R. E., Snow, C. C., and Pfeffer, J. "Organization-Environment: Concepts and Issues," *Industrial Relations*, 13 (1974), 244–264.

[18]Mileti, D. S., and Gillespie, D. F. "An Integrated Formalization of Organization-Environment Interdependencies," *Human Relations*, 29 (1976), 85–99.

[19]Osborn, R. N. "The Search for Environmental Complexity," *Hu-*

man *Relations,* 29 (1976), 179–191.

20Osborn, R. N., and Bishop, K. C. "The Influence of Environmental Conditions and Unit Performance on External Relations Emphasis," *Organization and Administrative Sciences,* 6 (1976), 15–27.

21Osborn, R. N., and Hunt, J. G. "An Adaptive-Reactive Theory of Leadership: The Role of Macro Variables in Leadership Research," *Organization and Administrative Sciences,* 6 (1975) 27–44.

22Paulson, S. "Causal Analysis of Interorganizational Relations: An Axiomatic Theory Revised," *Administrative Science Quarterly,* 19 (1974), 319–337.

23Pfeffer, J. "Interorganizational Influence and Managerial Attitudes," *Academy of Management Journal,* 15 (1972), 317–330.

24Pfeffer and Salancik, 1978.

25Rogers, 1974.

26Selznick, 1949.

27Shortell, S. M. "The Role of Environment in a Configurational Theory of Organizations," *Human Relations,* 30, 3 (1977), 275–302.

28Smith, D. H. "Organizational Boundaries and Organizational Affiliates," *Sociology and Social Research,* 56 (1972), 494–512.

29Thompson, 1967.

30Warren, 1967.

31Wren, D. A. "Interface and Interorganization Coordination," *Academy of Management Journal,* 19 (1967), 69–81.

B. Uncertainty in the Specific Environment

1Aldrich, H. E. "An Organization-Environment Perspective on Co-operation and Conflict in the Manpower Training System." In A. Negandhi (ed.), *Conflict and Power in Complex Organizations.* Kent, Ohio: Center for Business & Economic Research, 1972.

2Ashby, W. R. *An Introduction to Cybernetics.* New York: Wiley, 1957.

3Burns, T., and Stalker, G. M. *The Management of Innovation.* London: Tavistock, 1961.

4Child, J. "Managerial and Organizational Factors Associated with Company Performance," *Journal of Management Studies,* 12 (1975), 12–27.

5Conrath, D. "Organizational Decision Making Behavior Under Varying Conditions of Uncertainty," *Management Science,* 13 (1967). 487–500.

6Dill, 1958.

7Downey, H. K., Hellriegel, D., and Slocum, J. W. "Environmental Uncertainty: the Construct and its Operationalization," *Administrative Science Quarterly,* 20 (1975), 613–629.

8Duncan, R. "Characteristics of Organizational Environments and Perceived Environmental Uncertainty," *Administrative Science Quarterly,* 17 (1972), 313–328.

9Emery and Trist, 1965.

10Fiedler, F. "Engineer the Job to Fit the Manager," *Harvard Business Review,* 43 (1965), 115–122.

11Ford, J. D. "The Interaction of Size, Technology, and Uncertainty on Dimensions of Structure." Working paper, The Ohio State University, 1975.

12Hunt, J. G., and Osborn, R. N. "A Multiple Influence Model of Leadership," Army Research Institute Grant No. DAHC 19-78-G-0010, 1978.

13Keller, R., Slocum, J., and Susman,

G. "Uncertainty and Type of Management System in Continuous Process Organizations," *Administrative Science Quarterly,* 17 (1974), 56–67.

[14]Lawrence and Lorsch, 1967.

[15]Lev, B. "Environmental Uncertainty Reduction by Smoothing and Buffering," *Academy of Management Journal,* 18 (1975), 864–871.

[16]Meyer, 1975

[17]Nebecker, O. "Situational Favorability and Perceived Environmental Uncertainty: An Integration Approach," *Journal of Personality and Social Psychology,* 10 (1968), 479–486.

[18]Negandhi, A., and Reimann, B. "A Contingency Theory of Organizations Reexamined in the Context of a Developing Country," *Academy of Management Journal,* 15 (1972), 137–146.

[19]Osborn and Hunt, 1974.

[20]Osborn, R. N., Hunt, J. G., and Bussom, R. S. "On Getting Your Own Way in Organizational Design: An Empirical Investigation of Requisite Variety," *Organization and Administrative Sciences,* 8 (1976), 295–310.

[21]Pfeffer, 1972.

[22]Terreberry, 1968.

[23]Tosi et al, 1973.

C. Development in the Specific Environment

[1]Aldrich, 1971.

[2]Blumberg, 1975.

[3]Domhoff, G. W. *Who Rules America.* Englewood Cliffs, N. J.: Prentice-Hall, 1967.

[4]Evan, 1966.

[5]Glueck, W. "A Note on the American Soft Drink Industry." In W. Glueck, *Business Policy: Strategy Formulation and Management Action.* New York: McGraw Hill, 1976, 482–488.

[6]Green, M. (ed.). *The Monopoly Makers.* New York: Grossman, 1973.

[7]Hall, R., Clark, J., Giordano, P., Johnson, P., and Roekel, M. "Patterns of Interorganizational Relationships," *Administrative Science Quarterly,* 22 (1977), 457–474.

[8]Kriplan, H. S., and Bolce, J. W. "Interinstitutional Cooperational Cooperation in Higher Education," University of California at Berkeley: Ford Foundation Report #41, 1973.

[9]Leifer, R., and Huber, G. "Relations Among Perceived Environmental Uncertainty, Organization Structure and Boundary Spanning Behavior," *Administratitive Science Quarterly,* 22 (1977), 235–247.

[10]Lavin, B. "Major Variables Related to Interorganizational Cooperation." Unpublished thesis, Kent State University, 1969.

[11]Levine, S., White, P., and Paul, B. D. "Community Interorganizational Problems in Providing Medical Care and Social Services," *American Journal of Public Health,* 53 (1963), 1183–1195.

[12]McNaul, J. P., Sathe, V., and Shapiro, M. "Organization and Environment: Some Neglected Variables." Paper presented at the Thirty-fourth Annual Meeting of the Academy of Management, Seattle, Washington, 1974.

[13]Osborn, 1976.

[14]Osborn and Bishop, 1976.

[15]Pfeffer, 1972

[15]Reid, W. J. "Interorganizational Cooperation: A Review and Critique of Current Theory." In P. E. White and G. J. Vlasak (eds.), Interorganizational Research in Health:

Conference Proceedings. Washington: U.S. Government Printing Office, 1971, 102–111.

[17]Samuelson, P. A. *Economics*. New York: McGraw-Hill, 1973.

[18]Selznick, 1949.

[19]Van de Ven, A. "On the Nature, Formation and Maintenance of Relations Among Organizations," *The Academy of Management Review,* 1 (1976), 24–36.

[20]Wilcox, C. *Public Policies Toward Business*. Homewood, Ill.: Richard D. Irwin, 1971.

IV. Measurement Module

[1]Child, 1975.

[2]Downey, H. K., and Slocum, J. W. "Uncertainty Measures, Research, and Sources of Variation." Paper presented at the Annual Meeting of the Academy of Management, August 1975.

[3]Duncan, 1972.

[4]Ford, 1975.

[5]Freeman, 1972.

[6]Hunt and Osborn, 1978.

[7]Kochran, 1975.

[8]Lawrence and Lorsch, 1967.

[9]Osborn and Hunt, 1974.

[10]Pennings, J. M. "The Relevance of the Structural Contingency Model for Organizational Effectiveness," *Administrative Science Quarterly,* (1975), 393–410.

[11]Sathe, V. "Duncan's Structural Adaption Model: A Theoretical Extension and Empirical Test." Paper presented at the Annual Meeting of the Academy of Management, Kansas City, August 1976.

[12]Tosi et al, 1973.

[13]Williams, E. E., and Findlay, M. C. *Investment Analysis*. Englewood Cliffs, N. J. Prentice-Hall, 1974.

chapter 7 A CONTINGENCY APPROACH TO ORGANIZATIONAL ENVIRONMENTS

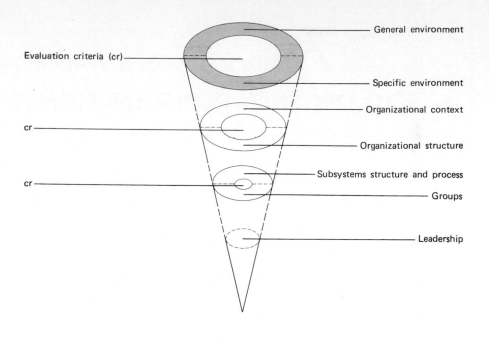

Detailed analyses of organizational environments shed considerable light on how and why organizations act as they do. It is also important to develop an overall view consistent with more detailed analyses. Why an overall view? Simply because the environment of an organization is but one set of factors you need to understand. Environmental conditions should be incorporated with other factors to explain and predict organizational actions and success.

In this contingency chapter, then, we will integrate material from the general and specific environments. Remember our analysis is quite speculative and likely to be controversial. Following our contingency theme, we note differences between large, complex organizations and small, simple organizations.

INTERDEPENDENCE, UNCERTAINTY, AND DEVELOPMENT IN THE GENERAL ENVIRONMENT

We found the concepts of interdependence, uncertainty, and development very useful in analyzing the specific environment. So let's use them to describe the general environment as well.

When analyzing the general environment it is often difficult to empirically separate interdependence and development. As development increases, all aspects of society tend to increase in specialization. For instance, some cities, like Washington D.C., specialize in legal-political affairs. Various geographic areas capitalize on their comparative advantage.[3] For example, Iowa is a farm state and imports most of its industrial products from other states. As areas become specialized, they are more dependent on others. Thus, for all practical purposes measures of development and interdependence in the general environment yield the same relative rankings.[6] To measure one is to measure the other. Since it is easier to measure development let's concentrate on it.*

Development in the economic and educational sectors and its impact on organizational criteria is straightforward. Higher GNP per capita and a more well-educated population means that most organizations have potentially better raw materials for reaching their goals and a more receptive environment for their outputs.[7] However, larger, complex organizations are often in a better position to take advantage of economic and educational development.[7]

Development in the legal-political sector yields a more complex and differentiated set of rules, regulations, and procedures.[1] Many consider this red tape. But a large complex system can benefit from knowing the exact rules of the game. Large systems can also play one specialized governmental unit against another.[8] And they may be able to substantially influence those governmental units designed to control their activities.[2] In contrast, smaller organizations can rarely afford to hire specialists to deal with the very technical rules, policies, and procedures stemming from legal-political systems. In summary, the overall benefits of legal-political development may be small or even slightly negative for small organizations.[5]

The second facet of development in the specific environment dealt with the change of resources. Growth was considered beneficial and indicated a better climate for organizations. To some extent this argument appears to hold at the societal level. The society is a system. Like all systems It Is plagued by the tendency to decay and disintegrate.[4] If there is no change in the cultural, economic, educational, or legal-political conditions, we can argue the nation is stagnating and in the process of decay. While the nation may appear stable, it becomes less viable. Small jolts become magnified into major problems. This can be called the paradox of stability. A low constant velocity permits organizations to predict and plan accurately for future events while keeping the society viable. With steady growth, organizations can continue specialization, increase their interdependence, and expect to grow and survive.

*It is virtually impossible to measure cultural development because of the interrelationship between values and culture. Organizations, however, would probably prefer scientific to postscientific patterns.

Uncertainty in the General Environment

What happens when the general environment becomes volatile? Recall, volatility centers on changes in trends. Cyclical changes introduce some uncertainty. But lack of directional stability dramatically increases uncertainty. Volatility in the general environment has much the same impact on organizations as does volatility in the specific environment.[3,10]

Large organizations can partially offset the damaging effects of volatility with "buffering units" and "early warning systems."[5] The development of a special consumer contact unit by Ford Motor Company is an example of a buffering unit. An example of an early-warning system is the effort by General Electric to estimate long-term changes in the noneconomic sectors of our nation.[9] Smaller organizations rarely have the excess resources to invest in either buffering units or early-warning systems. They must be more flexible, adaptive, and responsive. Rather than absorb volatility, they move with changing trends. Note that both large and small organizations are hurt by volatility in the general environment.

We should also make a distinction between short-term and long-run directional volatility.[1] Short-run disturbances often result from an attempt by one societal group or set of institutions to control another. For instance, under the Nixon administration the federal government established wage and price controls to stem inflation. The program was a disaster and was quickly abandoned. We argue that large complex organizations can withstand such short-term instability and weather the storm. Smaller units, however, are more vulnerable. They may collapse before the threat has passed.

Long-run directional instability is a different matter. Here the goal structure and ideology of organizations are undercut. Both large and small systems are affected. Long-term instability is particularly tricky. The effects on any one type of system are likely to be uneven. For instance, pollution control will become, we think, an important derived goal for all manufacturing organizations. But the emphasis on pollution control is uneven.[9] Part of this may stem from ignorance on the part of government agencies and scientists. Acceptable levels of pollution are difficult to establish. However, part of the uneveness may be due to the reluctance of manufacturers to accept this derived goal and follow through with the needed investment. If one manufacturer does make the investment in pollution control and competitors do not, it may be at a serious competitive disadvantage. All may want to institute pollution control. But none wants to be the first.

Disparity. So far we have assumed that conditions in the cultural, economic, educational, and legal-political sectors of the general environment are all very similar. Yet the pattern of development may not be the same across sectors.[6] There can be a mixed pattern. Moreover, changes in one sector may leave others untouched in the short run. Such disparity limits the ability of an organization to fully capitalize on opportunities for growth and goal attainment. It limits the flexibility of the system. Disparity also shows imbalance in the society.[8] Some types of systems are gaining greater resources at the expense of others. Weaker units are unable to complement the efforts of organizations in the more developed sectors. For instance, a temporary spurt in the economy of a developing nation cannot be sustained over the long-term unless the nation also invests in education.[4]

We think the impact of general environment disparity on large and small organizations is similar to that of disparity in the specific environment and depends upon the overall development of the nation. In underdeveloped countries, small organizations may be in a better position to deal with disparity than large complex systems. Smaller organizations tend to be more self-contained.[8] They can cope with traditional values and supplement inadequate education with informal relations.[6] Via personal contacts they may offset many of the limitations of primitive governmental arrangements. Large complex systems find it more difficult to surmount cultural and educational barriers. The reliance on informal relations runs counter to specialization. Unless locally owned, large organizations may also have difficulty working with local governmental units not designed to serve complex systems.[6]

In developed nations, disparity is still a problem. However, organizations rarely face prescientific value systems or a reactionary legal-political system. Even rural areas of highly developed nations are far ahead of the underdeveloped nations.[4] Thus, large complex organizations are in a position to offset the negative effects of traditional values and poorly developed legal-political systems. As they import resources they stimulate development and alter cultural values as well as the legal-political system. Small organizations, however, find it difficult to alter cultural and legal-political constraints. Unlike large systems, small organizations often cannot fully capitalize on a spurt in the economy, changes in cultural values, more sophisticated legal-political mechanisms, or an increase in knowledge until all begin to occur simultaneously.[7]

Let's take an example. Assume a rich ore deposit is discovered in rural Alabama. Miners, engineers, and managers are needed. Capital is required to build processing facilities. But locals still want to maintain control. We argue that a large conglomerate can provide the needed personnel and capital. It will assure the locals strict adherence to tradition. But the influx of workers will allow the organization to ease local restrictions. The balance between traditional and individualistic values will favor the organization. We are also struck by the willingness of many cities to provide large organizations tax holidays, free access roads, and zoning variances. Such concessions would rarely be given to a local merchant.

Large complex systems may be able to surmount many of the negative effects of disparity. But not all can be avoided. A disparity between dominant cultural values and economic development, for instance, can seriously hamper efforts to maintain high employee satisfaction.* Professionals, managers, and technicians may demand quality schools, adequate shopping, and cultural activities less-developed regions cannot provide.[1] If lower-level employees are locals, while managerial personnel are imported from other areas, the organization may face great conflict between managers and nonmanagers, high turnover within both groups, and suspicion from those outside the system.[2] Many professors are aware of such negative impacts of disparity under the term "town-gown split." Some professors with individualistic values may find it difficult to tolerate a traditional culture surrounding their university.

The Favorability of the General Environment

To incorporate analysis of the general environment into a more comprehensive framework, we need an overall index of favorability. Figure 7-1 shows our estimate of the survival potential for small and large organizations.

We think the degree of development is the most important aspect of the general environment.[2] This is an estimate of the opportunities and resources available to all organizations. Volatility is important and has substantial negative impacts on both small and large organizations.[6] But we argue that high volatility in a developed nation is preferable to certainty in an underdeveloped nation.

In a similar fashion, we argue that while disparity is important, development and volatility are more critical in determining the survival potential of large and small systems. Here we are arguing that disparity limits the ability of an organization to capitalize on opportunities. Disparity may lead to some serious internal problems of dissatisfaction, turnover, and the like.[5] But it has less impact on the survival potential of the system.

The top half of Figure 7-1 summarizes our contingency arguments concerning the impact of the general environment on large and small organizations. In general, we have argued that small systems have a greater chance of survival in less hospitable climates. In contrast, larger, more complex systems

---

*When the disparity is extreme, we often speak of cultural lag. Multinational corporations operating in underdeveloped nations often confront cultural lag and find themselves in the middle between old and emerging value systems. Nationals working for these firms may find that dominant cultural values are inconsistent with their roles as organizational members. They may suffer from isolation, anomie, normlessness, and an inability to link their organizational career and their private life.

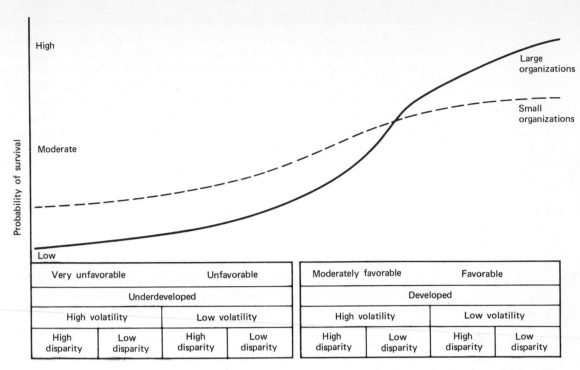

Figure 7-1 Chance of survival for large and small organizations under different degrees of favorability in the general environment.

Very unfavorable		Unfavorable		Moderately favorable		Favorable	
Underdeveloped				Developed			
High volatility		Low volatility		High volatility		Low volatility	
High disparity	Low disparity	High disparity	Low disparity	High disparity	Low disparity	High disparity	Low disparity

need greater external support and are less flexible than smaller units. However, a favorable general environment does not ensure the survival of any one organization. This is an important point. It is too easy to assume that the survival of an organization is externally determined.[4] The favorability of the general environment only makes it more or less difficult to survive and reach goals.

This is only a guide in estimating the overall favorability of the general environment on organizations collectively. When considering the environment of any one organization, a whole series of additional ideas needs to be considered. We have already offered some suggestions on this in the previous two chapters. We consider others in the remaining parts of this book. But several should be handled at this point.

First, conditions relevant to the societal contribution of the system are more important than development, volatility, or disparity in other sectors of the general environment.[3] Economic conditions are more important to business firms, educational conditions to universities, and so forth. Second, the relative importance of conditions in the general environment may differ depending upon which criteria are selected. For estimates of short-term performance, volatility may be more important than development.[6] Disparity may loom large when predicting satisfaction. But disparity is less important than development when attempting to predict long-term survival. We would like to list the factors in the general environment relevant for predicting different criteria in different types of organizations, but we cannot do so. At this time, we are still speculating about the overall impact of the general environment on all organizations. Third, one factor in the environment may negate the positive impact of all others. For instance, there may be high development, low volatility, and low disparity. But a new legal constraint could result in the death of the system.

ORGANIZATIONAL CHOICE: A KEY DIFFERENCE BETWEEN THE GENERAL AND SPECIFIC ENVIRONMENT

So far we have drawn several parallels between analyses of the general and specific environment. Theoretically we noted that the concepts of interdependence, uncertainty, and development could be applied to both. Yet we also noted that for all practical purposes, interdependence and development in the *general* environment folded into one variable. More developed general environments were more interdependent and vice versa. For simplicity we concentrated on development. Can we make the same argument in analyzing the specific environment? No. We don't think so. Let us explain.

Except for a very small number of multinational corporations, organizations cannot escape pressures from their national setting. Nor do they have much influence over general conditions in the society. In more eloquent terms, conditions in the general environment are a constraint, not a contingency.[4]

Quite the opposite may be the case when dealing with the specific environment. To a greater or lesser extent all organizations have some control over their domains.[1] They have some degree of choice concerning the members of the specific environment. Note, a change in domain indirectly yields a different specific environment, while a change in membership is more direct. To the extent top managers have the ability to change the domain of an organization and the membership of the specific environment, they can change the degree of interdependence, uncertainty, and development.[2] For instance, if obtaining supplies is fraught with uncertainty, a firm may vertically integrate to make sure it has greater control.[3] In this instance vertical integration may reduce uncertainty and interdependence in the specific environment.

We estimate that larger organizations will have more opportunities to alter conditions in their specific environment. Smaller systems have less choice once a domain decision has been made. But both large and small organizations do have the option to select a domain. Conditions in the specific environment are not totally beyond the control of management.

FAVORABILITY IN THE SPECIFIC ENVIRONMENT

In Chapter 6, we noted that the combination of interdependence and uncertainty was particularly important. We have just argued that top management may have some control over these factors. Now we want to add the notion of development and derive an overall estimate of favorability in the specific environment.

While development in the specific environment has a favorable impact on most organizations, it should not be considered in isolation from interdependence and uncertainty. Analyses suggest that the impact of uncertainty and interdependence differs in developed and underdeveloped specific environments.[6]

There are several reasons for the interplay among development, uncertainty, and interdependence. Perhaps it is easier to get an understanding of the interplay by returning to the idea of an interorganizational set.[3] Collections of interrelated organizations (a set) can partially offset the negative impact of the high interdependence-high uncertainty combination. All can move to moderate change and systematically maintain a favorable series of exchange relationships. Each realizes that what hurts one member of the set can ultimately hurt the others. Changes instituted by any one member can boomerang. For instance, both suppliers and users of the sugar substitute, saccharin, lobbied Congress when it was about to be taken off the market because it might cause cancer.

Figure 7-2 summarizes our estimate of favorability in the specific environment under different combinations of development, uncertainty, and inter-

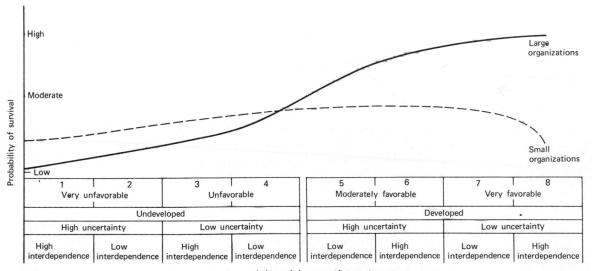

Figure 7-2 Favorability of the specific environment.

dependence. In the under-developed specific environment, high uncertainty is harmful, particularly if it is matched with high interdependence (Cell 1). A reduction of interdependence (movement to Cell 2) is beneficial to the system. For developed settings, however, note that high interdependence is preferred. You can capitalize on the strength of the interorganizational set and the power of external units.

Favorability for Large and Small Organizations

Figure 7-2 also shows that small and large organizations do not benefit equally from favorability in the specific environment. Here our analysis parallels that of the earlier discussion concerning the general environment.

We predict that smaller organizations have a better chance of survival in less favorable settings than larger organizations. They are likely to be more flexible and less specialized than their larger counterparts. Larger organizations need a favorable climate to maintain their survival.[4] They appear slower to adapt to change.[3] They need to develop more extensive patterns of interdependence to maintain control over their domains.[7]

However, as the specific environment becomes more favorable, larger organizations are in a better position to capitalize on the more complex pattern of interorganizational relations found in the developed and interdependent setting.[6] They are in a better position to buffer themselves from uncertainty with specialized units.[5] They can pass on the costs of interdependence to other systems or ultimate consumers.[1,2] We estimate that when the specific environment becomes very favorable the survival potential of small organizations may even deteriorate. They are likely to be incorporated into larger organizations.

Obviously, these are our speculations. Later, after a more thorough discussion of the internal operations of organizations, you may want to challenge these estimates. You might also want to change the criterion from survival potential to employee maintenance. We would expect quite the opposite than that depicted in Figure 7-2 for this criterion. The maintenance of employees in large, complex organizations is likely to be much less sensitive to conditions in the specific environment. Uncertainty may cause ulcers in managers, but lower-level employees in large organizations are likely to be buffered from all but the most serious outside forces. For instance, changes in EPA regulations for autos may result in headaches for managers at General Motors, but assembly-line personnel may not even be aware of the alterations.

In small organizations, however, much less buffering can take place. Employees are more likely to be familiar with slight changes that could alter their employment status or paychecks. On the other hand, it's likely they will share in at least the intrinsic benefits of a more favorable specific environment.

ENVIRONMENTAL COMPLEXITY

Now it's time to combine the conditions in the general and specific environment into an overall indicator of complexity. We will outline its components, and provide a format for deciding upon the degree of environmental complexity faced by any one organization.

The environment is more complex the greater the development, uncertainty, and interdependence. That is, the greater the opportunities and threats faced by an organization, the greater the complexity. These factors force managers and administrators to take the environment into account. In a simple environment the manager may close the boundaries of the organization and almost forget about external conditions. The one-best-way to organize the system can be sought. Improved efficiency is the touchstone. But in a complex setting the manager ignores external conditions only at great peril. Environmental forces quickly invade the domain. It is not enough to search for efficiency. The managerial practices and organizational structures applicable in simple environments may not work in a more complex world.

Depicting Complexity

To summarize the environmental conditions surrounding the organization, it is convenient to think of a continuum ranging from simple to complex. The key is to develop the notion of complexity so that you can compare the environments of organizations. Figure 7-3 graphically depicts this approach to estimating environmental complexity. Along the vertical axis are descriptions of the general environment. At the top are different degrees of volatility and disparity for developed areas. At the bottom are the combinations for underdeveloped areas. Note that the farther you move away from the center, the greater the threats and opportunities the organization faces. Along the horizontal axis are descriptions of the specific environment. To the left are combinations of uncertainty and interdependence for less-developed specific environments. The *distance from the origin reflects* the degree of *environmental complexity*.

For instance, assume the organization you are analyzing operates in a small underdeveloped nation that has been growing steadily for a number of years (underdeveloped general environment, low volatility, and low disparity). Furthermore, assume that it gathers inputs from a large number of suppliers, sells to several distributors, and does not contend with governmental regulations or a union. Its product has enjoyed steady sales growth even though it's a maverick in a depressed industry (low uncertainty and interdependence in the specific environment). It operates in a simple environment. It would be

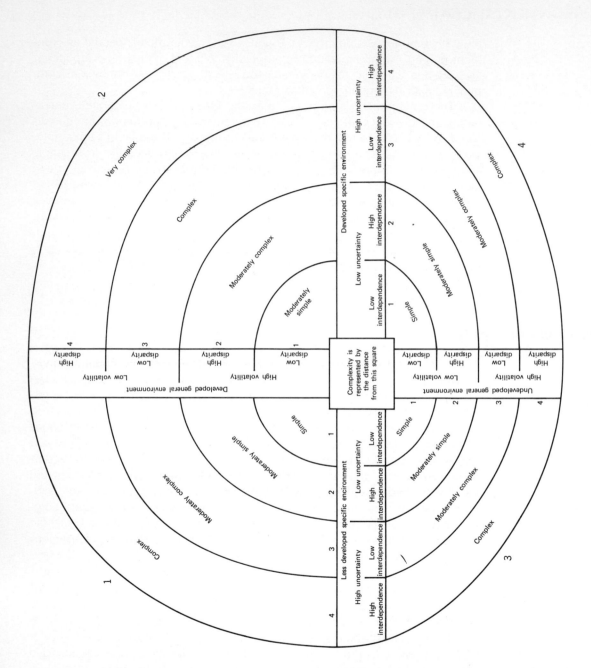

Figure 7-3 Environmental complexity.

placed in quadrant 3 (lower-left-hand portion of Figure 7-3). Now assume that it joins together with competitors to form a cartel (an increase in interdependence). On Figure 7-3 it moves into the moderately simple area in quadrant 3.

We think that if both the general and specific environments are low in uncertainty, the environment should be rated as simple or moderately simple. We assume that the organization should be rated as simple or moderately simple. We assume that the organization can learn from experience. Once a problem is successfully solved, the solution remains viable. Conversely, high uncertainty inhibits organizational learning. Once-successful solutions are no longer adequate. Further, uncertainty is likely to bring forth new threats and opportunities. When high uncertainty is coupled with high interdependence in the specific environment you have a candidate for complexity. If high disparity is added to the uncertainty and interdependence, the environment is complex. The organization is placed at the edge of Figure 7-3. Note that the degree of complexity is greater for developed environments than underdeveloped ones. Thus, in quadrant 2 where the general and specific environments are both developed, the levels of complexity are increased.*

Organizational Impacts

From Figure 7-3 you can generalize about environmental complexity. In later contingency chapters we use complexity as a global term. But here we want to specify the environmental impacts by examining the quadrant in which the organization lies.

In quadrant 1, the firm operates in a developed nation but still faces an underdeveloped specific environment. What types of problems and opportunities will be faced as the organization moves away from the origin of Figure 7-3? In the simple environment the firm may have considerable difficulty obtaining needed inputs and selling its outputs. As interdependence increases, the firm is in a weak position to reap the benefits of interorganizational cooperation. Moreover, the firms it must associate with are weak. Thus, the interorganization set provides only marginal help. Since the organization operates in a developed general environment, it finds more powerful organizations creeping in on its domain and challenging its legitimacy. It can, however, still maintain a moderate growth and moderately high survival potential by

*Our illustration of complexity does not show all the possible combinations of general and specific environment conditions. The figure assumes that high volatility in the general environment will be accompanied by high uncertainty in the specific environment. Such is not always the case. A firm can operate in a stable society yet be a member of a dynamic industry. Its specific environment might be very uncertain though the general environment remains stable. In such cases we would place the firm in the moderately complex category.

stressing internal efficiency and strict adherence to rules, policies, and por-
cedures. But if high uncertainty is piled on top of high interdependence, the
firm must scramble to keep ahead. Its strategy of stressing internal efficiency
may only serve to hasten its demise. In this complex environment the firm
must capitalize on the uncertainty in the specific environment. It must stress
flexibility and receptiveness to change. However, the prospects for growth are
not particularly good even if the firm is successful in adjusting to the high
interdependence. The lack of development in the specific environment cannot
be fully overcome.

The lack of opportunity from the environment is a major problem in
quadrant 1. Quite the opposite is the case in quadrant 2. Here, the organization
operates in a developed general and specific environment. Complexity causes
problems of adjustment and potential invasion by other systems if some response cannot be made. High interdependence pushes the organization toward establishing more buffering and liaison units (e.g., trade associations) to
coordinate the actions among members of the interorganizational set. The
benefits to be derived from cooperative efforts are substantial. Thus the possibilities for growth are considerable. If high uncertainty is added, the time
and resources needed to maintain cooperative relations under shifting conditions may become exorbitant and outweigh the benefits. It is possible that
uncertainty on top of high interdependence in this quadrant could trigger what
some have called turbulence. The organization loses control of its own fate.
A major portion of its resources is used to merely cope with external pressures.
The viability of the organization as a system might be questionable as powerful
external units begin to pull it apart.

Complexity in quadrant 3 presents some of the same problems as encountered in quadrant 1. However, there are likely to be few powerful systems
able to challenge the domain of the organization.   There is also some evidence
to suggest that *if* political conditions are stable, high interdependence among
weak organizations might partially offset high uncertainty. Why? Primarily because there may be few alternatives available. Something is better than nothing. Even if the organizations are grossly inefficient they may still survive by
joining together to ignore change. Those that do attempt to adapt, however,
might reap substantial benefits. They eventually swamp the less flexible and
adaptive organizations. Of course, if new organizations are allowed to enter
that have ties to more developed settings, the existing less-efficient organizations of quadrant 3 may quickly die.

In quadrant 4, uncertainty arises from shifting political fortunes and disparity between the degrees of cultural, economic, legal-political, and educational development. The major threats to the organization are nationalization
and social unrest.

Prescriptions

Generally, an organization can partially offset environmental complexity with more flexible internal structure. But there must be an emphasis on monitoring the environment. The organization might also directly reduce the degree of complexity by changing interdependence in the specific environment.[6] Or it may move into less volatile portions of its domain.[7] Both of these strategies for reducing complexity, however, call for alterations in its domain. This cannot be accomplished overnight.

In the face of greater environmental complexity, organizations appear to centralize operations to cope with shifting and interdependent conditions.[4] Who else but the top echelon can direct an organization through troubled waters? We estimate that this is exactly the wrong strategy for long-term growth and survival.[2] For as top management begins to move an organization toward a solution, conditions have already changed. There is a fair chance that an organization will move too slowly too late.[3] We think the key to growth and survival in a complex environment is the development of more autonomous simple organizations (i.e., divisions).[1] These subsystems face portions of the specific environment of the larger more complex organization. Some control may be lost. But adaptation to the environment is gained along with a dispersion of the high uncertainty and interdependence facing the organization as a whole.[5] But we may very well be incorrect for some organizations. There may be technological barriers to this strategy. We will return to this theme after a more complete discussion of the characteristics of organizations in Part III.

REFERENCES

I. Interdependence, Uncertainty, and Development in the General Environment

[1]Coleman, S. *Measurement and Analysis of Political Systems.* New York: Wiley, 1975.

[2]Domhoff, G. W. *Who Rules America.* Englewood Cliffs, N. J.: Prentice-Hall, 1967.

[3]Duncan, O. D. *Metropolis and Region.* Baltimore: Johns Hopkins Press, 1960.

[4]Emery, F. E., and Trist, E. L. *Towards A Social Ecology.* New York: Plenum Press, 1973.

[5]Evan, W. *Organization Theory: Structures, Systems and Environments.* New York: Wiley-Interscience, 1976.

[6]Nourse, H. O. *Regional Economics.* New York: McGraw-Hill, 1968.

[7]Osborn, R. "The Search for Environmental Complexity," *Human Relations,* 29 (1976), 15–27.

[8]Pfeffer, J., and Salancik, G. *The External Control of Organizations:*

A Resource Dependence Perspective. New York: Harper & Row, 1978.

A. Uncertainty in the General Environment

[1]Fischer, C. S. *The Urban Experience.* New York: Harcourt, Brace & Jovanovich, 1976.

[2]Gouldner, A. *Patterns of Industrial Bureaucracy.* New York: The Free Press, 1954.

[3]Hill, R. "Which Countries are Best for Investment," *International Management,* 12 (1974), 12–16.

[4]Johnson, H. G. *On Economics and Society.* Chicago: University of Chicago Press, 1975.

[5]Lev, B. "Environmental Uncertainty Reduction by Smoothing and Buffering," *Academy of Management Journal,* 18 (1975), 599–615.

[6]Morgan, T. *Economic Development, Concept and Strategy.* New York: Harper & Row, 1976.

[7]Nourse, 1968.

[8]Owens, E., and Shaw, R. *Development Reconsidered.* Lexington, Mass.: Heath, 1972.

[9]Steiner, G. *Business and Society.* New York: Random House, 1975.

[10]Tosi, H., Aldag, R., and Storey, R. "On the Measurement of the Environment: An Assessment of the Lawrence-Lorsch Environmental Uncertainty Questionnaire," *Administrative Science Quarterly,* 18 (1973), 27–37.

B. Favorability of the General Environment

[1]Blumberg, P. *The Mega Corporation in American Society: The Scope of Corporate Power.* Englewood Cliffs, N. J.: Prentice-Hall, 1975.

[2]Osborn, 1976.

[3]Osborn, R., and Hunt, J. "Environment and Organizational Effectiveness," *Administrative Science Quarterly,* 19 (1974), 231–246.

[4]Shortell, S. M. "The Role of Environment in a Configurational Theory of Organizations," *Human Relations,* 30 (1977), 275–302.

[5]Triandis, H. C., Malpass, R. S., and Davidson, A. R. "Psychology and Culture," *Annual Review of Psychology,* 24 (1973), 205–378.

[6]Tosi et al, 1973.

II. Organizational Choice: A Key Difference between the General and Specific Environment

[1]Meyer, M. "Organizational Domains," *American Sociological Review,* 40 (1975), 599–615.

[2]Osborn and Hunt, 1974.

[3]Pfeffer and Salancik, 1978.

[4]Thompson, J. D. *Organizations in Action.* New York: McGraw-Hill, 1967.

III. Favorability in the Specific Environment

[1]Evan, 1976.

[2]Negandhi, A., and Reimann, B. "A Contingency Theory of Organizations Re-examined in the Context of a Developing Country," *Academy of Management Journal,* 15 (1972), 137–146.

[3]Osborn, 1976.

A. Favorability for Large and Small Organizations

[1]Blumberg, 1975.

[2]Coleman, 1975.

[3]Evan, 1976.

[4]Johnson, 1975.

[5]Lev, 1975.

[6]Osborn, 1976.

[7]Sebring, R. "The Five Million Dollar Misunderstanding: A Perspective on State Government-University

Interorganizational Conflicts," *Administrative Science Quarterly,* 22 (1977), 505–523.

IV. Environmental Complexity

C. Prescriptions

¹Chandler, A. *The Visible Hand: The Managerial Revolution in American Business.* Cambridge, Mass.: Belkap, 1977.

²Evan, 1976.

³Galbraith, J. R., and Nathanson, D. A. *Strategy Implementation: The Role of Structure and Process.* St. Paul: West, 1978.

⁴Negandhi and Reimann, 1972.

⁵Osborn, 1976.

⁶Pfeffer and Salancik, 1978.

⁷Thompson, 1967.

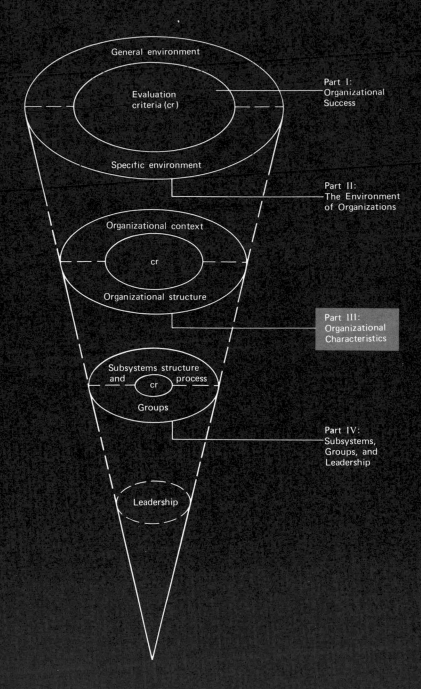

Figure III-1 A cone model for organizational analysis.

part

organizational
characteristics

One of the more popular approaches to the analysis of organizations centers on the structure of the system. Originally those studying organizations talked of developing the best structure for all systems. They used elementary "principles of management." For instance, each employee should have only one boss. This was a common principle. Contingency analyses of organizational structure then emerged. Both theorists and practitioners realized that the appropriate structure was partly dependent on the environment, size, technology, and administrative philosophy of the top-level executives. The basic thrust of contingency analysis involving organizational structure is illustrated well by those called developmental theorists.

STAGES OF ORGANIZATIONAL DEVELOPMENT*

Historical analyses of business organizations suggest some common patterns of size, technology, and structure during various stages of their development. Initially, firms are simple organizations. They rely upon the technical and administrative ability of one individual. Producing one major product, their key to survival lies in developing a munificent and stable domain that will accept the organization's exchanges. The structure is loose and informal. Managers attempt to estimate how the "great man" would solve a particular problem. Through trial and error, managers find the set of tasks they can do best. They work together on an informal basis to react appropriately to the daily technical and administrative problems of the small organization. For instance, how many people should be hired? Is there a better and more efficient way to produce the product? How can funds for new equipment be obtained? Will a new package, channel of distribution, or advertising campaign pay off? In short, can the organization produce a product or service that consumers are willing to pay for?

To summarize, the organization in this phase is typically small. It is mainly concerned with producing outputs to ensure survival. Most often it selects a loose-knit structure.

Assuming the corporation is successful in securing adequate growth and profits, it may evolve into a second stage. It becomes a complex organization. While the pattern of evolution is far from clear, the organization undergoes a number of substantial changes. It produces several products and/or services in one or more business sectors. In more technical terms, it has experienced vertical and/or horizontal integration. The system usually operates with a func-

*Much of this discussion is based on work by William Glueck at the University of Georgia.

tional structure. Employees are grouped into units on the basis of their outputs to the system, which yield production, finance, personnel, and marketing subsystems. Within the production subsystem there may be several plant managers, a staff of engineers, scheduling and maintenance personnel, and the like. The informal "one-boss" rule of the small organization has been replaced with a reliance upon rules, policies, and procedures. The organization is a developed bureaucracy complete with red tape.

The increased specialization in both technical and administrative areas brings forth problems of control and integration. Middle- and lower-level managers share the concerns of their counterparts in the smaller systems. However, successful adaptations have already been made. Many administrative and technical problems can be solved with minor alterations in existing methods. Top management becomes a unique and quite different world complete with an executive suite and a corporate airplane. A corporate staff emerges to integrate the functional specialties and provide technical assistance in such areas as legal affairs and governmental relations. However, the key to growth and survival probably still lies with one or a few key products and/or services.

In a third stage, the business may reach maturity. It evolves into the mammoth quasi-independent subculture known as the conglomerate. The organization is huge. Its volume of products and services may outstrip that of many nations. It may employ over 100,000 people. The range of products and services offered by the system is not likely to have any particular logic even though it may be well known for a popular industrial or consumer product. Its key problem becomes governance. For the very largest, maintaining a relative power position vis-à-vis the governments in several countries may become a major concern. For instance, ITT has had substantial difficulty in maintaining control over the assets of foreign subsidiaries. Lower, middle, and upper management are separate. Individuals are specifically recruited for one of these administrative levels. The firm has multiple divisions for multiple products and services. The system is also likely to be overlaid with a geographical hierarchy incorporating numerous subsidiaries, joint ventures, and franchises. Top management, through its corporate staff, is likely to maintain financial control. Survival for the system as a whole is no longer an overriding problem. The separation of ownership and control is complete.

Governmental bureaucracies appear to follow similar patterns as have, to a lesser degree, some churches and state university systems. There may be more than three stages and different ones for dissimilar organizations. Whether there are three, six, or sixteen stages, the overall pattern is clear; size, technology, and structure move together. They tend to reinforce each other. Larger size facilitates technological development. And this may require larger systems to capitalize on economies of scale. Administrative restructuring may be needed to handle larger volumes of products, services, and/or employees. Reorganization may facilitate growth in both size and technology. Of course these changes do not occur automatically. They must be initiated and directed by top management. Furthermore, attempts to transform the organization from one stage to the next may be prohibited or facilitated by environmental conditions. All of these in combination appear to have an important impact on organizational success.

For convenience we assume that size, technology, and administrative philosophy have a primary impact on organizational structure and criteria. That is, size, technology, and management philosophy may be viewed as "contextual variables" that partially determine the structure and outputs of an organization. Chapter 8 will focus on these contextual variables. First we delve into the deceptively simple analysis of organizational size. We are accustomed to dividing organizations into small, medium, and large categories without too much thought. But the analyst needs specific rules for putting a tag on an organization. We will note that size has a close association with a number of organizational characteristics. Direct comparison of organizations with different social functions and domains may be questionable, since some organizations are more labor intensive than others. When size is used to explain organizational success there is also the problem of causation. Is the organization successful because it is large? Or is it large because it is successful?

Technology is a frequently mentioned factor in explaining the success of an organization and its structure. But all too often the concept is described in vague terms. In Chapter 8 we attempt to nail down the concept of technology by concentrating on the major operations of the system. The analysis also attempts to reconcile apparently conflicting findings in the literature.

Chapter 8 also develops the concept of administrative philosophy. Organizations operating in similar settings of about the same size and using similar technologies may be quite different. The top managements may move their organizations in different directions. They march to the beat of different drummers. We will look at administrative philosophy in terms of patterns of attitudes toward an organization's domain and describe some implications of these attitudes.

Chapter 9 is concerned with organizational structure. Here we will provide a static picture of what organizations may look like. But we also discuss processes that occur within the structure. Thus, a major emphasis in the chapter is how designers break an organization into several parts, and how they provide for integration of these parts. This is viewed from the top down, across the organization, and from the bottom up. We also identify two internally consistent structural patterns—organic and mechanistic.

After discussing the influence of contextual factors on structure itself, the contingency chapter integrates environmental conditions, contextual variables, and structural factors in an attempt to predict various criteria.

As you will note, this part of the book moves you down another stage into our cone model (see Figure III-1). Thus, the unit of analysis is the organization itself.

chapter 8 CONTEXTUAL VARIABLES: SIZE, TECHNOLOGY, AND ADMINISTRATIVE PHILOSOPHY

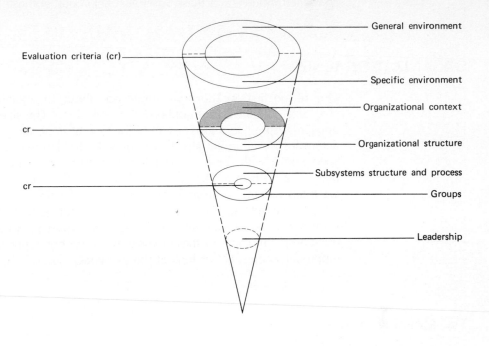

Evaluation criteria (cr) ——————————— General environment

—— Specific environment

—— Organizational context

cr ——————————— Organizational structure

—— Subsystems structure and process

cr ——————————— Groups

—— Leadership

We have defined an organization as a collection of individuals able to enter into a legally binding contract. Organizations are recognized by others, and they can act as a collectivity. We have also noted that the more predominant organizations in our society are complex. That is, they contain a number of legal entities. This is helpful for a gross distinction between organizations and other collective efforts. But more detail is needed.

In this chapter we will discuss three important organizational characteristics. They are size, technology, and administrative philosophy. These have been called contextual variables. They are constants for most managers and help provide important distinctions among organizations. These variables are treated before a discussion of an organization's anatomy because they limit the structure this entity can adopt, and they help mold the formal relationships among its participants.

In combination with environmental factors and organizational structure, we think that size, technology, and administrative philosophy help explain and predict substantial aspects of an organization's functioning and effectiveness.

The success of the system, in other words, in large part depends upon the combined influence of these variables. Let's look at these in more detail.

ORGANIZATIONAL SIZE

One of the first questions we might ask about an organization concerns its size. Size data are easy to obtain.[1,5,6,7,8,10,11,12,13,14] The size of an organization appears to provide a gross estimate of several important organizational characteristics.[2,9] We might also feel intuitively that larger organizations are more specialized, with more complicated administrative frameworks. The task of managing 50 is much less difficult than if 1000 are in the unit.[4] Furthermore, we often picture the large organization as a faceless bureaucracy that treats both employees and outsiders as numbers, not people. It's no wonder that some claim organizational size is the single most important feature of organizations.[3] But some of these expectations are not supported by more recent empirical studies. Let us look at the evidence.

The Meaning of Size

For most organizational analysts size means the number of full-time employees.[3,15,22] Even with a simple count of employees we need some gross division among small, medium, large, and huge. Caplow argues that interaction possibilities could be used to make rough size categories.[5] In units from 2 to 50, individuals have the opportunity (at least statistically) to interact with one another. These small units contrast with medium units of some 50 to 200, in which the individual has an opportunity to develop only limited contact with every other member. Large units of from 200 to 1000 don't allow the individual to interact with all other members. Instead, a key member or members may be recognized by all. In huge systems of over 1000 employees only a few personalities may be recognized with the aid of mass communication.*

Huge organizations beyond that of the military and the church are a recent development. The biggest industrial corporations at the turn of the century would merely be rated as large.[26] Few universities prior to World War II were even close to the "large" category in terms of full-time faculty. Now many may be considered huge systems. Tables 8-1, 8-2, and 8-3 provide size information about selected business, government, and university systems.

*The exact cutoffs are not identical to those of Caplow but follow the logic of his argument.[5]

Table 8-1 The Twenty-Five Largest U.S. Companies (Selected Years, by Annual Sales)[a]

Company	1938–1939 Number Employed	1975 Dollar Sales in Millions	1975 Number Employed
Exxon Corporation[a]	48,500 (in 1940)	47,795.5	133,000
General Motors Corporation[d]	220,434	35,724.9	734,000
American Telephone and Telegraph[b,d]	13,790	28,957.2	999,795
Texaco[d]	32,032	24,507.5	76,420
Ford Motor Company[d]	117,000	24,009.1	464,731
Mobil Oil Corporation[d]	34,270	22,135.3	73,100
Standard Oil of California[d]	18,748	17,523.6	38,722
Gulf Oil Corporation[d]	23,000	15,838.0	52,700
International Business Machines[d]	11,200	14,436.5	292,350
Sears, Roebuck & Company[d]	57,000	13,639.9	437,000
General Electric Company[c]	62,797	13,399.1	404,000
Chrysler Corporation[d]	5,400	11,598.4	255,929
International Telephone and Telegraph[b,d]	77,955	11,338.1	409,000
Standard Oil Company (Indiana)[d]	31,221	11,034.2	47,200
Safeway Stores, Inc.[d]	19,450	9,716.9	121,355
Shell Oil Company[d]	25,114	8,876.2	32,287
U.S. Steel Corporation[d]	223,844	8,167.2	187,503
Atlantic Richfield Company[d]	12,192	7,746.5	28,800
Penney (J. C.) Company[d]	31,181	7,678.6	193,000
Continental Oil Company[d]	5,195	7,500.3	41,174
du Pont de Nemours (E. I.)[d]	54,800	7,221.5	136,866
Kresge (S. S.) Company[d]	35,060	6,798.1	134,000
Great Atlantic & Pacific Tea Co.[e]	90,000	6,537.9	105,000
Proctor & Gamble[d]	13,500	6,081.7	33,600
General Telephone & Electronics[d]	6,900	5,948.4	196,000

Sources:

[a]*The World Almanac and Book of Facts, 1977* (Newspaper Enterprise Association Inc., New York—Cleveland), 123.

[b]*Moody's Manual of Investments, American and Foreign, Public Utility Securities, 1940* (Moody's Investors Service, New York, 1940–1975).

[c]*Dun and Bradstreet—Principle International Businesses* (New York, 1976), 1539, 1941.

[d]*Moody's Industrial Manual, 1939–1976* (Moody's Investors Service, Inc., New York).

Table 8-2 The Nineteen Largest U.S. Colleges and Universities (Selected Years)

Rank	1939[a]		1972[b]	
	Number of Full-Time Students	Number of Full-Time Faculty	Number of Full-Time Students	Number of Full-Time Faculty
1 State University of New York	12,585	2,192	226,623	N/A
2 California State Colleges	N/A	N/A	181,328	N/A
3 City University of New York	8,680	983	117,288	N/A
4 University of Wisconsin System	11,397	566	108,040	N/A
5 University of California	9,043	388	103,874	5,775
6 University of Texas	10,091	681	56,768	3,877
7 University of Minnesota	15,167	1,609	51,245	5,707(in 1975)
8 University of Illinois	13,551	1,680	48,778	4,110
9 Ohio State University	12,980	1,108	46,644	3,694(in 1975)
10 Indiana University	6,322	398	43,247	2,375
11 University of North Carolina	3,935	354	40,153	3,016
12 Pennsylvania State University	6,765	1,480	40,051	3,467
13 University of Missouri	6,128	444	37,137	2,810
14 Michigan State University	2,614	206	35,053	2,195
15 University of Maryland	4,277	800	33,920	
19 Southern Illinois University	2,136	141	28,259	1,712 (in 1975)

Sources:

[a]Walters, R., "Statistics of Registration in American Universities and Colleges 1939–1940," *School and Society* (Vol. 52, No. 1355, 1940).
[b]Parker, G. G., "College and University Enrollments in America, 1971–1972," *School and Society* (Vol. 100, No. 2339, 1972).

As these tables reflect, there has been a tremendous increase in the size of major institutions in the United States. Some if this can be attributed to population growth. But the data also suggest a greater concentration of employees under one administrative roof.

Organizational Size as an Indicator of Effectiveness. To many managers the larger the organization the more effective it has been.[3,28] Largeness connotes prestige,[8] power,[22] and, last but far from least, higher executive salaries.[29] As Yuchtman and Seashore note, since size reflects the discretionary resources available within the system, it is a measure of autonomy.[31] Organizational growth is often an important systems goal implicitly related to survival.[30] If the

Table 8-3 U.S. Government and Selected State Civilian Employment (Selected Years)

U.S. Government	1939[a]	1976[b]
Treasury	N/A	124,680
U.S. Postal Service	314,478	665,679
Army	189,839	326,562
Navy	125,202	311,210
Air Force	N/A	248,219
HEW	N/A	153,245
Total, all branches of federal government	953,891	2,846,844

Selected States	1937[c]	1974[d]
California	26,000	440,827
Texas	9,000	161,695*
Pennsylvania	N/A	147,021*
Ohio	21,271	426,437
New York	42,631	234,388*
Illinois	N/A	135,430*
Michigan	22,818	113,097*
Florida	7,200	136,164
Total state and local government	3,090,000	10,830,000

Sources:

[a]*Historical Statistics of the U.S.: Bicentennial Edition* (U.S. Department of Commerce, Bureau of the Census, 1976.

[b]*Readers Digest Almanac and Yearbook, 1977* (The Reader's Digest Association, Inc., Pleasantville, New York), 969.

[c]*Financial Statistics of States, 1938* (U.S. Department of Commerce, Bureau of the Census), 21.

[d]*Employment and Wages* (U.S. Department of Labor, Bureau of Labor Statistics), 76.

*State employees only—does not include university or community college personnel

organization does not grow it may be starting a decline that will lead to its demise.[7,11,14]

However, these arguments might be countered by realizing that the larger organization also needs a greater infusion of resources to maintain itself.[20] As England and Lee show in studies of firms in the United States, Korea, and Japan, managers in larger corporations express more concern over efficiency, growth, and profits than managers in smaller businesses.[9] Haas and Drabek note that growth may come in several areas of an organization's domain that do not lead to an increase in the number of employees.[13] Moreover, growth that threatens to upset the balance of power may initiate countermoves by external systems.[25] For instance, if business organizations are becoming too large and powerful, then government may intervene.[23] Huge organizations may also have difficulty adjusting to uncertainty.[10] They may believe that through their power they can alter their environment, when in fact they cannot.[21] In short, larger organizations are more powerful than smaller ones, holding all other factors constant.[24] But whether they can turn this clout toward mission attainment, output goals, and/or employee maintenance is quite another question.[13]

Advocates of larger systems point to economies of scale.[2] Size may be associated with some aspects of specialization.[4] But there is some question as to the relationship between organizational size and administrative efficiency. Several studies suggest that the proportion of administrators to workers increases as organizational size increases.[*,4,13,16,17,18] Other studies of administrative efficiency seem to suggest that larger systems have comparatively fewer administrators.[6] But, the savings in administrators may be somewhat deceiving. The proportion of secretaries, clerical staff, and technical specialists seems to increase with size.[27,19]

Large organizations may only appear more effective since they are more likely to alter the working definition of their mission more than smaller systems.[1] There is more of a tendency to confuse means and ends of larger organizations. The amount spent, for instance, may be used to document achievement even though dumping money on a problem may not provide a solution. Huge systems are apt to publicize aspects of the mission that favor larger systems. For instance, large state universities are fond of talking of general education for the masses. They may claim to do a better job for "the people" than private colleges catering to the "intellectual elite."

Organizational Size and Employee Maintenance

There is also a myth surrounding the large organization concerning employee satisfaction. Everyone knows employees in large organizations are less satisfied than their counterparts in small organizations.[2] Not so! The size of the total

*Kimberly notes that a statistical quirk when relating number of employees and the ratio of administrators to workers may have produced these results. He also provides some caveats that aggregate measures of size may have different meanings for different purposes. For our purposes here, it is easier to conceive of size in the four broad categories of small, medium, large, and huge.

organization is not a good predictor of employee satisfaction.[6] However, many large organizations do tend to have large subsystems.[1] And subsystem size is negatively associated with employee satisfaction.[4,7]

Ingham also found that organizational size was positively related to absenteeism but not turnover.[5] Again, however, the association seems to be traceable to subsystems, not organizational size.

There are some data suggesting that organizational size and managerial satisfaction might be related. One factor is fairly obvious. Since managers of larger organizations tend to receive higher salaries, they also tend to be more satisfied with their pay.[8] However, Cummings and El Salmi, among others, found that managers in large business organizations (500 to 1000 employees) were more satisfied than those in small or huge ones.[3,2] They argue that the small- and medium-size organizations do not provide adequate mechanisms for managerial satisfaction. Huge organizations are too impersonal and bureaucratic. In slightly different terms, the association between organizational size and satisfaction seems to depend upon how size affects other variables. For instance, are larger organizations more impersonal and bureaucratic? To answer this question we must switch to a more neutral view of size.

Organizational Size and Structure

Size can be treated as a direct measure of an organization's scope of operations.[1,8,12] As such it is assumed to have a direct or primary impact on the structure of the system. In this sense, then, size is viewed as a contextual variable. Larger organizations may not be better than smaller ones. But they do appear to be structured in a different manner. Specifically, larger size has been related to specialization (the number of different occupational specialists in the system and the number of separate departmental units),[4,5,10,2] more formalization (the use of rules, policies, and procedures),[7] and less centralization (the locus of decision making).[*,3,9,11,14] Much of the reasoning behind the analyses of size and organizational structure is based on implicit hypotheses. Namely, particular combinations of size and structure should be more effective.[6] These are treated in Chapter 10.

The exact association between size and structure and various criteria also appears to be dependent upon the environment of the system, its administrative philosophy, and its technology.[3,8] So let's take a closer look at technology, then turn to administrative philosophy.

*More detailed definitions of these structure variables are provided in Chapter 9.

TECHNOLOGY

Organizations bring together the necessary materials, knowledge, and techniques that form technology. This technology is used to transform inputs to outputs. Thus, there's a direct link between technology and performance. The organization's technology also has an important and enduring impact on its anatomy and behavior.[3] And the technology an organization selects has a direct bearing on employee maintenance criteria.[1]

However, there has been considerable controversy over exactly which aspects of technology are most influential, and precisely how technology works in combination with other variables. On one side of the controversy is a group suggesting a "technological imperative."[4] The most successful organizations balance size, structure, leadership, and motivational patterns to fit technological dictates. Conversely, another group argues that technology is not a particularly important consideration in large, modern organizations.[2] Instead, size and environment conditions swamp the "technological imperative." Both groups provide data from field studies to support their contention. Here we will provide an analysis of technology consistent with the data from both groups. First we will describe various types of technology, and the choice among types, and then briefly explore the controversy mentioned above to help develop our integrated view.

Types of Technology

A technology is formed with a particular combination of materials (human and nonhuman), knowledge and techniques (processes) in an attempt to produce desired outcomes. It's often assumed that organizations know how to produce desired outcomes. But Thompson notes that the technology may be far from "instrumentally perfect."[26] Many organizations can systematically sequence the work and assign specific jobs to each and every worker. But many other organizations must put together teams of individuals to produce an outcome. Technologies also differ on interdependence.[14] In some cases workers and/or work units can act independently. In other instances, workers and work units must act as a team. Some organizations attempt to produce goods or change the psychological states of clients. Others merely act as a liaison between collections of individuals and store goods and information. (Different utilities are provided.) By rating the organization on instrumental perfection, interdependence among tasks, and utility provided, it is possible to identify three different kinds of technology—intensive, mediating, and long-linked. Each has its own advantages and disadvantages.*

*This discussion relies heavily on the work of Thompson.[26]

The Intensive Technology. In many cases an organization is not sure how to produce desired outcomes (low instrumental perfection). It must bring together a group of specialists with the hope they can find a solution. A variety of techniques is normally employed by a team of specialists to solve problems (high interdependence). Frequently this technology is used to treat physical and psychological problems. It is often found in general hospitals and some mental health facilities. Research and development organizations, graduate schools, and top managements also use this technology.

In the intensive technology the critical administrative problems often revolve around efficiency, coordination, ideology, and the measurement of effectiveness.[17,20] The organization is not sure how to transform inputs to desired outputs. So standard operating procedures may be difficult to develop.[19] Most of the effort may be expended in just finding a workable solution. Thus, it may be difficult, if not impossible, for administrators to effectively mesh together the operations of specialists in a meaningful fashion. Coordination and integration often is a matter of mutual adjustment among those trying to solve the problem and produce the desired outcomes.

Where the intensive technology dominates, technical personnel have a nasty tendency of subverting the organization toward their own professional ends. Administrators may not be technically competent.[22,25] So professionals may be able to justify the subversion by developing an ideology that links their desires to organizational effectiveness.[12,15] Finally, the measurement of effectiveness may center on outside evaluations reflecting prestige. For instance, how do we know Quark State is an excellent university? We usually ask professors In other universities.

The Mediating Technology. In the mediating technology there is a different combination of instrumental perfection, interdependence, and utility. Mediating technology is used to link parties desirous of becoming interdependent. Those using this technology "store" the medium of interdependence. The linkage methods are typically known (instrumentally perfect). And a change in the physical or psychological characteristics of inputs is not intended. Banks, wholesalers, retailers, and real estate agencies are examples of organizations using a mediating technology. Banks, for instance, match creditors and depositors and store money and information to facilitate exchanges. They assign the parties to categories and treat all members of a category in a similar fashion. Borrowers are assigned credit ratings. Bank deposits are placed in several categories such as demand deposits, long-term certificates of deposit, and short-term savings accounts. While all depositors and creditors are interdependent, the reliance is *pooled* through the bank. Thus, if one creditor defaults on a loan, no one depositor is injured. In much the same manner an employment security agency uses applications to match employers and job applicants.

While wholesalers and retailers also provide linkage, they often store goods to facilitate exchange.[27,28] Storage provides time and place utility. In much the same manner, some mental health units and nursing homes merely store individuals (even though their social function may suggest an attempt at altering the physical and psychological characteristics of their clients).[7]

There are comparatively few ideological problems within organizations dominated by a mediating technology.[7] There are two possible exceptions. One, outside units may bar an organization from developing categories, or require new ones. For instance, jobs were once routinely divided into race and sex categories. The EEOC frowns on such categories for employment agencies. Yet it requires employers to report the race, sex, and national origin of their employees.[11] Two, employers in direct contact with outsiders may begin to identify with their peers and/or one of the linkage groups *instead* of the organization. Members of regulatory groups, for instance, may become more closely identified with the industry they are to control than the government agency they work for.[15,16,24]

Measures of effectiveness in mediating technologies may also be somewhat misleading. The focus tends to be on efficiency. Frequently the volume of transactions per employee is used as a measure. But to increase efficiency the unit may concentrate on those matches that are easily established with a minimum of effort.[6] Matches that are more difficult to make (e.g., finding jobs for the hard-core unemployed) may be given a lower priority.[18] To increase efficiency, organizations using mediating technologies often ask clients to pre-sort themselves to cut costs. For instance, for bulk mailing, letters must have ZIP codes and be presorted by region. Telephone users should dial calls direct for long distance. While outsiders do the work, the organization may claim it is more efficient. The mediating technology is essential in a complex, differentiated society if for no other reason than it allows for the more complete development of long-linked technology.[27,28]

The Long-linked Technology. The long-linked technology is also called mass production or industrial technology.[23] Here the organization assumes it knows how to produce the desired outcomes (instrumentally perfect). It can break down the total task into a series of steps.[21] Interdependence results primarily from the sequencing of tasks. The auto assembly line is a classic example. Most long-linked technologies involve physical transformations (production). It is also used by some organizations attempting to alter the psychological characteristics of clients. Many elementary schools once used to teach reading and spelling by rote. Even in the more modern era, elements of the long-linked technology dominate some educational systems in that they use programmed learning and computerized instruction.[4]

The hallmark of long-linked technologies is a sequential flow of work. The performance on one task is dependent upon successful completion of the previous step. Jobs are broken down into their most elementary components.[5] An attempt is made to standardize inputs, materials, and outputs. The fully automated chemical plant, with its instantaneous alterations in the refining process, is the ultimate long-linked technology.[29]

Some advantages of this technology are efficiency, lower skill requirements for employees, the production of standard outputs from identical inputs, and flexibility to substitute machines for employees.[5] Some argue, for example, that the steady increase in the productivity of manufacturing organizations is primarily due to more efficient machinery and techniques.[5]

Critical problems in long-linked technologies often stem from the rigidity needed to increase efficiency.[9] Raw material must flow into the system at a predictable pace. The organization must be assured of adequate demand for a comparatively small range of products. Thus, organizations using this technology often develop a series of "buffering" units to ensure a consistent flow of raw materials and sales. For instance, few large manufacturing firms using a long-linked technology are without marketing departments.[10] Even top-level executives of large corporations are likely to be replaced when assured sources of supply are threatened.

Employees must also subordinate their desires for autonomy and independent judgment to the logic of the assembly line.[1,3] For instance, industrial engineers often work out detailed procedures for the most efficient way to perform routine tasks. Employees must pace themselves to the speed of the line. They cannot follow a more natural cyclical pattern. Some jobs in long-linked technologies thus appear routine, fractured, and meaningless.[2] However, later we will notice that some jobs here have quite different characteristics.[8]

Technological Choice

So far we have treated the three technologies as if an organization were forced to select just one. Actually, it may be in a position to substitute elements of the intensive technology where the mediating or long-linked technology would appear more appropriate.[2]

The intensive technology may be used to produce both goods and services even where an organization knows how to produce desired outcomes. It is, so to speak, the technology of last resort. Where demand is insufficient or machinery is too expensive, the organization may be forced to forego the efficiency of the long-linked technology.[6] It can adopt a handicraft mode.

In a handicraft mode the organization could use an assembly line. Instead, it forms work teams to produce custom products. For instance, cargo vessels are typically produced with a custom or handicraft mode. Kaiser Industries, though, demonstrated that long-linked technology could be used. When large numbers of "liberty" ships were needed in World War II, Kaiser developed an assembly line operation using standardized parts and procedures. Houses, railroad cars, and spaceships are examples of products that can be made with either a handicraft or long-linked technology. This interface is graphically displayed in Figure 8-4.

Figure 8-4 also shows an interface between the intensive and mediating types. When linking parties or storing goods and information there may be insufficient volume to implement the mediating technology. A more intensive mode, called technical services, may be found. This mode may also be used when storage is specialized and one or each party must be treated as a separate category. The technical services mode is often used in industrial sales and by executive recruiting firms.

Organizations selecting a technical services mode may be eliminated by their more efficient counterparts using a mediating technology. For instance, the vast bulk of the auto, liability, fire, and windstorm insurance was sold by technical service units—independent insurance agents. Theoretically, an agent tailor-fits coverage to the specialized needs of a particular client. But many individuals prefer cheaper standardized policies. They cover the bulk of their insurance needs, even though the fit may not be particularly good. Thus, mass merchandisers sell standardized policies by mail, at retail stores, or through

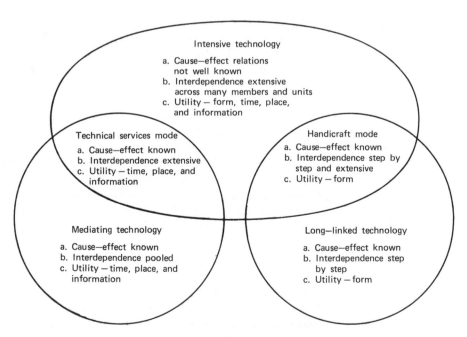

Figure 8-4 Types of technologies and their major characteristics.

minimally trained agents. Individuals are merely placed in one of a few broad categories. All are issued virtually identical policies. Note that such standard policies may be cheaper but not necessarily better.

As Figure 8-4 indicates, there is no substitution between mediating and long-linked technologies. Each is intended to provide a different type of utility. However, large-scale, long-linked technology is dependent on a well-developed mediating technology either inside the organization or within the specific environment.[5] For instance, if channels of distribution are not well developed, the organization may be forced to revert to custom work as is often the case in underdeveloped nations.[3]

Note that the substitute modes of handicraft and technical services are partly functions of demand and quality.[1] If the volume of transactions is low, and the organization seeks to offer quality, customized outputs lend themselves to these two approaches. And if distribution is weak (thus a low derived demand for output), with no mediating technology available, then the handicraft mode of long-linked technology can be substituted. Therefore, the choice of these technologies may be a function of strategy regarding quality and demand considerations.[4] This is a question of administrative philosophy that we will discuss later.

Dominant and Multiple Technologies and the Technical Core

Again, the three technologies are used in different circumstances to produce different kinds of outputs. So it's not unusual to find organizations using all three simultaneously.[5] If one technology is dominant, then a description of that technology is adequate to characterize the system as a whole.[6] Generally speaking, only small- and moderate-sized organizations have one dominant technology. Large and huge organizations typically have at least two and usually all three.[1]

Organizations with multiple technologies pose a problem of the "unit of analysis."[2] Should the whole organization be studied or just those parts with a common technology? This makes a tremendous difference in research findings. Analyses of organizations with multiple technologies do not support the technological imperative.[4] To resolve this potential confusion we need to introduce another "level of analysis." It is neither clearly the organization nor a group. Again we follow the pioneering analyses of Thompson and Parsons.[6,3]

Thompson argued that organizations have a "technical core."[6] Essentially, the technical core is the collection of line units that perform the basic transformations called for by the mission of the system. For business firms the technical core of an organization is often readily apparent as in Figure 8-5. This shows a partial organization chart for a medium-size manufacturer of

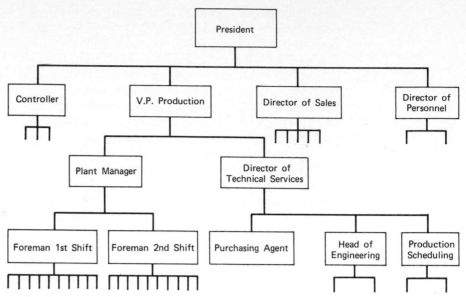

Figure 8-5 Partial organization chart for Playground, Inc. (1975). Number of employees = 73.

playground equipment. Those units reporting to the plant manager constitute the technical core. Note that within this long-linked technology there is a technical service unit (scheduling). Engineering probably uses an intensive technology. Here is an example of a dominant long-linked technology. The vast proportion of people and effort is involved with production. Figure 8-6 shows a revised organization chart five years later. The firm decided to market its products through independent wholesalers and retailers. Both production and marketing are line units in the classical sense. But they have different technologies. Furthermore, with the growth in size the staff areas are more specialized. We will have more to say about technology and structure in Chapter 9. For now, you should recognize that organizations may use several technologies, and the technical core is composed of the basic line units. Now that we have defined the types of technologies, we can take a brief look at the controversy alluded to at the beginning of our discussion of technology.

The Controversy over the Technological Imperative

In the 1950s and 1960s Joan Woodward attempted to empirically examine classical management principles in some 100 British manufacturing plants.[12]

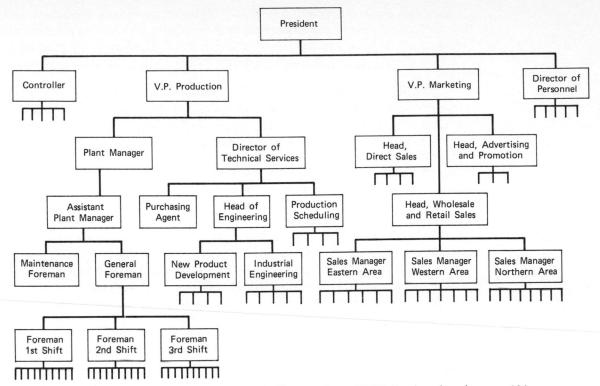

Figure 8-6 Partial organization chart for Playground, Inc. (1979). Number of employees = 104.

The data made little sense until the plants were organized by the nature of the work they performed. Originally eleven different categories were formed. But these seemed to boil down to three different and distinct groups.

The first group, labeled unit or small-batch production, made custom products. The techniques used in the transformation were generally not very sophisticated mechanically, but called for considerable craftsmanship. Work on one product could proceed without too much concern for what else was being produced, so that different production units operated in an almost independent fashion. A wide variety of tools, techniques, and skills were needed and used. The second group consisted of mass-production operations à la the Detroit assembly line. Here the techniques were more sophisticated, with machines replacing craftsmen. Standardized inputs were used to produce a large volume of a few products. The work of one group was highly dependent upon that of another. While interdependence was cut with inventories of partially manufactured parts and subassemblies, a prolonged shortage of but one part could shut down the plant completely. The third group was composed of continuous-process manufacturers using automated equipment to produce a very small range of products. A chemical plant is an example of this. The techniques and machinery were very sophisticated and the work flow was almost completely integrated.

Moving from custom to mass to continuous processing, Woodward found that the number of administrative levels increased, there were larger spans of control (numbers of employees per supervisor) at the top, plus the number and use of committees rose. In many regards, however, unit and continuous-processing systems were much alike. In both, work groups at the bottom of the organization were small; there was considerable flexibility in their administrative structures; line-staff conflict was minimal, and the jobs of most employees appeared challenging and nonroutine. Mass-production operations were quite different with large work groups, inflexible formal structures, considerable line-staff conflict, and a predominance of simple, routine jobs.

When the organization matched its structure to that most typical of others in its group, it was rated more effective. For instance, mass-production operations that attempted to develop flexible structures, small work teams, or highly varied jobs were lower performers. The technological imperative was born. Partial replications by several researchers appeared to confirm the notion of a technological imperative.[1,5,13]

The controversy surrounding Woodward's technological imperative stems from the problem that several different variables are combined to place an organization in one of the three categories.[1,4] That is, unit and small-batch operations are quite different from continuous-process manufacturers in a number of ways. This would not be particularly upsetting if all the variables used to classify organizations had virtually identical effects on structure, performance, and employee maintenance. Unfortunately they do not. For example, work-flow interdependence (independence of the units in the technical core) systematically differs across Woodward's categories. But it does not appear to be a particularly important aspect of technology in manufacturing organizations.[3] Research work coming out of a series of studies by the Aston group shows that work-flow interdependence does not explain the structure of organizations using long-linked technologies.[6,9] Instead, size and dependence upon others in the specific environment were more important in their study of British organizations. Similar results are reported by Reimann for U.S. firms.[7] Such data have been used to dismiss the notion of a technological imperative.[2]

To reduce the controversy, we provide an integrative analysis. We can combine Woodward's analyses with those of several other scholars to examine two aspects of technology useful in explaining criteria of organizational effectiveness and employee maintenance.[11,8,10] We call these two *sophistication* and *variability*. (Again, this analysis is somewhat speculative.)

Sophistication and Variability across Technologies

Within a type of technology there appear to be substantial differences in the way organizations transform inputs to outputs. Yet, the structure and operations of some mediating technologies appear quite similar to those of some long-linked ones. Handicraft and technical services seem to require different skills. Yet one finds organizations that use these two different technologies facing similar problems and being structured in much the same manner.

We argue that many of these similarities are due to the degrees of sophistication and variability of the technology employed.[7,2] Sophistication is the difficulty of making the desired transformation. Transformation becomes more difficult when: (1) there is less knowledge of the process;[6] (2) more individuals are needed in a team effort to produce desired outcomes;[4] and (3) linkage among parties is more intricate[3] and/or machinery replaces individuals.[1] Variability is the number of different combinations of knowledge, materials, and processes an organization uses in the transformation process.[5,6,8,9]

Remember, the work performed in the three technologies is essentially different. Thus different aspects of sophistication and variability are important in the intensive, mediating, and long-linked modes. Therefore, the indicators of sophistication and variability are not identical across the three modes even though the effects of these two variables appear similar. In the Measurement Module you will see how these two variables may be looked at in each of the three technologies. But here, let's see how sophistication and variability in different technologies influence effectiveness and employee maintenance.

Technology and Criteria of Organizational Effectiveness and Employee Maintenance

Long-linked Technologies. Sophistication in this technology centers on the use of machines.[3] What appears to be a very simple repetitive task for humans often requires very intricate machinery. Thus, the greater the proportion of capital to labor the more technically sophisticated long-linked technology becomes. If capital is comparatively cheap, then substitution (greater sophistication) will increase productivity. Following the old dictum from classical economics, organizations should substitute capital for labor until their marginal productivity is roughly equal.[23]

Variability in long-linked technologies includes the number of different inputs introduced into the system, the number of transformations made, and the number of outputs produced.[17,22] For instance, a job shop uses a wide variety of inputs and processes to produce several different products. Variability is the nemesis of long-linked technologies. It cuts the economies of scale that are provided by long production runs and limits the substitution of capital for labor.[32] For example, as the number of basic models of autos (and options available) increases, the production run is confounded: Setup time increases and different types of raw materials must be available.[19] Whenever possible, organizations using the long-linked technology will attempt to ensure standardized inputs, transformation, and outputs.[27] For instance, producers will move to help suppliers provide virtually identical raw materials and subassemblies to the point of vertical integration. In regard to outputs, an organization may attempt to alter consumer preferences to reduce variability and/or magnify slight differences within the capability of the technical core. In marketing terms, organizations using sophisticated long-linked technologies will use product differentiation to minimize variability. For instance, General Motors once advertised the Oldsmobile Rocket engine as a unique product feature. Yet it was virtually identical to engines used in Chevys.

While an organization may wish to ignore potential variability, it does so only at the risk of its own survival. Ashby, among others, argues that for an organization to survive it must contain as much internal variety as in its specific environment.[1,7] Thus, organizations using a long-linked technology, when customers require individual products, will lose business to those selecting a handicraft mode.

The impact of sophistication appears generally positive for employee maintenance in long-linked technologies.[6,13] More sophistication allows for progressively more interesting, challenging, and less physically strenuous tasks.[3] However, the substitution of labor for capital does not automatically make jobs less routine. A line of research by Trist and those following the sociotechnical system view, indicates that within long-linked technologies, group and social interaction considerations may loom large.[29] Alterations in sophistication upset employee relations.[28] Change the social structure and you often destroy highly productive and cohesive work crews. But by allowing workers the opportunity to maintain social relationships and build cohesive teams, both satisfaction and productivity can increase.[20] It appears that variability may be a partial substitute for sophistication in long-linked technologies, to enhance employee maintenance criteria.[4] For instance, handicraft operations are technically unsophisticated, but they do call for continual slight adjustments by individual workers. Thus jobs are varied and complete. The variability and completeness seem to substitute for the intellectual complexity embodied in highly sophisticated technologies.[4] As numerous studies show, however, when the technology provides jobs that are neither varied nor challenging, employee maintenance becomes a substantial problem.[5] Satisfaction is low and absenteeism high.

Mediating Technologies. The work of the mediating technology is to link parties and store the medium for exchange. A mediating technology is more sophisticated as: (1) the number of matches needed to connect the parties increases;[7] (2) it becomes more difficult to estimate if a match is acceptable;[21] and (3) the medium of exchange becomes harder to store. For instance, the linkages provided by a bank involve comparatively few matches for interdependence. It is easy to measure acceptable matches since the bank decides when a linkage is made. The medium of exchange (money) is comparatively easy to store. Conversely, an executive recruiting firm may have a very sophisticated technology. The parties need to mesh together in several different areas. Often they are unsure of how to estimate whether a match is acceptable. And together they must decide if there are enough matches to become interdependent.

A parallel between sophistication in long-linked and mediating technologies is beginning to develop as the use of the computer increases.[3] The least sophisticated mediating technologies are able to substitute computers for labor in many aspects of their operations in much the same manner as machines replace labor in long-linked technologies.[14] Those mediating technologies using computer matching begin to look more like their more sophisticated counterparts. It's expected that the continual decline in computer costs will result in increased substitution of computers for workers. Given sufficient volume, we predict this substitution will increase the efficiency of organizations that rely on mediating technologies.*,[18]

Variability in mediating technologies centers on the number of categories needed to link parties and the number of exceptional cases that defy grouping.[9,31] Mediating technologies are more efficient when all parties fall into a few categories.[18] Well-developed rules, policies, and procedures can be developed.[3] Clients can be processed as mere numbers. This eliminates individual processing, and developing interdependencies one at a time is expensive.

Thus, just as organizations with long-linked technologies attempt to standardize inputs, those with mediating technologies attempt to deal with large sets of homogeneous clients.[25] Standardized matching, however, ignores individual differences. The organization may be undercut by others approaching a technical services mode.

As with long-linked technology, it appears that sophistication and variability are partial substitutes for one another in regard to employee maintenance.[16,4] Sophisticated but routine matches provide challenge and completeness, facilitating higher satisfaction and involvement.[24] Conversely, high variability with low sophistication provides tasks that are nonroutine and individualized.[15] Again, satisfaction and involvement are facilitated. Jobs with neither sophistication nor variety are associated with high absenteeism, turnover, and lower satisfaction.[2,15,24]

---

*At this time, the computer frees specialists to work on more complicated matches. As computer capability increases, it may perform more sophisticated linkages of parties.

Intensive Technologies. As we noted earlier, intensive technology may overlap with long-linked and mediating ones. Sophistication and variability in these overlapping areas follows that of either the long-linked or mediating technology. But, in some cases organizations are forced to use the intensive mode to produce outcomes consistent with their social function.[3] Since the work of those employing this technology is different, let's see how sophistication and variability work here.

Sophistication in intensive technologies centers on two related factors. One, to what extent does the organization know how to produce the desired outcomes?[21,27] Two, how many different occupational specialists must be drawn together in a team effort to produce these outcomes (i.e., how many individuals are involved interdependently)?[10] The less information concerning cause-effect relations, and the more individuals involved in interdependence, the more sophisticated the intensive technology. For instance, a law firm may be able to match each client with one lawyer. While considerable judgment is needed and the organization can't exactly prescribe how the legal interests of a client should be served, there is little team effort needed. Conversely, the technology of some law firms is more sophisticated in that teams of lawyers (extensive interdependence) must be developed to solve particularly knotty legal problems. No one lawyer can be expected to deal with all the intricacies of the case. Several highly specialized individuals may be needed.

It is difficult to estimate the association between sophistication and effectiveness in intensive technologies. The technical specialists themselves may be the only ones in a position to accurately estimate the relative degree of effectiveness. And they may define effectiveness so that it is consistent with existing performance. A frequently used indirect measure of performance is the amount of information gained.[26] If used, greater sophistication is associated with greater performance by definition. You should also realize that the ultimate solution, such as a cure for cancer or a workable theory of organizations, may only be the result of hundreds of apparently unsuccessful efforts, which only indicated where the solution could *not* be found.[14]

Variability in intensive technologies may be seen as the number of different combinations of materials, knowledge, and processes used by an organization.[12,30] More specifically, how many different teams and combinations of individuals are needed to produce desired outcomes? As in the other technologies, variability seems to have a negative impact on effectiveness.[25] As variability increases an organization must seek different ways of integrating and using various specialists. But this is most difficult to do as variability increases, for specialists may resist being placed on a variety of different teams.[18]

Greater sophistication in intensive technologies appears to have a positive association with employee maintenance.[4] But, increasing sophistication appears to loosen ties between professionals and the organization.[8] By attempting to solve the problems given to them by their organization, specialists become involved with advancing the knowledge in their profession. Hence, they become involved with others outside the system.

Moderate variability within intensive technologies appears to have a functional impact on experts and professionals.[25] Extensive variability may be damaging if individuals are moved from one project to another before the fruits of their efforts can be seen. Extensive variability may also leave individuals without the social support of a small cohesive group.[11] As with greater sophistication, increasing variability drives the individual away from the organization toward identification with a more stable professional group. For the organization, this may involve a trade-off between effectiveness and employee attachment. That is, the organization may choose to increase variability for effectiveness by transferring specialists in and out of work teams. But this may reduce the attachment of professionals to their organization.

Summary

Through the discussion of variability and sophistication we have assumed that an organization will select the technological mode needed to produce desired outcomes. Furthermore, it was assumed that organizations generally improve the quality of their outputs by increasing sophistication. Higher quality may not be translated into effectiveness unless it matches the degree of sophistication and volume desired in the environment. Thus, the automated plant generally produces higher quality products within narrower tolerances than the mass-production assembly line.[1] But this greater quality may or may not be needed in sufficient quantities to warrant a substantial capital investment. In a similar way, an insurance agent can tailor-make policies, but the mass marketing of standard policies is cheaper. Variability, on the other hand, clearly reduces efficiency and is often associated with lower quality.

As noted, sophistication and variability appear to play complementary roles when predicting employee maintenance. Within limits, sophistication and variability have a positive impact on satisfaction and involvement. Also, one may be a partial substitute for the other. Both sophistication and variability push an organization toward a more organic and diverse structure.* These concepts force it to rely more on the judgment of lower-level employees and managers. The subordinates' actions cannot be prescribed by rules, policies, and procedures. Individuals must be allowed flexibility to adapt.

*These structures are explained in more detail in Chapter 9.

These expectations are summarized in Table 8-7 along with the measures for sophistication and variability for the three types of technology. These are noncontingent associations. They assume environmental factors and size are not important. And they assume the technical core and the organization are one and the same. At this point you should realize that both size and environmental conditions limit the technology potentially available to an organization (and also have an influence on structure and performance as well). Combinations of environment and contextual factors are more fully discussed in Chapter 10.

Table 8-7. Sophistication and Variability Associations across Technological Modes

	Technological Mode		
	Long-linked or Handicraft	Intensive	Mediating or Technical Services
Sophistication			
a. Measure	Ratio of labor to capital	Education level; search analyzability	Number of matches; difficulty of matching
b. Effectiveness association	Positive	Positive	Positive
c. Employee maintenance association	Positive	Positive	Positive
d. Impact on structure	Organic with greater sophistication	Organic with greater sophistication	Organic with greater sophistication
Variability			
a. Measure	Number of products	Number of different teams of specialists; overtime	Number of exceptions and number of categories
b. Effectiveness association	Negative	Negative	Negative
c. Employee maintenance association	Positive	Positive	Positive
d. Impact on structure	Organic with greater diversity	Organic with greater diversity	Organic with greater diversity

In sum, we argue that the technological imperative holds for the structure of the technical core under two conditions: (1) it can be buffered from environmental disturbances; and (2) the organization can select the technology best suited to produce desired outcomes.[4] That is, if huge, automated, continuous processing plants are needed, and the organization has the resources, we estimate a more flexible organic formal structure will emerge and be more effective than a mechanistic one.[3]

As we have thus far outlined, technology is an important variable for explaining organizational effectiveness and employee maintenance. As with size, we have briefly mentioned that technology is a contextual variable that influences structure. This will be fully addressed in Chapter 10.

ADMINISTRATIVE PHILOSOPHY

Now let's turn to the third contextual variable of interest—administrative philosophy. In this section, the impact on effectiveness and maintenance criteria is one of value orientations. But we also note the structural tendencies resulting from administrative philosophies. This begins to provide a linkage between the other contextual variables of size and technology to an organization's structure.

As with values, administrative philosophy is a slippery concept that is difficult to conceptualize and measure. Our treatment here is molded into the overall view taken in earlier parts of the text. That is, administrative philosophy is the set of attitudes of the administrative elite directed toward key aspects of an organization's domain. We will focus our attention on a set of consistent orientations toward goals, the environment, technology, and employees. We also note the structural tendencies consistent with these sets of attitudes. Three questions are addressed. First, whose attitudes should be considered? Second, what profiles are commonly found? Third, just how important is administrative philosophy?

The Administrative Elite

Since organizations are hierarchical, some individuals have more clout than others.[1] Those at the top are held accountable for the effectiveness of the organization as a whole.[7] They are normally given the authority to substantially influence the domain of the organization.[1] They can color the goals of the system, modify its technology, develop (or not develop) programs to improve employee maintenance, and, of course, alter its formal structure.[2,11] Even in the largest and most technically complex organizations, senior administrators set the tone of the system and guide the actions of subordinates.[9] Typically, they control the flow of funds within the organization, select future members of top management, and represent it in its interface with other systems.[7,2,12]

To the uninitiated, the chief executive officer is the individual who determines the philosophy of an organization. This may be true for small systems.[5] However, a more realistic view for large and huge organizations would suggest that coalitions of senior administrators form an "inner circle."[3,12] Collectively, their attitudes toward the domain constitute the organization's administrative philosophy.[13]

Several investigations suggest that individuals become members of the administrative elite when it appears they can handle critical problems facing the organization.[8,15] For instance, John Dean emerged as a member of the "inner circle" of the Nixon administration when it appeared he might be in a position to keep a lid on Watergate. Members of the administrative elite frequently hold important organizational positions.[4,10] Sometimes they do not. For instance, Kissinger was a member of the inner circle when he was just an advisor for National Security Affairs.

Organizations may also add outsiders to the administrative elite.[12] Corporations that are highly dependent on banks may select a banker for their board of directors. The banker may become a member of the administrative elite if his or her advice is solicited before and during the development and implementation of corporate strategy.* Government agencies often do much the same by bringing in outsiders for their governing boards. Selznick, for instance, argued that the Tennessee Valley Authority (TVA) used this strategy to gain acceptance in a traditionalistic culture.[14] Representatives of powerful community groups and local organizations were systematically incorporated in the TVA's administrative elite. Selznick called this process "cooptation." The TVA was successful in changing the attitudes of outside members—assuring favorable treatment for the agency. Of course, outsiders also had an influence on the administrative philosophy of TVA officials.

The philosophy of the administrative elite is supported and maintained to the extent that organizational members accept that philosophy. As Mann suggests, there is a "pragmatic acceptance" of the rights, privileges, and decisions of top-level administrators.[9] In Barnard's terminology, there is a zone of indifference by organizational members.[1] Yet, you should recognize that professionalization and an erosion of the work ethic may be closing the "zone of

---

*Board membership alone does not mean the banker is in the "inner circle." As Pfeffer shows, membership on corporate boards may be used merely as a mechanism to facilitate interorganizational communications.[11]

indifference." Some argue that individuals are becoming more difficult to socialize.[16] Likert and Likert note that resistance to change and subordinate inflexibility are becoming serious problems.[9] While top-management values are not the only relevant set of attitudes in an organization, their attitudes still appear to dominate the system.

Thus, the analysis of administrative philosophy centers on the set of attitudes held by the administrative elite. As with size and technology, management philosophy is not an independent variable. It is influenced by environmental forces and other contextual variables. Furthermore, it may dramatically change with a turnover of top management.[6]

Patterns of Attitudes toward the Organization's Domain

There are many possible sets of attitudes directed toward the domain of an organization.[15] Elements of three types have received attention in the literature. Table 8-8 outlines these three patterns, including the orientation toward goals, the environment, technology, and employees. Organizational structures consistent with these philosophies are also noted. Following the analysis of cultural values, they are called traditionalistic, moralistic, and individualistic (see Chapter 5). These tags are descriptive. They are not designed to imply that any one philosophy is inherently superior to another. Nor should you expect to find these "pure" types consistently followed in an organization.

The Traditionalistic Philosophy. In this case the administrative elite places considerable emphasis on the social function of an organization.[32] For instance, profits would be seen as an indicator of how efficiently an organization is producing desired products and services.[23] As such, profitability becomes a major indicator of its achievements.[15] Derived goals would be considered constraints on improving profits.[5] Growth and power would be natural by-products of performing an organization's social function.[13] Top management is "results oriented" and "hard nosed" in evaluating alternatives with regard to "the bottom line."

As Reimann indicates, administrative elites tend to hold unified orientations toward a specific environment. For the traditionalistic philosophy, the specific environment is characterized as unfavorable. Unions are seen as "out to get management."[27] Suppliers are to be carefully monitored to ensure adequate quality. Customers (clients) are assumed to be fickle, and the notion of competition also plays an important role. Interestingly enough, Reimann found it difficult to find anything but a traditionalistic philosophy toward government and unions in his sample of manufacturing organizations.[27]

Table 8-8 Three Administrative Philosophies

	Traditionalistic	Moralistic	Individualistic
Goal emphasis	Social function— output goals	Quality of life; derived	Growth and power
Environment	Unfavorable	Dynamic and favorable	Indeterminant
Technology	Dynamic and favorable	Dynamic yet unfavorable	Dynamic and favorable
Employees	Static and unfavorable	Dynamic and favorable	Static but neither favorable nor unfavorable
Structural tendencies[a]	Centralized, specialized, and formalized	Decentralized, contingent upon employer, informal	Contingent upon assumed cause-effect relationships

[a]See Chapter 9 for details.

Those following a traditionalistic philosophy are likely to view technology as both dynamic and favorable.[30] It may seem paradoxical that traditionalists see change as favorable.[7] But think of the substantial technological developments over the last fifty years. Traditionalists tend to see technological evolution as *a,* if not *the,* primary means for obtaining greater social contribution.[19] New processes, equipment, and products are welcomed if costs are outweighed by benefits. We are not proposing that organizations following a traditionalistic philosophy will be more innovative than others. But those following this philosophy will look toward technology to solve organizational problems. Innovation in traditionalistic firms seems to be stifled by emphasis on cost effectiveness and the centralization in decision making, which often accompanies this set of attitudes.[9]

The emphasis on technology is also reinforced by the view with regard to employees, taken by those subscribing to a traditional management philosophy. That view closely corresponds to McGregor's Theory X and Likert's description of Systems I and II.[16,20] That is, employees are seen as inherently lazy, unwilling to voluntarily assume leadership roles, and lacking the motivation to manage. Thus, employees are seen as being induced into exchanging their labor for money, and perhaps recognition. Of course, a few selected individuals are quite the opposite. They rise to managerial positions and can become members of the administrative elite. Furthermore, unions can turn this "neutral force" into a very unfavorable group that demands less work for higher pay.

Many scholars have chastised administrators for their unfavorable attitudes toward employees.[11] Few have recognized that this attitude facilitates changes in an organization's technology, structure, and outputs. For instance, assume that automated equipment can be installed and that a substitution of capital for labor would dramatically increase profits. In a traditionalistic philosophy, the plight of displaced workers would not be a major concern that could block automation. Of course, numerous studies show that the traditional attitude toward employees breeds subordinate resistance to change.[22] Those favoring a traditionalistic philosophy may have substantial problems implementing desired changes.[16]

The Moralistic Philosophy. The hallmark of the moralistic philosophy is the emphasis on employee maintenance.[12] Instead of stressing the social function of an organization, those following a moralistic philosophy are primarily concerned with attachment to the organization and quality of working life.[6] As suggested in the tag given this philosophy, the desired conditions are clearly outlined in terms of some ideal conditions (often espoused with the moral fervor of an evangelist).

The view of outsiders appears to complement the attitudes toward goals. The specific environment is considered dynamic yet basically favorable to the overall emphasis on employee attachment.[14] Unions are considered mechanisms for employee participation and representation.[21] Government is viewed as moving toward the quality of working life, albeit too slowly. Competition is not stressed.[17] Suppliers are not expected to provide anything but material consistent with contract specifications. As members of an organization's specific environment move toward the social ideal, change is expected and welcome.[8]

Technology is not the answer to the problems of an organization. It is a necessary evil that must be tolerated on the path to a better world. Engineering, for instance, should take a backseat to personnel development. Technical changes that reduce the quality of working life should be rejected. Those that alter the social configuration of an organization should be studied in detail before implementation is considered.[12] For instance, automation would generally be favored if it improved employee maintenance and if displaced workers would be assured of more interesting and challenging jobs with greater promotion potential and security. Thus, technology is considered dynamic, but essentially an unfavorable force within the organization.

As you might expect, the assumptions concerning employees are consistent with McGregor's Theory Y and Likert's System IV.[20,16] Employees are the most potent and dynamic force within an organization. They can become committed to organizations committed to them.[1] Lower-level employees and middle-level managers are to provide the system with a continual flow of new ideas.[35] This improves both the quality of outputs and systems efficiency. You need only tap this powerful, latent force within organizations to achieve greatness. Employees are willing to take leadership positions and are drawn to organizations that allow them to meet their full potential.[17]

The Individualistic Philosophy. Even as the moralistic philosophy is being more fully articulated, a third set of attitudes is identified. Here, it is called individualistic. In the individualistic philosophy, growth and power are the paramount goals.[13] To the extent that an organization is a more powerful force in society, the administrative elite may perceive themselves as more important, influential, and valuable members of society.[26]

In this philosophy, the administrative elite does not have any particular orientation toward the environment. That is, those subscribing to the individualistic philosophy do not color their perception of external units.[25] Instead, they actively search for information concerning the nature of the environment.[15] They attempt to monitor and forecast changes in the specific environment. This stance has been called proactive by several researchers.[15,32]

Those following an individualistic philosophy see technology as a dynamic and positive force for their organization. But they place less faith in the ability of technology alone to provide continued growth and development.[24] Technological developments are to be incorporated into the social system of the organization to minimize the problems of implementation.[15]

A parallel concerning employees may also be found. The Theory X-Theory Y dichotomy makes little sense to those subscribing to the individualistic philosophy. They see ample evidence to support both sets of assumptions.[28] Employees are viewed as useful so long as it appears they contribute to the potential growth of the organization.[29] If an orientation toward employee maintenance is needed to keep valuable employees, such programs would be considered. If the technology calls for highly routine, boring, and repetitive jobs, then employee maintenance concerns may be dismissed.[11] The orientation toward the environment and employees is Machiavellian.[29] For instance, employee participation would be encouraged so long as employees are willing to accept the decision premises of the administrative elite.[21] Employee participation in goal formation isn't even considered.[10] Participation concerning means is used, but only to facilitate a smooth transition to a new series of policies, strategies, or formal structure.[4]

Those familiar with the misuse of management by objectives (MBO) recognize the essence of this administrative philosophy. In some MBO systems, employees are to specify their objectives for the coming year so that they fit into the overall strategy established by higher-level management. Rewards are to be based on "objective performance" in accordance with MBO statements submitted by each subordinate manager. However, the rewards to be given for successfully meeting MBO objectives are rarely spelled out. Superiors are to "stretch" subordinates to gain additional performance. They refrain from directly comparing subordinates with one another. As Bishop suggests, however, progress up the organizational ladder is not always based on MBO performance measures.[2] Other less objective measures are used. Further, some critics see MBO as just another way of manipulating employees.[10]

Data on managerial values by England and Lee among others, suggest that a substantial proportion of U.S. managers may subscribe to the individualistic philosophy.[5] They call this "pragmatic." Whyte, Reich, and a number of other social critics have also identified this profile of attitudes.[35,26] But they view it as a potential threat to society.

Administrative Philosophy—Some Additional Concerns. The three patterns outlined above are not likely to be clearly identifiable.[18] They're "ideal" categories of internally consistent attitudes. Administrative elites rarely mention the more unfavorable side of the philosophies outlined above.[29] Henry Ford was willing to say that jobs must be broken down into their simplest form to fit the limited capabilities of employees. Few managers would risk such pronouncements today. Furthermore, the actual administrative philosophy is likely to be a mix of three ideal types.[32] But we estimate one will predominate.

The strategic actions and the emphasis put on various aspects of an organization's domain may allow you to gauge the management philosophy operating within it. For instance, interviews with chief executives centering on the strategy of the organization often suggest that a particular philosophy is in effect. The corporate president may stress automation of manufacturing processes to beat the "stiff" competition. Conveniently dismissed is the fact that workers in the northeast were terminated when the new plant was opened in the Sun Belt. Another chief executive may focus on new efforts to upgrade employees to minimize turnover, absenteeism, and the like. A third may discuss how changing environmental conditions and new technological breakthroughs are necessitating new growth and development. You should note what is not said, just as the astute purchaser of a car becomes suspicious when styling is stressed without any mention of the car's mileage or reliability record.

We think the administrative philosophy sets the tone and "personality" of an organization. Some refer to this as the "climate" of the organization.[11] As we noted earlier, the employees (or clients in some cases) often accept this philosophy. Recruiting practices and socialization may also serve to maintain the climate. Thus, one administrative philosophy may pervade an organization. Once established, it may take on a life of its own; that is, organizations do have various images. This suggests that similar to nations or regions, large and huge organizations within the same industry may vary substantially in their value orientations.[32] All firms in the oil industry are not alike. All colleges are not the same. Hospitals are not homogeneous. Differences exist partly as a reflection of administrative philosophy.[27] This is important for you as an organizational analyst. As a student of organizations, you should recognize the subtle but important differences in administrative philosophy.[3] And when you begin a job search, recognize that you may be more comfortable and/or more productive in one setting than another.

MEASUREMENT MODULE

Here, we provide some suggested indicators for measuring context—size, technology, and administrative philosophy.

MEASURING SIZE

Kimberly has recently argued that there tends to be some lack of agreement about how to measure size.[2] The number of employees, the log of that, and net assets have all been used. But as indicated, numbers of full-time employees is the measure most commonly used by organization analysts.*

To the financial analyst, sales volume, budget allocations, or assets listed on the books are more likely to be used. In educational systems the most frequently used measure is the number of full-time students. Hospitals are rated on the number of beds, prisons on the number of inmates, and government agencies on their budgets. When comparing organizations with similar missions and technologies, any one of a number of size indicators is likely to yield the same relative ranking of organizations. As Hall notes, several authors have reported virtually identical rankings by size, using student enrollment and full-time faculty equivalents for universities, number of employees and assets for business organizations, and patient loads and the total labor force for hospitals.[1]

Thus, size seems to present few measurement problems. Getting at technology and administrative philosophy, though, is quite another matter.

MEASURING TECHNOLOGY—SOPHISTICATION AND VARIABILITY

We can attack the measurement of technology in several different ways. For instance, Harvey used the number of product changes over a ten-year period to estimate the form of technology and the degree of change within his sample of manufacturing firms.[1] Other researchers have used questionnaires to esti-

---

*Hall, among others, recommends using full-time equivalent workers by adjusting for differences in part-time and volunteer workers.[1] The log of size is used by most researchers to adjust for the diminishing relationships discussed earlier.

mate the degree of task difficulty and task variability. The more employees reporting difficult and varied tasks, the more sophisticated and varied the organization's technology. We will discuss these questionnaire measures in Chapter 12.

We suggest the following procedure when estimating the degrees of technological sophistication and variability for an organization as a whole. For each major aspect of an organization's operations, clinically estimate the dominant mode of technology. Is it long-linked, mediating, or intensive? Once having determined the dominant form of technology we suggest you use the measures outlined in Table 8-7. Let's discuss these in more detail.

Long-linked Technologies. Recall that sophistication here represents the substitution of machines for human labor. The measure of sophistication, then, is quite straightforward—the ratio of labor to capital. As more labor is involved, long-linked technology is considered less sophisticated. As more capital is used for intricate machinery, the sophistication increases. Variability can be measured by the number of products produced. As this increases, the number of job changes, setups, inputs, processes, and scheduling goes up. As the number of operations performed rises, the number of motions required by a worker or machine goes up, and the number of different tools required to do a job increases as does variability. These are relatively easy to measure compared to intensive and mediating technologies.

Mediating Technologies. Since the work here requires matching parties, sophistication can be partially measured by a count of the number of matches needed. Measuring the acceptability of a match can be gleaned indirectly by asking to what extent rules and policies can be used for decisions about clients matching categories. If these procedures cannot be used, more sophistication is involved. The storage of medium of exchange involves a clinical judgment.

Variability in the mediating technology is addressed by determining the number of categories and exceptions dealt with. Recall, this technology requires matching clients to categories.

Intensive Technologies. One way to get at sophistication in this technology is to analyze the educational level of employees. Since this technology is often labor intensive, and there is considerable judgment involved, higher education levels connote more sophistication. However, when comparing professional organizations, this approach may not lead to distinguishing among levels of sophistication. Thus, a direct measure of "search analyzability" may be used. Perrow argued that technologies might be rated on the search analyzability needed to produce outcomes.[2] At one extreme, problems might be solved with prescribed techniques, existing rules of thumb or current professional standards (i.e., conventional logic could be used). In such cases Perrow says the organization makes, "incremental adaptations from existing programs or parts of existing programs" (p. 76). This has been called a "programmed" approach.

Conversely, problems may not be amenable to existing solutions and an organization must rely upon other processes. Since creativity is not well understood, we often refer to the experience, judgment, wisdom, or intuition of individuals to describe "nonprogrammed" decision making. Some researchers have approached the measurement of this by asking respondents to indicate whether rules, procedures, or written policies exist to help make decisions in certain areas of the organization. While this has often been used as a structural measure of "standardization," it seems to also relate here as an indicator of search analyzability.* To the extent that few policies or formal standards exist for making decisions about work flow, the intensive technology will be more "sophisticated." That is, less is known about how to produce outcomes. More search is needed. This requires greater sophistication. You cannot rely on prescribed "programmed" decisions.

Related to search analyzability is another aspect of sophistication. Namely, how many different perspectives (specialists) are needed to develop a workable solution. The number of specialists is an aspect of sophistication when all members must act as a team. As the number of team members increases arithmetically, the number of interactions required to achieve interdependence increases geometrically. Greater effort and cooperation is needed to arrive at a decision about how to do the work. Greater numbers increase the likelihood of disagreement about appropriate means-ends relationships.

The number of teams may also reflect a measure of variability. However, variabilty connotes less stability in the continuing composition of these teams. Thus, the greater the movement of occupational specialists in and out of teams, the greater the variabillty. This might be measured indirectly by the average length of time occupational specialists stay on projects or teams.

MEASURING ADMINISTRATIVE PHILOSOPHY

Since philosophy reflects values and personalities, it is difficult to assess it in a tangible way. There have been some attempts to measure McGregor's Theory X and Y notions. This would give you an idea of attitudes toward employees. However, the instruments have not been well developed or validated.

---

*Measures of standardization in a structural sense are included in Chapter 9. See Table 9-7 for specific items.

Exhibit 8-9 Concepts and Scales of PPQ (Public Policy Questionnaire)

	Concepts	
Publics		Reference Concepts

The national government	Yourself
Labor unions	Executive
Your firm's suppliers	Servant
Your firm's consumers	Friend
Your firm's community	Leader
Your firm's stockholders	Criminal
Your firm's creditors	Enemy
Your firm's competitors	
Your firm's employees	

Scales

1. Disloyal	—: —: —: —: —: —: —	Loyal
2. Hostile	—: —: —: —: —: —: —	Friendly
3. Unconcerned	—: —: —: —: —: —: —	Concerned
4. Uncooperative	—: —: —: —: —: —: —	Cooperative
5. Unfair	—: —: —: —: —: —: —	Fair
6. Stable	—: —: —: —: —: —: —	Unstable
7. Slow	—: —: —: —: —: —: —	Fast
8. Passive	—: —: —: —: —: —: —	Active
9. Ineffective	—: —: —: —: —: —: —	Effective
10. Weak	—: —: —: —: —: —: —	Strong

Point values (most negative) 1 2 3 4 5 6 7 (most positive)

Source: Reimann, B. C. "The Public Philosophy of Organizations," *Academy of Management Journal,* 17 (1974), 418–427. Reprinted by permission of the author and Academy of Management Publications.

Note: Scales 1–5 are "evaluative" and scales 6–10 "dynamism" measures. Scales were randomly changed in both order and direction for each concept throughout the questionnaire.

To use the PPQ to tap the degree to which administrative philosophy is traditionalistic, moralistic, or individualistic some adjustments must be made. First the reference concepts would be dropped. Additional "publics" for relevant goals, and technology must be added.

Scoring would follow Reimann's suggestions. The profile indicating a traditionalistic philosophy would be consistent with that outlined in Table 8-8. Unfavorable would be an average score of 1 to 2.5. Indeterminant would be an average score of 2.6 to 5.5, while a favorable score would be an average of 5.6 to 7. Similar cutoffs would be used for dynamism.

We are not aware of any instruments that directly tap the administrative elite's attitudes toward goals, environment, technology, and employees, as outlined in Table 8-8. One approach, of course, is to rely on published statements about these areas. However, official pronouncements may not reflect operative philosophies. While this might be said about responses to questionnaires, we highlight one approach that attempts to minimize that problem. And from it, the philosophy might be gleaned. Exhibit 8-9 presents Reimann's Public Policy Questionnaire.[6] You will note that the respondent is asked to complete the semantic differential scales for each of nine publics and seven reference groups. Reimann's data suggest that these scales do differentiate managerial philosophies among business firms. The approach could be applied to other organizations as well. And it can be used to categorize administrative elites as we did in Table 8-8. But you should be cautious about self-report data, just as you should be cautious about using public pronouncements to categorize managers' philosophies.

There are some measures that may indirectly indicate the effects of philosophy on an organization's "personality." These are the so-called "climate" indicators referred to earlier. There are several designed for businesses and hospitals (see the references for this section). Instruments have also been developed specifically for analyzing climate and subcultural differences among colleges and universities. (College and University Environment Scale and College Characteristics Index.)[4,8] These have been used to study differences in the environment and to show how student culture has an impact on academic effort and outcomes. These climate scales are only partially developed and are not generalizable. Furthermore, development of the climate is a reflection of factors other than administrative philosophy. Thus, we do not include examples here. But you may want to use the references to see what they look like.

We now turn to a description of structure and process. Chapter 10 integrates these context variables with the structural concepts outlined in Chapter 9.

REFERENCES

I. Organizational Size

[1]*Dun and Bradstreet—Principle International Businesses.* New York: Dun & Bradstreet, 1976.

[2]Kimberly, J. R. "Organizational Size and the Structuralist Perspective: A Review, Critique, and Proposal," *Administrative Science Quarterly*, 21 (1976), 571–597.

[3]Luthans, F. *Organizational Behavior* (2nd edition). New York: McGraw-Hill, 1977.

[4]Melcher, A. *Structure and Process of Organizations—A Systems Approach.* Englewood Cliffs, N.J.: Prentice-Hall, 1976.

[5]*Moody's Industrial Manual, 1939–1976.* New York: Moody's Investors Service.

[6]*Moody's Manual of Investments,*

American and Foreign, Public Utility Securities, 1940. New York: Moody's Investors Service.

[7]Parker, G. "College and University Enrollments in America, 1971–1972," *School and Society,* 100, No. 2339 (1972).

[8]*Readers Digest Almanac and Yearbook, 1977.* Pleasantville, N.Y.: Reader's Digest Association, 1977.

[9]Scott, W. "Organizational Structure," *Annual Review of Sociology,* (1975), 1–20.

[10]*The World Almanac and Book of Facts, 1977.* New York: Newspaper Enterprise Association, 123.

[11]U.S. Department of Commerce, Bureau of the Census, *Financial Statistics of States, 1938.* Washington, D.C.: U.S. Government Printing Office, 1938, 21.

[12]U.S. Department of Commerce, Bureau of the Census, *Historical Statistics of the U.S., Bicentennial Edition.* Washington, D.C.: U.S. Government Printing Office, 1976.

[13]U.S. Department of Labor, Bureau of Labor Statistics, *Employment and Wages.* Washington, D.C.: U.S. Government Printing Office.

[14]Walters, R. "Statistics of Registration in American Universities and Colleges 1939–1940," *School and Society,* 52, 1355 (1940).

A. The Meaning of Size

[1]Bass, S., and Barrett, G. *Man, Work and Organization.* Boston: Allyn and Bacon, 1972.

[2]Baumol, W. *Economic Theory and Operations Analysis.* (2nd edition). Englewood Cliffs, N.J.: Prentice-Hall, 1965.

[3]Becker, S., and Gordon, G. "An Entrepreneurial Theory of Formal Organizations, Part 1." *Administrative Science Quarterly,* (1966) 315–344.

[4]Blau, P. "A Formal Theory of Differentiation in Organizations," *American Sociological Review,* 35 (1970), 201–218.

[5]Caplow, T. "Organizational Size," *Administrative Science Quarterly,* 1 (1957), 484–505.

[6]Coats, R., and Updegraff, D. "The Relationship Between Organization Size and the Administrative Component of Banks," *Journal of Business,* 46 (1973), 576–588.

[7]Coffey, R., Athos, A., and Reynolds, E. *Behavior in Organizations.* Englewood Cliffs, N.J.: Prentice-Hall, 1975.

[8]Downs, A. *Inside Bureaucracy.* Boston: Little, Brown, 1967.

[9]England, G., and Lee, R. "Organizational Size as an Influence on Perceived Organizational Goals: A Comparative Study Among American, Japanese and Korean Managers," *Organizational Behavior and Human Performance,* 9 (1973), 48–58.

[10]Galbraith, J. *Designing Complex Organizations.* Reading, Mass.: Addison-Wesley, 1973.

[11]Greiner, L. "Evolution and Revolution as Organizations Grow," *Harvard Business Review,* 50 (July 1972), 37–46.

[12]Haas, E., Hall, N., and Johnson, N. "The Size of the Supportive Component in Organizations: A Multi-Organizational Analysis," *Social Forces,* 42 (1963), 9–17.

[13]Haas, J., and Drabek, T. *Complex Organizations: A Sociological Perspective.* New York: Macmillan, 1973.

[14]Haire, M. "Biological Models and

Empirical Histories of the Growth of Organizations." In M. Haire, (ed.) *Modern Organization Theory.* New York: Wiley, 1959.

[15]Hall, R. *Organizations: Structure and Process.* Englewood Cliffs, N.J.: Prentice-Hall, 1977.

[16]Hendershot, G., and James, T. "Size and Growth as Determinants of Administrative-Production Ratios in Organizations." *American Sociological Review,* 37 (1972), 149–153.

[17]Holdaway, E., and Bowers, T. "Administrative Ratios and Organization Size: A Longitudinal Examination," *American Sociological Review,* 36, (1971), 278–286.

[18]Indik, B. "The Relationship Between Organizational Size and Supervision Ratio," *Administrative Science Quarterly,* 9 (1964), 301–312.

[19]Kasarda, J. D. "Effects on Personnel Turnover, Employee Qualifications, and Professional Staff Ratios on Administrative Intensity and Overhead," *The Sociological Quarterly,* 14 (1973), 350–358.

[20]Katz, D., and Kahn, R. *The Social Psychology of Organizations* New York: Wiley, 1966.

[21]Khandwalla, P. M. "Mass Output Orientation of Operations Technology and Organizational Structure," *Administrative Science Quarterly,* 19 (1974), 74–89.

[22]Kimberly, 1976.

[23]Osborn, R., and Hunt, J. "Environment and Organizational Effectiveness," *Administrative Science Quarterly,* 19, No. 2 (1974), 231–246.

[24]Pfeffer, J. *Organizational Design.* Arlington Heights, Ill.: AHM Publishing, 1978.

[25]Pfeffer, J., and Salancik, G. *The External Control of Organizations.* New York: Harper & Row, 1978.

[26]Revans, R. "Bigness and Change," *New Society,* January 2, 1964, 31–48.

[27]Rushing, W. "Organizational Size and Administration: The Problems of Causal Homogeneity and a Heterogeneous Category," *Pacific Sociological Review,* (1966), 100–108.

[28]Seashore, F., and Yuchtman, E. "A Systematic Resource Approach to Organizational Effectiveness," *Administrative Science Quarterly,* 32 (1967), 377–395.

[29]Starbuck, W. H. *Organizational Growth and Development: Selected Readings.* Harmondsworth, England: Penguin, 1971.

[30]Starbuck, W. "Organizations and Their Environments." In M. Dunnette (ed.), *Handbook of Organizational and Industrial Psychology.* Chicago: Rand McNally, 1976.

[31]Yuchtman, E., and Seashore, S. E. "A System Resource Approach to Organizational Effectiveness," *American Sociological Review,* 32 (1967), 891–903.

B. Organizational Size and Employee Maintenance

[1]Blau, 1970.

[2]Cummings, L., and Burger, C. "Organization Structure: How Does It Influence Attitudes and Performance?" *Organizational Dynamics* (Autumn 1976), 34–49.

[3]Cummings, L. L., and ElSalmi, A. M. "The Impact of Role Diversity, Job Level, and Organizational Size on Managerial Satisfaction," *Administrative Science Quarterly,* 15 (1970), 1–10.

[4]Hare, A. P. *Handbook of Small Group Research*. New York: The Free Press, 1976.

[5]Ingham, G. *Size of Industrial Organization and Worker Behavior*. Cambridge: Cambridge University Press, 1970.

[6]Mahoney, T. A., Frost, P., Crandall, N. F., and Wetcel, W. "The Conditioning Influence of Organization Size Upon Managerial Practice," *Organizational Behavior and Human Performance*, 8 (1972), 230–241.

[7]Melcher, 1976.

[8]Porter, L. W., and Lawler, E. E., III. "Properties of Organization Structure in Relation to Job Attitudes and Job Behavior," *Psychological Bulletin*, 64 (1965), 23–51.

C. Organization Size and Structure

[1]Blau, 1970.

[2]Blau, P., and Schoenherr, R. *The Structure of Organizations*. New York: Basic Books, 1971.

[3]Child, J. "Organizational Structure, Environment and Performance: The Role of Strategic Choice," *Sociology*, 6 (1972), 1–22.

[4]Child, J. "Predicting and Understanding Organization Structure," *Administrative Science Quarterly*, 18 (1973), 168–185.

[5]Child, J., and Mansfield, R. "Technology, Size and Organizational Structure," *Sociology*, 6 (1972) 369–380.

[6]Ford, J., and Slocum, J. "Size, Technology, Environment and the Structure of Organizations." Working paper, The Ohio State University, 1976.

[7]Gouldner, A. *Patterns of Industrial Bureaucracy*. New York: The Free Press, 1954.

[8]Hall, 1977.

[9]Hinings, C., and Lee, G. "Dimensions of Organization Structure and Their Context: A Replication," *Sociology*, 5 (1971), 83–93.

[10]Hrebiniak, L., and Alutto, J. "A Comparative Organizational Study of Performance and Size Correlates in Inpatient Psychiatric Departments," *Administrative Science Quarterly*, 18 (1973), 365–382.

[11]James, L., and Jones, A. "An organizational model: Components and measurement." Paper presented at a symposium on "Men in Social Systems: Results of a Three-Year Multiorganization Study," American Psychological Association, New Orleans, 1974.

[12]Pugh, D., Hickson, D., Hinings, C., and Turner, C. "The Context of Organizational Structures." *Administrative Science Quarterly*, 14 (1969), 91–114.

[13]Warner, M., and Donaldson, L. "Dimensions of Organization in Occupational Interest Associations: Some Preliminary Findings." Third Joint Conference on the Behavioral Sciences and Operational Research, London, 1971.

[14]Weed, F. "Centralized and Pluralistic Structures in Public Welfare," *Administration and Society*, 19, 1 (1977), 111–136.

II. Technology

[1]Fullan, M. "Industrial Technology and Worker Integration in the Organization," *American Sociological Review*, 35 (1970), 1028–1089.

[2]Pugh et al., 69.

[3]Thompson, J. *Organizations In Action*. New York: McGraw-Hill, 1967.

[4]Woodward, J. *Industrial Organization: Theory and Practice*. Lon-

don: Oxford University Press, 1965.

A. Types of Technology

[1]Argyris, C. *Integrating the Individual and the Organization.* New York: Wiley, 1964.

[2]Blauner, R. "Work Satisfaction and Industrial Trends in Modern Society." In W. Galerson and S. M. Lipset (eds.), *Labor and Trade Unionism.* New York: Wiley, 1960.

[3]Blauner, R. *Alienation and Freedom.* Chicago: University of Chicago Press, 1964.

[4]Broudy, H. "Didactics, Heuristics, and Philetics." Paper presented at the Midwest Academy of Management, 1972.

[5]Burack, E. *Organization Analysis: Theory and Applications.* Hinsdale, Ill.: The Dryden Press, 1975.

[6]Clark, K. *A Relevant War Against Poverty.* New York: Metropolitan Applied Research Center, 1966.

[7]Clausen, J. "Mental Disorders." In R. Merton, and R. Nisbet, (eds.), *Contemporary Social Problems.* New York: Harcourt Brace, 1976, 103–140.

[8]Fullan, 1970.

[9]Galbraith, 1973.

[10]Glueck, W. F. *Management.* Hinsdale, Ill.: Dryden, 1977.

[11]Haimann, T., Scott, W., and Connor, P. *Managing the Modern Corporation.* Boston: Houghton-Mifflin, 1978.

[12]Herrick, N., and Maccoby, M. "Humanizing Work: A Priority Goal of the 1970's." In L. Davis, and A. Cherns, (eds.), *The Quality of Working Life, Volume One.* New York: The Free Press, 1975.

[13]Jauch, L. R., Osborn, R. N., and Martin, T. H. "The Role of Strategy, Performance and Environ-

ment in Managerial Succession," *Academy of Management Proceedings '78,* 398.

[14]Jelinek, M. "Technology, Organizations, and Contingency," *Academy of Management Review,* 2, 1 (1977), 17–26.

[15]Katz, D., and Kahn, R. *The Social Psychology of Organizations.* New York: Wiley, 1978.

[16]Knejer, A., Gittings, H., and Conway, J. *Serving Two Masters.* Summarized in *Front Line,* Washington, D.C., 2, 6, 8. And in D. Katz, and R. Kahn, *The Social Psychology of Organizations.* New York: Wiley, 1978.

[17]Mahoney, T., and Frost, P. "The Role of Technology in Models of Organizational Effectiveness," *Organizational Behavior and Human Performance,* 14 (1974), 122–38.

[18]Osborn, R. N. "Organizational Effectiveness: A Model and a Test." Unpublished dissertation, Kent State University, 1971.

[19]Perrow, C. *Organizational Analysis: A Sociological View.* Belmont, Calif.: Wadsworth, 1970.

[20]Pfeffer, 1978.

[21]Pugh et al., 1969.

[22]Ritti, R., and Funkhouser, G. *The Ropes to Skip and the Ropes to Know.* Columbus, Ohio: Grid, 1977.

[23]Scott, 1975.

[24]Steiner, G. *Business and Society.* New York: Random House, 1975.

[25]Taylor, J. "Technology and Supervision in the Postindustrial Era." In J. G. Hunt and L. Larson (eds.), *Contingency Approaches to Leadership.* Carbondale: Southern Illinois University Press, 1974.

[26]Thompson, 1967.

[27]Walker, B., and Haynes, J. *Marketing Channels and Institutions:*

Readings on Distribution Concepts and Practices. Columbus: Grid, 1973.

²⁸Walters, G. *Marketing Channels.* Santa Monica, Calif.: Goodyear, 1977.

²⁹Woodward, 1965.

B. Technological Choice

¹Burack, 1975.

²Child, 1972.

³Higgins, B. *Economic Development.* New York: W. W. Norton and Company, 1968.

⁴Reimann, B. "Dimensions of Organizational Technology and Structure: An Exploratory Study," *Human Relations,* 30, 6 (1977), 545–566.

⁵Thompson, J. D. "Technology, Polity, and Societal Development," *Administrative Science Quarterly,* 19, 1 (1974), 6–22.

⁶Woodward, 1965.

C. Dominant and Multiple Technologies and the Technical Core

¹Child, J. *Organization.* New York: Harper & Row, 1977.

²Ford, J., and Slocum, J. "Size, Technology and the Structure of Organizations," *Academy of Management Review,* 2, 4 (1977), 561–575.

³Parsons, T. *Toward A General Theory of Action.* New York: The Free Press, 1962.

⁴Pugh et al., 1969.

⁵Scott, 1975.

⁶Thompson, 1967.

D. The Controversy over the Technological Imperative

¹Aldrich, H. "Technology and Organizational Structure: A Reexamination of the Findings of the Aston Group," *Administrative Science Quarterly,* 17 (1972), 26–43.

²Blau, P., Falbe, C., McKinly, W., and Tracy, P. "Technology and Organization in Manufacturing," *Administrative Science Quarterly,* 21 (1976), 20–30.

³Child, J., and Mansfield, R. "Technology, Size and Organization Structure," *Sociology,* 6 (1972), 369–393.

⁴Ford and Slocum, 1977.

⁵Harvey, E. "Technology and the Structure of Organizations," *American Sociological Review,* 33 (1968), 247–259.

⁶Hickson, D., Pugh, D., and Pheysey, D. "Operations Technology and Organization Structure," *Administrative Science Quarterly,* 14 (1969), 378–97.

⁷Negandhi, A., and Reimann, B. "Correlates of Decentralization: Closed and Open Systems Perspectives," *Academy of Management Journal,* 16 (1973), 570–581.

⁸Perrow, 1970.

⁹Pugh et al., 1969.

¹⁰Trist and Bamforth, 1951.

¹¹Van de Ven, and Delbecq, A. "A Task Contingent Model of Work-Unit Structure," *Administrative Science Quarterly,* 19 (1974), 183–197.

¹²Woodward, 1965.

¹³Zwerman, W. *New Perspectives on Organizational Theory.* Westport, Conn.: Greenwood Publishing Company, 1970.

E. Sophistication and Variability Across Technologies

¹Burack, 1975.

²Ford and Slocum, 1977.

³Galbraith, 1973.

⁴Hall, 1977.

⁵Litwak, E. "Models of Bureaucracy Which Permit Conflict," *American Journal of Sociology,* 67 (1961), 177–184.

⁶Perrow, 1970.

[7]Scott, 1975.

[8]Thompson, 1967.

F. Technology and Criteria of Organizational Effectiveness.

[1]Ashby, W. *Design for a Brain*. New York: Wiley, 1952.

[2]Bass, B., and Barrett, G. *Man, Work and Organizations*. Boston: Allyn and Bacon, 1972.

[3]Burack, 1975.

[4]Chung, K., and Ross, M. "Differences in Motivational Properties Between Job Enlargement and Job Enrichment," *Academy of Management Review*, 2, 1 (1977), 113–122.

[5]Cummings and Burger, 1976.

[6]Fullan, 1970.

[7]Galbraith, 1973.

[8]Gouldner, 1957–58.

[9]Hage, J., and Aiken, M. "Routine Technology, Social Structure, and Organizational Goals," *Administrative Science Quarterly*, 14 (1969), 366–376.

[10]Hall, 1977.

[11]Hare, A., Borgatta, E., and Bales, R. *Small Groups*. New York: Knopf, 1966.

[12]Hrebiniak, L. "Job Technology, Supervision and Work," *Administrative Science Quarterly*, 19, 4 (1974), 395–410.

[13]James, L., and Jones, A. "Organizational Structure: A Review of Structural Dimensions and their Conceptual Relationships with Individual Attitudes and Behavior," *Organizational Behavior and Human Performance*, 16 (1976), 74–113.

[14]Katz and Kahn, 1976.

[15]Kidron, A. G. "Individual Differences, Job Characteristics and Commitment to the Organization." Doctoral dissertation, Ohio State University, 1976.

[16]Lichtman, C. M., and Hunt, R. C. "Personality and Organization Theory: A Review of Some Conceptual Literature," *Psychological Bulletin*, 76 (1971), 271–294.

[17]Litwak, 1961.

[18]Lucas, H. *Information Systems Concepts for Management*. New York: McGraw-Hill, 1978.

[19]Melcher, A. *Structure and Process of Organizations—A Systems Approach*. Englewood Cliffs, N.J.: Prentice-Hall, 1976.

[20]Miller, E. "Socio-Technical Systems in Weaving 1953–1970: A Follow-Up Study," *Human Relations*, 28, 4 (1975), 546–553.

[21]Perrow, 1970.

[22]Rushing, W. A. "Hardness of Material as an External Constraint on the Division of Labor in the Manufacturing Industries," *Administrative Science Quarterly*, 13 (1969), 229–245.

[23]Samuelson, P. *Economics*. New York: McGraw-Hill, 1977.

[24]Sekaran, U. "The Dynamics of Job Involvement: A Study of the Congruence among Personality, Job and Organization Factors in the Context of Changing Demographic Variables." Unpublished doctoral dissertation, University of California, Los Angeles, 1977.

[25]Sutherland, J. *Systems: Analysis, Administration and Architecture*. New York: Van Nostrand Reinhold, 1975.

[26]Steers, R. M. "Problems in the Measurement of Organizational Effectiveness," *Administrative Science Quarterly*, 20 (1975), 546–558.

[27]Thompson, 1967.

[28]Trist, E. *Organization Theory: Structures, Systems and Environments*. New York: Wiley, 1976.

[29]Trist, E. and Banforth, K. "Some So-

cial and Psychological Consequences of the Long Wall Method of Coal-Getting," *Human Relations,* 4 (1951), 3–38.

[30]Udy, 1959.

[31]Wheeler, S. "The Structure of Formally Organized Socialization Settings." In O. Brim, Jr., and S. Wheeler (eds.), *Socialization After Childhood.* New York: Wiley, 1966.

[32]Woodward, 1965.

G. Summary

[1]Burack, 1975.

[2]Chandler, A. *Strategy and Structure.* Cambridge, Mass.: M.I.T. Press, 1962.

[3]Lawrence, P., and Lorsch, J. *Organization and Environment.* Boston: Harvard Business School, 1967.

[4]Thompson, 1967.

III. Administrative Philosophy

A. The Administrative Elite

[1]Barnard, C. *The Function of the Executive.* Cambridge, Mass.: Harvard University Press, 1938.

[2]Child, J. *Organization.* London: Wheaton, 1977.

[3]Cyert, R., and March, J. *A Behavioral Theory of the Firm.* Englewood Cliffs, N.J.: Prentice-Hall, 1963.

[4]Evan, W. *Organization Theory.* New York: Wiley, 1976.

[5]Glueck, 1977.

[6]Helmich, D. "Executive Succession in the Corporate Organization: A Current Integration," *Academy of Management Review,* 2 (1977), 252–266.

[7]Jauch, L., Osborn, R., Martin, T., and Glueck, W. "CEO Succession, Performance and Environmental Conditions." Paper presented at the Annual Meeting of the Academy of Management, San Francisco, August 1978.

[8]Khandwalla, P. *The Design of Organizations.* New York: Harcourt Brace Jovanovich, 1977.

[9]Likert, R., and Likert, J. *New Ways of Managing Conflict.* New York: McGraw-Hill, 1976.

[10]Mann, M. "The Social Cohesion of a Liberal Democracy," *American Sociological Review,* 35 (1970), 423–439.

[11]Osborn and Hunt, 1974.

[12]Pfeffer, J. "Size and Composition of Corporate Boards of Directors," *Administrative Science Quarterly,* 17 (1972), 218–228.

[13]Pfeffer, 1978.

[14]Reimann, 1978.

[15]Selznick, P. *T.V.A. and the Grass Roots.* Berkeley, Calif.: University of California Press, 1949.

[16]Smalter, D., and Ruggles, R., Jr. "Six Lessons from the Pentagon." *Harvard Business Review,* 44, 2 (1966), 64–75.

[17]Van Maanen, J. "Breaking In: Socialization to Work." In R. Dubin (ed.), *Handbook of Work, Organization and Society.* Chicago: Rand McNally, 1976.

B. Patterns of Attitudes toward the Organization's Domain

[1]Argyris, C. *Integrating the Individual and the Organization.* New York: Wiley, 1964.

[2]Bishop, R. "The Relationship between Objective Criteria and Subjective Judgment in Performance Appraisal," *Academy of Management Journal,* 17 (1974), 558–563.

[3]Child, 1972.

[4]Child, 1977.

[5]England and Lee, 1973.

[6]Georgiou, P. "The Goal Paradigm,"

Administrative Science Quarterly, 18 (1973), 291–310.

[7]Ericson, R. "Organizational Cybernetics and Human Values." In J. S. Jun and W. B. Storm (eds.), *Tomorrow's Organization: Challenges and Strategies.* Glenview, Ill.: Scott, Foresman, 1973, 213–225.

[8]Haas and Drabek, 1973.

[9]Hage, J., and Dewar, R. "Elite Values Versus Organizational Structure in Predicting Innovation," *Administrative Science Quarterly,* 18 (1973), 279–291.

[10]Hall, 1977.

[11]Hellriegel, D., and Slocum, J., Jr. "Organizational Climate: Measures, Research and Contingencies," *Academy of Management Journal,* 17 (June, 1974), 255–280.

[12]Herrick, 1975.

[13]Jauch et al., 1978.

[14]Katz and Kahn, 1978.

[15]Khandwalla, P. *The Design of Organizations.* New York: Harcourt Brace Jovanovich, 1977.

[16]Likert, R. *The Human Organization.* New York: McGraw-Hill, 1967.

[17]Likert and Likert, 1976.

[18]Litzinger, R., and Schaifer, W. "Perspective: Management Philosophy Enigma," *Academy of Management Journal,* 9, 3 (1966), 337–343.

[19]Luthans, 1977.

[20]McGregor, D. *The Human Side of Enterprise.* New York: McGraw-Hill, 1960.

[21]Miner, J., and Miner, M. *Personnel and Industrial Relations* (3rd edition). New York: Macmillan, 1977.

[22]Mirvis, P., and Berg, D. (eds.). *Failures in Organizational Development.* New York: Wiley, 1972.

[23]Negandhi, A., and Reimann, B. "Correlates of Decentralization: Closed and Open Systems Perspectives," *Academy of Management Journal,* 16, (1973), 570–582.

[24]Nightingale, D. V., and Toulouse, J. "Toward a Multilevel Congruence Theory of Organization," *Administrative Science Quarterly,* 22 (1977), 264–280.

[25]Osborn and Hunt, 1974.

[26]Reich, C. *The Greening of America.* New York: Random House, 1970.

[27]Reimann, B. "The Public Philosophy of Organizations," *Academy of Management Journal,* 17 (1974), 418–427.

[28]Ritti and Funkhouser, 1977.

[29]Seider, M. "American Big Business Ideology: A Content Analysis of Executive Speeches," *American Sociological Review,* 39 (1974), 802–815.

[30]Sloan, A. P. *My Years with General Motors.* New York: Sidgwick and Jackson, 1965.

[31]Simon, H. "On the Concept of Organizational Goal," *Administrative Science Quarterly,* 9 (1964), 1–22.

[32]Sturdivant, F., and Ginter, J. "Corporate Social Responsiveness: Management Attitudes and Economic Performance," *California Management Review,* 19, 3 (1977), 30–39.

[33]Taylor, 1974.

[34]Whyte, W. H. *The Organization Man.* New York: Anchor Books, 1957.

[35]Whyte, W. F. *Organizational Behavior: Theory and Application.* Homewood, Ill.: Irwin and Dorsey, 1969.

IV. Measurement Module

A. Measuring Size
  [1]Hall, R. *Organizations: Structure and Process.* Englewood Cliffs, N.J.: Prentice-Hall, 1972.
  [2]Kimberly, 1976.
B. Measuring Technology—Sophistication and Variability
  [1]Harvey, 1968.
  [2]Perrow, 1970.
C. Measuring Administrative Philosophy
  [1]England and Lee, 1973.
  [2]Hellriegel and Slocum, 1974.
  [3]Khandwalla, P. "Effect of Competition on the Structure of Top Management Control," *Academy of Management Journal,* 16 (June, 1973), 285–295.

[4]Pace, C. R. *College and University Environment Scales.* Princeton: Educational Testing Service, 1962.
[5]Pace, C. R. "The Influence of Academic and Student Subcultures in College and University Environments," Cooperative Research Project No. 1083, University of California, Los Angeles, 1964.
[6]Reimann, 1974.
[7]Sanford, N. (ed.) *The American College: A Psychological and Social Interpretation of the Higher Learning.* New York: Wiley, 1962.
[8]Stern, G. *Studies of College Environments.* Syracuse, N.Y.: Psychological Research Center, 1966.

chapter **9** **ORGANIZATIONAL STRUCTURE**

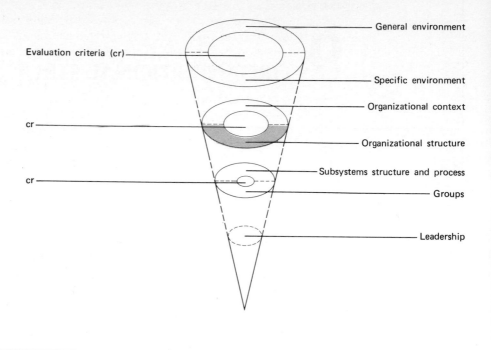

General environment

Evaluation criteria (cr)

Specific environment

Organizational context

cr

Organizational structure

cr

Subsystems structure and process

Groups

Leadership

The organization's structure is its anatomy. This anatomy prescribes formal roles and relationships for people and groups within the system. (Groups include such units or subsystems as departments, divisions, and so on). The structure is an attempt to arrange these roles and relationships so that the work of an organization is directed toward accomplishing the goals and mission of the system.

There are several ways to look at this anatomy—horizontally and vertically (and top down or bottom up). We will describe these shortly. But several key themes run through each view. One, the roles people and groups are assigned are often restricted to the performance of a narrow range of activities. That is, formally assigned roles often become specialized. This is often done under the assumption that more specialized roles allow for more effective performance. Two, the roles, once specialized, need to be coordinated and controlled through various mechanisms. Specialized roles need to be integrated in order to get synergy and consistency of action toward goals. Third, the roles differ in terms of their power and authority to control and coordinate the activities of those performing other roles. That is, some units can make decisions about what work will be performed by other units, and they control and coordinate that work. This is often termed centralization. Here, the greater the centralization, the fewer the number of units that are given this power. Another aspect of centralization is a "location" question. Where are the decisions made? Where are the units placed—both physically, and in terms of the reporting relationships?

A host of patterns or anatomies can result when these aspects of specialization, formalization, and centralization, are combined. No one pattern is better than others. Nor is the "best" structure totally dependent on the size of an organization, its technology, *or* its administrative philosophy. Each of these contextual variables has an influence, as do its goals and environmental conditions.

Before looking at these structures, let's look at an historical analysis to highlight some common themes.

THE WEBERIAN VIEW OF STRUCTURE—THE CONCEPT OF BUREAUCRACY

Weber attempted to show how and why modern organizations stemming from the Industrial Revolution are quite unlike their historical counterparts.[14,15] Since he stressed the more machinelike characteristics of organizations, we know him best for the concept of bureaucracy and the very negative public image of an organization's hierarchy, red tape, and impersonality.[7] To Weber, these characteristics were advantages of the bureaucracy when compared to earlier forms. To understand Weber's view it is important to realize that he attempted to describe ideal types much like a human-anatomy text outlines the perfect human form. This is important to keep in mind. Some of Weber's critics claim he is too idealistic.[1] And by design he is.

Weber started his analysis with the idea of different bases for authority. Three were enumerated: charismatic, traditional, and legal.[15] Charismatic domination stems from the "personality" of a leader. Traditional domination has its seeds in basic cultural patterns. Weber accurately predicted that a legal base would dominate since it concentrated on scientific rationality and efficiency. In the legal base, the authority figure (manager) dominates via a "legal" procedure followers generally consider just. According to Weber, bureaucracy was the natural outgrowth of legal authority.

A bureaucracy can be seen as a series of reinforcing conditions that stress efficiency, rationality, and security.[14] In an ideal formulation, impersonality and formal role relationships are stressed. The personality of a position-holder is not particularly important. Relationships among members are to be guided by a series of "rational" rules, policies, and procedures.[13] These are used to standardize operations, show the best methods available, and protect individuals from unequal treatment. Note that subscription to a dominant ideology as in a charismatic base of authority is outmoded. Gone, too, are the reliance upon past successes and kinship as in the traditional base.

In the ideal bureaucracy there would be a hierarchy of positions. Each position is to have limited authority. And each position-holder would be held accountable for the actions of subordinates. There would be a complete separation of ownership and position so that individual and organizational concerns are separate. Officials don't own their jobs. They are expected to pursue a career. A person's position within an organization and the privileges given would be based on technical competence. To bolster the chances of developing careers and to promote efficiency, an organization would divide work up into specific tasks based on the technical competencies required. Thus, the hard-working individual could ascend the organizational ladder.

Each aspect of bureaucracy reinforces the others. For instance, specialization, the development of rules, policies, and procedures, plus the separation of ownership and control places emphasis on careers. Likewise, career-oriented individuals reinforce an emphasis on specialization, rules, policies, and procedures.

According to Weber, bureaucracy should promote technical efficiency. It should protect the member from the ideological whims of superiors. Critics of Weber usually zero-in on the mechanistic nature of bureaucracies.[9] Some claim that Weber, as well as his followers, is insensitive to human needs.[2] Weber, himself, was concerned that the ideal type was inhumane and gave too much weight to security over individual freedom.[14] Yet it is difficult to believe Weber would agree with Likert's suggestion that organizations with nonbureaucratic characteristics would be more effective.[9]

Bureaucracies have also been criticized because they lead to inflexibility.[10] There are too many rules, policies, and procedures. Bureaucracy may also lead to too much conflict and a subversion of means and ends, say other critics.[12] Others argue that bureaucracy leads to mediocrity.[16] Rules, policies, and procedures only indicate minimum requirements.[5] However, few critics have gone as far as Warren Bennis who predicted the demise of bureaucracy as an organizational form.[2] Like so many others, he has been forced to recognize that something akin to Weber's ideal type will be with us for some time.[3]

It is important to note three important factors. One, within Western cultures the concept of bureaucracy appears well accepted. It forms the basis for many, if not most, large organizations.[7] It reinforces dominant religious, economic, legal-political, and educational forces.[11] The second point stems from the first. With the widespread acceptance of the bureaucratic model, it isn't a very useful way of describing the structure of large and huge organizations.[6] All are bureaucracies. However, it is particularly useful in comparing small organizations, where growth often triggers a critical problem—separation of ownership and management—with the accompanying increase in bureaucratization (movement toward the ideal type).[4] Third, Weber centered his discussion of organizations on: (1) rules, policies, and procedures versus personal direction by a charismatic leader; (2) equal treatment based on performance versus personal, kinship, or emotionally based rewards; (3) division of labor and a stress on expertise versus multiple job assignments; (4) a concentration on roles in a hierarchical structure versus personalities; (5) career commitment versus temporary association; and (6) the separation of ownership and control.[8] These six issues keep recurring, albeit in different forms, in the bulk of the literature on structure.[6]

SOME BASIC STRUCTURAL CONSIDERATIONS

When discussing organizational structure it is useful to get a visual picture of an organization and go over a few basic terms. Since there is such a wide variety in titles and position descriptions, let's provide a common base. Figure 9-1 graphically depicts the skeleton of large organizations.

Larger organizations can be hierarchically divided into three levels as in Figure 9-1.[8,14] The top positions are often called the institutional level of management. Here, the essential tasks are to develop the domain of the organization.[14] Officers guide the development of its goals, property, outputs, personnel, and structure.[8] Furthermore, top administrators also manage the organization's interface with the specific environment and establish the administrative climate for subordinate managers.[20] Below this level is middle management. We call this the administrative level.* At the top of this level, many of the organization's policies, rules, and regulations are formulated (to be authorized by top management).[5] As you move toward the bottom of this level, existing policies are interpreted to fit the day-to-day operations of the

*Others refer to this level as a bureaucratic or managerial level. We will also call this middle management.

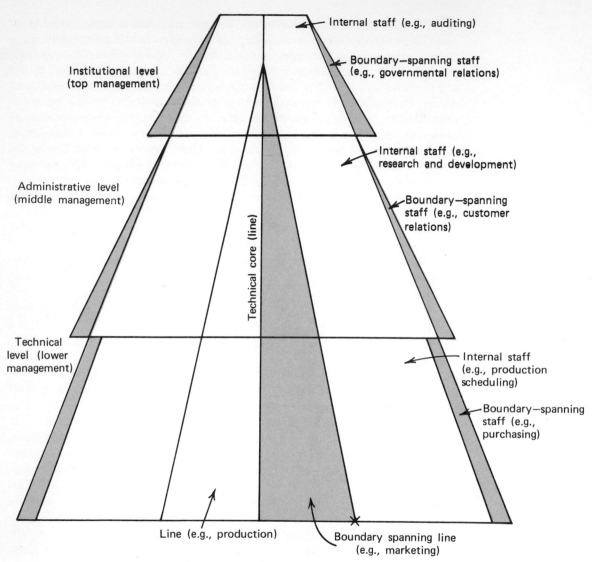

Institutional level
(top management)

Administrative level
(middle management)

Technical
level (lower
management)

Technical core (line)

Internal staff (e.g., auditing)

Boundary—spanning staff
(e.g., governmental relations)

Internal staff (e.g.,
research and development)

Boundary—spanning
staff (e.g., customer
relations)

Internal staff
(e.g., production
scheduling)

Boundary—spanning
staff (e.g.,
purchasing)

Line (e.g., production)

Boundary spanning line
(e.g., marketing)

Figure 9-1 The basic skeleton of an organization.

organization.[19] Throughout middle management you find the planning, organizing, and controlling functions stressed in many introductory management texts.[9] At the bottom of the managerial hierarchy you find the lower or the technical level. It is at this level that products are produced; services rendered; and rules, policies, and procedures are put into effect.[21]

To many top-level managers the institutional, administrative, and technical levels are linked by the organization's means-ends chain.[9,11] The chain starts with the overall mission of the system.[20] The mission is operationally stated by top management in the form of systems, output, and derived goals.[4] These are subdivided and given to subordinate units. Note that "goals" are divided into "means" that are the "goals" for subordinate units. Obviously, organizations develop methods for assuring that the intentions of top-level managers are implemented by others.[10] Thus, much of what we call structure is often seen as a direct outgrowth of the means-ends chain.[1] Not so obvious is the need for greater control, as the organization has a longer and more complex means-ends chain.[12] Longer means-ends chains require greater vertical specialization.[2] And the more extensive the vertical specialization, the more extensive must be the controls.[12]

You can also see that size, technology, and management philosophy may have much to do with the exact pattern selected by any one organization.[3,6] Larger organizations tend to be "taller," with more administrative levels.[7] Furthermore, as the technology requires more individual direction and control, it seems likely that an organization will develop more levels of administration.[18] However, the direct relationship between size and structure and technology and structure is often weak.[18] This partially stems from an organization's ability to substitute managerial techniques, formal control, and formal information systems for managers.[17] Moreover, organizations need not just add additional levels of management. They can also react to and/or anticipate technological and size changes by adding specialists, expanding line units and/or establishing new staff units.[15]

Line units perform the transformations implied by the basic mission of an organization.[20] The focus may be internal (such as the production of aspirin) or external (marketing the aspirin). Thus you can see traditional line units (e.g., production) as well as boundary-spanning line units (e.g., marketing).*

Staff units assist the line by performing tasks that support the main function of the system. Traditionally, the staff role centered on providing services, technical information, and the like.[21] The old dictum was that staff advised but never decided.[9] Obviously, staff units may act much like the lawyer to the ignorant client. The lawyer can "decide" merely by selecting the alternatives given to the client.

Again, staff units may be located at the institutional, managerial, or technical level. For instance, Auditing may be at the institutional level in a large

---

*Depending on the mission of an organization, boundary-spanning units (e.g., marketing) may or may not constitute a separate technical core. For instance, the marketing units of integrated oil companies are considered to be technical core units. Greater vertical integration leads to greater likelihood that marketing is a boundary-spanning technical core unit (Thompson, p. 41).[20]

business corporation. Research and development may be at the managerial level. The placement of staff units is, as we will see, a critical decision in developing an organization's structure.

Where the primary contact or focus for the staff unit is outside an organization, it may be called a staff boundary-spanning unit. Governmental relations is an example of this at the institutional level of some large organizations. In comparison with internal staff, boundary-spanning staff more often process environmental information, represent the organization to specific outside units, and "absorb uncertainty" by drawing inferences from external information sources.[20,16] For instance, Marketing Research, after conducting a brief informal survey of selected consumers, may tell a top manager a particular product won't sell.

So far we have provided only the broadest outline of an organization's structure. Now we will go into more detail on the vertical and horizontal aspects of structure. Our discussion follows two assumptions: vertical specialization must be matched with more control; horizontal specialization must be matched with more coordination.[10,2] In each of the following parts of this chapter, we first explore the notion of specialization and then the diversity in patterns that can exist.

VERTICAL SPECIALIZATION AND CONTROL (TOP-DOWN VIEW)

It is necessary to go beyond a simple assessment of levels in order to get a more accurate picture of the manner in which an organization divides effort vertically. A convenient way of doing this is to look at how planning, implementation, and control are accomplished. (Our treatment here takes a top-down view. The bottom-up view is discussed later in the chapter.)

Methods of Planning, Implementation, and Control

Essentially three techniques are available to an organization for planning, implementation, and control.[22] First, the organization can use individual judgment. That is, it can use managers. Second, it may rely upon a whole series of procedures loosely tagged managerial techniques. These include MBO (management by objectives), PERT (program evaluation and review technique), CPM (critical path method), PPBS (planning, programming, and budgeting system). Also included are cost-benefit analysis, break-even analysis and a whole range of capital budgeting techniques. Third, the organization can develop sophisticated control systems.[19] We expect organizations to use a combination of these three methods. But for the moment, let's look at each separately.

Using Managers and Specialists. All organizations can and do use managers and specialists for planning, implementation, and control. However, there are several different ways an organization can arrange managers and specialists.[9] At one extreme they can be stacked one on top of the other in the organization's hierarchy. This leads to many organizational levels, with a comparatively small span of control (number of subordinates to supervisors) and a high ratio of managers to employees. Conversely, an organization can develop a large central staff at the institutional level. Here, specialized units and/ or individuals would be held accountable for one or more aspects of the organization's domain. For instance, there might be a specialized planning unit, centralized personnel, and the like. This approach yields fewer administrative levels, a broad span of control (at least within the technical core), and a low ratio of managers to employees. However, it also yields a high ratio of specialized staff to the number of employees.

As the organization gets larger you can expect it to use a combination of these two approaches.[11] Many larger organizations use specialized institutional staff for planning and controlling long-term capital commitments, personnel policies, et cetera.[23] Managers in the technical core and middle-management staff concentrate on operations (technology) on a week-to-week basis. We think the most appropriate combination depends upon a number of factors, particularly the use of the other methods. So let us look at these.

Using Managerial Techniques. The use of managers is frequenty supplemented by the development of specialized decision and control techniques.[7] Managerial techniques are often used to make routine decisions, formulate alternatives for nonroutine decision making, and establish boundaries for the decisions of subordinate managers.[25] Most techniques attempt to establish the premises upon which decisions are made and the process for developing and evaluating alternatives.[6] On occasion, these techniques give detailed procedures for evaluating the results of implementation. One of the oldest and most common techniques is the planning-budgeting process. Let's use it as an illustration.

Organizations often develop five-year rolling plans where the latest year "drops out" as a detailed budget.[7] These five-year plans frequently outline expected environmental conditions such as long-term economic and industry forecasts.[4] Projections are made of externalities and current strengths and weaknesses within the organization. Based on these, plans often estimate expected major capital purchases, provisions for technical advances, and perhaps new products as well as anticipated alterations in personnel costs and requirements.[3] While estimates for the fifth year may be very general, the budget is often a very explicit outline of goals, property, and technological and personnel expectations.

Just as an organization has choices concerning the deployment of managers, it may select various approaches to the planning-budgeting process. At one extreme, a centralized staff and/or senior management may attempt to develop all the estimates and a full-blown budget. At the other extreme the budget may be "built-up" from estimates by subordinate managers. Most frequently a combination of these two is used.[15] Top management and central staff establish overall policies and strategies for the planning-budgeting procedure.[14] Their emphasis is often on long-term commitments such as the purchase of plant and equipment.[3] Detailed estimates for raw materials, personnel, and the like are provided by subordinate managers so that they fit within the planning guidelines established above.[3]

Note that the planning-budgeting process can provide an indication of an organization's goals, structure, property, technology, and personnel intentions, in monetary form.[2] To the extent that the monetary form provides for adequate control, the managerial techniques, such as the planning-budgeting process, are a partial substitute for additional managers. Instead of controlling every facet of an organization's operations, managers can concentrate on exceptions.[7] Those units within budget, for instance, can be left alone. Those outside a specific percentage, say 10 percent, receive "managerial attention." The budget also helps select alternatives and provides a format for evaluating them.[14] Thus it is a partial substitute for individual judgment.

In addition to the planning-budgeting process, organizations also have a whole series of other techniques such as internal rate of return or PPBS.[25] These can be used to eliminate alternatives. At the same time, they can provide the primary goal a lower-level manager must use in evaluating specific actions and expenditures. However, neither internal rate of return nor PPBS is a direct substitute for managerial judgment. Neither recognizes conflicting goals that cannot be quantified and neither provides for implementation.[24] If you're skeptical, we need only remind you of the "management" of the Vietnamese War, where the substitution of techniques for judgment led to very costly errors.

Using Control Systems. A wide variety of managerial techniques as well as managerial judgment are often supplemented with sophisticated control systems. Control systems establish standards, provide the measuring instruments for judging performance, and yield the criteria for allocating rewards and penalties.[19] To nonmanagerial personnel, the planning-budgeting process may be indistinguishable from the control system. They only see standards, measuring instruments, and rewards/penalties. But to top-level administrators it can be a separate tool for linking the various levels of administration.

It is useful to look at the control system on a continuum ranging from simple to sophisticated. At the simple end the organization does *not* attempt to establish specific standards, systematically measure individual performance, and adjust rewards or sanctions to individual goal attainment. In essence individuals are asked to "do their best" and "keep their nose clean."[16] That is, don't rock the boat. Many of you are already familiar with this simple control system in elementary schools. Those of you in state colleges or universities may see the same thing. Instructors are asked to "do their best" in teaching. Yet pay and promotions may be based more on the number of years of education and service to the school.[1,10,12,17] Performance may be estimated once a year at most. But it makes comparatively little difference since the control system is only as strong as its weakest link.

At the other extreme, an organization may have a very elaborate control system. It may set standards for each position.[20] Elaborate mechanisms for judging outcomes and rewards (positively or negatively) are established strictly on the basis of outcomes.[21] As we noted in Chapter 3, measuring individual performance is sticky even for nonmanagers performing comparatively simple, routine tasks. Even here you must attempt to balance quality, quantity, and cost considerations.[5]

As you move up the organizational ladder the control system may appear less sophisticated.[1] This is because it is more difficult to estimate appropriate standards, provide detailed measuring instruments, and match performance with rewards.[1] Toward the top of the system, the time period of discretion may indicate the degree of sophistication in the control system.[19] The shorter the time between reviews, the more sophisticated the system. For instance, typically you expect to find some "controls" over managers, even if they are only "do your best standards."[19]

Subscription to policy is the major way of measuring executive output. Often policy will attempt to specify objectives, set parameters for decision making and outline appropriate steps for implementation.[8] Moreover, prohibited behavior is often outlined. But how often are the actions of the manager checked? The shorter the review period the closer the control.[13] Of course, without standards and measuring instruments backed up with rewards and/or penalties, frequent checking may do little good. Without support, frequent checking only indicates management's frustration with current operations.

Like management techniques, the control system is a partial substitute for managers. By specifying outputs, managers can concentrate on exceptional cases. The knowledge of periodic review also keeps the focus of activities centered on the concerns of superiors. But just as techniques cannot substitute for managers when it comes to implementation, neither can control systems.

Diversity in the Pattern of Vertical Specialization and Control

We have argued that the use of managers, techniques, and control systems are partial substitutes for each other.[4] This leads to structural diversity and has plagued organizational theorists for some time.[2] Some researchers have all but abandoned attempts to provide a unified estimate of vertical specialization and control for large and huge organizations.[13] The patterns are too diverse to apply any one description.[5] Instead, they prefer to divide these larger organizations into separate geographic units.[20] Thus, some researchers describe the structure of a plant or sales office as if it were an organization.[6]

There is no perfect resolution to this problem.[23] But we think you can estimate patterns for the major levels outlined in Figure 9-1. While substitution of managers, techniques, and control systems is possible, this may not occur.[10] Some of the patterns are, of course, dependent on context and environment.[11,3] But take a look at a common pattern for each level. At the top, managers often prefer to rely on their own judgment.[14] They could use programmed techniques or control systems.[15] But the decision making may often be more political or judgmental than "rational."[14] As you move to the middle level, more emphasis may be placed on techniques.[16] Judgment and control systems are used. But judgment is used to a lesser degree than at the top level, and control systems are used less than at the lower level.[17] Finally, the lower level places more emphasis on controls.[18] Again, the other two methods can be, and are used.

Another aspect of diversity is particularly important when you incorporate environmental conditions and structure to predict organizational effectiveness. It is diversity by aspect of domain of the system. General Systems Theory suggests that an organization's structure should contain more diversity as the disparity of the environment increases.[1]

An organization may attempt to control the various aspects of its domain in a different fashion.[9,21] For instance, it may want to maintain tight financial control while allowing individuals considerable freedom in devising new products and/or technologies.[24] Organizations can and do vary the use and amount of managers, techniques, and control systems across different aspects of their domains.[25,7] This is a second aspect of diversity.

Table 9-2 provides a format for analyzing the degree of diversity across the various aspects of an organization's domain. Across the top are the methods—managers, techniques, and control systems. Down the side are the areas of the organization's domain—goals, technology, structure, property, person-

Table 9-2 Analyzing the Diversity in the Pattern of Vertical Specialization and Control

Domain Area	Method of Vertical Specialization and Control		
	Managers	Managerial techniques	Control System
Goals a. Planning b. Implementation c. Control			
Technology a. Planning b. Implementation c. Control			
Property a. Planning b. Implementation c. Control			
Personnel a. Planning b. Implementation c. Control			
Outputs a. Planning b. Implementation c. Control			

nel, and outputs (goods and services). You can ask the extent to which organizational goals are planned, implemented, and controlled by managers, techniques, and/or control systems. Then this answer is compared to that for the other areas of domain in the table. The larger the difference across the various aspects of an organization's domain, the larger the diversity.*

Increased diversity in the pattern of vertical specialization and control is one important way organizations with extensive specialization and control can adapt to changing environmental circumstances.[3] By changing the emphasis

*This is, of course, hard to operationalize. We include some other suggestions for analyzing diversity in the Measurement Module.

from one area to another in the use of techniques and/or the control system, the energies of several organizational units can be redirected.[8] If you're familiar with equal opportunity for females and minorities, you should see this clearly. Calculate the number or ratio of a minority to evaluate the extent to which equal opportunity is being used. Then require the organization (unit) to indicate how (what techniques) it intends to ensure equal opportunity. If these new standards and procedures are given priority over others, the organization can quickly reach toward equal opportunity. Once a change is identified (say a recession) the organization can also redirect management techniques and control systems.[19] In the case of a recession it may place efficiency at the top of the priority list.[19] Thus, the ability to react can be built into organizations with apparently rigid hierarchical structures.[2]

Astute managers in an organization with high diversity and extensive vertical specialization and control are particularly alert to subtle changes in the emphasis placed on techniques and control systems.[22] Often the astute manager must quickly shift gears or quickly move into a different organizational position as his or her organization shifts priorities. Ritti and Funkhouser have a particularly interesting name for this—"skating fast over thin ice."[22]

Contextual Factors and Vertical Specialization and Control

Contextual factors appear to have an influence on the usage of all three methods for planning, implementation, and control.[3,4] As size increases, organizations tend to become more vertically specialized and increase control to both gain efficiency and cope with the greater volume of operations.[1,12]

More than any other factor, a larger scope of operations allows an organization to substitute managerial techniques and control systems for managers.[1] The reason is quite simple. Managerial techniques and control systems are cheaper when the initial time and expense to establish these substitutes can be spread across a large number of units.[19] To a lesser extent greater technological sophistication appears to foster more extensive use of managerial techniques and control systems, but for a different reason.[5] As technological sophistication increases, management loses more control over operations, particularly in the technical core.[10] Managerial techniques and control systems allow management to reassert itself throughout an organization.[4,20] Implementing these partial substitutes for managers also means that technically qualified individuals may be hired to operate sophisticated technologies.[9,21] Managerial judgment need not be a prime characteristic for all lower- and middle-level managers.

Technological variability limits the substitution of managers. Neither procedures nor control systems can cover unanticipated situations.[4] With substantial change, their cost advantage also drops, since new circumstances often call for new techniques and control systems.[7] The greater the variability the greater the chance unanticipated situations will occur.[13] Lastly, greater variability makes techniques and control systems much more complicated and expensive; it also limits the cost effectiveness of these managerial substitutes.[26]

Of course the use of substitutes in large part depends on what top management wants.[3] The preceding paragraphs assume that management is interested in efficiency and output goals. Thus, you saw arguments for cost-effectiveness and the limited applicability of techniques and information-control systems as variability increases.[22] But what if top management is more interested in derived goals and/or not particularly concerned with efficiency, output, or systems goals?[2] We expect the substitution of managerial techniques and information-control systems for managers may not occur. Perhaps the best example is found in some political organizations. The ostensible goal is to effectively manage a governmental unit. But an important derived goal may be more important. To the extent that managers and specialists vote for those who hire them, there is substantially less pressure for substitution.[23] The organization may use as many managers and specialists as possible. Conversely, if management is more interested in stability, it may institute control and information systems even where volatility would suggest otherwise.[6]

Administrative philosophy typically appears to have more influence on how managers and techniques will be used than the balance among managers, techniques, and control systems.[15] Overall it appears that a traditionalistic managerial philosophy favors a greater reliance upon centralized staff, more emphasis on control systems, and generally less inputs by subordinates.[16] The moralistic philosophy seems to favor the opposite except for the possible emphasis on managerial techniques.[17] As we indicated earlier, there doesn't appear to be a particular structural preference for those following the individualistic administrative philosophy.

Administrative philosophy has also been linked to the concentration of managers, techniques, and control systems at various levels of an organization's hierarchy.[14] Overall we expect those with a traditionalistic philosophy to concentrate managers at the top, develop numerous managerial techniques for middle managers, and implement sophisticated control systems for those at the technical level.[18,8] In larger organizations, then, you might expect a large centralized staff plus numerous levels of management if the technology is sophisticated.[1] For organizations dominated by a moralistic philosophy you would expect a pattern consistent with views of employees and the environment. Essentially this boils down to more decentralization.[16] Specifically, we expect that staff will be placed lower in an organization's hierarchy.[25] And middle-level managers should be actively engaged in the development of managerial techniques and control systems.[11] However, with a moralistic philosophy, employees (nonmanagers) may or may not see decentralization.[24] They may see just the techniques and control procedures developed by middle management.[10] (This is developed later in this chapter in the bottom-up view).

As we indicated before, we don't expect organizations dominated by an individualistic administrative philosophy to favor any particular structure. Thus, for these organizations the substitution is more likely to follow size and technological dictates.

HORIZONTAL SPECIALIZATION AND COORDINATION

Analyzing vertical specialization and control only provides part of the structural picture. Organizations also develop extensive horizontal specialization. In conjunction with this, they often have considerable problems with coordinating the efforts of quite varied units. So let us take a more detailed look at horizontal specialization and coordination. We assume that additional horizontal specialization must be matched with greater coordination much as greater vertical specialization must be matched with greater control. To get a better handle on this it is important to review the various patterns of departmentation organizations can use.

Forms of Departmentation

Both scholars and managers have identified some basic ways of dividing the total task of an organization.[1,9,24] Four can be identified as: (1) functional, (2) divisional, (3) matrix, and (4) legal.

Division of labor by function is the development of units and departments on the basis of specialized knowledge, skill, and action.[14] Most of you are familiar with this form through course work in "functional areas" of marketing, production, finance, and personnel. Functional specialization may be the most popular form in business organizations and established our view of line and staff units.[15,16] Functional departmentation is used in a wide variety of organizations.[11] Often liberal arts colleges are organized by function.[2,28] For instance, your college may have departments of psychology, art, music, and the like.[4]

In divisional specialization, an extra management layer is added, and functions are designed around products, clients, or territories.[2] If units perform almost all the activities needed to produce a product or service, then there is product divisionalization.[27] In complex organizations, this is a typical pattern.[13] For example, multidivisional firms (like GE or Eaton) may have several decentralized profit centers that sell a whole line of products (e.g., consumer appliances).[8] Yet even here, the top corporate level often maintains control over legal functions or may exercise tight financial control.[19,12] Pure product specialization for large organizations may also be found.[9] Here functional units are often assigned the bulk of the physical transformation and/or information processing for a specialized line of products. For instance, large department stores often specialize by asking buyers to purchase and merchandise a related line of goods.[11] However, these firms often have centralized warehouse facilities and specialized units for personnel and advertising. Hence, these are more functionally oriented. The differences between functional and divisional forms can be readily seen in Figure 9-3.

Divisionalizing by client or territory is another common form of departmentation.[11] They may be divisions at the top of the hierarchy or exist within the functions. For instance, an organization might divide its marketing operations into industrial sales, governmental sales, and consumer sales divisions. Most large organizations geographically dispersed also use specialization by territory.[15] That is, individuals are grouped into units on the basis of where they are located or where the location of their effort is targeted.

The matrix form is a unique combination of functional and divisional types.[7] It is most often found for special projects of fairly limited time duration.[23] For example, assume the organization in Figure 9-3 decides to make a

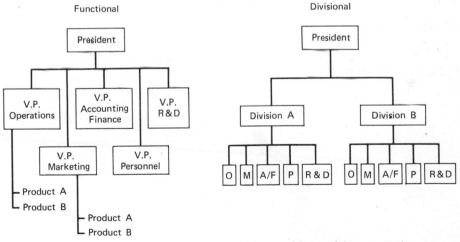

Figure 9-3 Comparison of functional and divisional forms of departmentation.

particular Product C under a short-term contract. Specialists from several departments might work together under a special-project manager even though they retain their positions in the "old" structure.[22] We will comment more on this later.

The last pure form, specialization by legal entity, is not new.[1] But it has recently received considerably more attention. As organizational analysis has spread to governmental units, legal entity has been recognized as a pure form.[10] Legislation often establishes administrative units.[4] Furthermore, a whole series of merger "waves" has produced huge conglomerates that use this form.[20] In effect, the huge organization sets up divisions of autonomous entities composed of several legal entities.[12] There is no particular rationale for this form save a legal requirement to establish a separate unit.[25]

A confusing point is that these forms of departmentation often reinforce and overlap one another.[18] For instance, a large conglomerate may have a separate international division with a separate name. It may be a legal entity producing and selling but one product. Thus, departmentation by product, territory, and legal entity are all used simultaneously.

Organizations would prefer as much overlap and reinforcement in the pattern of departmentation as possible. For when there is overlap, coordination can take place within a unit.[17] When an organization cannot develop overlap,

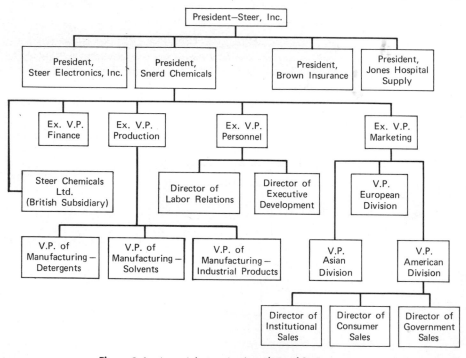

Figure 9-4 A partial organization chart of Steer, Inc.

then it must coordinate the actions of various units and individuals across functions or divisions.[21,26] As you will see shortly, coordination can be extremely difficult and expensive.

You are likely to hear that an organization is "functionally" organized or divisionalized by product group when you know it also uses departmentation by territory and legal entity as well.[6] That description is probably the dominant form of the organization. Often the first form of departmentation below the chief executive officer is called the dominant form.[9] This is used to describe the entire organization even though several forms may be used. You will notice that on the abbreviated organization chart for Steer, Inc. (see Figure 9-4), the corporation is a conglomerate. It owns Steer Electronics, Snerd Chemicals, Brown Insurance, and Jones Hospital Supply. Snerd Chemicals would be called "functionally organized" even though all the basic forms of departmentation are used. But note that Steer, Inc., at the president's level, is divisionalized.

Selecting the Best Pattern of Departmentation

The combination of forms any one organization should select rests on a number of different factors. Organization theory has not yet developed to the point where specific combinations can be predicted or linked to organizational success. The best we can provide are some basic guidelines.

A number of people suggest that the pattern of departmentation is better when it both recognizes the most critical problems of an organization and minimizes coordination costs.[25,18,17] Yet rarely can an organization simultaneously meet both of these requirements. Selecting one basic form typically means that problems will occur in other areas, and units will need to be linked on other bases.[14] For instance, if a functional pattern is selected, the territorial or product concerns may be slighted. The organization may need to link functionally departmentalized units to ensure appropriate treatment across products, territories, and/or clients. So let's take a look at the strengths and weaknesses of each basic form.

Pros and Cons of Functional Departmentation. Functional departmentation provides for clear task assignments often consistent with the previous training of specialists.[18,19] It helps provide individuals with a pool of knowledgeable co-workers.[2] Yet, it is often difficult to integrate units with different functional specialties since functional specialization only reinforces the narrow academic training of professionals.[21] Further, if carried deep within an organization, functional specialization often leads to long, complex communication channels.[22] The contribution of the individual manager may also be hidden as is performance across different products and territories.[6]

Functional specialization does have two major advantages from the organization's point of view. One, it places considerable emphasis on the technical aspects of transforming inputs to outputs.[8] Two, it focuses attention and activities vertically.[21] Much of the coordination must be made at the top of an organization where the various functional concerns merge.[9]

We should note that functional specialization may lead to extremely narrow, routine, and boring jobs in organizations with routine technologies.[5,22] It is not a particularly good dominant form for huge organizations with a highly variable technology facing very complex environments.[20] The contextual conditions place too much pressure on top-level personnel.[26] When environmental and contextual variables call for extensive flexibility, adaptability, and change, more coordination must be done at lower levels than can be accomplished under the functional pattern of departmentation.[4,13,21]

Pros and Cons of Divisional Departmentation. The choice of this form of departmentation may almost be prescribed by the variety of products, clients, or territories within the domain of an organization.[16] A divisional form places major attention on external conditions.[4] And it facilitates integration across different specialties.[1] But it does not provide a pool of highly trained specialists who can train new employees for other parts of the organization.[9] There is less attention paid to efficiency from a total organizational perspective.[20] The focus is on divisional goals rather than coordination of the entire system.[28] This comes at the possible expense of overall systems efficiency.[26] Decentralized decision making is stressed, but it makes it more difficult for specialized staff to help with administrative problems.[11] Compared to functional departmentation it is less likely to yield narrow, routine, and boring jobs.[5] However, it is often difficult to coordinate the functions of units concentrating on outsiders.[18,20] Organizational personnel may become more closely attuned to the desires of outsiders than the organization.[15] Unless the organization is large or huge, this form may also lead to undue duplication of effort.[2] Its hallmarks, however, are (1) adaptability and flexibility in meeting outside demands, and (2) a greater likelihood of detecting changes in external demands.

Pros and Cons of the Matrix Structure. As organizations have become larger, technologies more sophisticated and varied, and environments more complex, more organizations are facing conflicting pressures to use the matrix structure.[7,23] This is done by favoring coordination (horizontal linkages) over control (vertical linkages).

The matrix structure exists where individuals have two superiors and are members of more than one administrative unit.[24] For instance, engineers may be members of a functional engineering group and a special project team. Their permanent home may be in the engineering unit while they may be on temporary assignment with a project team. Note that the engineers have two superiors—a functional boss and a team boss.[10]

In the matrix form, unity of command is lost.[9] And the means-ends chain for an organization becomes muddled.[18] However, it can be used to gain the advantages of two forms. In our example the strengths of the functional and divisional forms are matched. Several scholars favor this hybrid form in large organizations where the environment is very complex and technology is very sophisticated and variable.[7,24,27] We would add it may be more useful where combining two forms actually yields a reinforcing pattern. For instance, assume product, client, and territorial departmentation yield similar units. Perhaps all customers wanting a particular product are located in the same geographic area. If the organization faces a complex environment and must rely upon a very sophisticated and highly variable technology, then the matrix form is likely to be appropriate.

While the matrix structure does facilitate coordination, it's a very expensive way of horizontally linking the actions of various specialists.[25] Organizations are more likely to try cheaper means.

Pros and Cons of the Legal Entity Form. The chief advantages of departmentation by legal entity appear to be in the limitation of liability, a possible reduction of taxes (particularly for corporations), and the appearance of autonomy for various divisions. The legal entity form appears to favor systems survival and growth over technical concerns or flexibility. It can be the most inflexible form if carried deep within an organization.[12] With a legal entity form, it may be virtually impossible to alter programs, personnel, territories or even the specific environment of an organization.[28] The law determines what decisions will be made regarding domain questions. We could detail many of the problems of this form of specialization if carried down within an organization. But let's just say it has the least advantages and the greatest potential limitations.[3]

Methods of Coordinating Horizontal Specialization

As we've noted, it is virtually impossible to eliminate all interdependence across units in an organization. Regardless of the departmentation pattern selected, vertical linkages through a common boss will not always be sufficient to link highly interdependent units. A change in the pattern of departmentation is likely to just change the location of the problem. Thus, organizations use information systems, staff units, and other methods to provide necessary coordination across the system. Table 9-5 presents these mechanisms.[1]

As noted in the table, these methods of coordination can be done at the

Table 9-5 Mechanisms for Horizontal Coordination

	Individual	Group
	INFORMAL	
Impersonal	Values (e.g., professionalism)	Norms
Personal	Grapevine	Grapevine
	FORMAL	
Impersonal	Formal information systems Rules, policies, procedures, forms, schedules	Matrix structure
Personal	Gangplank	Committees Staff units

individual and/or group level. They may be informal or formal. That is, a formal system is one intentionally created by organizational designers. The informal system emerges. It is not officially established as part of the structure. These methods can also be personal or impersonal.[13] Personal methods require more direct face-to-face interpersonal interaction among people. Impersonal approaches do not require personal interaction; they are detached and programmed. Each approach is designed to link individuals and units across an organization that has been separated due to horizontal specialization.

Let's take a closer look at several of these. Every organization has a grapevine.[11] A lot of personal and organizational information is transmitted along this network.[7] It can be used by groups or individuals to link departments across an organization. While this is an inexpensive mechanism, it is less predictable than more formal methods of information exchange.[7] Individual values and group norms can provide ways to coordinate specialists in an organization.[10] For instance, a value of professionalism may help individuals in different parts of an organization interact in ways they would not in the absence of such a value.[9] Shared values or norms held by a group can act in the same way.[10] We will have more to say about these mechanisms in Chapter 12.

The organization often develops formal ways to integrate across departments.[14] Managers at or near the same organizational level must and do meet to solve common problems. Fayol suggested a gangplank effect here, when specialists in separate departments work together formally.[5] An example might be that a director of purchasing needs to periodically meet with the head of the production scheduling department. Both need each other's assistance to accomplish their work.

Direct exchanges among managers can take several different forms. Less sophisticated and less expensive approaches involve direct contact between unit heads.[16] If much of the interdependence is predictable, then a staff assistant may be assigned to act as a liaison.[19] But where several units must be coordinated, it's often necessary to establish temporary task forces.[4] For recurring problems an organization may need to set up a more permanent team (staff unit) to represent the interests of several units.[6] If none of these is sufficient, it may have need to implement a matrix structure complete with a full-time coordinator and staff.[17] The latter methods of direct exchange among managers are particularly expensive. These are group forms of coordination often calling for extensive meetings of several expensive executives.[15]

The staff units mentioned above may be helpful in developing the rules, policies, procedures, and forms that can provide coordination.[7]

Many organizations design information systems to connect highly interdependent units.* We can rate the sophistication of the information system on three criteria.[14] One, to what extent are there multiple linkages outside of the chain of command? Two, how many different forms are available? Some organizations may rely solely upon informal gatherings. Others may ask for written reports, group meetings, suggestion systems, newsletters, and the like. Three, in some organizations there is an attempt to keep all information current (on a real-time basis). In others, data may be weeks or months old. Finally, the matrix structure, as discussed earlier, can serve to coordinate teams of specialists from many units in an organization.[17]

Several analyses suggest that organizations attempt to use these formal coordinative mechanisms to link interdependent units that the pattern of departmentation has separated.[3,8] These are the horizontal counterparts of control systems.[19] Similar to those, they are often partial substitutes for one another. But there is one important difference. Control systems reinforce vertical means-ends chains. This adds to the legitimacy of those at the top who specify standards, measures, and rewards (punishments) for those below.[8] Coordinative mechanisms don't often have such clout. They rely mostly on the need to coordinate action across the system. Merely establishing an information system, for instance, rarely has the potential influence that control systems do.[14]

We expect that as an organization becomes more horizontally specialized it's more likely to develop formal coordination mechanisms. The logic is quite simple. The more units there are, the more likely that highly interdependent groups have been developed. Thus there is a need for more sophisticated

*We use the term information systems since we rely heavily on the work of Melcher.[14] Others combine what we have called control and information systems and call it the management information system, or MIS.

formal mechanisms.[2] However, this does not come cost free. Thompson argued that "rational" organizations will try to coordinate their operations as efficiently as possible.[20] We estimate that informal mechanisms are less expensive even though less predictable. And we think individual approaches are less expensive than group methods. But they may be less effective. Finally, we estimate that personal approaches are more costly than impersonal ones. These are tentative statements. We are not aware of any research that has attempted to measure the cost-benefit of various coordination mechanisms.

As you may already be thinking, larger organizations with sophisticated technologies are likely to have very severe coordination problems. For instance, one staff unit could be piled on top of another. If you are the head of one of these staff units, you might think it would be easier to coordinate if you had but a little bit of vertical authority.[19] It would be nice to be a pseudoline unit.[18] Then you could claim to be part of an organization's primary means-ends chain. As we have suggested, the placement of staff units is a critical question, since staff units will act as top-level managers when they can. If the staff units are concentrated at the institutional level, their activities often turn from coordination to control.[18] They attempt to act as a surrogate for top-level line managers.[18] When placed at the middle, however, it is difficult for staff units to claim this surrogate authority.[18] They must attempt to sell their wares.[16] They typically cannot require prior approval of decisions nor audit the procedures and outcomes of middle-level managers. The nature of these subsystems relationships is so important we'll take a detailed look at them in Chapter 11. For now it is important to recognize that placement in the hierarchy is an extremely important consideration.

Now let's turn our attention to diversity evident from this horizontal view before we look at the impact of contextual variables.

Diversity in Horizontal Specialization and Coordination

Within the managerial and technical levels of an organization, you may or may not find the same pattern of departmentation.[9] The larger the number of forms of departmentation used, the more diverse is the organization's horizontal specialization.[3] Organizations often appear to use a more diverse form of departmentation before moving to an entirely different dominant form of departmentation.[5] For example, functionally organized companies often form specialized units at the managerial and technical levels to serve specialized clients, products, and/or territories.[7] Some of these may be staff units attached to traditional line operations such as production or marketing. With growth, many of these organizations evolve into a divisionalized structure since it becomes cheaper and more effective in directing system activities.[1,11]

Diversity in the coordination used by an organization may go hand in hand with greater diversity in the pattern of horizontal specialization.[6] While almost all organizations rely upon informal mechanisms, there may be substantial differences in the formal mechanisms they employ across any one zone.[4] Some units may rely upon rules and policies while others may place more emphasis on committees and liaison units.[8] As the dominant pattern of coordination varies, the pattern of coordination across units is more diverse. Thus, within huge organizations it is not uncommon to find quite different dominant patterns of coordination in middle- and lower-level management.[2] Furthermore, it seems quite obvious that as the huge organization adopts more divergent technologies, customers, and suppliers, it is likely to increase both the degrees of diversity in horizontal specialization and coordination. So let us take a closer look at the association among contextual variables and the horizontal aspects of an organization's anatomy.

Contextual Variables and Horizontal Specialization

Recall that size, and to a lesser extent technology, are associated with vertical specialization and control. In a similar way, these contextual factors also press an organization to increase horizontal specialization and coordination.

Technological sophistication pressures an organization toward a more elaborate form of departmentation and a greater reliance on staff units to coordinate the activities of disparate units (greater diversity).[3] Technological variability pushes an organization toward a matrix structure.[2] The greater reciprocal interdependence forces it toward small work groups even though larger ones may be needed to successfully complete a project.[11,10] As a result, committees and verbal communications are used more extensively since they help coordinate the groups.[6] To a lesser extent size is also related to horizontal specialization and control.[1,7] Larger organizations tend to be more horizontally specialized (larger number of units).[4,9] And they have more staff units than smaller systems.[4,9] Furthermore, increasing technological variability makes standard rules and procedures less and less appropriate—more coordinative divisions are needed to maintain the integrity of the system.[5,12,8]

As for administrative philosophy, we think that those with a traditional orientation will use less horizontal specialization. They are more likely to prefer vertical control mechanisms. To the extent horizontal specialization is used, the emphasis will more likely be placed on formal and impersonal coordination mechanisms. Conversely, those with a moralistic philosophy will emphasize personal coordinative mechanisms, even though they may be more expensive. Finally, we think that technology will be a dominant factor influencing horizontal specialization in organizations where the primary administrative philosophy is individualistic.

TOWARD AN INTEGRATED VIEW OF ORGANIZATIONAL STRUCTURE: MECHANISTIC AND ORGANIC ORGANIZATIONS

We haven't identified all the various aspects of an organization's structure mentioned in the literature. There are probably as many dimensions of structure as designers of organizations. But enough is enough. What you need is a simpler version that can be integrated with environmental conditions and an organization's context.

Let us assume that an organization has balanced vertical specialization and control plus horizontal specialization and coordination. Also assume that control and information systems are consistent with one another, and it has struck a balance between the costs and benefits of coordination. Is the structure appropriate? Unfortunately it may not be.

Burns and Stalker and their followers suggest that organizations should match their structure to environmental conditions as well as contextual variables.[2,9,8] Chapter 10 will discuss the interplay of these variables and various aspects of organizational effectiveness and employee maintenance. But parts of the Burns and Stalker analysis are particularly useful in tying together the vertical and horizontal views of structure.

Burns and Stalker borrowed a page from Weber to simplify their analysis of organizations. They argue that some successful organizations tend to favor vertical specialization and control *or* horizontal specialization and coordination. When an organization stresses rules, policies, procedures, specifies the techniques for decision making, and develops an elaborate control system backed by a centralized staff, it can be called "mechanistic." In mechanistic organizations you expect that staff units will be placed toward the top of the system, and this placement reinforces a vertical emphasis. While a consistent pattern of departmentation is the functional form, it may not be the dominant pattern when an organization is huge. The divisional form may be employed below the chief executive office.[3]

Burns and Stalker called the opposite type "organic." Here the strategy is to increase horizontal specialization and coordination. While there may be numerous policies and procedures and an extensive information system, staff units are placed toward the middle of an organization. There are comparatively few rules. Consistent forms of departmentation are the divisional and the matrix.

To us, both of these provide consistent patterns that can be altered to fit pressures from contextual variables. Of course each of the two "ideal" patterns appears to have its own strengths and weaknesses. The mechanistic pattern appears more suited to low technological variability conditions, where organizations are most interested in efficiency.[9] Conversely, where there is high variability, and an organization is less sure of how to transform inputs to outputs, the organic form may be preferred.[13] However, either may yield high effectiveness if you adjust the amount of structural diversity.

The strength of the mechanistic organization lies in its concentration on consistency and problem solving to gain higher efficiency.[9] The problem, of course, is that some flexibility is lost in the concentration over control. Some of the flexibility may be regained by developing a more vertically diverse pattern of specialization and control. By selectively concentrating on one or a few areas of its domain, an organization places priorities and resources in those areas. Of course, if an organization decides to concentrate on the wrong aspect of its domain or overemphasizes one area, the effectiveness of its system could be severely damaged.

The strength of the organic organization is its flexibility, adaptability, and early recognition of external change.[2] Its weakness is its inability to quickly respond to the dictates of top management. In other words, the organic organization is likely to spot problems first and be the first to develop viable alternatives. But the mechanistic organization may wind up implementing a solution first even though it was late in spotting a problem and developing an alternative.

Just as the mechanistic organization can use diversity to gain flexibility, the organic organization often uses it to reassert some degree of control over operations.[5] Few organically structured organizations decentralize every decision.[6] For instance, you expect organic organizations to maintain a tight, centralized rein on part of one critical aspect of the domain. Those at the institutional level are apt to be very concerned with the degree of horizontal diversity. They often take an active hand in deciding where additional units will be developed.[6]

Burns and Stalker also suggested that the match between environmental complexity and structure could be particularly critical.[2] Lawrence and Lorsch followed their lead in an analysis of organizations operating in either comparatively simple or comparatively complex environments.[8] Lawrence and Lorsch's clinical analysis suggested, as did Burns and Stalker's, that as the environment became more complex, organic structure was superior. In the language of architecture, the anatomy of a system should be flexible enough to withstand substantial external variations and pressures. In somewhat less complex settings, particularly stable industries with comparatively simple technologies, organizations with a mechanistic structure were deemed more successful. Essentially, these systems were more efficient and did not have to develop coordinative mechanisms to buffer external changes. Lawrence and Lorsch were also careful to point out that success also depended on matching specialization and control-coordination. In their terms, differentiation and integration needed to be matched. In the large corporations they studied, high differentiation (specialization) and high integration (control-coordination) were needed for economic success.[8]

We should note that some scholars initially felt that to be successful, organizations should match structure and environment and match differentiation with integration.[8] More recent analyses by Child, Pennings, and Melcher, among others, suggest that matching structure and environment may not be sufficient to assure high effectiveness.[4,11,10,7] Other patterns may also be successful.[14] Thus, the simple contingency notion of matching environment and structure is being replaced with more complex and, we think, accurate descriptions.

ORGANIZATIONAL STRUCTURE—THE VIEW FROM THE BOTTOM

Our analysis has implicitly taken the perspective of top-level management. The majority of the discussion has been targeted toward organizational effectiveness with little concern for employee maintenance. But does the organization look the same from the bottom up? No! If you are an employee, is effectiveness likely to be more important than maintenance? We think not. Several scholars have asked employees and lower-level executives to describe the structure of organizations. And while they find employees describing organizations much the way managers do, lower-level members combine things a little differently.

First, employees do not see the subtle difference between vertical and horizontal specialization. Instead an overall specialization index appears to make more sense to lower-level managers and employees. Further, the degree of centralization appears to play a dominant role in describing the anatomy of an organization. Let's take a closer look at the centralization-decentralization question.

Centralization

We have discussed centralization in terms of how planning, implementation, and control procedures will be established and where the staff units will be placed. To some individuals, however, the degree of decentralization is a rough measure of an organization's interest in employee-maintenance issues.[18] For instance, if employees are considered dynamic, helpful, and generally capable, then decentralization should occur.[14]

We, like several others, make a distinction between the locus of decision making and control (often called locus of control) and participation.[5] Both of these have been described as decentralization. Locus of control refers to where, in the vertical hierarchy, most of the decisions are made.[20] Participation, however, refers to the extent to which subordinates are allowed to contribute to the choice-making process.[21] When viewing an organization as a nonmanagement employee, the locus of control and participation can be quite different.[11] For instance, assume your boss is empowered to make substantial choices in several aspects of the organization's domain. Your boss may or may not ask for your advice. Conversely, your boss's superior may be at the locus of control and may or may not ask for your advice (or your boss's advice, for that matter). Even if your advice were sought, existing procedures, policies, and rules might severely constrain the available alternatives. You could wind up having little if any impact on the choices made. A good example of the latter is often found in student government. The advice and counsel of student government officials may be sought, but these hardly make any difference to the outcome in most cases.

Thus, when asking employees to describe structure, centralization is often positively related with the use of written documents.[5] There is little evidence that the number of organizational levels or management descriptions are highly related to employee reports of locus of control.[26] While some indicate this is a difference between intended (formal) and actual (formal and informal) structure, you should recognize the following.[25] One, when combining employee reports of centralization, the analyst assumes that the organization has one technical core (or at least that all technical cores have virtually identical characteristics). Two, managers may or may not follow the pattern of delegation established by superiors. Even though a manager might be told to allow subordinate managers to choose among alternatives, the manager may not. There are several good reasons. Subordinate managers may be incompetent. Such instructions may not be appropriate (i.e., a misguided attempt at participation). Some managers may be unable to instruct subordinates in how choices may be made and/or the priority that should be given partially conflicting goals.

It is not unusual for top-level managers to think they are promoting decentralization when they aren't.[12] For instance, they may establish few levels of management and a large centralized staff, arguing that this is a decentralized form of administration.[13] If the staff acts as a surrogate for top brass, however, then the pattern facing middle- and lower-level managers is likely to appear quite centralized.[24] Who cares if headquarters line or staff personnel make choices or establish the techniques to be used—it is centralization in any event.

When asked to describe the structure of their organization, employees are likely to estimate the extent to which they think their bosses can act on their own.[7,9,22] A favorite item in assessing centralization-decentralization is to ask employees to estimate if their boss must clear a particular decision, or whether they can make it on their own.[16] Thus, the top-down, vertical, or horizontal view may or may not fit bottom-up employee descriptions of centralization-decentralization.[*,25]

Formalization and Standardization

There is another link between two other predominately mentioned "bottom up" structural characteristics and our presentation. Here, several people have identified the degree of formalization and standardization as important aspects of structure.[1,7,8,22,23] Formalization is often estimated by asking employees the extent to which rules, procedures, instructions, and communications are written and the extent to which jobs are explicitly defined, such as in a manual.[22,6,7,9,1] Formalization, then, appears to be a rough but combined measure of the sophistication of control and information systems plus coordination activities calling for simple rules, policies, and procedures. It harkens back to Weber's concern with the impersonality of organizations. Another popular bottom-up dimension is standardization. Standardization, following James and Jones, among others, is the degree to which there are standard operating procedures, and the degree of task specification.[10,22,7,1] This appears quite similar to our discussion of the use of managerial techniques. (These are often seen by employees as just standard operating procedures.) Thus, we expect that the more an organization relies upon specified decision techniques, the more likely subordinates will report high standardization.

We have taken particular care in separating vertical and horizontal specialization. Not all analyses are quite so elaborate. Often the two are combined into some measure of overall specialization.[3] That may be easier, but it fails to reveal the complexity of organization structure. Many appear unconcerned with how the organization specializes. As you have seen, it's a very critical decision in the design of organizations.

*See Sathe for a detailed discussion of this point.[25]

MEASUREMENT MODULE

Our discussion of organizational structure has included several different views such as the top-down and bottom-up approaches to specialization. Different views, obviously, often lead to different measurement approaches. To compound the problem we have mixed what traditional scholars call structure and process. That is, we have partially combined "what" and "how" questions. Combining aspects of structure and process provides a clearer picture of what happens in organizations. Unfortunately, measurement of some aspects of structure becomes more complex. Much like the analysis of social contribution, we think some clinical judgment may be needed in assessing the structure of organizations. Taking the top-down approach you will be making the judgments supplemented with information from an organization chart. Taking a bottom-up view there are several instruments that rely upon employee judgments. Let us take a look at each of these.

VERTICAL SPECIALIZATION AND CONTROL

Theoretically we are interested in assessing the extent to which planning, implementation, and control are specialized down through an organization. Yet to assess vertical specialization and control it is often helpful to combine indirect estimates based on the organization chart, with direct clinical assessments.[5,6]

The easiest estimate of vertical specialization is the number of organizational levels in the longest chain of command.[5] This provides a rough estimate of tall or flat structures. This assumes that tall organizations are more vertically specialized than flat ones.[6] Since there may be some differences across the institutional, administrative, and technical levels, you could make separate estimates for each.

Closely related to the number of levels is the so-called span of control concept.[3] This refers to the number of supervisors assigned to each manager. You may also calculate the ratio of managers to employees for an entire organization.[1] This ratio partially controls for size and thus allows you to more directly compare different-sized systems. Again you can think in terms of a tall or flat organization with a smaller span of control yielding a taller organization.

As we suggested earlier a simple numerical count does not always indicate the degree of vertical specialization and control.[4] Organizations also substitute managerial techniques and control systems for managers. Unfortunately, gaining information about managerial techniques and control systems can be difficult and time consuming.[2] You should also realize that if you ask managers whether they use advanced techniques, they are most likely to suggest they use the most advanced procedures available for their particular task. They are likely to see such questions as partial measures of their competency. Unfortunately, we cannot provide a magic wand to circumvent this problem. The best you may be able to do is derive a clinical estimate of the uses of various techniques such as MBO, PERT, PPBS, and the like. Several judgments by higher-level personnel, regarding those two or three levels below, may be particularly helpful if you can cover the major operations of the system.

Estimating the sophistication of an organization's control system appears a bit easier. Here you ask the extent to which standards are available, performance is measured and rewards are tied to individual action.[2] If there are no formal approaches to evaluating personnel or subunit performance, the control system is quite simple (several performance evaluation instruments are in the Measurement Module of Chapter 3). The control system becomes more elaborate as the following occurs to more individuals and units: (1) specific standards cover quality, quantity, and cost; (2) fixed and relatively short review periods are used; (3) specific instruments are used to measure quality, quantity, and cost; (4) salary differentials are related to differences in individual and/or unit performance.[2]

Diversity in Vertical Specialization and Control

Our discussion of diversity in the pattern of vertical specialization stressed two aspects. First, we found the difference in the use and sophistication of planning, implementation, and control in the institutional, administrative, and technical levels of an organization. Again we are forced to recommend a clinical estimate since we know of no good measures. The notion is simple. Merely evaluate the difference in the pattern by level. Actual measurement, we recognize, is extremely difficult. The best you might hope for is a consistent set of judgments from those who are familiar with the operations of the organization.

The second aspect of diversity also requires considerable judgment. Here we suggested that there may be differences across various aspects of the organization's domain. We suggest that differences by major organizational functions may be an indirect indicator. Unfortunately, this assumes a functionally organized system. Where other forms of departmentation dominate, you will, in all likelihood, be forced to make the final determination judgmentally. As before, you should use knowledgeable sources recognizing that their descriptions reflect both structural differences and differences in perception.

HORIZONTAL SPECIALIZATION AND COORDINATION

As with vertical specialization and control there are both indirect and clinical estimates that can be used to measure horizontal specialization and coordination. The most frequently used indicator of horizontal specialization is the number of different job titles.[3] However, Dewar and Hage suggest that this measure may be erroneous.[1] They argue that more title distinctions are made for lower-skilled positions than higher-skilled ones. Thus, they propose that the indirect measure should be the number of different occupational specialties. Occupational specialties come closer to estimating distinct and separate kinds of knowledge.

Dewar and Hage also note that the number of job titles, the number of departments, the level of training, and the extent of professional activity have been used to tap various portions of horizontal specialization.[1] We opt for the number of occupational specialties and the number of separate departmental units. However, these may not always be highly related. Only in large systems, where functional departmentation is used at the first level, might you expect a close correspondence between the number of occupations and the number of units. Furthermore, both of these indicators reflect the size of the organization and should be adjusted for the number of full-time employees.

More direct measures may be based on an assessment of an organization chart and observers' opinions.[5] A basic concept of an organization's structure is to describe its form of departmentation.[6] As we discussed, this conveys some of the advantages and disadvantages an organization is likely to encounter. About all we can add to our earlier description is that you can clinically categorize departmentation on the basis of how its tasks have been divided. Frequently, an organization chart provides the basic data for this.[6] Remember, the dominant form is that used at the level directly below the chief executive. This is your basic description. But also recall that many organizations use a number of combined forms.

Recall that Table 9-5 provided a variety of mechanisms used for coordination. The measurement of aspects for many of these is covered in later chapters. For example, mechanisms such as group norms and values are treated in Chapter 12. Instruments are available for detecting what these might be. But you must clinically interpret how these are used for coordination purposes. For instance, you may be able to detect that individuals across several units are homogeneous based on a measurement of their values or other characteristics. On this basis, you may be able to infer that an organization *can* rely on them for coordination of the units of which they are members. Similarly, the "gangplank" coordination among managers may depend on the degree of interdependence seen to exist among them or their units.[2] Measures are provided in Chapters 11 and 13 that establish predispositions of managerial behavior toward coordination with other units. Again, you will have to clinically evaluate the extent to which managers are actually used to provide these linking functions.

You can tell whether a matrix structure is being used by determining whether there are teams of specialists from several units in the organization working together. You should also be able to detect whether committees are frequently used or if staff units are established for the purpose of aiding coordination among units.

Finally, the extent to which rules, policies, and procedures exist can be readily measured. Reference to organization documents should reveal whether procedures manuals, job descriptions, forms, rules, written reports, and the like are in existence and how detailed they are. For example, are written reports required? Are copies of minutes of meetings required to be distributed? How extensively? How many forms are in use, and so on. However, you might want to determine if these are used or ignored. The existence and greater detail of large numbers of documents are likely to connote greater formal coordination and specialization. But if unused, you may get a different picture of the situation. The informal mechanisms may, in fact, be those relied upon.

Finally, you can estimate whether the information system is extensive and used.[4] For example, is it sophisticated? Are there specialized personnel operating it? Is it computerized? How many managers are tied into the system? Are they required to provide data and receive reports? How extensive and detailed are the reports?

Diversity of Horizontal Specialization and Coordination

As before, the greater the different number of forms of departmentation used by an organization, the greater the diversity of horizontal specialization. Similarly, as different patterns of coordination are used, diversity increases. An organization could rely entirely on managers for coordination. This would imply very low (or no) diversity. If it also has extensive rules, formal information systems, formal committees, and a matrix structure, greater diversity results. Recall that these are partially functional substitutes. But they are also complementary. They are not mutually exclusive.

Finally, we think an indirect measure of diversity might be made by a count of the number of staff units at each organization level. Further, you can measure the number of units concentrated on one aspect of the domain of an organization. As these increase, diversity goes up.

BOTTOM-UP MEASURES

The following exhibits represent standardized instruments to measure various aspects of structure. You will note some similarity to the suggestions made above. These have been adapted from several sources. Other references are provided at the end of the chapter if you wish to see how other researchers have measured structure.* Again, the emphasis has been to ask lower-level participants to describe these various dimensions.

Formalization

Exhibit 9-6 taps the extent to which a variety of documents are available. The more of these there are, the more formal the organization.[13,15] This is quite similar to the use of formal policies, rules, and procedures used for coordination.

Standardization

Exhibit 9-7 is quite similar. It asks the respondent to indicate the extent to which standard operating procedures are used.[5,18] Higher scores reflect more reliance on these for control and coordination.

Centralization

Exhibit 9-8 indicates the degree of centralization perceived in the organization.[3,13] Higher scores indicate greater decentralization (assuming the respondent is at a lower level in the hierarchy).

*See references 1, 2, 4, 6–12, 14, and 16.

Exhibit 9-6   A Formalization Scale

The questions below consider whether documents are available irrespective of whether they are actually used. A document is at a minimum a single piece of paper with printed, typed, or otherwise reproduced content—not handwritten.

1. Who is given a copy of the organization chart? (Check *one* of the alternatives below.)
   a. _____ No one.
   b. _____ Head of organizational unit only.
   c. _____ Head of organizational unit plus one other supervisory employee.
   d. _____ Head of organizational unit plus most or all other supervisors.
   e. _____ All employees in organizational unit.

2. What percentage of nonsupervisory employees are given written operating instructions? (Check one.)
   a. _____ 0 to 20%
   b. _____ 21 to 40%
   c. _____ 41 to 60%
   d. _____ 61 to 80%
   e. _____ 81 to 100%

3. Are written terms of reference or job descriptions given to the following? (Check your answer.)
   a. Head of organization unit: yes _____ no _____
   b. Supervisory employees: yes _____ no _____
   c. Nonsupervisory employees: yes _____ no _____

4. Is a manual of rules and regulations available? (Check one.)

_____ yes

_____ no

5. Is a written statement of policies available? (Check one.)

_____ yes

_____ no

6. Is a written work flow schedule available? (Check one.)

_____ yes

_____ no

7. What percent of employees in your organizational unit turn in a written report on a regular basis? (Check your answer.)

a. _____ 0 to 20%

b. _____ 21 to 40%

c. _____ 41 to 60%

d. _____ 61 to 80%

e. _____ 81 to 100%

Scoring

For items 1, 2, and 5, a = 1, b = 2, c = 3, d = 4, e = 5. For all other items a yes = 2 and a no = 1. The sum of the item scores is the degree of formalization.

Source: Sathe, V. J. "Structural Adaptation to Environment: Study of Insurance Company Departments and Branch Banks" (unpublished dissertation, The Ohio State University, Columbus, Ohio, 1974). Based on Pugh, D. N., Hickson, D. J., Hinings, C. R., and Turner, C. "Dimensions of Organizational Structure," *Administrative Science Quarterly,* 13 (1968), 65–105. Reprinted by permission of Sathe.

Exhibit 9-7   A Standardization Scale

1. How many written rules and procedures exist for doing your major tasks. (Check one.)
   a. _____ Very few
   b. _____ Small number
   c. _____ A moderate number
   d. _____ A large number
   e. _____ A great number

2. How precisely do these rules and procedures specify how your major tasks are done? (Check one.)
   a. _____ Very general
   b. _____ Mostly general
   c. _____ Somewhat specific
   d. _____ Quite specific
   e. _____ Very specific

3. To what extent did you follow standard procedures or practices to do your major tasks in the last three months? (Check one.)
   a. _____ To no extent.
   b. _____ Little extent
   c. _____ Some extent
   d. _____ Great extent
   e. _____ Very great extent

4. When considering the various situations that arise in performing your work, what percent of the time do you have written or unwritten procedures for dealing with them? (Check one.)
   a. _____ 0 to 20%
   b. _____ 21 to 40%
   c. _____ 41 to 60%
   d. _____ 61 to 80%
   e. _____ 81 to 100%

Scoring

For all items a = 1, b = 2, c = 3, d = 4, e = 5. The sum of the item scores is the degree of standardization.

Source: Adapted by Hunt, J. G., and Osborn, R. N. *A Multiple Influence Model of Leadership* (proposal funded by the U.S. Army Research Institute for the Behavioral and Social Sciences, May 1978). Based on work by Van de Ven, A. H., and Ferry, D. L. *Measuring and Assessing Organizations* (New York: Wiley-Interscience, 1979). By permission of Van de Ven.

Exhibit 9-8   A Centralization-Decentralization Scale

	None	Little	Some	Great	Very Great
1. Listed below are some common decisions and actions concerning the work of your work unit. How much influence does the typical supervisor at your organizational level have over each. (Circle answer at right.)					
a. Establishing a budget for the unit	A	B	C	D	E
b. Hiring and firing personnel	A	B	C	D	E
c. Promoting and demoting personnel	A	B	C	D	E
d. Establishing a new project or program	A	B	C	D	E
e. Setting work quotas	A	B	C	D	E
f. Establishing rules and procedures	A	B	C	D	E
g. Determining how work exceptions are to be handled	A	B	C	D	E
h. Purchase of supplies and equipment	A	B	C	D	E
	0–20%	21–40%	41–60%	61–80%	81–100%
2. Approximately what percent of the budget for your unit is directly under your control?	A	B	C	D	E
3. Approximately what percent of your budget could you cut without specific approval by a higher-up (e.g., a cut which would mean firing an employee)?	A	B	C	D	E
4. Approximately what percent of the merit raises given to subordinates are under your control?	A	B	C	D	E

5. Where you do not have the formal authority to make a decision, what percent of the time is your immediate superior authorized to make decisions (rather than being required to refer them to a higher level)?

                   A   B   C   D   E

6. If you were to describe your part of the organization to an outsider would you call it (check one):
   A. _____ Very centralized
   B. _____ Somewhat centralized
   C. _____ About as centralized as decentralized
   D. _____ Somewhat decentralized
   E. _____ Very decentralized

Scoring

For all items A = 1, B = 2, C = 3, D = 4, E= 5. The larger the sum of the item scores, the greater the decentralization at a particular organizational level.

Source: Ford, J. D. "An Empirical Investigation of the Relationship of Size, Technology, Workflow Interdependence, and Perceived Environmental Uncertainty to Selected Dimensions of Subunit Structure" (unpublished dissertation, The Ohio State University, Columbus, Ohio, 1975). Based on work by Sathe, V. J., "Structural Adaptation to Environment: Study of Insurance Company Departments and Branch Banks" (unpublished dissertation, The Ohio State University, Columbus, Ohio, 1974). Based on Pugh, D. N., et al., "Dimensions of Organizational Structure," *Administrative Science Quarterly,* 13 (1968), 65–105. Reprinted by permission of Ford.

Suggested Use of Bottom-up Measures

It is not unusual to average the superiors' score with the average of subordinate responses when using employee perceptions of structure.[17] This weights the superior and the total of the subordinates equally. The weighting procedure is arbitrary even though it attempts to strike a balance between perceptions of employee and superior. Van de Ven recommends averaging when attempting to describe subsystems.[17]

The weighting problem partially centers on the consistency of descriptions. If subordinates and managers always saw the same structural characteristics, there would be no problem. However, assume that the structure is diverse. Then you would expect those under one manager to see the same structure.[15] But you would expect different perceptions across groups. We estimate that diversity is partially reflected in the diversity of average group scores across any given level of an organization. Furthermore, we expect different perceptions by those in the institutional, administrative, and technical levels. Part of the difference may be due to perceptual bias and part due to inadequate measurement. However, considerable differences are expected because the degree of specialization, formalization, and centralization is probably different by level.

REFERENCES

I. The Weberian View of Structure— The Concept of Bureaucracy

[1] Bennis, W. *Changing Organizations.* New York: McGraw-Hill, 1966.

[2] Bennis, W. "Organizational Developments and the Fate of Bureaucracy," *Industrial Management Review,* 7 (1966), 41–55.

[3] Bennis, W. "A Funny Thing Happened on the Way to the Future," *American Psychologist,* 27, 7 (1970), 595–608.

[4] Glueck, W. *Management.* Hinsdale, Ill.: Dryden, 1977.

[5] Gouldner, A. *Patterns of Industrial Bureaucracy.* New York: The Free Press, 1954.

[6] Hall, R. *Organizations, Structure and Process.* Englewood Cliffs, N.J.: Prentice-Hall, 1977.

[7] Jackson, J., and Morgan, C., *Organization Theory: A Macro Approach for Management.* Englewood Cliffs, N.J.: Prentice-Hall, 1978.

[8] Katz, D., and Kahn, R., *The Social Psychology of Organizations.* New York: Wiley, 1978.

[9] Likert, R. *The Human Organization.* New York: McGraw-Hill, 1967.

[10] Melcher, A. *Structure and Process of Organizations—A Systems Approach.* Englewood Cliffs, N.J.: Prentice-Hall, 1976.

[11] Perrow, C. "The Short and Glorious History of Organizational Theory," *Organizational Dynamics,* 2 (1973), 2–16.

[12] Selznick, P. *TVA and the Grass Roots.* Berkeley: University of California Press, 1949.

[13] Scott, W. G., and Mitchell, T. R. *Organization Theory: A Structural and Behavioral Analysis.* Homewood, Ill.: Irwin, 1972,

[14] Weber, M. *The Theory of Social and Economic Organization.* Translated by A. M. Henderson and H. T. Parsons. New York: The Free Press, 1947.

[15] Weber, M. *Max Weber: Essays in Sociology.* Translated and edited by H. H. Gerth and C. W. Mills. New York: Oxford University Press, 1958.

[16] Wieland, G., and Ullrich, R. *Orga-*

nizations: Behavior Design and Change. Homewood, Ill.: Irwin, 1976.

II. Some Basic Structural Considerations

[1]Chandler, A. *Strategy and Structure*. Cambridge, Mass.: MIT Press, 1962.

[2]Chandler, A. *The Visible Hand: The Managerial Revolution in American Business*. Cambridge, Mass.: Belknap Press, 1977.

[3]Child, J. "Organizational Structure, Environment and Performance: The Role of Strategic Choice," *Sociology*, 6 (1972), 1–21.

[4]Etzioni A. *A Comparative Analysis of Complex Organizations*. New York: The Free Press, 1975.

[5]Glueck, 1977.

[6]Hall, 1977.

[7]James, L., and Jones, A. *An Organizational Model: Components and Measurement*. Paper presented at a symposium on, "Men in Social Systems: Results of a Three-year Multiorganization Study," American Psychological Association, New Orleans, 1974.

[8]Katz and Kahn, 1978.

[9]Koontz, H., and O'Donnell, C. *Principles of Management: An Analysis of Managerial Functions*. New York: McGraw-Hill, 1976.

[10]Lawrence and Lorsch, 1965.

[11]Litterer, J. *The Analysis of Organizations*. New York: Wiley, 1973.

[12]Melcher, 1976.

[13]Meyer, M. W. "Size and the Structure of Organizations: A Causal Analysis," *American Sociological Review*, 37 (1972), 434–441.

[14]Parsons, H. T. *Structure and Process in Modern Societies*. New York: The Free Press, 1960.

[15]Paulson, S. "Causal Analysis of Interorganizational Relations: An Axiomatic Theory Revised," *Administrative Science Quarterly*, 19 (1974), 319–337.

[16]Pfeffer, J. *Organizational Design*. Arlington Heights, Ill.: AHM Publishing, 1978.

[17]Reimann, B. "On the Dimensions of Bureaucratic Structure: An Empirical Reappraisal," *Administrative Science Quarterly*, 18 (1973), 462–476.

[18]Scott, W. "Organizational Structure," *Annual Review of Sociology*, 1 (1975), 1–20.

[19]Tannenbaum, A. S. *Hierarchy in Organizations*. San Francisco, Calif.: Jossey-Bass, 1974.

[20]Thompson, J. *Organizations in Action*. New York: McGraw-Hill, 1967.

[21]Weber, R. *Management: Basic Elements of Managing Organizations*. Homewood, Ill.: Irwin, 1975.

III. Vertical Specialization and Control (Top-down View)

A. Methods of Planning, Implementation, and Control

[1]Bishop, R. "The Relationship Between Objective Criteria and Subjective Judgment in Performance Appraisal," *Academy of Management Journal*, 17 (1974), 558–563.

[2]Burack, E. *Strategies for Manpower Planning and Programming*. Morristown, N.J.: General Learning, 1972.

[3]Buffa, E. *Operations Management: The Management of Productive Systems*. New York: Wiley, 1976.

[4]Cross, H. "New Directions in Corporate Planning." Address to Operations Research Society of America, Milwaukee, Wis., 1973.

[5]Cummings, L. L. and Schwab, D. P. *Performance in Organizations: Determinants and Appraisal.* Glenview, Ill.: Scott, Foresman, 1973.

[6]Cyert, R., and March, J. *A Behavioral Theory of the Firm.* Englewood Cliffs, N.J.: Prentice-Hall, 1963.

[7]Drucker, P. *Management.* New York: Harper & Row, 1974.

[8]Glueck, W. F. *Business Policy.* New York: McGraw-Hill, 1976.

[9]Glueck, 1977.

[10]Haas, L., and Collen, L. "Administrative Practices in University Departments," *Administrative Science Quarterly,* 8, 2 (1963), 44–60.

[11]Henry, H. *Long Range Planning Practices in 47 Industrial Companies.* Englewood Cliffs, N.J.: Prentice-Hall, 1967.

[12]Hodgkinson, H. L. "Assessment and Reward Systems," *Current Issues in Higher Education,* 26 (1971), 47–54.

[13]Jacques, E. *Equitable Payment.* New York: Wiley, 1963.

[14]Katz and Kahn, 1978.

[15]Koontz and O'Donnell, 1976.

[16]Lawler, E., and Rhode, J. *Information and Control in Organizations.* Santa Monica, Calif.: Goodyear, 1976.

[17]Luthans, F. *The Faculty Promotion Process.* Iowa City: The University of Iowa, Bureau of Business and Economic Research, 1967.

[18]Mansfield, R. "Bureaucracy and Centralization: An Examination of Organizational Structure," *Administrative Science Quarterly,* 18 (1973), 477–488.

[19]Melcher, 1976.

[20]Odiorne, G. *Management by Objectives.* New York: Pitman, 1965.

[21]Ouchi, W. G., and Maguire, M. A. "Organizational Control: Two Functions," *Administrative Science Quarterly,* 20 (1975), 559–569.

[22]Reimann, 1973.

[23]Ringbakk, K. A. "Organized Planning in Major U.S. Companies," *Long Range Planning,* 2 (1969), 25–32.

[24]Schick, A. "A Death in the Bureaucracy: The Demise of Federal PPB," *Public Administration Review,* 22 (1973), 142–158.

[25]Sutherland, J. *Administrative Decision-Making: Extending the Bounds of Ratonality.* New York: Van Nostrand Reinhold, 1977.

B. Diversity in the Pattern of Vertical Specialization and Control

[1]Ashby, W. R. *Design for a Brain.* New York: Wiley, 1952.

[2]Blau, P. M., and Schoenherr, R. A. *The Structure of Organizations.* New York: Basic Books, 1971.

[3]Child, J. "Organizational Structure, Environment and Performance: The Role of Strategic Choice," *Sociology,* 6 (1972), 1–21.

[4]Child, J. "Predicting and Understanding Organizational Structure," *Administrative Science Quarterly,* 18 (1973), 168–185.

[5]Donaldson, L., Child, J., and Aldrich, H. "The Aston Findings on Centralization: Further Discussion," *Administrative Science Quarterly,* 20 (1975), 453–459.

[6]Ford, J., and Slocum, J. "Size, Technology, Environment and the Structure of Organizations." Working paper, The Ohio State University, 1976.

[7]Hage, J., and Aiken, M. "Routine Technology, Social Structure and Organizational Goals," *Adminis-*

trative *Science Quarterly,* 14 (1969), 366–376.

[8]Hall, 1978.

[9]Hall, R. H. *Occupations and the Social Structure.* Englewood Cliffs, N.J.: Prentice-Hall, 1975.

[10]Hendershot, G., and James, T. "Size and Growth as Determinants of Administrative Production Ratios in Organizations," *American Sociological Review,* 37 (1972), 149–153.

[11]Hrebiniak, L. "Job Technology, Supervision and Work-Group Structure," *Administrative Science Quarterly,* 19 (1974), 395–410.

[12]Jackson and Morgan, 1978.

[13]James, L., and Jones, A. *An Organizational Model: Components and Measurement.* Paper presented at symposium on "Men in Social Systems: Results of a Three-year Multiorganization Study," American Psychological Association, New Orleans, 1974.

[14]Katz and Kahn, 1978.

[15]Khandwalla, P. *The Design of Organizations.* New York: Harcourt Brace Jovanovich, 1977.

[16]Khandwalla, P. "Mass Output Orientation of Operations, Technology and Organizational Structure," *Administrative Science Quarterly,* 19 (1974), 74–97

[17]Likert, 1964.

[18]Melcher, 1976.

[19]Osborn, R., Jauch, L., Martin, T., and Glueck, W. "CEO Succession, Performance and Environmental Conditions." Working paper, Department of Administrative Sciences, Southern Illinois University at Carbondale, 1978.

[20]Pugh, D. S., Hickson, D. J., Hinings, C. R., and Turner, C. "Dimensions of Organizational Structure," *Administrative Science Quarterly,* 13 (1968), 65–105.

[21]Reimann, 1973.

[22]Ritti, R., and Funkhouser, G. *The Ropes to Skip and the Ropes to Know.* Columbus, Ohio: Grid, 1977.

[23]Sathe, V. "Measures of Organizational Structure: A Conceptual Distinction between Two Major Approaches." Paper presented at the Academy of Management, Thirty-Fifth Annual Meeting, 1975.

[24]Sloan, A. P. *My Years with General Motors.* New York: Sidgwick and Jackson, 1965.

[25]Wieland and Ullrich, 1976.

C. Contextual Factors and Vertical Specialization and Control

[1]Blau, P. M., and Schoenherr, R. A. *The Structure of Organizations.* New York: Basic Books, 1971.

[2]Buchele, R. *The Management of Business and Public Organization.* New York: McGraw-Hill, 1977.

[3]Child, 1972.

[4]Child, 1973.

[5]Dewar, R., and Hage, J. "Size, Technology, Complexity, and Structural Differentiation: Towards a Theoretical Synthesis," *Administrative Science Quarterly,* 23 (1978), 111–136.

[6]Edstrom, A., and Galbraith, J. "Transfer of Managers as a Coordination and Control Strategy in Multinational Organizations," *Administrative Science Quarterly,* 22 (1977), 248–263.

[7]Ford and Slocum, 1976.

[8]Hage and Dewar, 1973.

[9]Hall, 1975.

[10]Hall, 1977.

[11]Hellriegel, D., and Slocum, J., Jr. "Organizational Climate: Meas-

ures, Research and Contingencies," *Academy of Management Journal,* 17 (1974), 255–280.

[12]Hendershot and James, 1972.

[13]Hrebiniak, 1974.

[14]Khandwalla, 1974.

[15]Khandwalla, 1977.

[16]Likert, 1967.

[17]Likert, R., and Likert, J. *New Ways of Managing Conflict.* New York: McGraw-Hill, 1976.

[18]Luthans, F. *Organizational Behavior.* New York: McGraw-Hill, 1977.

[19]Melcher, 1976.

[20]Ouchi, W. G. "The Relationship between Organizational Structure and Organizational Control," *Administrative Science Quarterly,* 22 (1977), 95–113.

[21]Ouchi and Maguire, 1975.

[22]Perrow, C. "A Framework for the Comparative Analysis of Organizations," *American Sociological Review,* 32 (1967), 194–208.

[23]Poland, O. F. "Program Evaluation and Administrative Theory," *Public Administration Review,* 14 (1974), 333–338.

[24]Sathe, 1975.

[25]Viola, R. *Organizations in a Changing Society: Administration and Human Values.* Philadelphia: Saunders, 1977.

[26]Wieland and Ullrich, 1976.

IV. Horizontal Specialization and Coordination

A. Forms of Departmentation

[1]Berge, N. "What's Different about Conglomerate Management?" *Harvard Business Review,* 47 (1969), 110–118.

[2]Blau, P. "A Formal Theory of Differentiation in Organizations," *American Sociological Review,* 35 (1970), 201–218.

[3]Blau, P. M. *The Organization of Academic Work.* New York: Wiley, 1973.

[4]Buchele, 1977.

[5]Child, 1972.

[6]Child, J. "Parkinson's Progress: Accounting for the Number of Specialists in Organizations," *Administrative Science Quarterly,* 19 (1973), 328–348.

[7]Davis, S., Lawrence, P., Kolodny, H., and Beer, M. *Matrix.* Reading, Mass.: Addison-Wesley, 1977.

[8]Duncan, W. J. *Essentials of Management.* Hinsdale, Ill.: Dryden Press, 1978.

[9]Drucker, P. M. *The Practice of Management.* New York: Harper & Row, 1954.

[10]Evan, W. M. *Organization Theory: Structures, Systems and Environment.* New York: Wiley, 1976.

[11]Galbraith, J. *Designing Complex Organizations.* Boston: Addison-Wesley, 1973.

[12]Glueck, 1977.

[13]Hrebinak, L. G. *Complex Organizations.* New York: West, 1978.

[14]Jackson and Morgan, 1978.

[15]Koontz and O'Donnell, 1976.

[16]Lawrence and Lorsch, 1965.

[17]Litterer, J. *The Analysis of Organizations.* New York: Wiley, 1973.

[18]Melcher, 1976

[19]Payne, L., and Mansfield, R. "Organizational Structure, Organizational Control, Hierarchical Position and Perceptions of Organizational Climate," *Administrative Science Quarterly,* 18 (1973), 515–526.

[20]Pfeffer, J., and Salancik, G. *The External Control of Organizations: A Resource Dependence Perspective.* New York: Harper & Row, 1978.

[21]Reimann, B. "Dimensions of Struc-

ture in Effective Organizations," *Academy of Management Journal,* 17 (1974), 693–708.

[22]Sayles, L. "Matrix Management: The Structure with a Future," *Organizational Dynamics,* 5 (1976) 2–17.

[23]Sayles, L., and Chandler, M. *Managing Large Systems: Organizations for the Future.* New York: Harper & Row, 1971.

[24]Sloan, 1965.

[25]Sutherland, 1977.

[26]Thompson, 1967.

[27]Walker, A. H., and Lorsch, J. "Organizational Choice: Product or Function," *Harvard Business Review,* 46 (1968), 129–138.

[28]Weick, K. E. "Educational Organizations as Loosely Coupled Systems," *Administrative Science Quarterly,* 21 (1976), 1–19.

B. Selecting the Best Pattern of Departmentation

[1]Aldrich, H., and Hecker, D. "Boundary Spanning Roles and Organization Structure," *Academy of Management Review,* 2 (1977), 211–230.

[2]Blau, 1970.

[3]Buchele, R. *The Management of Business and Public Organizations.* New York: McGraw-Hill, 1977.

[4]Burns, T., and Stalker, G. M. *The Management of Innovation.* London: Tavistock, 1961.

[5]Cummings, T., and Berger, C. "Organization Structure: How Does It Influence Attitudes and Performance?" *Organizational Dynamics,* (Autumn 1976), 34–49.

[6]Cummings and Schwab, 1973.

[7]Davis et al., 1977.

[8]Duncan, 1978.

[9]Drucker, P. *Management: Tasks, Responsibilities, Practices.* New York: Harper & Row, 1974.

[10]Galbraith, 1973.

[11]Glueck, 1977.

[12]Grafton, C. "The Creation of Federal Agencies," *Administration and Society,* 7 (1975), 328–365.

[13]Hrebiniak, 1978.

[14]Jackson and Morgan, 1978.

[15]Keller, R., and Holland, W. "Boundary-Spanning Roles in a Research and Development Organization," *Academy of Management Journal,* 18 (1975), 388–393.

[16]Koontz and O'Donnell, 1976.

[17]Lawrence and Lorsch, 1965.

[18]Litterer, 1973.

[19]Phelps, T., and Azumi, K. "Determinants of Administrative Control: A Test of Theory in Japanese Factories," *American Sociological Review,* 41 (1967), 80–94.

[20]Pitts, R. "Diversification Strategies and Organizational Policies of Large Diversified Firms," *Journal of Economics and Business,* 28 (1976), 181–188.

[21]Price, J. "The Impact of Departmentalization on Interoccupational Cooperation," *Human Organization,* 27 (1968), 362–367.

[22]Reimann, B., and Negandhi, A. "Strategies of Administrative Control and Organizational Effectiveness," *Human Relations,* 28 (1975), 475–486.

[23]Sayles, 1976.

[24]Sayles and Chandler, 1971.

[25]Thompson, 1967.

[26]Walker and Lorsch, 1968.

[27]Weick, 1976.

[28]Wildavsky, A. *The Politics of the Budgetary Process.* Boston: Little, Brown, 1964.

C. Methods of Coordinating Horizontal Specialization

[1]Allen, T. J. *Managing the Flow of Technology.* Cambridge, Mass.: M.I.T. Press, 1977.

[2]Blau and Schoenherr, 1971.

[3]Connelly, T. "Information Processing and Decision Making in Organizations." In B. Staw, and G. Salancik. *New Directions in Organizational Behavior.* Chicago: St. Clair Press, 1977.

[4]Davis et al., 1977.

[5]Fayol, H. *General and Industrial Administration.* New York: Pittman, 1949.

[6]Galbraith, 1973.

[7]Glueck, 1977.

[8]Hage, J., Aiken, M., and Manett, P. "Organization Structure and Communications," *American Sociological Review,* 36 (1971), 860–871.

[9]Hall, 1975.

[10]Hare, A., Borgatta, E., and Bales, R. *Small Groups.* New York: Knopf, 1966.

[11]Knipper, J. "Grapevine Communication: Management Employees," *Journal of Business Research,* 2 (1974), 42–58.

[12]Lucus, H. *Information Systems Concepts for Management.* New York: McGraw-Hill, 1978.

[13]McMahon, J. T. "Participative and Power Equalized Organizational Systems: An Empirical Investigation and Theoretical Integration," *Human Relations,* 29 (1976), 203–214.

[14]Melcher, 1976.

[15]Melcher, A., and Beller, R. "Toward a Theory of Organization Communication: Consideration in Channel Solution," *Academy of Management Journal,* 10 (1967), 39–52.

[16]Sayles, L. *Managerial Behavior: Administration in Complex Organizations.* New York: McGraw-Hill, 1964.

[17]Sayles, 1976.

[18]Sayles, L. *Leadership.* New York: McGraw-Hill, In press.

[19]Schwartz, D., and Jacobson, E. "Organizational Communication Network Analysis: The Liaison Role," *Organizational Behavior and Human Performance,* 18 (1977), 158–174.

[20]Thompson, 1967.

D. Diversity in Horizontal Specialization and Coordination

[1]Chandler, 1976.

[2]Drucker, 1974.

[3]Ford and Slocum, 1976.

[4]Gouldner, A. W. *Patterns of Industrial Bureaucracy.* Glencoe, Ill.: The Free Press, 1954.

[5]Glueck, 1977.

[6]Katz and Kahn, 1978.

[7]Koontz and O'Donnell, 1976.

[8]Perrow, C. *Complex Organizations; A Critical Essay.* Glenview, Ill.: Scott, Foresman, 1972.

[9]Scott, 1975.

[10]Van de Ven, A. "A Framework for Organizational Assessment," *Academy of Management Review,* 2 (1976), 64–78.

[11]Walker and Lorsch, 1968.

E. Contextual Variables and Horizontal Specialization

[1]Blau and Schoenherr, 1974.

[2]Davis et al., 1977.

[3]Dewar and Hage, 1978.

[4]Ford and Slocum, 1976.

[5]Hage and Aiken, 1969.

[6]Heydebrand, W. V. (ed). *Compara-*

tive Organizations. Englewood Cliffs, N.J.: Prentice-Hall, 1973.

[7]Jackson and Morgan, 1978.

[8]Lawrence and Lorsch, 1965.

[9]Scott, 1975.

[10]Thompson, 1967.

[11]Woodward, 1965.

[12]Van de Ven, 1976.

V. Toward an Integrated View of Organizational Structure: Mechanistic and Organic Organizations

[1]Aiken, M., and Hage, J. "The Organic Organization and Innovation," *Sociology,* 5 (1971), 63–82.

[2]Burns and Stalker, 1962.

[3]Chandler, A. D., Jr. *Strategy and Structure.* Cambridge, Mass.: M.I.T. Press, 1962.

[4]Child, 1972.

[5]Child, J. "Managerial and Organizational Factors Associated with Company Performance," *Journal of Management Studies,* 11 (1974), 175–189 and 12 (1975), 12–27.

[6]Drucker, 1974.

[7]Jelinek, M. "Technology, Organizations and Contingency," *Academy of Managerial Review,* 2 (1977), 11–26.

[8]Lawrence and Lorsch, 1965.

[9]Litterer, 1973.

[10]Melcher, 1967.

[11]Pennings, J. "The Relevance of the Structural-Contingency Model for Organizational Effectiveness," *Administrative Science Quarterly,* 20 (1975), 393–410

[12]Reimann, B. C. "Dimensions of Structure in Effective Organizations: Some Empirical Evidence," *Academy of Management Journal,* 17 (1974), 693–708.

[13]Reimann, B., and Negandhi, A. "Strategies of Administrative Control and Organizational Effectiveness," *Human Relations,* 28 (1975), 475–486.

[14]Van de Ven, 1976.

VI. Organizational Structure—The View from the Bottom

[1]Child, 1972.

[2]Child, 1973.

[3]Ford and Slocum, 1977.

[4]Hage and Aiken, 1969.

[5]Hall, 1977.

[6]Hickson et al., 1969.

[7]Hinings, C. R., and Lee, G. L. "Dimensions of Organization Structure and Their Context: À Replication," *Sociology,* 5 (1971), 83–93.

[8]Inkson, J., Pugh, D. S., and Hickson, D. J. "Organizational Context and Structure: An Abbreviated Replication," *Administrative Science Quarterly,* 15 (1970), 318–329.

[9]Inkson, J., Schwitter, J., Pheysey, D., and Hickson, D. J. "A Comparison of Organizational Structure and Managerial Roles." *Journal of Management Studies,* 7 (1970), 347–363.

[10]James and Jones, 1974.

[11]Lammers, C. "Self-Management and Participation: Two Concepts of Democratization in Organizations," *Organization and Administrative Sciences,* 5, 4 (1975), 35–53.

[12]Litterer, 1973.

[13]Lorsch, J., and Morse, J. *Organizations and Their Members.* New York: Harper & Row, 1974.

[14]McGregor, D. *The Human Side of Enterprise.* New York: McGraw-Hill, 1960.

[15]McMahon, 1976.

[16]Melcher, 1976.

[17]Pennings, J. "The Relevance of the Structural-Contingency Model for Organizational Effectiveness," *Administrative Science Quarterly,* 20 (1975), 393–410.

[18]Perrow, L. "The Short and Glorious History of Organizational Theory," *Organizational Dynamics,* 2 (1973), 2–16.

[19]Prien, E. P., and Ronan, W. W. "An Analysis of Organizational Characteristics," *Organizational Behavior and Human Performance,* 6 (1971), 215–234.

[20]Price, J. *Handbook of Organizational Measurement.* Lexington, Mass.: Heath, 1972.

[21]Pierce, J., and Delbecq, A. "Organizational Structure, Individual Attitudes and Innovation," *Academy of Management Review,* 2 (1977), 27–37.

[22]Pugh et al., 1968.

[23]Reimann, B. "On the Dimensions of Bureaucratic Structure: An Empirical Reappraisal," *Administrative Science Quarterly,* 18 (1973), 462–476.

[24]Sayles, L. *Leadership: What Effective Managers Really Do and How They Do It.* New York: McGraw-Hill, in press.

[25]Sathe, 1975.

[26]Scott, 1975.

VII. Measurement Module

A. Vertical Specialization and Control

[1]Blau and Schoenherr, 1971.

[2]Melcher, 1976.

[3]Pugh et al., 1968.

[4]Scott, 1975.

[5]Van de Ven, 1976.

[6]Weber, 1975.

B. Horizontal Specialization and Coordination

[1]Dewar and Hage, 1978.

[2]Fayol, 1949.

[3]Ford and Slocum, 1976.

[4]Melcher, 1976.

[5]Van de Ven, 1976.

[6]Weber, 1976.

C. Bottom-up Measures

[1]Blau and Schoenherr, 1971.

[2]Child, 1973.

[3]Ford, J. D. "An Empirical Investigation of the Relationship of Size, Technology, Workflow Interdependence and Perceived Environmental Uncertainty to Selected Dimensions of Subunit Structure." Unpublished dissertation, The Ohio State University, Columbus, Ohio 1975.

[4]Hellriegal and Slocum, 1974.

[5]Hunt, J. G., and Osborn, R. N. *A Multiple Influence Model of Leadership.* Proposal funded by the U.S. Army Research Institute for the Behaviorial and Social Sciences, May 1978.

[6]James and Jones, 1974.

[7]Lawrence and Lorsch, 1965.

[8]Mansfield, 1973.

[9]Melcher, 1976.

[10]Paulson, 1974.

[11]Perrow, 1967.

[12]Price, 1972.

[13]Pugh et al., 1968.

[14]Relmann, 1973.

[15]Sathe, V. J., "Structural Adaption to Environment: Study of Insurance Company Departments and Branch Banks." Unpublished dissertation, The Ohio State University, Columbus, Ohio, 1974.

[16]Scott, 1975.

[17]Van de Ven, 1976.

[18]Van de Ven, A. H., and Ferry, D. L. *Measuring and Assessing Organizations.* New York: Wiley-Interscience, 1979.

chapter 10 A CONTINGENCY VIEW OF ORGANIZATIONAL DESIGN

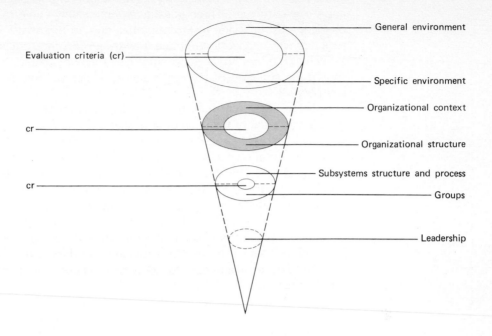

General environment

Evaluation criteria (cr)

Specific environment

Organizational context

cr

Organizational structure

Subsystems structure and process

cr

Groups

Leadership

As the new president of Hunch Engineering, Ron checked off a number of pluses and minuses. The firm had dramatically expanded into several rapidly changing areas and managed to stay ahead of its competition. As a technical leader Hunch had a long history of financial and technical success. Its human-relations record was sound as was its management training and development program. Yet there were some minuses. Several of the brightest young managers had left. The remaining ones complained that their superiors were too busy to explain the firm's game plan or their role in the organization's future. Warehousing, Sales, and Purchasing were always at each other's throats in meetings, confronting the same problems over and over again.

Ron's predecessor had taken considerable pride in developing a lean, hard-driving management team. The current functional arrangement did provide unity of command, an adequate span of control and a clear-cut chain of command. Technical development matched with tightfisted financial controls characterized the firm. This structure had served the firm well. Yet, Ron knew it was time for a change. The old structure was out of step with the firm's more complex environment, more sophisticated technology, and larger size. Before launching two new engineering services, Ron wanted to change the horse-and-buggy structure. Three questions immediately came to mind. One, what changes must be made just to minimize current problems? Two, what kind of structure was needed to continue growth, profitability, engineering excellence as well as their record of good employee relations. Three, how much can and should the structure of the organization reflect his own style and that of his key people?

These three important questions keep recurring in the area called organizational design. Organizational design goes far beyond just deriving an internally consistent structure. The heart of the design problem is to develop a structure that allows an organization to capitalize on opportunities and minimize problems. The structure should be an aid to managers not a stumbling block, a barrier of red tape, or just a chart at the bottom of everyone's desk. A structure that matches the environmental, contextual, and goal requirements of an organization helps managers identify and solve problems. A number of different aspects of environment, context, and structure need to be molded. Thus our normative discussion is divided into three areas.

The first area attempts to address a deceptively simple question: How much structuring should the organization develop? We think the easiest way to answer this question is to focus on the problem of survival. We think each organization should build a strategic advantage. That is, it should emphasize one combination of environment and context over others. However, it is also important to recognize that all aspects of the environment and context should be considered simultaneously. Thus we develop the notion of contextual and structural complexity to complement the concept of environmental complexity. The outcome of our analysis is a simple decision rule. How much structure is needed for survival? "The structure should be as complex as the context and environment." Our second question centers on the linkage among environment, context, structure, and effectiveness. We build upon the notion that environmental, contextual, and structural complexity should be similar. Specifically, the structure needed to increase the chances of goal attainment should also match the specific opportunities and demands emanating from the environment and context. Specific aspects of environment and context can place similar demands upon the structure. In such cases the structure can do double duty by helping the organization cope with environmental and contextual concerns. However, changes in structure will not solve every problem. There may be no structure that can simultaneously meet the stresses and opportunities provided by environmental and contextual conditions. At times management should consider changing its size, technology, and/or environment.

Our analysis is intricate, but the underlying message is still simple. Structure is a tool. The organization needs different tools for different jobs. The wrong tool, no matter how well built, will not help management succeed.

Our last question focuses on the role of administrative philosophy in fine tuning the structure. Our discussion centers on long-run issues. We will pay particular attention to which types of administrative philosophy match different combinations of environment, context, and structure.

You should recognize that as a lower-level or middle-level manager many of your problems and opportunities will be a microcosm of the organization's problems and opportunities. You will need to recognize when the structure is inappropriate and how you can minimize the problems facing you. Understanding which structure should be used under different environments and contexts is a major step in assessing the conditions facing your unit.

THE AMOUNT OF STRUCTURE NEEDED FOR SURVIVAL

To estimate the amount of structure needed, we analyze the combined impact of environment, context, and structure on the survival potential of an organization. To do this we introduce the notions of strategic advantage and contextual and structural complexity.

Strategic Advantage

In our analysis of size and technology we noted an interesting characteristic of organizations in developed nations. They are becoming larger, more technically sophisticated, *and* more technically varied. Why this drive toward larger scale and more intricate technologies? Part of the answer lies in the greater probability of survival offered by development of these three variables. As each increases, the survival potential increases when organizations can operate in more complex environments.[8] But another part of the answer lies in the reinforcing influence of the contextual variables.[5] Let's look at the advantages and problems an organization receives from emphasizing size, technological sophistication, and/or technological variability.

Building upon Size. An organization may develop an advantage over similar systems by building upon the advantages of size. Larger organizations can develop specialized units to take advantage of all modes of technology.[2] They can have units which use long-linked, intensive, mediating, handicraft, and technical services modes. With more modes, larger organizations can fit unit size and technological requirements to increase both the quantity and quality of outputs. Further, the larger scope of operations allows larger organizations to invest in new technology specifically suited for their operations.[3]

For instance, assume economies of scale call for a large computer operation. Larger organizations can develop an internal staff unit to institute a computer based information and control system. By comparison, smaller organizations have limited abilities to divert precious resources into such a specialized staff area.

Larger organizations may also be able to use their size to alter their environment.[14] They may block the development of competitors. Historically, the post office is an example of a huge organization that has used its environmental clout.[1] While quasi-private, it has a monopoly over mail service. And it has effectively blocked the development of competing methods of mail delivery. Larger systems may also ignore some environmental demands. For instance, General Motors does not produce a convertible; smaller firms convert existing models, and a few European and Asian manufacturers export roadsters. Some larger organizations can tilt the balance of exchanges in their favor.[9] The Internal Revenue Service, for instance, has a special legal status. When facing the IRS, you are assumed guilty and must prove your innocence. Exactly the opposite is the case when confronting other governmental agencies. For corporations, the theory of monopoly shows how and why larger firms can directly tilt the pattern of exchange in their favor.[15] In much the same fashion, larger unions can use their environmental muscle. Larger organizations may also use their size indirectly. For instance, they can promote legislation that substantially increases fixed costs and/or minimum quality standards. Such legislation favors larger systems that can more easily cover additional fixed costs with high volume.[14] In sum, the organization can build directly and indirectly upon economies of scale.

Larger systems (size) also bring additional problems in that they may be more likely targets for external groups.[13] Actions taken to reap the benefits of economies of scale can reduce flexibility. Of course, the environment may not be sufficiently developed for a larger organization to survive (see Chapters 5 and 6). And those in charge of the system may be unable to cope with structural problems.[16] Greater size does bring advantages, but it also brings problems.

Building upon Technology. Are smaller organizations doomed? No. Organizations may also build upon technological sophistication and technological variability.

Building upon economies of scale assumes the organization knows what outputs it wants and how these outputs can be produced.[17] For many organizations such as universities, hospitals, and aerospace firms, cause-effect relationships are clouded and standards of desirability may be unclear. Furthermore, building upon economies of scale yields outputs that are essentially similar. The organization may not want to produce standardized outputs.

For instance, assume you are the head of a small, handicrafts manufacturing firm. All the talk of altering the environment and economies of scale makes little sense. While you would like to be larger, you can't expand without anticipated sales or you soon would go broke. There may not be a very large market for any one of your products. But most of all you want to maintain the individuality of your "art works."

By emphasizing technological sophistication an organization has a better chance of producing products and services. In fact, stressing technological sophistication may be the only way it can produce acceptable products and services.[4] Of course, technological sophistication brings problems as well. The search for answers is rarely efficient and the organization may be forced to surrender some control to technical experts.[11] Hospital administrators, for example, may not be as powerful as physicians in determining who will be helped and how they will be served.

To cope with uncertain settings, organizations may stress technological variability.[6] With greater variability organizations may be in a better position to pool risk across a broad spectrum of inputs, transformations, and outputs. They can expand into areas of demand while dropping or putting less emphasis on outputs the environment no longer desires. They can also individually tailor outputs to better serve clients. The clearest examples are small organizations that provide a wide variety of services—none of which requires a sophisticated technology. However, larger organizations, such as retail chains and cooperatives can build upon the ability to provide a broad range of products and services. Some organizations, such as city governments, find technological variability not only an advantage but a necessity.

As with size and technological sophistication, stressing technological variability also brings problems. The organization may be unable to compete with more specialized systems that provide similar outputs at lower cost. And it may not be flexible enough to rapidly adapt to changing demands. Lastly, it may be unable to divert sufficient resources to any one area to produce outputs of sufficient quality and/or quantity.

Building upon Balance. As our discussion of size and technology suggests, these contextual factors are not totally separate.[10] An organization may attempt to build upon a combination of size, technological sophistication, and technological variability.[11] In reaping economies of scale, the large organization can increase its technological variability via creating specialized staff units.[2] Smaller organizations may not have sufficient resources to substantially increase technological sophistication.

In our computer example, the larger organization can benefit more because it gets the combined effect of size, technological sophistication, and technological variability. The larger organization can develop a computer system individually tailored for its needs (technological variability), hire experts to design, run, and improve the system (technological sophistication), and cover these fixed costs with high volume (economies of scale). By comparison, the smaller firm might be forced to purchase standard computer packages that are not individually tailored to its needs, use a generalist to interpret computer outputs, and have a higher cost per report. The smaller firm cannot reap the combined benefits of economies of scale, the ability to produce higher quality outputs, or the ability to develop individually tailored products and services.

The balance among size and technological characteristics may be small size, with low sophistication and variability (e.g., a dry cleaner). At the opposite extreme it may be huge size with high sophistication and variability as with General Electric. At first glance, it appears strange to talk of a dry cleaner and General Electric as if they had the same combination of size, technological sophistication, and technological variability. Obviously, they do not. Each has balance in the sense that the advantages and problems from each of its contextual variables is about equal. When and why can a balance among contextual factors lead to success? We will explain this in greater detail later in this chapter. For now let's build on our contingency view of organization environments.

We suggested that as the environment becomes more complex it offers both more challenges and opportunities.[12] As the degrees of development, interdependence and uncertainty increase, larger organizations with more sophisticated and variable technologies have a better chance of survival. We outlined our size argument in Chapter 7. Larger systems have a better chance of influencing the environment and molding it. Furthermore, they can capitalize on the larger markets provided by a more complex environment.

At the same time the more complex environment provides larger markets, there is often a call for higher quality outputs as well as new products and services.[12] For instance, greater economic development often brings forth demands for more elaborate government services. But at the same time the more developed setting may hold the resources (personnel, tax base, and ideas) needed to increase technological sophistication. On top of increased calls for elaborate products and services, the more complex environment places more disparate demands on an organization. Greater heterogeneity in demand favors organizations that can individually tailor outputs. That is, it favors the more technologically variable system. Note the combined demands and how the balanced strategy can fit with environmental complexity.

If you remember that organizations may have considerable choice in selecting their specific environment, you can see why some small, technologically less sophisticated and less variable organizations survive.[18] Their context fits the demands and opportunities of their setting. There may be fewer opportunities for these small balanced systems. But there may also be fewer problems.

In sum, an organization can improve its chances of survival by developing one of four strategic advantages. It can: (1) build upon size; (2) stress technological sophistication; (3) emphasize technological variability; or (4) strike a balance between size and technology.* As our analysis of the balanced strategic advantage suggested, contextual factors should not be considered in isolation of one another. So before moving on let's develop the notion of contextual complexity.

Contextual Complexity

Larger, more technically sophisticated and variable organizations have greater opportunities and challenges. The impact of contextual variables is not just additive. There is a combined impact.3 Large organizations with high sophistication and variability are much more difficult to manage than medium-size organizations with moderate sophistication and variability.

Table 10-1 provides example combinations for the four types of strategic advantage. We have identified four degrees of contextual complexity. If we had a scale of 1 to 100 our simple category might range from 1 to 10, the moderately complex could run from 11 to 30, the complex range might be from 31 to 60, and the very complex range could be from 61 to 100. The midpoints of these categories could be: Simple = 5; moderately complex = 15; complex = 45; and very complex = 80. These example midpoints represent the degree of complexity stemming from the combined impact of size, technological sophistication, and technological variability. As the example scale suggests, the simple and moderately complex categories are more alike than the complex and very complex ones.

As you study Table 10-1, It's obvious that different combinations may yield similar ratings for contextual complexity. No one factor is dominant. It is the interaction that Is stressed. For instance, look down the complex category. Here we find a railroad, the AFL-CIO, an electronics manufacturer, and a Chinese farm commune. Each of these has a different set of opportunities and problems stemming from the profile of contextual variables. The strategic advantage of the railroad is balance, while the AFL-CIO relies upon the economies of scale and its ability to influence the environment. Note the railroad is large while the AFL-CIO is huge. The large electronics manufacturer relies upon technological sophistication while the farm commune uses its technological variability.

---

*As we show later, the choice among these may reflect the influence of prior strategy, administrative philosophy, and environmental conditions, among other factors.

Table 10-1 Examples of Organizations with Different Degrees of Contextual Complexity and Strategic Advantage

Strategic Advantage	Degree of Contextual Complexity			
	Simple to Moderately Simple	Moderately Complex	Complex	Very Complex
Balanced	Size = small Technological sophistication = low Technological variability = low For example: 1. Dry cleaners 2. ABC Bakery	Size = medium Technological sophistication = moderate Technological Variability = low For example: 1. Furniture manufacturing 2. Finance company	Size = large Technological sophistication = moderate Technological variability = moderate For example: 1. Railroad 2. Public school system	Size = huge Technological sophistication = high Technological variability = high For Example: 1. General Motors 2. AT&T
Size	Size = moderate Technological sophistication = low Technological variability = low For example: 1. Real estate agency 2. Employment service	Size = large Technological sophistication = low Technological variability = low For example: 1. Fast-food chain 2. Direct Mail Life Insurance Co.	Size = huge Technological sophistication = moderate Technological variability = low-moderate For example: 1. AFL-CIO 2. Diamond mine	Size = huge Technological sophistication = moderate Technological variability = moderate For example: 1. Post office 2. State junior college system

Technological sophistication	Size = small Technological sophistication = high Technological variability = low For example: 1. Jones and Jones, Attorneys at Law 2. CPA office	Size = medium Technological sophistication = high Technological variability = moderate For example: 1. Medical clinic 2. Consulting firm	Size = large Technological sophistication = high Technological variability = moderate For example: 1. Electronics manufacturing 2. Pharmaceutical manufacturing	Size = huge Technological sophistication = high Technological variability = moderate For example: 1. American Motors 2. Citibank
Technological variability	Size = small Technological sophistication = low Technological variability = high For example: 1. Pa's General Store 2. Jim's Fix-it Shop	Size = moderate Technological sophistication = low Technological variability = high For example: 1. City government of small town 2. General merchandise wholesaler	Size = huge Technological sophistication = low Technological variability = high For example: 1. European consumers' cooperative 2. Chinese farm commune	Size = huge Technological sophistication = moderate Technological variability = high For example: 1. Federated department store 2. HUD

Two other aspects of contextual complexity may strike you as you study Table 10-1. First, size, technological sophistication, and technological variability are not completely independent.[1] None of the organizations with very complex contexts is of small or medium size. None has low technological sophistication or variability. Thus, the argument for strategic advantage is a relative one. For the organization relying upon technological sophistication, there is higher sophistication than other types of organizations with the same overall degree of contextual complexity. Second, organizations within the same category of contextual complexity would not receive identical complexity scores if we could provide a precise scale. For instance, GM has a more complex context than American Motors.

To summarize, contextual complexity is the combined impact of size and technological factors. Akin to environmental complexity, it is an attempt to chart the magnitude of the opportunities and problems stemming from the context of the organization. While a global rating hides considerable information, it can be very useful in predicting the survival potential of an organization.[2]

Structural Complexity

Following the review of the literature on structure, it is also possible to develop an overall estimate of structural complexity. The structure is more complex as the degrees of vertical specialization, control, horizontal specialization, coordination, and diversity increase. To simplify matters, let us assume that organizations will match vertical specialization and control. Also assume they equalize horizontal specialization and coordination as suggested in the previous chapter.

Figure 10-2 illustrates structural complexity. The degrees of each dimension of structure for an organization can be plotted on the figure using as an example a bakery or pharmaceutical firm. To a greater or lesser extent all of these elements are present in an organization. The degree of structural complexity is represented by the distance from the origin (O) to the centroid of the resulting triangles (X for the pharmaceutical firm, Y for the bakery).

As with contextual complexity, a more complex structure provides more opportunities and problems. Also, as with contextual complexity, the combined effect is most important. For structural complexity we concentrate on the *combination* of vertical specialization (and control), horizontal specialization (and coordination), and diversity. As each increases, an organization's

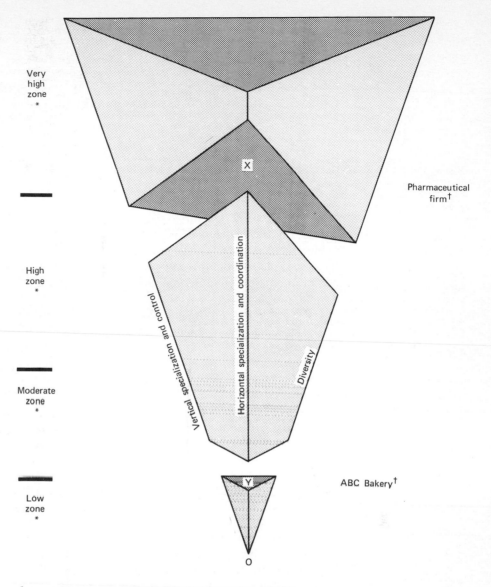

*These are the measurement zones for variables and complexity.

†OX represents the degree of structural complexity for the Pharmaceutical firm; OY is complexity for ABC Bakery (distance from origin O).

Figure 10-2 Structural complexity.

structure becomes more complex.* For instance, the matrix form of departmentation is often more difficult to administer because of the overlay of vertical and horizontal specialization, as well as the diversity of control and coordination systems that are likely to be used in different parts of an organization.[1] Of course, the matrix form allows it to cope more successfully with some problems even if it is more expensive to operate.

Matching Environmental, Contextual, and Structural Complexity for Survival

Now that we have developed the general notions of contextual and structural complexity, let's integrate them with environmental complexity. Recall, the environment is more complex as the degrees of development, interdependence, and uncertainty increase. As with contextual and structural complexity, a more complex environment offers more opportunities and presents more difficult problems.

We argue that an organization, to survive, must develop a reasonable fit among the degrees of environmental, contextual, and structural complexity. As the environment becomes more complex, a more complex context allows an organization to capitalize on environmental opportunities and cope with the problems associated with greater environmental complexity.[4] For instance, assume your firm is a small employment service that attempts to contract for all employee placement with a large conglomerate. Your chances of obtaining the contract are slim. Even if the conglomerate did make such a choice, you would be forced to dramatically alter size, technological sophistication, and variability to meet its needs. At the opposite extreme, assume you wanted to develop a refinery in rural Argentina to process crude oil from a new discovery. The total costs are likely to be prohibitive even if you could obtain governmental support, hire skilled technicians, and secure sufficient buyers.

Matching environmental and contextual complexity is not enough to insure survival.[3] An organization must establish an anatomy that allows it to take advantage of the opportunities provided by its environment and context.[6] An inadequate structure does not permit an organization to capitalize on economies of scale, develop synergy from greater technological specialization, or integrate customer needs with production capacity.[1,2,4] Even if an organization's environment allows it to increase its scope of operations, calls for higher

*As with contextual complexity the combined impact of the structural components can dramatically increase the degree of structural complexity.[2] Furthermore, the three aspects of structural complexity are not completely independent.

quality or new products, and forces the organization to tailor its outputs, the structure must be adequate to handle these new demands and opportunities. We should note an interesting phenomenon Litterer calls overstructuring.[5] When the structure of an organization is more complex than that of the environment and context, it faces problems similar to those emanating from understructuring. Its efficiency declines, it appears unresponsive to external demands, and there's a loss of control and coordination. Thompson noted a similar phenomenon and called it bureaupathology.[8] It would be much like trying to structure a small men's shop using Sears-Roebuck as a model. Perrow also suggests that managers and employees often disregard the structure when it becomes overly complex.[7] Thus, control and coordination become major problems.

ENHANCING THE POTENTIAL FOR GOAL ATTAINMENT

For many managers a vague discussion of survival is inadequate. They administer or operate in organizations that have already developed a rough correspondence among environmental, contextual, and structural complexity. They, as you, are probably more interested in increasing the capacity for goal attainment. To develop this type of argument, let us take a more detailed look at the dimensions of environment, context, and structure. We will build the analysis by noting combinations of environment and context; then we will include structure.

To get a better idea of environment-context matches, let us plot environmental and contextual complexity in three-dimensional space. Of course, we will lose some of the detail outlined in Figure 7-3 and Table 10-1, but we must keep the analysis manageable. Figure 10-3 depicts contextual complexity. The distance from the bottom of the figure represents the degree of contextual complexity. Thus, ABC Bakery has a simple context, while the pharmaceutical manufacturer has a complex context. Note also that the context of the bakery is balanced. Small size is matched with low technological sophistication and low variability. The bakery's strategic advantage is balance. By comparison, the strategic advantage of the ethical drug firm centers on technological sophistication. While it is large with moderately high technological variability, its technological sophistication is very high.

Similarly, we can plot the degree of environmental complexity. For simplicity, let's assume that the specific environment of an organization is most relevant and that we are describing those that operate in developed general environments. Figure 10-4 depicts environmental complexity for the ABC Bakery and the ethical drug firm. As before, the distance from the bottom of the

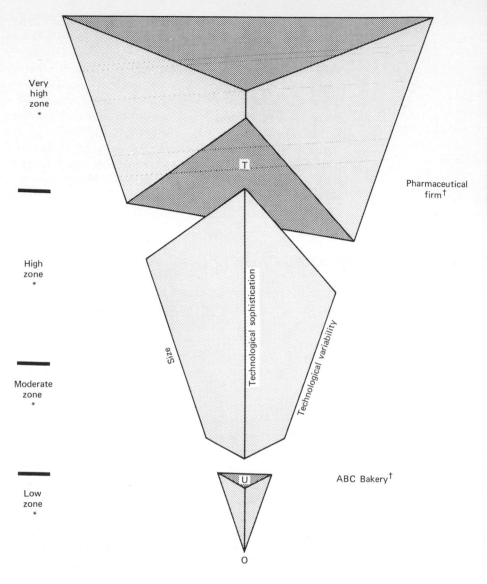

Very
high
zone
*

High
zone
*

Moderate
zone
*

Low
zone
*

T

Pharmaceutical
firm†

Size

Technological sophistication

Technological variability

U

ABC Bakery†

O

*These are the measurement zones for variables and complexity.
For Size, the measurement zones are Huge, Large, Medium and Small.

†OT represents the degree of contextual complexity for the Pharmaceutical
firm; OU is complexity for ABC Bakery (distance from origin O).

Figure 10-3 Two patterns of contextual complexity.

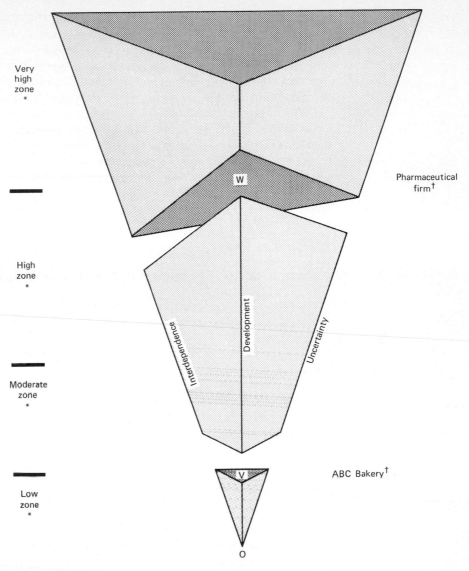

Very
high
zone
*

High
zone
*

Moderate
zone
*

Low
zone
*

W

Pharmaceutical
firm[†]

Interdependence

Development

Uncertainty

V

ABC Bakery[†]

O

[*]These are the measurement zones for variables and complexity.

[†]OW represents the degree of environmental complexity for the
Pharmaceutica firm; OV is complexity for ABC Bakery
(distance from origin O).

Figure 10-4   Two patterns of environmental complexity.

figure represents the degree of complexity. The ABC Bakery is in a balanced environment in that degrees of interdependence, development, and uncertainty are low. The drug manufacturer operates in a more complex environment and one where the degree of development is higher than that of interdependence or uncertainty. (The plane cut for the pharmaceutical firm is not parallel to that for the figure, while the plane for ABC Bakery is parallel.)

We have not introduced the strategic advantages of building on the environment for a simple reason. We think that firms that match their environment with their context have a far better chance of reaching their goals. We have chosen our examples to reflect this estimate. To get a better picture of this, let's look at the pressures and opportunities provided by each dimension of the environment and context. Since structure is a tool for dealing with the environment and context, we need to include it as well.

Associations among Dimensions of Environment, Context, and Structure

There are simply too many possible combinations among the dimensions to present a reasonably simple analysis. Thus, we will shift gears to take a normative stance. That is, we will suggest how organizations *should* respond to improve their chances of goal attainment. Some may respond as we suggest, some may not.

We argue that each aspect (dimension) of the environment and context provides an organization with slightly different opportunities and problems. An organization can increase its chances of success if it can adjust its structure to capitalize on these opportunities and solve the major problems posed by a particular environmental or contextual condition. Recognize, too, that a change in environmental or contextual conditions is most likely to call for several different types of structural alterations. But some changes are needed more than others. In our terms, there should be primary, secondary, and tertiary adjustments.

Table 10-5 systematically presents the primary (most important), secondary, and tertiary (least important) effects of the environmental and contextual dimensions on the anatomy of an organization wanting to improve its chances of goal attainment. Furthermore, we have estimated the pattern of appropriate response. To keep the analysis from becoming too abstract we only discuss secondary and tertiary effects for one contextual variable. However, the table specifies our estimates for each.

Interdependence and Size. We argue that the primary impact of environmental interdependence and size is on vertical specialization and control.[3]

Table 10-5 Primary, Secondary, and Tertiary Effects of Environmental and Contextual Factors: A Normative Estimate

Structural[a] Dimension	Environment[b]			Context[b]		
	Interdependence	Development	Uncertainty	Size	Technological Sophistication	Technological Variability
Vertical specialization and control	Primary	Secondary	Tertiary	Primary	Secondary	Tertiary
Horizontal specialization and coordination	Secondary	Primary	Secondary	Secondary	Primary	Secondary
Structural diversity	Tertiary	Tertiary	Primary	Tertiary	Tertiary	Primary

[a] The structural dimension is on the vertical axis for each graph.

[b] Environment, or context, is on the horizontal axis for each graph.

As Blau and his associates argue, larger organizations can capitalize on economies of scale by increasing formalization and instituting more managerial decision techniques.[14] More sophisticated controls are needed to ensure consistency.[11] Greater size also appears to have a lesser, secondary impact, horizontally.[5] The greater magnitude of operations often causes some problems of coordination even as it allows an organization to add some specialized units to increase decision quality and efficiency.[14] Lastly, with greater specialization and the creation of new units, an organization should not treat all subsystems in an identical fashion.[8] For instance, slightly different patterns of departmentation may be needed to build upon the strengths of the new specialized departments.[9] Thus, the tertiary effect of greater size is an increase in structural diversity.*

Several people argue that long-term exchange relationships among organizations are established at the institutional levels of organizations.[2,15] Once established, these interdependencies must be managed to ensure that the pattern of exchange conforms to the original agreements and still provides for adequate flexibility.[16] A contract is an example. It details the exchanges to be made, the time-frame for exchange and, often implicitly, the conditions under which the parties may alter the agreement. In our terms, the administration of environmental interdependence calls for more formalization, more detailed managerial techniques, and more detailed control systems. Thus, there should be an increase in vertical specialization and control. A secondary adjustment to higher interdependence is an increase in horizontal specialization and coordination.[1,18] The tertiary response should come by increasing structural diversity.[8]

Note that greater size and environmental interdependence have a primary impact on vertical specialization and control. As Table 10-5 indicates, this pattern is not identical at all levels of size or interdependence.[10,1] We estimate the needed response diminishes as size and environmental interdependence increase.[15] Thus, the pattern of response calls for substantial changes as size and interdependence increase for smaller organizations with lower degrees of interdependence.[20] But for huge organizations with high degrees of interdependence, substantial changes in size and interdependence are needed to alter vertical specialization and control.[20]

Note the pattern for the secondary impact of greater size and environmental interdependence. In smaller organizations with comparatively low interdependence, small changes in size and interdependence have a very modest impact on horizontal specialization and coordination.[20] In the middle range, the pattern changes. Small changes in size and interdependence trigger the development of specialized units and more elaborate coordination mechanisms.[4] For instance, it is in this "middle" range that organizations feel the pressure to move from a functional to a divisional pattern of departmentation. For huge organizations with high degrees of interdependence the pattern of appropriate response flattens.[19] For these systems, structural diversity is needed.[17] Structural diversity should increase when an organization is huge and faces a highly interdependent environment. We realize that our recommendations are getting quite involved. But as we suggested, organizations facing more complex environments and contexts are more difficult to administer.[14] Developing an appropriate structure for these complex settings is no exception.

*You may also notice that a substantial increase in size also allows an organization to increase technological sophistication and variability.[13]

Development and Technological Sophistication. Now let us turn to development and technological sophistication. In Chapters 6 and 7, we showed that increasing development in the environment of an organization provides more opportunities for growth and success. It provides slack for investment in the future as well. It also allows the organization to expand its domain by developing new outputs and by serving new customers and clients.[17] The primary impact on structure is the development of new units and an increase in the number of different specialists.[6] The organization is investing in the future. Of course, these new types of specialists and specialized units must be integrated into existing operations, thus the call for more coordination.[18] The secondary impact of more development in the environment is an increase in vertical specialization and control,[16] while the tertiary impact is in diversity.[1]

✓ Greater technological sophistication has similar effects on the structure of organizations wanting to increase their chances of goal attainment.[20] As we showed earlier, greater technological sophistication may be needed just to increase the chances of producing a product or service. Often it is needed to increase the quality of outputs. Additional types of specialists and specialized units are needed as the technology becomes more sophisticated.[6] Moreover, an organization must increase its emphasis on coordination to reap the synergistic benefits from the greater number of specialized units.[18] Of course, greater technological sophistication is also felt to a lesser degree vertically, and it calls for slight adjustment in structural diversity.[20]

Table 10-5 summarizes the pattern of desired response to greater development and technological sophistication. Both have a diminishing impact on horizontal specialization and coordination.[20] In a similar fashion their secondary effect on vertical specialization and control diminishes as the environment becomes more developed and the technology becomes even more sophisticated.[20]

Uncertainty and Technological Variability. As we might suspect from Ashby's law of requisite variety, greater uncertainty and technological variety call for a more diverse structure. Remember, environmental uncertainty is more than just change. It is change without a predictable pattern. Both the magnitude and direction of change are shifting, so an organization must develop a better early-warning and forecasting system and prepare itself to alter internal operations quickly.[7] We previously indicated that an organic structure (high horizontal specialization and coordination vis-à-vis vertical specialization and control) was better in detecting change and developing the detailed information needed to make appropriate adaptation.[12] However, the organic structure was inferior to the mechanistic arrangement for quickly instituting changes in production, marketing, and the like.[12] Thus, an organization facing greater uncertainty needs to become more organic *and* more mechanistic.

How? In boundary line and staff units, it needs to stress horizontal speciali-zation and coordination.[2] Planning units need to scan the environment to detect emerging patterns. Boundary line units such as marketing should be in a position to chart small changes in demand and/or preferences. But internal staff and line units need to be in a position to quickly change inputs, trans-formations, and outputs once a new pattern has been detected.[14]

Thus they need to be mechanistically structured with higher degrees of vertical specialization and control. We should note that the greater vertical specialization should not come in the form of more elaborate rules, policies, and procedures. Instead we would recommend additional levels of adminis-tration and more elaborate managerial techniques. The control system also needs to be more flexible and comprehensive to recognize that implementa-tion of change means that old standards, measuring instruments, and rewards may be quickly outmoded.[11]

Of course, simply altering the degree of diversity in the structure is not enough. As the preceding suggests, greater environmental uncertainty calls for additional managers and units.[16] We think that detection of external changes is more important than quick response. Therefore, we recommend that the secondary impact of greater environmental uncertainty should come in hori-zontal specialization and coordination.[15] Greater vertical specialization and control is a tertiary response stemming primarily from the need to quickly adapt once an organization has decided how it wants to alter inputs, trans-formations, and/or outputs.[9]

Technological variability appears to have a similar impact on the desired structure of an organization.[20] But greater technological variability also appears to put pressure on both internal and external units.[6] The administration of an organization with a varying pattern of inputs, transformations, and outputs needs to be attuned to the requirements of each technology. Some parts of the technical core may not require as much horizontal specialization and coor-dination as others. Some may be simple, routine operations calling for a me-chanistic treatment. Of course, the efforts of diverse units must be coordinated; thus, we see a secondary impact on horizontal specialization and coordina-tion.[18] Lastly, greater technological variability may call for some additional levels of administration, more elaborate managerial decision techniques, and a slightly more elaborate control system (tertiary impacts).[20]

While our analysis is quite detailed, we can make some summary state-ments using the notions of mechanistic and organic structures. Where an or-ganization's strategic advantage is balance among environmental and contextual conditions, it should balance its structure. It should be neither clearly organic nor clearly mechanistic. Instead the degrees of vertical spe-cialization (and control), horizontal specialization (and coordination), and di-versity should be similar. Where size and environmental interdependence are an organization's strategic advantage, its structure should be mechanistic. Those organizations relying upon technological sophistication should be organically structured and should stress horizontal specialization and coordination. Finally, where technological variability and uncertainty are high, an organization should develop a highly diverse structure. Parts of an organization should be mechanistically structured and other parts should conform to an organic mode. The analysis of secondary and tertiary effects reinforces our earlier prescription that the overall degrees of environmental, contextual, and structural complexity should be matched.

So far we have assumed that the pressures from environment and context are similar. What happens if size places more pressure on the structure than interdependence? Let's examine gaps between paired dimensions of environment and context.

Matching the Pressures and Opportunities of Various Aspects of Environmental and Contextual Complexity

Figure 10-6 graphically combines environmental and contextual complexity. Note the dimensions of environment and context are matched on the basis of their primary impact on the structure of an organization. Thus, there are paired dimensions. Remember our analysis is normative. The figure itself does not describe how organizations develop a particular structure, but suggests how we can analyze their environment and context. From this analysis, we can prescribe a structure that has a higher probability of goal attainment.

Where structural pressures from components of "paired dimensions" (matched) are equal, then the prescription concerning structure is quite clear. For instance, look at ABC Bakery. Environmental interdependence and size are matched. Size is small and interdependence is low. Both components indicate that ABC Bakery should have low vertical specialization and few formal controls. For the technological sophistication-environmental development pair we find another match. Both are low. ABC Bakery should have little horizontal specialization and few formal coordinative mechanisms. Technological variability and uncertainty are also matched. Thus there should be little diversity in the structure of the organization. The structure has low complexity and it should be balanced. ABC Bakery has a high probability of reaching its goals vis-à-vis other organizations with a simple environment and context. The bakery can develop a structure that does double duty.

Now take a look at our sample pharmaceutical firm. While environmental and contextual complexity are similar, the components of the paired dimensions are not equal. Size is calling for more vertical specialization and control

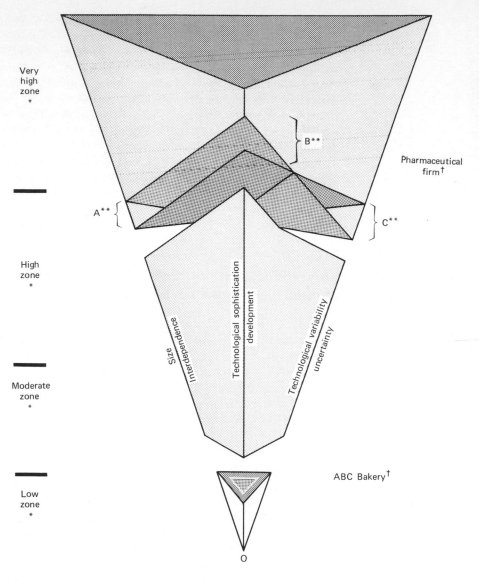

Very
high
zone
*

B**

Pharmaceutical
firm†

A**

C**

High
zone
*

Size

Interdependence

Technological sophistication
development

Technological variability
uncertainty

Moderate
zone
*

ABC Bakery†

Low
zone
*

O

*These are the measurement zones for variables and complexity; for
Size, the zones are Huge, Large, Medium and Small.

†Dark shaded slice through the cone represents environmental complexity.
Light shaded slice through the cone represents contextual complexity.

**A is the size–interdependence gap; B is the technological sophistication–
development gap; C is the technological variability–uncertainty gap.

Figure 10-6 Combining environmental and contextual complexity.

than the degree of environmental interdependence (A in Figure 10-6). The very high degree of technological sophistication is calling for more horizontal specialization and coordination than the degree of development (B in Figure 10-6). Finally, uncertainty is greater than technological variability (C in Figure 10-6). These mismatches or gaps make it difficult for the firm to develop a structure that simultaneously capitalizes on the opportunities provided by the environment and context. The structure needed to cope with environmental problems is slightly different than that called for by the context. As the gaps increase, the organization will find it increasingly difficult to develop an appropriate structure. If the structure is attuned to an environmental dimension, then it is less appropriate for the contextual pressures and opportunities. (An organization can be both "understructured" and "overstructured," if it chooses an anatomy that is a compromise between the environmental and contextual pressures and opportunities.) Note, these gaps are not considered nearly as serious as a mismatch between the overall degrees of environmental and contextual complexity. They do not threaten survival potential. But as they increase, the potential goal attainment of an organization declines.

TOP MANAGEMENT DISCRETION AND STRUCTURE

Now we can start answering our third question. How much discretion can and should top management have over the structure of an organization? We can break this question into several parts. First, let's look at fine tuning a structure where the demands and opportunities from the environment and context are similar. Next we look at a more difficult situation. Can management develop an effective structure where the demands of the environment and context are inconsistent? We suggest that, in the long run, changes in all three should be considered. We also recognize that in the long-run the match among environment, context, and structure favor some administrative philosophies over others. Finally, we summarize by noting what types of adjustments top management can make. Let us look at the most favorable condition first.

Fine Tuning the Structure

If the gaps between paired components of the environment and context are small, an organization can make minor adjustments in its structure that will capitalize on its strategic advantage.

Earlier in our chapter on structure we noted that various aspects of vertical specialization were partial substitutes for one another. We argued much the same for horizontal specialization and for structural diversity. Further, there were several different ways of increasing control and coordination. When faced with small gaps on paired dimensions, an organization can adjust the form of vertical specialization, horizontal specialization, control, or coordination. We argue that the form should address the problems and opportunities provided by that aspect of paired dimensions that is yielding greater complexity.

In our sample ethical drug firm, those aspects of horizontal specialization most suited for technological sophistication should be used. In the case of the size-interdependence pair, those forms of vertical specialization and control needed to cope with size should be stressed. For the uncertainty-technological variability pair, horizontal diversity should be stressed over vertical diversity. Why? Because horizontal diversity is more attuned to coping with environmental uncertainty.

Generally, the balanced organization would stress developing a balance among vertical specialization (and control), horizontal specialization (and coordination), and diversity. But the pattern of gaps may favor those forms that are more mechanistic. For instance, policies, procedures, and managerial techniques may be substituted for managers, and more formal coordinative mechanisms may be selected over informal ones. Thus, a successful organization building upon a balanced strategic advantage may appear centralized, formalized, and standardized.[1] Conversely, the gaps could favor the organic mode. It is also possible for a successful firm building upon the balanced strategic advantage to be decentralized and less formalized, with comparatively little standardization.[1]

Minor alterations in the form of the structure may not make much difference in terms of reaching output goals. But they can have a tremendous impact on the ability of an organization to increase employee maintenance.[2] Where more organic forms of structure are selected, an organization increases its employee maintenance. Obviously, however, the strategic advantage of an organization places limits on the extent to which it can move toward an organic structure.[4] An organization building upon size has more limited prospects for employee maintenance than one building upon technological sophistication.[4] Those building upon technological variability may find that they can boost employee maintenance in some units but not others.[3]

Strategic Choices in the Long Run

In the long run we argue that top management can have considerable influence on the type of match the organization develops.[4] That is, the environment, context, and structure can be molded. Developing a consistent match calls for a combination of short-term adjustments and long-term investments. This can be more easily seen if we develop some normative guidelines for developing matches that increase the chances of goal attainment.

It is important to remember the direct impact of environmental and contextual variables. First, greater environmental development and interdependence are preferred to less. Uncertainty has a negative impact. Assuming the environment is conducive, larger size, greater sophistication, and greater variability generally increase the chances of goal attainment. Second, an organization should not sacrifice a strategic advantage just to bring components of the environment and context into line.[4] Third, when analyzing the fit between the environmental and contextual dimensions, coping with mismatches involving an organization's strategic advantage should be considered first.[8] These decision rules ensure that it will capitalize on its strategic advantage and not dissipate its resources. Fourth, the basic thrust of an organization's structure should follow its strategic advantage.[5] This is to ensure that the structure is capable of allowing it to capitalize on its strengths and offset potentially dangerous problems. Fifth, top management should concentrate its efforts on those gaps that are widest and most difficult to change.[7] In structural terms this translates to centralization of those functions directly involved in closing the widest and most important gap. In more theoretical terms, this gap constitutes the critical contingency for an organization.[10]

Sixth, environmental conditions are often more difficult to change than contextual factors. Organizations can make dramatic changes in size by mergers, acquisitions, and/or the sale of divisions.[7] By adding or dropping new products and/or services, organizations can alter technological variability.[9] Increasing sophistication is a more difficult matter, but it may be easier than altering environmental uncertainty or development.[3] Remember, alterations in environmental conditions often call for the cooperative efforts of several organizations.[2] Seventh, a dramatic change in any of the environmental or contextual factors may threaten the survival of an organization.[6] Moving into a new industry or moving operations to a different country are risky, since these may drastically change the environment. Eighth, alterations in environment, context, and structure are likely to have short-run negative effects on goal attainment even though they may enhance the chances of longer-term goal attainment.[11] Ninth, no organization has unlimited resources. Each must target its efforts to a limited number of problems.[5] An attempt to simultaneously change all dimensions of the environment, context, and structure is quite risky.[3] Tenth, an organization may be forced to create gaps between the paired components of environment and context and/or maintain an inappropriate structure to ensure short-term survival. The best examples of these are short-term corporate layoffs and efficiency campaigns during recessions. Organizations may be forced to retrench and gear up before they can consider the longer-term matching of environment, context, and structure.

Let us clarify these recommendations by using them to analyze the choices available to our ethical drug firm. Refer back to Figure 10-6. We will highlight the three mismatches among the paired environmental and contextual dimensions, and apply our decision rules.

Looking at the patterns, the firm has forged a fairly close match between environmental and contextual complexity, both of which are high. Thus the structure of the organization should be complex. Note also that the strategic advantage of this firm centers on technological sophistication. Hence, this organization should have a complex organic structure.

Since technological sophistication is the firm's primary strategic advantage it should not be lowered to match the degree of development (see B in Figure 10-6). Unfortunately, environmental development is extremely difficult to change. Therefore, the organization faces a gap that is difficult to close without upsetting its strategic advantage. Here we argue the organization should focus the attention of top management on the discrepency between very high technological sophistication and high development. Specifically, those functions dealing with an increase in technological sophistication and increasing development in the environment should be attached to top management. For our ethical drug firm, research and development would rate a vice presidential post and considerable staff support.

The gap between size and interdependence is a different story (see A in Figure 10-6). Here the organization may have some freedom to increase interdependence to match size, without substantially altering its structure. Increasing interdependence could be accomplished by closer ties with key members of the specific environment. For instance, the firm might hire a former member of the Food and Drug Administration (FDA). The higher ranking the member the better. The drug firm could also increase interdependence indirectly by diverting more resources to an industry association. This could increase the interdependence among members of the specific setting.

The gap between environmental uncertainty and technological variability is quite another matter (see C in Figure 10-6). Here an organization should increase the number and types of its products and/or markets to spread the risk. In the case of the ethical drug firm, it is extremely difficult and expensive to get FDA approval for new products. However, standards in Europe, Asia, and South America are different. Test marketing in foreign nations already served can be less expensive, less time consuming, and still yield more than adequate data. Note that if the changes in both interdependence and technological variability are made, the balance between environmental and contextual complexity is still maintained. The structure needs to become more diverse, but the higher environmental uncertainty is already calling for a more diverse structure.

The danger is in the secondary impact of alterations in interdependence and technological variability. The ethical drug firm must move incrementally to ensure that problems of coordination do not overwhelm the advantages of developing more consistent matches between size and interdependence on the one hand and uncertainty and technological variability on the other.[10]

We should note that our recommendations center on the long-term. If our ethical drug firm faced a recession, it might be forced to cut expenditures just to minimize losses. Analysis of paired dimensions does not suggest where cuts should be made. However, the strategic advantage does indicate where they should *not* come. In our example, the ethical drug manufacturer should not cut research and development. Similarly, organizations building upon size should be wary of cost-cutting measures that damage their ability to capitalize on economies of scale and manipulate the environment. The last place to cut for these organizations is at the middle- and top-management levels. Organizations whose advantage is technological variability should be careful not to eliminate products or markets. Instead, they should consider reductions. Only where a balanced strategic advantage is the key should balanced cuts be considered.

Our recommendation to test market drugs in a foreign nation with lower standards may shock you. Some pharmaceutical firms would reject this alternative as unethical. They would be willing to sacrifice some increase in profits, flexibility, and adaptability to maintain ethical standards. In other words, top management does have a choice.[1] How it chooses is part and parcel of what we've called administrative philosophy.

Administrative Philosophy in Complex Settings

To simplify our analysis let us assume that an organization has developed a match among environmental, contextual, and structural complexity. Where the profile is a simple environment with simple context and a simple structure we have a simple setting. Where all are complex we have a complex setting. Furthermore, let's continue to use our short-hand in describing the strategic advantage of an organization. It can build upon balance, size, technological sophistication, or technological variability. Now let's look at where you would expect to find different administrative philosophies and the chances an organization has in reaching goals most likely to be set by top management.

As we indicated in Chapter 8, administrative philosophy is the orientation of top management toward goals, environment, technology, and employees. We identified three ideal profiles: traditionalistic, moralistic, and individualistic. Assuming that the survival of the system is assured, we can deduce the goal priorities of organizations following one of the three administrative philosophies. For organizations dominated by the traditionalistic philosophy the goal priorities are likely to be: (1) output goals (2) systems goals (3) derived goals and (4) employee maintenance.*

For organizations with a moralistic administrative philosophy, the goal priorities are different. Consistent with the positive view of employees and the orientation toward the quality of working life, we expect employee maintenance will be given priority (1) after survival appears assured, followed by: (2) systems goals, (3) derived goals, and (4) output goals.

The goal priorities for the individualistic philosophy are likely to be: (1) systems goals (2) derived goals (3) output goals and (4) employee maintenance. Remember that growth and power are systems goals. They are the primary interest of those with an individualistic philosophy.

The structural tendencies of the three philosophies can also be derived from their orientations toward the environment, technology, and employees. The logic underlying our predictions is in Chapter 8. But now with a more detailed discussion of structure we can be more specific. Organizations dominated by the traditionalistic philosophy tend to favor vertical specialization and control. Furthermore, they will substitute rules, policies, and procedures for managers as often as possible. In the moralistic philosophy you find exactly the opposite. The organic form is preferred. Where vertical specialization and control is needed, you're more likely to see additional managers and some substitution of managerial techniques for managers. Rules, policies, and procedures will be held to a minimum. Finally, in the individualistic philosophy there is no particular structural tendency. The structure will be attuned to increase the chances of growth and greater power.

Table 10-7 gives our estimate of which administrative philosophies are likely to dominate organizations with different types of strategic advantages and degrees of complexity in the setting. Our estimates are based on combining the goal priorities of top management, the likelihood a strategic advantage can meet the priorities of management, and the chances top management will develop a structure consistent with the environment and context. To simplify matters we've combined the simple and moderately simple categories.

First, let us explain why we think *very complex* settings will be dominated by the individualistic philosophy. An organization with a complex setting provides the greatest opportunities for those adhering to the individualistic philosophy to reach their top priority goals of growth and power. Thus, they may gravitate toward these systems.

Second, regardless of their strategic advantage, organizations with a very complex setting are in a position to "invest" resources in members of the

*While employee maintenance can be a derived goal, we think it deserves special treatment.

Table 10-7 Consistent Patterns Between Administrative Philosophy and Complexity in the Setting

Degree of complexity in the setting	Simple and Moderately Complex				Complex				Very Complex			
Type of strategic advantage	Balance	Size	Technological Sophistication	Technological Variability	Balance	Size	Technological Sophistication	Technological Variability	Balance	Size	Technological Sophistication	Technological Variability
Consistent administrative philosophy (in order of dominance where appropriate)	1. T 2. M	T	T	I	I	1. I 2. T M	T I	I M	I	I	I	I

T = Traditionalistic.

M = Moralistic.

I = Individualistic.

specific environment.[1] The more complex the environment and context the higher the payoff of these "investments." Further, their size and power tilts the balance of exchange in their favor and increases the chances of collecting an adequate return.[7] While these opportunities are open to all organizations with a complex setting, those dominated by traditionalists and moralists are less likely to make these external investments.[5] Traditionalists are likely to concentrate on technological improvements. Organizations dominated by the moralistic philosophy are too concerned with employees. Third, organizations with a very complex setting tend to be older than their less-complex counterparts.[4] And a key to the dominance of any one administrative philosophy is its longevity.[6]

If top managers can remain in the executive suite, they can have a substantial impact on who gets promoted. And they can groom their replacements. The literature on corporate succession suggests that a primary factor in executive turnover is growth and power.[6] Firms that grow faster (via merger for instance) and select actions directly related to growth (expanding internationally, for example) are more likely to have a stable top management. The stress on growth and power favors the dominance of the individualistic philosophy.[7,8]

For organizations with a less-complex setting we see a more varied pattern in the prevalent administrative philosophy. A key factor may be the type of strategic advantage. The organization's strategic advantage suggests both the type of goals the system can most easily reach and the type of structure needed to increase the chances of goal attainment. First, let's look at organizations with a complex setting (opposed to very complex). Where the strategic advantage is balanced, we expect the individualistic philosophy to have some advantages. Why? These organizations provide the opportunity for growth and power. Moreover, the balanced strategy calls for investments in the environment, technology, as well as in employees. Assume greater investment in one area yields increasingly smaller returns. With a balance, you want approximately equal investment in the environment, technology, and employees. Those with the traditionalistic philosophy are likely to put too much into the technology, while the moralistic organization may overinvest in employees.

Where there is balance, the structural tendencies of the traditionalistic and individualistic philosophies are only partially consistent with that required. The problem with the traditionalistic-dominated organization is inadequate development of horizontal specialization and coordination. For the moralistic system it is the opposite problem—too little attention to vertical specialization and control. Without any structural predispositions, the tendencies for the individualistic philosophy are consistent by definition.

We should note that the pattern of gaps between paired dimensions of the environment and context may allow organizations with a balanced advantage to tilt the structure to be more consistent with a moralistic or traditionalistic philosophy. Thus, the dominance of the individualistic philosophy is not clear-cut.

In organizations with a complex setting, building upon size, the traditionalistic philosophy can dominate. Why? This pattern can yield high efficiency and high product/service quality. The structural tendencies of the traditionalistic philosophy are consistent with the pressure for a mechanistic anatomy. Continual investment in technology can substantially increase efficiency. Where the organization with a complex setting builds upon technological sophistication, we think the moralistic philosophy can dominate. While there may be inadequate attention to technological development, the moralistic philosophy is consistent with organic structural tendencies. Where technological variability is the strategic advantage, the required structure favors the individualistic philosophy.

As we move toward organizations with simple and moderately complex settings we find a slightly different pattern. In these smaller systems there are fewer demands on the anatomy of the organization. Furthermore, technical and personal factors loom larger. Thus, the traditionalistic philosophy can dominate where the strategic advantage is technological sophistication, even though there may be too much vertical specialization and control. One technical breakthrough can provide sufficient slack to compensate for inadequate structure and still provide sufficient resources for continued research and development.

If you look at Table 10-7, a subtle but important factor may cross your mind. As an organization moves from simple to very complex, the dominant administrative philosophy changes. For instance, in the simple setting where an organization builds upon technological sophistication, continual success calls for a change in administrative philosophy. A once-successful top management is no longer appropriate.[3] To maintain the chances of success a moralistic rather than a traditionalistic philosophy may be needed. This is one explanation for the crises organizations face as they move through various stages of development. It is also one reason why organizations may remain in a particular developmental category. Top management may realize that continued growth coupled with more technological sophistication and variability may be inconsistent with its desires.

Finally, we should note that large and huge organizations contain many subsystems. Each of these has its own strategic advantage and may provide the type of climate suitable for those with traditionalistic and moralistic philosophies.[2] You may or may not want the rewards provided top managers of organizations with a complex setting. If you're more traditionalistic or moralistic, heading a huge conglomerate may not be your cup of tea. You can, we think, operate successfully within these systems with a traditionalistic or moralistic philosophy.

Molding the Structure to the Desires of Top Management

So far we have argued that top management does have latitude for substantial long-term adjustments. Yet, administrative philosophy reinforces the type of match needed for an organization to succeed. That is, organizations often promote an administrative philosophy consistent with the needed match among environment, context, and structure. But we have yet to fully address our key question raised at the beginning of the chapter. Just how much influence can and should top management have in molding structure to suit its own style?

We think top management has very little room to maneuver when it comes to the *amount* of structure. To ensure survival, an organization must build a structure that accommodates its strategic advantage and the scope and magnitude of its operations. Environmental and contextual complexity call for an equally complex structure. The penalty for failing to respond could be the demise of an organization.

The issue becomes much more complicated when we look at the chances of goal attainment. We suggested that there were "paired dimensions" of environment and context that called for virtually identical structural responses. Specifically, when environmental interdependence and size increase, an organization should respond with greater vertical specialization and control. However, the exact way in which vertical specialization and control should be adjusted can easily reflect the administrative philosophy of top management. While alterations in technological sophistication and environmental development should be met with greater horizontal specialization and coordination, the desires of top management may be reflected in the exact type of change. A more diverse structure is needed to cope with greater environmental uncertainty and technological variability. But again the philosophy of top management may dictate how this is done. In different terms we propose the following: Where the environment and context put similar pressures on the structure, top-level managers can have considerable influence over the form of response and the priority among various goals. The extent to which the structure actually matches the dominant philosophy of top management will depend upon several factors. Two appear particularly important. First, to what extent does top management recognize that structure can be used to direct an organization toward different goals? That is, does top management consider structure a useful tool? Second, does top management believe that it has sufficient resources to overcome short-term inefficiencies stemming from a structural change? As we will note in the next part of the book, the formal structure does not completely specify all of the interconnections needed to successfully run an organization. Thus, a change in structure is inevitably followed by a period of readjustment when all members of the organization must help make the new structure work.

Where the environment and context yield inconsistent demands on the structure of an organization, we think top management has considerably less discretion. To improve the chances of success, top management should attempt to reconfigure the match involving environment, context, and structure while still maintaining a strategic advantage. Such reconfiguration is difficult, time-consuming, and may sap an organization's capacity to emphasize those goals most desired by top management. In short, developing a match may take precedence. Of course, many organizations can survive with an inconsistent match and even direct their energies toward the priorities of top management. Why? Simply because some unique factors ensure a steady stream of resources. Such unique factors may be a patent, legal mandate and support, or the lack of competition. However, such short-term success may not carry into the longer run if the unique advantage disappears.

For instance, Coors has been a successful regional brewery for almost a century. It has traditionally stressed product quality, a conservative approach to marketing, and an emphasis on one product. However, changes in the industry and new technology as well as the emergence of low-calorie beer as an important product have placed top management in a serious predicament. Its traditional management philosophy and existing management structure are inconsistent with the new environment, technological sophistication, and tech-nological variability pervading the industry. Coors is likely to survive, but top management is being forced to reassess its expectations and style of manage-ment. Changes outside of the firm may be substantially reducing the organi-zation's ability to reach those goals most cherished by its owner-managers.

Now let's return to the three questions we asked at the beginning of the chapter. How much structuring should an organization develop? It should develop as complex a structure as dictated by the environment and context, if it is to survive. What kind of structure is needed to increase the chances of goal attainment? The structure should match the opportunities and require-ments of the environment and context and allow It to capitalize on its strategic advantage. Minor inconsistencies between the structural pressures from the environment and context may be subject to a structural solution. However, as the environment and context continue to diverge, management should con-sider alterations in the environment and context. At times there is no structural solution.

Our last question was how much can and should the structure of an organization reflect the desires of top management? Over the long run we argued that organizations tend to attract and promote those managers whose philosophy is consistent with the match among environment, context, and structure. For any one top-management group the discretion over structure was problematical if they wanted to ensure survival and goal attainment. We suggested there was comparatively little choice over how much structure was needed. Top management had considerably more discretion over how the structure should be molded to match consistent demands from the environ-ment and context. If demands from environment and context were inconsist-ent, we suggested that the structure may not be as susceptible to fine tuning by top management.

Understanding the match involving environment, context, and structure is important in forecasting survival and organizational success. In Part IV we will also see how it is important in predicting the types of problems and opportunities facing middle- and lower-level managers. With this in mind let's move down the cone model and into the organization where we look at subsystems, groups, and leadership.

REFERENCES

I. The Amount of Structure Needed for Survival

A. Strategic Advantage

[1]Biggart, N. "The Creative-Destructive Process of Organizational Change: The Case of the Post Office," *Administrative Science Quarterly*, 22 (1977), 410–426.

[2]Blau, P., and Schoenherr, R. *The Structure of Organizations*. New York: Basic Books, 1971.

[3]Buffa, E. *Operations Management: The Management of Productive Systems*. New York: Wiley, 1976.

[4]Burack, E. *Organization Analysis: Theory and Applications*. Hinsdale, Ill.: Dryden Press, 1975.

[5]Child, J. "Organizational Structure, Environment and Performance: The Role of Strategic Choice," *Sociology*, 6 (1972), 1–22.

[6]Dewar, R., and Hage, J. "Size, Technology, Complexity and Structural Differentiation: Toward a Theoretical Synthesis," *Administrative Science Quarterly*, 23 (1978), 111–136.

[7]Hall, R. *Occupations and The Social Structure*. Englewood Cliffs, N.J.: Prentice-Hall, 1975.

[8]Jelinek, M. "Technology, Organiza-tions, and Contingency," *Academy of Management Review*, 2 (1977), 17–26.

[9]Kimberly, J. R. "Organizational Size and the Structuralist Perspective: A Review and a Critique," *Administrative Science Quarterly*, 21 (1976), 571–597.

[10]McKelvey, W. "Guidelines for the Empirical Assessment of Organizations," *Administrative Science Quarterly*, 21 (1976), 571–597.

[11]Melcher, A. *Structure and Process of Organizations: A Systems Approach*. Englewood Cliffs, N.J.: Prentice-Hall, 1976.

[12]Osborn, R. "The Search for Environmental Complexity," *Human Relations,* 29 (1976), 179–191.

[13]Perrow, C. *Complex Organizations: A Critical Essay*. Glenview, Ill.: Scott, Foresman, 1972.

[14]Pfeffer, J. *Organizational Design*, Arlington Heights, Ill.: AHM, 1978.

[15]Samuelsen, P. *Economics*. New York: McGraw-Hill, 1967.

[16]Sutherland, J. *Administrative Decision-Making: Extending the Bounds of Rationality*. New York: Van Nostrand Reinhold, 1977.

[17]Thompson, J. D. *Organizations in Action*. New York: McGraw-Hill, 1967.

[18]Weick, K. E. *The Social Psychology of Organizing*. Reading, Mass.: Addison-Wesley, 1969.

B. Contextual Complexity

[1]Child, J. *Organization*. New York: Harper & Row, 1977.

[2]Haas, J., and Drabek, T. *Complex Organizations: A Sociological Perspective*. New York: Macmillan, 1973.

[3]Melcher, 1976.

[4]Pugh, D., Hickson, D., Hinings, C., and Turner, C. "The Context of Organizational Structures," *Administrative Science Quarterly*, 14 (1969), 91–114.

C. Structural Complexity

[1]Galbraith, J. *Designing Complex Organizations*. Reading, Mass.: Addison-Wesley, 1973.

[2]Haas and Drabek, 1973.

D. Matching Environmental, Contextual, and Structural Complexity for Survival

[1]Arlen, T. J. *Managing the Flow of Technology*. Cambridge, Mass.: M.I.T. Press, 1977.

[2]Blau and Schoenherr, 1971.

[3]Greiner, L. "Evolution and Revolution as Organizations Grow," *Harvard Business Review*, 60 (1972), 37–46.

[4]Haas and Drabek, 1973.

[5]Litterer, J. *The Analysis of Organizations*. New York: Wiley, 1973.

[6]Nightingale, D. V., and Toulouse, J. "Toward a Multilevel Congruence Theory of Organization," *Administrative Science Quarterly*, 22 (1977), 264–280.

[7]Perrow, C. *Organizational Analysis: A Sociological View*. Belmont, Calif.: Wadsworth, 1970.

[8]Thompson, V. *Modern Organizations*. New York: Knopf, 1961.

II. Enhancing the Potential for Goal Attainment

A. Associations among Dimensions of Environment, Context, and Structure

[1]Aiken, M., and Hage, J. "Organizational Interdependence and Intraorganizational Structure," *American Sociological Review*, 33 (1968), 912–930.

[2]Aldrich, H. "Resource Dependence and Interorganizational Relations: Relations Between Local Employment Service Offices and Social Services Sector Organizations," *Administration and Society*, 7 (1976), 419–454.

[3]Blau and Schoenherr, 1971.

[4]Child, 1977.

[5]Child, J., and Mansfield, R. "Technology, Size and Organizational Structure," *Sociology*, 6 (1972), 369–380.

[6]Dewar and Hage, 1978.

[7]Galbraith, 1973.

[8]Haas and Drabek, 1973.

[9]Jackson, J., and Morgan, C. *Organization Theory: A Macro Perspective for Management*. Englewood Cliffs, N.J.: Prentice-Hall, 1978.

[10]Kimberly, 1976.

[11]Lawler, E., and Rhode, J. *Information and Control in Organizations*. Santa Monica, Calif. Goodyear, 1976.

[12]Litterer, 1973.

[13]Meyer, M. "Size and the Structure of Organizations: A Causal Analysis," *American Sociological Review*, 37 (1972), 434–440.

[14]Melcher, 1976.

[15]Osborn, R., and Hunt, J. G. "The Environment and Organizational

Effectiveness," *Administrative Science Quarterly,* 19 (1974), 231–246.

[16]Pfeffer, 1978.

[17]Pitts, R. "Diversification Strategies and Organizational Policies of Large Diversified Firms," *Journal of Economics and Business,* 28, (Spring – Summer, 1976) 181–188.

[18]Thompson, 1967.

[19]Scott, W. "Organizational Structure," *Annual Review of Sociology,* 1 (1975), 1–20.

[20]Van de Ven, A. "A Revised Framework for Organizational Assessment." In E. Lawler, A. Nadler, and C. Cammann (eds.), *Organizational Assessment: Perspectives on the Measurement of Organizational Behavior and the Quality of Working Life.* New York: Wiley, in press.

III. Top Management Discretion and Structure

A. Fine Tuning the Structure

[1]Child, 1977.

[2]Cummings, L. L., and Berger, C. "Organizational Structure: How Does It Influence Attitudes and Performance," *Organizational Dynamics* (Autumn 1976), 34–49.

[3]Hellriegel, D., and Slocum, J. "Organizational Climate: Measures, Research and Contingencies," *Academy of Management Journal,* 17 (1974), 255–279.

[4]James, L., and Jones, A. "Organizational Structure: A Review of Structural Dimensions and Their Conceptual Relationships with Individual Attitudes and Behavior,"

Organizational Behavior and Human Performance, 16 (1976), 74–113.

B. Strategic Choices in the Long Run

[1]Ackoff, R. *A Concept of Corporate Planning.* New York: Wiley-Interscience, 1970.

[2]Aldrich, 1976.

[3]Biggart, 1977.

[4]Child, 1977.

[5]Greiner, 1972.

[6]Osborn and Hunt, 1974.

[7]Pfeffer, 1978.

[8]Pitts, R. "Diversification Strategies and Organizational Policies of Large Diversified Firms," *Journal of Economics and Business,* 28 (1976), 181–188.

[9]Scott, 1975.

[10]Thompson, 1967.

[11]Weed, F. "Centralized and Pluralistic Structures in Public Welfare," *Administration and Society,* 19 (1977), 111–136.

C. Administrative Philosophy in Complex Settings

[1]Aldrich, 1976.

[2]Child, 1977.

[3]Glueck, W. *Management.* Hinsdale, Ill.: Dryden, 1977.

[4]Greiner, 1972.

[5]Moch, M. "Structure and Organizational Resource Allocation," *Administrative Science Quarterly,* 2 (1976), 419–454.

[6]Osborn, R. N., Jauch, L., Martin, T., and Glueck, W. F. "CEO Succession, Performance and Environmental Conditions." Working paper, Southern Illinois University, 1978.

[7]Pfeffer, 1978.

[8]Sutherland, 1977.

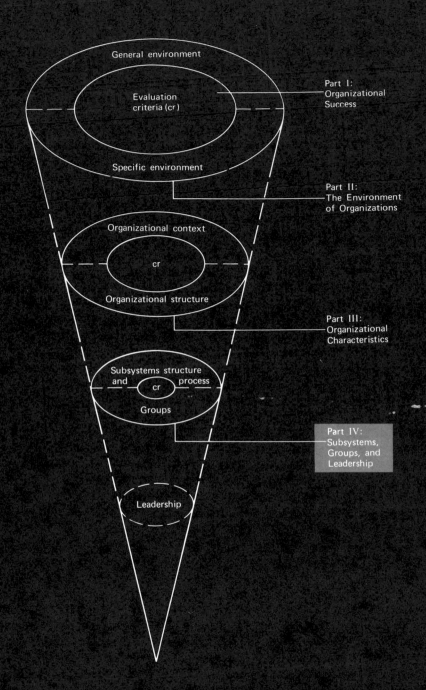

Figure IV-1 A cone model for organizational analysis.

subsystems, groups, and leadership

At last Sam was alone in the executive suite of Mammoth Chemicals and Insurance. It had been a long fight. Sam's desire to become "the man" at Mammoth had been well hidden. A year ago the final step seemed far away. Either Joe Rice, president of Insurance, or Pete Corbin, president of Chemicals, seemed certain to ascend to the presidency. Sam was but a lawyer and merely head of Legal and Governmental Relations. Sure, a cousin was a major stockholder; and the president of the bank Mammoth owed 15 million dollars, was an uncle. But Sam wasn't in on the action. Good old Sam was just corporate staff. Now Joe and Pete were gone. Most of their lieutenants would be leaving, too.

Sam knew there was a chance when Leslie Brick, the old chairman and CEO, had his third heart attack and would not favor either Joe or Pete. They both set out to move toward the presidency. But since neither could get the upper hand the board of directors had no choice. One had to go. Just when it appeared Pete Corbin was going to be the man, the bombshell hit. Chemicals had paid almost a million dollars in commissions to secure a monopoly on fertilizer in Sauba. The Sauba foreign minister failed in his bid to overthrow the government and spilled the beans. The million dollars in Mammoth commissions had actually been used to buy arms and munitions. The press got to Pete, and he denied the whole affair only to recant some 24 hours later when additional incriminating evidence came out. Congress called for a complete investigation and the Securities and Exchange Commission (SEC) started a complete audit. Through three hard months in Washington, Sam had diverted the congressional investigation and worked closely with an old friend at the SEC to shepherd the audit. Sam and Leslie Brick tried to save the image of Mammoth; their efforts drew attention toward Sam.

Sam and Leslie centralized all foreign operations in a new division. It cut across the traditional insurance-chemical divisional arrangement that Mammoth had used since Leslie had put the unlikely conglomerate together. By an astute accounting transaction, Sam had Chemical and Insurance carry most of the overhead for the new division. The new division also got most of the developmental people and all the external relations units, and it reported directly to the "old man." Sam was careful to make sure that most of the overhead and the costs of the litigation were born by Insurance.

Joe made his fatal mistake at the June board meeting. He openly challenged Pete, suggesting that he should be replaced as division president and indicated Insurance did not want to hold bonds for the Sauba project. An argument ensued and Leslie just shook his head. He turned to Sam and muttered, "If these [expletive deleted] can't get along, they both ought to go." When Joe brought up the matter of overhead for the new division, Leslie finally interceded. He appointed a review committee of board members to work with Sam in a complete investigation of Mammoth's organization structure and operations for the 1980s. Further, all senior personnel changes were to be cleared first by the review committee. Later he told Pete to submit his resignation. It was presented to the board just hours before the old man's last heart attack.

Chief Executive Officer and Chairman of the Board! "The man" at Mammoth—Samantha Burklin. She would make sure the Chemical and Insurance divisions cooperated. There would be no more "politics" at Mammoth. Of course, the first order of business would be to quietly sell the bonds for the Sauba project.

Our example is a bit farfetched. But it is intended to show the rise of a politically astute manager who used a basic knowledge of subsystems structure and processes to ascend the organization ladder. Chapter 11 focuses on this. It goes into much greater detail about interunit relations, conflicts that may result, and the power involved in coalition development among units.

In the previous part of the book we outlined the formal structure using the entire organization as the unit of analysis. As you will see, subunits and groups may support or refute the tenets and premises of the formal structure. This part, then, moves you down our cone model further into the organization (see Figure IV-1). The unit of analysis is split into two parts—subsystems and groups. In both cases we are talking about units within the organization. In a sense, the environment of most of these units is the broader organization. However, some units (boundary-spanning) interface directly with the specific environment. And there are general and specific environmental forces operating on an organization as a whole that affect units within it.

Chapter 12 explores groups and group behavior. Individuals in organizations almost always function together in groups in one way or another. But groups are more than mere collections of individuals. They are affected by their membership and by other groups and subsystems with which they interact.

The third chapter in this section explores leadership. Leaders attempt to influence others to accomplish organizational goals. They frequently must work with groups and through groups. But they also work one-on-one with individuals, both vertically with subordinates, and laterally with peers. As such, it doesn't fit neatly into the top-down approach. Leadership goes on at all levels of the organization. It is both a group and an individual phenomenon. But the influence which leaders exercise gives rise to their ability to carry out the earlier functions we have described.

The final chapter (14) is our last contingency view of an organization. We integrate the material from this part of the book with those preceding it.

As we move through the chapters in this part you may notice a subtle but important change from earlier ones. Previous chapters tended to use global concepts justified by deductive logic and relatively few empirical studies. In this part, however, (with the exception of the contingency chapter) there are many empirical studies. So many in fact that much of the literature deals with trying to derive integrating constructs from the divergent findings. If the first approach is deductive, then the second is inductive (recall the discussion of these in Chapter 1).

You will find these differences in the organization of the chapters in this part and in the greater number of names cited in them. For example, a number of contingency models of leadership are associated with individual authors. These are then used to inductively "build up" to our own multiple influence leadership model.

chapter **11** **SUBSYSTEMS**

RELATIONSHIPS

I. **Basic Types of Subsystems**

   A. **Vertical Splits**
   B. **Horizontal Splits**

II. **Relationships among Units**

   A. **Balanced Relationships**
      1. **Work-flow Relationships**
      2. **Service Relationships**
      3. **Advisory Relationships**
   B. **Asymmetrical Relationships**
      1. **Auditing Relationships**
      2. **Approval Relationships**
   C. **The Drive toward Power**
   D. **The Path to Power**
      1. **Combinations Enhancing Power**

III. **Functional and Dysfunctional Consequences of Conflict**

   A. **Goals, Ideology, and Terminal Conflict**
      1. **Terminal Conflict**
   B. **Factors Increasing the Probability and Severity of Conflict**
      1. **Interdependence among Units**
      2. **Power Imbalances**
      3. **Means-ends Ambiguity**
      4. **Confict Management**

IV. **Organizational Politics**

   A. **Managers as Politicians**
   B. **Organizational Politics and Ideology**
   C. **Managing Coalitions**

V. **Measurement Module**

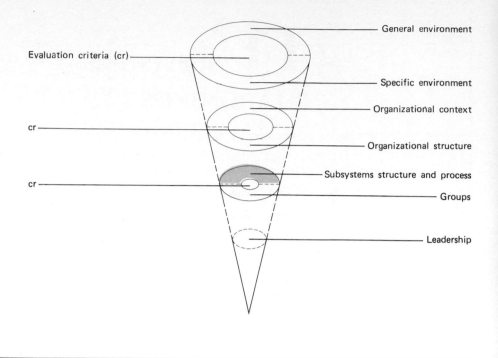

Evaluation criteria (cr) ——————

cr ——————

cr ——————

General environment

Specific environment

Organizational context

Organizational structure

Subsystems structure and process

Groups

Leadership

In the introduction to Part IV we showed how Samantha used her understanding of subsystems and organizational power to her advantage. This chapter focuses on interunit relations and organizational politics.

The analysis of interunit relations begins with a review of some basic types of subsystems. We then move to a description of relationships among units. Subsystems, like organizations, attempt to grow and survive. So it is natural they will upset the balanced pattern of influence suggested by the formal structure. Thus we discuss conflict, noting that it can be both functional and dysfunctional. Along with this, several important factors that appear to increase the chances of conflict are discussed. We conclude by first delving into organizational politics from the viewpoint of interunit development and growth. We then follow with the Measurement Module.

BASIC TYPES OF SUBSYSTEMS

Before we delve into an analysis of subsystems it's important to quickly review some material and recast it into an interunit framework. Subsystems of organizations are just that—systems. As such they have a domain and may be viewed as input-transformation-output mechanisms complete with goals, technology, structure and individual members. Unlike organizations, however, subsystems rarely guide their own destiny. They rarely contain all the components necessary to operate as an independent unit. Put in a slightly different way, they are not the legal entities we discussed in Chapter 6. As long as the system responds appropriately, few outsiders care which subsystem they are dealing with. They tend to treat all subsystems as representatives of an organization. For instance, say you contact the university for material concerning graduate programs. You would probably care less whether the unit responding was the graduate school or an academic department, as long as you got the required information. The function and role of the responding unit does make a substantial difference. But few outsiders can quickly spot the key features that differentiate one type of outside contact unit from another. Thus, let's take a look at some of the types of subsystems within large organizations. First we will vertically dissect the organization. Then we will slice it horizontally.

Vertical Splits

Figure 11-1 outlines some of the major types of subsystems you would expect to find in large and huge organizations. At the top of the modified pyramid are the institutional subsystems.[5] They are designed to guide the overall development of an organization, manage the interface with the environment, and hold the key positions of power within the system.[2] Here you find the organizational elite described in Chapter 8. Moving down into the organization you find the managerial subunits that help formulate and interpret the policies and strategies ratified at the institutional level. These are the bureaucrats and administrators who plan, organize, and monitor the day-to-day operations of the organization. At the bottom are the technical units, which produce the outputs of the system. Here you find the work crews, production groups, and sales units.

As noted in the analysis of organizational criteria in Chapter 3, it is useful to look at a series of vertical means-ends chains that tie the units of an organization together. As suggested by Figure 11-1, technical units are subordinate to managerial ones and managerial units to those at the institutional level. As

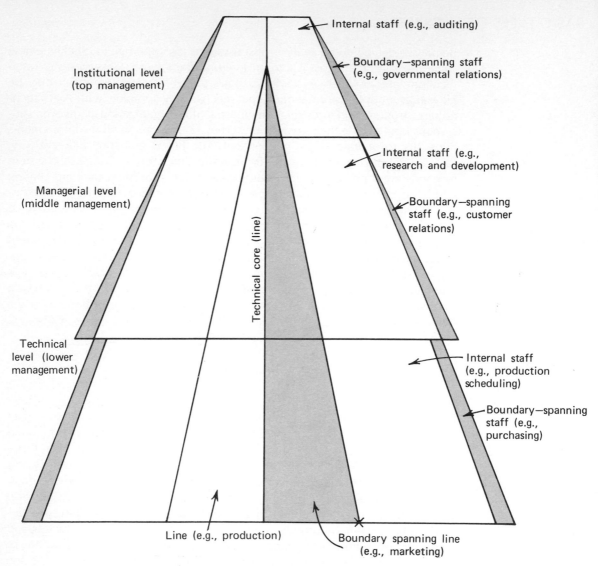

Institutional level
(top management)

Managerial level
(middle management)

Technical
level (lower
management)

Technical core (line)

Internal staff (e.g., auditing)

Boundary—spanning staff
(e.g., governmental relations)

Internal staff (e.g.,
research and development)

Boundary—spanning
staff (e.g., customer
relations)

Internal staff
(e.g., production
scheduling)

Boundary—spanning
staff (e.g.,
purchasing)

Line (e.g., production)

Boundary spanning line
(e.g., marketing)

Figure 11-1 Major types of organizational subsystems.

we pointed out earlier, often the means-ends chain is presumed to start with overall systems and output goals established by institutional units. These are then divided into tasks and given to managerial units as goals. These "goals" are further subdivided into tasks and assigned to units at the technical level. If each unit does its assigned task, theoretically the organization should have a good chance of reaching its systems and output goals. However, organizations just do not operate on this simple rational model.[3] Goals are often conflicting.[1] The division of tasks naturally leads to gaps and inconsistencies. Few organizations can clearly specify their goals. Even fewer have such a clear-cut view of ways to reach goals that the means-ends process yields a harmonious, well-operating, efficient machine. To further complicate matters, individuals do not subordinate their lives to organizations and may manipulate the system to their own ends.[4]

Horizontal Splits

The inherent conflict of goals and means between units within an organization can be seen more clearly if we consider the tasks they must perform. Running through the middle of Figure 11-1 is the technical core—also known as the "line."[7] These units produce and market the outputs of the system. Some, such as marketing, can be called boundary spanners, since much of their contact is with outsiders.[5] Units outside the technical core are called "staff."

Staff units can also roughly be divided on the basis of their interaction with external units. Traditional internal staff units theoretically assist the line by providing specialized services and/or information.[4] As noted in the figure, internal staff may be at the institutional, managerial, or technical level of an organization. For instance, auditing is often attached to the institutional level to ensure its independence. Many large organizations have specialized research and development units attached to a high-level production manager.[5] Day-to-day information and consultation by production scheduling and organizational development units occurs at the technical level.[7] We should note that staff units often appear on the organization chart as if they were all at the institutional and managerial levels.[7] This is due to the shorter chain of command (fewer hierarchical levels) typically found in the staff. Furthermore, staff units themselves and even many line units may see the staff as higher in the organization due to specialized skills and their access to those at managerial and institutional levels.[3] Yet, by contact across the organization, as we show later in the chapter, such is not always the case.

A primary contact for some staff units may be with those outside the boundaries of the organization. These units are tagged "staff boundary spanning units." They may also be found at the institutional, managerial, and technical levels.[2] Governmental Relations, for instance, is often attached to an institutional-level manager. Government officials expect an organization to speak through one voice of authority. Some units, such as that of Customer Relations in an auto manufacturer, are attached to middle management. They buffer (protect) institutional units and the technical core from outside harrassment.[1] At the technical level you find units designated to perform specialized tasks such as purchasing and personnel selection.

Staff boundary-spanning units often perform diverse activities, but most center on processing information from the environment and representing the organization to outside constituencies.[1] One of their major functions is often "uncertainty absorption."[9] They collect, process, and draw inferences from their contacts with outsiders and pass on only the inferences.[8] These opinions often became "solid" data concerning the environment.[1] For example, the legal department "tells" plant managers what the OSHA standards mean and how they will be enforced. The marketing research group tells the production units an item will or won't sell. As we also noted above, boundary-spanning units represent the organization to others. They are often charged with developing a favorable image with governmental units, customers, suppliers, and distributors. Marketing, for instance, performs this representative function in small organizations. In very large organizations, staff units may even buffer boundary-spanning line units.[2] For instance, a governmental relations unit may protect marketing from direct contact with government.

As this brief description implies, units with different functions must interface and respond to different pressures to achieve their subsystems goals.[9] We have stressed the role of staff and boundary-spanning units because they can upset a developing harmony among units in their attempts to match the organization to its environment. In all larger organizations there are tricky problems of power and influence.[10] Each subsystem is likely to overestimate its importance, see some of its goals in conflict with others, and perform activities that disturb the smooth functioning of other units.[10] To get an overall picture of the interplay among subsystems it's helpful to enumerate some common types of relationships.

RELATIONSHIPS AMONG UNITS*

We may roughly divide the relationships among subsystems into two categories. First, are interrelationships that are balanced. The units exchange resources in a more or less free market. The power of these units is relatively equal. The second category consists of those interrelationships in which there's an imbalance in either the resources being exchanged or in the power of one group in an exchange. First let us take a look at the more balanced interdependencies.

*This discussion is based heavily on Sayles,[2] and Hall and Leidecker.[1]

Balanced Relationships

Within any large organization you expect to find staff departments busy peddling their wares to other units. In the executive dining room the head of the operations research department has lunch with the plant manager to extol the virtues of a computerized inventory system. She is selling an on-line package. Her people can install the computer, program it, train plant personnel to operate it, and modify the programming to meet the changing demands of the plant manager. At another table, the assistant vice-president of personnel is talking with the assistant vice-president of finance about improving the "quality of working life." Personnel wants to set up a series of workshops on transcendental meditation (TM). The production manager may buy the services of the operations research group. The assistant finance vice-president doesn't seem interested in TM. These meetings can be called missionary work. It involves widely dispersed contacts throughout the organization to seek potential "buyers" and "sellers."[8]

Support units are anxious to have services used to justify their existence. Much of their time may be spent in "selling." Essentially, these sellers must convince those in the technical core and in other staff units that their services will be beneficial. Buyers, on the other hand, know that accepting services is not free. It must be purchased with the time of subordinates, alterations in standard operating procedures, legitimization of the staff unit, and support of an activity that may or may not prove to be beneficial.

After an initial contact, actual "terms of trade" may be discussed. Both parties will attempt to uncover possible defects, problems, and limitations. Each may jockey for better terms from the other party. To return to the operations research (OR) and production example, the production manager may want the OR group to use its equipment budget. The OR head may want the production department to finance the computer system. If terms of trade appear favorable, then both parties may provide more complete information concerning their needs and capabilities. For instance, the production manager may reveal he has enough discretionary investment funds to finance half of the computer needed to implement the proposed inventory control system. The OR manager may admit she doesn't have enough excess personnel to assign an individual full-time to the project. Throughout this process either party may withdraw. Neither has the power to force the other into the exchange.

When such exchanges are within the technical core, you have what we call work-flow relationships.[8] When such trading relations emerge between technical core units and internal staff, you typically differentiate between exchange of services and information. Let us look more carefully at these three balanced interdependencies among units.

Work-flow Relationships. Work-flow relationships involve interdependencies among two or more units at different stages of a transformation process.[8] The simplest work-flow relationship involves sequential interdependence. One unit is dependent directly upon only one other unit. For example, assume two units in a small insurance company process policies for independent agents. A clerical unit must check the policies for procedural details before they go to an actuarial unit for a price quotation. The manager of the actuarial unit is accountable for providing a price quotation. But it won't be done until the application is processed by the clerical unit. At the same time the agent is pressuring the actuarial manager for a price quotation, the actuarial manager is pressuring the manager of the clerical unit. Each stage feeds sequentially into the next. Timing is particularly important.

As you might expect, when the processing is clear-cut and there is sufficient slack, the two managers are likely to trade personnel and duties to speed-up the process. For instance, the actuarial manager may give a list of standard price quotations to the clerical group so that it may tentatively total a price quotation. In exchange, the actuarial manager may comment favorably on the performance of the clerical unit in discussions with their common supervisor.[7]

Such simple trading between two parties becomes more difficult as the work flow becomes more complex.* However, the essential nature of the relationship is much the same. A mutually satisfactory trade is negotiated and maintained because both parties benefit. Imbalance may be corrected by "side payments" to the head of the unit or its members.†

One important feature of work-flow relationships is their duration.[9] Short-term contacts typically involve merely an exchange of relatively unambiguous information. Parties are expected to cooperate as a matter of course without expecting any specific compensation. Moderately long-term contacts often involve routine reports concerning cooperation and coordination as well as balancing the terms of exchange and the resources of the units. Here, support for additional resources is expected (an important side payment). Long-term contacts often develop where ambiguity with regard to the implementation of a new technique or process must be resolved.[8] Here, both parties may change the operations of their units in order to help the other. Managers must often "bank resources" in a work-flow partner to help them through a transitionary period.[3] Only later will the manager get a return on this "investment." Above all, both parties must strive toward a balanced exchange to maintain a long-term relationship.

---

*Other work-flow relationships include independent, reciprocal, or team approaches. See Exhibit 11-4 in the Measurement Module.

†Side payments may come in many forms including: (1) personal favors, such as tickets to a sporting event or recommending a relative for a job; (2) organizational support, such as a favorable comment on the performance of another unit; or (3) external support, such as telling a client how hard another unit has worked to overcome difficulties unknown to the outsider.

Service Relationships. Service relationships involve exchanges of goods and services outside the flow of work.[8] In small organizations service units are often within the technical core. For instance, the computer unit may be under the plant manager. In larger organizations, service units are typically outside the technical core under one or more staff specialties. Printing and duplicating, purchasing, and computer programming are examples of units that hold valuable resources several units may need to accomplish their tasks. Service groups manage scarce resources needed by many units. Thus, they have some power over which unit receives favorable treatment. For example, a printing and duplicating unit handles a routine, predictable task needed by many organizational units. Sheer economies of scale often dictate a centralized computer programming operation. Astute managers cultivate the heads of such service units.[7] For when there is a sudden demand for the service, various line units will vie for preferential treatment. Service managers can "pay off" some by putting their orders ahead or by reclassifying them into a high-priority group. They can deny favorable treatment and fall back on formal rules and procedures. For example, many a manager has heard the following from the head of the secretarial pool: "Look at all the requests ahead of yours. You know the standard time for a letter is three days. Sorry." As we note later, service interdependencies may have more inherent friction than any other.

Advisory Relationships. Advisors provide one party with expert advice from a specialist in areas where generalists need help.[8] The exchange is balanced directly by the recognition and legitimacy the generalist provides the specialist. Indirectly, the exchange can be balanced when the specialist seeks expansion of the advisory unit.[10] The most common form of advisory relationships are between line and internal staff units. Theoretically, the line manager requests help from staff specialists upon identifying a problem or opportunity.[6] Of course, the staff may help identify problems and opportunities. The staff unit investigates and provides the line manager with several alternatives complete with advantages and disadvantages.

As you can probably anticipate, there is a tricky balancing problem involved. The staff unit must not provide "too much" or "too little" advice. If "too much" advice is given, the generalist may think the staff is encroaching on line turf.[1] The relationship may be terminated or the line may not support the staff in its attempts to grow. If insufficient advice is given, the generalist won't get enough help to solve the problem. The exact balance depends upon a number of considerations, two of which are the desires of the generalist and the scope of the problem.[1] Some generalists want internal staff units to solve problems by providing *the* optimal, workable solution. They expect staff to follow through the implementation of changes and suggest modifications. Others merely want a series of alternatives. From the organization's viewpoint the scope of the problem should guide the role of staff advice.[4] Staff recommendations are typically focused around a particular specialty or narrow view of a problem. Thus, the narrow problems with minimal consequences in other areas call for extensive staff consultation where "too much" staff advice is all but impossible. Conversely, broader problems or those with substantial ramifications call for the generalists to integrate several staff recommendations.

Several authors indicate that advisors should not usurp generalists' authority.[2,5] And they should make sure that the generalist gets the credit for any improvements stemming from staff consultation. Generalists are admonished to support staff units by granting them credit and supporting them in attempts to gain an expanded domain. This mutual backscratching maintains the balance of exchange needed to keep relationships viable. It also helps explain a congenital problem of growing organizations—staff proliferation.

Work-flow, service, and advisory relationships most frequently occur among units at or near the same organizational level. They are horizontal in that the interacting units are at the technical, managerial, or institutional level. Furthermore, both units can voluntarily withdraw from the exchange if it's not mutually beneficial. While one unit may have somewhat more clout than another, both play in the same league. Such is not the case with a second series of interunit relationships. These are asymmetrical in that one party is dominant.

Asymmetrical Relationships

In most organizations there is an elaborate network of checks and balances.[13] This limits the authority of subsystems' managers and serves to evaluate the performance of their units. Much of this network is represented in the formal organization chart by the chain of command. Yet managers must also contend with specialized units that attempt to control their operations. Let us take a look at these two asymmetrical relationships—auditing and approval.

Auditing Relationships. In almost all organizations you find units concerned with keeping tabs on how other units are performing.[8] Budgeting, quality control, and, of course, financial auditing are examples. Both internal staff and boundary-spanning units must often submit auditing reports to units dealing with equal opportunity employment, health and safety, personnel development, and the like. Essentially, the auditing manager checks the performance of other units to determine the extent to which their activities and/or outputs are consistent with those specified by the organization. Most frequently the auditing group is one or more levels above the units it is checking.[3]

The exchange is heavily one-sided in favor of the auditing group. The criteria used by various auditing groups usually aren't consistent with one another. The criteria may or may not be consistent with the apparent function of the unit being examined.[8] For example, budgeting may evaluate a sales department on the percentage of expenditures over or under estimate. Being under budget could be just as bad as being over budget. Consumer relations may judge the sales department solely on customer satisfaction, while financial auditors may check for a detailed accounting of expenditures. Yet the vice-president of marketing may merely use sales volume for granting promotions and raises.

Auditors are also taught not to fraternize with the "enemy." This makes it particularly difficult to develop a more balanced exchange relationship.[9] Theoretically, they are to report their findings "up the line," without giving the units a chance to correct a deficiency. The astute auditing manager, however, realizes that accurate information from subsystems' managers is important. Bogus data can be developed to deceive the auditor. And the subsystem's manager may make it difficult to obtain records by inaction.[7] Thus, many auditors work with subsystems' managers to spot deficiencies and allow them to make corrections before final reports are submitted. Further, they may solicit promises of improvement in exchange for vaguely stated evaluations.[8] For instance, more than one auditing report has read, "This unit is making substantial improvement and embarking on a new program to ensure meeting organizational standards." This may sound acceptable, but it doesn't indicate the current level of performance.

Approval Relationships. Subunit managers also deal with units that require advanced approval before action can be taken.[8] These approval relationships block the subsystem from acting as an organization. You might normally think that the vertical chain of command delineates the flow of authority within an organization. Yet it does not provide the full network.[5] Approval units are an organization's political arm. They generate and allocate power to keep one subsystem from overpowering another, help to prevent suboptimization of units, and initiate changes detrimental to subsystems. In many organizations the legal department has such power. In the old General Motors divisional arrangement it was a finance unit.[12]

Approval relationships are blatantly unequal. The approval unit may establish its own bases for decisions, change standards at the drop of a hat, and/or institute application procedures that suit its purposes.[10] The exchange may be partially balanced by allowing subunit members to participate in decisions.[11] For instance, banks use a loan committee to establish policy and approve unusual loan applications.

As with auditing units, the approval unit is typically one or more levels above the unit seeking approval.[3] However, the approval relationship requires more contact and quick clearance if an organization is to avoid excessive red-tape delays. Thus, approval units are often stacked on top of one another with clearance authority consistent with that of a line manager.[3] For instance, a conglomerate may consider capital investment such an important decision that approval relationships are needed before committing the organization. A division president may be given the authority to approve capital investments up to $5 million with the advice of a financial planning unit. This unit reports to headquarters financial planning. It may recommend against an investment under $5 million and be overruled by the division president. Above the $5 million level, the division president may need approval from headquarters financial planning. However, one does not want a division president seeking approval from a unit in middle management. Thus, you either balance the authority, here at $5 million, or move the staff unit to corporate headquarters. If such balance is not developed, you can expect substantial conflict between line and staff as well as a predominance of staff versus line decisions.[14,4]

If you think such approval relationships are restricted to corporations, consider a typical state personnel unit. To control patronage while giving the appearance of a merit system, some states have a centralized personnel department with members assigned to many state facilities. To hire a state worker the manager submits a request and receives a list of approved candidates. Three candidates are often listed in priority. These individuals must be contacted before the hiring of anyone. Justification must be provided if they are not acceptable. To balance the power of the personnel department representative (read patronage chief), the unit head may recommend individuals to be considered for the list. It is expected that one of these will be approved and that the unit head has "talked over" the recommendations with the local patronage chief.

Approval relationships aren't limited to internal staff units. Boundary-spanning units can develop an approval relationship if they appear to be dealing with a critical contingency.[1] For example, equal opportunity is a critical contingency for some universities that rely heavily upon federal funds. Before an academic unit may hire faculty, it may be required to show an internal equal employment unit that it made substantial efforts to hire applicants from minorities.

The problems with approval units are legion.[2] They are surrogate bosses without the onus of matching responsibility.[4] Thus, they often appear to act as if they make their own rules just to frustrate managers.[7] Such conflict may be partially reduced if approval units incorporate subordinate managers and provide advance notice about new standards, procedures, and bases for decisions.[6] Yet the role of these units invites conflict.

The Drive Toward Power

Our description of subsystems relations is oversimplified. It seems to imply that each unit has only one kind of lateral relationship. What you really find is a mixture of many lateral relationships where the role of the subsystem favors one type of relationship over another.[1] You can also expect to find different relationships among the same units.[7] For example, the budgeting unit may be required to seek approval from the unit in charge of equal opportunity hiring. But the situation is reversed when it comes to financial affairs. Cynics argue that subsystems' managers look for favorable imbalances among units and trade favors to enhance the performance of their units and their own career progression.[4] Some probably do. But it's important to realize that the network of relationships suggests that no one subsystem is invulnerable.[7] All must cooperate to some extent. No subsystem can alienate everyone and survive.

A number of authors have suggested, however, that subsystems' managers jockey for position in an attempt to improve their relative standing.[5,6,9] The shifts may be partially explained as follows. The low unit on the totem pole is the service unit, which must respond to the demands of others.[5] These units will attempt to shift toward an advisory role or at least incorporate this role in their relationships with others. It is more prestigious and easier to give advice than balance conflicting demands. Advice may be accepted or rejected, and a developed alternative may not be implemented properly. So advisory units often shift toward a work-flow relationship.[5] Recall, the advisory unit must "sell" its wares to survive and grow. By developing a work-flow relationship it has gained equal footing with the traditionally more influential line units. This relationship is particularly beneficial for the staff unit. It won't be held fully accountable for poor performance but often receives the kudos if the line unit is successful.[4]

The staff unit may reduce the risk of being incorporated into the line by shifting from a work-flow relationship to an audit role.[5] The integrity of the staff subsystem Is assured. Furthermore, it is generally more desirable to appraise the work of others and report to prestigious organizational members than to merely provide advice. Lastly, the performance of the units and the audit unit are separate. The audit unit is in a much better bargaining position to get its ideology and programs accepted.[3]

While the auditing relationship gives the unit security and leverage, the approval role cements its power and prestige.[5] Others initiate contact with the unit and seek preferential treatment. This power base also allows the unit to expand into new areas where an organization is facing problems, for in the approval role you normally find substantial slack resources.[2]

The Path to Power

The desired relationships are easy to see. But the path a subunit takes toward increasing its power is more complex. Different subunits can travel slightly different paths at different times. Hinings and his associates have identified two paths followed.[2] These are based on the help a subunit can give others and the organization. Other routes involving political alliances and personal relationships are also available and are discussed under the topic of organizational politics. For now let's examine two "legitimate routes."

As our discussion of subsystem relations indicates, interdependence is the key to analyzing subsystems. The structure, technology, or, on occasion, environmental conditions favor some subunits over others. Specifically, some units are interconnected with many others and have an immediate impact on their actions and performance. Many units are less intertwined with others and find their actions have little direct impact on others. The more reliant others are upon a subunit for day-to-day operations the greater its immediacy.[2] Units with high immediacy can build power by dealing with uncertainty facing the organization as a whole or other subunits. The subunit must cope effectively by providing valuable information, clarifying expectations, and/or reducing the variety of demands and inputs. As it copes with uncertainty its power may be reduced if other subunits are seen as viable substitutes. Thus, a unit must appear to acquire specialized skills in an effort to reduce uncertainty. Lastly, the unit must expand its domain by increasing the number of contacts within the organization and undertake new activities needed by other units. In different terms, it can build on its existing power base by becoming a more pervasive force throughout the organization. The key here is in having already acquired a favorable position within the organization. Units in the technical core at the institutional level are probably in the best position to use this path.[2]

For instance, some liberal arts colleges facing declining enrollments have started programs in more "applied" areas such as business. For these emerging business programs to bloom, they must cope with uncertainty posed by declining enrollments, hire specialized faculty (to maintain uniqueness), and develop closer ties with more traditional social science units (e.g., economics, political science, psychology, and sociology). In this way they can increase pervasiveness and demonstrate how they are helping traditionally powerful academic units (immediacy).

But what if you are not in a good position? A similar approach can be used by staff and boundary-spanning units.[2] The path is to identify an area of high uncertainty, cope with the uncertainty by using specialized skills (to enhance nonsubstitutability), and to expand the network of interdependencies more extensively throughout the organization.[2] Again, this is similar to the first path. But in the first situation the unit was already in a position of importance.

In the latter case, the unit tries to expand its domain to gain immediacy. Our vignette concerning Samantha's rise to the executive suite is one example. Another is evident when some subsystems have used a computerized management information system (MIS) to build power.[1] MIS units can tackle an area of high uncertainty. MIS can be used to provide reliable estimates for sales and production scheduling as well as to track the performance of selected units. If its reports can reduce uncertainty, it is effectively coping. The computer provides a natural means for developing specialized skills. And the success in providing accurate forecasts for sales and production can be extended into other areas.[4]

Combinations Enhancing Power. As Hinings et al. point out, immediacy, uncertainty reduction, substitutability, and pervasiveness should not be considered separately.[2] For instance, accounting units may be able to reduce uncertainty and have contacts with almost all subsystems within an organization. But they lack immediacy. Their actions can be ignored for some time before substantial negative effects are noticed. Similarly, the power of a subunit can be partially managed by altering its degree of immediacy. For example, alterations in the environment, structure, or technology of an organization may shift the types of help it needs to remain viable. Once-powerful units may be eased out by asking them to concentrate more on long-range innovations and development projects. Since long-range planning and strategic development are typically considered top-management functions, the subsystem may readily move into an innovative role.[3] Then, the subsystem can be extricated from day-to-day operations without an immediate loss of stature. Talented and useful members may be subsequently reassigned as if it were part and parcel of their career progression. In essence, the unit is moved up and then out.

Of course such jockeying for power, growth, and prestige automatically leads to conflict among units. There are likely to be substantial disagreements over the goal priorities of the system, the best means to accomplish the goals, and exactly what share of the resources various subsystems should be getting in order to adequately perform their duties. So let's take a closer look at conflict among subsystems.

FUNCTIONAL AND DYSFUNCTIONAL CONSEQUENCES OF CONFLICT

Conflict and integration have positive and negative effects on an organization.[7,9] On the functional side, conflict between units is a mechanism that helps keep an organization responsive to external change.[8] It provides a climate for a shift of power among units. Interunit conflict also helps maintain unit cohesiveness and partially offsets individual anxiety and frustration.[9,3] At the same time, conflict tends to reduce efficiency; lower the risk-propensity of units; drive institutional, administrative, and technical levels away from one another; and bring a distortion of information.[4,1] As you will see shortly, conflict can also break an organization into rival camps. Infighting replaces integration as the dominant theme of interunit interaction.[2]

Given the positive and negative consequences of interunit conflict it is not surprising that many scholars argue that too much as well as too little conflict should be avoided. Janis is perhaps the most well-known advocate of conflict in organizations.[6] He argues that organizational norms for harmony, loyalty, and agreement backed up by organizational rewards may lead to a mindless consensus called "groupthink." Groupthink paves the way for disaster. Plans, strategies, and commitments are developed without considering all the implications and are continued even when it is apparent they are damaging the organization. For instance, Janis blames much of the Vietnam disaster and the Bay of Pigs fiasco on groupthink.

In a complementary analysis, Caplow notes the debilitating effects of terminal conflict where most, if not all, of the resources of the unit are directed toward defeating another subsystem.[2] Even the winning unit may find that it is isolated and has fostered a perverted view of outsiders. Furthermore, the winning unit itself may split and another round of terminal conflict may ensue. Caplow's analysis of terminal conflict as well as analyses by several other authors suggest that organizational goals and ideology play a critical role in keeping conflict within acceptable boundaries.[8,9] So let's take a closer look at terminal conflict. Our description will also indicate why many managers and others see conflict as potentially damaging and why they are often less afraid of groupthink than terminal conflict (a fight to the death of one unit).

Goals, Ideology, and Terminal Conflict

Some years ago Sherif empirically demonstrated what managers find in everyday practice.[9] The existence of mutual superordinate goals constricts conflict and brings out functional effects. For organizations with complex means-ends chains, however, superordinate goals, such as the organization's mission, are too vague and remote for effectively containing conflict among subsystems. But goals do form the base for an organization's ideology. This in itself is used to contain disputes among units.[10]

An organization's ideology is a blend of its mission, technological thrust, structural logic, and administrative philosophy. It is the day-to-day expression of the desired ends and acceptable means. Such ideology is often referred to as a series of core values, guiding principles, or tradition. This gives a larger meaning to the routine tasks of an organization. In Chapter 8 we discussed the ideology at the institutional level. We called it administrative philosophy. However, those at the administrative and technical levels also have an ideology.

As a set of shared values, concerns, beliefs, and myths, the ideology indicates the relative importance of various units and the limits on acceptable means. That is, it can govern the way in which power is achieved and exercised. Most managers need not be told that certain actions are unacceptable.[6] It is understood that actions should appear to be consistent with the dominant ideology. Socialization helps build and maintain these belief systems.[5] However, ideologies are like cultural value systems. They are composed of a series of dominant and contradictory elements. Consider, for instance, these two statements: "Manufacturing is the most important aspect of our operations." "Without marketing there would be no need for production." These ideologies would seem to conflict.

When environmental conditions are stable, the technology remains essentially unchanged, and the structure of an organization remains within narrow limits. Here there is likely to be a fairly well-developed ideology that is generally accepted by managers at every level.[1] In such cases, managers would no more think of violating the ideology than a baseball manager would think of putting ten players on the field.[6] However, the stresses and strains from alterations in environmental and organizational conditions typically block ideological consensus. Different units must cope with ambiguity and change. But they tend to place somewhat different priorities on the primary and contradictory elements of the dominant ideology. Conflict of understanding or ideology may emerge.[4]

Organizations also reinforce the ideological splits across units at the same time they reinforce a common ideological viewpoint. For instance, the performance of a manufacturing unit may be based on efficiency. A sales unit might be judged on sales volume. Long production runs yielding identical products improve production efficiency. But sales often increase when products are tailored to each customer. These criteria for judging manufacturing and sales are inconsistent.[3] Thus you may expect conflict even though top-level management reinforces harmony and consensus. Where a dominant ideology is widely held you may expect this conflict to yield solutions that help the organization as a whole.[7] Note that neither unit maximizes its goals. As long as conflict remains within an organization's ideology, it will most likely be considered functional, just as most football fans like a clean, hard-fought game.*,[2]

*We should note that the ideology may not fit with emerging environmental or technical demands and, thus, an organization may be led astray.

Terminal Conflict.* Where the ideology of the units becomes disparate, contact between units can quickly degenerate into terminal conflict.[2] In terminal conflict the antagonists believe they are defending cherished values by crushing the opposition. A weaker unit may defeat a stronger foe by mobilizing its resources properly. All the resources of the unit may be directed toward victory regardless of the short-run consequences. Mobilization is defensive. But outsiders see it as an offensive move and automatically begin to plan their defense. Again defense is confused with offense and a destructive cycle begins.†

To gain a temporary advantage the unit in question encroaches on the boundaries of the dominant ideology by using questionable means to increase its power. For instance, promotions often include some consideration of technical competence and past performance; however, allegiance to one of the warring parties may be the sole criterion. Once loyalty is used for promotions by one unit it will be used by the other warring party. The cycle may continue as a unit uses loyalty to decide who should or should not be fired. Once the cycle begins and the organization's ideology is ignored the conflict quickly degenerates into a struggle in which victory is paramount. The units may even violate the ideology they seek to "protect." The perverted logic of terminal conflict is perhaps best represented by a quote from a soldier in Vietnam, "We had to destroy the village to save it."

In sum, conflict is much like dynamite. Comparatively small amounts that are controlled are quite beneficial, but the potential for disaster is always present. If conflict over resources, means, or power goes beyond the accepted ideology of an organization, it becomes quite dysfunctional. It is impossible to forecast precisely when a contest between units may erupt into terminal conflict.[8] So it's important to look at the factors that increase the probability and severity of interunit conflict.

Factors Increasing the Probability and Severity of Conflict

There are a number of environmental and organizational factors that appear to increase the probability and severity of interunit conflict.[4,7,14,18,23] Essentially these can be boiled down into three general propositions. One, as uncertainty increases, the probability of conflict between units increases.[22] The units must establish new interfaces to cope with changing conditions. Such alterations may stem from changes in the environment, contextual factors, or structure.

---

*This discussion is based on Caplow's treatment of this topic.[2]
†Note: The criterion here is survival.

The second proposition follows the same logic. Increases in interdependence appear to increase the probability and severity of conflict.[7,12,26] Increasing interdependence forces units to adjust more internal operations to meet external demands. Third, additional resources (development) seem to be an important factor in keeping conflict within acceptable bounds.[3,21] In regard to interunit conflict we often talk of organizational slack.[13] Slack resources allow units to grow without taking resources away from others. All can have a bigger slice of the pie. Further, more slack in an organization seems to foster a broader range of contacts among units, where there's a greater likelihood of building ideological consensus.[6] Thus, a reduction in interunit conflict is a side benefit of organizational growth. Increases in resources to units decreases the severity of conflict. While these propositions await empirical testing, they are consistent with a number of clinical descriptions of interunit conflict.[26]

There are also a series of factors that are often unique to a particular set of subsystems. These factors can be roughly classified as dealing with the nature of the interdependencies among units, the balance of power, and the ambiguity surrounding the subsystems. Since these factors are associated with conflict, they may be altered to help manage it.

Interdependence among Units. As the interdependence among units increases you expect more conflict among the parties for much the same reasons outlined above. A common mistake many managers make is to assume that forced integration will lead to the eventual development of mutual problem solving.[12] We need to remember that there are strong ethnocentric tendencies that form a natural barrier between units.[2] Members see their groups as superior and others as inferior much as Americans see the United States as superior to Russia (see Table 11-2). Thus, upon initial contact, unit representatives may look for ideological differences rather than seek common ground.

Table 11-2 Ethnocentric Attitudes and Behavioral Predispositions toward Outsiders

They are contemptible, inferior, and perhaps immoral.

One should maintain social distance from them.

The absence of cooperation with other groups is sanctioned by members.

There is an unwillingness to join and/or fight for other groups.

Other groups are used as bad examples.

Other groups are blamed for current problems.

There is a general distrust and fear of other groups.

Source: Adapted from Levine, R. A., and Campbell, D. T. *Ethnocentrism* (New York: John Wiley, 1972). Based on work by Sumner, W. G., *Folkways* (New York: Ginn, 1906).

Demographic differences between units may reinforce ethnocentrism.[23] For example, staff units with young, highly educated members often degrade line units in which members are older and not as well educated. Conversely, new ideas initiated by staff may be automatically rejected by the line as too idealistic and theoretical. Rejection by the line only reinforces the staff's ethnocentric views.[5]

Without clear expectations of mutual benefit, forced integration turns to conflict as ethnocentric attitudes are reinforced.[21] Researchers have often noted the cool, formal, and tense relationships among units that are forced to cooperate without apparent benefits to either unit.[16] Furthermore, forced interaction may build a climate for terminal conflict. Contact may highlight more differences than similarities.

Power Imbalances. Our analyses of interunit relations and the drive toward unit power suggest another potent force influencing the amount of conflict within an organization. Specifically, as the balance of power between units becomes more asymmetrical, conflict is expected to increase.[25] The nature of the relationship is one potential type of power imbalance.[17] The position in the hierarchy is another.[25] However, there are several other forms of imbalance that increase the chances of conflict. One of these is a disparity between hierarchical position and relationship. For instance, assume that a senior production vice-president was forced to obtain clearance for moving machinery from a low-level safety unit. Here, an institutional level unit would be forced into an approval relationship with a staff unit at the managerial level. Unless the safety unit always acquiesces, one would expect conflict.[17]

A particularly sticky problem of power imbalance occurs when environmental or technological changes have not been recognized in the formal structure. Declining units will often attempt to regain lost ground by relying upon outmoded rules, policies, and procedures. As emerging units cope with uncertainty and become more pervasive, they run head-on into the declining unit's red tape.[10] The units quickly get immersed in an apparent conflict over means. Really, though, it's a cover for an imbalance in power.[19]

A common form of power imbalance is found when members of a lower status initiate contact with those of a higher status subsystem. Conflict is expected here. Higher status members think they should initiate and control the timing of such interactions.[17] To prevent this, organizations often create barriers between units such as liaison personnel, contact by appointment only, et cetera. Whyte notes an interesting case of this in restaurants.[24] Cooks were in conflict with waitresses. They were giving food orders to cooks who had higher status. Whyte installed a circular check minder. The cooks could take food orders off the check minder rather than directly from the waitresses.

Interestingly, an imbalance of power vertically in an organization is also expected to increase interunit conflict. This is the modern version of Machiavelli's weak kings, strong barons.[11]

Without a strong source of power at the top of the system, underlings quarrel and jockey more for position. Thus, less conflict is expected in centralized than decentralized organizations.

Visibility of the exchanges among units is another factor. The less visible the relationships among the units, the lower the probability of conflict, since the relative standing of each unit is not broadcast. Each may keep the appearance of having the upperhand and adequately representing its members.[1] When exchanges are highly visible, however, each unit representative must fight for more favorable terms or face sanctions from unit members.[9]

Means-ends Ambiguity. The last factor deals with organizational means and ends. More conflict is expected as mean-ends linkages become more intricate. Confusion and semantic difficulties make the task of each group more difficult. Substantial communication barriers are erected.[4,14,19]

When means are ambiguous, units are likely to propose strategies that lead to an increase in their size, power, and status.[15]

Table 11-3 summarizes the factors that appear to increase the probability of conflict among units. Without information concerning environmental conditions, contextual variables, or organizational structure we can only estimate

---

Table 11-3

Environment and Organizational Factors
1. Uncertainty
2. Interdependence
3. Development (resource decline)

Interunit Factors
1. Interdependence among units
   a. Increases in interdependence
   b. Narrow range of interdependency
2. Imbalance among units
   a. Imbalance of formal authority
   b. Imbalance of power
   c. Imbalance of formal authority and power
   d. Imbalance of status
   e. Weak control at the top
   f. Visibility of relationships
3. Means-ends ambiguity

---

a vague curvilinear relationship between unit conflict and organizational effectiveness. Too much and too little conflict appears dysfunctional.

Conflict Management. While some people speak of resolving conflict, it's more appropriate to think in terms of conflict "management." Here, since a certain amount of conflict is useful, one would try to manage it rather than eliminate it completely. Conflict at the interunit level, which has been our key focus, can be managed by altering the environmental, organizational, or interunit factors in Table 11-3. Discussion of interpersonal rather than interunit conflict is treated by Filley, among others.[8] Some interpersonal conflict management strategies are also summarized there and by Thomas as well.[21]

ORGANIZATIONAL POLITICS

So far we have dealt with functional or rational relationships among units. It was assumed the unit was seeking organizational goals via unit elaboration. But there is another side to interunit relations often called organizational politics. It is unfortunate that organizational politics has such bad press. It can and often is quite useful for an organization and its members.[2]

As Peters explains, political actions may or may not be self-serving; but they normally center on the allocation, distribution (or redistribution) of resources, and the regulation of behavior.[3] Glenn et al. would add, the development of ideology.[1] Thus, Peters classifies actions into four categories: legitimate; client-directed; kinship- and peer-directed; and illegitimate.[3] Legitimate relationships were discussed under types of interunit relations. Illegitimate behaviors are those that are clearly illegal. For instance, when Gulf Oil executives authorized payments to the Nixon reelection campaign, this was illegal behavior. Client, kinship- and peer-directed behaviors are the ones normally called organizational politics.[4]

Managers as Politicians

In political terms managers represent several constituencies. These are clients, kin, and/or peers. Managers represent subordinates and are expected to fight for their interests.[1] At the same time they are members of groups and are expected to protect their peers.[7] They also represent themselves and their families within institutions that expect them to devote their energy toward the good of the organization. Actions that *appear* to benefit clients, kin, or peers more than the organization are called political.[2] Note that beneficiary rather than intent is stressed. Thus, behaviors intended to serve the organization but actually helping clients, kin, or peers will be deemed political.[2]

Most blatant political activities are usually sanctioned by an organization.[4] For instance, it's taboo for a boss to have an affair with a subordinate. This would appear to result in preferential treatment.[4] Conversely, some political actions are actually promoted by the organization. For example, organizational rationality would dictate merit promotion based on factors that predict future job success. Yet, under external pressure an organization may use race or sex as the basis for promotion.

Political behavior is difficult to measure accurately because few organizations have clear-cut goals or means.[6] Most managers can legitimize political actions by showing how they are, in reality, in the organization's best interests even though clients, peers, or kin also benefit.[5] Furthermore, most managers realize that "favors" to clients or peers are forms of "investment" that may later be used to help the organization.[3]

Organizational Politics and Ideology

Political behaviors that violate organizational rules, policies, or procedures are the easiest to detect but rarely the most important.[4] For instance, the supervisor may ignore a no smoking rule or tardiness to help satisfy subordinates. In our opinion, the more important political behaviors involve the development of an ideology.

A dominant and stable ideology emerges by direction from the top of an organization through the development of stable coalitions.[3]

Essentially, institutional-level managers put together coalitions where there's a balance among interests: organization, client, kin, and peers. According to Drucker, ideologies that emerge from the technical and administrative levels do not recognize external factors and may kill an organization.[2] Callon and Vignolle stress the importance of having an ideology that appears to mesh with those of powerful units in an organization's environment.[1]

Managing Coalitions

For most administrators, even at the institutional level, managing existing coalitions and preventing the uncontrollable formation of new ones is a persistent political problem. As Pettigrew notes, it's the involvement of subsystems in a demand-support process that constitutes the most critical aspect of organizational politics.[5] Each subsystem expects the dominant coalition to allow divergent individuals to live together, to provide them with privileges, to enforce minimal standards of performance in others, and to enhance the stability of intragroup relations.[2] At the same time, remember, each unit is attempting to improve. This upsets the balance and stability it expects the ideology to provide. Thus a manager must continually revise and tailor the existing ideology to maintain a balance among units.

Managers can maintain coalitions by altering the relationships among subsystems, changing the function and composition of the units, and/or changing the managers of the units.[7] The best technique may well be dictated by external factors, such as the opportunity to change managers. But recent research suggests that a manager's lateral contacts are particularly important in building and maintaining coalitions.[3]

For years political scientists have cautioned against equating power and potential power. Conditions may favor a particular coalition. But it may never emerge unless the group representatives seek contact. In much the same manner, where several units may be candidates for membership in a coalition, the actual membership may partially reflect the willingness and skill of the managers at lateral relationships.

Since lateral relationships are inherently political, many managers tend to view them with suspicion and disdain as if they were nonprofessional.[6] Yet several research studies suggest that the development and maintenance of lateral relations is a critical part of a manager's job. Specifically, studies by Osborn and Hunt and Duffy suggest that as managers become more willing to develop contacts with related units, the performance and satisfaction of their unit increases.[1,3] The unit head seems to establish the climate for interaction by subordinates. Where there are systematic attempts to exploit opportunities for interface with others, it appears subordinates are more willing to be flexible and express less ethnocentrism. Osborn and Bishop also indicate that the willingness of unit heads to develop lateral relations increases as both slack resources become available and interdependence provides the opportunity for substantial benefits to interacting units.[4] Thus, managers can encourage lateral relations by increasing slack and mutual payoffs.

In the discussion of leadership in Chapter 13 we develop the concept of lateral relations in a more systematic way. For now it's important to understand that individual action by the manager is important in developing and maintaining unit coalitions. The potential for coalitions and ideological consensus must be made a reality by individuals. It does not just occur from environmental, structural, or technological conditions. Finally, the development of coalitions is, we think, another way to manage interunit conflict. Terminal conflict signals a political failure within an organization. To paraphrase Lyndon Johnson, the art of organizational politics is compromise, which enhances an organization's chances of success.

MEASUREMENT MODULE

Interrelationships among subunits involve interactions of people. As such, the measures here require instruments that tap perceptions of how work is performed, and how other units relate to the work of the focal unit of analysis.

A quite direct way to measure work-flow interdependence is to ask the unit head to indicate the type of flow between units. Exhibit 11-4 provides an illustration. The respondent indicates what proportion of work flows in a sequential, independent, or team work-flow approach.[4] Note that this does not indicate the nature of the relationship in terms of whether it is service, advisory, auditing, or approval. But it does indicate the kinds of exchanges that the focal unit must deal with.

In the introduction to Part IV we noted that a parallel can be drawn between the organization and its environment and the subunit and the organization. Specifically, the environment of the subunit is primarily other subunits of an organization. As such, another way to measure interunit relationships is by applying the instrument in Exhibit 6-2 (see Chapter 6). There, the concern was primarily with the organization as the unit of analysis. The respondents indicated the units in the environment that were important to their organization's activities. Here, the important units would be those within the organization. Once again, using subsystems relationships as the unit of analysis, you can measure the degrees of interdependence, uncertainty, and development of the other units relating to yours. Note that this incorporates several of the concepts discussed in this chapter. For instance, under development note the items that reflect perceptions of slack and favorable policies. There are quite different relationships possible among interdependent units where the "development" is more positive. These kinds of questions give you an idea of the perceived balance among the focal unit and those with which it interacts. Recall that these can be used to estimate the probability of conflict among units.

As we also noted in this chapter, the actions of unit leaders are important in developing and maintaining subsystems relationships. Lateral relationships are used to help manage coalitions. Furthermore, the attitudes and behavioral predispositions toward "outsiders" help explain and predict the probability and severity of interunit conflict (as does interdependence, uncertainty, and development measured above). Exhibit 11-5 illustrates a way to measure the leader's predispositions toward interunit relationships.[1] Note there are items dealing with coalition formation and conflict resolution among important groups. And there are items involving the appropriateness of certain behaviors for providing service, advisory, auditing, or approving functions. Your instructor has scoring instructions available for different purposes.

These measures don't completely resolve issues of how coalitions are formed or how power is obtained. But they do provide important indicators of the kinds of relationships that are likely to develop, the balance among units, and the conflict potential among subunits.

Exhibit 11-4   Work-flow Interdependence

Instructions:

These questions are about the work flow BETWEEN organizational units. Respond to the item that most accurately describes the flow of work between units in your organization.

How Much Work Normally Flows Between the Organizational Units in This Manner?

	Almost None of the Work	Little	About 50% of the Work	A Great Deal	Almost All of the Work
1. Independent work-flow case—your unit receives work from one or a number of different units and sends it on to several others after processing.	A	B	C	D	E

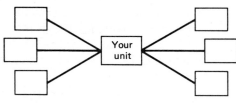

	Almost None of the Work	Little	About 50% of the Work	A Great Deal	Almost All of the Work
2. Sequential work-flow case—your unit receives the work from one unit and processes it for another as one unit in a series.	A	B	C	D	E

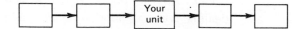

---

3. Reciprocal work-flow case—the work of your unit and other units flows back and forth over time; your imput is their output, and vice-versa.

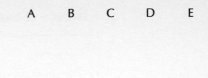

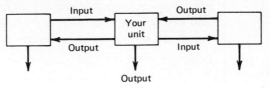

4. Team work-flow case—your unit collaborates with others to diagnose problems and solve them.

A   B   C   D   E

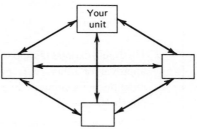

Scoring

For each item: A=1, B=2, C=3, D=4, E=5. To obtain an overall score for work-flow interdependence, compute the following: score for item 1 × 0 + score for item 2 × 0.33 + score for item 3 × 0.66 + score for item 4 × 1.0. The higher this score, the higher the interdependence.

Source: Hunt, J. G., and Osborn, R. N. *A Multiple Influence Model of Leadership.* Proposal funded by the U.S. Army Research Institute for the Behavioral and Social Sciences, May 1978. Adapted from Van de Ven, A. H., and Ferry, D. L. *Measuring and Assessing Organizations.* (New York: Wiley-Interscience, 1979). By permission of Van de Ven.

Exhibit 11-5   Predispositions Toward Internal Relationships

Instructions

The items below are concerned with HOW A LEADER IN YOUR POSITION should interact with the units in your organization. From your work experience and viewpoint, answer each of the following questions as if you were recommending a general policy for leaders in your position.

	Always	Often	Occa-sionally	Seldom	Never
1. He (the leader) should initiate contact with other units as opposed to waiting for their unit personnel to come to him.	A	B	C	D	E
2. He should express his approval or disapproval of other units by complimenting achievements and pointing out shortcomings.	A	B	C	D	E
3. Where he thinks that close contact with other units is necessary, he should develop the contact himself as opposed to having others develop the contact.	A	B	C	D	E
4. He should stress building the image of his unit in his relationship with other units as opposed to letting the actions of his unit speak for themselves.	A	B	C	D	E
5. When the interests of other units conflict with those of his own unit, he should make immediate adjustments to these pressures.	A	B	C	D	E
6. He should exert pressure on other units to obtain closer enforcement of policies, procedures, and rules concerning existing projects.	A	B	C	D	E
7. He should exert pressure on other units to exceed existing performance standards or plans (as opposed to accepting performance that is just up to existing standards or plans).	A	B	C	D	E

	Always	Often	Occa-sionally	Seldom	Never
8. He should exert pressure on other units to develop a series of evaluation criteria for existing programs and projects.	A	B	C	D	E
9. He should try to discourage open discussion of issues and problems with other units.	A	B	C	D	E
10. He should try to persuade the leaders of other units to agree to broadly stated policies and procedures on common projects (as opposed to detailed instructions that clarify exactly what each unit is expected to do).	A	B	C	D	E
11. When the overall interests of the organization come into direct conflict with those in his own unit, he should make immediate adjustment to these pressures.	A	B	C	D	E
12. He should place roughly equal responsibility on all the units participating in a given project rather than on one or more of the main contributors.	A	B	C	D	E
13. When developing new programs or projects, he should rely principally upon his own judgment rather than the judgment of other units.	A	B	C	D	E
14. In operating existing programs or projects, he should rely principally upon his own judgment rather than the judgment of other units.	A	B	C	D	E
15. He should maintain tight control over his unit's resources.	A	B	C	D	E
16. He should spend time obtaining information from other units that provide services to his unit.	A	B	C	D	E
17. He should concentrate on serving a relatively few units which need ser-					

vices that help develop his people or lead to extra 'know how' (as opposed to providing routine services to many units).

	Always	Often	Occasionally	Seldom	Never
	A	B	C	D	E

18. He should spend time maintaining contacts with widely dispersed units that might someday need his unit's services.

	A	B	C	D	E

19. When his unit's advice is not accepted by the head of another unit he should not stop but try to 'sell' the advice to others in that unit.

	A	B	C	D	E

20. He should encourage his subordinates to offer advice to other units beyond that which the other units ask for.

	A	B	C	D	E

21. He should be concerned that his unit, rather than the unit that it has helped, receive credit for resulting improvements.

	A	B	C	D	E

22. He should encourage his subordinates to assist other units by helping their people to understand their problems and developing skills in taking action.

	A	B	C	D	E

23. He should provide opportunities for other units to call for help from his unit.

	A	B	C	D	E

24. In dealing with units which routinely check or audit the performance of his unit he should initiate and maintain contact with the checking units.

	A	B	C	D	E

25. He should encourage the separateness and independence of his unit (as opposed to encouraging interaction with other units).

	A	B	C	D	E

26. He should emphasize the authority of his position when dealing with other units.

	A	B	C	D	E

	0–20%	21–40%	41–60%	61–80%	81–100%
27. What percent of time should he spend in interacting with other units as opposed to spending time administering his own unit.	A	B	C	D	E

Instructions

These three questions concern only those units that are MOST IMPORTANT to your operation.

	Always	Often	Occasionally	Seldom	Never
28. When the overall interests of the organization come into direct conflict with those of the 'important units' he should support the organization.	A	B	C	D	E
29. He should allocate considerable time to developing a very close working relationship with the 'important units' as opposed to allocating time to developing subordinate relationships in his own unit.	A	B	C	D	E
30. He should attempt to form coalitions with the 'important units' as opposed to working with each separately.	A	B	C	D	E

Scoring Instructions for different purposes are available from your instructor.

Source: Hunt, J. G., and Osborn, R. N. *A Multiple Influence Model of Leadership.* Proposal funded by the U.S. Army Research Institute for the Behavioral and Social Sciences, May 1978. By permission of the authors.

REFERENCES

I. Basic Types of Subsystems
A. Vertical Splits
[1]Hall, R. *Organizations: Structure and Process.* Englewood Cliffs, N. J.: Prentice-Hall, 1977.
[2]Katz, D., and Kahn, R. *The Social Psychology of Organizations.* New York: Wiley, 1978.
[3]Litterer, J. *The Analysis of Organizations.* New York: Wiley, 1973.
[4]Melcher, A. *Structure and Process of Organizations: A Systems Ap-*

proach. Englewood Cliffs, N. J.: Prentice-Hall, 1976.

[5]Parsons, T. *Structure and Process in Modern Societies.* New York: The Free Press, 1960.

B. Horizontal Splits

[1]Aldrich, H., and Herker, D. "Boundary Spanning Roles and Organization Structure," *Academy of Management Review,* 2 (1977), 217–231.

[2]Boddewyn, J. "External Affairs: A Corporate Function in Search of Conceptualization and Theory." In A. Negandhi (ed.), *Organization Theory and Interorganizational Analysis.* Kent, Ohio: Kent State University Press, 1973.

[3]Dalton, M. *Men Who Manage: Fusions of Feeling and Theory in Administration.* New York: Wiley, 1959.

[4]Filley, A. C., House, R. J., and Kerr, S. *Managerial Process and Organizational Behavior.* Glenview, Ill.: Scott, Foresman, 1976.

[5]Galbraith, J. *Designing Complex Organizations.* Reading, Mass.: Addison-Wesley, 1973.

[6]Katz and Kahn, 1978.

[7]Litterer, 1973.

[8]Pettigrew, A. "Information Control as a Power Resource," *Sociology,* 6 (1972), 187–204.

[9]Thompson, J. D. *Organizations in Action.* New York: McGraw-Hill, 1967.

[10]Zald, M. (ed.). *Power in Organizations.* Nashville, Tenn.: Vanderbilt Press, 1970.

II. Relationships among Units

[1]Hall, J. L., and Leidecker, J. K. "Lateral Relations in Organizations: Theory and Application," *Advanced Management Journal,* 12 (1975), 11–16.

[2]Sayles, L. *Managerial Behavior: Administration in Complex Organizations.* New York: McGraw-Hill, 1964.

A. Balanced Relationships

[1]Brown, P., and Cotton, C. "The Top-down-underdog Syndrome in Line-Staff Relations," *Personnel Journal,* 27 (1975), 23–27.

[2]Drucker, P. *Management: Tasks, Responsibilities, and Practices.* New York: Harper & Row, 1974.

[3]Hall and Leidecker, 1975.

[4]Holder, J. "What is Line? What is Staff?," *Supervisory Management* (1973), 37–40.

[5]Koontz, H., and O'Donnell, C. *Principles of Management: An Analysis of Managerial Functions.* New York: McGraw-Hill, 1972.

[6]Litterer, 1973.

[7]Ritti, R., and Funkhouser, G. *The Ropes to Skip and the Ropes to Know.* Columbus, Ohio: Grid, 1977.

[8]Sayles, 1964.

[9]Sayles, L. *Leadership: What Effective Managers Really Do and How They Do It.* New York: McGraw-Hill, in press.

[10]Strauss, G. "Tactics of Lateral Relationships," *Administrative Science Quarterly,* 7 (1962), 161–186.

B. Asymmetrical Relationships

[1]Aldrich and Hecker, 1977.

[2]Buchele, R. B. *The Management of Business and Public Organizations.* New York: McGraw-Hill, 1977.

[3]Drucker, 1974.

[4]Koontz and O'Donnell, 1972.

[5]Landsberger, H. "The Horizontal Dimension in Bureaucracy," *Administrative Science Quarterly,* 6 (1961), 299–322.

[6]Lawrence, P., and Lorsch, J. *Organization and Environment: Man-*

aging *Differentiation and Integration.* Homewood, Ill.: Irwin, 1969.

[7]Ritti and Funkhouser, 1977.

[8]Sayles, 1964.

[9]Sayles, in press.

[10]Schmidt, S. M. "Interunit Tension: Incompatible Goals-Interdependency Model." Paper presented at the Thirty-Fourth National Academy of Management Meeting, 1974.

[11]Scharpf, F. "Does Organization Matter? Task Structure and Interaction in the Ministerial Bureaucracy," *Organization and Administrative Sciences,* 8 (1977), 149–168.

[12]Sloan, A. P. "My Years with General Motors—Part II, " *Fortune,* 68 (1963), 145–148.

[13]Urban, T. F., and Rose, G. L. "Asymmetric Relationships and Arbitration Effects on Negotiation Outcomes." Unpublished manuscript, Institute of Industrial Relations, University of Iowa, 1973.

[14]Zald, M. N. "Power Balance and Staff Conflict in Correctional Institutions," *Administrative Science Quarterly,* 7 (1962), 22–49.

C. The Drive Toward Power

[1]Baldridge, J. V. *Power and Conflict in the University.* New York: Wiley, 1971.

[2]Cyert, R., and March, J. *A Behavioral Theory of the Firm.* Englewood Cliffs, N.J.: Prentice-Hall, 1963.

[3]Pettigrew, A. *The Politics of Organizational Decision Making.* London: Tavistock, 1973.

[4]Ritti and Funkhouser, 1977.

[5]Sayles, 1964.

[6]Strauss, 1962.

[7]Tuschman, M. L. "A Political Approach to Organizations; A Review and Rationale," *Academy of*

Management Review, 2 (1977), 206–216.

[8]Warwick, D. and Reed, T. *A Theory of Public Bureaucracy.* Cambridge, Mass.: Harvard Press, 1975.

[9]Zald, 1970.

D. The Path to Power

[1]Burack, E., and Sorensen, P. "Computer Technology and Organizational Design," *Organization and Administrative Sciences,* 8 (1977), 223–236.

[2]Hinings, C. R., Hickson, D. J., Pennings, J. M., and Schneck, R. E. "Structural Conditions of Intraorganizational Power," *Administrative Science Quarterly,* 49 (1974), 22–44.

[3]Sayles, 1964.

[4]Whisler, T. L. *The Impact of Computers on Organizations.* New York: Praeger, 1970.

III. Functional and Dysfunctional Consequences of Conflict

[1]Blake, R. R., Shepard, H. A., and Mouton, J. S. *Managing Intergroup Conflict in Industry.* Houston: Gulf, 1964.

[2]Caplow, T. A. *Principles of Organizations.* New York: Harcourt, Brace and World, 1964.

[3]Fiedler, F. "The Effect of Inter-group Competition on Group Member Adjustment," *Personnel Psychology,* 20 (1967), 33–44.

[4]Filley, A. C. *Interpersonal Conflict Resolution.* Glenview, Ill.: Scott, Foresman, 1975.

[5]Halberstam, D. *The Best and the Brightest.* Greenwich, Conn.: Fawcett, 1973.

[6]Janis, I. L. *Victims of Groupthink.* Boston: Houghton Mifflin, 1972.

[7]Lawrence and Lorsch, 1969.

[8]Schmidt, S. M., and Kochan, T. A. "Conflict: Toward Conceptual

Clarity," *Administrative Science Quarterly,* 17 (1972), 359–370.

[9]Thomas, F. W. "Conflict and Conflict Management." In M. D. Dunnette (ed.), *Handbook of Industrial and Organizational Psychology.* Chicago: Rand McNally, 1976.

A. Goals, Ideology, and Terminal Conflict

[1]Callon, M., and Vignolle, J. P. "Breaking Down the Organization: Local Conflicts and Societal Systems of Action," *Social Science Information,* 16 (1977), 147–167.

[2]Caplow, 1964.

[3]Dalton, 1959.

[4]Glenn, E. S., Johnson, R. H., Kimmel, P. R., and Wedge, B. "A Cognitive Interaction Model to Analyze Culture Conflict in International Relations," *Journal of Conflict Resolution,* 14 (1970), 35–48.

[5]Korman, A. *Organizational Behavior.* Englewood Cliffs, N. J.: Prentice-Hall, 1977.

[6]Ritti and Funkhouser, 1977.

[7]Scott, W. G., and Mitchell, T. R. *Organization Theory.* Homewood, Ill.: Irwin, 1972.

[8]Schmidt and Kochan, 1972.

[9]Sherif, M. "Superordinate Goals in the Reduction of Intergroup Conflict," *American Journal of Sociology,* 43 (1958), 345–356.

[10]Thomas, 1976.

B. Factors Increasing the Probability and Severity of Conflict

[1]Blake et al., 1964.

[2]Campbell, R., and LeVine, D. *Ethnocentrism: Theories of Conflict, Ethnic Attitudes and Group Behavior.* New York: Wiley, 1972.

[3]Caplow, 1964.

[4]Coser, L. "Social Conflict and the Theory of Social Change," *The British Journal of Sociology,* 7 (1957), 197–207.

[5]Dalton, 1959.

[6]Druckman, D., and Zechmeister, K. "Conflict of Interest and Value Dissensus: Propositions in the Sociology of Conflict," *Human Relations,* 26 (1973), 449–446.

[7]Dutton, J. M., and Walton, R. E. "Interdepartmental Conflicts and Cooperation: Two Contrasting Studies." In J. Lorsch, and P. Lawrence (eds.), *Managing Group and Intergroup Relations.* Homewood, Ill.: Irwin, 1972.

[8]Filley, 1975.

[9]Hills, R. J. "The Representative Function: A Neglected Dimension of Leadership Behavior," *Administrative Science Quarterly,* 8 (1963), 83–101.

[10]Hinings et al., 1974.

[11]Jay, A. *Management and Machiavelli: An Inquiry into the Politics of Corporate Life.* New York: Holt, Rinehart and Winston, 1968.

[12]Lawrence and Lorsch, 1969.

[13]March J., and Simon, H. *Organizations.* New York: Wiley, 1958.

[14]Miller, J. "Toward a General Theory for the Behavioral Sciences," *American Psychologist,* 10 (1955), 513–531.

[15]Pfeffer, J., and Salancik, G. R. *The External Control of Organizations: A Resource Dependence Perspective.* New York: Harper & Row, 1978.

[16]Ritti and Funkhouser, 1977.

[17]Sayles, 1964.

[18]Seiler, J. A. "Diagnosing Interdepartmental Conflict." In J. Lorsch, and P. Lawrence, (eds.), *Manag-*

ing *Group and Intergroup Relations*. Homewood, Ill.: Irwin, 1972.

[19]Strauss, 1962.

[20]Sumner, W. G. *Folkways*. New York: Ginn, 1906.

[21]Thomas, 1976.

[22]Thompson, 1967.

[23]Walton, R., and McKersie, R. *A Behavioral Theory of Labor Negotiations*. New York: McGraw-Hill, 1965.

[24]Whyte, W. "The Social Structure of the Restaurant," *American Journal of Sociology*, 54 (1949), 302–310.

[25]Zald, 1962.

[26]Zald, 1970.

IV. Organizational Politics

[1]Glenn et al., 1970.

[2]Mayes, B., and Allen, R. "Toward a Definition of Organizational Politics," *Academy of Management Review*, 2 (1977), 672–677.

[3]Peters, G. "Insiders and Outsiders: The Politics of Pressure Group Influence on Bureaucracy," *Administrative Science Quarterly*, 9 (1977), 191–217.

[4]Tuschman, M. "A Political Approach to Organization: A Review and Rationale," *Academy of Management Review*, 2 (1977), 206–216.

A. Managers as Politicians

[1]Hills, 1963.

[2]Mayes and Allen, 1977.

[3]Osborn, R., and Bishop, R. C. "The Influence of Environmental Conditions and Unit Performance on External Relations Emphasis," *Organization and Administrative Sciences*, 6 (1976), 15–27.

[4]Quinn, R. E. "Coping with Cupid and the Formation, Impact, and Management of Romantic Relationships in Organizations," *Administrative Science Quarterly*, 22 (1977), 30–45.

[5]Ritti and Funkhouser, 1977.

[6]Thompson, 1967.

[7]Tuschman, 1977.

B. Organizational Politics and Ideology

[1]Callon, M., and Vignolle, J. P. "Breaking Down the Organization: Local Conflicts and Societal Systems of Action," *Social Science Information*, 16 (1977), 147–167.

[2]Drucker, 1974.

[3]March and Simon, 1963.

[4]Mayes and Allen, 1977.

C. Managing Coalitions

[1]Duffy, P. J. "Lateral Interaction Orientation: An Expanded View of Leadership." Unpublished doctoral dissertation, Southern Illinois University, Carbondale, 1973.

[2]Katz and Kahn, 1978.

[3]Osborn, R. N., and Hunt, J. G. "An Empirical Investigation of Lateral and Vertical Leadership at Two Organizational Levels," *Journal of Business Research*, 2 (1974), 209–221.

[4]Osborn and Bishop, 1976.

[5]Pettigrew, 1973.

[6]Sayles, in press.

[7]Wahba, M. A., and Lirtzman, S. I. "A Theory of Organizational Coalition Formations," *Human Relations*, 25 (1972), 515–527.

V. Measurement Module

[1]Hunt, J. G., and Osborn, R. N. *A Multiple Influence Model of Leadership*. Army Research Institute Grant No. DAHC 19-78-G-0010, 1978.

[2]Van de Ven, A., and Ferry, D. *Measuring and Assessing Organizations*. New York: Wiley-Interscience, 1979.

chapter 12 GROUPS AND GROUP BEHAVIOR

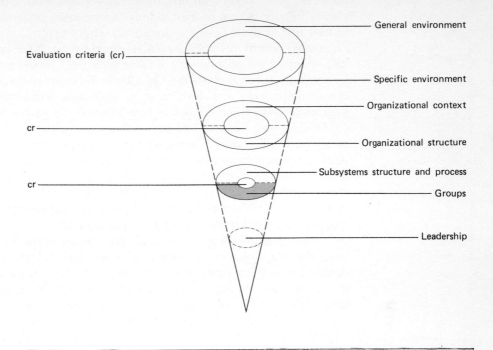

Evaluation criteria (cr) ─────────

cr ─────────

cr ─────────

General environment

Specific environment

Organizational context

Organizational structure

Subsystems structure and process

Groups

Leadership

Consider two sets of prisoners of war who have just been freed. In the first set, the POWs are filled with jubilation. In the second set, there is a sullen quietness and many POWs appear highly anxious. Upon further investigation you find that in the first set, there had been many escape attempts, little collaboration with the enemy, and a relatively low death rate from illness. In the second set there had been few escape attempts, many deaths from disease, and many instances of apparent collaboration with the enemy. Indeed, the two sets are so different that it is as if they are from two different countries. Yet both sets were American POWs. The first, from World War II, was captured by the Nazis. The second, from the Korean conflict a scant half dozen years later, was captured by the Chinese. Indeed, the behavior of these latter prisoners became a national scandal. Many interpreted this as indicating a deterioration of U.S. moral fiber. How could such marked differences between the two sets of POWs occur?

In the first set, the Nazis required the POWs to organize themselves in a military structure similar to that from which they came. Rank was strictly recognized. American officers were responsible for policing and maintaining the POW unit. Along with this, the prisoners had food, clothing, and shelter clearly inferior to that of their guards. Interrogated prisoners were sent back to their unit to serve as an "example" to other POWs.

Now contrast this with conditions faced by the POWs in the Korean conflict. Many of the prisoners were taken after the Chinese entered the conflict by suddenly surging across the Yalu River. This was perhaps one of the most demoralizing routs in U.S. history. As they were being marched into China they were constantly reminded of how fortunate they were that they had been captured by their Chinese "friends" rather than the North Koreans, who would surely have killed them. Along with this, living conditions during the march were not very different between the POWs and their captors. Both were far from comfortable. At the prison camps officers were separated from enlisted men. Sometimes those with lower ranks were placed in charge of those with higher ranks. Units were frequently broken up and reconstituted. After interrogation, prisoners were sent back to a new unit.*

These examples serve as dramatic illustrations of the influence groups can have over the behavior of people who are, individually, probably not very different from each other. It sets the stage for our discussion of groups and group behavior. We start by defining what we mean by groups and discussing some different types of groups. We then examine the usefulness of groups for task accomplishment. This gets us into a comparison of groups versus individuals, for various kinds of tasks. Next we look at some interworkings of groups within organizations. We then examine in some detail the impact of a number of aspects of group composition. The various stages of group development are considered next. We conclude with some applications of these notions to committees, the group's environment, and measurement.

WHAT DO WE MEAN BY GROUPS?

Suppose there is an automobile accident and you join a number of other people gathered around the wreck. Or suppose you join several others waiting for an elevator. Are these groups? Not in the way most social scientists define the term. A representative definition is, "A group is a collection of people who interact with each other regularly over a period of time and perceive themselves to be mutually dependent with respect to the attainment of one or more

*These descriptions are based on Schein.[3]

common goals."[4] Note the key elements—interaction, time, and feeling of mutual dependence for goal accomplishment. Neither the aggregation of people at the wreck nor those waiting for the elevator would meet all of these characteristics. They would be considered an aggregation or collection of individuals but not a group.

What if the collection of individuals waiting for the elevator were at the eighty-third floor at ten o'clock at night during the dead of winter and there was an extended power failure? Then such an aggregation might become a group as they interacted in an effort to determine ways (common goals) to deal with the emergency.

The definition used here also raises by implication the question of whether groups are real or not. Can we speak meaningfully about a group's feeling or reaction to various things? There are psychologists who would argue that only individuals are real. To them, groups are merely artificial collectivities. It is meaningless to speak about a group reaction to anything. You can only speak of the reactions of individuals within the group.[1] A more moderate view, and the one to which the previous definition leads, is that groups are "real" to the extent to which they are seen as "entities" as opposed to mere collections of individuals.[2] Thus, in the power failure situation we might speak of the effect of the elevator group on the feelings of a pregnant secretary. However, that would not be very meaningful in the more typical situation when a group of strangers is routinely waiting for an elevator.

Keeping in mind these notions, let's look at some different types of groups. And let's also further restrict these to groups within organizations.

TYPES OF GROUPS WITHIN ORGANIZATIONS

Formal Groups

The organizational groups with which you are probably most familiar are supervisor-subordinate work groups. These are established by an organization to accomplish goals. As we pointed out earlier, these groups become necessary as means-ends chains are established to accomplish organizational objectives. Some common examples are departments or divisions, boundary-spanning units, and various committees or task forces. We discussed several of these in earlier chapters. Boundary-spanning units such as purchasing are set up to cut across other organizational units. These units are typically composed of a formally designated superior together with a number of subordinates.

Committees or task forces can either be permanent (standing) or ad hoc when they are established to deal with a special problem and then dissolved. They may also have a formally designated chairperson or members may be allowed to choose their own.

Informal Groups

Informal groups are those that spring up without being formally specified by someone in authority. In organizations these are often found as subgroups or cliques within formally designated groups. Thus, you may find that the same people eat together, go on break together, or engage in other informal activities on the job. Other people in the group may form a separate informal subgroup. It is also possible that the informal subgrouping can take place *across* as well as within formally designated units. You might find, for instance, secretaries from one department eating lunch with those from another. These subgroupings can take many forms as can formal groups. The key difference is that informal groups arise spontaneously, whereas formal ones are designated by someone other than the members.

We shall have more to say about these points later in the chapter. For now you simply need to remind yourself that these differences do exist.

Task and Process Groups

Within both the formal and informal categories we can also include task groups and process groups. Task groups are those whose major goal is to turn out some end product. Hence, group process is incidental to this goal. Process groups on the other hand, are those whose product is the process itself. Therapy groups or the currently popular encounter groups or sensitivity groups are examples of process groups as are many "rap sessions." All have been set up with the process itself as the prime consideration.

Figure 12-1 shows a simple framework for classifying and combining the different kinds of groups just discussed. Most of our concern will be with the four output cells.

Figure 12-1. A Matrix of Different Kinds of Organizational Groups.

	Output	Process
Formal	1A Boundary spanning 1B	
	2A Nonboundary spanning 2B	
Informal	3A Between units 3B	
	4A Within units 4B	

USEFULNESS OF GROUPS FOR TASK ACCOMPLISHMENT*

What evidence do we have concerning when a group might be better than an individual or vice versa in terms of task accomplishment? We will look at this in organizational situations where there is some choice concerning whether an individual or a group should be appointed to handle a task. (In many cases, of course, technology and other considerations require a group.) Virtually all the evidence we have on this point comes from laboratory settings.

Whether to use individuals or a group differs as a function of the kind of task to be done. The tasks are generally of three kinds: judgment, problem solving, and learning. In addition, there is some evidence about idea generation and risk taking.

---

*This discussion is based primarily on a literature review by Shaw.[1] This section and much of the rest of the chapter relies heavily on evidence from artifical laboratory studies. For our purposes, we assume these results can be generalized to apply to existing organizations.

Judgment Tasks

Suppose you are asked to estimate or judge the weights of a number of objects. In one case you do this alone. In another you are part of a group that is asked to come up with a group decision. In which case is the judgment likely to lie closer to the "true" weight of the objects? For judgment-type decisions, group judgments are seldom less accurate than the *average* individual judgment. They are often better.[1] In contrast, some studies indicate that group judgments are not generally likely to exceed those of the most proficient member of the group.[1] Thus, on judgment tasks, group versus individual performance seems to differ as a function of expertise. If you could identify the most proficient person ahead of time, you would be better off to simply have that person make the judgment. However, if you're not sure about the expertise of various group members concerning a given judgment, you will generally get a more accurate decision from a group.

Problem Solving Tasks

Does the same thing hold true with problem solving? Here we are concerned with performance on such assignments as complex deductive reasoning (discussed in Chapter 1), solving simple puzzles, and so on. Evidence suggests that groups tend to be superior to individuals in problem solving on tasks with the following characteristics: (1) there can be a division of labor; (2) the creation of ideas or the remembering of information is required; and (3) it is possible for other group members to recognize and correct individual errors. There is also evidence suggesting that groups will be better when: (1) the influence of the ablest member is greater; (2) influence of the most confident member is greater; (3) interest in the task aroused by group membership is greater; and (4) the amount of information available to the group is greater.[1]

Does this mean you should try to use a group whenever you have these conditions? Maybe. But we haven't yet considered the amount of effort or time required. When you consider the total time required of each group member, evidence suggests that groups will generally require more than that required for an individual. Thus it appears that problem solving quality and quantity may be enhanced by groups. But cost and total time will be increased. Effectiveness may be greater, but efficiency may be lower.

Learning Tasks

Suppose we switch now from problem solving to learning? Again groups appear to possess some advantages. Evidence is quite consistent in showing that groups generally learn faster than individuals. This is true in both natural settings and laboratory studies.[1]

Group Idea Generation and Risk Taking

How do groups compare with individuals for generation of new and radical ideas? One widely heralded approach to this is the notion of "brainstorming." The technique involves group participation to produce novel ideas.[2] It is touted as showing the superiority of groups over individuals in generating creative ideas. While group participation is involved, it is participation of a very special kind. The participation conforms to the following rules: (1) ideas are expressed regardless of quality; (2) no idea is evaluated until all ideas are expressed; and (3) elaboration of one person's ideas by another is encouraged. Given these rules, the question arises as to whether the process of group participation or its nature as specified by the rules is the key. The evidence is not entirely consistent on this. It does suggest, though, that it is possible for individuals in so-called nominal groups (where they work alone but have their results compared and pooled) to fare better than when group interaction occurs. Maybe then, it is the rules and *not* the group participation that is the key. Thus, Shaw[3] hypothesizes that a suspension of evaluation during the production of ideas may lead to more new and radical ideas for *both* groups and individuals.

In direct opposition to the belief that group process leads to more novel ideas is the belief that groups tend to be *less* innovative or creative. There seems to be a widely held belief that groups tend to make relatively less novel, perhaps even mediocre, decisions compared to individuals. This contention has led to a series of studies examining the riskiness of groups as compared to individual decision making. The question is whether decisions made after group discussion are more risky than decisions made by the average person prior to group discussion. This is the so-called "risky shift" phenomenon.[4] Hare[1] suggests that there does indeed appear to be such a phenomenon. Why might this be so? Three factors seem to be particularly important. The first is concerned with the diffusion of responsibility that occurs with a group as compared with an individual decision. The second is the influence of the most risky individual member. The third is the cultural value associated with risk taking. It is argued that people (in the United States at least) appear to value risk. The group interaction may cause less risky members to accept more risk to conform to perceived expectations of other group members.[3]

On balance, contrary to the opinions of many: there may not be much difference in the creativity of groups and individuals when the same rules are used; and groups may take more risks than individuals.

Summary

The high points of the material just discussed are summarized in Table 12-2.

Table 12-2 Summary of Performance of Groups and Individuals on Different Kinds of Tasks

Judgment tasks	Group better than *average* individual, but not *most proficient* individual.
Problem solving tasks	Groups more effective, though not necessarily more efficient, when: (1) There is division of labor (2) Creation of ideas or remembering of information is required (3) It is possible for other group members to recognize and correct individual errors (4) Influence of ablest member is greater (5) Influence of most confident member is greater (6) Task interest aroused by being group member is greater (7) Amount of available information is greater
Learning tasks	Groups learn fast.
Tasks involving idea generation and risk taking	Groups and individuals may both be superior where critical evaluation of ideas is suspended. Groups make more risky decisions than individuals.

ORGANIZATIONAL REQUIREMENTS AND GROUP RESPONSES

So far we have assumed you could use individuals or a group for task performance. Now let's assume you must use a formally designated group. What are some important considerations in understanding how such groups operate? A good starting point in answering this question is to think in terms of a set of required and emergent factors operating within the group.*

Required and Emergent Factors

Required factors are simply those required of employees by an organization. For example, managers designate task objectives so the organization can survive and grow. Emergent factors, on the other hand, are those that informally emerge over and above those formally required. You can expect to find these in virtually any formally organized work group. Note that even though these groups fall in the formal cells of Figure 12-1, they still include informal factors. Let's get more specific. We can divide these required and emergent factors into activities, interactions, and sentiments.[2]

Activities. These are what a person does (e.g., runs, talks, etc.). The required activities are specified by the organization. They are influenced by the environmental and organizational variables previously discussed as well as by individual-difference variables. Over and above these required activities a number of emergent activities are also likely to occur. Some of them will almost surely be functional for performance and maintenance criteria. Others will not. Some may be functional for one but not the other. For example, lunch breaks might be dysfunctional for performance, but they might provide useful maintenance functions.

Interactions. These are based on communication or contact between two or more people such that the activity of one responds to the activity of the other. The most common form of interaction is talking. But this is only defined as an interaction if it meets the response aspect of this definition. There are also many nonverbal interactions. Perhaps one of the better known of these is the famous wire service photo of a few years ago that showed American

*We have borrowed these general notions from Homans[1] and Turner,[2] though our treatment of them is not identical with theirs.

POWs with upraised middle fingers. There was clearly a nonverbal interaction with the American public.

Again, interactions are both required and emergent. Like activities, they can be either functional or dysfunctional in terms of performance and maintenance (or functional for one but dysfunctional for the other). Frequent "shooting the breeze" by two people may lower performance but increase their satisfaction.

Sentiments. These are considered to be beliefs, feelings, attitudes, or values held by an individual.* In addition to required and emergent sentiments, there are *given* sentiments. These are sentiments an individual brings into the group from outside. (Note the impact of the environment and culture here.) Feelings about the value of hard work or about the proper role of female coworkers are two examples. Given sentiments like these can be as important as required or emergent ones in terms of their impact on the group.

There is a special kind of emergent sentiment called a "norm." This is defined as an idea or belief about what the sentiments, activities, or interactions in a particular group *should* be. Norms develop in any group, with greater or lesser degree of consensus. They define how a member in good standing should behave relative to, other members, outsiders, the job, and emergent factors.

The degree to which a group member conforms to these norms helps influence that person's standing within the group (called "internal subgrouping"). This internal subgrouping consists of subsets of members within a group according to how closely they conform to group norms. Three rough categories are "regulars," "deviants," and "isolates."[2] *Regulars* are those who most closely conform to and influence group norms. *Deviants* are those whose interaction with group members is relatively frequent but who are denied regular group membership because they are unwilling or unable to accept dominant norms. *Isolates* are those whose interactions with other members is relatively infrequent. For whatever reason, they do not conform to the norms of either regulars or deviants. It is possible that all work group members could be regulars. Probably a more common situation is to find a mix of different subgroups and individuals as indicated above.

Consistency. We have described what we mean by required and emergent activities, interactions, and sentiments. Now it is important to consider the degree of consistency between and among them. For example, let us assume your job required you to interact with a person of the opposite sex and

*Though these are sometimes differentiated, for our purposes they can be grouped together under the broad label of "sentiments."

you felt that people of that sex should not be working in your group. There would be an inconsistency between a required interaction and either a given or emergent sentiment. It is possible, of course, for the degree of consistency to range from perfect (all factors in-line) to the exact opposite. A more likely situation is to have some mix of consistency and inconsistency among the factors. For example, you might find general consistency except that talking is formally restricted (required interaction) on an interdependent task (required activity). Or there might be consistency except that a person volunteers to give the boss a ride (emergent activity) even though the boss is heartily disliked (emergent sentiment). With a moment's reflection you can think of many other possibilities.

Based on Homans[1] we can argue that performance and employee maintenace will be enhanced with more consistency. We expect inconsistencies of various kinds to influence performance and/or employee maintenance negatively. Thus, it's important to be on the lookout for such inconsistencies. Depending on the nature of that inconsistency, it may be possible to alter one or more factors to change the pattern.

Required and Emergent Factors and Group Cohesiveness

These required and emergent factors can also be related to the key concept of group cohesiveness. Before making the link, let's briefly consider what is meant by group cohesiveness and examine its consequences.

What Is Group Cohesiveness? Definitions of group cohesiveness differ somewhat. Here are two representative ones: "attraction to the group and resistance to leaving it"[5]; and "the resultant of all forces acting on the members to remain in the group."[1] A cohesiveness measure is shown in the Measurement Module.

Group cohesiveness has a substantial bearing on the synergistic impact in a group. Synergy, as you recall, was described as the effect in an organization or group over and above the sum of its parts. It is this effect that helps differentiate groups from mere aggregations discussed earlier. The more cohesive a group, the higher the level of synergy.

Cohesiveness Consequences. Evidence suggests at least four consequences of group cohesiveness. These are: (1) greater interaction; (2) greater social influence; (3) consistent performance; and (4) greater employee maintenance.

There is a widely held assumption, confirmed by data, that interaction is greater in highly attractive groups than in less attractive groups.* Not only is there likely to be more interaction in highly cohesive groups; that interaction is likely to be more positive in nature. Members tend to be more friendly and cooperative and to stress group integration behaviors. They act less like aggregates of people.[2]

In terms of social influence, data suggest that the higher the group cohesiveness, the greater: (1) the response to influence attempts by group members; (2) the likelihood of an opinion change to agree with a partner's; and (3) the likelihood of agreement with majority judgments.[2]

In terms of goal achievement and performance, highly cohesive groups tend to be more effective than low-cohesive groups.[5] This finding, coupled with the one concerning social influence, suggests that the relationships of cohesiveness to performance, *as defined by management,* may be more difficult to predict than you might first imagine. The relationship can be *either* positive or negative.

If group norms are oriented toward productivity as defined by management, cohesiveness should promote productivity. On the other hand, if group norms are not consistent with management's productivity expectations, you would expect a negative relationship with performance. What we can predict is that whatever the level of performance, it will be more consistent in high- than low-cohesive groups. This is because the social influence impact is high. The level of performance is determined by other factors, of course. But the variability about a given level will be influenced by cohesiveness.[4]

Shifting to employee maintenance, as we might predict, there is a tendency for members of more cohesive groups to be more satisfied than members of less cohesive groups. They are likely to be more satisfied with the group itself and what the group produces.[5] Furthermore, absenteeism and turnover are likely to be less when groups are more cohesive.[3] Finally, there may be less work-related tension.[4]

Consistency and Cohesiveness. Let us link these considerations together now. We can argue that where there is perfect consistency among the required and emergent factors discussed earlier, there should be high cohesiveness. That should lead to high performance and high values on employee maintenance measures. Where there's a fit among the emergent factors, but not a fit between these and the required factors, we would argue that there will be

*The reverse is also likely to be true. Cohesiveness may be greater in groups with much interaction. The treatment here of cohesiveness as the causal variable is consistent with a good bit of experimental evidence.

high cohesiveness and favorable employee maintenance, but not high performance (as defined by management). Situations with inconsistencies among the required factors or inconsistencies among the emergent factors are likely to show low cohesiveness. Or at least we expect lower cohesiveness than where there is a perfect consistency. As a result we would predict lower performance in the required inconsistency case. And we expect lower employee maintenance in the emergent inconsistency case. Performance might be more variable with inconsistency among emergent elements if we assume, as in our earlier discussion, that internal subgrouping occurs. This suggests that cohesiveness is important. And it may have different relationships with criteria depending on the nature of the required and emergent consistencies.

GROUP COMPOSITION

The previous discussion provides a way of analyzing the impact on criteria of actions, interactions, and sentiments in groups. Now it will be useful to consider the relationship of a number of aspects of group composition to selected criteria. Several of these aspects are roughly analogous to those treated earlier at the organizational level. They are: group size (including an odd versus even number of members)*; group task; and group structure or work-flow configurations. In addition, the literature suggests we should consider the fit among different group member characteristics. Fit is related to consistency discussed earlier, though in a little different way. In some cases such a fit involves similarity of group members. In others it involves dissimilarity.

A key consideration running through the treatment of group composition is balancing the trade-off between the resource requirements and the communication/coordination requirements to perform the group's task (see Figure 12-3).[1] Thus, for example, additional group size or heterogeneity may provide more potential resources for the group. But these are likely to lead to an additional need for more communication or coordination. Hence, a trade-off between these two considerations is involved in composing groups. It would be nice if the empirical evidence concerning group composition effects were tied to these considerations. Since it isn't, we will make inferences where necessary.

*This is size of the group as opposed to that of the organization as a whole. Our review of organization size in Chapter 8 shows its effects are separate from and not always consistent with those of work-group size.

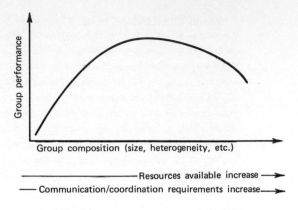

Figure 12-3 Trade-offs in group composition.

Group Size

Let's start our discussion of group size by considering what happens to the possible number of relationships in the group as size increases. The number of potential relationships between individuals in a group is

$$x = \frac{n^2 - n}{2}$$

where x is the number of mutual relationships and n is the number of individuals. Note that the number of relationships increases much faster than the number of group members. With two members there is one potential mutual relationship. If the group increases to five, the number of potential relationships increases to ten.

Further, we should include not only the number of relationships between individuals. We should also include relationships between subgroups, and between an individual and a subgroup as well. If we do this, the number of potential relationships increases even faster. The formula is

$$x = \tfrac{1}{2} (3^n - 2^{n+1} + 1)$$

The potential relationships increase astronomically as group size goes up.[4]

This sharply increasing number of potential relationships is one reason for the increased communication/coordination requirements shown in Figure 12-3. The increase also illustrates why the feeling of intimacy disappears as group size increases. With this in mind, let's briefly highlight findings concerning the impact of size.

Size and Performance. Conclusions here are mixed, probably because other variables such as the nature of the task intervene. One comprehensive review of ten experimental studies concluded that both quality of performance and group productivity were positively related to group size under some conditions. *There was no case* where smaller groups were better.[9] Group sizes varied from 2 to 96 members, though most had less than 10. These results vary from those of a field study that showed that group productivity *decreased* with size.[5] There could be many reasons for this difference, not the least of which might be differences in task complexity, task interdependence, and the like.

There is also considerable evidence that, at least for discussion and similar type groups, performance may increase up to about five members. It then drops off, fast at first and then at a slower rate.[3,4,6] These results are in conformance with those of the preferences of experienced executives for five-member committees.[3]

These conclusions are also related to the diminishing returns argument of Figure 12-3. Five members may be the point at which the resource-communication/coordination trade-off is balanced.

Size and Employee Maintenance. There are two basic conclusions with regard to satisfaction. First, satisfaction drops as group size increases.[4,9] Second, at least for discussion-type tasks, satisfaction may increase up to a group size of about five members.[6,9] It then drops off above that number.

Evidence concerning turnover generally shows that the larger the work group the greater the turnover.[7] One exception to this was a study that showed a curvilinear relationship, with medium-sized units (20 to 30 members for combined units) having the most turnover.[1] Similarly, the relationship between size and absenteeism is usually positive. The larger the size, the greater the absenteeism.[7]

On balance, it appears that larger groups tend to be associated with lower satisfaction, and higher absenteeism and turnover. However, as with performance, a very small amount of evidence suggests that these associations could be curvilinear.

Size and Odd Versus Even Numbers. Groups of two (dyads) appear to be unique when compared to those of other sizes.[10] Among other things, they tend to have high rates of tension, show low disagreement, and high rates of information-seeking behavior.[2] It has been argued that the dyad may be viewed as having an implicit agreement that the two members will stay within areas on which they can agree.[4]

As we move above the dyad size, odd-even differences become important. Evidence suggests that even-sized groups (four, six) as compared with odd-size groups (three, five, seven) show disagreement and antagonism. They also have lower rates in seeking suggestions. These differences apparently occur because in odd-size groups it is easier to form coalitions and use a majority vote for decision making.[3,4] Such behavior would seem to be functional where speed was required. But this is not so where careful deliberation is desirable. There, in spite of the greater difficulty of agreement, the end product may be better unless the group deadlocks.

Group Task

Earlier we talked about the usefulness of groups versus individuals in performance on various kinds of tasks. Here we extend this by looking at task accomplishment within a group. A means-ends chain is followed such that different tasks are taken on by the group's members. Similar to our discussion in Chapter 9, differentiation within the group occurs. Whether the tasks are formally assigned or informally selected by each group member, different jobs need to be done to accomplish goals.

There has been substantial debate in the literature about how to look at task differentiation in the group. One popular way is to examine the nature of the jobs performed based on perceptions of those performing them. Two recent instruments have been used to tap several "core" job dimensions believed to be crucial in differentiating among tasks. The first of these is the Job Diagnostic Survey (JDS).[5] The second is the Job Characteristics Inventory (JCI).[14] Four core dimensions common to both are: variety, autonomy, task identity, and feedback.

Variety is the extent to which a job requires employees to perform a wide range of operations in their work and/or the degree to which employees must use a variety of equipment and procedures. *Autonomy* is the extent to which workers have a major say in scheduling their work, selecting the equipment they will use, and deciding on procedures. *Task identity* is the degree to which employees do a whole piece of work and can clearly identify the result of their efforts. *Feedback* is the extent to which workers receive information as they are working, which reveals how well they are performing on the job.[14] A copy of the JCI, which taps these dimensions, is included in the Measurement Module. It has been shown that the JDS and JCI give similar results when measuring these four dimensions.[9]

Coming from a different theoretical base, a number of other researchers have concentrated on dimensions variously termed task structure, task programmability, task variability, task difficulty, task predictability, and the like. These dimensions bear remarkable empirical similarity to some of those above.[9] Thus, task variety and task variability were found to be highly related to each other. So were task feedback and task predictability. We have included in the Measurement Module task variability and task difficulty, or predictability measures.[15] Some people have used task structure measures that seem to embody both variability and difficulty.[4]

So far so good. It looks as if there are at least four separate core job dimensions that can be measured in different ways. However, some recent work has questioned whether these dimensions are really separate or not.[2] In other words, they question whether workers see jobs as multidimensional.[3] There are data suggesting that workers see only an overall "job complexity" type dimension rather than more specific dimensions such as those above.[11]

There may be many reasons for these differences in results, including the different kinds of technologies in which the studies were conducted. We won't attempt to reconcile the debate. But we think it is fruitful to look at group tasks in a fashion similar to our treatment of environment, technology, and structure. That is, complexity of tasks increases with task difficulty, interdependence, and variability. These terms should be familiar by now. But let us briefly go over what they mean in terms of our discussion of groups.

As shown in the Measurement Module, task difficulty implies that it is hard to find a clearly known way to do the task.[15] You are unsure of how to proceed. You can't readily get help in handling the work problems. A high degree of intellectual competence and effort may be needed to arrive at an answer.

Interdependence, of course, means the degree to which group members must cooperate in a team effort to get the job done or find a solution. One measure of interdependence is shown in the Measurement Module.[15]

Variability, as shown in the Measurement Module, deals with the many different kinds of things necessary to accomplish a task.[15] Goal ambiguity, uncertainty, and change will also increase task variability. As before, we argue that these aspects of tasks performed by groups increase the complexity of the job.

You may have noted that part of the dilemma surrounding task dimensionality is due to the question of the unit of analysis. That is, are you looking at the individual's perception of his or her own job, or are you looking at task complexity from a group point of view? Remember that the group is more than a collection of individuals. Yet the individuals making up the group perform different jobs in order to accomplish group goals.

Effects of Task Complexity. Logic and evidence support the idea that group performance decreases with increasing task complexity.[13] This appears to be particularly true for quality of performance. While the types of tasks noted previously may alter this generality, complexity makes it harder for the group to accomplish its goals.[6,7,12] As we will show shortly, the way a group is structured can have a bearing on this. And as we show presently, so can characteristics of group members (whether they are homogeneous or heterogeneous, for instance).[1] But there is evidence that as the task demands greater cooperation and interdependence, quality declines.[13] As the task becomes more difficult, reaction time and performance quality decreases. Variability lowers performance in that group members must distribute their activities more broadly. Thus they cannot focus attention on one or a few aspects of the task.*

We are more tentative about the job complexity relationships with employee maintenance criteria. This is because the conclusions rely on the job dimensionality research referred to earlier. But generally, there is an indication that maintenance criteria improve as complexity increases.[1] Job satisfaction seems to increase with complexity, at least so long as the job is not too difficult. (Note the possibility of an inverted U relationship here). Turnover and absenteeism decline with complexity. And Walton argues that complexity aids the quality of working life.[16] Job enrichment and job enlargement design strategies have been touted as ways to enhance quality of work life and employee maintenance.[8] Essentially, these approaches increase complexity. As before, we note that trade-offs seem to occur between performance and employee maintenance when it comes to job design and complexity.

Group Structure

Structuring of relationships is important at the organizational level and formed the basis for Chapter 9. So too is it important in groups. Here, following the available literature, we are concerned with various configurations that have been used in setting up laboratory experiments. There are a large number of potential group structures. These vary to some extent with the number of group members.[2] The structures about which we have the most information are based on five-member groups (see Figure 12-4). In laboratory studies, group members were required to send and receive communications following only the channels indicated in each of the configurations. They had to perform different kinds of tasks. Thus the nature of the structure determined the work-flow. The structures in Figure 12-4 are arranged in terms of openness. The all-channel structure is the most open in terms of communication. All members are allowed to communicate with all other members. The wheel is the least open. All communications are restricted to the central person.

Effects of Structure. Some effects of variations in structure are summarized in Tables 12-5 and 12-6. Table 12-5 shows that the more open (lower degree of centralization) the structure, the more difficult it is to predict who

*Note the notion of specialization here as a corollary to that in Chapter 9.

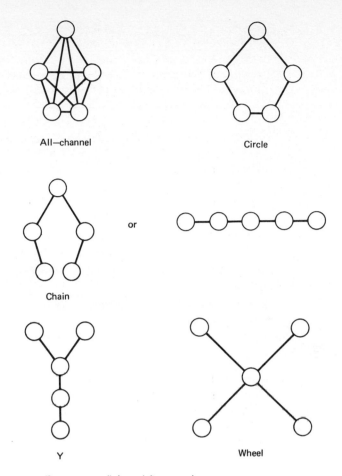

All—channel   Circle

Chain   or

Y   Wheel

Figure 12-4 Selected five-member group structures.

will assume a leadership role. It also shows that the average member satisfaction level is higher. And the range in satisfaction is lower under less centralized structures than in the more centralized Y and wheel structures. In the centralized networks, a clearly designated central person tends to control the communication process and hence is seen as the leader. That individual also tends to be more satisfied than other group members. In the more decentralized structures, satisfaction is more evenly distributed among the members.

The reason for this difference in satisfaction between the central person and other group members can be better understood if we look at the communication process within a wheel structure. All five group members are involved in transmitting information, and receiving and reporting answers.

Table 12-5 Some Effects of Five-Member Group Structures

	Type of Structure				
	All-Channel	*Circle*	*Chain*	*Y*	*Wheel*
Degree of centralization	Very low	Low	Moderate	High	Very high
Number of possible channels	Very high	Moderate	Moderate	Low	Very low
Leadership predictability	Very low	Low	Moderate	High	Very high
Average group satisfaction	High	Moderate	Moderate	Low	Low
Range in satisfaction among members	Very low	Low	Moderate	High	High

Source: Reproduced by permission from Hellriegel, D., and Slocum, J. *Organizational Behavior: Contingency Views.* Copyright © 1976, West Publishing Company. All rights reserved.

However, only the person in the central position compiles data, forms solutions, and transmits answers. Those in peripheral positions spend most of their time receiving information and answers.[1]

What about performance? Table 12-6 shows three different measures: time to solve a problem; number of messages sent in a given time period; and number of errors in a problem solution. Performance is also broken down by the complexity of the task—in this case, simple or complicated. Simple tasks were those requiring the collating of information. This involved such things as identifying which of several symbols (e.g., stars or triangles) appeared on cards held by group members. Complicated tasks required that operations be performed on information. This involved arithmetic, word arrangement, sentence construction and discussion-type problems. The table shows that for simple tasks the centralized structure was faster. The additional information opportunities were apparently necessary to provide the resources to handle the task rapidly. In terms of number of messages sent, as you might expect, the decentralized structure sent more regardless of the nature of the task. As for errors, there were less for the decentralized structure when the task was complicated but less for the centralized network when the task was simple.

Table 12-6 Some Differences in Performance in Decentralized (All-Channel, Circle) and Centralized (Chain, Y, Wheel) Structures as a Function of Simple and Complicated Tasks

Type of Performance Measure	Type of Problem[a]	Type of Structure	
		Decentralized	Centralized
Time to solve problem	Simple		Faster
	Complicated	Faster	
Messages to solve problem	Simple	Sent more	
	Complicated	Sent more	
Errors in solution	Simple		Less
	Complicated	Less	

Source: Summarized from Shaw, M. E. "Comunication Networks." In L. Berkowitz (ed.), *Advances in Experimental Social Psychology,* Vol. 1 (New York: Academic Press, 1964).

[a]*Simple* problems (require only collation of information): Identify symbols, letters, numbers, or colors. *Complicated* problems (require that operations be performed upon information): Arithmetic, work arrangement, sentence construction, and discussion problems.

These findings are explained with a concept called "saturation."[3] In centralized structures, the central person can quickly become saturated or overloaded with information in complicated tasks. Hence, solutions are slower and contain more errors. Saturation is less a problem for complicated tasks in decentralized networks. When the task is simple, saturation is not a problem in either network. Thus, the more direct, centralized structure has an advantage.

Finally, it is of interest to note that the nature of the task made no difference in terms of average member satisfaction. The higher level for the decentralized structure held regardless of whether the task was simple or complicated. However, on complex tasks, if group members can freely communicate their satisfaction about progress toward the goal, performance is enhanced.[3]

Mode of Operation. We have shown a number of effects of five-member group structures. Let us now consider group mode of operation as a function of structure. One aspect is the identification of a leader. We have already shown this occurs more readily in a centralized structure. Another aspect is the development of a consistent pattern of information exchange in solving a problem. You can think of this as the informal information exchange pattern that emerges within the limits established by the original, formally designated structure.

First, the centralized structures predisposed groups to develop informal exchange patterns more rapidly than did decentralized setups. In the less formally structured groups it took longer for the group to decide on a consistent work-flow relationship than it did where the original structure was more centralized. Second, the centralized structures predisposed groups to develop more centralized patterns of information exchange. Thus, chain, Y, and wheel structures developed patterns that funneled information through one person, who solved the problem and distributed the answer to other group members. The less centralized structures developed informal patterns whereby all available information was transmitted to all group members, each of whom solved the problem independently.[3]

Implications. It would be possible to talk about the implications of these structures in terms of the structures of the entire organization. But our primary interest here is with groups. The results demonstrate that the way in which individuals in groups are arranged, or arrange themselves, has an important impact on performance, satisfaction, and other variables. Thus, for example, the wheel pattern, though commonly used, is obviously more suitable for some circumstances than others. And structures such as the all-channel, though they appear inefficient and chaotic, can offer some real advantages for more complex tasks.

Fit among Group Member Characteristics

In addition to aspects of group composition such as size, task, and structure, the fit among group member characteristics is important. Looking at this fit among group member characteristics we note that sometimes such a fit calls for similarity among group members on one or more characteristics ("birds of a feather flock together"). In other cases, a fit calls for dissimilarity among group members on one or more characteristics ("opposites attract"). For example, a dyad might function better if there were one dominant and one submissive member than if there were two dominant or two submissive members. The issue is further complicated because there are innumerable characteristics that might be important in terms of group member fit. We first consider fit in terms of compatibility-incompatibility. Then we look at it from a homogeneity-heterogeneity point of view. Finally we explore fit in terms of status congruence-status incongruence.

The Concept of Compatibility.* Here the available evidence is concerned with compatibility in two ways—compatibility on the basis of needs, and on the basis of group behavior. In the former, a compatible group might consist of combining individuals with, say, a high need for assertiveness with those with a high need for submissiveness. In each case, the interaction process should lead to mutual satisfaction. Where group behaviors are considered, it is the compatibility of the behaviors that is of primary concern. The group situation must allow for the behaviors to be clearly demonstrated. For example, an authoritarian leader in charge of authoritarian followers would be more compatible than would an authoritarian leader in charge of democratic followers. The leader would be in a better position to behave autocratically. With democratic followers autocratic behaviors would have to be tempered. Hence, there would be less compatibility.

Most of the evidence about compatibility comes from laboratory studies of college students. Much of it is not very systematic. There is little similarity in the variables studied. What evidence there is, though, tends to support the notion that compatible groups are more likely to have satisfied members. And they will be more effective in accomplishing group goals than incompatible groups. The rationale is that groups compatible in terms of needs and behaviors tend to have less anxious members, function more smoothly, and devote less energy to holding the group together. Hence, they tend to be better at goal accomplishment than those low in compatibility.

Unfortunately, the available evidence does not allow us to go much further in specifying which *specific* variables should be compatible and which incompatible, in terms of predicting group criteria.†

Homogeneity-Heterogeneity. In the discussion above, the compatibility relationships among particular characteristics or behaviors were emphasized. There is another body of literature, though, that concentrates on the concept of homogeneity-heterogeneity, as such. The general assumption is that most group activities require a variety of skill and knowledge. Hence, in many cases, heterogeneity will be required, at least up to the trade-off point, where the communication/coordination requirements brought on by increased heterogeneity counterbalance the additional resources needed (see Figure 12-3).[6]

Two ways of looking at homogeneity-heterogeneity are found in the literature. In the first, homogeneity is looked at in terms of a single characteristic. Thus, groups with members of the same general educational background might

*Much of the following discussion is based on Shaw.[6]

†For those interested in *individual* criteria, some recent field studies concerned with "life-style compatibility" may be of interest.[5]

be compared to those with members of varied backgrounds. Of course, other characteristics could be used as well. The second approach considers a profile of several characteristics. Here, a homogeneous group might be formed of people with a similar profile of scores on a psychological test. A heterogeneous group would be composed of members with different profiles.

Again, most of the evidence in this area comes from laboratory studies of students. A couple of broad generalizations are possible from these. First, groups of members with *diverse abilities* are likely to perform better than more homogeneous groups.[6] Second, groups that have members with *heterogeneous* psychological profiles are likely to perform better than groups with more homogeneous profiles.[6] There is an interesting study qualifying this second generalization.[7] It was found that dyads were more creative when they had members who were heterogeneous in terms of attitudes and homogeneous with respect to ability. As in Figure 12-3, it appears as if homogeneity on both attitude and ability profile dimensions, while decreasing communication/coordination requirements relative to the more heterogeneous dyads, did not provide enough diversity for creative decisions. Too much heterogeneity, though, apparently made it too difficult to communicate. A mix of heterogeneity and homogeneity seems to provide the appropriate balance for creative tasks.

Status Congruence. An additional body of evidence concerning the fit among characteristics is that based on "status congruence." A person's status is his or her standing in a group or social system. That standing is based on a number of different characteristics such as age, seniority, occupation, and so on. These are called status factors. *Status congruence* is concerned with the extent to which a person's standing on one factor is *consistent* with his or her standing on other factors (individual status congruence). The extent to which persons within a group have the same standing on corresponding status factors with respect to other people within the same group is group status congruence. High individual status congruence implies high group congruence. The reverse does not necessarily hold. A group of sixteen-year-old bank presidents with a third-grade education would be an extreme example of high group status congruence but low individual status congruence.

Evidence from a number of studies suggests that status congruence may operate as shown in Figure 12-7 in influencing the response categories shown there.* These responses appear to be self-explanatory except for the fourth category of status equalization. One example might be a highly competent manager with relatively low formal authority who tries to equalize the authority-competence incongruence through empire building.

*The evidence here and below does not always differentiate between group and individual status congruence. For our purposes, it might well be either.

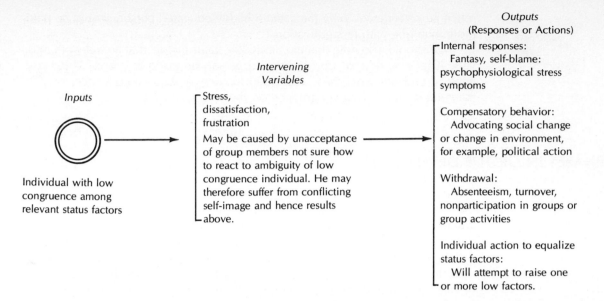

Inputs

Individual with low
congruence among
relevant status factors

_Intervening
Variables_

Stress,
dissatisfaction,
frustration

May be caused by unacceptance
of group members not sure how
to react to ambiguity of low
congruence individual. He may
therefore suffer from conflicting
self-image and hence results
above.

Outputs
(Responses or Actions)

Internal responses:
Fantasy, self-blame:
psychophysiological stress
symptoms

Compensatory behavior:
Advocating social change
or change in environment,
for example, political action

Withdrawal:
Absenteeism, turnover,
nonparticipation in groups or
group activities

Individual action to equalize
status factors:
Will attempt to raise one
or more low factors.

Figure 12-7 Summary of status congruence relationships. _Source:_ Hunt, J. G. "Status Congruence in Organizations: Effects and Suggested Research." In R. W. Millman, and M. P. Hottenstein (eds.), _Academy of Management Proceedings_ (1967). Reprinted by permission of Hunt and Academy of Management Publications.

Status congruence has been shown to have a possible inverted U relationship with performance. Performance is higher at middle levels of congruence than at either very high or very low levels.[3,4] One possible explanation for this curvilinear relationship is in terms of factors concerned with communication and facilitation of coordination. Improved interpersonal relations from increased status congruence may lead to better communication and coordination and better performance. This holds until the relations become so good that too much time is spent socializing and not enough performing.[1] A variation is that the conflict inherent at very low levels of congruence is so great that performance suffers. Then as congruence increases, the conflict leads to a healthy generation of ideas and resources and finally drops as congruence becomes "too high."[2]

At a more general level, status congruence reactions are sometimes explained in terms of various balance or cognitive consistency theories.[4] Essentially these theories argue that individuals expect various characteristics to be "balanced." People are uncomfortable when they are not. Or persons have a sense of justice such that they expect a certain equity or fairness relative to the way in which resources are allocated. For example, in many situations it might be considered "only fair" that a highly educated person should be paid more than one with less education.

We should also note that the particular status factors that are relevant may vary at least somewhat from person to person or group to group. Thus, you need to find out what these are when looking at status congruence, or you may end up measuring congruence on the wrong factors.

PHASES IN GROUP DEVELOPMENT

Up to now we have treated groups as static entities, implicitly assuming that the nature of the group stays the same over time. However, newly formed groups exhibit quite different behavior patterns from mature ones. It is, therefore, quite important to know the stage of development of a given group. This should help you to predict the kinds of behavior most likely to occur and to help understand why one group acts one way and one, another. A synthesis of the small group literature suggests that there are four distinct phases of group development.* The description of these phases is more meaningful if process groups are separated from task or organizational work groups (Figure 12-1). These four phases are: (1) the forming stage; (2) the storming period; (3) the initial integration phase; and (4) the completion of integration.†

Forming Stage

This includes the process by which an individual identifies with the group. What can individuals get from a relationship with the group? What do they have to contribute to the group? What is the congruence between the needs of the individual and the needs of the group?

Along with this is a concern with discovering what is acceptable behavior in the group and what the *real* task of the group is. Here, defining group boundaries and ground rules in terms of the set of expectations among group members is important. In the organizational task group this identification process is likely to be affected by many more factors than in other small groups. The group is generally composed of individuals who have been in the organization for substantial time periods. Such things as multiple group memberships and identifications, experience with task group members in other

*You may find it useful at this point to reread the earlier discussion of stages of organizational development (see Part III).

†This discussion is based primarily on Heinen and Jacobson.[2]

contexts, and conceptions of organization philosophies, goals, and norms may all be important in newly formed organizational task groups. The new group starts as an undifferentiated global mass. The organization, through its structure, technology, and division of labor, spells out the basis for group activity in terms of required interdependence among members. These requirements provide for an initial definition of the group by its members.

Storming Period

This second stage is seen as a period of high emotionality, especially in therapy- and sensitivity process-type groups. There are likely to be overt expressions of hostility and infighting. Evidence suggests that these kinds of behavior will not be as dramatic in task groups. But this second phase is still one of relatively high tension.

Accompanying these changes in affective relations are changes in group structure. Group activities are elaborated upon based on the definition of the group in the forming stage. Attention is also likely to be directed toward attacking obstacles standing in the way of group goals.

In process groups, the situation is structured so that individuals can examine the impact of their different interpersonal styles, primarily in relation to authority. Hence there is a tendency for interpersonal conflict. In task groups the emphasis will be on finding appropriate ways to accomplish the task that will also satisfy individual needs.

Demands from outside the group may tend to increase interaction for certain individuals within the group. Coalitions or cliques are likely to form to improve group "rewards" and reduce group "costs." Frequently there will be some conflict and competition aroused as individuals try to impose their definition of the situation on the group and attempt to gain a desired position in the group's structure.

Initial Integration

While phase 2 emphasized role differentiation, this phase stresses integration. Bales[1] describes this as the "equilibrium process." The group is coordinated into a task unit. The probes and jockeying for position of phase 2 lead to a precarious balancing of forces. There will be a tendency to try to maintain this balance. The group will tend to closely regulate individual member behavior. There is likely to develop: a strong (though possibly superficial) closeness; a communication system that integrates differentiated roles into a task unit; and standardization of behavior to try to protect the group from possible disintegration. Indeed, holding the group together may become more important to group members than task accomplishment. Minority viewpoints may be strongly discouraged. As we pointed out earlier, this process has been called "groupthink."[3] An example was the reaction of President Kennedy's advisors before the ill-fated Bay of Pigs invasion. Even when they had misgivings they were hesitant to express them. They feared rejection by Kennedy and other group members.

Completion of Integration

This final phase is considered to be that of a mature, well-integrated group. The integration, started in the previous phase, is now completed. The group is now well enough developed to deal with difficulties and disagreements in innovative ways. There is stability of structure along with the capability of reorganizing to adapt to changing conditions.

Additional Considerations

Our description above might seem to imply that all groups go neatly through these phases exactly as described. It is possible, though, for a group to take some actions described in later phases, earlier. Also, all groups may not go through all the phases. Have you ever been in a group that seemed stuck at phase 3 or maybe even phase 2? The question of time is also important. We know very little about this. It appears, though, that the time periods for each of these phases could vary considerably among different groups. Some groups might move from 1 to 2 quickly and then from 3 to 4 more slowly. Others could move through all four phases quickly or slowly for that matter.

Finally, do these stages appear in discrete steps? Or are they more continuous so that there is gradual movement through one phase and into the next. We are not sure. We need more data on this and the preceding questions. In the meantime, this knowledge of stages, rough as it is, can help you better understand group behavior. In closing, we might ask what the relationship is between group maturity and contribution to managerial objectives. As with cohesiveness, there is no *necessary* relationship. Mature groups can function better than those in earlier stages. They can also be very good at subverting managerial objectives.

A SCENARIO FOR THE ANALYSIS OF ORGANIZATIONAL GROUPS

Now that we have discussed some key aspects of groups, let's see how these might be applied in an organiztion. We can first look into the formation and development of committees and task groups and then at the environment of a group.

Committees and Task Forces

Part of your work life is likely to be involved with committees, project groups, or task forces formed to handle special assignments. Given a choice, how should these groups be formed and allowed to evolve?

First, the chapter material suggests that the size of the group should probably be from five to seven members to balance specialization on the one hand and coordination/control costs on the other. Assuming you can tap individuals with relevant expertise, then if there were judgment tasks they could be assigned to individual members. The exception is judgments cutting across areas of expertise. Furthermore, let's assume that the group is required because high-quality problem solving is needed. If efficiency is paramount, the chapter suggests you should probably not use a group. If it is a group of managers, you can usually assume that there is considerable interest in the task and that members have access to as much relevant information as can be obtained. If these are problems, commissioning by a senior executive and clearance to get data should be obtained. To minimize the chances of a "risky shift" you probably want the outcomes of the group given to a senior executive for confirmation.

With these considerations taken into account, then what? You will probably be concerned with status congruence. Status incongruity will quickly upset the chances of the group emerging around the nature of the task. For instance, the most technically qualified individual is unlikely to have the most influence in groups with high status incongruence.

Given a reasonable degree of status congruence, then by specifying the agenda and altering among written and oral presentations, and open discussion, you can initially establish the formal communication pattern. The degree of specialization flows naturally from the nature of the task, subject to size limitations.

Yet perhaps the stickiest question of all still remains. Exactly who will be in the group? To aid in the development of the group, earlier material suggests you would like homogeneity in terms of attitudes and heterogeneity in terms of skills. This pattern facilitates group development by providing a base for emergent sentiments. Skill heterogeneity is not particularly difficult to measure or develop, but homogeneity in attitudes is. In many larger organizations the apparent attitudes of managers play a particularly important role in selecting individuals for managerial posts. Now you should see an important reason why subscription to the dominant philosophy of the organization can be particularly important. The organization wants to develop groups with individuals of different skills knowing their attitudes are homogeneous.

You should also be aware that with experienced managers, and perhaps others as well, it will be virtually impossible to fake the "real" task of the group.[1] If the group is to merely ratify the opinions and decisions of others, this will quickly be discovered in the forming stage of the group. Also, expect some interpersonal conflict as the group moves out of the forming stage into the storming period. The key is to allow the group's interpersonal communications channels to develop and to encourage a changing of patterns of those who lose out in the jockeying for position that typically goes on during this period. Recognize that, though this period is messy and time consuming, it is probably crucial before integration can be attempted.

From this point on, evolution of the collection into a group can be stopped dead or may move on quickly as various actions are integrated. Holding the group together is particularly important and the absence of a minority opinion holder can be quite functional.

Of course, there are a number of other factors, but these appear to be some key ones that will help move these committees or task forces toward evolution into mature groups.

The Environment of the Group

When working with groups, you also need to be aware of "external" factors that can affect them. We call this the group's environment. This consists of those aspects from the organization's setting (environment, context, and structure) that are salient to a particular group within that organization. For the group in question, this is analogous to the specific environment for the organization as a whole. For example, different groups in an organization may be affected by different portions of the structure, whereas some contextual variables might affect all groups. But the most likely impact on the group comes from other groups.

We think an overall estimate of the group's environment can be obtained by treating the group as a small subsystem.[3] Then you can plot the environmental complexity for a given unit using the measures provided earlier. We recommend that you be particularly aware of unusual factors in the environment of the organization, its context and structure. Realize that not every group within the same organization faces an identical setting.

Generally what do we expect as the complexity of the group's environment increases? Remember we said that complexity for organizations was a mixed bag, but it generally favored organizational survival and many aspects of organizational effectiveness. It is just the opposite for groups.* Interdependence in the group's environment makes it particularly difficult to develop a consistent pattern of required actions, interactions, and sentiments.[2] Also, interdependence often pulls group members away from each other as they attempt to respond to outside demands. External uncertainty also has a devisive effect.

Again the negative impact is two-sided. First, it is harder to develop consistency among required actions, interactions, and sentiments. Second, it makes it difficult for group members to develop a reinforcing pattern of emergent actions, interactions, and sentiments. Essentially, uncertainty disrupts existing patterns and reduces the expected value of working toward consistency.

Along with interdependence and uncertainty is munificence (development in the group environment). For analysis of units we emphasize the amount of resources available to the group and its power potential. We think that munificence has a positive effect on groups. Dumping resources on a group will be functional for employee maintenance, and it can partially offset high interdependence and uncertainty.

Just operating in a setting with many resources does not always allow you to develop a balance among requirements or soothe employees facing conflicting and rapidly changing external demands. However, operating in a lean environment can be devastating. Faced with a hostile setting that does not provide for many returns to the group, members may form into a cohesive group.[1,4] But the norms of the group are not likely to favor high performance.[1,4]

Figure 12-8 shows the estimated combined effect of the three variables in the group's environment. Notice the combination is similar to that provided earlier for the organization.

While not shown here, we think that there may be a different result for the leader faced with these combinations. Specifically, high uncertainty in the group's environment provides the leader an opportunity to build the long-term power of the group. Thus, a factor that causes problems within the group is also a potential factor in its development. To understand how a manager may build upon uncertainty in the group's environment, you need a deeper understanding of leadership. We turn to that in the next chapter. For now, rec-

*Organizational factors may place counterpressures on a group. The same factors that make the group's task sophisticated, varied, and interdependent may also lead to a setting that is interdependent and uncertain. While internal task complexity is functional, external interdependence and uncertainty are not.

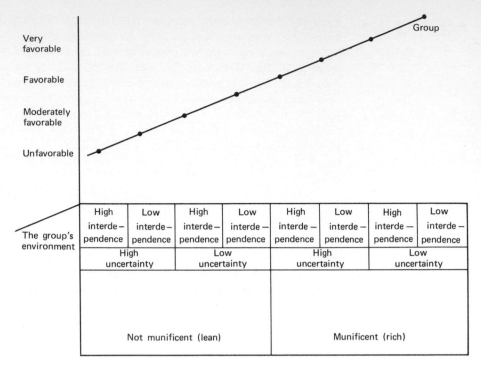

Figure 12-8 Favorability in the group's environment.

ognize that the environment of the group can affect performance and satisfaction and the actions of the leader.

Also, the nature of the group itself is important. That is, the cohesiveness and consistency among actions, interactions, and sentiments, and the composition of the group (size, task, structure, and member characteristics) may be influenced by its environment. We will use the nature of the group as a summary term. Now, let's try to pin down some of these group concepts with our Measurement Module. Then we will turn to leadership and influence.

MEASUREMENT MODULE

Here we first treat the measurement of group cohesiveness. Then we present measures of various aspects of group member tasks using the Job Characteristics Inventory, along with measures of task difficulty, interdependence, and variability. Finally we get into one aspect of group homogeneity by showing a couple of ways of determining status congruence.

Exhibit 12-9 is a measure of group cohesiveness by Scott and Rowland.[3] They report developmental data for the instrument, and it's been used in recent work by Hunt and Osborn,[1] among others.

Exhibit 12-9   A Measure of Group Cohesiveness

Please place a check mark in the most appropriate space below for each of the nine pairs of adjectives best describing your feeling about your fellow workers most of the time.

My Fellow Workers

	Extremely	Quite	Slightly	Neither One Or The Other	Slightly	Quite	Extremely	
Cooperative	___	___	___	___	___	___	___	Uncooperative
Pleasant	___	___	___	___	___	___	___	Unpleasant
Quarrelsome	___	___	___	___	___	___	___	Congenial
Selfish	___	___	___	___	___	___	___	Unselfish
Belligerent	___	___	___	___	___	___	___	Peaceful
Vigorous	___	___	___	___	___	___	___	Feeble
Efficient	___	___	___	___	___	___	___	Inefficient
Wise	___	___	___	___	___	___	___	Foolish
Obstructive	___	___	___	___	___	___	___	Helpful

Scoring

Cooperative, pleasant, vigorous, efficient, and wise from extreme left=7 to extreme right=1. Other adjectives are scored in opposite direction. Cohesiveness score is sum of the above.

Source: Scott, W. E., and Rowland, K. M. "The Generality and Significance of Semantic Differential Scales as Measures of Morale," *Organizational Behavior and Human Performance,* 5 (1970), 576–591. Reprinted by permission of Scott and Academic Press.

A short version of the Job Characteristics Inventory is shown in Exhibit 12-10.[4] As indicated in the figure, this version taps variety, autonomy, task identity, and feedback. The longer version taps some additional dimensions not shown here. In addition to the extensive developmental data reported by Sims, Szilagyi, and Keller,[4] Pierce and Dunham,[2] among others, provide support for the instrument.

Task difficulty, interdependence, and task variability measures are shown in Exhibits 12-11, 12-12, and 12-13. Developmental work on these is reported in Van de Ven.[5] They have also been used by Hunt and Osborn.[1] The interdependence measure is a within-group variation of the earlier one used in Chapter 11.

Finally, we consider a couple of ways of determining status congruence. Assume that you have determined that age, education, and job grade are important status factors for the people in the group(s) with which you are concerned. If you also assume that all three are of roughly the same importance, then one simple way to calculate status congruence is to rank the individuals in the group in terms of their standing on each of these factors. Suppose Jones is 57 years old, with 14 years of education and holds a job grade 12 with ranks relative to others in the group on these factors of 1, 1, and 1. Smith's standing on these same factors is 49, 10, and 10, with ranks of 2, 3, and 2. To compute status congruence for each of the two individuals simply add the difference between the rank on each factor and the rank on each other factor. For Jones there are no differences, so his congruence index is 0 (the lower the score, the higher the congruence). For Smith the difference between: age and education ranks is 1; age and job is 0; and education and job is 1. His status congruence index is 2. If you were interested in status rather than status congruence, you'd simply add the ranks with the lower rank having higher status.

Another approach is to assign arbitrary point values to different standings on each factor. For example, you might say for education: 8 years and below = 1 point; 9 to 12 years = 2 points; up to 2 years of college = 3 points; 2 to 4 years = 4 points; and more than 4 years = 5 points. You then assign points similarly for other factors (differentially weighted if you desire). Differences in standings across the point values for each individual are then calculated as above.

If you calculate the differences by individual across status factors, you have a measure of individual status congruence for each person. If you use these same values but calculate differences across individuals on each factor and then sum these totals across factors, you have one measure of group status congruence.

There are other ways in which congruence can be calculated. The key is to determine similarity in factor standings. The greater the similarity or the less the variability in standings, the greater the congruence.

Exhibit 12-10   Job Characteristics Inventory[a]

Respondents are asked to describe their job situation in terms of the items below.

1. How much variety is there in your job?

2. How much are you left on your own to do your own work?

3. How often do you see projects or jobs through to completion?

4. To what extent do you find out how well you are doing on the job as you are working?

5. How repetitious are your duties?

6. To what extent are you able to act independently of your supervisor in performing your job function?

7. To what extent do you receive information from your superior on your job performance?

8. How similar are the tasks you perform in a typical work day?

9. To what extent are you able to do your job independently of others?

10. The feedback from my supervisor on how well I'm doing.

11. The opportunity to do a number of different things.

12. The freedom to do pretty much what I want on my job.

13. The degree to which the work I'm involved with is handled from beginning to end by myself.

14. The opportunity to find out how well I am doing on my job.

15. The amount of variety in my job.

16. The opportunity for independent thought and action.

17. The opportunity to complete work I start.

18. The feeling that I know whether I am performing my job well or poorly.

19. The control I have over the pace of my work.

20. The opportunity to do a job from the beginning to end (i.e., the chance to do a whole job).

Scoring

For items 1 – 9: Very little = 1; little = 2; a moderate amount = 3; much = 4; very much = 5. For items after 9: A minimum amount = 1; some = 2; a moderate amount = 3; much = 4; a maximum amount = 5. Variety equals the sum of items: 1, 5, 8, 15, 21; autonomy equals the sum of items: 2, 6, 9, 12, 16, 19; task identity equals the sum of items: 3, 13, 17, 20; feedback equals the sum of items: 4, 7, 10, 14, 18.

Source: Sims, H. P., Szilagyi, A. D., and Keller, R. T. "The Measurement of Job Characteristics," *Academy of Management Journal*, 19 (1976), 195–212. Reprinted by permission of Sims and Academy of Management Publications.

[a]Though this instrument is not quite as well known as the Job Diagnostic Survey by Hackman and Oldham, there is some evidence suggesting it may be more valid.

Exhibit 12-11 Task Difficulty Scale

1. To what extent is there a CLEARLY KNOWN WAY to do the major types of work you normally encounter?

No Extent	Little extent	Some extent	Great extent	Very great extent
A	B	C	D	E

2. HOW EASY is it for YOU to KNOW whether you do your work correctly?

Very difficult	Quite Difficult	Some-what Easy	Quite Easy	Very Easy
A	B	C	D	E

3. What percent of the time are you GENERALLY SURE OF WHAT the OUTCOME of your work efforts will be?

40% or less	41–60%	61–75%	76–90%	91% or more
A	B	C	D	E

4. In the past 3 months, HOW OFTEN did DIFFICULT PROBLEMS ARISE in your work for which there were no immediate or apparent solutions?

Once a week or less	About 2–4 times a week	About once a day	About 2–4 times a day	5 times or more a day
A	B	C	D	E

5. About HOW MUCH TIME did you spend solving these WORK PROBLEMS?

Less than 1 hr/week	About 1–4 hours/week	About 1 hour/day	About 2–3 hours/day	4 hours or more hours/day
A	B	C	D	E

6. How often can you solve these types of specific work problems BY GOING to SOMEONE in this organization for an answer?

Very seldom	Sometimes	About half the time	Quite often	Most of the time
A	B	C	D	E

Scoring

For items 1, 2, 3, 6: A = 5, B = 4, C = 3, D = 2, E = 1; for items 4, 5: A = 1, B = 2, C = 3, D = 4, E = 5. Task difficulty equals the sum of the six items.

Source: Van de Ven, A. H., and Ferry D. L. *Measuring and Assessing Organizations* (New York: Wiley-Interscience, 1979). Reprinted by permission of Van de Ven.

Exhibit 12-12   Within Group Work-flow Interdependence Scale

Please indicate HOW MUCH of the NORMAL WORK in your unit FLOWS BETWEEN THE EMPLOYEES in a manner as described by EACH of the following cases:	*HOW MUCH WORK NORMALLY FLOWS Between the Employees in Your Unit In This Manner*				
	Almost None of the Work	*Little*	*About 50% of All Work*	*A Great Deal*	*Almost All of the Work*
1. INDEPENDENT WORK-FLOW CASE, where work and activities are performed by employees separately and does not flow between them. 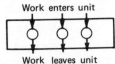	A	B	C	D	E
2. SEQUENTIAL WORK-FLOW CASE, where work and activities flow between subordinates, but mostly in one direction only. 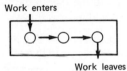	A	B	C	D	E
3. RECIPROCAL WORK-FLOW CASE, where work and activities flow between subordinates in a back-and-forth manner over a period of time. 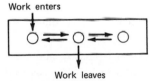	A	B	C	D	E
4. TEAM WORK-FLOW CASE, where work and activities come into your unit and subordinates diagnose, problem solve, and collaborate as a group AT THE SAME TIME in meetings to deal with the work. 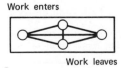	A	B	C	D	E

Exhiblt 12-13 Task Variability Scale

1. To what extent do you perform THE SAME TASKS from day-to-day?

Almost all my tasks are the same day-to-day	Many of my tasks are the same day-to-day	About half my tasks are the same day-to-day	Some of my tasks are the same day-to-day	Almost no tasks are the same day-to-day
A	B	C	D	E

2. How much the same are the day-to-day situations, problems, or issues you encounter in performing your major tasks?

Very much the same	Mostly the same	Quite a bit different	Very much different	Completely different
A	B	C	D	E

3. During a normal week, HOW FREQUENTLY do EXCEPTIONS ARISE in your work which require SUBSTANTIALLY DIFFERENT methods or procedures?

Very rarely	Occa-sion-ally	Quite often	Very often	Con-stantly
A	B	C	D	E

4. HOW OFTEN do you FOLLOW about the SAME WORK METHODS OR STEPS for DOING your major tasks day-to-day?

Very seldom	Sometimes	About half the time	Quite often	Very often
A	B	C	D	E

Scoring

For items 1, 2, 3: A = 1, B = 2, C = 3, D = 4, E = 5; for item 4: A = 5, B = 4, C = 3, D = 2, E = 1. Task variability equals the sum of the four items.

Source: Van de Ven, A. H., and Ferry, D. L. *Measuring and Assessing Organizations* (New York: Wiley-Interscience, 1979). Reprinted by Permission of Van de Ven.

REFERENCES

I. What Do We Mean By Groups?

[1]Allport, F. H. *Social Psychology.* Boston: Houghton Mifflin, 1924.

[2]Campbell, D. T. "Common Fate, Similarity, and Other Indices of the Status of Aggregates of Persons as Social Entities," *Behavioral Science,* 3 (1958), 14–25.

[3]Schein, E. "The Chinese Indoctrination Program for Prisoners of War," *Psychiatry,* 19 (1956), 149–172.

[4]Wexley, K. N., and Yukl, G. A. *Organizational Behavior and Personnel Psychology.* Homewood, Ill.: Irwin, 1977.

III. Usefulness of Groups for Task Accomplishment

A. Judgment Tasks

[1]Shaw, M. E. *Group Dynamics: The Psychology of Small Group Behavior* (2nd edition). New York: McGraw-Hill, 1976.

B. Problem Solving Tasks

[1]Shaw, 1976.

C. Learning Tasks

[1]Shaw, 1976.

D. Group Idea Generation and Risk Taking

[1]Hare, A. P. *Handbook of Small Group Research.* New York: The Free Press, 1976.

[2]Osborn, A. F. *Applied Imagination.* New York: Scribners, 1957.

[3]Shaw, 1976.

[4]Wallach, M. A., Kogan, N., and Bem, D. J. "Group Influence on Individual Risk Taking," *Journal of Abnormal and Social Psychology,* 65 (1962), 75–86.

IV. Organizational Requirements and Group Responses

A. Required and Emergent Factors

[1]Homans, C. C. *The Human Group.* New York: Harcourt, Brace & World, 1950.

[2]Turner, A. N., "A Conceptual Scheme for Describing Work Group Behavior." In P. R. Lawrence and J. A. Seiler (eds.), *Organizational Behavior and Administration.* Homewood, Ill.: Irwin, 1965.

B. Required and Emergent Factors and Group Cohesiveness

[1]Festinger, L. "Informal Social Communication," *Psychological Review,* 57 (1950), 271–282.

[2]Hare, 1976.

[3]Mann, R. D., and Baumgartel, H. "The Supervisor's Concern with Costs in an Electric Power Company." Ann Arbor: Survey Research Center, University of Michigan, 1953.

[4]Seashore, S. E. *Group Cohesiveness in the Industrial Work Group.* Ann Arbor: University of Michigan Press, 1954.

[5]Shaw, 1976.

V. Group Composition

[1]Hare, 1976.

A. Group Size

[1]Argyle, M., Gardner, G., and Cioffi, F. "Supervisory Methods Related to Productivity, Absenteeism, and Labor Turnover," *Human Relations,* 11 (1958), 23–40.

[2]Bales, R. F., and Borgatta, E. F. "Size of Groups as a Factor in the Interaction Profile." In A. P. Hare, E. F. Borgatta, and R. R. Bales (eds.), *Small Groups: Studies in Social Interaction.* (New York: Knopf, 1955).

[3]Bass, B. M. *Organizational Psychology.* Boston: Allyn and Bacon, 1965.

[4]Hare, 1976.

[5]Marriott, R. "Size of Working Group and Output." *Occupational Psychology,* 26 (1949), 47–51.

[6]Melcher, A. J. *Structure and Process of Organizations: A Systems Approach.* Englewood Cliffs, N.J.: Prentice-Hall, 1976.

[7]Porter, L. W. and Steers, R. M. "Organizational, Work, and Personal Factors in Employee Turnover and Satisfaction," *Journal of Applied Psychology,* 80 (1973), 151–176.

[8]Thomas, E. J., and Fink, C. F. "Effects of Group Size." In L. L. Cummings and W. E. Scott (eds.), *Readings in Organizational Behavior and Human Performance.* Homewood, Ill.: Irwin, 1969).

[9]Thomas and Fink, 1969.

[10]Weick, K. E., and Penner, D. D. "Triads: A Laboratory Analogue," *Organizational Behavior and Human Performance,* 1 (1966), 191–211.

B. Group Task

[1]Brief, A. P., and Aldag, R. J. "Employee Reactions to Job Characteristics: A Constructive Replication," *Journal of Applied Psychology,* 60 (1975), 182–186.

[2]Dunham, R. B. "The Measurement and Dimensionality of Job Characteristics," *Journal of Applied Psychology,* 61 (1976), 404–409.

[3]Dunham, R. B, Aldag, R., and Brief, A. "Dimensionality of Task Design as Measured by the Job Diagnostic Survey," *Academy of Management Journal,* 20 (1977), 209–223.

[4]Fiedler, F. E. *A Theory of Leadership Effectiveness.* New York: McGraw-Hill, 1967.

[5]Hackman, J. R., and Oldham, G. R. "Development of the Job Diagnostic Survey," *Journal of Applied Psychology,* 60 (1975), 159–170.

[6]Lanzetta, J. T., and Roby, T. B. "Effects of Work Group Structure and Certain Task Variables on Group Performance," *Journal of Abnormal and Social Psychology,* 53 (1956), 307–314.

[7]Lanzetta, J. T., and Roby, T. B. "Group Learning and Communication as a Function of Task and Structure 'Demands,' " *Journal of Abnormal and Social Psychology,* 55 (1957), 121–131.

[8]Lawler, E. E., Hackman, R., and Kaufman, S. "Effects of Job Redesign: A Field Experiment," *Journal of Applied Social Psychology,* 3 (1973), 49–62.

[9]Pierce, J. L., and Dunham, R. B. "An Empirical Demonstration of the Convergence of Common Macro and Micro Organization Measures," *Academy of Management Journal,* in press.

[10]Pierce, J. L., and Dunham, R. B. "The Measurement of Perceived Job Characteristics: The Job Diagnostic Survey Versus the Job Characteristics Inventory," *Academy of Management Journal,* 21 (1978), 123–128.

[11]Sekaran, U., Trafton, R., and Jauch, L. R. "Factor Analysis in Organizational Research: Some Suggested Guidelines and a Case in Point," Working paper, Department of Administrative Sciences, Southern Illinois University, Carbondale, 1978.

[12]Shaw, M. E., and Briscoe, M. E. "Group Size and Effectiveness in Solving Tasks Varying in Degree of Cooperation Requirements." Technical Report No. 6, ONR Contract NR 170-266, Nonr-580 (11), University of Florida, 1966.

[13]Shaw, M. E., and Blum, J. M. "Group Performance as a Function of Task Difficulty and the Group's Awareness of Member Satisfaction," *Journal of Applied Psychology,* 49 (1965), 151–154.

[14]Sims, H. P., Szilagyi, A. D., and Keller, R. T. "The Measurement of Job Characteristics." *Academy of Management Journal,* 19 (1976), 195–212.

[15]Van de Ven, A. H. *Organizational Assessment Measurement Manual.* Philadelphia: Wharton School, University of Pennsylvania, 1977.

[16]Walton, R. "Criteria for Quality of Working Life." In L. E. Davis and A. B. Cherns (eds.), *The Quality of Working Life, Volume One.* New York: The Free Press, 1975.

C. Group Structure

[1]Guetzkow, H., and Simon, H. A. "The Impact of Certain Communication Nets Upon Organization and Performance in Task-oriented Groups," *Management Science,* 1 (1955), 233–250.

[2]Shaw, M. E. "Communication Networks." In L. Berkowitz (ed.), *Advances in Experimental Social Psychology, Volume One.* New York: Academic Press, 1964.

[3]Shaw, 1976.

D. Fit among Group Member Characteristics

[1]Adams, S. "Status Congruency as a Variable in Small Group Performance," *Social Forces,* 32 (1953), 16–22.

[2]Exline, R. V., and Ziller, R. C. "Status Congruency and Interpersonal Conflict in Decision-Making Groups," *Human Relations,* 12 (1959), 147–161.

[3]Hunt, J. G. "Status Congruence in Organizations: Effects and Suggested Research." In R. W. Millman and M. P. Hottenstein (eds.), *Academy of Management Proceedings, 27th Annual Meeting.* University Park, Pa.: Pennsylvania State University, 1967.

[4]Hunt, J. G., and Bishop, R. C. "Implications of Status Congruence in Organizations." Unpublished manuscript, Southern Illinois University, Carbondale, 1974.

[5]Norton, S. D., and DiMarco, N. "A Comparison of the Predictive Models of Job Satisfaction and Performance." Unpublished manuscript, School of Business Administration, University of Missouri, St. Louis, 1977.

[6]Shaw, 1976.

[7]Triandis, H. E., Hall, E. R., and Ewen, R. B. "Member Heterogeneity and Dyadic Creativity," *Human Relations,* 18 (1965), 33–55.

VI. Phases in Group Development

[1]Bales, R. F. *Interaction Process Analysis: A Method for the Study of Small Groups.* Cambridge, Mass., Addison-Wesley, 1950.

[2]Heinen, J. S., and Jacobson, E. "A Model of Task Group Development in Complex Organizations and a Strategy of Supplementation," *Academy of Management Review,* 1 (1976), 98–111.

[3]Janis, I. L. *Victims of Groupthink.* Boston: Houghton Mifflin, 1972.

VII. A Scenario for the Analysis of Organizational Groups

A. Committees and Task Forces

[1]Ritti, R. R., and Funkhouser, G. R. *The Ropes to Skip and the Ropes to Know.* Columbus, Ohio: Grid, Inc., 1977.

B. The Environment of the Group
[1]Hare, 1976.
[2]Litterer, J. A. *The Analysis of Organizations* (2nd edition.) New York: Wiley, 1975.
[3]Osborn, R. "The Search for Environmental Complexity," *Human Relations,* 29 (1976), 179–191.
[4]Shaw, 1976.
IX. Measurement Module
[1]Hunt, J. G., and Osborn, R. N. *A Multiple Influence Model of Leadership.* Proposal funded by the U.S. Army Research Institute for the Behavioral and Social Sciences, May 1978.
[2]Pierce and Dunham, in press.
[3]Scott, W. E., and Rowland, K. M. "The Generality and Significance of Semantic Differential Scales as Measures of Morale," *Organizational Behavior and Human Performance,* 5 (1970), 576–591.
[4]Sims, Szilagyi, and Keller, 1976.
[5]Van de Ven, 1977.

chapter **13** **LEADERSHIP AND INFLUENCE**

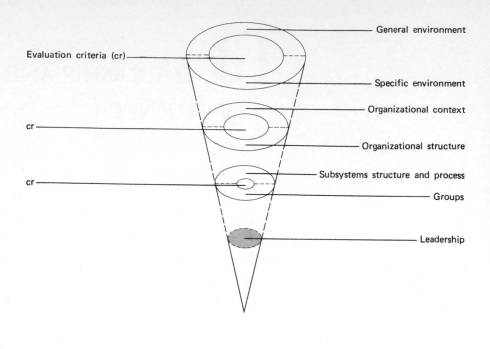

He comes riding out of the setting sun, high in the saddle, on his magnificent white stallion. As the sun illuminates his white hat, everyone knows he is somebody. Everything will be all right. He is special. He is the leader. His square jaw, well-built frame, and magnetic personality assure the people of secure peace, harmony, and everlasting joy. He rides to the next village before the townspeople can even thank him. All realize that they have seen a true leader.

This example is clearly exaggerated. However, it does focus on the intuitively appealing "great man" or trait approaches to leadership and it seems a good place to start the chapter. After a discussion of leadership traits we examine leader effectiveness versus who gets to be leader; we then move into a discussion of informal versus formal leadership.

With this as a background, we consider approaches emphasizing leader behavior, as contrasted with traits, and discuss the difference between power, authority, and leadership—all ways in which one person exerts influence over others. Next, we elaborate on the notion of lateral relations discussed in Chapter 11. The lateral focus is in sharp contrast to the vertical superior-subordinate focus typically emphasized in treatments of leadership.

All of these set the stage for an examination of some current approaches to leadership. These are contingency approaches and were selected to illustrate the different directions current contingency thinking is taking in the leadership area. We then build on these contingency notions in discussing our own more comprehensive "multiple influence approach" to leadership. Here we very generally link this approach with previously discussed organizational variables. Then, in the final contingency chapter (Chapter 14), we elaborate on the multiple influence approach and apply it systematically as a number of different organizational characteristics are varied.

GREAT MAN AND TRAIT APPROACHES

What makes a person a great leader? Is leadership related to traits that only a few privileged individuals are born with? Are you the great leader that nobody has yet recognized? Should you run out and get elevator shoes (leaders selected by their peers tend to be taller), buy a white hat, and sign up for a physical fitness course? All of these recommendations are consistent with the "great man" approach to leadership.

The first attempts to understand leadership were based on this great man approach to leadership. Attempts were made to determine those unique qualities separating great men in history from the masses. The notion that the leader is endowed with superior qualities led quite naturally to a search for these qualities—the so-called trait approach to leadership.[1]

The great man and trait approaches have not held up well when subjected to research. There has been little consistency in the traits identified. No one trait explains very much of what it is that separates leaders from others.[1] There is no denying, though, that these approaches have a certain intuitive appeal. Thus, in spite of the largely unpromising research findings, you will still find a heavy emphasis on these approaches in the popular media.[2]

Actually, if you think about it a bit, you shouldn't be surprised that great man or trait approaches have not been more successful in predicting leadership. Just as there is no one organization structure that identifies superior organizations, so there is no one trait or set of traits that identifies leaders in all situations.

LEADERSHIP EFFECTIVENESS AND WHO WILL BE THE LEADER

The central focus of the great man approach to leadership is: Who will be the leader? Specifically, it attempted to predict the type of individual people would select as their leader.[5] While this is an important question, analysis of leadership in organizational settings has tended to take a different tack. Subordinates rarely elect their leaders in work organizations. So much of the literature concentrates on improving the leadership effectiveness of the manager in terms of organizational, work unit, or individual subordinate performance and maintenance criteria.[2] Concentrating on the formal leader (the individual selected by management) does not preclude consideration of traits or attitudes. But traits and attitudes have been more frequently used in separating leaders from nonleaders.[5]

Before restricting our focus strictly to formal leadership, though, it is important to consider a variation of the leader-nonleader dichotomy—namely, informal versus formal leadership. This variation often is discussed in the organizational literature.[1]

Informal or Peer Leadership

Informal or peer leadership exists anywhere where nonsupervisory employees exert influence over one another. Typically, one or more people will be recognized as having more influence than others and these may be called "informal leaders." Thus, there may be one, or more than one, informal leader in a given work group. It is possible, for example, that one individual may be looked to for his or her task knowledge; another may be influential in helping members take care of their social and emotional needs. Or perhaps one of these leaders is formal and the other informal. It is also possible that different individuals can be informal leaders depending upon ways in which group activities change over time. Other possibilities also exist. But these should illustrate the point.

The importance of informal leadership was demonstrated in a study of industrial work groups.[4] Here the findings suggest that where workers saw their supervisors as providing inadequate leadership, informal leaders stepped in to fill the vacuum. Others found that when subordinates were asked to complete questionnaires describing their supervisor, a number of those in supervisory roles were not described by anyone. The researchers attributed this to the lack of demonstrated leader behaviors by such supervisors.[3] Stogdill found, in a study of the organization of aircraft carriers, that frequently leadership influence was not exerted along formal organizational lines. In many cases such influence came from someone other than an individual's designated supervisor.[7]

A related point centers on the relative impact of both formal and informal leadership in the same organizational setting. Some work suggests the importance of both formal and informal leadership, but does not identify one person(s) as the informal leader(s).[1,2,5] In one study it was found that peer leadership and formal leadership were about equal in the number of times each predicted a given aspect of satisfaction better than the other.[1] A more recent study found that formal and peer leader behavior each significantly predicted five components of satisfaction plus overall satisfaction in a manufacturing firm. However, peer leadership significantly predicted only three of six satisfaction measures when formal leadership was controlled. But formal leadership predicted five of six measures when peer leadership was controlled. The magnitude of the correlations for formal leadership was generally greater as well.[5] In other words peer leadership helped predict beyond formal leadership in some cases. But given a choice of one or the other, formal leadership was the better predictor.

One study compared formal and informal leaders. Reaser, was concerned with the relative impact of formal ("officials" in his terms) and informal leaders. However, some formal leaders were also informal leaders. Thus, he looked at the behavior of officials who were not sociometrically chosen as "leaders" by group members versus the leader behavior of officials *and* nonofficials who were chosen as leaders (endorsed). In other words, how important is it to examine leadership in terms of sociometrically endorsed leaders (both official and nonofficial) versus merely considering leadership in terms of officials only? A key finding was that various aspects of satisfaction were significantly predicted by the leadership of officials over and above endorsed leaders, but not vice versa.[6]

We conclude from these studies that both formal and informal leadership are important. However, when the impact of both is compared in the same study, the results suggest that formal leadership may be more important in terms of its effect on criteria. And that is what we concentrate on in the remainder of this chapter.

LEADER BEHAVIOR

With a concentration on formal leadership, there was a shift away from traits to behaviors. In the late 1940s to about the early 1960s most leadership researchers concentrated on finding the set of leader behaviors associated with high performance and employee maintenance.[4] One set of findings suggested that leaders who were employee-centered rather than production-centered had work units with higher production.[3] Initially, supporting evidence was found; but later more sophisticated studies revealed that this view was too simple.

This first set of studies tended to look at employee centeredness and production centeredness as opposite ends of a continuum.[3] Another set examined two aspects of leadership that were considered to be independent of each other rather than being opposite ends of a continuum. The first of these concerned actions related to the task of individuals and the group. The second was concerned with actions relating to the social aspects of organizational membership.[4]

With a wide variety of approaches, the field quickly developed into a terminological jungle. Each scholar looked at slightly different aspects of the task and social actions of leaders, and each developed a separate series of terms. Table 13-1 is one attempt to piece this jungle together.

Generally this literature suggested that leaders who were more considerate (supportive, facilitating interaction, sensitive, employee-oriented with good human relations skills) headed groups with higher employee maintenance.[4] While this relationship did not hold in all circumstances, it fit common sense and supported the human relations movement that was receiving considerable attention in the 1950s and 1960s.[3] Some studies also showed that leaders who initiated more structure had more productive groups.[4] Again there were numerous terms, including goal emphasis, work facilitation, objective attainment behavior, enabling goal achievement, and the like. Here results were not as consistent as for social actions. Finally, a few studies suggested that leaders who were active in both areas headed more productive and satisfied groups. The "high-high" leader behavior belief was born. It suggested that "successful" leaders should be high in both task and social behaviors if they wanted high productivity and satisfaction. The combination was important. Both were required.[4]

Later evidence suggested that the high-high recommendation is a myth.[2] As more studies were published it became apparent that leaders who were high on either or both task and social aspects could be either successful or unsuccessful. No one set of leader behaviors was equally successful in all situations.[2]

While the search for universal leader behaviors leading to success was not successful, it did clarify some important issues. First, it gave us a much better understanding of the types of leader actions that might sometimes be taken to increase performance and employee maintenance. And that served as a point of departure for the contingency approaches discussed later in this

Table 13-1 Comparison of Leadership Dimensions Used by Different Investigators

Bowers and Seashore (1966)	Hemphill and Coons (1957)	Halpin and Winer (1957)	Katz et al. (1950)	Katz and Kahn (1951)	Kahn (1958)	Mann (1962)	Likert (1961)	Cartwright and Zander (1960)
Support	Maintenance of membership character	Consideration	Employee orientation	Employee orientation	Providing direct need satisfaction	Human relations skills	Principle of supportive relationships	Group maintenance functions
				Closeness of supervision			Group methods of supervision	
Interaction facilitation	Group interaction facilitation behavior	Sensitivity		Group relationships				
Goal emphasis	Objective attainment behavior	Production emphasis	Production orientation		Structuring path to goal attainment	Administrative skills	High-performance goals	Goal achievement functions
					Modifying employee goals			
Work facilitation		Initiating structure		Differentiation of supervisory role	Enabling goal achievement	Technical skills	Technical knowledge, planning, scheduling	
				Closeness of supervision				

Source: Bowers, D. G., and Seashore, S. E. ''Predicting Organizational Effectiveness with a Four Factor Theory of Leadership,'' *Administrative Science Quarterly,* 11 (1966), 233–263. Reprinted by permission of *Administrative Science Quarterly.* Copyright © 1966, Cornell University.

chapter. Second, it led to a more detailed analysis of what leadership is and how it differs from management and such related notions as power and authority. We now turn to that point.

LEADERSHIP AND RELATED CONCEPTS

Up to now we have loosely treated leadership as a form of influence without being very specific. The term is used even more loosely in the literature. Some see leadership as a process; some as a set of behaviors; some see it as abilities people possess.[4] Some people use organizational position as one of the ways to define a leader, others do not.[4] The common element running through the definitions is influence, without regard to organizational position. In many cases, the definition is further narrowed to face-to-face influence or influence via personal interaction. That definition is consistent with our treatment of leadership.[3]

This notion brings us to the question of whether leadership is the same as management. Most management scholars would probably argue that the two are not the same. One school of thought is that management is a broader concept than leadership.[1] Filley and House[2] distinguish between management and leadership by defining management "as a process, mental and physical, whereby subordinates are brought to execute prescribed formal duties and to accomplish certain given objectives" (p. 391). In contrast, they define leadership as "a process whereby one person exerts *social influence* over the members of a group" (their emphasis). Included within the definition of management are such functions as planning, organizing, staffing, directing, and controlling, whereas the essence of the leadership definition is interpersonal influence.

If the essence of leadership is interpersonal influence, how does this differ from the commonly used notions of power and authority?

Power

Power is not always defined in the same way. But a widely accepted definition is given by French and Raven.[1] They define it as "the control which a person possesses and can exercise over others." Defined in this way, it is virtually the same as our leaderhip definition. Thus, as in our discussion of formal and informal leadership, power can be entirely independent of organizational position. You have probably attended a group meeting where you tended to listen to and do what one individual said more than others, even though that person held no official leadership position.

What makes French and Raven's discussion of power so interesting is not their definition, but their attempt to explain the power base of individuals. They provide five bases of power:

1. *Reward Power.* To what extent can an individual grant extrinsic rewards such as money, promotions, and compliments to others?
2. *Coercive power.* While an individual may not be able to give another individual extrinsic rewards, he or she may be able to punish that individual. For example, a supervisor may be in a position to fire a subordinate or withhold his or her pay raise.
3. *Legitimate power.* This is power that stems from the internalized values of one person that dictate that another person has a legitimate right to influence the second person, and that that person has an obligation to accept the influence. Usually associated with cultural values, legitimate power may be institutionalized in terms of rank such as in the army.
4. *Referent power.* Referent power is based on an individual wanting to identify with another individual. This identification can be sustained if the second person behaves, perceives, or believes as the first person does.
5. *Expert power.* The knowledge one individual possesses that another person does not have but needs is another basis for power. It is likely to be evaluated in terms of a person's own knowledge as well as some absolute standard. One example of the exercise of expert power is when a patient follows a physician's "advice."

Authority

Power and authority are often discussed together because authority may be seen as institutionalized power. The willingness of individuals to accept the directions of others is so pervasive in societies that authority and power have received considerable attention. Weber[2] and Barnard[1] are only two of the many scholars who have commented on authority and power in organizational settings. Their contributions are particularly interesting because they help us understand why a leader may be able to influence subordinates.

Weber argues that authority does not necessarily rest on coercive power. Authority is most closely associated with a combination of legitimate, referent, and expert power. That is, bosses are followed because they *should* be (legitimate power), *should know more* (expert power), and are to be emulated (referent power). In Weberian terminology, there is legal authority (legitimate power), traditional authority (expert power—assuming one thinks that superiors know best), and charismatic authority (referent power).[2]

Barnard's discussion of authority is similar. He argues that subordinates are generally willing to accept direction. However, if orders are not apparently based on legitimate, expert, or referent power, they may be ignored almost regardless of the rewards or sanctions.[1] For example, in Vietnam, U.S. prisoners of war were ordered to divulge military secrets and admonished not to talk among themselves. In spite of the severe consequences, many refused to give information to their captors and the prisoners devised ingenious ways of communication.

The willingness to accept direction may be expressed in terms of a zone of indifference. The larger the zone of indifference, the more direction a subordinate will accept.[1]

What does all this have to do with leadership? Plenty. The formal leader in an organization is given formal authority as a boss. Merely putting him or her in charge initially gives legitimate, expert, and perhaps referent power. But how much power and authority?

The ability of the supervisor to provide extrinsic rewards and sanctions is often limited. It is limited both by organizational policies and societal norms. For example, a first-level supervisor may be able to *recommend* promotions, raises, or demotions. But this is often only a recommendation, not the decision. A supervisor cannot bring in a whip and threaten subordinates. However, in all probability the supervisor can compliment subordinates on a good job, listen to their concerns, and even attempt to rectify some apparent injustices.

More than anything else, the boss can build and use legitimate, expert, and referent power and expand a subordinate's "zone of indifference." The boss may also see this zone expanded or contracted by the organization. For example, assembly line workers who only "follow the book" have a limited zone of indifference. We suspect that many supervisors have difficulty expanding influence beyond that provided in the union contract.

Thus leadership is influence. But influence of a very special kind. Leadership is the influence an individual gains over and above that bestowed to a specific position.

Leadership as an Exchange Process

Extending the above discussion, Jacobs uses the notion of social exchange to explain leader-follower relationships.[1] He argues that individuals are in an exchange relationship where group members and an organization depend upon each other. The organization must rely on employees to help meet its objectives, while employees depend on it to provide intrinsic and extrinsic rewards. The leader may be seen as an organizational representative. Benefits can be provided with proper inducements to work toward organizational objectives. Also, we normally expect that the "goals" given to employees are socially acceptable. If not, the exchange view of leadership must be replaced with an emphasis on coercion.

Jacobs also introduces the concept of expectation into his approach to leadership. It is assumed that the organization, the boss as a representative of the organization, and subordinates have expectations concerning changes. These expectations must be met before an exchange will be considered fair. Dissatisfaction will result from unfair exchanges and efforts will be made to alter the agreement. If a mutually beneficial arrangement cannot be made, one of three things will happen: (1) the relationship will terminate; or (2) coercion will be used to enforce the existing agreement; or (3) the parties will change their expectations.

Monetary or similar kinds of exchanges are easy to see and understand. For example, the employee works at a lathe producing finished products in exchange for money. Labor unions bargain with management to arrive at a "fair exchange." However, Jacobs argues that psychological exchanges are perhaps more important in understanding leadership. Both the leader and the follower specialize in job-related activities. The followers depend upon the leader to do the things they cannot. The boss is endorsed and "paid" when he or she does these things well. Some psychological kinds of pay include status, esteem, and of course, influence. In return the boss can help subordinates satisfy some of their needs, accomplish their given task, and buffer them from organizational pressures.

As the discussion of leadership, power and authority implies, leadership by those in formal managerial positions is not necessarily confined to subordinates. The leader may make exchanges with those at or near his or her own level within the organizational hierarchy. Let's take a look at these attempts at influence.

LATERAL LEADERSHIP AND EXTERNAL ORIENTATION

Discussion of lateral leadership in the literature has received little emphasis compared with vertical leadership. As indicated, lateral leadership emphasizes horizontal influence. While our earlier discussion of informal leadership also implied horizontal influence from one individual to another, the definition of lateral leadership is somewhat different. It refers to leadership of the formal leader in dealing with peers *outside* his or her own work group. This notion would range from relationships of a first-level supervisor with other staff or nonstaff units, which would be necessary to get a job done, all the way to relationships of a chief executive with organizations in the specific environment.

Lateral Leadership within Organizations

Aside from the work of Sayles,[3,4] emphasized in Chapter 11, empirical studies of lateral leadership have been largely neglected. Two recent studies, however, tend to emphasize the importance of the concept. Duffy utilized data from the first two managerial levels in two state mental health organizations.[1] Osborn and Hunt used data from one of these same organizations using different criterion measures than Duffy.[2] In both, lateral leadership was a measure of the leader's orientation toward lateral relations. Managers at each of the levels were asked to indicate the extent to which they thought managers in their position should become actively involved in relationships with other units inside their organization. The scale was similar to the one shown in the Measurement Module for Chapter 11. In general, there were differences by organization and sometimes by level as well. But there was a tendency for lateral leadership to predict some aspects of satisfaction beyond vertical leadership (consideration and/or initiating structure dimensions similar to those in Exhibit 13-12). There were also some significant interactions. These interactions suggest the importance of the combination of vertical and lateral leadership. One implication is that you are not likely to be successful if you concentrate on one at the expense of the other. Lateral and vertical leadership are necessary.

More sophisticated studies, among other things, would examine not only the impact of lateral leadership in general, but its impact for different kinds of units. Our previous discussion of Sayles' work suggests that exchange relationships will be important for all units. But the relative importance of the different kinds of exchange relationships (work-flow, service, etc.) will vary as a function of the type of work unit. The general importance of lateral relations, though, seems to have been reinforced in the two studies discussed.

External Orientation

Lateral leadership between units within an organization is important. But the chief executive must also be concerned with relations between the organization and members of its specific environment. Such relations are one means by which an organization is able to carry out its necessary exchanges with the environment. The chief executive, through example, sets the stage for environmental interaction by subordinates. The interaction strategy can range from a calculated attempt to exploit the environment systematically all the way to ignoring external units. There is evidence that the interaction strategy chosen will influence the overall effectiveness of the organization.[1]

The data we have suggest that overall organizational success is favorably influenced by a strong external (as compared with an internal) orientation on the part of the chief executive. Of course, we might expect that the type of environment in which an organization operates would influence the importance of external orientation. So far, however, we have little "hard" data on this.

What do we mean by an external orientation? Externally oriented chief executives tend to feel that those in their position should be actively involved with important outside organizations. Thus they indicate a preference for trying to influence these organizations in a number of ways. And they try to buffer their own organization against outside pressures.

It is obvious, of course, that the chief executive, like our earlier mentioned managers, also has important internal responsibilities besides these external ones. Therefore, the executive is faced with a delegation problem. There is some evidence suggesting that faced with a choice, the chief executive should probably delegate internal rather than external duties. Many chief executives of organizations in the specific environment desire to interact with a chief executive rather than a subordinate. Hence, where a large number of external interactions with specific environment members have been delegated, it is quite likely that the delegating organization will lose much of its ability to influence the other specific environment members. Faced with an external-internal choice, then, it appears that the chief executive should opt for taking an active external role and delegating many internal functions.

CONTINGENCY APPROACHES TO LEADERSHIP

Figure 13-2 summarizes the major trends in studying leadership. Panels *A* and *B* might be considered "precontingency approaches." Panel *C* captures some key aspects of the contingency approaches to be discussed in this section. This discussion then leads to the treatment of a more comprehensive "multiple influence" approach to leadership, summarized in the next section.

Note in Panel *C* that the current contingency leadership models use variables, such as task and subordinate personality, that are generally seen to

"Great man" and trait approaches (Panel *A*)

Leader behavior approaches (Panel *B*)

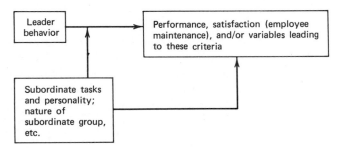

Most contingency approaches (Panel *C*)

Figure 13-2   Key relationships stressed in different approaches to leadership.

moderate the relationships between leader behavior and criteria. They may sometimes have a direct effect as well (as shown by the right-hand arrow). In contingency terminology we might say, for example, *if* the task has certain characteristics, *then* a given type of leader behavior is associated with higher performance.

In discussing these approaches three important concerns are: (1) the unit of analysis (i.e., does a given contingency model focus on groups or individuals*); (2) the kinds of leadership measures used; and (3) the nature and scope of the contingency variables considered. We will focus on unit of analysis as the major way of categorizing the approaches, and briefly compare and contrast the other points as a part of our discussion.

To be effective, the leader must adjust attempts at influence to meet the

*Current contingency models emphasize groups or individuals rather than subsystem or total organization units of analysis.

"situation." However the term "situation" is seen quite differently by different leadership scholars. Our discussion of contingency approaches will start with group and leader situational factors. That is, how should the leader adjust influence attempts to mesh with the nature of the group? Then our discussion will incorporate some of the more popular individual approaches. Here the focus is on the interaction between a boss and a subordinate. We will note, however, that more and more group and organizational factors are being considered by those interested in the individual actions of a leader. We will close the discussion with our multiple influence model of leadership. Here we argue that the "situation" of the leader should be broadly defined. In some cases, the leader cannot have a dramatic impact on criteria. In other cases, the leader may have considerable discretion and be in a position to increase group and individual performance and satisfaction. In all of the contingency approaches you do find a common theme. The effective leader is the one who adjusts influence attempts to the challenges and opportunities of the situation.

Group Approaches

Fiedler's Leadership Contingency Model. Fiedler's model is the "grand daddy" of all leadership contingency approaches. Insightful people have argued for many years that leadership requirements will vary as a function of the situation within which a leader operates. But Fiedler's approach was the first to define the situation in operational terms. Because of its seminal nature, we discuss it in some detail.

Before we discuss Fiedler's operational framework, we temporarily digress to explore his measure of leadership, for it is quite different from any other. He uses a measure of leadership style rather than leader behavior per se. His style measure is akin to the attitude or philosophy variables discussed earlier in Chapter 8 in that it is not a measure of behavior. An individual is asked to describe the person with whom he or she has been able to work with least well (the least-preferred co-worker or LPC). The person does not have to be someone with whom the individual presently works, but can be anyone in the organization. Once the items are completed, the LPC questionnaire is scored by adding the individual item responses.

Those individuals in the top portion of the scoring distribution (generally the top one-half or top one-third) are classified as high LPC persons and those in the bottom one-half or one-third are low LPC individuals.* Thus, Fiedler

---

*See the Measurement Module in this chapter for a sample LPC questionnaire.

begins by administering LPC questionnaires to group leaders and classifying the leaders as high or low LPC.[6] At this point many people ask if we can convert this abstract LPC measure into something more concrete such as leader behavior. The answer is maybe, and we discuss it further.

The heart of Fiedler's contingency model is what he calls the "favorableness for the leader" continuum. This is a continuum that is defined in terms of how favorable it is in allowing the leader to exert influence in getting a group task accomplished. Fiedler has used a number of different ways to measure the favorableness notion.[1] In this sense Fiedler's model relies heavily on the functional equivalency concept that we discussed earlier. It is also concerned with our other frequently stressed notion of "fit." Group performance is postulated to be influenced by the fit between a given leadership style and Fiedler's favorability continuum.

Measuring Favorability. The most frequently discussed way of measuring favorability is in terms of three variables: leader-member relations, task structure, and position power.

The leader-member relations variable is concerned with either group member acceptance of the leader or the leader's *feeling* of acceptance by group members.* Task structure is concerned with the degree to which the job duties of group members are clearly spelled out (high structure) versus being vague and undefined. Position power is concerned with power inherent in the leader's position.[3] This corresponds closely to our notion of authority or French and Raven's legitimate, expert, reward, and coercive power bases.

These dimensions were inductively derived from more than 12 years of research with over 800 groups, comprising more than 60 separate studies. Figure 13-3 shows the way in which Fiedler ordered the dimensions into eight different cells or "octants" on the favorableness for the leader axis. He accomplished this ordering by making two sets of assumptions. First, he assumed leader-member relations was the most important variable and that position power was the least important. As the arrangement of the cells on the favorability axis in the figure shows, leader-member relations are actually weighted twice as much as position power. Second, Fiedler assumed that leadership would be easier to implement when the leader is accepted or feels accepted, when the task is clear, and when he or she has the power to entice or coerce group members into action.

Given these assumptions, the figure shows that under very favorable (all three dimensions positive) *and* very unfavorable conditions (all three dimensions negative) low-LPC leaders tend to have high-performing groups and vice

*These may or may not be the same, though Fiedler tends to use the two interchangeably.

Figure 13-3 Relations Predicted by Fiedler's model

High LPC	Low Performance			High Performance			Low Performance	
Low LPC	High Performance			Low Performance			High Performance	
	I	*II*	*III*	*IV*	*V*	*VI*	*VII*	*VIII*
	Favorable for leader			Moderate Situation			Unfavorable for leader	
Leader-member relations	Good	Good	Good	Good	Poor	Poor	Poor	Poor
Task structure	Structured		Unstructured		Structured		Unstructured	
Leader position power	Strong	Weak	Strong	Weak	Strong	Weak	Strong	Weak

Source: Adapted from Fiedler, F. E. *A Theory of Leadership Effectiveness* (New York: McGraw-Hill, 1967).

versa for high-LPC leaders. However, in moderately favorable conditions, high-LPC leaders obtain better results.[6]

Why is there a difference in the way groups perform under high- and low-LPC leaders as favorableness changes? To answer this question a description of the behavior of the high- and low-LPC leaders is necessary. In the high favorability situation (Octants I, II, and III) the superior performing low-LPC leader perceives the "ease" of the situation and the likelihood of task attainment. Feeling secure that his or her needs will be met, the leader feels able to attend to interpersonal relationship factors. That is, "socio-emotional" behaviors are used to reinforce appropriate subordinate task behaviors, while maintaining a "normal" level of task-directive behavior. The result is effective group performance. To the high-LPC leader, the situation "looks good" In terms of meeting a need for acceptance by his or her members. Therefore, task factors are focused on. This is done by using directive, "initiating" or "structuring" behaviors, while maintaining a "normal" level of interpersonal relationship-oriented behaviors. The result is poor performance since the structuring behaviors are not rewarding to subordinates. It is more appropriate for the leader to place heavier emphasis on relationship-oriented behaviors. The task is, by situational definition, progressing smoothly.

In Octants IV, V, and VI (moderate favorability), high-LPC leaders have better performing groups than low-LPC leaders. Here, the leader becomes aware that his or her needs may not be satisfied. The high-LPC leader responds by focusing behaviors on interpersonal relationships—the primary means for need satisfaction here. Fiedler argues that a major factor in these moderate favorability situations is a concern with interpersonal relations. So the result of the high-LPC behavior is good performance. However, the low-LPC leader's focus on task-directive behavior is inappropriate. Poor group performance results.

Finally, in the highly unfavorable Octant VIII, only highly directive leader behavior can get anything accomplished. And this is the behavior that the low-LPC leader will tend to emphasize in this situation.*

At this point many people want to know more about what variables LPC may be related to. What does this mysterious variable measure?

What is LPC Related To? Almost since the inception of LPC, people have been asking this question. The answer has not been easy to come by. Unfortunately, it does not appear to correlate directly or consistently with personality variables.[4,1] Neither has it been related in any simple way with leader behavior measures. Instead, its relationships with leader behavior appear to be complex.

One of the earlier interpretations of LPC was that a leader with a high LPC score was primarily oriented toward interpersonal relations. A low-LPC leader was primarily oriented toward successful task completion.[3] The latest, and more complex interpretation, is that the LPC score reflects a hierarchy of goals. High-LPC leaders have the establishment and maintenance of interpersonal relations as a primary goal, with prominence and self-enhancement as a secondary goal. A low-LPC leader has a primary goal of achievement of task and material rewards, with a secondary goal the development of good interpersonal relations. An individual will attempt to achieve both primary and secondary goals in situations where his or her influence is relatively great. However, in a stressful or unfavorable situation, where it is not possible to obtain both goals, only the primary goal will be stressed.[6] Thus, there is a situation in which the behavior of both high- and low-LPC leaders changes as favorability changes. You should recognize that this is essentially the explanation that was used in the previous section in describing why the relationship between LPC and group performance changed as favorability changed.

Importance of the Model. One key measure of the importance of a model is how well it holds up under empirical testing. Fiedler's model has now been tested numerous times with some, but by no means complete, support. Fiedler has summarized the results of over 30 studies, which tend to show substantial support.[5] Others have been highly critical of these studies and some of the assumptions of the model.[9] On the other hand, Chemers and Rice after reviewing a number of studies on both sides of the issue conclude "that after over twenty years of research [Fiedler's] model is alive and well" (p. 123).[6]

*We have relied heavily on Sashkin, Taylor, and Trepathi[8] for this behavior summary.

Regardless of whether the model is verified or not we consider its most important contribution to be the development of contingency models in general. Much of our current contingency thinking has developed as a result of Fiedler's model.

Farris' Five-Factor Contingency Approach. Another group leadership model is that of Farris.[2] As you will see, it's quite different from Fiedler's. Farris treats leadership as influence in much the way we have earlier. He argues that such influence can come from both supervisors and subordinates and can be distributed differently between the two sources. The appropriateness of a given kind of leader behavior is hypothesized to be contingent upon five factors: (1) supervisory competence concerning the issue at hand; (2) group member competence concerning the matter; (3) importance of acceptance of a given decision to the supervisor; (4) importance of decision acceptance to group members; and (5) time pressure. Farris hypothesized that these would influence the relationship between leader behavior and group innovation as a measure of performance; this relationship is summarized in Table 13-4.

Table 13-4 shows four leader-behavior dimensions (collaboration, domination, delegation, abdication) that are an indication of the relative amount of influence exerted by the supervisor and group member. The first factors considered in the table are concerned with the competence of the supervisor and group member to deal with the matter of organizational relevance. If both are competent to exert influence concerning the matter, then collaboration, domination, *or* delegation could be appropriate behaviors for the leader. If the supervisor is competent but the group member is not, then domination is more appropriate. If the group member is competent but the boss is not, then delegation is most appropriate.

If both parties are competent to exert influence, the importance of acceptance of the results becomes a key determinant of the appropriate leader behavior. If acceptance by both is important, then collaboration should be used. And so it goes, according to the various cells in Table 13-4. Note also that when time pressure is high, then domination or delegation becomes the preferred alternative.

This approach allows not only for supervisory leadership but for subordinate influence, which is related to peer leadership treated earlier in this chapter. Farris reports data from three research studies that provide some support for his hypotheses. Results are most consistent for supervisor competence as a contingency variable.[*,2]

---

*A well-known current approach that examines some of the same kinds of variables as this one is by Vroom and Yetton.[10] We don't treat it here because it is normative (treats what a leader should do in a set of hypothetical situations), whereas the other approaches are descriptive or analytical.

Table 13-4 Farris' Five-Factor Contingency Approach

Supervisor (S) Competence	Group Member (GM) Competence	
	High	Low

High	Appropriate leadership behavior:
	
	Collaboration:
	    S and GM each exert substantial influence
	Domination:
	    S exerts high influence
	    GM, low influence
	Delegation:
	    S exerts low influence
	    GM, high influence
		Domination

Low	Delegation	Abdication: S and GM each exert low influence

Importance of Acceptance by Supervisor	Importance of Acceptance by Group Member	
	High	Low
High	Collaboration	Collaboration Domination[a]
Low	Collaboration Delegation[a]	Collaboration Domination[a] Delegation[a]

Source: Adapted from Farris, G. F. "Leadership and Supervision in the Informal Organization," In Hunt, J. G., and Larson, L. L. (eds.), *Contingency Approaches to Leadership* (Carbondale, Ill.: Southern Illinois University Press, 1974) Copyright © SIU Press, 1974, by permission.

[a]Preferred leader behavior when time pressure is high.

Individual Approaches

While contingency analysis began with an attempt to interrelate leadership, group factors, and group performance, much of the more recent work has focused on the one-on-one exchange between a leader and a follower. Generally, individual approaches start with some underlying assumptions about individual behavior and then incorporate selected situational characteristics. As a whole, individual approaches are rich in describing the dimensions of leader behavior and explaining how and why a leader can increase individual performance and satisfaction. We will start with the most popular approach (a path-goal view) and then progress to views that attempt to incorporate a wider variety of nonindividual contingencies. This sequencing will give you an idea of the progression in much of the leadership literature and a feel for the individual emphasis found in most contingency views of leadership.

Path-Goal Models. Path-goal approaches are based on path-goal or expectancy motivation theory, now treated in virtually all organizational behavior texts.* Essentially, a path-goal approach is one way of looking inside the "black box" of leadership to discover some of the ways in which a leader's behavior can influence individual subordinates. From this you can get an idea of what kind of relationship there is between a specific kind of leader behavior and certain criteria. And you can get some idea as to *why* that relationship exists.

The term "path-goal" is used because the approach concentrates on how a leader influences subordinates' perceptions of work goals, personal goals, and the linkages or *paths* between these two sets of *goals*.[10] House, based on the work of others,[2,3] has gone farthest in extending and testing this general approach. His work has been evolving since 1971.†[8]

House assumes that a leader's chief function is to complement the setting within which a worker operates. For example, if the task is fuzzy or ambiguous, then the leader should help remove some of this ambiguity unless other factors make this unnecessary. If they do, then clarifying behavior on the part of the leader will be redundant. If they don't, then such behavior is likely to be quite helpful. The leader "compensates" for something lacking in the setting. Where this is the case, employees should be satisfied with the leader. And, they should be willing to put forth more effort because they can see the path by which effort leads to performance and performance leads to valued rewards. Where the leader's behavior is repetitive, it is likely to have either a less positive or possibly even a negative effect on these criteria.[9]

What are some of the factors that might make the leader's behavior repetitive? House and Mitchell argue that these can be grouped into subordinate characteristics and work-setting factors. They further contend that there are four kinds of leader behaviors that are likely to be particularly important.[9] Thus House's model postulates, in essence, that employee attitudes and motiva-

*See, for example, Reitz.[14]

†The latest version as set forth in House and Mitchell[9] is summarized here. We draw heavily on that article in our discussion.

tional behavior will be a function of these four leader behaviors moderated by the contingency variables of employee characteristics and the work setting within which subordinates operate.

Let's get more specific by discussing Figure 13-5. We will start by looking at each leadership dimension separately.*

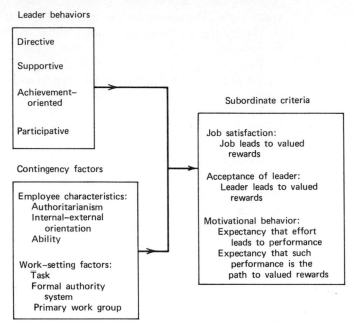

Figure 13-5 Summary of major path-goal relationships in House's path-goal leadership model.

Leader Directiveness. This dimension is concerned with letting subordinates know what is expected, spelling out what and how tasks are to be done, and so forth. It is similar to the Initiating Structure dimension summarized in Table 13-1 and discussed in the Measurement Module. It is also related to task behavior discussed earlier in the chapter. A number of studies show it to have a positive relationship with satisfaction and expectancies of subordinates who have ambiguous tasks, and a negative association with these criteria when tasks are clear. In line with our earlier discussion, the reasoning is, when task demands are ambiguous and the formal authority system does not provide

*Note that this as well as other approaches in this chapter assume that a leader can engage in several different behaviors that will in varying degrees be independent of each other. Hill,[7] among many others, has shown support for this contention. It is in marked contrast to the argument that leaders behave on an autocratic-democratic continuum.

clarification, leader directiveness is needed to compensate. However, when the opposite is true, directiveness is seen as a hindrance.

Where these findings have not been confirmed, House and Mitchell argue that employee authoritarianism may be a key (see Figure 13-5).[9] Sometimes authoritarianism and ambiguity operate simultaneously. That is, authoritarian (close-minded, rigid) subordinates and ambiguous tasks in combination may call for directive leadership. Ambiguous tasks by themselves may not always call for directive leadership.

Leader Supportiveness. This is characterized by being friendly and approachable, concerned with subordinate well-being and needs, and so on.[9] It is similar to human-relations orientation (discussed earlier in the chapter) and Consideration, treated in Table 13-1 and the Measurement Module. The model postulates that supportiveness will have its most positive impact on subordinate satisfaction for those who work on stressful, frustrating, or dissatisfying tasks. House and Mitchell report a substantial amount of support for this hypothesis.

Achievement-oriented Leadership. This is characterized by the leader's setting of challenging goals, expecting subordinates to perform at their highest level, and showing a high degree of confidence in their ability to do these things.[9] The model hypothesizes that achievement-oriented leadership will cause subordinates to strive for higher performance standards and have more confidence in their ability to meet challenging goals. One study provides partial support. It shows that for subordinates with ambiguous, nonrepetitive jobs there was a positive association between achievement-oriented leadership and subordinate expectancy that effort would lead to performance. For those with moderately ambiguous, repetitive tasks, these relations did not hold. One possible explanation is that there is more room for leadership to affect expectancies in ambiguous jobs than those where many things are already spelled out.[9]

Participative leadership. This is characterized by a leader who consults with subordinates and considers their suggestions in decisions.[9] The model predicts that on nonrepetitive tasks, which allow for subordinate ego-involvement, employees will be more satisfied under a participative than under a nonparticipative style. On the other hand, on repetitive tasks allowing for little ego involvement, only *low*-authoritarian subordinates will be more satisfied under a participatory leader. Once again we see authoritarianism operating in combination with the nature of the task. House and Mitchell cite one study that confirms these hypotheses. Participation here is presumed to complement the ego-involving potential of the nonrepetitive task and the participatory desires of low authoritarians on repetitive tasks with little ego involvement.[9]

If you look closer at Figure 13-5 you will note that it includes internal-external orientation, ability, and primary work group variables. These have not yet been tested within the context of the model but are considered by House to be some potentially important, additional variables. Ability is considered important since, when it is present, it can serve to provide clarity in much the same way as, for example, the formal authority system. Hence it may make the clarification of leader behavior less important or even redundant.[9]

External-internal orientation is hypothesized to affect the impact of participative leadership. Internals (those who feel they can exert strong control over their own actions) as contrasted with externals (who feel their actions are controlled primarily by outside forces) can be predicted to respond more favorably to participation than externals.[9]

Finally, the primary work group is believed to have a potentially significant impact on the need for leader behavior. As we showed in the group chapter, group members can exert a substantial influence on each others' attitudes and behaviors.[9]

It may also have occurred to you in what you have just read that all of the criteria for all of the leadership dimensions were not discussed. To date, there are no reported studies that test all of the variables shown in Figure 13-5. So complete information on this is not available. The most that can be said, based on empirical support, is what we have just presented. We hope future work will help fill in these gaps. We might also note that performance is not directly measured. Instead, effort to perform is measured. The implicit assumption is that if a leader can increase task-directed effort, performance should increase. Although not always true, in general this is a reasonable assumption.

Even in its incomplete state of development, House's theory, like Fiedler's, has had a substantial impact on helping us understand the importance of contingency variables in the study of leadership. Furthermore, it appears flexible enough to allow for the addition of new variables should future work suggest these. We invite you to read House and Mitchell[9] for a much more detailed treatment of the model.

The Graen VDL Approach. Another individually oriented approach to leadership is that by George Graen and his associates.[6] Graen has labeled this the VDL (vertical dyad linkage) approach. (Graen has been known to wear a shirt given to him by his graduate students with "VDL" emblazoned across the front.)

The VDL approach takes the individual level of analysis and concentrates on one-to-one relationships between supervisor-subordinate dyads. It thus allows for differences in leader behavior toward each subordinate and differences in individual subordinate reactions to such behavior.[4] This mode of conceiving leader-subordinate relations has led to a number of recent studies by Graen and his associates. A summary of many of these is included in Hunt and Larson.[12] This forms the basis for much of the following discussion.

All of these studies are longitudinal in nature (see a later section of this chapter for more detail on longitudinal studies) and concentrate not only on inputs and outputs but on the development of superior-subordinate dyadic relations. Thus, unlike many leadership approaches, there is an emphasis on the on-going leadership process and not just static relations at one point in time.

Among the more interesting of Graen's studies are those that look at in-groups and out-groups and consider Jacob's exchange theory of leadership touched upon earlier in the chapter.[13] In these studies leader-subordinate dyads were investigated over a nine-month period. It was found, based on the compatibility of combinations of leader-member characteristics, that over time leaders developed in-group or out-group exchanges with each of their subordinates. Those in-group subordinates were allowed more negotiating latitude with their supervisors than were those in the out-group.* Furthermore, these in-group, out-group exchanges were found to relate to member performance, satisfaction, and job problems (with in-group members having more favorable responses). The exchanges were also found to be relatively stable over time.[4]

A supervisor allowing a subordinate considerable negotiating latitude was considered to be using "leadership" in Jacob's terms (influence without resort to authority); whereas a supervisor allowing little negotiating latitude was considered to be using "supervision" (influence based primarily on authority).

Graen and his associates have recently extended the in-group versus out-group notion from first-level manager-subordinate dyads to second-level manager-first-level manager dyads. Preliminary findings suggest that subordinates of in-group first-level managers tend to be in a more favorable situation than subordinates of out-group first-level managers.[5]

The major contributions of this work appear to be three. First, it concentrates on one-to-one leader-member relations. It raises by implication the question of when these are likely to be more important than an emphasis on the group, and vice versa. Second, it considers relationships over time. Third, it puts heavy emphasis on the process variables involved in leadership.

Bass' Systems Approach. Still another approach using an individual unit of analysis is one by Bass and his associates.[1] Ironically, though the unit of analysis is an individual one, the model considers a wider range of organizational variables than any other approach treated in this section. The systems model in Figure 13-6 summarizes this approach. You can readily see that it

*Negotiating latitude was concerned with the relative openness of a leader to individualized assistance for a subordinate.

Figure 13-6 Bass' model of manager-subordinate system.

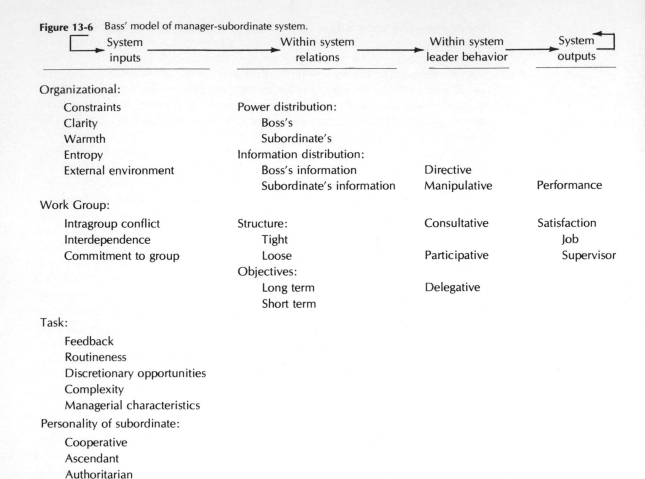

Organizational:
- Constraints
- Clarity
- Warmth
- Entropy
- External environment

Work Group:
- Intragroup conflict
- Interdependence
- Commitment to group

Task:
- Feedback
- Routineness
- Discretionary opportunities
- Complexity
- Managerial characteristics

Personality of subordinate:
- Cooperative
- Ascendant
- Authoritarian
- Introverted

Source: Adapted from Bass, B. M., and Valenzi, E. R. "Contingent Aspects of Effective Management Styles." In Hunt, J. G., and Larson, L. L. (eds.), *Contingency Approaches to Leadership* (Carbondale, Ill.: Southern Illinois University Press, 1974). Copyright © SIU Press, 1974, by permission.

considers both external and internal variables and other systems notions discussed throughout the text. In addition to the broad scope, the research is notable for its elaborate efforts at instrument development.

It is instructive in going through the figure to consider the following points based on a discussion by Bass and Valenzi.[1] First, consistent with Graen's VDL approach, a manager and his or her subordinates are viewed as an open social system consisting of two persons. This system is open to organization, group, task, and personality variables. What takes place within the system is based on power and information differences between manager and subordinate, the structure of the system, and the objectives of the manager. These affect which leader behavior dimension(s) will be most appropriate for effective systems functioning (outputs). These criteria, in turn, feedback on other systems components.

To transform inputs to outputs, a power flow and an information flow occur within the system. An input, transformation, output cycle is completed. The outputs result in a new wave of inputs and a new cycle. At the beginning of a designated cycle the manager-subordinate power will have been established by outside authority or mutual expectations of legitimacy. Here many of the power and authority notions discussed earlier appear appropriate, as do Farris' notions concerning the distribution of influence between supervisor and subordinate.

Informational differences between manager and subordinate are based on such things as relative ability, education, and so on.

The structure is defined by the formal and informal manager-subordinate relations. Such relations may be tight or loose, mechanistic or organic. The structure is seen as a consequence of organizational, group, task, and/or personality variables. Managerial goals are also important and seen as influenced by these same inputs.

Five leader behavior dimensions are specified. They are proposed to be influenced by a joint manager-subordinate power and information difference, as well as structural relations and objectives. These leadership dimensions are, in turn, hypothesized to influence the outputs. They imply different superior-subordinate influence distributions. Let's look at the behaviors included in the dimensions.

1. *Direction:* Telling subordinates what is expected of them, seeing that they work to capacity, emphasizing meeting deadlines, setting standards, ruling with an iron hand, encouraging uniformity, scheduling their tasks, telling them to follow rules and regulations, changing duties without first talking it over with them.
2. *Manipulation:* Doing personal favors for subordinates, changing behaviors to fit the occasion, persuading, promising, making them compete with each other, timing the release of information, making political alliances, maintaining social distance, bending rules, reassigning tasks to balance the work load.
3. *Consultation:* Being candid and open to questions, listening to subordinates, trying out their ideas, giving advance notice of changes.
4. *Participation:* Sharing decision making, making attitudes clear, arranging meetings, putting group suggestions into operation, treating subordinates as equals, being approachable and friendly.
5. *Delegation:* Exhibiting confidence in subordinates, leaving members free to follow their own course, permitting them to make their own decisions.[1]

These measures are important refinements and extensions of dimensions such as those shown in Table 13-1 as well as others. Note also their similarities to some of those of Farris and House.

As reported here, the model is in a very preliminary stage. Some results based on system inputs, leader behavior, and system outputs are summarized in Table 13-7. The results are based on three of the five leadership dimensions that were ready for testing. All inputs but those for personality were included. Only the seven in the table had any influence at all on the leadership-criterion

Table 13-7 Predictability of Leader Behavior Dimensions and Differences in Predictability of Leader Behavior Dimensions for High- and Low-System Input Values

System Input	System Output								
	Satisfaction with:						Performance		
	Supervisor			Job					
	Direction	Manipulation	Participation	Direction	Manipulation	Participation	Direction	Manipulation	Participation
Organizational									
Entropy(organized/ disorganized)	X		*			X			X
Constraints (loose/ tight)						X			
External environment	X		*						
Group									
Conflict								X	
Commitment	*		*						
Task									
Routineness (varied/ routine)							X		
Managerial characteristics (planning and coordination)	X		*		X		X		

Note: An asterisk (*) indicates a significant leadership-output relationship, regardless of whether the input is high or low. An X indicates that the leadership-output relationship differs depending upon a high or low input value.

relations.[1] Of these it is obvious that the relationships differ as a function of criterion and leadership dimension. The complexity of the model is apparent when you realize that these results are only for inputs and outputs and do not include the relations studied within the system as compared with the other variables. Bass and his colleagues also report additional work on this model, which is not discussed here.*

Summary Comparisons

Our grouping of the approaches contrasted them in terms of the unit of analysis. Some other similarities and differences were pointed out in our discussion. Let us summarize here by highlighting the kinds of measures used and the nature and scope of the contingency variables considered, along with a brief word about criteria.

Fiedler's model uses the LPC attitudinal measure, while all the others use some aspects of the perceived leader behavior. The House, Farris, and Bass models all use four or five dimensions that are at least conceptually somewhat independent of each other. Furthermore, there appears to be considerable similarity in the nature of the dimensions. Directiveness and participation are two common threads, and it doesn't take much imagination to see others as well. Graen's measure of negotiating latitude appears to be relatively unique, but even it might be related to participation, consultation, or the like. Thus, though the models use quite different theoretical frameworks, there are surprising similarities in the leadership dimensions used.

In terms of the contingency variables, the broadest is Bass' approach. It explicitly includes some 17 variables in 4 categories. It is the only one of the models explicitly incorporating organizational variables, though House does discuss them. Farris' model includes the narrowest range of variables since, with the exception of time pressure, they are all boss-subordinate variables. Graen too has tended to concentrate on boss-subordinate variables but uses a wider range. While Fiedler uses only three variables, they cover aspects of the task as well as formal power and boss-subordinate relations.

In terms of criteria, it's interesting to note that Fiedler and Bass use a performance measure only. Graen uses performance, satisfaction, and job problems, while Bass uses performance and satisfaction. Finally, House uses satisfaction (but treated a little differently than the others) and motivation. His is the only approach that does not utilize performance.

*See Hunt and Larson.[11]

Causality

The part and parcel of contingency thinking is the question of causality. While the various approaches were discussed in terms of leadership causing satisfaction/performance, and so forth, there is now considerable evidence that a "process" point of view is more appropriate. Such a view considers the process involved in leadership. And it allows for leadership to cause performance/employee maintenance, performance/maintenance to cause satisfaction, or for "reciprocal causation"—where each partially "causes" the other via feedback loops. Graen's work treats this line of thinking directly. Bass' systems approach calls for it in future tests of the model. Most of the other approaches also are consistent with it.

We should note that research designed to get at causality calls for a more sophisticated design than the more typical studies that simply examine several variables at a single time period and then look for associations among them.* One example of this additional sophistication is an experimental study. For instance, performance might be manipulated (the leader may be told that subordinates performed poorly during a previous period) and leader behavior is measured before and after manipulation.

Another example, and one that is usually more feasible in actual or realistic settings, is the longitudinal study. Here, data are obtained at more than one time period. From this it is possible to infer whether leadership influenced the criterion, whether the criterion influenced leadership, whether there might have been some combination of both or whether, perhaps, a third unmeasured variable may have been responsible. Longitudinal studies are also important if you want to determine whether there has or has not been a change in leadership over time.

Let's look at some recent work with causality as a central focus. Farris and Lim suggest that high past performance can increase leader supportiveness, interaction facilitation, goal emphasis, and work facilitation.[2] Similarly, Lowin and Craig showed that performance affects leader consideration, initiating structure and closeness of supervision.[5] Finally, Dawson, Messi, and Phillips conducted a classroom investigation.[1] The instructor (leader) deliberately varied consideration and initiating structure behavior across different sections of the same class. They showed that leader behavior influenced various performance measures.

What can we conclude? The common assumption that leader behavior influences performance appears to be true. It also appears that performance influences leader behavior. This conclusion is reinforced by two recently conducted longitudinal studies by Greene.[3,4] He obtained data at two different

*As you may remember, we treated research designs and problems in more detail in Chapter 1.

time periods for managers and subordinates in several organizations. He found that performance was a more important determinant of leader emphasis on consideration and initiating structure than vice versa. However, for satisfaction, leader consideration was identified as the causal variable.

Other longitudinal studies have been conducted to examine leadership change. A very extensive body of work has been done at the University of Michigan in conjunction with planned organizational development changes.[6] These investigations are too complex to go into here. But they, as well as the other work described here, support quite strongly the notion that studies at more than one time period can add much beyond "one shot" investigations in our understanding of leadership. Hence, you can expect to see many of these kinds of studies done over the next few years.

A MULTIPLE INFLUENCE APPROACH

While each of the group and individual views of leadership effectiveness adds considerable information, they need to be integrated with a more comprehensive view of the organization and its environment. So far each approach has assumed that the leader alone decides on how he or she will act. Yet our discussion of causality suggests that leadership alters and is altered by situational, performance, and individual factors. In simple terms the leader is in the middle of the action. As shown in Figure 13-8, our multiple influence approach (Panel B) treats leadership as being embedded within the organization. The more popular view (Panel A) of most contingency approaches is also diagrammed to highlight our perspective of leadership. In this section we will provide some highlights of the multiple influence approach. At the end of the last contingency chapter we will use it to suggest how to use leadership to enhance your chances of success.

In the multiple influence approach, four broad classes of variables are considered to have an impact on criteria. Some of the variables have an indirect effect in that they are considered to affect variables directly related to criteria. Leader individual characteristics are the class of variables highlighted in Figure 13-8. The setting, leader behavior, the environment of the group, and the nature of the group all appear to have both direct and indirect effects on criteria. The figure shows only a few of these we think are particularly important.

The setting, we argue, influences not only the leader's behavior, but the environment of the group as well as the nature of the group. Furthermore, in combination with other variables, the setting influences criteria. The arrows are drawn to reflect three additional estimates. One, the combination of setting, group environment, nature of the group, and leadership is likely to be partic-

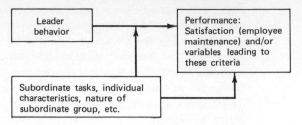

Most contingency approaches (Panel *A*)

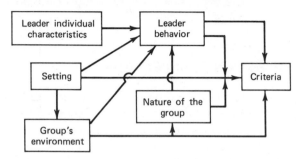

Multiple influence approach (Panel *B*)

Figure 13-8 Key relationships stressed in contrasting contingency approaches to leadership.

ularly important. Two, the nature of the group, its environment, and the setting have an impact on the behavior of the leader. Three, the setting, leader behavior, the group's environment, and the nature of the group have a direct influence on performance and maintenance criteria. Some relationships can be documented. We know that each class of variables has a direct impact on criteria. A few of our studies suggest that setting variables and the nature of the group have an influence on leader behavior.[1,2,5] The combined (interaction) effects among all the variables have not been documented. Here we are speculating.

We can simplify the multiple influence approach with the addition of two concepts. The first is the notion of the gap. The first gap is the difference between performance requirements of management and existing outcomes. A second is the gap between employee desires and the current level of satisfaction. Let's call the first a performance gap and the second a satisfaction gap. We see the job of the leader as closing both gaps. We argue that setting conditions plus group and subordinate factors are the most important determinants of the gap. There are probably others, but let's concentrate on these.

The second concept is the notion of discretionary leadership. This is considered to be a measure of the leader's clout or ability to fill the gaps. It consists of those leader behaviors or influence attempts that are at the discretion of the manager. Most leadership approaches seem to imply that all leadership is at the manager's discretion. However, some portion of the manager's behavior is nondiscretionary or dictated by the kinds of variables shown in Panel B.

The amount of discretionary behavior available to a manager is thus considered to vary as a function of the particular combination of setting, group environment, and nature of the group. In some cases there is much, in others, little. Where most of a leader's behavior is nondiscretionary, we hypothesize that he or she will have less clout than when there is more discretion. A couple of our own studies suggest that subordinate reactions to nondiscretionary and discretionary behavior will be different.[3,4,5] For example, if your boss rewards you because the system requires it, you will probably react differently than if you are rewarded because he or she wants to.

Furthermore, the two kinds of leadership have different organizational implications.[3] If a manager's leadership is primarily discretionary, then leadership training to alter his or her behavior may be appropriate. However, if most of that is nondiscretionary, then training to alter behavior would be a waste of money. Instead, training could be devoted to teaching the leader to diagnose those situations where he or she might have some discretion. Perhaps even more appropriate would be changes, where possible, in those variables affecting discretion.

We can summarize this discussion and simplify the earlier treatment of the multiple influence approach in Figure 13-9.

Up to now we have used the term leader behavior in a global sense. Let's now break down the behavior a little. Dimensions reflecting the well-known task and human-relations or consideration-type behaviors are good starting points. We also believe these can be supplemented in some cases with lateral leadership to help narrow the gap(s). For example, a leader with little inherent vertical clout may be able to add to his or her discretion through informal lateral trade-offs with other managers. For instance, assume a manager of a mechanized assembly line has trouble maintaining scheduled outputs. Discretion may be restricted by technology (setting) and union activity (nature of group). If lateral influence can be exercised with, say, personnel managers, who may be able to influence overtime scheduling or union relations, then

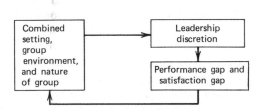

Figure 13-9 Simplified view of the multiple influence approach to leadership.

the performance gap may be reduced. Undoubtedly there are other specific behaviors in addition to these. Further research will need to address that question.

Since the multiple influence model is quite new and yet to be fully tested, we will reserve a more detailed discussion for the final contingency chapter. For now it is important to recognize that the multiple influence approach considers a broad range of contingency factors. It can be used to integrate many of the current contingency models.

We have seen that leadership is an exchange process that occurs within an organizational and group setting. Fiedler's pioneering work in linking group, leadership, and performance variables clearly indicates that both the nature of the group and the position of its leader should be used to select the leadership pattern most likely to increase group performance. Farris' approach requires careful consideration of both leader and follower expertise. Specifically, the Farris approach suggests that the leader should intervene most where his or her competence is needed by the group. In groups where follower competence is high, the leader needs to stress collaboration, for instance. Farris' analysis also suggests that leadership cannot always be used to increase performance. Where both leader and followers are incompetent, more leadership is unlikely to increase performance.

Several contingency models stress the pattern of exchange between a leader and a subordinate. As a whole these approaches suggest that the leader has a wide variety of behaviors that might be used to stimulate individual performance and increase satisfaction. House, for instance, argues that the leader's chief function is to complement the setting in which the worker operates. Graen's unusual perspective alerts us to the subtle role of group dynamics in the long-term process of trying to alter the actions of individual workers. If Graen is correct, perhaps only a comparatively few individuals are actually involved in an exchange process with a leader. Many members of the group may be outside the leadership sphere of the manager. Of course, the "out-group" members might be linked to the manager via the "in-group." We take a close look at this in the next chapter.

Bass and our multiple influence model raise a more complex yet still important series of issues. The leader does not operate in an organizational vacuum. The leader's group is but part of the organization. We will argue in the next chapter that organizational factors can play an important role in the potential success of the leader. While the individual approaches often assume that the skillful use of leadership can induce better performance and satisfaction, we are not so sure. Often, leadership can be used to improve the chances of success, though at times it cannot. One point seems clear, however. The chances of success improve when the leader adjusts behavior to the situation. No one pattern of leadership is universally successful.

MEASUREMENT MODULE

Here we discuss some commonly used ways of measuring leadership and some differences and similarities among the dimensions.

FIEDLER'S LPC SCALE[1]

This scale is shown in Exhibit 13-10. To determine an individual's LPC score simply record the value corresponding to the space checked, and then sum this value for each of the 16 items.

MICHIGAN FOUR-FACTOR SCALE[1]

Table 13-1 showed the four dimensions of support, interaction facilitation, goal emphasis, and work facilitation. The table suggests that these dimensions appear to be fairly general in that they parallel those in a number of other studies. Because of this, we include the measurement of these four dimensions here (see Exhibit 13-11).

OHIO STATE LBDQ SCALES

The most widely used leadership dimensions in the leadership literature today are *initiating structure* and *consideration,* from the Ohio State Leader Behavior Description Questionnaire.[1] Although they are similar to two of the Michigan Four-Factor dimensions, as shown in Table 13-1, we think they bear reproducing because of their widespread use. Thus, they are summarized in Exhibit 13-12. The two dimensions shown in the exhibit come from the Form XII version of the LBDQ.[2,3] It is called Form XII because there are twelve leadership dimensions altogether. Space precludes showing any but the initiating structure and consideration dimensions. If you are interested in the others, see Stogdill.[2,3]

Exhibit 13-10 Fiedler's LPC Scale

Think of the person with whom you can work least well. He may be someone you work with now or someone you knew in the past. He does not have to be the person you like least, but should be the person with whom you had the most difficulty in getting a job done. Describe this person as he appears to you.

| Pleasant | ____ : ____ : ____ : ____ : ____ : ____ : ____ : ____ | Unpleasant |
| | 8   7   6   5   4   3   2   1 | |

Pleasant ____ : ____ : ____ : ____ : ____ : ____ : ____ : ____ Unpleasant
           8   7   6   5   4   3   2   1

Friendly ____ : ____ : ____ : ____ : ____ : ____ : ____ : ____ Unfriendly
         8   7   6   5   4   3   2   1

Rejecting ____ : ____ : ____ : ____ : ____ : ____ : ____ : ____ Accepting
         1   2   3   4   5   6   7   8

Helpful ____ : ____ : ____ : ____ : ____ : ____ : ____ : ____ Frustrating
        8   7   6   5   4   3   2   1

Unenthusiastic ____ : ____ : ____ : ____ : ____ : ____ : ____ : ____ Enthusiastic
        1   2   3   4   5   6   7   8

Tense ____ : ____ : ____ : ____ : ____ : ____ : ____ : ____ Relaxed
      1   2   3   4   5   6   7   8

Distant ____ : ____ : ____ : ____ : ____ : ____ : ____ : ____ Close
       1   2   3   4   5   6   7   8

Cold ____ : ____ : ____ : ____ : ____ : ____ : ____ : ____ Warm
     1   2   3   4   5   6   7   8

Cooperative ____ : ____ : ____ : ____ : ____ : ____ : ____ : ____ Uncooperative
       8   7   6   5   4   3   2   1

Supportive ____ : ____ : ____ : ____ : ____ : ____ : ____ : ____ Hostile
      8   7   6   5   4   3   2   1

Boring ____ : ____ : ____ : ____ : ____ : ____ : ____ : ____ Interesting
      1   2   3   4   5   6   7   8

Quarrelsome ____ : ____ : ____ : ____ : ____ : ____ : ____ : ____ Harmonious
      1   2   3   4   5   6   7   8

Self-assured ____ : ____ : ____ : ____ : ____ : ____ : ____ : ____ Hesitant
      8   7   6   5   4   3   2   1

Efficient ____ : ____ : ____ : ____ : ____ : ____ : ____ : ____ Inefficient
      8   7   6   5   4   3   2   1

Gloomy ____ : ____ : ____ : ____ : ____ : ____ : ____ : ____ Cheerful
      1   2   3   4   5   6   7   8

Open ____ : ____ : ____ : ____ : ____ : ____ : ____ : ____ Guarded
    8   7   6   5   4   3   2   1

Source: Fiedler, F. E. *A Theory of Leadership Effectiveness* (New York: McGraw-Hill, 1967). Reprinted by permission of McGraw-Hill, Copyright © 1967.

Exhibit 13-11 Michigan Four-Factor Leadership Scale

1. *Support.* Enchancement of someone else's feeling of personal worth and importance.
   To what extent is your immediate supervisor:
   a. Friendly and easy to approach?
   b. Willing to listen to your problems?
   c. Attentive to what you say?

2. *Interaction Facilitation.* Encouragement of group members to develop close, mutually satisfying relationships.
   To what extent does your immediate supervisor:
   a. Encourage people who work for him to exchange opinions and ideas?
   b. Encourage the persons who work for him to work as a team?
   c. How often does your supervisor hold group meetings where he and the people who work for him can really discuss things together?

3. *Goal Emphasis.* Stimulation of enthusiasm for meeting the group's goal(s) or achieving excellent performance.
   To what extent does your immediate supervisor:
   a. Set an example by working hard himself?
   b. Encourage people to give their best effort?
   c. Maintain high standards of performance?

4. *Work Facilitation.* Helping achieve goal attainment by such activities as scheduling, coordinating, planning, and by providing resources such as tools, materials, and technical knowledge.
   To what extent does your immediate supervisor:
   a. Encourage members to take action without waiting for detailed review and approval from him?
   b. Show you how to improve your performance?
   c. Provide the help you need so that you can schedule work ahead of time?
   d. Offer new ideas for solving job-related problems?

Scoring

All items above use a one-to-five response mode (one least favorable, five most favorable). The score for each dimension is based on the sum of its items. The following descriptors are used: to a very great extent (5 points); to a great extent (4 points); to some extent (3 points); to a little extent (2 points); to a very little extent (1 point). With a slight change in wording these same items have also been used to measure peer leadership and are scored in the same way.

Source: Taylor, J. C., and Bowers, D. G. *Survey of Organizations* (Ann Arbor: Center for Research on Utilization of Scientific Knowledge, Institute for Social Research, University of Michigan, 1972). By permission of Taylor.

LATERAL LEADERSHIP

Refer back to Exhibit 11-5 in the Measurement Module for Chapter 11. You will see there the items that can be used to measure lateral leadership. Specifically, these items describe the leader's predisposition to the establishment of relationships with other internal units. Of course, these can also be used as an indicator of external orientation. Merely alter the instructions to reflect that the respondent should refer to units outside the organization as the focal point for responses. These give you important clues about how the leader is predisposed to behave toward other units both in the organization and outside it.

Exhibit 13-12   Ohio State Leader Behavior Description Questionnaire*(LBDQ)—Form XII

Purpose of the Questionnaire

On the following pages is a list of items that may be used to describe the behavior of your supervisor. Each item describes a specific kind of behavior, but does not ask you to judge whether the behavior is desirable or undesirable. Although some items may appear similar, they express differences that are important in the description of leadership. Each item should be considered as a separate description. This is not a test of ability or consistency in making answers. Its only purpose is to make it possible for you to describe, as accurately as you can, the behavior of your supervisor.

Note: The term, "group," as employed in the following items, refers to a department, division, or other unit of organization that is supervised by the person being described.

The term "members" refers to all the people in the unit of organization that is supervised by the person being described.

Initiating Structure

Clearly defines own role and lets followers know what is expected.

4. He lets group members know what is expected of them.
14. He encourages the use of uniform procedures.
24. He tries out his ideas in the group.
34. He makes his attitudes clear to the group.
44. He decides what shall be done and how it shall be done.
54. He assigns group members to particular tasks.
64. He makes sure that his part in the group is understood by the group members.
74. He schedules the work to be done.
84. He maintains definite standards of performance.
94. He asks that group members follow standard rules and regulations.

Consideration

Regards the comfort, well-being, status, and contributions of followers.

   7. He is friendly and approachable.
  17. He does little things to make it pleasant to be a member of the group.
  27. He puts suggestions made by the group into operation.
  37. He treats all group members as his equal.
  47. He gives advance notice of changes.
 *57. He keeps to himself.
  67. He looks out for the personal welfare of group members.
  77. He is willing to make changes.
 *87. He refuses to explain his actions.
 *97. He acts without consulting the group.

Source: Stogdill, R. M. *Manual for Leader Behavior Description Questionnaire—Form XII* (Columbus: Ohio State University, Bureau of Business Research, 1963). Reprinted by permission of College of Administrative Science, The Ohio State University. Copyright © 1963, by The Ohio State University.

*This exhibit shows 2 of the 12 dimensions of the 100-item questionnaire. All items use a 5-point response format describing how often the supervisor in question engages in the behavior described by an item. A - Always, B - Often, C - Occasionally, D - Seldom, E - Never. Except for items with an asterisk, *Always* is scored as "5," *Often* as "4," down to *Never* as a "1." Items with an asterisk are scored in the opposite direction. Though grouped together here, items are not placed together nor labeled in the instrument. They are set up in numbered sequence. Scores for each dimension are summed (e.g. 4, 14, 24, 34, 44, etc., are summed for a score for initiating structure).

REFERENCES

I. Great Man and Trait Approaches

[1]Stogdill, R. M. *Handbook of Leadership.* New York: The Free Press, 1974.

[2]"In Quest of Leadership," *Time,* July 15 (1974), 21–25, 28, 33–35.

II. Leadership Effectiveness and Who Will Be the Leader

[1]Etzioni, A. "Dual Leadership in Complex Organizations," *American Sociological Review,* 30 (1965), 688–698.

[2]Fiedler, F. E. *A Theory of Leadership Effectiveness.* New York: McGraw-Hill, 1967.

[3]Jennings, H. H. "Leadership and Sociometric Choice." In E. Maccoby, J. M. Newcomb, and E. L. Hartley (eds.), *Readings in Social Psychology* (3rd edition). New York: Holt, Rinehart and Winston, 1958.

[4]Morris, R. T., and Seaman, M. "The Problem of Leadership: An Interdisciplinary Approach," *American Journal of Sociology,* 56 (1950), 149–155.

[5]Stogdill, 1974.

A. Informal or Peer Leadership

[1]Bowers, D. G., and Seashore, S. E. "Predicting Organizational Effectiveness with a Four Factor Theory of Leadership," *Administrative Science Quarterly,* 11 (1966), 238–263.

[2]Comrey, A. L., Pfiffner, J. M., and High, W. S. "Factors Influencing Organizational Effectiveness: A

Final Report," University of Southern California, Office of Naval Research, 1954.

[3]Fleishman, E. A., Harris, E. F., and Burtt, H. E. *Leadership and Supervision in Industry.* Columbus: Ohio State University, Bureau of Educational Research, 1955.

[4]Katz, D., and Kahn, R. L., "Human Organization and Worker Motivation." In L. R. Tripp (ed.), *Industrial Productivity.* Madison, Wis.: Industrial Relations Research Association, 1952.

[5]Larson, L. L., and Allen, A. E. "The Relationships of Formal and Peer Leadership to Job Satisfaction." In A. F. Sikula, and R. L. Hilgert (eds.), Proceedings of the Nineteenth Annual Midwest Academy of Management Conference, St. Louis, Washington University, 1975.

[6]Reaser, J. M. "The Relationship between Official and Leader Behaviors and the Performance and Job Satisfaction of Mental Health Employees." Unpublished dissertation, Southern Illinois University, Carbondale, 1972.

[7]Stogdill, R. M. "Leadership, Membership and Organization," *Psychological Bulletin,* 47 (1950), 1–14.

III. Leader Behavior

[1]Bowers and Seashore, 1966.

[2]Larson, L. L., Hunt, J. G., and Osborn, R. N. "The Great Hi-Hi Leader Behavior Myth: A Lesson from Occam's Razor," *Academy of Management Journal,* 19 (1976), 628–641.

[3]Likert, R. *New Patterns of Management.* New York: McGraw-Hill, 1961.

[4]Stogdill, 1974.

IV. Leadership and Related Concepts

[1]Donnelly, J. H. Gibson, J. L., and Ivancevich, J. M. *Fundamentals of Management: Functions, Behavior, Models* (revised edition). Dallas: Business Publications, Inc., 1975.

[2]Filley, A. C., and House, R. J. *Managerial Process and Organizational Behavior.* Glenview, Ill.: Scott, Foresman, 1969.

[3]Fox, W. M. "An Analysis of Military Leadership in a Realistic Field Setting," ONR Technical Report 70–6, 70–7. Organizational Effectiveness Research Programs, Office of Naval Research, Code 452, Arlington, Va., 1974.

[4]Reaser, 1972.

A. Power

[1]French, J. R. P., and Raven, B. "The Bases of Social Power." In D. Cartwright (ed.), *Studies in Social Power.* Ann Arbor: Institute of Social Research, 1959.

B. Authority

[1]Barnard, C. *The Functions of the Executive.* Cambridge, Mass.: Harvard University Press, 1938.

[2]Weber, M. *The Theory of Social and Economic Organization.* Translated and edited by A. M. Henderson and T. Parsons. New York: The Free Press, 1947.

C. Leadership as an Exchange Process

[1]Jacobs, T. O. *Leadership and Exchange in Formal Organizations.* Alexandria, Va.: Human Resources Organization, 1970.

V. Lateral Leadership and External Orientation

A. Lateral Leadership within Organizations

[1]Duffy, P. J. "Lateral Interaction Orientation: An Expanded View of Leadership." Unpublished doc-

toral dissertation, Southern Illinois University, Carbondale, 1973.

[2]Osborn, R. N., and Hunt, J. G. "An Empirical Examination of Lateral and Vertical Leadership at Two Organizational Levels," *Journal of Business Research,* 2 (1974a), 209–221.

[3]Sayles, L. R. *Leadership: What Effective Managers Really Do and How They Do It.* New York: McGraw-Hill, in press.

[4]Sayles, L. R. *Managerial Behavior.* New York: McGraw-Hill, 1964.

B. External Orientation

[1]Osborn, R. N., and Hunt, J. G. "Environment and Organizational Effectiveness," *Administrative Science Quarterly,* 19 (1974b), 231–246.

VI. Contingency Approaches to Leadership

[1]Hunt, J. G., and Larson, L. L. (eds.). *Contingency Approaches to Leadership.* Carbondale, Ill.: Southern Illinois University Press, 1974.

A. Group Approaches

[1]Chemers, M. M., and Rice, R. W. "A Theoretical and Empirical Examination of Fiedler's Contingency Model of Leadership Effectiveness." In J. G. Hunt and L. L. Larson (eds.), *Contingency Approaches to Leadership.* Carbondale, Ill.: Southern Illinois University Press, 1974.

[2]Farris, G. F. "Leadership and Supervision in the Informal Organization." In J. G. Hunt and L. L. Larson (eds.), *Contingency Approaches to Leadership.* Carbondale, Ill.: Southern Illinois University Press, 1974.

[3]Fiedler, 1967.

[4]Fiedler, F. E. "Personality and Situational Determinants of Leader Behavior." In E. A. Fleishman and J. G. Hunt (eds.), *Current Developments in the Study of Leadership.* Carbondale, Ill.: Southern Illinois University Press, 1973b.

[5]Fiedler, F. E. "Validation and Extension of the Contingency Model of Leadership Effectiveness: A Review of Empirical Findings," *Psychological Bulletin,* 76 (1971), 128–148.

[6]Fiedler, F. E., and Chemers, M. M. *Leadership and Effective Management.* Glenview, Ill.: Scott, Foresman, 1974.

[7]Hunt and Larson, 1974.

[8]Sashkin, M., Taylor, F., and Tripathi, R. "An Analysis of Situational Moderating Effects on the Relationship between Least Preferred Co-Workers and Other Psychological Measures," *Journal of Applied Psychology,* 59 (1974), 731–740.

[9]Schriesheim, C. A., and Kerr, S. "Theories and Measures of Leadership: A Critical Appraisal of Current and Future Directions." in J. G. Hunt and L. L. Larson (eds.), *Leadership: The Cutting Edge.* Carbondale, Ill.: Southern Illinois University Press, 1977.

[10]Vroom, V. H., and Yetten, P. W. *Leadership and Decision-Making.* Pittsburgh: University of Pittsburgh Press, 1973.

B. Individual Approaches

[1]Bass, B. M., and Valenzi, E. R. "Contingent Aspects of Effective Management Styles." In J. G. Hunt and L. L. Larson (eds.), *Contingency Approaches to Leadership.* Carbondale, Ill.: Southern Illinois University Press, 1974.

Evans, M. G. "The Effects of Supervisory Behavior on the Path-Goal Relationship," *Organizational Behavior and Human Performance, 5* (1970), 277–298.

[3]Evans, M. G. "Extensions of a Path-Goal Theory of Motivation," *Journal of Applied Psychology, 59* (1974), 172–178.

[4]Graen, G., and Cashman, J. F. "A Role Making Model of Leadership in Formal Organizations: A Developmental Approach." In J. G. Hunt and L. L. Larson (eds.), *Leadership Frontiers.* Kent, Oh.: Comparative Administrative Research Institute, Kent State University, 1975.

[5]Graen, G., Cashman, J., Ginsburgh, S., and Schiemann, W. "Effects of Linking-Pin Quality Upon the Quality of Working Life of Lower Participants: A Longitudinal Investigation of the Managerial Understructure," *Administrative Science Quarterly, 22* (1977), 191–202.

[6]Graen, G., Dansereau, F., Jr., and Minami, T. "Dysfunctional Leadership Styles," *Organizational Behavior and Human Performance, 7* (1972), 216–236.

[7]Hill, W. A. "Leadership Style Flexibility, Satisfaction, and Performance." In E. A. Fleishman and J. G. Hunt (eds.), *Current Developments in the Study of Leadership.* Carbondale, Ill.: Southern Illinois University Press, 1973.

[8]House, R. J. "A Path-Goal Theory of Leader Effectiveness," *Administrative Science Quarterly, 16* (1971), 321–338.

[9]House, R. J., and Mitchell, T. R. "Path-Goal Theory of Leadership," *Journal of Contemporary Business, 3* (Autumn 1974), 81–87.

[10]Hunt, J. G. "Leadership in the Media Profession: Some Vertical and Lateral Considerations." In L. W. Cochran (ed.), *Leadership Development for the Media Profession.* Iowa City: Audio Visual Center, University of Iowa, 1973.

[11]Hunt, J. G., and Larson, L. L. (eds.). *Crosscurrents in Leadership.* Carbondale, Ill.: Southern Illinois University Press, in press.

[12]Hunt, J. G., and Larson, L. L. (eds.). *Leadership Frontiers.* Kent, Oh.: Comparative Administration Research Institute, Kent State University, 1975.

[13]Jacobs, 1970.

[14]Reitz, H. J. *Behavior in Organizations.* Homewood, Ill.: Irwin, 1977.

D. Causality

[1]Dawson, J. A., Messe, L. A., and Phillips, J. L. "Effects of Instructor-Leader Behavior on Student Performance," *Journal of Applied Psychology, 56* (1972), 369–376.

[2]Farris, G. F., and Lim, F. G. "Effects of Performance on Leadership Cohesiveness, Influence, Satisfaction, and Subsequent Performance," *Journal of Applied Psychology, 53* (1969), 490–497.

[3]Greene, C. N. "A Longitudinal Analysis of Relationships among Leader Behavior and Subordinate Performance and Satisfaction." In T. B. Greene and D. F. Ray (eds.), *Proceedings of the Thirty-Third Academy of Management Annual meeting.* State College: Mississippi State University, 1974.

[4]Greene, C. N. "The Path-Goal Theory of Leadership: A Replication

and an Analysis of Causality," Paper presented at the Thirty-Fourth National meeting of the Academy of Management, Seattle, August, 1974.

[5]Lowin, A., and Craig, J. R. "The Influence of Level of Performance on Managerial Style: An Experimental Object Lesson in the Ambiguity of Correlation Data," *Organizational Behavior and Human Performance,* 3 (1968), 440–458.

[6]Taylor, J. C., and Bowers, D. G. *Survey of Organizations.* Ann Arbor, Mich.: Institute for Social Research, University of Michigan, 1972.

VII. A Multiple Influence Approach

[1]Hunt, J. G., and Osborn, R. N. "A Multiple Influence Approach to Leadership for Managers." In J. S. Stinson and P. Hersey (eds.), *Perspectives in Leader Effectiveness.* Athens, Ohio: Center for Leadership Studies, Ohio University, in press.

[2]Hunt, J. G., and Osborn, R. N. "A Multiple Influence Model of Leadership," Army Research Institute Grant No. DAHC 19-78-G-0010, 1978.

[3]Hunt, J. G., Osborn, R. N., and Schuler, R. E. "Relations of Discretionary and Nondiscretionary Leadership to Performance and Satisfaction in a Complex Organization," *Human Relations,* 31 (1978), 507–523.

[4]Osborn, R. N., and Fohr, B. E. "Organizational Environments, Nondiscretionary and Discretionary Leadership." Unpublished paper, Department of Administrative Sciences, Southern Illinois University at Carbondale, 1976.

[5]Osborn, R. N., and Hunt, J. G. "Environment and Leadership: Discretionary and Nondiscretionary Leader Behavior and Organizational Outcomes." Unpublished paper, Department of Administrative Sciences, Southern Illinois University at Carbondale, 1978.

VIII. Measurement Module

A. Fiedler's LPC Scale
[1]Fiedler, 1967.

B. Michigan Four-Factor Scale
[1]Taylor and Bowers, 1972.

C. Ohio State LBDQ Scales
[1]Hunt, J. G., Osborn, R. N., and Schriesheim, C. A. "Some Neglected Aspects of Leadership Research." In C. N. Greene and P. H. Birnbaum (eds.), *Proceedings of the Twenty-Second Annual Midwest Academy of Management Conference.* Bloomington/Indianapolis, Ind.: Graduate School of Business, Indiana University, 1978.

[2]Stogdill, 1974.

[3]Stogdill, R. M. *Manual for Leader Behavior Description Questionnaire—Form XII.* Columbus: Ohio State University, Bureau of Business Research, 1963.

chapter **14** **LAST THINGS LAST:**
TOWARD AN INTEGRATED
CONTINGENCY VIEW

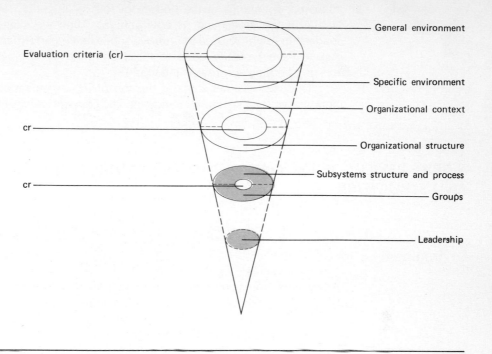

General environment

Evaluation criteria (cr)

Specific environment

Organizational context

cr

Organizational structure

cr

Subsystems structure and process

Groups

Leadership

In Part IV of this book we have progressed through a thicket of empirical studies and viewpoints. As we noted in our analysis of groups and leadership, much of the empirical support came from laboratory studies. They appeared quite far afield from day-to-day organizational operations. We know comparatively little about how and why subsystems, groups, and leadership influence and are influenced by organizational and environmental factors. Yet as a manager you will operate in an organizational setting that affects your leadership and the operation of your group. Thus, in this chapter we will integrate information concerning the organization and its environment with our understanding of subsystems, groups, and leadership.

Rather than attempt to develop a formal model, we will analyze top management to illustrate how these factors intermingle in the operations of complex organizations. To accomplish this we think it's important to review key concepts developed in earlier chapters. Then we will show how an organization can use subsystems' representatives to capitalize on its strategic advantage.

To integrate group and leadership factors into our perspective we will focus on operations at the bottom of the organization. We will discuss the nature of the group and its environment. Then we suggest how and when leadership might be used to improve subordinate performance and satisfaction. As we have typically done in these contingency chapters, we will extend existing findings to provide integration.

Thus, the chapter starts at the top of the organization, then goes to the bottom. Let's get started by reviewing key concepts developed in earlier parts.

A BRIEF REVIEW OF THE ORGANIZATION'S ENVIRONMENT, CONTEXT, AND STRUCTURE

Environment

An organization's environment is divided into two segments. The first is called the general environment. It deals with overall cultural, economic, educational, and legal-political conditions facing all organizations operating within a given area. We argue that the most important measure for this part of the environment is its degree of development. More developed general environments are more interdependent and growing. We argue that more development provides a better (more favorable) climate for organizations.

We also noted that the specific environment of an organization was important. The specific environment is defined as the set of organizations with which a particular organization interacts in its attempts to survive. Much of our previous contingency discussion centered on developing linkages among the development provided by the specific environment, the interdependence between and among organizations, and the extent of uncertainty.

We combined the analysis of the general and specific environments by developing the notion of environmental complexity. A more complex environment is one in which an organization operates in a developed general environment and faces high interdependence and uncertainty in the specific environment. More complex environments cut both ways for an organization. On the one hand, more opportunities for survival are available and more organizations with needed resources can be tapped. On the other hand, the organization has less control over its own destiny. External change, for instance, may severely disrupt smooth internal functioning and reduce efficiency.

Not all organizations are affected by environmental complexity in exactly the same fashion. Some are better able to cope than others. One factor determining how an organization can operate in a complex environment (or for that matter in a simple environment) is how it configures various aspects of its context.

Context

The context of an organization is its size, technology, and administrative philosophy. While size is easy to measure (the number of full-time equivalent employees), it has multiple interpretations. For the analysis of units and leadership within organizations, organizational size can be combined with organizational success into an overall estimate of favorability. That is, larger size and past success provide more opportunities and resources for groups and leaders. We also noted that size has a direct impact on the structure of the system such that larger organizations are more difficult to administer. Thus, size, like environmental complexity, is a double-edged sword.

Our analysis of technology attempted to reconcile contradictory findings by stressing sophistication and variability regardless of whether an organization is producing goods and services or linking parties for an exchange. Essentially, sophistication is the intricacy used in transforming inputs to outputs. This may stem from substituting machines for labor, the number of different matches needed to link parties, and/or the knowledge and skill needed to produce a satisfactory output. Not only does greater technological sophistication make production more difficult, it also means greater interdependence within an organization. Often greater sophistication improves the chances of survival. But it also tends to drive various parts of an organization apart and makes it more difficult for the organization to control events at the administrative and technical levels.

Variability in an organization's technology parallels the notion of environmental uncertainty. However, we placed much more emphasis on the number of different activities performed. For instance, the number of different products and services has often been used to estimate technological variability. It is assumed that different products require different methods of production. Much as environmental uncertainty is the nemesis of organizations, technological variability cuts an organization's potential efficiency. However, it may be critical to organizational survival, since more complex settings often call for more variable technologies.

Administrative philosophy was the third part of an organization's context. Three basic types were described. First, the traditionalistic philosophy stresses technical development and output goals. The environment is viewed as hostile and employees are seen as static and unfavorable. The second administrative philosophy was called moralistic since employee maintenance is stressed above organizational effectiveness. Employees are viewed as dynamic and positive, while technology is seen as just the opposite. The environment is most likely to be seen in negative terms. The third administrative philosophy was tagged individualistic. Here perceptions of the environment and employees are neutral, neither dynamic nor static, neither positive nor negative. The primary goal in this administrative philosophy is growth.

Structure

Our discussion of organizational structure stressed the point that vertical specialization should be matched with control and that horizontal specialization should be matched with coordination. We also noted that subordinates could rarely distinguish between vertical and horizontal specialization. Furthermore, they often see little distinction between coordination and control. Instead, subordinates appear more interested in the degree of specialization (either vertical or horizontal), the extent to which the organization is centralized or decentralized, and the amount of formalization (either from attempts to control or to coordinate). Finally, we suggested that organization structures may be diverse. That is, a variety of techniques for control and coordination may be used and substituted for one another, and the emphasis on vertical or horizontal specialization can be shifted among subsystems.

We suggested that it's often convenient to partially summarize structure by noting the emphasis on vertical specialization or on horizontal specialization. A more organic structure is one where horizontal specialization and coordination are favored over the vertical aspects of structure. To employees in the middle of an organization, the organic tilt may be seen as decentralized. On the other hand, the organization may be more mechanistic by stressing vertical specialization and control. To those in the middle of an organization, the anatomy may appear more centralized.

We noted that the structure of an organization appears to be influenced both by environmental conditions and contextual factors. Greater environmental development and larger size pressure an organization to become more vertically specialized and to increase formal controls. Technological sophistication and environmental interdependence pressures are primarily horizontal. Organizations can cope with this by increasing horizontal specialization and coordination. We also noted that as technological variability and environmental uncertainty increase, organizations can increase their chances of success by increasing structural diversity. That is, they can vary the degree of vertical and horizontal specialization as well as the degrees of control and coordination across different major subsystems.

Combining Environment, Context, and Structure

We also suggested that when predicting organizational effectiveness and employee maintenance, it's important to recognize the combined impact of environment, context, and structure. To analyze combined effects we developed the notions of contextual and structural complexity. The context is more complex as an organization becomes larger and as its technological sophistication and variability increase. The structure of an organization becomes more complex as the degrees of horizontal specialization (and coordination), vertical specialization (and control), and diversity increase.

For an organization to survive we suggested that it should seek equivalence among degrees of environmental, contextual, and structural complexity. To the extent these conditions are similar, the organization can capitalize on the opportunities provided by the environment and context. Moreover, to offset problems from the environment and context, an organization needs to develop an appropriately complex structure. As environment, context, and structure increase in complexity, the setting becomes more complex.

To get a better picture of the goal attainment potential of organizations it was necessary to go beyond the notions of environmental, contextual, and structural complexity. We suggested that an organization may build upon one of four strategic advantages. It can: (1) build upon size; (2) use its technological sophistication; (3) capitalize on technological variability; or (4) develop a balance. We noted that each strategic advantage combines environmental and contextual conditions. Thus, *size* and *interdependence* are matched, *technological sophistication* and *development* are coupled, the organization counters *uncertainty* with *technological variability,* or the organization can *balance* environmental and contextual forces. Each strategic advantage calls for a slightly different structure and gives an organization an advantage in reaching some goals. Building upon size calls for a mechanistic structure, which provides an edge in reaching efficiency goals. The advantage of technological sophistication calls for an organic structure and allows an organization to most easily reach product/service goals. Where technological variability is the strategic advantage, an organization has a leg up on flexibility if it can develop a diverse structure. Balance doesn't favor any particular goal. But we noted that most complex and very complex organizations are dominated by the individualistic administrative philosophy. Thus, these balanced organizations often emphasize the systems goals of growth and greater power.

We also noted that it is extremely difficult for an organization to completely match all environmental, contextual, and structural conditions regardless of its strategic advantage. Gaps between those aspects of environment and context calling for similar structural adjustments were highlighted. Where these "paired dimensions" call for different structural adjustments, an organization has a problem. It can become "over" and "under" structured. The result might be less efficiency or effectiveness, less responsiveness to the environment, and/ or problems with control and coordination. We indicated that the problems with too much or too little structuring appear quite similar.

To summarize, there are several different ways organizations can survive and become more successful. Now that you have been exposed to an analysis of subsystems relations, it's obvious that different paths to success place some subsystems at the center of the action, while others become less important. Thus, more fine tuning can be done to compensate for structural problems noted before. So let's turn to the question of strategic advantage and subsystems relations.

STRATEGIC ADVANTAGE AND SUBSYSTEMS

Without substantially changing the degrees of specialization and control or coordination, an organization can make some changes to close the gaps between environmental and contextual conditions. We see two different but interrelated strategies. One concerns the vertical placement of staff- and boundary-line units in an organization's hierarchy. A second concerns the placement of subsystems heads on key policy committees at the top of this structure.

Placement of Subsystems

If an organization follows its strategic advantage, placement of staff- and boundary-line units is comparatively easy to project for organizations building upon size, technological sophistication, and technological variability. Units needed to build upon strategic advantage should be placed at the top of the organizational hierarchy. Such placement allows these subsystems to deal with critical contingencies and develop the auditing and approval relationships needed to capitalize on the organization's strategic advantage.[2]

Where size is the strategic advantage, internal staff units dealing with efficiency and boundary staff should be elevated. Thus, they have and can build more approval relationships. Where technological sophistication is the strategic advantage, internal staff dealing with research and development should be elevated. Boundary-line units should be given priority when an organization builds upon technological variability. In other terms, those functions most critical to an organization's strategic advantage should be more centralized than the others.*

For organizations building upon balance, there's some evidence suggesting that they select one of two different ways of placing staff and boundary units. In analysis of huge corporations, Pitts cites two different types of firms.[1] One collection of conglomerates has grown primarily via acquisition. He cites ITT, Gulf and Western Industries, and SCM as examples. At the top, these behemoths appear to have an organic structure. Division presidents act much as if they headed independent corporations. Related information suggests that boundary-staff units at the top of these systems may have considerable organizational clout. In the case of ITT there is evidence that governmental relations (a boundary-staff unit) had considerable influence.

Scattered information concerning some of these corporations suggests a somewhat different pattern below the division presidents. Here we find internal staff to ensure that an adequate volume and quality of outputs is being produced. Furthermore, these internal staff units help the division build upon possible synergy across different product and market areas. There are comparatively few boundary-staff units and boundary-line units, and they often appear to take a back seat to internal staff.

Comparatively little is known about the structure at the bottom of these systems, and the structure is quite diverse. But our analysis would suggest the following: (1) boundary-line units are powerful and modifications of a matrix form of departmentation may be used extensively; (2) with internal staff functions concentrated at upper middle management, boundary-line units and internal line units may operate on work-flow relationships that are fairly evenly balanced.

Note the pattern throughout the hierarchy. At the top, boundary staff help keep these behemoths attuned to the interests of other large systems. They are politically responsive as opposed to technically innovative. At the administrative level the focus changes to the technical side to maintain the balance of the structure. At the bottom, the organization has established a structure that is responsive to the specific demands for particular products and services. These lower-level units are constrained, though, by the approval relations held by higher-level staff units.

Pitts also identified a second collection of firms that are as large, technologically sophisticated, and variable as the first.[1] But these firms have grown primarily through internal diversification. They use top-level technical staff to link the technical opportunities of different divisions. Corning Glass Works,

*The question focuses on what should be centralized more than whether the locus of control for all activities should be placed at the top or middle of the system. For instance, when General Motors was heralded as a decentralized firm, finance was centralized.

Borg Warner, and General Electric are examples.[1] In this analysis internal staff has considerable clout at the top of these systems. Division presidents, for instance, are more interdependent with one another. They are much less like heads of independent corporations than their counterparts in the acquisitive diversifiers.

Scattered information concerning these corporations suggests they "decentralize" boundary staff toward the division level. It appears that internal staff units have comparatively little clout in the middle of the organization. They appear to act more as liaison between line managers and the powerful internal staff at the top. These organizations also appear to carry the divisional form farther down into the organization. General Electric, for instance, has some 500 different business units centered on different products and industries. This pattern compensates for the internal, vertical orientation found at the top of the organization. Thus, these firms appear to balance their structure, but in a different manner than the more clear-cut conglomerate forms.

There is some question as to which pattern is more successful. Sutherland argues that both types may be too large.[3] Clearly, each collection has survived and very few huge systems appear to be a mix of these two structural patterns. For our purposes it's interesting to note that each type has developed a structure appropriate for its environment and context. The placement and power of subsystems is, however, quite different.

Subsystems at the Top of the Organization

So far we have suggested that the placement of subsystems can be used to help an organization capitalize on its strategic advantage. But it may also be possible to make more subtle adjustments at the top of an organization. Specifically, it can tilt the balance of power toward some subsystems by placing their heads on key policy committees. To understand this more fully you need to recognize that at the top of larger organizations you find a matrix form of departmentation.

As we examine the top two or three levels of many large and huge organizations, there are a great number of individuals. It's not unusual to find ten to fifteen people on a corporate board of directors.[6] Similarly, hospitals and universities have boards of directors or trustees. Government agencies are overlaid with congressional committees whose function is to oversee and guide the agency's actions.[2] At the top of the larger systems you frequently find a matrix consisting of formal positions and policy committees.[4] Corporations provide good examples with their finance and operations committees. Later in the chapter we will take a closer look at those individuals who have multiple membership on top-level policy committees. For now recognize that multiple membership by a subsystems head ensures that the views of the unit will be represented.[9] Furthermore, the subsystem has a better chance of developing more approval relationships and becoming a more pervasive force in an organization.[3]

The organization can use several methods of selecting the membership of the top policy committees.[5] Here we are interested in the proportion of boundary line, boundary staff, and internal staff members. Approximately equal representation provides a rough balance among the different types of units. Disproportional representation, however, tilts the balance of power without changing the formal structure.

We suggest that an organization may improve its chances of success by adjusting the membership on these committees.[8] Specifically, disproportional representation can be used to help close an important gap between important paired dimensions. Let's take a look at organizations building upon technological sophistication, size, and variability.

For organizations building on technological sophistication, we argued earlier that the gap between technological sophistication and development in the environment was particularly important. If technological sophistication lags behind development, we suggested the organization could be both under and over structured. Centralization of the research and development functions could help mitigate gap-related problems. Now we are suggesting that the placement of internal staff (e.g., R&D) could further close the gap. Why? Primarily because the interests of research and development are represented at the highest levels and because it allows this staff unit to become an even more pervasive force. Specifically, a disproportionate number of internal staff heads could be placed on high-level policy committees. Where technological sophistication outweighs development, we suggest exactly the opposite. Line unit heads (e.g., division managers) should be disproportionately represented on the top-level policy committees. Why? To facilitate altering the domain of an organization into a more developed environment.

Now let's look at organizations building upon size. The principle is the same, but the gap and the key subsystems are different. Recall, the gap considered most critical is that between size and environmental interdependence. Where size outweighs interdependence we suggest an organization may help close the gap by favoring internal staff on policy committees. This placement is apt to put more emphasis on internal operations than suggested by the formal structure. Where interdependence is outweighed by size, an organization can compensate by tilting the membership of top-level committees toward boundary staff personnel. This can result in more attention devoted to the critical interdependencies.[7]

Where an organization builds upon technological variability we argued that the match between technological variability and environmental uncertainty was particularly important. Boundary-line units were considered the key to increasing the range of outputs needed to match variability and uncertainty. Thus a tilt toward boundary-line units, such as marketing, is suggested in organizations in which technological variability lags behind uncertainty. The development of Gillette is an example. Where variability outstrips environmental uncertainty, internal line units should be favored so that an organization can cut the range of outputs.

We have been very careful to use the words should, could, and can in our discussion because we have clearly provided normative recommendations. Further, we suspect it may be extremely difficult for some organizations to substantially alter the composition of policy committees. Let's combine information concerning top management and groups to explain some of the dynamics at the top of an organization.

THE "IN-GROUP" AT THE TOP OF THE ORGANIZATION

The collection of people holding formal positions at the top of an organization has been called its *dominant coalition*.[8] Individuals in these top positions can represent an organization (as in the case of top management) or one of a number of interests it needs for growth and survival.[1] For instance, it has been shown that members of corporate boards of directors may be used to link an organization with important members of the specific environment.*[5] Selznick argues that membership on governing boards is one way organizations can "co-opt" potentially hostile organizations.[7] Participation on governing boards is also used to ensure that the interests of a key contributor are represented. European corporations, for instance, may have representatives of organized labor on their governing boards.[3] Banks holding a corporation's debentures are often represented on the board of directors.[1]

Not all members of an organization's dominant coalition are equal. You typically find an "inner circle" or "in-group" forming around the chief executive officer.[8] These in-group members do not only have a high formal position within an organization; they may also be found on several high-level policy committees.[2] This small collection of individuals come as close as any set of individuals to running an organization.

Members of the "in-group" are in a politically delicate position. They represent their subsystems, the interests of those who rely upon their subsystems, the organization as a whole, those who rely upon it, and last, but far

*As we noted in our discussion of administrative philosophy, not every member of the dominant coalition has a formal role in the organization.

from least, themselves.[3] The "in-group" must keep other members of the dominant coalition attached to the organization and actively participating in but still willing to defer to, the "in-group" judgment.[6] Stated differently, the "in-group" must keep other members of the dominant coalition within their zone of indifference.

We think the key to this balancing act is using an organization's strategic advantage to build slack. As Cyert and March, among others, suggest, slack resources allow the "in-group" to maintain a viable coalition by backing-up ideological claims with resources.[2,6] No one goal is maximized. Once satisfactory performance in one high-priority area is expected, an organization can direct its efforts toward lower-priority goals.[4] For instance, consider the organization building upon size. Slack from internal efficiency can be used to improve the quality of outputs, develop greater flexibility, and/or expand operations. However, minimum performance in areas of interest to the dominant coalition must be maintained (i.e., goals are also constraints).[2]

Constraints on Building Slack

The composition of the "in-group" and the membership of the dominant coalition help to establish goal priorities and to limit the range of choices open to an organization.[9] Alternatives that would severely undercut the power of "in-group" members or repel members of the dominant coalition out of their "zone of indifference" must be rejected.[2] While the "in-group" must be kept small to ensure smooth functioning, it needs a variety of skills and a homogeneity of attitudes.[7] Moreover, individuals in the dominant coalition should feel they have access to "in-group" members and that they could become a member if they were willing to make the additional commitment.[4]

While you might think the "in-group" would constitute a future-oriented "think-tank," it doesn't. Top-level executives act as if they are under severe time constraints.[7] Information, activities, and interaction come in short bursts.[9] Few appear to take the time for reflection.

It is often quite difficult to track-down when the "in-group" makes a choice among alternatives. Alternatives associated with problems and opportunities appear to be discussed together so that a clear-cut separation of means and ends becomes difficult.[1] The "in-group" does not appear to use sophisticated decision-making techniques.[7] Instead, it seems to rely upon the collective wisdom of its members. As some consensus begins to emerge among the "in-group," it appears that the chief executive officer ratifies and anoints the emerging position.[10] After an apparent pause, the consensus position, with some modifications, becomes policy. You often find this pause between meetings of high-level policy committees.[10] At the end of one meeting little appears accomplished. But at the beginning of the next, some consensus policy or position seems to have emerged.[10]

Note we have described the outcomes of the "in-group" in terms of policies or positions that appear to evolve from a process of creeping commitment. It's important to understand that precedent plays an important role in the dynamics of the "in-group." Radical departures from existing positions could upset the dominant coalition.[5] Also, lower-level executives often attempt to follow the posture established by the "in-group." Alterations in the posture of the "in-group" limit the ability of lower-level executives to follow a consistent interpretation of top-management intentions.[9] When top management appears to vacillate, the control and coordination in the middle of an organization suffers.

It is also important to recognize that the inner circle is a mixture of elite specialists who are trying to maintain their credibility and managerial generalists who may not have the technical expertise to question the cause-effect linkages made by a specialist.[7] Norms of reciprocity operate such that specialists do not question one another's expertise.[3] After all, if the specialists were not knowledgeable how could they be in the "in-group"?

Furthermore, members of the "in-group" may also color the information shared with their colleagues.[6] Their status in the "in-group" partially rests on the appearance of successfully managing their own subsystems. Even though their subsystem is experiencing considerable difficulty they may not admit it. Moreover, the personal and organizational lives of "in-group" members are often difficult to separate. Thus, much of the information they receive is filtered and colored by similar forces.

What is the outcome of these constraints? Time pressures, the inability to clarify cause-effect relations, the ambiguity of desired outcomes, the need for stability, and the role of precedent often mean that only a limited number of alternatives and consequences is considered.[8] Positions are likely to be quite similar to or extensions of existing policy.[1] Implementation is not comprehensive. As Wieland and Ullrich suggest, executives select targets of opportunity.[11] Where events force a change, such as a retirement or a scheduled review period, executives take the opportunity to install modified programs, policies, and procedures.

Advantages for the "In-Group"

While the "in-group" faces a number of obstacles and problems it is by no means powerless. A well-developed administrative philosophy can be an important source of power and serve as a defense for the "in-group." The chief executive officer can use it to develop a common language that minimizes conflicts. It also can provide broader social significance for the actions, sentiments, and norms of "in-group" members. On the other side of the coin, an administrative philosophy can be a positive force for change, for it can establish a series of ideals toward which the "in-group" can strive as well as evaluate itself and its members.

We should also note that the very position of the "in-group" at the top of an organization provides some often hidden strengths.

First, lower-level executives will not only accept the "decisions" of the "in-group," but they will also try to make them work. Without challenging the authority of top management, executives near the top will modify, expand, and mold the choices of the "in-group" into a more detailed plan for action. These plans may then be ratified and/or modified by the "in group."[1] Second, if a decision is incorrect, failure may not be placed on the shoulders of top management. It is rarely blamed for "wrong" decisions—conditions change, unforeseen events occur, subordinates are overzealous, and the like.[3] Of course, should a choice yield expected results, success is attributed to the wisdom and judgment of top management. Third, by adjusting the way in which outcomes are eveluted, many apparently poor choices can be made to appear more favorable.[2] Finally, the "in-group" may simply rewrite history. Positions are reinterpreted; a major position was but a contingency plan; or top management was just sending up a "trial" balloon.[2]

Trauma in the "In-Group"

While a listing of constraints and advantages for top management helps in understanding their actions, it is not sufficient to predict the demise of an "in-group." Predicting the demise of an "in-group" is important since it often signals a fundamental change in the whole administration of an organization.[2] When an "in-group" dies, several analyses suggest that organizational changes can be swift and brutal.[1,3] In corporations, for instance, the sale of unprofitable divisions, entering new products in new markets, and the rise of internal staff units into the "in-group" can accompany succession.[2]

Analyses of organizational succession suggest that poor performance and changing environmental conditions may place sufficient strain on the "in-group" to force its demise.[2] Yet we should also add that abundant slack or the anticipation of abundant slack may be sufficient to keep an "in-group" in power.[2] A poor match among environment, context, and structure alone may not trigger a change in the dominant coalition.

However, a slight change in external conditions can set the stage for succession. If environmental change makes it appear that an organization's action may become inappropriate, outsiders in the dominant coalition can quickly solidify to overthrow the existing "in-group."[4] It is also possible that the squabbling of the "in-group" and its challengers may evolve into terminal conflict, in which case both could lose. One point seems clear: If the terminal conflict persists, the organization may lose.

One other clear conclusion emanates from recent succession studies of corporations. The coupling of an inappropriate strategy with a reluctance to change is a particular threat to the "in-group."[2] With its limited ability to change, the "in-group" may die of shock if it confronts a unified challenge from outsiders in the dominant coalition.

There is no assurance that incumbents fare better than the old "in-group."[2] Dramatic changes may bring a match among the environment, context, and structure of an organization. However, the organization can also seesaw across the balance of environmental, contextual, and structural conditions needed for success.[4]

At least one study also suggests that a few organizations can forestall succession by appropriate adaptation to changing environmental conditions.[2] In many cases a reorientation is in response to well-known and well-understood changes in the environmental setting. For instance, corporations were able to forestall succession when facing a recession by launching an efficiency campaign. Yet, many corporate "in-groups" were unable or unwilling to meet such challenges and found themselves being replaced.

We have taken a fairly comprehensive look at top management. Environmental, contextual, structural, and group factors all appear to both free and confine top management. The inner circle of an organization can be led astray and not be able to detect or cope with alterations in its setting. If it violates the zone of indifference of other members of the dominant coalition it can be vulnerable. Succession studies suggest a variety of interest groups can coalesce to topple the "in-group." Once it is displaced, an organization may experience sudden changes that may or may not increase the chances of organizational success.

As an aspiring middle manager you should be aware of the nature of top management and the types of conditions likely to yield a change at the top. More than one career has been stifled simply because the manager was on the wrong side in a top-management change. Yet, to become a middle manager you must first show the management and leadership abilities needed for promotion. So let's move to the bottom of an organization and use our knowledge of organizations, groups, and leadership to suggest how you might adjust to unfavorable, moderately favorable, and favorable settings.

USING ORGANIZATION THEORY TO IMPROVE YOUR CHANCES OF SUCCESS

Analyzing Groups

Your first managerial job may well be as a supervisor of a small group of employees. What are some key considerations to keep in mind? We think a good starting point is the analysis of required and emergent actions, interactions, and sentiments in terms of their relationship to cohesiveness and the receptiveness of the group to management. We noted earlier that cohesiveness is a two-edged sword. If group norms are consistent with those of management (the group is receptive), then cohesiveness is a boon. If not, a cohesive group can cause subtantial problems.[1]

In making this analysis you are concerned with analyzing the context (size and task) and structure of the group in terms of its effects upon required and emergent factors and their consistency with each other. We assume you would like to get as close to a perfect fit as possible since we've argued earlier that this should enhance performance and employee maintenance.

Analysis of Group Context and Structure. The first question in this analysis is, how big is the group? The larger the size the more difficult it is to develop a perfect fit. Two reasons stand out. First, the larger the group the more difficult it is for all members to interact. Thus, the chances of finding shared emergent sentiments, actions, and interactions decline. Second, the larger the group the less likely all individuals will agree on anything.[2] Thus, size, after that magic number of five, is likely to be dysfunctional for developing a perfect fit.[2]

The next factor to check out is the required task of the group. For our purposes let's assume that the task of the group can meaningfully be rated in terms of difficulty, Interdependence, and varlability. Difficulty, we estimate, is functional for developing a fit. Difficult tasks provide a mechanism for task-related exchanges among individuals that supercedes personal eccentricities. In other words, you put up with a nonconformist when he or she can help solve a particularly knotty problem. Task difficulty also tends to increase satisfaction, thus facilitating group cohesiveness.[2,4] Task interdependence, by requiring more teamwork, facilitates development of consistency among actions, sentiments, and interactions. Tasks that are both difficult and interdependent, however, can be a double-edged sword. When group members are technically competent, the challenge facilitates consistency. When even a few members are incompetent, quite the opposite is the case. Let's assume you are lucky. The members of your group are technically competent.

Some task uncertainty in terms of variety facilitates consistency. It provides new challenges. But where the task is difficult and calls for extensive team-work, change can be a very devisive force. If a group is already cohesive, uncertainty will probably not be a particularly critical factor since a group faces the problem together, and each member derives support from the others. When just forming, even moderate amounts of uncertainty can prohibit group development.[3] In short, task uncertainty is a devisive factor prohibiting the development of consistency. But if it were the only negative factor, and a group were otherwise stable, it could be offset.

Let's summarize quickly. Overall, the larger a group the less the chance of developing consistency. Groups involved in more complex tasks (difficult, interdependent, and uncertain tasks) have a better chance of developing consistency. However, unplanned changes in the pattern of work can be potentially quite disruptive. Note that a group's task establishes many of the required actions and interactions.

The structure of a group is also an important element. Studies of groups stress the formal channels of communication among members.[4] But the degree of specialization is also likely to be important. That is, to what extent is each member expected to have a set of specialized skills? Often, specialization can be measured by the required level of education and/or training.

We think that the structure of a group has direct influence on emergent factors and employee maintenance. Thus, more open and specialized structures should facilitate the development of consistency. However, we think it's even more important to fit the structure with task requirements and group size. Complex tasks (those that are difficult, call for interdependence among group members and involve more change) require a more open and specialized structure. Thus, it's not surprising that those interested in the quality of working life call for complex tasks and an open structure to build work teams.[1]

Where tasks are simple, however, the all-channel network with extensive specialization is not needed. The costs of coordination are not offset by higher quality, quantity, or efficiency. Thus, less specialization is found, and the wheel and modifications of the Y (see Chapter 12) are expected. We should note that the linkage among group members should be particularly sensitive to task interdependence. If the flow of work is independent, the wheel is more appropriate. But if the workflow is sequential, then the Y provides a better fit. If the workflow calls for team action, then the open channel is preferred. Where there is a mix of independent, sequential, and interdependent tasks, we think a combination of channels should be used. Many of these combinations will involve a Y with "wheels" at the ends. The exact pattern should, in large part, fit the size of the group. The larger the size the more complex the pattern, so that small collections of members can fully interact. Connections among members in larger groups is often via informal leaders who occupy key positions in the network.

Let's assume that your predecessor had enough savvy to fit size, tasks, and structure. Essentially you find that required actions and interactions are consistent with one another. Now we come to the more difficult question of required sentiments. Our discussion of required sentiments was very brief. One reason for our brevity is our lack of understanding of the sentiments required of various groups. Managers often speak of commitment, loyalty, and willingness to work. Many people consider these as outcomes of the work experience. You can expect management to require a minimum of commitment to the mission of the organization, a willingness to work at assigned duties, and some indications of attachment to the job. You can expect that most of the required sentiments are within an employee's "zone of indifference." Of course, as you move up the organizational hierarchy, the required sentiments may loom as a more important consideration. For instance, the chief executive may be expected to do or die for the organization.

So far we have looked at matching required and emergent actions, interactions, and sentiments in various forms. In doing this we have assumed that you could vary the group context to try to promote this consistency. Now let's focus on leadership. In our analysis, we will incorporate the environment and the nature of the group so that you can reduce gaps in satisfaction and performance.

Using Leadership to Improve Your Success Potential

We have studied the executive suite and the way in which it is influenced by the setting. We have also taken a similar look at subsystems. Finally, we have briefly considered the nature of groups at the bottom of an organization. Let's go one step further and consider the impact of all of these things on leadership and the role of the lower-level leader.

Before we do, we should quickly review some of the leadership highlights discussed in Chapter 13. There we showed that leadership need not be an inborn trait. Nor was one combination of behaviors best in all situations. That lead to an analysis of various kinds of contingency approaches and culminated in a quick look at a multiple influence approach to leadership. Within that approach we utilized three broad leader-behavior categories stemming from earlier work. These could be summarized under: (1) initiating structure or task-orientation; (2) consideration or a human-relations orientation; and (3) lateral leadership. Each of these three categories appears to have numerous subdimensions and includes only a portion of what a leader is called upon to do. Yet, for simplicity we will concentrate on these categories when we combine leadership with environment and group conditions.

We showed earlier that distinctions among authority, power, and influence were useful in understanding leadership. A key part of such understanding was the notion of exchange. Here it was argued that rather than relying on an arbitrary order as the only way of exerting influence, an astute leader recognized that social quid pro quos were involved. In other words, leaders recognize that they must "scratch subordinates backs" to get them to go beyond minimal compliance with orders.[7]

If exchange is indeed an integral part of a leader's success, then it's necessary to look at factors altering the resources available for exchange. With fewer resources leaders find it more difficult to reinforce desired subordinate actions. At the same time, the same conditions that affect a leader's clout also have a direct bearing on criteria. We summarize this again in Figure 14-1. As you look at the figure, it may be helpful to elaborate the points we made earlier.

First, each variable can have a direct impact on criteria. Second, each of the variables has an indirect impact as they influence other variables directly related to the criteria. We simplified the multiple influence approach with the addition of two concepts. First was the idea that the leader had to close both performance and satisfaction gaps. The second concept was discretionary leadership. Here, the leader's ability to influence (discretion) may be restricted by the setting (e.g., a subsystem in the process of reorganization), the group's environment (e.g., limited resources), or the nature of the group (e.g., a cohesive antimanagement group). Put in a different way, discretionary leadership consists of those leader behaviors that the manager selects in an attempt to influence subordinates. We argued this can be looked at as a global construct or by separate leadership dimensions.

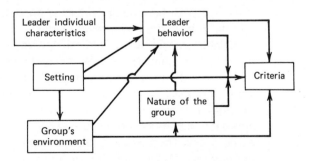

Figure 14-1 A multiple influence model of leadership.

There are several methods we can use to estimate the gaps the leader is expected to close. We will focus on a group's environment and the nature of its interaction with initiating structure, consideration, and lateral leadership behaviors.* This approach highlights the role of leadership as an intermediate predictor (one operating between a group's environment, its nature, and criteria). Furthermore, it allows for short-term inconsistencies between the environment and the nature of the group. For instance, a group's environment may have turned poor even though it remains cohesive and receptive to management.

Earlier we talked of favorability in the group's environment. Where there were few external opportunities and resources, a group's environment was not particularly favorable (see Figure 12-8). If interdependence and uncertainty were piled on top of a lean environment, its environment was called very unfavorable. Let's look at leaders facing a lean group environment. We start here simply because many leadership analyses paint a very optimistic picture. They assume the leader can make a big difference. In our view many leaders cannot close the performance and satisfaction gaps. (We will treat the favorable group environment later.)

Leadership in an Unfavorable Environment.

Discretion. The worst group environment is the combination of few outside resources and high interdependence on others, coupled with uncertainty (substantial external change is an important aspect). How much discretion does the leader have? Very little. The boss is not the master of the ship. The leader gains little from attempting to develop exchanges with other leaders (lateral behavior). There are few opportunities, and even considerable efforts are unlikely to pay substantial dividends. As Osborn and Bishop show, lateral leadership drops as the environment becomes less favorable.[9]

We recognize that in the lean setting, higher managers want more lateral contact by subordinate managers to help improve efficiency and cut redundancy. While many subordinate leaders recognize this, they may still cut lateral exchanges to avert losses. Why lose internal resources for the benefit of others?

The discretion the leader has in initiating structure for subordinates is undercut in the unfavorable environment in at least two ways. First, the leader must continually change instructions given to subordinates and often rearticulate the role of the group and its members. To group members this may be seen as inconsistent leadership—a lack of clear direction. Evidence suggests subordinates don't respond well to substantial variation in leader behavior.[1,10]

*We assume that a lateral orientation will result in appropriate behaviors.

Second, the leader must often pass-on conflicting instructions and desires from more powerful outside groups. For instance, the leader may be in the difficult position of instituting efficiency campaigns at the same time benefits to employees are not being increased. Thus the leader may be instructing an employee in a more efficient method, while that employee suspects that greater efficiency will mean a reduction in staff.

Existing data run counter to intuitive notions when it comes to discretionary consideration.[6] In an unfavorable environment it appears that leaders should compensate with more employee consideration. We are not sure why, but it appears they don't. One explanation is perhaps that the situation is one in which leaders have fewer tangible rewards to dispense and therefore they are separate from subordinates. Complimenting subordinates for a good job seems inconsistent with distributing few or no tangible rewards. Yet in the unfavorable situation it appears that leaders should fight the tendency to withdraw from the group. Greater consideration can probably be beneficial in closing the satisfaction gap.

Nature of the Group. Now let's take a look at the nature of the group when the environment is not favorable. Earlier analyses suggested that in the unfavorable environment the group may be cohesive but hostile. That is, the group may have a consistent pattern of emergent actions, interactions, and sentiments that are in direct conflict with required actions, interactions, and sentiments. The leader who faces both an unfavorable environment and a cohesive but hostile group is in serious trouble. We doubt such a leader can close the satisfaction gap. Subordinates may look to themselves for support. Attempts to change sentiments may be viewed with suspicion. If the hostility of the group also has its seeds in routine, unsophisticated tasks, and if it is large, we see an almost untenable situation. Perhaps the best the leader can do is attempt to work out a relationship with informal leaders and work to improve the group's environment. While the boss may be the titular head of the group, informal leaders are likely to have the upper hand. We also think that leaders operating in a lean environment should be particularly careful to offset as much interdependence and uncertainty as possible. If the lean environment is matched by high uncertainty and interdependence, we estimate that the favorable combination of required and emergent actions, interactions, and sentiments may disappear quickly. The once favorable, cohesive group could turn into the hostile, cohesive group.

Yet a focus on subordinates can backfire on the leader. Employees may want higher satisfaction. But it's likely management is more interested in performance. In the unfavorable environment, actions that help protect the group from higher interdependence or uncertainty may appear to run counter to management's desires for higher performance. Thus, the leader runs the risk of alienating management in attempts to protect the group.

We suspect that unfavorable environments place more requirements on leaders to initiate structure and contact other managers. Such contacts are probably not very helpful in closing either the satisfaction or performance gap. For example, we noted that continually changing the instructions given to subordinates did not reduce uncertainty, clear paths to goal accomplishment, or remove roadblocks. In a similar fashion, just getting managers to talk doesn't mean they will make changes needed to help one another. As we showed earlier, conflict and cooperation are *both* forms of managerial exchange.

When analyzing leader consideration you might automatically think all of these influence-attempts would be under the discretion of the leader. Being friendly and approachable, for instance, appears as a difficult requirement. A more careful look at consideration, however, suggests the following. Via human relations training many managers have been instructed to keep open channels of communication with employees and to appear concerned with their personal welfare. "How are the wife and kids?" is an example. To encourage consideration, organizations may stage events such as company picnics. Attendance is not formally required, but even the dullard knows that it would be a mistake to be absent. The leader is expected to smile, appear concerned, and stress participation in all situations. Note, required consideration is not based upon subordinate actions. Neither is it backed up with leader action or change.

Can required (nondiscretionary) leadership attempts make a difference? In unfavorable environments we think they may be of little value. Continual contact with peers and subordinates may only serve to widen the performance and satisfaction gaps. Laterally, these attempts may induce conflict rather than cooperation. Vertically, they may build roadblocks to task accomplishment and sow seeds of misunderstanding and hostility.

Expanding the Range of Leader Behaviors to Gain Discretion. Separate analyses of House's support and participation dimensions (Chapter 13) help us understand more of the specific actions open to leaders in various situations. For instance, in the unfavorable environment just described, the leader could use supportive actions. Participation by subordinates is another matter. It's not open to leaders facing cohesive, hostile groups nearly as much as it is when one such group has more favorable emergent sentiments. For example, assume that the environment is lean, but that the task of the group is sophisticated. Participation can be used to build on the ego involvement of subordinates and thus help close the satisfaction gap. We also estimate that participation may be helpful in closing the performance gap. It could not only clarify paths and/

or circumvent roadblocks but also help to evolve new methods and procedures. However, participation is not universally good for closing either gap.

House's work has also led him toward analyzing new dimensions of leadership that are not apparently related to either task (like initiating structure) or human relations (consideration) dimensions. One of these is charismatic leadership.[3] House is particularly interested in the influence the leader has on the goals subordinates set for themselves and their co-workers. His recent research, then, is starting to expand the definition of leadership to incorporate the most difficult to understand portions. Why and how can some individuals turn an apparently dismal situation into a better environment? Perhaps charismatic leadership is a key for leaders facing dismal environments and hostile, cohesive groups. In unfavorable settings, managerial skills related to vertical and lateral aspects of leadership may be especially important. For instance, the leader's technical skills, knowledge of the bureaucracy, persuasiveness, and planning skills may be important. Each of these may allow the leader to get additional resources for the group, reduce the involuntary changes by subordinates, and/ or tilt the balance of lateral exchanges in its favor. As an "in-group" member of the unit headed by the leader's boss, the leader may also modify some of the negative pressures on the group.

Leadership in Moderately Unfavorable Environments. It is not unusual to find fairly responsive groups operating in unfavorable environments. One typical combination is a lean environment combined with low uncertainty and high interdependence. If there's consistency between required and emergent group factors, the leader has a chance to build discretion. For instance, assume the group performs a sophisticated but not highly varied task. It is more than possible that subordinates are craftsmen or quasi-professionals who gain a good bit of satisfaction from performing the task itself. The leader probably finds few direct benefits from lateral leadership. The environment is too lean. But the leader may use initiating structure and consideration.

Structuring may be used to take innovations from one member and pass them to others. We assume the leader can recognize the technical requirements. Where there is high task interdependence with the group, leader consideration can help build cohesiveness. Even where the tasks of group members are not highly interrelated, leader consideration may act as a reward for good performance. Here we think the combination of high consideration and initiating structure may be important. Structuring helps clarify paths in doing a complex job and may help avert roadblocks, particularly for new employees. Consideration can partially act as a reward and facilitate group development by raising the stature of lower-status members. But we should also be aware of the "manure hypothesis." Too much consideration may be like too much manure. When spread indiscriminately or in too heavy a dose, it just begins to stink. Furthermore, the leader's ability to back up consideration is limited by the lean environment.

Let's turn now to more favorable environments that we hope you will encounter in your managerial career. Here, the environment of the group is more munificent (rich).

Leadership in a Favorable Environment. Extending House's thinking, we believe the leader should compensate for deficiencies that widen either the performance and/or satisfaction gap.[4] For instance, if subordinates are not clear in how a task should be performed, the leader should initiate structure to clarify the path.

There are two points that need to be discussed. One is where the environment is favorable and the nature of the group is not. For example, assume the group is hostile toward management yet in recent years the environment of the group has switched from lean to rich. We suspect the group will remain suspicious of management. Its members are likely to believe that one robin does not make a spring. Over the long haul the leader may use discretionary structuring and consideration to alter the norms of the group. But that may be difficult in the short run. Since the leader is often judged on short-term results it may be necessary to trade high short-term productivity for longer-term satisfaction. Since the leader is most interested in closing the performance gap, we suggest that Fiedler's recommendations be followed.[2] That is, the leader might emphasize task structuring and bear down on the group. He or she won't be popular and employee satisfaction may not be outstanding, but if that leader gets promoted soon enough, this short-term strategy may have its most negative effects on the career of the next formal leader.

Since favorable environments provide for discretion and generally lower the gaps the leader needs to close, a different type of question often surfaces. Specifically, what mix of leader-influence attempts is most likely to yield higher performance and satisfaction? To a large extent the specific problems facing the group and its members dictate the mix among various vertical behaviors. But an important question is the mix between vertical and lateral leadership.

We noted earlier in the analysis of groups that some favorable settings are better for the leader than the group (Chapter 12, p. 431). Specifically, where interdependence and uncertainty in the environment are high, you can expect a somewhat larger satisfaction gap. Yet, the leader has an opportunity to build the power of the group and its size. How? By coping with uncertainty and moving the group into a more powerful position vis-à-vis others. Where the group is cohesive we think the leader should take full advantage of this opportunity. Specifically, lateral leadership should be emphasized. The group's satisfaction and performance may suffer somewhat, but substitutes for leadership may be operating.[8] If the setting, the group's environment, and the nature of the group all complement each other, we expect high satisfaction and performance.

In this case, the leader has substantial discretion, but doesn't need it. Thus, the leader can focus on lateral relations as opposed to vertical behaviors. Note the paradox. When the leader needs it most, discretion is lowest. That is, the unfavorable environment widens the very gaps the leader is expected to close.

We close with two additional points. First, leadership is not management nor does it entail the technical aspects of moving the group toward its goal.[5] Leaders who can build discretion and develop a narrow performance and satisfaction gap can devote energies to other matters. They can, for instance, work on establishing new and better techniques for administering the organization and/or their area of responsibility. Second, careful tuning of environment, context, structure, and leadership does not ensure group, subsystems, or organizational effectiveness. Thus, organization theory is not the only important point of view. The well-run organization, subsystem, or group also rests on performing the technical aspects of the task. Your task as a manager will be to integrate knowledge of organizations with other information and apply your skills and knowledge.

REFERENCES

II. Strategic Advantage and Subsystems
A. Placement of Subsystems
[1]Pitts, R. "Diversification Strategies and Organizational Policies of Large Diversified Firms," *Journal of Economics and Business,* 28 (1976), 181–188.
[2]Sayles, L. *Leadership: What Effective Managers Really Do and How They Do It.* New York: McGraw-Hill, in press.
[3]Sutherland, J. *Administrative Decision-Making and Extending the Bounds of Rationality.* New York: Van Nostrand Reinhold, 1977.
B. Subsystems at the Top of the Organization
[1]Behling, C., and Schriesheim, C. *Organization Behavior: Theory, Research and Application.* Boston: Allyn and Bacon, 1976.

[2]Buchele, R. B. *The Management of Business and Public Organizations.* New York: McGraw-Hill, 1977.
[3]Chapple, E., and Sayles, L. *The Measure of Management: Designing Organizations for Human Effectiveness.* New York: Macmillan, 1961.
[4]Katz, D., and Kahn, R. *The Social Psychology of Organizations.* New York: Wiley, 1978.
[5]Koontz, H. *The Board of Directors and Effective Management.* New York: McGraw-Hill, 1967.
[6]Pfeffer, J. "Size and Composition of Corporate Boards of Directors: The Organization and Its Environment," *Administrative Science Quarterly,* 17 (1972), 218–228.
[7]Pfeffer, J., and Salancik, G. *The Ex-*

ternal Control of Organizations: A Resource Dependence Perspective. New York: Harper & Row, 1978.

[8]Thompson, J. D. Organizations in Action. New York: McGraw-Hill, 1967.

[9]Zald, M. N. "The Power and Function of Boards of Directors: A Theoretical Synthesis," American Journal of Sociology, 75 (1969), 97–111.

III. The "In Group" at the Top of the Organization

[1]Allen, M. P. "The Structure of Interorganizational Elite Cooptation: Interlocking Corporate Directorates," American Sociological Review, 39 (1974), 393–406.

[2]Cyert, R. M., and March, J. G. A Behavioral Theory of the Firm. Englewood Cliffs, N.J.: Prentice-Hall, 1963.

[3]Katz and Kahn, 1978.

[4]Pennings, J. M., and Goodman, P. S. "Toward a Framework of Organizational Effectiveness." In P. S. Goodman and J. M. Pennings (eds.), New Perspectives on Organizational Effectiveness. San Francisco: Jossey-Bass, 1977.

[5]Pfeffer, 1972.

[6]Pfeffer and Salancik, 1978.

[7]Selznick, P. Leadership in Administration. Evanston, Ill.: Row, Peterson, 1957.

[8]Thompson, 1967.

A. Constraints on Building Slack

[1]Braybrooke, D., and Lindblom, C. E. A Strategy of Decision. New York: The Free Press, 1963.

[2]Cyert and March, 1963.

[3]Gouldner, A. W. "The Norm of Reciprocity: A Preliminary Statement," American Sociological Review, 25 (1960), 161–179.

[4]Hall, R. N. Organizations: Structure and Process. Englewood Cliffs, N.J.: Prentice-Hall, 1978.

[5]Janis, I. L. Victims of Groupthink. Boston: Houghton Mifflin, 1972.

[6]Karas, T. H. "Secrecy as a Reducer of Learning Capacity in the U.S. Foreign Policy Bureaucracy," Policy Studies Journal, 3 (1974), 162–166.

[7]Katz and Kahn, 1978.

[8]March, J. G., Olsen, J., Christensen, S., Cohen, M., Enderud, H., Kreiner, K., Romelaer, P., Rommetveit, K., Stava, P., and Weiner, S. Ambiguity and Choice in Organizations. Berger, Norway: Universitetsforlaget, 1976.

[9]March, J. G., and Simon, H. A. Organizations. New York: Wiley, 1958.

[10]Osborn, R. N. "The Process of Creeping Commitment." Working paper, Department of Administrative Sciences, Southern Illinois University at Carbondale, 1978.

[11]Wieland, G., and Ullrich, R. Organizations: Behavior, Design and Change. Homewood, Ill: Irwin, 1976.

B. Advantages for the "In-Group"

[1]Hofer, C. W. "Toward a Contingency Theory of Business Strategy," Academy of Management Journal, 18 (1975), 784–809.

[2]Ritti, R. R., and Funkhouser, G. R. The Ropes to Skip and the Ropes to Know: Studies in Organizational Behavior. Columbus, Ohio: Grid, 1977.

[3]Swanberg, W. A. Luce and His Empire. New York: Scribners, 1970.

C. Trauma in the "In Group"

[1]Helmich, A. D. "Leader Flows and Organizational Process," Academy of Management Journal, in press.

[2]Osborn, R., Jauch, L., Martin, T., and

Glueck, W. "CEO Succession, Performance and Environmental Conditions." Working paper, Department of Administrative Sciences, Southern Illinois University at Carbondale, 1978.

[3]Pfeffer and Salancik, 1978.

[4]Sutherland, 1977.

IV. Using Organization Theory to Improve Your Chances of Success.

[1]Seashore, S. E. *Group Cohesiveness in the Industrial Work Group.* Ann Arbor: The University of Michigan Press, 1954.

A. Analyzing Groups

[1]Davis, L. E., and Chernes, A. E. (eds.). *The Quality of Working Life, Volumes One and Two.* New York: The Free Press, 1975.

[2]Hare, A. P. *Handbook of Small Group Research.* New York: The Free Press, 1976.

[3]Heinen, J. S., and Jacobson, E. "A Model of Task Group Development in Complex Organizations and a Strategy of Implementation," *Academy of Management Review,* 1 (1976), 98–111.

[4]Shaw, M. E. *Group Dynamics: The Psychology of Small Group Behavior.* New York: McGraw-Hill, 1976.

B. Using Leadership to Improve Your Success Potential

[1]Aldag, R. J., and Brief, A. P. "Relationships Between Leader Behavior Variability Indices and Subordinate Responses." O. C. Behling and J. G. Henderson (eds.)., *Proceedings of the Twentieth Annual Conference: Midwest Academy of Management.* Columbus, Ohio: Ohio State University, 1977.

[2]Fiedler, F. E., and Chemers, M. M. *Leadership and Effective Management.* Glenview, Ill.: Scott, Foresman, 1974.

[3]House, R. J. "A 1976 Theory of Charismatic Leadership." In J. G. Hunt and L. L. Larson (eds.), *Leadership: The Cutting Edge.* Carbondale: Southern Illinois University Press, 1977.

[4]House, R. J., and Mitchell, T. R. "Path-Goal Theory of Leadership," *Journal of Contemporary Business,* 3 (1974), 81–87.

[5]Hunt, J. G., and Larson, L. L. (eds). *Crosscurrents in Leadership.* Carbondale: Southern Illinois University Press, in press.

[6]Hunt, J. G., Osborn, R. N., and Schuler, R. S. "Relations of Discretionary and Non-Discretionary Leadership to Performance and Satisfaction in a Complex Organization," *Human Relations,* 31 (1978), 507–523.

[7]Jacobs, T. O. *Leadership and Exchange in Formal Organizations.* Alexandria, Va.: Human Resources Research Organization, 1970.

[8]Kerr, S., and Jermier, J. M. "Substitutes for Leadership: Their Meaning and Measurement," *Organizational Behavior and Human Performance,* 22, 3 (1978), 375–403.

[9]Osborn, R. N., and Bishop, R. C. "The Influence of Environmental Conditions and Unit Performance on External Relations Emphasis," *Organization and Administrative Sciences,* 6 (1976), 15–27.

[10]Osborn, R. N., Hunt, J. G., and Bussom, R. S. "On Getting Your Own Way in Organizational Design: An Empirical Illustration of Requisite Variety," *Organization and Administrative Sciences,* 8, 2–3 (1977), 295–310.

part

applications:
cases and exercises

In this part of the book you will find a set of materials designed to aid you in applying the concepts you have learned in other parts of this book. Some ask you to analyze organizations using the framework we have provided in the text. Others are descriptions of different kinds of organizations (all of them real) faced with various problems. Using these materials, you will be able to learn how to analyze organizations and make prescriptions for their improvement. The exercises and cases are consecutively numbered and preceded by a numeral that tells you to which part of the text that material is primarily related. Therefore, Exercises 1-1 and 1-2 and Cases 1-3 and 1-4 relate to Chapter 1, I-5 through I-10 relate to Part I, and so on. Cases C-26, C-27, and C-28 are comprehensive cases that integrate all the material.

Exercise 1-1   The Scientific Approach and Your Personality

This exercise will give you a chance to apply the scientific approach to evaluating something with which you are already very familiar—your personality. You should start by spending a few minutes to complete the well-known Composite Personality Test shown below. Use a separate sheet of paper to record your answers for each of the 30 questions and give this sheet to your instructor. The instructor will then score your results and go over them with you. In the process you will learn about the scientific approach.

Composite Personality Test

	Yes A	No B
1. Have you enjoyed reading books as much as having company in?	___	___
2. Are you sometimes afraid of failure?	___	___
3. Do you sometimes feel self-conscious?	___	___
4. Does it annoy you to be interrupted in the middle of your work?	___	___
5. Do you prefer serious motion pictures about historical personalities to musical comedies?	___	___

	Agree A	Disagree B	Uncertain C
6. I am going to Hell.	___	___	___
7. I sometimes get pink spots all over	___	___	___
8. The sex act is repulsive	___	___	___
9. I like strong-minded people of the opposite sex.	___	___	___

10. Strange voices speak to me.   ___ ___ ___
11. My father is a tyrant.   ___ ___ ___
12. You have been waiting patiently for a salesperson to wait on you. Just when she's finished with another customer a woman walks up abruptly and demands to be waited upon before you. What would you do?

    A ___ Nothing, B ___ Push the woman aside, C ___ Give her a piece of your mind, D ___ Comment about her behavior to the salesperson.

	Agree A	Disagree B
13. Prostitution should be state supervised.	___	___
14. Modern art should not be allowed in churches.	___	___
15. It is worse for a woman to have extramarital relations than for a man.	___	___
16. Foreigners are dirtier than Americans.	___	___
17. "The Star Spangled Banner" is difficult to sing properly.	___	___

Which word goes best with the word in capitals?

18. UMBRELLA A ___ rain, B ___ prepared, C ___ cumbersome, D ___ appeasement
19. RED A ___ hot, B ___ color, C ___ stain, D ___ blood
20. GRASS A ___ green, B ___ mow, C ___ lawn, D ___ court
21. NIGHT A ___ nude, B ___ sleep, C ___ moon, D ___ morbid
22. NAKED A ___ nude, B ___ body, C ___ art, D ___ evil
23. AUTUMN A ___ fall, B ___ leaves, C ___ season, D ___ sad
24. What would you do if you saw a woman holding a baby at the window of a burning house?

    A ___ Call the fire department, B ___ Rush into the house, C ___ Fetch a ladder, D ___ Try and catch the baby.
25. Which do you think is the best answer for an executive to make in the following situation? Worker: "Why did Jones get the promotion and I didn't?"

    Executive: A ___ "You deserved it but Jones has seniority," B ___ "You've got to work harder," C ___ "Jones' uncle owns the plant," D ___ "Let's figure out how you can improve."

	Agree A	Disagree B
26. A worker's home life is not the concern of the company.	___	___

27. Good supervisors are born, not made. ____ ____

28. It should be company policy to encourage off-hours participation by employees in company-sponsored social gatherings, clubs, teams. ____ ____

29. When you look at a great skyscraper, do you think of: A ____ Our tremendous industrial growth, B ____ The simplicity and beauty of the structural design.

30. Who helped mankind most? A ____ Shakespeare, B ____ Sir Isaac Newton.

Source: From White, W. H., Jr. *The Organization Man* (Garden City, N.Y.: Doubleday & Co., 1956). Copyright © 1956 by White, W. H., Jr. Reprinted by permission of Simon & Schuster, a Division of Gulf & Western Corporation.

Reprinted with permission.

Exercise 1-2   Organizational Analysis Exercise

For each part of the book there will be an organizational analysis exercise (see later exercises). Should your instructor choose to assign them, these exercises will give you a chance to apply the concepts you have learned to actual organizations. We think that such application can be among the most meaningful parts of the course. Make no mistake about it, though; doing a good job on the exercises is hard work! But very well-spent hard work, we would argue.

These exercises can be assigned in different ways by your instructor. For example, the instructor might use different organizations for each part or ask you to follow the same one or ones through each of the assignments. At the same time, your instructor may or may not want you to consider all the questions in each exercise. The exact way in which your instructor will want the assignments prepared will also differ. Your instructor will thus supplement the general instructions given for each of these exercises.

Here, your assignment is quite straightforward. Simply select two organizations of a similar kind to be used for one or more future organizational analysis exercises. Student organizations such as student government, fraternities, sororities, professional organizations, or clubs are possibilities. So are churches, scouting organizations and various volunteer systems with which you may be familiar. Part- or full-time work organizations are obvious candidates. Even grocery stores, dry cleaners, or eating establishments that you frequent are possibilities. The key is to choose organizations from which you can get clinical and/or questionnaire data to make the later analyses called for by your instructor. If you are somewhat familiar with one or both organizations that will prove very helpful.

Case 1-3

PONDER'S PREDICAMENT

Professor Ponder had just returned to the office with note cards from the 25 students in BA 500. They provided personal data about their academic backgrounds and work experience. This was their first course at the graduate level in organization theory in the MBA program. Dr. Ponder began analyzing the data and discovered some interesting facts.

Thirteen students had undergraduate degrees in business administration. They were about equally split in their former majors between accounting, finance, marketing, and management. Two students had degrees in economics. One student each had majored in psychology, political science, chemistry, English, and home economics. The other five students had majored in engineering fields.

When asked about career objectives, most students indicated that they planned to seek employment with industrial, commercial, or accounting firms after graduation. However, two students indicated that they planned to return to their jobs in engineering firms where they had worked for three to four years after they had earned their bachelor's degree. The political science major indicated interest in pursuing a law degree in conjunction with the MBA. The home economics student indicated interest in hospital or other institutional food service work. And two indicated they might be interested in pursuing doctoral work after the MBA.

As mentioned, two of the engineers had previous work experience. Of the business undergraduates, two had 2 or 3 years experience with public accounting firms; one had worked at the university's business office for the past 12 years, and indicated the MBA would be an aid in promotion. Two of the students (one in English and the other in marketing) were veterans who had not been able to locate good jobs after leaving the service and decided to take advantage of the GI bill.

In a class discussion about the course and the students' interests on the first day, Dr. Ponder had also picked up some other interesting facts. The engineering, accounting, and chemistry students were used to courses where their instructor assigned lots of problems. They operated under the assumption that there was one and only one right answer to these problems. Many of the other students had been used to taking true-false and multiple choice exams for which they had to "parrot back" information from texts and lectures. Few of the students had had an opportunity to analyze case material or write essay questions on exams.

After class, one of the more courageous students had asked Dr. Ponder, "Is this going to be another one of those abstract theory classes where we do a lot of mental gymnastics that lead nowhere? Or are you going to tell us what organizations are really like so we can go out and apply this stuff?" Professor Ponder said, "Let's talk about that at the next class session."

Ponder pondered. How many other students were thinking the same thing? How can I approach this issue at the next class meeting? Can I alter student expectations about this course? Will they be more comfortable with a didactic or heuristic approach? Regardless of comfort or satisfaction, what's the best way to help them learn the material? Ponder could get by with stating questionable hypotheses as positive facts so long as they fit the experience of students who had been working. But should that be done? Or should he introduce ambiguity by qualifying much of what he taught so that it fit the "facts" available? Ponder knew that satisfaction and performance are not necessarily related in other work situations—should they be related in a university classroom? If the students learn but are not happy, will their ratings of Ponder's performance be considered by the department head as good or bad?

Case 1-4

PONDER'S STUDENTS

Two of Professor Ponder's BA 500 students had just completed their second class session and were leaving the class together. In that session Ponder answered a number of questions about the nature of the class. One of the students, Hank, had an undergraduate engineering degree. He had also worked for three years as an engineer and two years as a manager. The other, Tom, was a political science major as an undergraduate. By coincidence, both had briefly looked over the entire text before the start of the term. In spite of or maybe because of Ponder's efforts to clarify expectations, Hank was clearly concerned.

He had noted the heavy emphasis on theory in the book, the so-called measurement material and the "contingency" material. He also noted a number of cases and exercises at the end of the book. He was bothered by the "theory" because it seemed so detailed, complex, and wishy-washy, not at all

like that in the engineering texts he was used to. He thought he could probably handle the measurement material. Still he wasn't sure he understood why it was important for practicing managers. Why would it be so hard to measure the commonsense notions of people he worked with?

Perhaps the biggest question was the contingency material. It looked complicated, and it did not seem to apply to any one organization, specifically. It seemed to be quite general and abstract. It wasn't at all like the models that he was used to applying from his engineering textbook. He wasn't sure how well it fit with his previous work experience. He had often wished he knew more about organizations than he did. But this could be overkill. Finally, he had a sense of uneasiness because the material looked so much harder than that of the previous management course he had taken as an undergraduate. That course too was vague, but at least it was light and easily understood. This course seemed to be vague but didn't appear light—and certainly was not easy. What did it all mean?

Tom was not too comfortable either, but for different reasons. And he was even more uncomfortable after listening to Ponder and talking to Hank. The theoretical material didn't bother him. He was used to it from his political science courses. There they couldn't come up with many definite conclusions either. And there too, so-called empirical studies were supposed to shed light on the material. He had learned to skim it and look for general conclusions, if there were any. Some of the measurement material looked interesting if he could figure out how to use it. Like Hank, though, he wondered why he couldn't just make up some questions himself to get at a lot of the concepts. If he remembered correctly, some of his previous professors or "poli sci" textbooks did that, but they weren't concerned with measurement at all.

Like Hank, though, the contingency material was most foreign to him. Earlier, he had hoped that Ponder would skip it. But after the class period just completed it was obvious that Ponder was going to stress it. In fact Ponder seemed almost in love with it. It looked like it would take a lot more effort to learn than the other material. How could he memorize that abstract stuff for an exam? Why couldn't the authors of the book (he couldn't remember who they were, but they sounded like a vaudeville team he'd once heard of) be more specific in the contingency material? Here, like Hank, he wanted application to specific, actual companies. But all it looked like the book was giving were some vague generalizations—and complicated ones at that. He didn't mind the theoretical jargon since he was used to that. But here he didn't quite know what to make of things.

After exchanging their concerns over a cup of coffee in the Student Union, Hank and Tom agreed to bring these issues up before Ponder. Ponder seemed like a good sort who might try to clarify some of these concerns for them. At the same time, though, tonight's class was particularly confusing, introducing even more ambiguity in their minds. Maybe Ponder would only confuse them further.

Exercise I-5 Evaluating Organizations

To stimulate your thinking about approaches to evaluating organizations, consider the following news release. The St. Louis district office of the Corps of Engineers is making a study to provide answers to questions including:

- Is the Mississippi a liquid superhighway to be used mainly as a convenient route for transporting goods?
- Is it a scenic wonder to be preserved at all costs in as natural a state as possible?
- Is it a natural hazard to be controlled and kept from harming life and property?
- Is it a force to be feared and avoided?

- Is it a fishing ground, a transportation route, a recreational area, or an economic resource?
- Who does the river belong to? Any of us? All of us?
- Whose job is it to plan, care for, develop, protect, and regulate uses and users?

Consider how these questions might be answered by a citizen's group, interested in preservation, and by a barge company, interested in industry. Note that the ways of judging the effectiveness of what the army corps does to the river (e.g., building dams or levees, planting trees, building marinas, etc.) will depend on the view of the group and which of the views outlined in Chapter 2 is relied upon.

Another useful exercise would be to provide an example of effectiveness criteria for each viewpoint outlined in Exhibit 2-5 for your college or university.

Exercise I-6   Organizational Analysis Exercise—Part I

Using the two organizations you selected in Exercise 1-2, address the concerns below. Discuss these concerns in terms of the concepts treated in the relevant chapters. The more direct this linkage and the more comprehensive your discussion, the higher your grade should be on this assignment.

1. How is success of each organization evaluated?
2. How is effectiveness linked via means-ends chains to lower-level performance?
3. How comprehensive are these effectiveness and performance measures in terms of those discussed in Chapters 2 and 3?
4. Which of the two organizations appears to be more effective, and is this superiority evidenced across the board? What trade-offs do you see between performance and maintenance criteria in each of the organizations?
5. As you look at the different measurement devices in Chapters 2 and 3, discuss which, if any, might be added to those already in use to evaluate how well these two organizations are doing.
6. Discuss the steps that you think would be needed in each of these organizations to set up a more comprehensive effectiveness and performance evaluation system than they currently have.

Case I-7

ACCOUNTABILITY IN PUBLIC SCHOOLS

Currently there is great concern over declining aptitude test scores and over high school graduates who can't read newspapers or fill out job applications. One response to this has been a movement to "run schools like a business": by setting learning goals, meeting quotas of students who have mastered predesignated skills, and making schools accountable for pupils who pass through their classes.

School districts have traditionally had curricula that teachers were supposed to follow. But the guidelines have often been fuzzy or not enforced by school administrators who have wanted to protect academic freedom in the classroom as well as the jobs of teachers. Under this system teachers have often taught what they wanted or what their students liked.

This push for accountability has also led to so-called competency testing on the part of states or local school systems. Under such testing, students must demonstrate a minimum level of competency on a standardized test before graduating from high school. Those advocating a goals approach to accountability argue that this is simply locking the barn after the horse is gone. They contend that under this system, schools simply certify those students who have learned rather than being held accountable for those who have failed.

One of the school systems that has moved farthest in a goals accountability

Source: Based on an article by W. M. Bulkeley in The Wall Street Journal, (May 30, 1978), 1, 15.

approach is that of Indian Hill, an affluent suburb of Cincinnati. Five years ago a committee of residents decided that the school system was inefficient. The curriculum was loose and there was no systematic evaluation of performance. The school board forced out the former superintendent and hired an accountability-oriented school head. "We know if we're failing," he says, "we can change the program, change the books or change the teachers."

The new superintendent's first task was to define general goals that could be turned into curricula. For this he established a committee of 50 school administrators, teachers, parents, and students. The committee spent a year obtaining and processing parent input and came up with a set of goals. Teachers then built a sequential elementary school program around these goals. First they concentrated on reading, writing, and arithmetic. Each subject is broken down into specific objectives. For example, fourth-grade students must be able to "interpret the basic emotions of the characters in a story." Quick, four-question multiple-choice tests are used as measuring devices. Movement is now underway to teach other courses in this way and to extend the system into the high schools.

Along with a letter grade, parents receive reports of the skills their children have mastered. They are also told the specific things a child will be able to do by the end of the year.

How are those treated who can't

master the skills? Eighty-five percent of the children in each class are expected to pass the skills tests. Those who don't are either given extra help or put in special classes. Money has been set aside for this.*

Teachers whose pupils consistently fail the skills tests are given help by the principal and/or other teachers. If that doesn't work they are "counseled out." Fifteen Indian Hill teachers have left in this manner in the last three years. The teachers are not supposed to be evaluated on the basis of test results. However, there is concern that the tests will become the yardsticks for measuring performance.

"The manifestation of accountability is making teachers responsible for things over which they haven't any con-

---

*The Indian Hill school system spends a total of $1530 per pupil compared with the Ohio average of $1400.

trol," says a National Education Association official. Teachers wonder about what will happen if they get a number of slow learners or disruptive students.

There are also a number of other issues. First, there is a considerable amount of record keeping and paperwork. How will the teachers have time to prepare and grade all those tests and keep a running record of each student's progress? Second, teachers may "teach to the tests" and ignore other things. Third, some parents wonder if all this emphasis on measurement isn't taking precedence over integration and if it won't harm some of the minority students. Finally, some of the teachers are concerned that they didn't have enough input into setting up the system. They wonder what parents and other lay people know about professional education? They also wonder how a teacher can maintain academic freedom within a system like this.

Case I-8

THE ROVING CHURCH CRITIC

Mr. George R. Plagenz, religion editor of the *Cleveland Press,* has become what may be the nation's only roving church critic. He drops in on churches unannounced and uses stars to evaluate the service in four different categories. These are: (1) worship service; (2) music; (3) sermon; and (4) friendliness of the congregation.

He awards up to 3 stars in each category. He then totals these and derives a score where: 4 to 6 is fair, below that

Source: Based on an article by M. N. Dodosh in *The Wall Street Journal* (June 12, 1978), 1, 27.

poor, and 10 or more is good to excellent. He looks at each church or synagogue in three ways: (1) how does the service impress him; (2) how do congregation members react; and (3) what is keeping people away from the church. He is most concerned with the third area. He feels that the worship service is the key evangelical tool to get individuals to come to the Lord and that if it is handled ineptly, people stay home.

Since his ratings are part of a newspaper religion column, he supplements them with descriptive narrative. In addition to a 12-star rating, he commented that a Baptist church congregation performed hymns "with more gusto than Schlitz." He also liked the preacher, who blasted "lily-livered clergymen who deny heaven and hell and never talk about the blood [of Christ]."

Mr. Plagenz is a graduate of the Harvard Divinity School and in the early 1950s was ordained a Unitarian minister. He later went into news broadcasting and secular journalism. He was once a copyboy and sportswriter for the newspaper where he is now the religion editor.

While he has only given two 12-star ratings, the lowest one he has given so far is 7 stars (average). He says he tends to be an easy rater who doesn't want to be too mean or nasty.

Ministers have tended to react as you might predict. Some have likened him to the late Duncan Hines, the culi-

nary expert who gave his seal of approval to selected eating establishments throughout the country. Others, whose churches have been criticized, have been quite defensive.

His pet peeves strongly influence his reviews and usually cost the church or synagogue at least one star. For example, he doesn't like the minister's admonition to "turn around and shake hands," which occurs at many churches. He also dislikes organists who make recitals out of their accompaniments.

Have these evaluations led to changes? Mr. Plagenz indicates only one known case where attempts to change were made. He attributes this lack of response to the headstrongness of ministers, and organists too. Nevertheless, he feels his column is worthwhile because it makes people think. He feels that is important in trying to find out why so many people don't come to church.

Case I-9
CONFESSIONS OF A RESTAURANT MANAGEMENT CONSULTANT

Janet Rainey from Fastrack Associates, Inc. had been called in as a consultant for $400 a day plus expenses to examine an expanding restaurant chain. The chain consisted of 20 units, 18 of which were in Illinois, with one each in a small central Indiana city and a large Kentucky city. The chain had recently merged with a nationwide conglomerate and Janet had been called in shortly after the merger to see what, if any, changes

Source: Adapted from a course assignment prepared by D. Yocum for Professor J. G. Hunt, Southern Illinois University, Carbondale. Copyright © Osborn, Hunt, and Jauch, 1980.

seemed to be in order. The conglomerate's top management was especially interested in her reactions to the performance evaluation system. The chain was started in 1963. Before merging it was family owned. Most of the top executives (these include chairman of the board, president, and vice-president) were and still are relatives and large share owners. Each unit (restaurant) is primarily operated by an owner-manager who invests $25,000 into the restaurant to earn 20 percent of the profits. These profits are paid out monthly as a bonus to each owner-manager. Janet was impressed when she found that the return on investment for one manager in the previous year was 70 percent on his initial investment.

Each owner-manager has a night manager and a relief manager to help. However, most night managers are considered trainees for the owner-manager spot. Thus, each owner-manager is primarily responsible for a given unit. He or she supervises employees, greets customers, orders supplies, handles the cash register and daily receipts, and regulates all supplies and equipment within the restaurant.

Each of the 20 units has undergone occasional area managerial changes due to the expansion of the company. Each owner-manager reports to an area manager. The area managers report to the Director of Operations—a vice-president. Other vice-presidents oversee finances and personnel. The main office is located in the northern part of Illinois.

In checking the current evaluation system, Janet found that each owner-manager was evaluated by the top executives on the basis of the monthly performance of his or her unit. This was determined by a point system based on management by objectives (see Exhibit V-1). A high score entitled each manager to buy 5 percent of another unit at the next company drawing. In addition to this point system, Janet found that a figure labeled "prime" was very important.

Exhibit V-1 Point System for Director of Operations, Area Managers, and Owner-Managers

	Mini- mum	Aver- age	Maxi- mum
1. Return on investment as stated in budget	2	3	5
2. Gross sales as stated in budget	2	3	5
3. Food costs as stated in budget	9	13	16
4. Labor costs as stated in budget	9	13	16
5. Supply costs as stated in budget	10	12	14
6. Operating costs as stated in budget	1	2	3
7. Customer service			
a. Speed of food	1½	2½	3½
b. Quality of food	1½	2½	3½
c. Master schedule complete	3	5	7
d. Cleaning report	3	5	7
e. Greeting and seating of customers	3	5	7
f. Dress code 100% by department (based on wearing specified outfits)	3	5	7
8. Audit report	2	4	6
Total	50	75	100

This prime, expressed as a percent, was summarized monthly for each unit. It consisted of direct costs divided by total sales (adjusted for sales tax) for each month. It ignored customer service, but showed the approximate productivity or profitability percentage-wise of each restaurant. These primes were published with great fanfare in the company newsletter to serve as an incentive to the owner-managers (see an example in Exhibit V-2). The newsletter suggested an emphasis by top management on low prime percentages. To get an idea of what a profile of "primes" might look like for three restaurants with similar sales volume, Janet put together the data in Exhibit V-3 for the five months pre-

Exhibit V-2 Example Newsletter for July, 19—

TIGER PAW, TIGER PAW, IT'S A TERRIFIC PLACE WHERE FOOD IS GREAT
Prime Standings

(These averages tell the job your unit did in all around performance in July.)

Southern Division: Lewis "Bud" Smith[a]—Area Supervisor

July 19__

Pearsons Grove	59.10	Bamle, Dej, Plumber*
Lafayette	59.12	Carlson, Stone, Painter*
Kuma	59.17	McKey, Delmer, Bunting*
Springdale	59.82	Goodwin, Syse,* and Metz
Osto	59.83	Oloe, Dern, Myers*
Spring Arbor	61.66	Peon, Horn, Stein*
Forestville	63.39	Shoat, Vers, Peters*
Sin City	66.43	Consekos
Connors Park	86.95	Vymer, Lynd, Kamikazie*

*Indicates Relief Manager

Central Division: Larry Sundal—Area Supervisor

Bison Grove	57.79	Bear, Conesti
Pt. Pleasant	59.35	Hull, Baldwin, Tom*
Deschutes	60.37	Ham, Johnson, Stroh*
Moosefield	60.52	Jock, Carly, Strupak*
Lake Forest	61.66	Luiji, Baume, Manfriedo*
Carol Brook	61.72	Kupple, Smyth, Shane*
Chestnut Park	62.20	Kuhn, Marzeti
Watson Glen	62.42	Sancho, Paltre, Derringer,* Jantz*
Alderson	62.45	Smythe, Dolb*

Northern Division: Andy Morning Star—Area Supervisor

| Farstar | 67.67 | Come, Patterson, Dom* |
| Edwina | 71.12 | Batz, Brown, Guerney,* and Peters |

The Southern Division reversed the standings. Last month, the Central Division had 6 below 60 percent, and this month they had 5 below the 60 mark. Look who was the leader by a hen's tooth. Mitch Bamle, Dej, and Plumber of our new Pearsons Grove unit. Then just two-tenths of a point in back of him comes Lafayette's Carlson, Stone, and Painter, and from then on it's so close again with Kuma's McKey, Delmer, and Bunting showing the way. One egg separates Osto and Springdale. Shoat, like the Cubs, had a rough July going from first to seventh place. Jock says they will be back for August.

Tiger's Bison Grove unit can't lick the office softball team, but they walloped the other 7 units and ended in No. 1 spot. Big Jim and Conesti are a rough team. Hul!, Baldwin, and Tom brought our new Pt. Pleasant unit into second. Deschutes and Moosefield were a close third. We understand Herb Johnson is doing a fine job as night manager at Deschutes, plus his crew leaves the unit spotless for the day shift. An orchid to all of you.

[a]All names of persons and cities have been changed.

ceding her visit. After careful consideration, Janet felt that the current evaluation system was a step in the right direction but didn't go far enough. She proposed the following changes.

First, employee turnover cost did not seem to be adequately represented in the current approach. Janet recognized a trade-off in direct cost here since new employees could be hired for minimum wage while experienced employees made as much as 70 percent more per hour. However, she was concerned by the increased training and customer reactions to inexperienced help that resulted from high turnover.

Second, in interviewing some of the company officials she discovered a concern with the turnover of management trainees. Although these officials had no direct figures, they felt that this was becoming increasingly costly.

Third, it was her judgment that if there were a sustained loss in sales over a one- or two-year period, something was wrong with management. Thus, she felt some method of evaluation should be provided on a monthly basis to help management correct potential problems. She reasoned that the dollar amount of profit and not just percentages should be considered. A high dollar amount of profit might indicate good business and a good manager. Likewise, a low profit might suggest a weak business and high costs.

Finally, it was her judgment that customer attitudes were important and should be reflected in an evaluation system.

She revised the current MBO system to reflect each of these concerns as negative point values to be subtracted from the originally designated overall values.

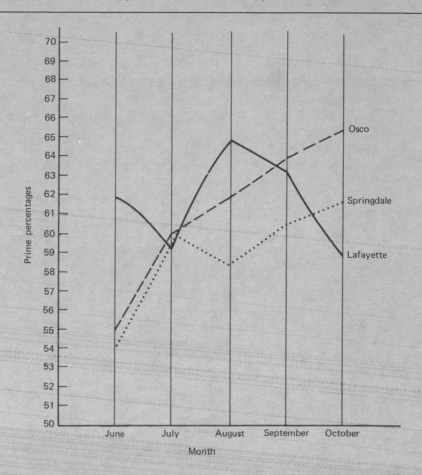

Although the weightings were arbitrary, they were designed to be heavy enough so that managers would take them seriously. The revised point system is shown in Exhibit V-4.

To determine point 7f in the exhibit, Janet proposed a random survey of customers taken at various peak and slow time periods. She proposed that five customers per unit per month would be ap-propriate. A copy of her proposed survey is shown as Exhibit V-5.

In discussing her report with her boss, Janet confessed that she was not really sure that even the revised evaluation system included enough kinds of criteria. Her boss said that though some might accuse her of "selling out to management," he felt that her recommendations went far enough.

Exhibit V-4 Revised Point System

	Mini- mum	Aver- age	Maxi- mum
1. Return on investment as stated in budget	2	3	5
a. Loss in store profits cost	−3	−5	−7
2. Gross sales as stated in budget	2	3	5
3. Food costs as stated in budget	9	13	16
4. Supply costs as stated in budget	10	12	14
5. Operating costs as stated in budget	1	2	3
a. High employee turnover cost	−3	−5	−7
b. Manager trainee turnover cost	−9	−13	−16
6. Labor costs as stated in budget	9	13	16
7. Customer services			
a. Speed of food	1½	2½	3½
b. Quality of food	1½	2½	3½
c. Master schedule complete	3	5	7
d. Cleaning report	3	5	7
e. Greeting and seating of customers	3	5	7
f. Unfavorable customer interview costs	−3	−5	−7
g. Dress code 100% by department	3	5	7
8. Audit report	2	4	6
Total	50	75	100

Exhibit V-5 Sample Survey

Personal interview, open-ended questions:
1. Does this restaurant appear clean and inviting to you?
2. What do you think of your waitress?
3. What do you think of your food?
   a. Size of portions?
   b. Quality of food?
   c. Appearance of food?
4. Will you return again as a customer soon? If not, why not?
5. In general, is this restaurant as good (or bad) as others where you have dined?

EARNING "WELL PAY"

Parson's Pine Products, Inc., in Ashland, Oregon, employs about 100 workers to cut lumber into specialty items, ranging from rattrap bases to bifold doors. It is believed to be the biggest U.S. producer of these items.

It offers an extra eight hours wages ("well pay") to workers who are neither absent nor late for an entire month. In addition to well pay, the firm offers retro pay, safety pay, and profit-sharing pay.

Retro pay is a bonus based on any reductions in premiums received from Oregon's accident insurance fund. Before this plan went into effect in 1976, the firm had an accident rate 86 percent above the statewide base and paid the fund accordingly. The workers were informed that they would recieve any retroactive refunds based on a lowered accident rate. The next year's accident bill dropped to $2500 from $28,500 the year before. After deducting administrative expenses, the state will refund about $89,000 of a $100,000 premium. The company president indicated that a number of other accident prevention measures were taken along with this retro pay.

Safety pay of two hours wages is given to any employee remaining accident-free for a month.

A profit-sharing bonus is based on everything the business earns over 4 percent, after taxes. Workers are rated in terms of four categories of excellence. The bonus is figured as a percentage of each person's wages multiplied by the category. The better employees usually get 8 to 10 percent bonuses, with a bonus one year of 16½ percent. Two-thirds of the bonus is in cash, the rest goes into the retirement fund.

The "well pay" brought lateness down close to zero. It also cut absenteeism, sometimes too much. Some workers came to work sick. The president then had to show them how much more accident prone they were, and how that would cut their retro pay.

The president has shown workers how they can contribute to profit. He sets up a pyramid of 250 rattrap bases, each representing $10,000 in sales. He knocks 100 onto the floor for raw materials. Another 100 drop to the floor for wages. Of the 50 left, he points out that that's where everything else, including profits, comes from.

After the last Christmas luncheon, the workers asked for the afternoon off. The president said fine but it would cost $3000. The workers voted almost unanimously to work that afternoon.

Source: Adapted from "How to Earn 'Well Pay,'" *Business Week* (June 12, 1978), pp. 143–146.

Exercise II-11   Organizational Analysis Exercise—Part II

Keep in mind the general instructions and admonitions for the previous organizational analysis exercises. Use the two organizations agreed upon with your instructor and address the concerns below.

1. Define the appropriate boundaries for the general environment of each of the two organizations.
2. Obtain the necessary information for the relevant general environment variables for each of these two organizations.
3. Assess the general degree of development, uncertainty, and disparity within the general environment for each of these two organizations.
4. Describe and obtain the necessary information for the specific environment for each of these two organizations.
5. Assess the degree of interdependence, uncertainty, and development within the specific environment for each of these two organizations.
6. Combining the general and specific environmental evaluations above, assess environmental complexity for each of these two organizations.
7. Which environmental variable(s) seems to be most important for each of these two organizations? Why?
8. What relationship do you see between environmental variables and efficiency/performance criteria in each of these organizations?

Case II-12

BRAZCO UTILITY

Brazco is an electric utility that operates in over 150 towns in the State of Parana (roughly the same size as the state of Texas), in southern Brazil. It is located in the capital of the state (about 600,000 inhabitants). The company, which was founded in 1954, has approximately 2000 employees. It is incorporated, with the majority of its stock being held by the government of the

State of Parana and the rest by private individuals. Its capital is approximately 90 billion cruzeiros ($30 million). Its top-level positions are filled with people appointed directly by the governor of the state. The other management positions of the various departments are occupied by people selected, hired, and trained according to the company's standards.

Brazco is a mixture of private and public enterprises. It is, in the language of the economists, a "mixed-economy" company. It has the freedom of action that private companies enjoy, and be-

Source: Adapted from a course assignment prepared by A. F. S. Lobo, for Professor J. G. Hunt, Southern Illionois University, Carbondale. Copyright © Osborn, Hunt, and Jauch, 1980.

cause it is disassociated from the general structure of the state administration, there is less bureaucracy to hamper its operations. On the other hand, being controlled directly by the government of the state, it receives the impact of current political events more sharply.

Brazco's role in the process of the economic development of the state is essential. It has undertaken, practically by itself, the urgently needed generation and transmission of electrical energy for the state. Since current needs far exceed the supply of electric power, Brazco, in spite of its gigantic programs of investment and projects, is frequently viewed by large segments of the public as a deceptive organism of the dominant political structure.

Thus, public opinion has always been a major concern for the top administration of the organization. As a result, special emphasis has been put on promoting the name of the company and its projects. The unit responsible for this key funtion is the *assessoria de relacoes publicas* (public relations department). It is this unit that is the focus of this case and covers a recent three-year period.

The department consisted of: a director, a layout man, an administrative assistant, an assistant news editor, a news analyst, a press release manager (the case writer), a typist, and an assistant layout man. The director, Jose Munez, was seen by his subordinates as extremely harddriving and demanding. He was deeply involved with all phases of the department and this was believed by many to contribute to the importance attached to the public relations function by the company president. Munez's subordinates were dissatisfied with him.

This was compounded by the fact that they felt underpaid.

Inflation was rampant, with a resulting continual erosion of purchasing power. Thus, a main preoccupation of a large segment of the employees was whether raises were keeping up with the runaway inflation. In many cases they were not, and that was the feeling of the public relations employees. Furthermore, they were paid less than other professional employees in the company. There were strongly demonstrated feelings about this issue, and it appeared to make most of the PR (public relations) people unconcerned about their individual productivity. At the same time, though they felt shortchanged by the company, there were very few places where they could expect to get equivalent salaries for similar work.

The PR department members had a feeling of superiority about their jobs in comparison with those of other administrative units. They felt their job required more creativity and mental activity. This feeling became stronger over time and added to the dissatisfaction with Mr. Munez. It was felt that his lack of clout with the directors was the reason for the inadequate pay increases.

All of this and more grew worse from day-to-day. Work piled up on the desks. The casewriter was called "the Slave," for trying to keep the work moving and not joining in the now almost hourly breaks taken by others in the department.

The situation might well have come to a head late in the year were it not for the upcoming governmental elections. Since government funds primarily supported the energy activities of Brazco, a major visitation campaign was launched by the PR department. The objective was to impress the populace and particularly public officials with the job that Brazco was doing. This campaign developed a great deal of enthusiasm within the PR department. However, after the elections passed, the previous situation returned, worse than ever, since the most recent pay raise caused the workers' buying power to fall even further behind the soaring inflation.

The casewriter's position required a great deal of contact with the heads of all the technical departments whose projects he was publicizing. As might be expected these people were generally very cooperative. Heads of administrative units whose work was not publicized by the PR department were another story, however. These individuals regarded the PR department as a pretty ineffective and completely dispensable unit. Their subordinates, however, envied the freedom of the people in the unit and the variety of tasks carried out.

The casewriter frequently visited the regional electrical systems Brazco operated throughout the state. His purpose was to handle institutional advertising through newspapers and radio stations. He perceived that the heads of these branches of Brazco had negative attitudes about the effectiveness of the PR department. Because of the severe inflation there was an almost constant round of electricity rate increases for consumers. The PR department's mission was to mold consumers' reactions to these rate increases by explaining the need for them. Unfortunately, even after these campaigns, consumers responded negatively to the rate increases, and their wrath was felt especially hard at the regional level of Brazco. There were also some utility companies that were able to keep their rates at a lower level than Brazco. All of these factors influenced the branch heads' perceptions of the PR department's effectiveness. In addition, Mr. Munez did not endear himself to these branch heads in his contacts with them.

Case II-13

THE ROAR OF THE CROWD

Two sociologists have recently studied the so-called home-field advantage and its relationship to athletic team success. They contend that this advantage is not because of familiarity with the playing area but because of the fans themselves. In fact, they go so far as to argue that the contribution of the fans is as important as the quality of the team

Source: Based on a column by J. Myers in the *St. Louis Post Dispatch* (May 18, 1978), 2D.

or the ability of the players. This works both ways. A wildly cheering crowd can be as helpful to a team's success as a home run. At the same time, a hostile crowd can be as detrimental as a fumble on a crucial play. The sociologists' data suggest that the fans are the main reason teams win more at home than on the road.

How much more? The researchers report that teams win the following percentage of time at home: 53 percent in pro baseball; 59 percent in pro football; 60 percent in college football; 64 percent in hockey (including ties); and 65 percent in pro basketball. Also, home teams have won 68 percent of the play-off games in pro basketball over the last 25 years.

Why is this? The researchers report that a crowd quick to show displeasure, if not hostility, produces a kind of schizophrenic team. Players' moods swing up and down and their play is affected. Likewise, if the fans strongly support the team, the players feel this and are encouraged in times of distress. A chicken and egg question emerges here: Which came first—the winning team or the enthusiastic fans? The researchers deduce that it is more likely that the fans cause the winning team than that the winning team causes the cheering fans. Probably it is some of both.

So perhaps you shouldn't be too surprised if the next time your favorite team loses, the players stride to midfield and boo the crowd in unison. For the crowd must share the blame for the defeat.

Case II-14

WHITHER ROCKWELL?

Al Rockwell, Jr., was the son of the founder of Rockwell International Corporation. He sat in his plush president's office in Pittsburgh contemplating some acquisitions to bolster the huge conglomerate's consumer products business. Rockwell's latest sales totaled $5.9 billion from automotive components, industrial goods, electronics, and consumer products. Of these, consumer goods sales totaled a bit under $470 million.

Rockwell's overall sales were up nearly 80 percent in the last four years. Earnings, during that same period, though, had gone from about $127 million down to almost zero to a bit over $144 million at latest count. Pretax income as a percent of sales dropped from about 7 percent to about 3.5 percent and was now at just under 5 percent.

Source: Adapted from Business Week (May 29, 1978), 60–66.

Mr. Rockwell was concerned about this erratic growth pattern and felt that strengthening consumer sales could help. This was despite the advice of many who told him to capitalize on the company's strengths rather than going with a loser. And the consumer products division had certainly been a loser. It lost $19 million during the latest fiscal year.

Rockwell would basically like to have a roughly equal balance among government, industrial, and consumer sales. This point was driven home with the recent government cancellation of Rockwell's B-1 bomber program and the previous spotty success in consumer product lines. Key examples of the spotiness are the aborted electronic calculator and digital watch ventures and the acquisition of the Admiral television and refrigerator-freezer lines.

On the former, Rockwell lost about $36 million when it was unsuccessful in trying to expand its semiconductor technology from its North American Aviation division to the consumer products. Its effort there peaked just as the 1974 recession hit and the Japanese aggressively entered the calculator and digital watch markets. Texas Instruments also came on aggressively at about this time, with remarkable success. On the latter, the data are not yet all in. Rockwell had hoped to increase the market penetration of the old-line Admiral brand name. It has spent the last four years trying to overhaul the Admiral product line. Yet the TV line has done so poorly that Rockwell himself says he would drop it if he could. On the other hand, Rockwell has just introduced nine new models in the refrigerator-freezer line. These are supposed to be more energy efficient than 95 percent of all models. The firm is also dickering with General Motors about acquiring its Frigidaire line. Should that be accomplished, Admiral would have close to 20 percent of that market.

How did the firm get where it is today? It started as an auto parts manufacturer, and in 1967 acquired North American Aviation. At that time Rockwell's sales were some $600 million, while North American's were some $2 billion. The acquisition was designed to build up high technology expertise from the vast flow of government research and development funds. It was hoped that the development of such technology would not only result in huge chunks of future government business, but would transfer to other product lines as well.

It was soon obvious, though, that there was so much uncertainty and volatility in business of this kind that diversification was needed. Rockwell then added Collins Radio and Admiral. Both were in trouble. Collins blended nicely with the highly sophisticated electronic capability of the Autonetics division, which developed guidance systems for the military. While Collins was successful, Admiral is still questionable. A multimillion dollar attempt to add electronic capability to knitting machines failed, and Rockwell has not yet been successful in mass producing electronic equipment.

One knowledgeable insider points out that no one in aerospace has transferred that technology to a high-volume consumer product. Based on its acquisitions, the major problem that appears to have plagued Rockwell has been lack of marketing savvy. It appears to lack the marketing expertise necessary to compete with entrenched and new domestic or foreign competitors. For example, it had been reasonably successful in its efforts at manufacturing electronic calculators for Sears. When it went to market its own, though, it could not weather the abrupt price drops and extreme competition.

In addition to its consumer product problems, the company has been hurt by the cancellation of the B-1 bomber project. Had the bomber gone into production, Rockwell would have been one of the premier aircraft manufacturers in the forseeable future. Instead, in addition to lost profits, it lost an experienced pool of workers capable of building large supersonic aircraft. On top of this, the firm's operations that build corporate planes have been losing money. It has joined forces with Fuji Industries in an attempt to strengthen this area. The market, though, is overcrowded and Rockwell has concentrated on a limited number of models rather than challenging industry leaders across the board.

A bright spot is the firm's space business. Over the last few years, Rockwell has been NASA's largest contractor, with contracts of more than $11 billion to date. It hopes to use its space-shuttle orbiter as a base for future industrialization of space.

Knowledgeable outsiders have expressed the opinion that Rockwell lacks the know-how to be successful in consumer products. Al Rockwell claims the company has learned valuable lessons from its previous problems and can become bigger and stronger in all the fields it is in. Some of Rockwell's people, on the other hand, argue that opportunities in the industrial and automotive areas are where the firm should sink its vast financial resources. These resources have been remarkably strengthened over the last couple of years by a hardnosed management approach.

Case II-15

BYE, BYE BI-STATE?

Nestled in the heart of one of the largest Standard Metropolitan Statistical Areas in the United States lies the Bi-State Development Agency. A key part of the mission of this agency is the provision of bus service on the Missouri and Illinois sides of the St. Louis metropolitan area. The agency is subsidized by a half-cent sales tax in Missouri as well as receiving support from Illinois. Bi-State recently consolidated its operations into the bus system headquarters in St. Louis, so that the executive director could be in closer contact with his subordinates.

The director, Barry M. Locke, was hired in December of a recent year. The case describes events transpiring over the next six to seven months. Locke's mission as defined by the Bi-State commissioners who set agency policy was to end the poor service that was characteristic of the bus system for many years. The commissioners indicated that they wanted heads to roll if necessary to carry out the mandate.

Locke moved aggressively to carry out his orders. As a result, political leaders and union leaders as well as others have been most upset with him. Among other things, he is accused of lowering morale at upper levels in the bus system. A recent action of his was to fire a black personnel director with more than twenty years experience.

On the other hand, most of those on the commission feel he is addressing previously ignored problems that were leading to deterioration of the system. One member stated that the system had not been efficient or effective. Service was poor and cost control was loose. Another commissioner stated that there were dirty, late, and broken-down buses, as well as discourteous drivers. There was also cheating on overtime, so that

Source: Based on material included in the *St. Louis Post Dispatch* (May 14, July 2, 3, 6, 1978).

some drivers were paid as much as $600 a week. One worker would arrange with a partner not to work. The partner would get overtime. Then later they would reverse roles.

The commissioner went on to point out that maintenance had been so bad that some buses would not start in the mornings. Late-night drivers would leave the buses idle all night. That caused fuel-cost problems. Locke fired the maintenance director at the same time he did the personnel director.

A commissioner indicated that these firings were well within the authority granted Locke. However, if Locke should alienate important community groups such as labor unions, blacks, and others, to the point where he should become a hindrance to the commission, then he would be forced to leave. The commissioner indicated he didn't think this point had been reached. In fact, he praised Locke for bringing more blacks in at all levels.

Black state legislators from Missouri were upset by the firing of the personnel director. They threatened to oppose the half-cent sales tax subsidy when it came up for renewal the following year.

Along with this there was a wildcat strike by the union. Drivers were upset over an impasse in contract negotiations. Locke had made public a letter in which he said he felt it unnecessary to abide by conditions in the old contract. He had also made public statements about sabotage of buses. These statements particularly annoyed an influential black as well as the president of the transit workers local to which the drivers belonged. The wife of the black was a leader of the legislative black caucus and had been critical of Locke for his handling of blacks in middle-management positions.

Some have argued that even though driver salaries are good ($16,000 to $19,000 a year) internal dissension within the union is causing much of the union turmoil. Locke contends that such dissension is largely due to black-white rivalries in the union. However, the union head and a black leader within the union argue that the rivalries and divisions are due to age. Younger drivers concerned with higher wages are clashing with older drivers concerned with pensions and other fringes. Most younger drivers are black, most older drivers are white.

Locke unilaterally lowered the pay of starting drivers from 85 percent to 70 percent that of experienced drivers. He did this even after the union had rejected this as a proposal. He also caught flak for releasing some information on matters covered in negotiations. There had been an agreement not to do this. To all this Locke indicates that his critics have failed to come up with responsible alternatives, and he isn't going to "capitulate to inefficiency and ineffectiveness."

In the meantime, the St. Louis County Supervisor (similar to a city mayor), his transportation commission, and the county council have involved themselves in the problems of Bi-State. The county and city levy the half-cent tax and control the money for the agency. However, Bi-State assumes responsibility for operating the system. This leads to the temptation to use political pressure to control the agency. Thus, the county supervisor, council, and transportation commission have forced Bi-State to discontinue zone fares and to provide services often unneeded and unused. On top of this, the county has withheld several million dollars in revenues from the agency and is looking for ways to use these funds on pork-barrel projects. Meanwhile, Bi-State's plans for additional drivers and maintenance personnel have been curtailed.

Watching all this with extreme interest has been the mayor of St. Louis. He has proposed to follow the county's lead. At its most recent meeting, the county council discussed the problem of irate customers on nonair-conditioned buses. During a 100-plus degree heat wave, as high as 15 percent of the buses had nonfunctioning air conditioners. Locke, last winter, had ordered that all air conditioners be repaired by May 15. Nearly 400 new buses were found to have defective units. Some mechanics have been working more than 60 hours a week repairing the air conditioning. The Bi-State maintenance director has said that if the county doesn't give the agency the funding it requested (and for which subsidy money is available) he can't keep up with air-conditioner repairs. County representatives are arguing, in effect, that if the agency can't provide good service it shouldn't get the full subsidy.

Keep in mind the general instructions and admonitions for the previous organizational analysis exercises. Use the two organizations agreed upon with your instructor and address the concerns below.

1. Specify the size of each of the two organizations.
2. Describe the dominant technologies in these two organizations.
3. Estimate the dominant administrative philosophy of top management in each of these two organizations.
4. Assess the degree of contextual complexity in each of these two organizations.
5. Assess key aspects of as many of these as feasible:
   a. Vertical specialization and control.
   b. Horizontal specialization and coordination.
   c. Bottom-up structure.
6. Discuss the relative importance that you think each of the above variables has on criteria in each of these two organizations.
7. Assess the overall degree of structural complexity in each of these two organizations.
8. Discuss the matches between environment and contextual variables, and comment on whether structural variables are appropriate for each of these two organizations.
9. Discuss the impact that you think the strategic advantages have on criteria in each of these two organizations.
10. Generally, how might you proceed to obtain a better match among the above variables in each of these two organizations?

Case III-17

THE FRUSTRATED TRAVEL AGENTS

"You feel like an idiot because you're supposed to know what you're doing," replied a manager of a large travel agency, recently. The reason was the upsurge in airline discount fares with the easing of restrictions by the Civil Aeronautics Board (CAB). Most airlines now have a minimum of 20 different categories of discount fares, each with complex conditions, and with new fares being introduced constantly. American Airlines, for example, now offers a systemwide total of 86 varieties of fares. In

Source: Based on the article "More Work, Less Profit for Travel Agents," *Business Week* (June 19, 1978), 123–129.

many cases, the travel agencies read about the new fares in newspaper ads before the airlines explain them. Customers, of course, expect the agency to be able to get them the lowest discount fare with the least onerous restrictions.

At the latest count there were 13,459 travel agency *locations* in the United States, accredited by the Air Traffic Conference (ATC). The ATC is composed of all scheduled airline carriers and a key function is to ensure that blank tickets do not get into unauthorized hands. A key reason for using locations rather than companies is that there are a number of large, multilocation firms.

In earlier days, the ATC protected an agency's territory by not accrediting a new one that was too close. However, that time is long past. The number of new agencies is up 83 percent since 1970. One source estimated that the industry's total sales volume tripled to $15 billion since 1970. However, another source estimated it at $11.5 billion.

Agencies get their remuneration from commissions paid by the companies whose services the agent buys. These range from 7 to 11 percent domestically. However, internationally the commission structure has so many incentives built into it that the sky is almost the limit.

For the period ending June 30, 1977, U.S. travel agencies received commissions for domestic air travel totaling $420 million. The cost for this was $443 million. International air travel had $246 million in commissions and costs of $183 million. Commissions from hotels, car rentals, etc. brought in an additional $19 million. All this was back in the "stable days" before the CAB opened up the fare structure. One agency, with 100 locations, reported that with the new fare structure, it was selling 35 to 40 percent more tickets, but revenue was increasing only 20 to 25 percent. Some small agencies are having to hire office business managers for the first time, and that often absorbs their profit.

The new fares mean a greater need for employee education. Often, in small agencies, this can be a problem because it requires closing the office while the sessions are being conducted. Many agencies fear their reputation for professionalism has suffered since they have trouble keeping on top of the rates.

To try to keep abreast of the chaotic rate structure, agencies have increasingly been calling airlines reservations desks. This has meant getting busy signals and being put on hold, often for very long periods of time. Sometimes a phone is tied up for hours by a single large agency.

To alleviate this, some larger firms have leased terminals hooked up to an airline's reservations computer. There is also teleticketing whereby the ticket is prepared automatically. The average cost for each such terminal (one per airline) is roughly $1000 per month. An experiment using a multiple-access terminal, tied in with every major airline computer, is now being conducted.

One partial solution to this ever-changing fare structure is to deal with corporate clients. These customers do not require large amounts of time devoted to explaining discounts. In fact, until recently, few of them qualified. The problem, though, is that they tend to change their plans much more than vacationers. One agency reports that its average reservation for corporate clients is changed three times. Also, corporations often take months to pay an agency, while the agency must settle its accounts within seven days. Agencies get around this by requiring credit cards from corporate customers, but now the airlines have to add that fee to their commission payment.

Because of all this, some travel agencies are beginning to institute separate charges to their customers for services that have traditionally been included in the commission received from the airlines, car rental agencies, and the like.

Case III-18

THE DOE IN DISARRAY

The new headquarters of the Department of Energy (DOE), on the seventh floor of a modern government building, is in physical disarray. This physical disorder, though probably temporary, is representative of the operating plight of the $10 billion a year agency. It has been in operation eight months and employs 20,000 people.

A number of people use the terms, "shambles" and "disaster area" to describe the department. Some even claim it to be the most hated agency in Washington. All this in less than a year.

To begin with, DOE's employees are scattered among 20 Washington buildings. To call a meeting of top assistants, Mr. Schlesinger, DOE Secretary, must bring them in from all over town. Some have changed offices five or six times. Phone service has sometimes lagged behind the moves.

There are also policy and enforcement problems. There have been delays in staffing top jobs and presently only five of eight assistant secretary positions

Source: Adapted from an article by W. S. Mossberg in The Wall Street Journal (June 13, 1978), 1, 16.

are filled. DOE has little clout with Congress, and recently lost in a bout with White House budget advisors. Its regulatory and data-gathering programs are also catching flak from industry and consumer groups alike. It is also six months or more behind in amassing a strategic oil reserve.

The department was formed by combining several now-defunct agencies. Among these were the Federal Energy Administration, Federal Power Commission, and sections from the Department of the Interior. Some of these were so new they had operating bugs when they were acquired. Schlesinger, among others, complains that these former agencies are still placing too much emphasis on the routine functions they performed in the past. They are still behaving like old-line agencies.

To try to integrate these component agencies, DOE was organized with new lines of jurisdiction. It was hoped this would avoid or weaken the buildup of internal power blocs dedicated to particular forms of energy. However, conflicts and confusion are frequent. For example, the Conservation and Solar Energy Section began to use advertising agencies for ads concerning energy conservation. However, it turned out that DOE's Office of Public Affairs was already utilizing ad agencies to do this, free.

The old Federal Power Commission, one of the most firmly entrenched of the previous agencies, has been a particular problem. Even with a new name it still maintains its own public relations office and former stationery. Within DOE there is also an Economic Regulatory Commission, and pages of rules are being drafted clarifying the relationships between it and the former Federal Power Commission.

All these things caused Schlesinger to comment, "There are incipient signs of incipient coagulation. But we need a much higher degree of coordination." A good bit of the difficulties seem to be because Schlesinger has spent almost all his time trying to get a complex energy bill through Congress. That bill had not yet passed as of this writing.

The head man has also proposed a number of nominees for top positions, which Congress has failed to approve. At least one person argues that this has contributed to lack of policy changes. It's hard to work on policy changes when several top slots are unfilled. Schlesinger attributes many of the criticisms to DOE's lack of a constituency. He claims it satisfies none of the energy zealots.

Schlesinger did not help the department when he was unable to deliver to Congress a batch of energy supply initiatives he promised in testimony at the beginning of the year. The White House scuttled his plan for this, and some argue that the reason was because he didn't get influential White House officials involved early enough. He is believed to have lost considerable face with Congress over this.

As if all this were not enough, there have been court setbacks as well. For example, there has been a court ruling that some of the oil pricing rules set down by DOE's predecessor agencies are too vague to enforce. One case against nine major oil companies was thrown out because of self-contradictory regulations. DOE has a special team of lawyers and auditors to press ahead on alleged overcharging by big oil companies. However, the previous court reversals may take the teeth out of enforcement. Thus, there is a real question as to whether DOE will be able to use the authority given it by Congress. And as we indicated earlier, the department's regulatory activity is also under attack from consumer groups, big oil, and independent gasoline station operators.

A key part of DOE's mission is information gathering. It is running into trouble here as well. In trying to develop a new financial reporting form for large oil companies, DOE is encountering resistance because the firms are afraid the information will be picked up by the Justice Department and other law-enforcement agencies. Its response from a new survey of gasoline prices and sales sent out to service stations is only a bit over 40 percent. Although required by law to complete the form, the stations apparently find it too complex.

All of these difficulties and more have made it very difficult for DOE to hire bright young employees. Who wants to go with an outfit that doesn't know where it's headed?

Case III-19
BIRTH AND DEVELOPMENT OF A NEW WAVE MEDICAL SCHOOL

This case describes a new school of medical education. The school opened its doors to its first class of students in September 1971. At its inception, there were 86 other medical schools in the United States. Most of these schools were very similar in terms of organizational structure and curriculum. They had four-year programs in which the first two years consisted of basic science training (biochemistry, physiology, etc.) and the final two were spent in clinical training (direct contact with patients in the hospital setting). Generally, the basic science curricula involved discipline-oriented, lecture- laboratory experiences taught by professors in the particular disciplines. The students had no contact with patients during this time. That contact awaited the clinical training. While not our basic thrust here, it is interesting to speculate why these schools were so similar. Was it because of the impact of the far-reaching Flexner Report at the beginning of this century? Was it the date of founding? Or were other things involved? Regardless of the answer to the question of similarity, though, it is crucial to note that the school here was not only new but different. Its structure and curriculum deviated substantially from those of traditional medical schools.

BACKGROUND

Nationally, in the middle and late sixties, there was increased concern about the supply of physicians. Although there was considerable debate about whether a shortage of doctors actually existed, the federal government was persuaded and developed several policies designed to increase the number of new doctors. Particularly influential was its decision to provide federal funds to medical schools on a capitation basis, thus encouraging the schools themselves to admit and graduate increasing numbers of students. Funds were also provided from the federal government and a number of private foundations to help finance the establishment of new schools.

At the same time, there was a national debate among medical educators about the viability of traditional structures of medical education. This debate was influenced by more general educational issues being discussed at that time. Traditional values and structures were questioned. Students were demanding more "relevance." They also wanted a stronger voice in determining educational content. Traditional grading

Source: Adapted from J. R. Kimberly, Contingencies in Creating New Institutions: An Example From Medical Education. Unpublished manuscript presented at the Joint EIASM-Dansk Management Center Research Seminar on "Entrepreneurs and the Process of Institution Building" (1976).

systems were questioned, and pass-fail systems became popular.

Critics argued that the traditional, lockstep med school structure was one in which a four-year time period was the constant and learning was the variable. The two years of basic science were considered to have negative motivational effects because they were similar to undergraduate school. Relevance of these courses was denied because students did not see patients until the third year of medical school. At the same time, there was such an emphasis on specialization that few students considered general practice.

In a nutshell, increasing the supply of doctors became a priority. And there was widespread questioning of many of the basic assumptions about medical education.

Along with these, more general concerns issued at the state and local level. The university with which this new medical school was to be affiliated had a very large traditional medical school headquartered in a major midwestern metropolitan area. The medical school was very well-known and highly regarded. However, doctors and politicians outside the metropolitan area, where it was located, were concerned that the rest of the state was being neglected in terms of medical education. There were shortages of doctors outside the metropolitan area. Many doctors were leaving the state when they finished their training. All of these things and more led to a push for new state-supported medical schools.

To get involved in this push for new medical schools, the traditional medical school proposed establishing semiautonomous branches in three other cities along with increasing its own capacity. The branch that is the subject of this case was established at the major campus of the university. Here, there were a number of distinguished basic science departments, three hospitals, and a sizable medical community in a metropolitan area exceeding 100,000 people. The hope was strong that doctors who received their training in smaller urban areas such as this would remain in them or at least not leave the state.

The campus that was to be the site of this new med school branch viewed the potential school with mixed feelings. In the short run, the school should help generate new resources. In the long run there were some questions about how it would interface with the traditional med school in the metropolitan area.

THE DEAN

The new dean was a cardiologist by training. When he was brought in he was in full-time private practice and held a clinical faculty position at a leading medical school.

The med school with which he had been affiliated was somewhat nontraditional and encouraged innovation. He had previous administrative experience as a five-year member of a city board of education. He had also been on the executive committee of a prepaid group practice.

Five personal characteristics of his appear particularly important. First, he was dissatisfied with traditional medical education and was committed to something different. Second, he was a risk-taker and willing to try new things. Third, he was action-oriented and made quick decisions. Fourth, he sketched broad ideas and left details to others. Last, he was an optimist and astute enough politically to enhance his survival.

He started with a budget and an associate dean. He soon added an assistant dean, executive secretary, and two secretaries. The school was to begin as a one-year basic science program. The three years of clinical training to follow were then to be completed at one of the other med school branches. The dean was accountable to the traditional med school and to the campus at which his branch was located.

The new dean went to great lengths to utilize physicians in the local medical community to work with his students. These physicians were obtained cost-free by being granted clinical associate titles at the med school. Commitments to participate if called upon were obtained from a little over 100 such doctors.

The dean had strong views on curriculum matters. He felt learning should be individually paced and that basic sciences should be taught from a disease-centered rather than discipline-oriented point of view. He felt this one-year program could replace the traditional one of two years.

Sixteen students were admitted the first year. Classes were to stabilize at 128 students after the fourth year. Five innovation-oriented faculty members were hired to become involved with curriculum design. Each student was assigned to a community physician who was to expose the student to patients with diseases related to problems being studied. Another community physician did the evaluating using an oral exam. The faculty was to provide advice and expertise as needed.

The dean worked a number of 16 to 18 hour days. In a short time he developed a high degree of credibility in the local medical community. Those affiliating with the program cited the influence of the dean on their willingness to participate. He also was able to begin to build a state and national reputation due to the innovative nature of the school. Enrollment grew almost as rapidly as projected and amounted to 100 students in 1974 (this was a newly imposed ceiling). Faculty size more than tripled between 1971–74. Staff size more than quadrupled. A new building for the school opened in 1975. The students liked the program and performed as well as their peers in university-wide year-end basic science exams.

The school's first year was characterized by experimentation and mutual tolerance for errors by everyone involved. All wanted to see the school get off the ground and all helped. One example reflecting this was the 20 local doctors whom the dean convinced to spend at least four hours a week on a nonsalaried basis as advisers to students.

There was much uncertainty concerning what these doctors were to do. There was also much uncertainty in the minds of the first 16 students about the program in general. Everything was so unstructured that they had trouble knowing how well they were doing. The first year, the dean and his staff spent immense amounts of time with the students, attempting to reassure them.

After the first year, though, the number of students grew and the dean's administrative duties increased. The dean hired people to perform the outside linking role he himself had performed earlier. Along with this, tolerance for errors dropped.

Accompanying these things were other changes. In the first year the dean could focus heavily on internal problems. After that more and more time had to be spent on environmental and structural-bureaucratic relations. In a word, a loose, flexible, innovative, organization became less flexible and more bureaucratic, with less willingness to tolerate the uncertainty that accompanies innovation.

PRESSURES TOWARD STRUCTURING

As described, the self-paced learning and other ambiguous relationships led to a great deal of uncertainty for everyone concerned. This was true despite students' favorable performance on the year-end exams and on Part I of the National Medical Board exams. Thus, there were pressures for more structure. After all, the students' favorable performance might have been a fluke.

Over the next three years the following kinds of things occurred. To begin with, physician advisers were given job descriptions. Along with this, students were required to finish a designated number of problems in a specified amount of time. As the program began to receive national attention, requests for documentation of the curriculum were received. Also, the demands of accreditation bodies required a heavy amount of documentation.

Relations with individuals and units outside the school were especially critical. One such relationship involved the basic science departments on campus. All faculty involved with the new med school had joint appointments with these departments. During the first year, relationships with the science departments were not a key concern. People were trying to define their role. After that, though, the faculty wanted to take a more active, traditional, and clearly defined teaching, advising, and research role. Over time, this role became more like that of other departments in the university. Higher status accompanies this more traditional role.

Temporarily the school could deviate from other units in terms of what it did. Over the long haul, however, the faculty was expected to meet the same teaching, service, and research standards as the more traditional units. As a result, the faculty tended to focus more and more on research and publication and less and less on program innovation.

A second crucial external relationship was in the national arena. The dean was interested in building a national reputation, along with a local one, for the school. Such recognition could help in many ways, not the least of which were fund raising and ego enhancement. The dean felt that there was too much specialization in medical education. He felt that good general physicians were what was needed. And the program was originally set up to produce these, innovatively. However, in the eyes of the public it was hard to differentiate good general physicians from general practitioners. Furthermore, general practitioners ranked low in the status hierarchy of medical education. Thus, over time there developed a conflict between the original character of the school and some external realities.

This then is a description of the growth and development of an innovative new medical school.

Case III-20

FOUR ABORTION CLINICS

A dramatic effect of the liberalization of abortion laws, which started in New York in 1970, was the emergence of free-standing abortion clinics. Such clinics were devoted entirely to performance of abortions. A 1973 U.S. Supreme Court decision resulted in the establishment of these clinics in most major cities in the United States.

These clinics caught the attention of the public and medical observers. However, they had particular appeal to patients. With them there was the promise of a minimum of bureacratic process and delay, relative privacy (no hospital admission was required), and, finally, lower cost. Accompanying this, many people saw these clinics as advancing social service and advancing the feminist cause. Included here were physicians, lay counselors, social workers, nurses, ministers, and administrators. At the same time, many clinics offered high pay (especially for physicians) for an activity that had not had a high professional standing. Indeed, only recently the operation had been illegal, stigmatized, and clandestinely performed under sordid circumstances.

All this led to the question of how best to organize these clinics to provide their unique health care service. While a key part of this service was the operation itself, other aspects included the provision for information, education, birth control assistance, and emotional support. There were substantial differences in the relative emphasis to be put on these additional concerns, and these differences led to different patterns of clinic operation and organization. Four such patterns are illustrated in the clinics described in this case.

CLINIC A

This clinic was opened in an Atlantic Coast city in 1971. It was designed to be a model nonprofit abortion clinic. In addition to patient care, it was to provide an example of how a first-rate outpatient clinic should operate.

The clinic had a full-time medical director who was a highly qualified and experienced obstetrics-gynecology specialist. There was an intensive lay abortion-training counselor program. One-

Source: Based on an article by W. M. Hern, M. R. Gold, and A. Oaks, "Administrative Incongruence and Authority Conflict in Four Abortion Clinics," *Human Organization,* 36 (1977), 376–383.

to-one counseling of patients and group counseling of a patient's relatives and friends were emphasized.

The staff was aware of the clinic's role as a leader in providing abortion services as well as a model for other clinics. Morale was initially high, and there was strong commitment to the clinic's activities, particularly from the counselors.

After 18 months of operation the clinic had serviced about 15,000 patients. Fifty to sixty abortions per day were performed. The staff numbered nearly a hundred. The clinic had bureaucratized and routinized many of the professional functions in order to cope with the patient load. There was now widespread severe dissatisfaction among the staff, especially the counselors. The professional supervisors, such as the clinic director, nursing director, and director of counseling (all of whom had outstanding reputations), often were not informed or consulted about policy or administrative decisions of the executive director.

These supervisors had to carry out such decisions without input. The result was confusion, tension, delays, overwork, and anxiety. The supervisors feared retribution from the executive director for any criticism of the problems, her methods, or even requests for information.

The executive director was widely admired as an intelligent, committed, and talented leader with many positive qualities. She was seen as dynamic and one who cared about what happened. She was also seen as authoritarian, autocratic, paranoid, vindictive, and una-

ble to tolerate questions or complaints. She felt under great pressure from the overall director to perform as many abortions as possible and produce as much revenue as possible. The revenue was used to finance similar clinics in other cities and expand nonabortion services in clinic A.

Many staff members felt these pressures were jeopardizing good medical care for the patients. "[Clinic A] is on the verge of becoming an abortion mill and slighting the patients—especially if it's going to be bankrolling other operations." "Teaching people how to screw is fine after we get some of the other things taken care of."

When the executive director was absent she left telephone commands through her secretary, who essentially was in charge of the clinic. The professionals had no decision-making autonomy in her absence.

CLINIC B

This clinic was established in mid-1973 in a western college town. It came as a response to efforts by several interested women and two male physicians, neither of whom was a gynecologist. The clinic was managed by an activist sociology student, as executive director, and a doctor experienced in abortion clinics, as medical director. A board of directors was established, a loan was obtained, and plans moved ahead to hire a nurse, train counselors, and provide facilities. Clinic A served as the model. A head counselor was hired by one of the original doctors without knowledge of either the medical or executive director. This counselor had experience as an abortion counselor, but no professional qualifications or training.

When the clinic finally got off the ground in late 1973 it was caught in the middle of the "Right to Life" controversy. The county medical association attacked the medical director. He also was opposed by several local physicians who opposed abortion or saw the clinic's low-cost abortions as an economic threat.

The atmosphere at the clinic was charged with much excitement at the idea of starting the program against great odds. The medical director was seen by a number of staff members as a hero. Virtually all of the medical director's recommended policies were adopted. The clinic was successful in having both the appearance and substance of a first-rate medical program.

Within eight months of its opening, however, the medical director and head nurse were snowed under by the workload. There were 25 to 50 abortion patients per week in addition to screening, follow-up exams, cleaning, and clerical work. The executive director refused to take action, arguing that he was only a sociologist writing a book about the clinic. The medical director's requests for additional equipment were dismissed for lack of funds. Instead, he was told to work on his "relationship" with the head nurse to solve the problems.

In late 1974 the head nurse resigned. Most of the original members on the board of directors also resigned, a number indicating poor management of the clinic as their reason.

Meanwhile, the executive director, fearing charges of sexism, chose one of the female counselors as a co-director. This slowed down the decision making, which was already none too swift. The resignation of the head nurse brought the tension to a climax. Shortly after, the medical director met with the co-directors and stressed the need for the highest professional standards of medical care. The co-directors indicated that they "hated professionalism" and saw the main purpose of the clinic as the personal growth and maturity of the women working there. The patients were secondary and incidental to that. The medical director saw the goal to be that of providing safe abortion services for patients.

The following day the executive director violated the confidentiality of a patient's records. Consequently, the medical director requested the board to ask the executive director to resign. The head counselor viewed the clinic as part of a larger political movement and obtained the support of the other counselors. At the same time, the executive director got the backing of the new board. The medical director's request that there should be a single director with clear authority and responsibility was rejected. The feeling was that there should not be a staff hierarchy. The board voted to do away with the post of medical director and to replace it with that of a part-time physician.

CLINIC C

Clinic C was established in a northeast industrial city. Its owners were two absentee real estate investors who saw opening the first such clinic in the community as a profit-making opportunity. They recognized the commercial value of excellent facilities and medical care.

The first administrator, a minister, was known for his work in abortion counseling. He was highly visible and well-known, with a strong commitment to social progress. He concentrated on providing a strong counseling emphasis and provided an important liaison with the community.

The medical director was chosen by the owners and was highly regarded by colleagues in the community. He operated with relative autonomy from both the owners and administrator, and appointed the staff physicians, who were highly competent though not oriented toward the emotional needs of patients. They were almost completely autonomous since the medical director seldom appeared. The head nurse was hired by the medical director and functioned almost entirely without supervision.

After eight months the first administrator resigned to return to graduate school. The second administrator was also a minister. He commuted from some distance, found this difficult, and resigned after four months. The third administrator had a degree in public health administration.

This administrator obtained reports and figures from every department in order to design flowcharts and make projections. He was not able to obtain figures concerning money coming in or going out or where it went in between. The bookkeeper was the only one who knew. However, she was under orders from the owners not to reveal this information. The bookkeeper also conveyed orders from the owners to the administrator concerning medical, nursing, or administrative policies. After two months of this, the administrator resigned.

The staff was demoralized by all this. No one was really in charge. Supervisors made up policy as they went along. However, in terms of their work, the professionals found it highly satisfying. They were able to isolate themselves pretty much from the push for profit, which characterized the owners' approach.

CLINIC D

Clinic D was one of the busiest abortion clinics in the northeast. Its average volume was about 100 patients per day. It was a good place to get an abortion, but the boss was feared. There was one owner, an M.D., who also single-handedly administered the clinic. He was an expert abortionist and in absolute charge. The policies were very clear. Anyone not following them was immediately fired. There was no discussion of idealism, social change, or making the patients comfortable. The common objective was simply to perform abortions.

All personnel punched a time clock. They referred to the clinic as "the factory." The owner-administrator pressured subordinates to give information about colleagues. They called it "screw your buddy."

The patients were under general anesthesia during the abortion. They were group counseled, with little doctor-patient contact, and received efficient and competent custodial care during their recovery.

The owner-administrator wanted money from the clinic and demanded performance from his people. They performed with precision within the rules provided. A doctor here was a technician expected to perform a medically perfect abortion and nothing more.

Exercise IV-21 Organizational Analysis Exercise—Part IV

Keep in mind the general instructions and admonitions for the previous organizational analysis exercises. Use the two organizations agreed upon with your instructor and address the concerns below.

1. Depending on the size of the selected organizations choose from two to all of the subsystems in each and describe the kinds of relationships between (among) the units.
2. Where do the key interdependencies and power imbalances appear to exist in the units of these two organizations?
3. Evaluate the conflict or potential conflict found in the above analyses.
4. Analyze the units in terms of the group characteristics of:
   a. Size
   b. Group structure
   c. Group cohesiveness
   d. Group compatibility
   e. Group homogeneity
   f. An estimate of each group's stage of development
5. Analyze the heads of the units above in terms of their vertical leader behavior, using dimensions from one of the contingency leadership approaches.
6. Analyze the heads of the units in terms of their lateral orientation.
7. Apply one of the leadership approaches presented in Chapter 13 to each of the units above. Make sure you discuss the application of this approach in terms of unit and/or individual criteria.
8. Which of the above variables seem to be most important in terms of subsystems criteria?
9. Keeping in mind earlier chapters, what group aspects might you attempt to change in each of the two organizations to enhance performance and maintenance criteria?

THE FINANCE DILEMMA

PART 1—BEFORE

The Finance and Accounting Office at Camp Zama, Japan, handled almost all payroll records for Army personnel in Japan. The office was located in a brick building, called the Pentagon Building, in the south wing. The main duty of the Finance and Accounting office was to pay all Army personnel under its jurisdiction in Japan. The office was divided into five different sections: in-and-out processing, hospital records, travel section, quality assurance, and payroll section. A major was in charge of the office. Reporting to him was a master sergeant, who was responsible for the whole office. Each of the five sections was run by a SFC (sergeant first-class). The payroll section was divided into two subsections: computation clerks and payroll record maintenance clerks. There were no physical partitions between sections, and each section had its quota of desks, chairs, file cabinets, and adding machines.

The hospital records section served all soldiers that were wounded or hurt enough to be evacuated from Vietnam. Most med evacs (personnel evacuated from Vietnam) left Vietnam so fast that their pay records were left behind. These records often did not catch up with the

wounded soldier until he was about to be reassigned from Japan. So, the duty of the hospital records section was to make up temporary records for each hospitalized soldier and pay him using these records until his permanent records arrived, if they ever did. This section consisted of one SFC and three enlisted personnel of lower rank.

In-and-out processing was supervised by one SFC. The SFC had three subordinate enlisted personnel whose ranks were E-4 and/or E-5. The duty of this section was the processing of records and the paying of all Army personnel that arrived in Japan and were assigned there for duty, and those that left as well. The newly arrived records were updated and processed to go on the computerized payroll. The section typed travel vouchers for all newly arrived personnel and sent them to the travel section to be computed and made ready for payment. Reenlistments, retirements, and discharge vouchers were also prepared, computed, and processed for payment.

This section was considered the most desirable to work in, and the other workers in the office envied the personnel working in it, although these people had no higher status than anybody else. The reason for this envy was that the SFC in charge was very personable. He took an interest in the personnel he was in

Source: Adapted from a course assignment prepared by R. E. Mohler for Professor J. G. Hunt, Southern Illinois University, Carbondale. Copyright © Osborn, Hunt, and Jauch, 1980.

charge of and would listen to suggestions put forth by them. The section was very efficient, had no trouble getting its work done, and never had to work at night or on Saturdays.

After the pay records left the in-and-out processing section, they went to the quality assurance section. The quality assurance section was staffed by four staff sergeants and one SFC who was in charge. The main duty of this section was to audit all pay records to find any errors and note these so they would be corrected. The newly arrived pay records go to this section for an initial audit and then are transferred to the payroll section. Along with this, the quality assurance section was constantly taking records from the payroll section and auditing them. Reenlistments, retirements, and discharge payments were also checked for accuracy by this section. This section had a high degree of responsibility, and its sergeants were the ones who knew finance the best.

The payroll section consisted of five pay teams (with two specialists, E-5s or below, on each team.) Each team had a number of companies' pay records for which they were held responsible. One person was in charge of computing the pay and making changes in pay status, and another was in charge of the maintenance of the pay record itself. These two individuals worked in close cooperation and when possible helped each other. Information that was needed in performing their duties often came from the other clerk. The payroll computation team was supervised by a staff sergeant, and the payroll record maintenance personnel were supervised by another staff sergeant. Both of these sergeants reported to the SFC who was in charge of the whole section. The payroll section was the least-desirable section in which to work. The section often had to work at nights and Saturdays to keep up with the workload, and this was the main reason for its low desirability.

The travel section was staffed with three enlisted personnel (one SFC in charge of the section and two individuals, E-5 and below). This section's main task was to fill out and compute travel vouchers for newly arrived personnel and permanent party.

At the inception of the case, and for about six months afterward, the office was like "one big happy family." All sections cooperated with each other in the work process and there was no trouble getting the work done, except occasionally the pay section had to work Saturdays or nights. The sergeants and all other enlisted personnel got along very well. All the section chiefs took an interest in their subordinates and were liked very much.

The sergeants in charge of each section would listen to the suggestions of the lower-ranking personnel and often would use some of these suggestions. If the suggestions were not used, the reasons would be explained.

The office had a bowling league, in which practically everyone participated, sergeants and lower-ranking personnel alike. Also, at least once every two weeks, a big party was given at one of the sergeant's homes for all enlisted personnel. On weekends when there were no parties, most of the personnel from the office would go to one of the NCO clubs, put a number of tables together, and have a party there.

There were a number of work requirements within each section and between sections. As described, within the payroll section, the computation clerk and the payroll record maintenance clerk had to work closely with each other. The information that each clerk needed to do the job often had to be obtained from the other clerk, so working smoothly with one another was essential. Also, there were required duties between this section and in-and-out processing, travel, and quality assurance. Often, when information was needed from a different section, the clerk would go to another clerk in that section instead of going to the sergeant in charge of the section. Most of the required activities within the office were set at a level just strict enough to get the work done in an efficient and correct manner.

The group members freely talked when they wanted, ate snacks while working, and had social interactions on a person-to-person basis, not taking rank into consideration. Sometimes these actions got out of hand and there were reprimands, but usually everything worked out. The many social activities that brought everybody together, greatly influenced the group behaviors. Virtually everyone in the office respected each other.

The work was done fast and efficiently, and usually there was no trouble keeping up with the workload. Also, almost everyone was highly satisfied with the atmosphere and working conditions in the office.

Starting with the master sergeant, most of the supervisors had certain performance standards that had to be met, but they also were concerned with their subordinates' attitudes, problems, and ideas. A couple of the sergeants would often let their subordinates "run all over them" and do what they wished.

PART 2—AFTER

After about six months, new sergeants were assigned to the office and all of the present sergeants left for new assignments. A new master sergeant was assigned to take over the duties of the departing master sergeant, and two new SFCs were assigned to the office. (One was put in charge of in-and out-processing, and one in charge of the payroll section.) Also at this time, two new staff sergeants took the places of the two sergeants in charge of the computation clerks and payroll maintenance clerks in the payroll section.

The new master sergeant, who was in charge of the office—second only to the officer in charge (a major), started changing office procedures immediately. No snacking was allowed in the office, and unnecessary talking and roaming was forbidden. Before he arrived, fatigues could be worn to work, but now he ordered everybody to wear dress greens. Hair had to be cut shorter, and shoes were to be "spit shined."* The

*An explanation of stateside duty and overseas duty would be helpful here. Duty requirements overseas are more lenient than duty stateside. The "spit and shine" rule and other strict office rules of duty stateside are not the same overseas. These things are often overlooked and a more informal atmosphere is generally the rule.

benefit of taking a half day off once a month for personal business was promptly halted, too. Moreover, when the payroll section worked overtime, all the other sections had to as well.

At the same time that the new master sergeant was making changes, the two new staff sergeants (with ranks E-6), in charge of the computation clerks and payroll maintenance clerks in the payroll section, also decided to start making changes. First, the computation and the maintenance clerks were split into two different groups. All the computation clerks were put in one location and all the maintenance clerks were put in another. Since both clerks who worked on the same records needed much information from each other, talking and walking between sections started to become common. The master sergeant and the two staff sergeants did not care for this, so they decided to put the filing cabinets, which contained the payroll records, between the two sections. In this way, people in the two sections could not see each other and, therefore, could not talk to each other. Then a rule was made that if there was information or data any clerk needed, he or she would have to put a note in the supervisor's "in-box." The sergeant would then give the note to the sergeant in charge of the other section. The latter would then give the note to the clerk who helped handle those records, to get the information needed. The needed information would follow the same route back to the clerk who asked for it. Often, this procedure took two or three days. If there was a change in a person's pay status, often it would not get to the com-

putation clerk in time to be changed. Therefore, some people would get over- or underpaid. Complaints started and the clerks were blamed.

Some of the clerks, who had worked in the office for a while, started to give suggestions to the sergeants on how they thought the problem could be solved. But the sergeants would not listen. Their attitudes were: (1) our ways are the correct ways; (2) no person of lower rank can tell us what to do; and (3) I am a sergeant, I should know what is right, you are only an E-5 or E-4. Other little things were also changed in the section. The clerks began blaming each other for mistakes found in the payroll records, and each part of the payroll section fought each other. Coordination and communication soon went downhill. Sergeants threatened to take stripes (rank) away from the clerks. The clerks started talking about the sergeants behind their backs, and sometimes things were done the old way just to spite them. The high performance and satisfaction, which was typical before, was nowhere to be seen.

Meanwhile, in-and-out processing was undergoing a similar change. The new sergeant in charge of the section decided to try a new method for taking care of the payroll records of incoming personnel. Instead of completely processing a person's records while the individual was waiting and providing up-to-date pay, partial pay was provided and the rest of the processing of the record was done later when no one was waiting to be processed. By not taking time to completely process the record at once, the section started having to work overtime. The reasons for this were:

(1) people were constantly coming in to be processed; and (2) the section had to do reenlistments, retirements, and discharges, which had high priorities and were constantly interrupting the work on the records. As a result, records began piling up and overtime was quite common. The sergeant in charge partly blamed the lower-ranking personnel in the section plus the newness of the operation for being so far behind.

The other sections—hospital pay, travel, and quality assurance—did not undergo any changes. However the changes mentioned above had an effect on each. For instance, the failure of the in-and-out processing section to completely process the records and get them to the payroll section on time caused many problems with the payrolls of each company. Complaints of people not getting paid correctly and on time were common. Thus, because of the problems occurring in the payroll section and the in-and-out processing section, the whole office was indirectly affected.

The attitude of the whole office began to change. The E-5s and personnel of lower ranks began to stick together, rejecting the authority of most of the sergeants. Most of the sergeants started excluding lower-ranking personnel from parties. In turn, the office became divided. There was more quarreling between sections than before. Sometimes work was slowed down on purpose to get even with the sergeants. To the enlisted personnel that had worked in the office when it ran smoothly, it was a bad place to work. But for personnel that came after everything had changed, it did not seem to be so bad.

Social events were not held as often. If a sergeant threw a party, very few, if any, lower-ranking personnel were invited. The same situation was true if an E-5, or staff below this rank, threw a party. The personnel in the office were not as close as before. The clerks were used to talking, snacking, and wandering around almost at will. They knew work had been performed well before, and they resented the denial of these privileges. What the clerks were used to had been taken away. Before, they had liked and respected their sergeants, but now they talked about them behind their backs, were disrespectful of them, and often did things to spite them. The clerks in all sections were affected because of the new strict rules, which they thought were unjustified. They were very dissatisfied.

Case IV-23

THE SANTO COMPANY

The Santo Company was a multinational company with revenue in excess of $2 billion annually. The parent company was divided into four autonomous companies: The Commercial Company, The Chemical Company, The Polymer Company, and The Textile Company. The Santo Company had

Source: Adapted from a course assignment by W. P. Hilmes for Professor J. G. Hunt, Southern Illinois University, Carbondale. Copyright © Osborn, Hunt, and Jauch, 1980.

hundreds of products. Here we will look more closely at the Commercial Company.

The Commercial Company had five product areas; they were the Agriculture Division, Plastics Division, Electronics Division, Environmental Division, and Fabricated Products Division (see Exhibit V-6). Each division was treated as a profit center, with a vice-president responsible for that division's performance. Because of the size of the Santo Company, we can concentrate only on the Agriculture Division.

The vice-president of the Agriculture Division had three directors under him: the Director of Agriculture Technology, Director of Agriculture Marketing, and Director of Agriculture Manufacturing. Specifically we are concerned with the unit that was under the supervision of the Director of Agriculture Technology. The director of technology had three research managers who reported to him. These managers were in charge of the Screening, Process, and Testing Departments. It was the responsibility of these departments to screen, process, and test new agriculture products. There was a common educational background across the departments.

The Process Department had the responsibility of developing a manufacturing process to make new compounds that the Screening Department had said look promising. Two processes had to be developed for each new candidate. One process involved making the chemical in small quantities to be used as soon as possible by the Testing Department for field tests. If the field tests were favora-

ble, a profitable large-scale manufacturing process had to be developed.

A hypothetical example will help illustrate the functions of each department and how they were interrelated. The Screening Department looked for potential new herbicides, insecticides, and plant-growth regulators that would improve an existing product. The Screening Department would generally screen several thousand compounds per year, and the candidates would go through a number of steps depending on how promising they looked. A computer comparison study would then compare new compounds with ones that had a proven performance record.

A few of the criteria used for comparison were: biodegradability, soil-retention time, functional group activity, and solubility in various mediums. Candidates that looked promising on the comparison study would be further screened for theoretical soundness. The candidates that were left would be prepared in small quantities and tested in the greenhouses. If the greenhouse tests were favorable, all information pertaining to the compound would be sent to the Process Department for development of a preparation process.

The key to the development of this process was a simple analytical technique that could be used to quickly analyze the new compound. One batch had to be analyzed before another batch could be started. The development of this technique required months of work and a great deal of communication between the Process, Screening, and Testing Departments before a final method could be found.

Exhibit V-6 Partial Organization Chart for Santo Company

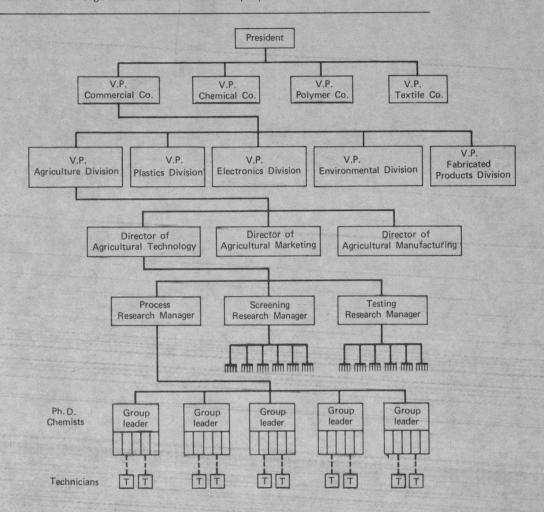

Once the process development was complete, all the relevant information was sent to the Testing Department for field testing under different soil and climate conditions. If the field test looked promising, the process group would now start to develop a profitable manufacturing process to make the compound. But if the tests were not favorable, all the relevant information would be sent to the Screening Department for evaluation of the results. These evaluations would be placed in the computer for help in future screening activities.

By and large, relations across these departments went smoothly, and the department members were satisfied with members of other departments. Group cohesiveness, though, was only moderate.

Most of the agriculture research personnel were located at the company's world headquarters in one large, modern, climate-controlled building. The research equipment at the world headquarters was the latest and best that money could buy. The Process Department had most of its analytical equipment tied into a CDC-1700 computer, which was located in the building. If an analysis was desired, information was typed into the computer (by way of CRT), then the sample was injected into another instrument. About fifteen minutes later, a computer printout described the mixture injected into the gas chromatograph.

In contrast, the manufacturing facilities for making the chemicals, developed by the research personnel, were located about twenty miles away in the heart of a large city. These facilities were built in the 1940s and most of the analytical equipment was nearly as old. Manufacturing had lower status and prestige than the research departments.

There were eight members in the group in which the casewriter worked, six Ph.D. chemists and two technicians (of which the casewriter was one). The group leader would tell associates what to do, in general terms, and leave the rest up to them. For example, he would say, "We need a process to make CP-42850." Then the person who was told this would begin to develop a process, knowing that if he or she needed any help or advice, the group leader was there to give it. A group member could go a week or more in some cases, with-out there being any communications with the group leader concerning the process being worked on.

In the group, the technicians were not assigned to any one chemist, but were there to help the group as a whole. Conflicts often arose as to whose work the technician should do first. It was not unusual for a technician to have four to five requests for help pending at any one time. Requests for the technician's help often came from outside his or her group. If another area was doing work on a compound that the technician had developed an analytical technique for, the technician might end up analyzing samples for other areas. Conflicts often arose over this, especially when agriculture manufacturing called up and asked for help. Agriculture manufacturing wanted this help immediately so another batch could be started. It was not a normal procedure for the Process Department to analyze samples for manufacturing, for it had its own equipment and chemists for analysis work.

The Process Department would develop an analytical technique for use by the Manufacturing Department. When someone from manufacturing called the person who developed the technique for help, he or she would say that the technique was no good. On further inquiry, it would be found that the individual from manufacturing had changed the method of analysis somewhat because it was felt that it would work better with the change. This is when things started getting hot. A typical comment from a process-personnel member would be, "You mean to tell me that I spent three months developing a technique for you to use, and you decide that you want to randomly change it?" The old-time manufacturing employee might respond by saying, "What do you mean telling me what to do. I was working in this plant, and doing all right, while you were still in grade school!"

Case IV-24

BEHAVIOR IN A CHANGING SETTING

PART 1—IN THE BEGINNING

This case describes a new-products department in a large industrial firm. The department was assigned responsibility for developing products that required sustained long-range attention. A key function was to bridge the gap between the Research Center, which generated products with marketability if developed further, and the Marketing Department, which distributed tested products.

Although many people were involved in the success of new products, two were especially important: marketing specialists, who provided information concerning requirements to be met to satisfy consumers, and research and technical personnel who created the product.

The department head, Harold P. Scott, was brought in from outside the firm. One of his first decisions was to devote sustained attention to Ferlin, a noncombustible synthetic fabric with great potential use in the garment industry.

Source: Based on an article by T. A. Kayser and A. J. Melcher. "Democratic Leadership in a Changing Environment: Behavioral and Organizational Consequences," *Human Resource Management,* 12 (Winter 1973), 24–35.

A six-member group of technical and marketing people was originally assigned to the Ferlin project. Exhibit V-7 summarizes the key organizational relationships. The company had a very strong technical manufacturing orientation. There was a widely held opinion that nobody could direct technical people except other technical people who had grown in the company. However, Scott, a nontechnical person brought in from outside, was held accountable for marketing a product requiring a great deal of support from different sources.

Many of these sources were either above him in the organization or outside his direct-authority hierarchy. A number of the operating divisions initially saw the new-products department as invading their jurisdiction. Also, the headquarters staff groups were oriented toward serving the operating divisions and were not anxious to divert resources to handle requests from Scott's group.

However, at its inception, Scott's group had the support of top management. Scott was given broad discretion in building an organization. His immediate superior had a marketing orienta-

Exhibit V-7 Initial Organization Relationship for the First Four and a Half Years

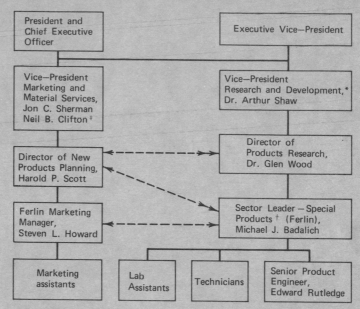

*All research facilities of Dunhill were located thirty miles from the main plant in Smallville.

†Ferlin was only one of several products within the section leader's responsibility.

‡After two years, Clifton replaced Sherman.

Note: Arrows indicate influence; double arrows indicate stronger influence.

tion. The initial resource commitment was relatively low, since there appeared to be no competitors working on a similar product.

Scott relied heavily on leadership to build a team. He emphasized voluntary cooperation and commitment rather than trying to demand or coerce. He stressed individual initiative and team spirit, emphasizing rewards and team goals. He supported informal interaction among team members and himself. He was also very active in representing his people and group to higher management, while at the same time delegating broadly and stressing participation when he made decisions. He went to great lengths to support his group in dealings with higher management. He also spent a great deal of time meeting with higher management and other groups to keep them informed on product developments and to make sure his people had the resources they needed. At the same time he stressed results and downplayed rules and policies. Frequently rules and policies were bent to facilitate results.

In motivating his people, Scott emphasized tying the goals of the individual to group goals. Successful group members were rewarded with salary increases, advancement, recognition, and special privileges. During the first four and one-half years of the project (called the "golden years" by some), there was high commitment, cooperative interpersonal relationships, and good relations between himself, his subordinates, and his superiors. He helped create a period of progress and harmonious relations.

PART 2—A CHANGING SETTING

During the golden years, the team's organizational setting remained relatively stable. Thereafter, however, Scott's team was faced with rapid change. Pressures increased from the market, and the resource commitment continued to increase. Concurrently, changes in top-level management took place that influenced the Ferlin project. First, Badalich was replaced as section leader. Second, the director of projects research was replaced. Third, the marketing vice-president was replaced. Finally, a new position of Ferlin project manager was established, along with some additional positions that in general tended to make the organizational setup more complex. The new people, with few exceptions, were wholly technical in orientation. Previously there was an appreciation of the marketing role in developing, producing, and selling a consumer product.

Now such appreciation was lacking. Also, whereas in the early stages there was no competition, now one company had already marketed a similar and very good quality product, and several others appeared to be close to market entry. Thus market pressure previously missing was now very great.

What was the reaction to all of these changes? At the lower levels the team continued to show high commitment, satisfaction, and cooperative working relations. At the upper levels, however, such was not the case. In the middle of the fifth year, conflict between the technical and marketing personnel developed higher up. As previously indicated, Scott was responsible for product development only; he had only a segment of the total group under his jurisdiction. With the separate chains of command, conflicts between technical and marketing personnel quickly jumped over Scott's head. The new, technically oriented vice-president did not represent Scott's viewpoint or involve him in decision making, as had his predecessor, who had an appreciation for the importance of marketing. While the dual-authority hierarchies could be bridged by Scott's leadership in the golden years, with low outside pressure and strong upper management support, now they created great difficulty. However, Scott's leadership was still functional at lower levels and helped buffer the pressures from above. The question is, is this enough, or must further steps be taken?

EAGLE AIRLINES

Eagle Airlines was a medium-sized regional airline serving the southwest quarter of the United States. The company had been growing rapidly in the last fifteen years, partially as a result of dynamic company activity, but also as a result of the rapid economic growth of the area which it served.

The most outstanding of the areas was Bartlett City. Bartlett City's growth since the middle 1940s had rested on two primary developments. One of these was the very rapid growth of manufacturing and research establishments concerned with defense work. Some firms located here at the urging of government agencies to build new defense plants and laboratories away from coastal areas. Others moved to this location because of the attractive climate and scenery, which was considered an advantage in attracting technicians, engineers and scientists for work on advanced military projects. Once some plants and research laboratories were developed, smaller, independent firms sprang up in the community for the purpose of servicing and supplying those which were established first. These developments encouraged the rapid growth of local construction and the opening of numerous attractive housing developments. The second basis for growth was the completion, also in the 1940s, of a major irrigation project that opened a large area for intensive cultivation.

Source: This case has been reproduced with the kind permission of its author, J. A. Litterer. Copyright © J. A. Litterer.

While the economy of Bartlett City had grown rapidly, it was in many ways tied to coastal areas, where parent firms or home offices of many of the local establishments existed. Also, since many of its industries serviced the national defense effort, they consequently had to be closely connected with matters decided on in Washington, or other places distant from Bartlett City. Lastly, it had many strong financial and business ties with major coastal cities, such as San Francisco and Los Angeles. As a result, executives, engineers, and scientists in Bartlett City industries were frequently in contact with the major business, political, and scientific centers of the country, particularly those on the West Coast. In making a trip, for example, to Los Angeles from Bartlett City, one was faced with using one of three alternative modes of travel: auto, private corporate jet, or commercial jet flight. Eagle Airlines had the sole route between Bartlett City and Los Angeles, which was found to be a most lucrative run and to which it gave a great deal of attention.

COMPANY MANAGEMENT

The rapid growth of Eagle Airlines was held by many to be in no small degree a result of the skill of its management. It should be pointed out that its top management had been particularly skillful in obtaining and defending its route structure and had been particularly successful in financing, at advantageous terms, the acquisition of modern aircraft, particularly jet-powered airplanes. Top management emphasized "decentralization," in which the lower members of management were given as much freedom as possible to fulfill their responsibilities in whatever way they thought best. This policy was thought to have built a dynamic, aggressive, and extremely able group of middle- and lower-level executives who had been particularly imaginative in finding ways to expand and improve the operation of the firm. This decentralization had always been accompanied by the understanding that the individual manager must "deliver." This policy, or actually philosophy, was conveyed and reinforced through letters, personal conversations, and example. Executives who increased sales or reduced costs, or in some manner made their operations more efficient, were rewarded in a number of ways. Praise, both public and private, was given to executives who improved their unit's performance. Bonuses for increased sales or cost reduction were both generous and frequent, and promotions came rapidly to those who managed outstanding units. The chairman of the board, who was also chief executive officer during this period of growth, frequently used words that were only half-jokingly claimed by other executives to be the company motto, "This company's success rests upon expansion and efficiency."

THE LOCAL UNIT

Eagle Airlines was organized as shown in Exhibit V-8. The three major divisions were: operations, which was involved in scheduling and operating the planes over the entire route system; sales, which was concerned with advertising all phases of airline service, maintaining ticket offices in all cities and airports, and also selling to institutional customers such as companies and government agencies; and service, which was concerned with activities at the airport, maintenance, handling baggage, loading passengers, and similar functions.

For all practical purposes, operations had no local offices in that it had to operate the entire system. Sales and service had both district and local or regional offices. The sales manager in Bartlett City, for example, was responsible for the ticket sales at the airport and in maintaining a downtown ticket office, as well as for institutional sales to the local companies and agencies. Service was usually broken into a number of subdivisions at the local level, so that at Bartlett City there was a ramp service manager who was responsible for handling everything pertaining to the airplane while it was on the ground, but not while it was under maintenance. The manager would, therefore, be responsible for the loading and the unloading of all baggage, mail, and passengers. That individual was also responsible for cleaning the planes between flights, having food put on board, getting baggage to the customers and picking it up from them, guiding passengers on and off the aircraft, and checking their tickets when they arrived at the terminal.

Consistent with company policy of decentralization and individual ac-

Exhibit V-8 Partial Organization Chart of Eagle Airlines

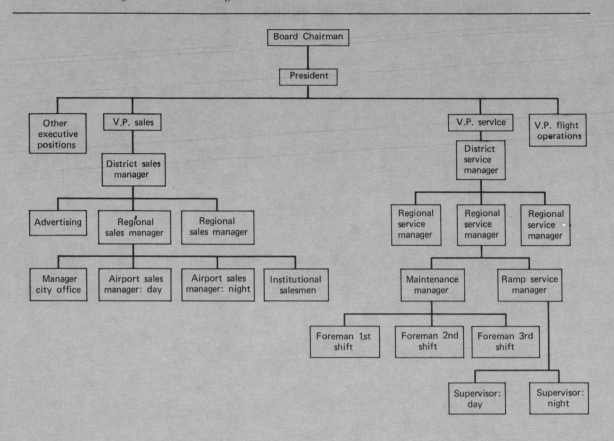

countability, each of these local people had an individual budget and standards of performance. A sales manager, for example, was given complete authority to hire, train, and fire whatever salespeople or any other personnel he or she thought necessary. The sales manager knew what his or her budget was and was expected to stick within it and reduce it if possible. Furthermore, the sales manager knew what the standards of performance relevant to sales volume were. The company placed great emphasis on an increase in sales rather than in absolute volume of sales. Hence, the sales manager at Bartlett City, as at all other local units, knew that individual performance would be evaluated, not on matching past sales volume, but by increasing it a certain percentage. The percentage would vary from one location to another depending upon the number of conditions: market potential, absolute volume, and similar items. Although the percentage increase might vary, it was always there and was known by the company as the "ratchet." The regional service manager had no actual sales figure to be held accountable for, but that manager did have costs that were expected to be controlled, and if at all possible, reduced. While there was no similar "ratchet," such as a percentage reduction of costs expected each year, there was continual pressure on the local ramp manager in the form of exhortation, suggestions, and illustrations of managers who had successfully found ways to reduce costs.

PLAN OF THE SALES MANAGER

Carl Dodds, sales manager in Bartlett City, had been with Eagle Airlines seven years, during which time he had had three promotions. Upon graduation from a western state university, he had started working for Eagle Airlines in the San Francisco office as a ticket clerk at the local airport. Within a year he had been made accounts salesman, selling airline service to local companies and institutions. Within two years he had become a district sales manager at San Jose, the smallest of the company's sales offices. Six months ago he had received his promotion to Bartlett City, the second largest sales office and, until recently, the one growing most rapidly. Dodds' superior looked at him as a particularly dynamic, inventive salesman and sales manager. He seemed gifted at finding spectacular ways of substantially increasing sales. In previous positions he had developed a number of attention-getting promotion packages that met with spectacular results. Higher man-

agement looked to him to again increase sales at Bartlett City, which had leveled out about a year ago with the decline in the economy. It was not known how long the decline would continue.

Some of Dodds' previous associates in the other parts of the company agreed that he had been imaginative in developing some spectacular promotion schemes, but also felt that success had always been of the short-run variety: he had made sudden bursts at the expense of long-term growth. They further claimed that he had been fortunate in always being promoted out of a position before the consequences of his activity caught up with him.

Since coming to Bartlett City, Dodds had been intensively studying the local market situation, making contacts with the various companies and big business executives, hiring some new salesmen, and training them after having, as he called it, weeded out some deadwood. He had also increased advertising and redecorated the downtown sales office. In spite of this activity, in his own mind, he had been largely getting ready for his major effort.

Dodds defined his sales situation this way. The airline had done well attracting customers who wanted speed and convenience. However, a considerable number of business executives drove or used a company plane. He adopted and embellished a popular local image of the Bartlett City executive as a dynamic, imaginative, administrator-scientist who represented a new type of business tycoon. In Dodds' mind, what he had to do was sell this young, dynamic, new type of tycoon the comfort and gracious service that, apparently, such a person thought should come to him or her in this new role. His new plan then was to do everything possible to give the "new tycoons" this sort of service. He therefore developed a plan to set up *Tycoon Specials* on certain of the flights carrying the greatest number of these business executives. This plan was to begin with the flight between Bartlett City and Los Angeles.

In this plan the customer-executive upon arriving at the ticket-checking counter for the *Tycoon Special* flight would be asked to select his or her own seat. This then would be reserved in the customer's name. Upon arriving at the ramp for boarding, the customer would be greeted by name by the gate attendant, usually dressed plainly but neatly in a white top, blue cap, and slacks, but now in a gold coat and a simulated turban. Stretching between the gate and the aircraft was to be a wide, rich-red carpet. Upon arrival, the customer's name would be announced through a special intercom to the plane. As the individual walked down the red carpet, the customer-executive would note that the flight hostess would appear smiling at the door, ready to greet him or her by name before being ushered to the appropriate seat, identified by a card with the executive's name, indicating, "This seat is reserved for Tycoon _____."

Once in flight this deluxe service would continue, with the hostesses changing into more comfortable and feminine-looking lounge dresses and serving a choice of champagne, wine, and other cocktails along with exotic and varied hors d'oeuvres. There were other details to the plan, but this will give you some idea of its general nature. In this way, Dodds thought surely that he would be able to not only match but exceed the services and comfort some executives thought they obtained by alternative means of transportation.

Dodds' great problem was in getting the plan operational. Almost all of the service had to be provided by people who did not report to him. This would be supplied by the local ramp service manager, to whom the gate clerk reported, and who would have to provide the red carpet, the additional gold uniforms, turbans, and the other paraphernalia necessary to create the impression that Dodds had in mind. The local ramp service manager, Chris Edwards, had been particularly abrupt in rejecting this proposal, insisting that it did not make sense and that he was going to have absolutely nothing to do with it. Dodds had in several meetings attempted to "sell," persuade, pressure, and finally threaten Edwards into accepting the plan. Edwards refusal had become more adamant and pointed at every step. Relationships between the two, never close or cordial, had deteriorated until there was now nothing but the most unrestrained hostility expressed between them.

REACTION OF THE SERVICE MANAGER

Chris Edwards was a graduate engineer who had worked for the company for about ten years. He had first started in the maintenance department of the firm and had gradually risen through several supervisory positions before being given this position as service manager with Eagle. It was the first position he had had in which he had an independent budget and was held individually accountable. After three years in this capacity, he personally felt and had been led to believe by several higher executives in the company that he had acquired as much experience in this position as was necessary. He was, therefore, looking forward to a new assignment, which probably involved a promotion in the very near future. He realized that this promotion would probably be based upon his earlier proven technical competence and his more recent experience as regional manager, when he had run a particularly efficient operation. This was evidenced by several reductions in his operating expenses, due to efficiencies he had installed, and by other measures of performance, such as a reduction in the time necessary to service, fuel, and load aircraft.

After having met with increasingly adamant refusals by Edwards, Dodds had gone to his superior, the district sales manager, pointing out that he was being hampered by Edwards in his effort to increase sales and advance the company. The district sales manager had made a point of seeing his counterpart, the district service manager, asking if something could not be done by the service people at Bartlett City to support the sales effort. Upon inquiry, the district service manager learned the details of the request from Edwards and the reasons for his refusal. Dodds kept insistent pressure on his superior, asking to have something done about the local service manager's obstinacy. Eventually, word of the continued arguments between Dodds and Edwards went up the chain of command to the vice-president of sales and later to the vice-president in charge of service. One day while discussing this issue, their conversation was overheard by the president. Upon hearing the story, he made the comment that these personality clashes would either have to be straightened out or one or both of the men either transferred or, for that matter, fired. He emphatically insisted that the company could not operate efficiently with an unnecessary expenditure of energy going into personal disputes.

Case C-26
SEVENTEENTH NATIONAL BANK, DATA PROCESSING DEPARTMENT

BACKGROUND

Described here is a computer programming department in an aggressive bank located in the Dallas-Fort Worth metroplex. Overall, the bank is experiencing moderate growth now and forecasts better than moderate growth in the future in both the data processing department

Source: Adapted from a course assignment prepared by W. D. Lincoln for Professor J. G. Hunt, University of Texas, Arlington. Copyright © Osborn, Hunt, and Jauch, 1980.

and other operations. The objectives of bank management are to make the bank competitive with the largest banks in the area and to expand the data processing department into a service bureau to handle the computer processing functions of banks and other financial outlets in addition to those of Seventeenth National (SN).

The exact goals of the data processing department as a service bureau have not been established. Currently, the department acts as a small service bureau and is doing computer processing for four banks other than SN. One of the four banks has already indicated that it intends not to renew its contract with the service bureau because the bank is getting its own computer and feels the work can be performed in-house less expensively.

Of the four banks being serviced, the three that will remain generate little revenue for the service bureau. One of the three is very small and is being serviced only because of its name. The service bureau uses it as bait to attract new customers.

The revenue earned from servicing outside companies is used by the service bureau to help offset the costs of doing its own bank's computer processing. In the future, management would like the data processing department to become a significant revenue source and, possibly, even separate from the parent bank acting as a subsidiary.

The data processing department employs people in three major departments: keypunch (15); computer operations (10); and programming (10). The department, as a whole, is managed by one person who has a private secretary. This gives the data processing department a total of 37 people, as shown in Exhibit V-9.

Prospective clients of the data processing department are interviewed by its manager to determine feasibility and profitability of the venture. If both sides agree to a contract, a date is set indicating when services will begin. The date chosen must conform to existing workloads and schedules of keypunch, operations, and programming. Work capacity for these departments is usually scheduled at least six months ahead of time, since new people may have to be hired and trained or new machinery purchased to accommodate servicing customers. The six-month schedule is revised frequently to adjust priorities of jobs.

The first major service performed by the data processing department for a new customer is to design the computer system that satisfies the client needs. Meetings are held between experienced programmers, the data processing manager, and the new customer to determine which programs and procedures will be required to meet those needs.

After the system is designed and agreed upon by all parties, programmers write the programs in the system. Depending on the size of the system, a staff of programmers will be chosen to manage the work on the project. Since most systems designed by this data processing department are usually small, one person is assigned the job of managing the project. The title given to this person is "project leader"; he or she will be responsible for making sure that programs

Exhibit V-9   Data Processing Department Structure

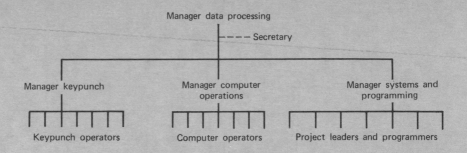

are written to conform to design specifications and that the project will be completed on time.

People selected to work on new systems are chosen by the data processing manager and the manager of systems and programming. Even though a person may hold a specific title assigned as a result of a promotion previous to this project (e.g., systems analyst, project leader, or programmer), this person may occupy one of several positions while working on this system. A "programmer" may be assigned as the leader of this project with other programmers working for him or her. This is done to train the person for a project leader position should he or she be promoted to that position later on.

The time that it takes to design and implement a system ranges anywhere from a few days to several years. Most major systems in this particular data processing department take three months to a year to complete. During this time, the programmers will write and test new programs, while the project leader coordinates their activities, answers their questions, monitors time and resources spent on the project, and initiates any changes required to the baseline design. People on the project are allowed much flexibility in the hours they work as long as milestones needed for the system are completed on time.

Frequently, small program maintenance jobs are given to project leaders and programmers while these people are assigned to a project. These maintenance jobs are usually unrelated to the project and need to be performed because an existing program was not set up to handle it, or the problem may be that a customer has requested that a change be made to comply with a new law. The reasons why program maintenance jobs originate are numerous, but nevertheless they require attention and completion.

Too many program maintenance jobs assigned to people working on projects can cause the original estimated project completion date to be missed. This happens quite frequently, and customers get very upset when they are told that their system won't be ready for another three weeks, or even longer.

Writing a new system for a customer is similar to constructing a bridge or a building. Much planning is required before any work actually takes place. After the workers are hired, a great deal of coordination and additional planning is required to keep the job on schedule and to make sure that the job is done according to engineer's specifications. Without the right controls, the final product can be a total disaster, and sometimes is.

SUMMARY CHARACTERISTICS

Size. The total size of this bank is 600 to 700 employees. At the first and second levels in the data processing department, the number of employees is 32 and 5, respectively. Overall, the bank is experiencing 10 to 15 percent annual growth and predicts that this growth will continue in the future.

Work Flow. Work flow in the data processing department is highly specialized in keypunch and computer operations, but the opposite is true in programming. Programmers perform a variety of tasks such as writing new programs, correcting problems in existing programs, documenting procedures, keypunching small amounts of data, meeting with customers, and teaching classes to customers and other programmers on technological changes and enhancements. Regardless of the task performed, it is almost always interdependent with the work of someone else.

Tasks. Task outcome predictability in programming is high in the long-term sense, but not necessarily so in the short term. Programmers usually (but not al-

ways) know what the eventual product of their work will be. A programmer must test programs that he or she writes or modifies before letting the program be used on customers' "live" data. Programs do not always function as intended at first. Different data are processed by the programmer through the program to test as many conditions as possible. Sometimes a program will malfunction because it handles a certain condition differently than intended. This is called a "bug" by computer people, and it results from not testing the program properly.

Even though a programmer may consult a more experienced programmer about how to handle a problem, the programmer is still not assured that the advice given is always reliable in all situations. There are usually many different ways to handle the same condition in a program, but many times each method depends on such things as the size of the computer, its speed, the amount of data being processed, and how often it is processed. Each time advice is given, these factors should be considered by all concerned.

Physical Surroundings. The programmers are all in one room and all of the project leaders are in another. Visual barriers in each room are strategically placed to reduce eye contact, but no barriers exist to prevent or reduce noise. Interruptions take place constantly, and some programmers have even had to take their work home in order to have enough peace and quiet to concentrate.

Delegation. Much discretion is given to programmers on how to handle a particular problem. Programmers are required to research certain topics selected for them by the programming manager and give a two-hour class to the rest of the programmers. The intent of the education program is to keep the programmers informed about new ways of handling program problems, technological enhancements that eliminate certain other problems, or a refresher course in selecting the best way among existing resources to handle them. The method chosen to handle the problem is left up to each programmer, and very few of the decisions are ever referred outside of the department.

Standards and Rewards and Penalties. Standards for programmers are set very high. They are exceptionally clear and can be measured quite accurately. Sometimes classes are held to let the programmers modify existing standards or add new ones. The programming department is very "standards" oriented and strongly encourages that each person follow these when writing programs.

Rewards and penalties are directly related to performance. Programmers are given salary reviews every six months. If the programmer did a good job during the previous six months, he or she is given a raise and possibly a promotion. Those who perform poorly get no raises or promotions and may be discharged if their performance continues to be less than satisfactory.

Supervision. Supervisory rule enforcement is strict only when actually writing programs; other rules are not strictly enforced. Close direction is usually given to all people in the department. Deadlines for work must be made and quality of work must be satisfactory. Inducements are usually in the form of rewards, with penalties used primarily for poor performers.

CURRENT CONCERN

The bank president has recently talked to the data processing manager about organization of the department. She (the president) is wondering if the department is organized as well as it should be, given its current internal and external data processing mission and other crucial variables. She is also wondering what the structure should look like two and five years from now if the bank and department growth-estimates are even approximately correct. She expects the department to aggressively pursue the outside business mentioned earlier and is willing to grant the department head as much authority as needed to accomplish his external and internal missions. She also has said she will grant reasonable budget increases if they can be justified. The department head knows she didn't get the name "Iron Nell" for nothing. She is a bear on efficiency and doesn't like high turnover even among programmers, who are known for their notoriously high turnover rate. The data processing manager knows that he must put together a report for her in the near future if he is to be able to get the increased budget he feels he needs.

THE JZZYZLPLKK COMPANY

PART 1—BEFORE

The Jzzyzlplkk Company was a manufacturing company in Midtown, that employed about 250 plant and office workers and fifty outside salesmen who covered most of the continental United States. Midtown is a midwestern town of about 15,000 people. The town's economic structure was based upon some 3000 industrial jobs. Midtown's economy was in a state of stagnation from closures and reductions in industrial activity. The town maintained a precarious economic equilibrium, though a new-industry recruiting program was initiated with the help of a nearby university.

The population of Midtown included three main segments. There were the descendents of the original settlers, with farm backgrounds. Many of these inherited small landholdings and augmented their farm income with industrial jobs. Then there were the people who had come north from the southern hill country to take railroad jobs in the 1920s; this group included many blacks. Finally, there were the oil-field workers who had followed a short-lived boom and then stayed on. All these groups were known for their commitment to the notions of hard work and thrift.

Source: Adapted from a course assignment prepared by J. Thompson for Professor J. G. Hunt, Southern Illinois University, Carbondale. Copyright © Osborn, Hunt, and Jauch, 1980.

The company was located in Midtown in 1927 by its founder Joseph Jzzyzlplkk (JJ). JJ had chosen the site for two main reasons. He was running away from a labor dispute in a nearby town, and the chamber of commerce offered a site grant worth $100,000 for him to do so. This site grant was a contingent deed that required that he operate in Midtown for a specified number of years and that he pay out a stipulated amount in payroll. By local reputation, the Jzzyzlplkk Company was known as a poor place to work. Working for the company had a certain adverse social stigma. Despite this, the company had little trouble recruiting the necessary manpower.

Two sons, Frank and Tim, had, by the 1950s, succeeded their father in control of the company. They had grown up in the business. The older, Tim, was the vice-president and treasurer, and Frank was the president and secretary. Tim headed marketing and administrative matters, and Frank ran the production operations. The three family members were the board of directors and owned all except 1 percent of the company's stock.

Although Tim was the official head of marketing operations, its acknowledged leader was actually Matt Uris. Uris tried unsuccessfully to organize a group to buy the company. Uris had the title of sales manager and owned no stock in the company.

Jack Newton, the assistant general manager, was the remaining main executive and headed all the administrative units except general accounting and finance. Both Newton and Uris reported to Tim who also held the title of general manager. The casewriter held the position of controller.

By the 1950s JJ was nearly 80. As a boy he had immigrated from Germany with his father. Starting in the 1920s with a new method of assembling porcelain, JJ founded a highly successful business. In 1927, after failing to settle with the labor union, he moved his business to Midtown.

JJ had all his cash invested in his firm when the Great Depression occurred. He was able to maintain the business throughout the Depression and by the end of World War II, the firm was highly successful. By that time too, Frank and Tim were in nominal charge of the business. Adding to the postwar success of the firm was a new product based on war-generated sales and marketing skills provided by Uris. In essence, the nucleus of a new business was established.

The business was a greater success than any of the Jzzyzlplkk family had ever hoped for. The net worth of the company increased from $300,000 at the end of World War II to over $3 million in the mid-fifties, even with the liberal salaries and bonuses taken by the Jzzyzlplkks. Actually, the success was a source of great concern to the Jzzyzlplkks. They could not see a way to take the profits out of the company without paying the confiscatory double taxes; and at the same time, they were certain that the bubble of postwar prosperity was to burst any day.

Tim and Frank often said that they did not hire any executives. They would come to the office at three in the afternoon twice a week. Then, at a few minutes before the five o'clock quitting time, they would call their key men into their office, break out a bottle of whiskey, and devote the next five or six hours listening to their ideas, attitudes, and problems. Sometimes these sessions got rowdy and were always tiring. They always involved a game of one-upmanship as the *de facto* executives vied with each other to express their views, for these meetings were the only time devoted to staff problems. Most of the major administrative, marketing, and production decisions were outcomes of these sessions. All the other major decisions were made in two other monthly meetings.

Once a month, a half day was spent reviewing the hourly paid employees. The rule of thumb for wage increases was a 2½-cent hourly increase for female employees and a 5-cent hourly increase for male employees. The rules pertained to both plant employees and hourly paid office employees. Each was reviewed every three months, and the increase was contingent on good conduct and good performance.

The other monthly meeting was held to decide what would be produced for the upcoming month and what employees would be used to produce it. Old JJ had a formula devised many years before for production: a man for each unit of daily production, and one salesman and one office clerk for every four production workers. Firm decisions were made to produce for the upcoming month two weeks before the beginning of the month. The company was to be committed for inventory purchases two months ahead of scheduled production to keep the pipeline filled: the plans all followed the minimum possible planning horizon.

After these decisions were made, the additional people needed were hired or the extra people not needed were fired. The meetings were always held on Thursdays; payday was Friday and that was also the day that the layoffs were announced. Company policy did not allow for severance pay. A union represented the factory employees, and any layoff was ordered on a reverse seniority basis, with the recalls to work on a seniority basis.

The office clerks, mostly young women, were not represented by a union. Extra office clerks were hired on a three-months, short-run basis, required by the seasonal nature of the company's product. The layoff of office clerks usually occurred once a year following the busy season. However, Newton also took advantage of the "layoff" to rid himself of his least-effective workers. So, to the office clerk, being laid off was equivalent to being fired.

At this time, office clerks' wages were about 85 to 90 percent of the competitive local scale, and 60 to 65 percent of the statewide mean rates. The factory wage scales were about 75 to 80 percent of the competitive local rates and 60 to 65 percent of the statewide mean rates.

Most of the female office clerks worked in a fairly large general-office

room. On a small, elevated platform, facing all the "girls," stood the old-fashioned desk of Newton. He kept the girls under his personal observation all day. A buzzer on his desk sounded at eight in the morning to signal the start of the day. It sounded again at noon to announce the 30-minute lunch break, at 12:30 to resume, and finally at 4:30 to quit for the day. The office girls, as well as the plant workers, worked six days: Monday through Saturday. With the six-days pay and the overtime bonus for Saturday work, the average hourly rate compared with the local average. Tim and Frank often said that they worked their people six days to keep them from looking for other jobs.

The office force was usually about 60 people, 35 women and 25 men. There was one rest room for each sex, and each was equipped with one stool and one lavatory. The morning "rush hour" also became the morning gossip session as the employees waited their turns, smoking and gossiping. The rest rooms and the adjacent areas were the only place that one could go without being observed by Newton. He did not smoke, though he allowed the men but not the women to smoke at their desks. Usually three or four women at a time could squeeze into the rest room, which measured about four by four; everytime the door opened the smoke billowed out.

Newton signed not only his own work, but everything prepared by the people who worked for him. In spite of Saturday work, the office was always behind schedule. The functions performed included: processing customers' orders, postshipping follow-up on orders, billing, accounts receivable, credit, and collections. In addition to these order-accounting functions, the office also performed the following production control work: inventory control, production material requirements, preparation of requisitions and purchase orders, expediting follow-ups, preparation of shop orders, and production-order closures.

The latter procedural system was fairly involved and worked reasonably well. The product itself was fairly complex and required an array of over 200 purchased parts and components as well as numerous fasteners and bulk-material purchases. A creditable job of control was performed through the use of the system, despite the tie-in coordination requirements among production, purchasing, and the general office.

The casewriter had installed the order and billing system. The system had been operating for about two years. The clerks had a good understanding of their assigned tasks. Under observed, timed studies, they performed competently and at a high rate of proficiency. Nevertheless, on Friday afternoons the office was behind in its work schedule, and Saturday overtime work was required to catch up.

The office employee voluntary turnover rate was about 65 percent, and mean length of service was about a year and a half. In addition, there was the involuntary turnover rate resulting from the policy of using seasonal help during the firm's busy season.

PART 2—AFTER

The business was sold in mid-November, and the takeover was immediate.

The buyers appointed Newton as first vice-president and authorized him to continue operations until Oscar Junkie, the new president, arrived the first of December. Tim, Frank, and JJ, as a condition of the selling agreement, were retained on a consulting basis for five years.

On the first of December, Junkie, the new president, showed up alone, except for his briefcase. He was a charming man who smiled easily. First, he called in Uris, Newton, Azrin—the plant superintendent, and the casewriter, and he talked to them. After serving coffee, he introduced himself and asked the others to do the same. After this, he asked each of them to make a list of no more than ten things that they thought they should do in their individual areas of responsibility. Then he dismissed the four after telling them to return with their lists in an hour. When Uris, Newton, and the casewriter returned with their lists, they found him with Azrin packing the liquor that Tim and Frank had used to "prime their meetings." He authorized the liquor to be given as a gift to Tim and Frank and said that it would not be needed anymore.

Junkie took the lists from each of the people and wrote the first three items from the top of each list onto a separate sheet of paper and wrote each individual's name alongside their recommendations. He then had the list typed and presented each of them with a copy saying that these would be the company's goals for the next month and that after a month they would reexamine their goals. He then asked for the staff to be assembled so that he could meet and talk to them.

When Junkie addressed the staff, he explained that the new owners had intended to "buy" the people who were working for the company. The buyers believed that people were the most important asset in any successful company. He told them not to be concerned over their jobs as no personnel changes were intended. He promised that they would be made when he understood the company better and promised that these would be for the betterment of the company and its personnel. He had coffee served and chatted with the various staff members. Later, he spent the remainder of the day talking to all the other company employees in groups of 25 to 50 throughout the plant complex. He gave each group the same message that he had given the staff. The next day, he prepared a letter for a mailing to the home of every employee. The letter covered the same points that he had made in his talks.

Within the next thirty days, a bewildering array of new titles began to be announced in the "administrative department" headed by Newton. The purchasing clerk became the purchasing director, the personnel clerk became the personnel director, the credit clerk became the credit manager, and so forth. About this time, Junkie sent for the casewriter to come to his office. Newton was with Junkie, and in his presence he asked the casewriter to assume the responsibility for the general office. The job was accepted on the conditions of hiring a new assistant controller to handle general accounting and of making changes in the office setup: more space, larger rest rooms, including a small lounge area for the female employees, permission for smoking and drinking coffee, and a survey to review and upgrade the salary and wage structure. The conditions were all accepted, and construction was started within three weeks and was finished within another month.

Under the new management, Uris was promoted to vice-president of marketing at the end of three months. Within a short time, new titles began appearing with the same degree of suddenness as seen in the administrative department. There were so many title upgradings that people joked about "generals of the Ruratanian Army." Even so, nameplates appeared on desks and doors. The shirtsleeve nature of the business faded; the men wore their coats *all day* while at their desks. Salary changes were minimal, as salaries for key people had always been competitive or better, in return for hard work.

Monthly staff meetings later became the custom. Here, key goals were determined. For example, a sales goal was established for 30 percent of the unit market and 55 percent of the dollar volume, a 3 percent average growth-rate goal was set, and centralized executive filing was to replace the scattered private files used by the various executives. At first, the firm started budgeting within an outline, to finish the fiscal year then in progress. This beginning was followed by a formalized and participative budgeting system that covered six-month planning horizons and a tentative additional six-month planning program beyond that. The budget was published every six months and distributed to the department heads. Special subunit budgets were sent to the section heads of all the various cost centers.

A new union contract was negotiated even though the old one still had a year to run of its original two-year life. Wage rates were adjusted to 90 percent of the local competitive rate, and progressive, 5 percent, six-month increments were provided for over the two-year life of the new agreement. The monthly union-management meetings were abolished and future union-management meetings were arranged to be held only on request; there was never another union-management meeting held that required the attendance of the president. From that time on, the personnel director, along with Newton and Azrin, the plant superintendent, handled the biennial labor negotiations.

The general office people seemed satisfied with the larger offices and rest rooms as well as the other privileges, but they were still behind in their work schedules. Junkie suggested that the office drop Saturday work and move to a five-day week. Though skeptical, the casewriter finally agreed to a five-and-one-half-day week on a trial basis. If the trial failed, then the six-day week would be resumed, but with an increased pay rate.

Later, the casewriter assembled the general office people and explained the plan and the contingencies: a five-and-a-half-day workweek with no reduction in pay, contingent on the work being kept up to schedule. At the end of the first trial week, the work was completely caught up, and similar results were obtained for three more consecutive weeks. When Junkie received the report of this, he laughed and said it always happens that way. After discussing it further, it was decided to make a similar trial of a five-day week on the same set of preconditions. The trial was made and the results were similar.

During the first year under the new owners, the state nearly completed construction of a large custodial-type institution in Midtown. The institution planned eventually to hire about 700 people. Salaries and wages were based on statewide surveys and equalization formulas, and there were generous holiday and sick leave provisions. In addition, two small branch factories had located in the local industrial park and planned to hire between 75 to 100 people each.

Given the entrance of these organizations into the community, management felt that the exodus from the Jzzyzlplkk Company would be massive.

Surprisingly, not one office employee was lost to the institution. The voluntary turnover rate declined to less than 10 percent. Although efforts were made to level the monthly rate of production to stabilize the level of employment, the problem of the short-term hiring and firing policy for meeting seasonal demand variations was never satisfactorily solved.

Later, and in conjunction with labor negotiations leading toward a new union contract, the five-day workweek was also made standard for the plant employees. This change to a five-day workweek later created an unforeseen problem. When the busy season arrived, it was difficult to get either office workers or factory workers to work overtime, especially on Saturdays. Attempts to line up work crews for Saturday would yield less than a 50 percent show-up rate. Frequently, fewer than half of those who promised to come in would actually show up for work.

By the time the company negotiated the first renewal of the labor contract, the turnover rate of factory employees had dropped to less than 25 percent of the rate before the business was sold. But the low-absentee rate that held before the business was sold nearly tripled. An additional 4 percent had to be hired to compensate for the increased absenteeism. Grievances filed against the company did not change, but they had never been significant under either one of the management groups. The personnel director could not sense any hostility when he interviewed the absentees: they merely said that they were sick. Absenteeism was no longer confined to the "old faithfuls," who continued their familiar patterns, but now it included people who had never missed work before and were beginning to miss a day or two a month.

When the union contract came up for renewal, the company did not get the usual "letter to Santa Claus." Instead, the fairly moderate wage increase of 20 cents an hour was asked. The established pattern was: the union would ask for 50 cents, the company would counter the offer with 5 cents, the union to a quarter, the company to a dime, then settle for 15 cents. This departure from the old pattern was tentatively interpreted as a condition of near satisfaction with wages. However, the employees did ask for Washington's Birthday, Co-

lumbus Day, Veterans' Day, and their own birthdays as additional paid holidays—the old contract provided seven paid holidays: New Year's Day, Memorial Day, Independence Day, Labor Day, two days at Thanksgiving, and Christmas Day. In addition, they asked for the second vacation week after 3 years rather than 4 years, the third vacation week after 7 years rather than after 10 years, and four weeks after 11 years rather than 15 years. They also asked for simultaneous department-wide work breaks rather than the system of staggered work breaks then in effect. The final request was for a simultaneous lunch break rather than staggered lunch breaks.

When the company countered the offer with a five-cent increase, another week on the vacations for three years and longer, and two additional paid holidays, the break times seemed to be the greatest source of resistance. It was explained that the company's rest room facilities were not adequate to handle simultaneous breaks; the argument got nowhere. After several negotiations, the contract was settled with a 7½-cent an hour increase, two additional paid holidays, the original, union-proposed vacation schedule, and the promise for the simultaneous work breaks. To deliver on this promise, it was necessary to spend over $75,000 to build the additional rest rooms needed to handle the simultaneous work breaks.

Within a few weeks, after the simultaneous work breaks were implemented, the individual coffeepots got to be such a nuisance that the company, to keep down the clutter and extra safety hazards, finally bought several urns and provided free coffee for the breaks.

THE CENTRAL JUNIOR COLLEGE SYSTEM

PART 1—THE SYSTEM

The Central Junior College System was started in 1911, when 28 students were enrolled in college-level courses at two public high schools. In the early sixties the system had nine branch colleges, with a combined enrollment of 25,000 students. (Recent estimates indicated that this enrollment would increase 86 percent by the early seventies, necessitating a 75 percent increase in the junior college administration, faculty, and staff.)

The primary purpose of the various branches of the college was to service the needs of the immediate community. The courses were designed to (1) provide a student with a two-year education that would "technically," emotionally, and intellectually prepare him or her for the employment selected; (2) prepare the student for further academic work at a four-year college or university; or (3) allow persons, other than regular college students, to pursue their special interests at the college level. In addition, special courses were offered as training sessions for several city departments such as fire, police, health, human relations, and public school food service.

Operating revenue was obtained from city and state taxes. New construc-

tion and expansion had sometimes been aided by special grants. Special programs were often instituted with grants from private foundations at no expense to the junior college system.

Recently, a student was able to receive a two-year college education for as low as $200, exclusive of books and materials. Obviously, the Central Junior College System gave many students an opportunity they would not otherwise have. This benefit was reflected either in the student's ability to extend his or her education beyond the high school level or in the student's completion of undergraduate work without depleting his or her financial security during the first two years of college. The system had no housing facilities, since it was designed to serve the students of the immediate community.

The student body was composed of extremes in economic, social, and educational status. For example, a branch might have had a retired college professor taking a course in a field foreign to his or her discipline or students in a remedial program because of inadequate preparation for college work. It was conceivable that a professor would meet some former students in the same class. Though a large portion of the student body was made up of students who had run into academic difficulty at other colleges or universities, academic standards

Source: Adapted from a course assignment prepared by K. Finley for Professor J. G. Hunt, University of Illinois, Urbana-Champaign. Copyright © Osborn, Hunt, and Jauch, 1980.

were considered to be relatively high, particularly for a junior college. A recent survey revealed that students from the junior college who completed their education at other colleges and universities did so with commendable grades, and that only a surprisingly small percentage were unsuccessful.

The Central Junior College System had worked extremely hard in the past few years to rid itself of the strongly ingrained "junior college" image the general public, the student body, the board of education, and even some of its administrative officers felt the various branches displayed. A new executive dean was appointed to coordinate the activities of the branch college deans and generally upgrade the system in order to improve its acceptance in the community.

The success had been great, and there was growing belief that the system was becoming a model junior college. National recognition had been received for the junior college system's educational television station, which was the first in the nation to offer regular full-credit college courses. Several hundred students had completed the necessary work for the Associate in Arts degree, the recognized degree for a two-year college course.

More recently, the emphasis was on keeping up with technological advances. Even with limited funds, a comprehensive electronics laboratory was installed in one of the branches. Food service and nursing curricula were also developed. But the real indication of broadening the course offerings came with the implementation of the data processing curriculum. A greater variety of courses in this field were taught here than at many of the more prominent colleges in the state.

Beyond these improvements in the "product," the executive dean was successful in receiving the active support, both financial and otherwise, of the city's chamber of commerce and several other associations and foundations. It became obvious that the dean was administratively competent, and he was given more or less full authority over the junior college system. Up to this time, the executive dean was considered to be a member of the central staff of the board of education. His main function was to advise the superintendent of higher education on junior college affairs. During this time the individual branch deans operated independently. Broad policy decisions or specific directives were passed down from above, but on the whole they had great freedom in operating their particular branch within these parameters (see Exhibit V-10).

With this new authority the executive dean felt coordination of the junior college system could become a fact rather than a product of someone's imagination. Prior to this time, the branches were dealt with independently where specific problems of the junior college system existed. Coordination was attempted, but much duplication of activity and resources continued to exist. There was no real standardization of operations, and the various branches were too dissimilar to be coordinated in such a loose fashion.

In implementing this change, the executive dean made it clear to the

Exhibit V-10 Top Administration Before and After Reorganization

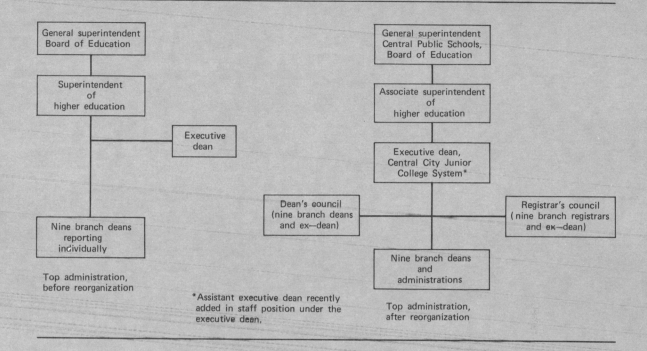

General superintendent
Board of Education

Superintendent
of
higher education

Executive
dean

Nine branch deans
reporting
individually

Top administration,
before reorganization

General superintendent
Central Public Schools,
Board of Education

Associate superintendent
of
higher education

Executive dean,
Central City Junior
College System*

Dean's council
(nine branch deans
and ex—dean)

Registrar's council
(nine branch registrars
and ex—dean)

Nine branch deans
and
administrations

*Assistant executive dean recently
added in staff position under the
executive dean.

Top administration,
after reorganization

branch deans that he would not interfere with the operation of the individual branches except where such matters conflicted with or unnecessarily duplicated operations of other branches. He stressed that the deans should be active, not only in administering the branch, but in advancing its achievement. He particularly stressed that they work closely with their community leaders and citizens, in general, to gain acceptance and support.

The executive dean felt that for effective coordination to be obtained, the deans would have to work actively toward the implementation of these principles. Furthermore, he felt this could not be accomplished without the deans assembling in a group to discuss such problems. As a result, he formed the Dean's Council. The meeting of the deans would also enable them to discuss and solve their own problems without his intervention. The executive dean and his new role were well accepted by the branch deans. They all started thinking not only in terms of their own particular branch, but in terms of the overall junior college system and their place within it (see Exhibit V-10).

Meetings were held monthly and special meetings were called in planning for such things as registration and expansion. The committee approach had been extended to the functional areas of the administration. Registrars and directors of student services had their own committees that met with or without the executive dean, as he or they requested.

PART 2—BRANCHES A AND B

Branch A of the junior college system was the largest, with about 9000 students. The administration consisted of a dean in charge of the overall operation and faculty affairs; department heads, and heads of all staff functions who report to the dean; an assistant dean in charge of registration, with an administrative assistant; an assistant dean in charge of property and finance, with an assistant; a director of student services; a registrar, with an administrative assistant; a placement director; a director of student activities; and a director of admissions. Nominally included in the administration were the librarian, the treasurer, and the maintenance engineer (see Exhibit V-11).

Exhibit V-11   Organization: Branch A

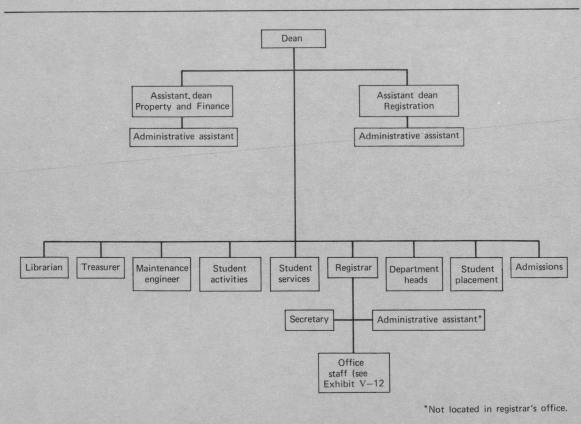

The registrar's office had 20 people performing various tasks essential to processing and maintaining student records (see Exhibit V-12).

Branch B was the newest branch of the junior college system. The administration consisted of a dean, an assistant dean, a director of student services, and a registrar. Nominally included were the building manager, the librarian, and the treasurer (see Exhibit V-13). The school had an enrollment of 4000. The registrar's staff consisted of ten people.

A comparison of these two registrar's offices will reveal some striking differences in the way their activities were carried out.

BRANCH A

In Branch A the activities of the clerks were highly confined to one part of the total area of functioning of the registrar's office. For example, the two clerks who worked on preparing the records for graduation never performed any other kind of work. They also did not work in the registration process, since this coincided with the peak in the cycle of their work. Generally, the only clerks to be

Exhibit V-12 Registrar's Office: Branch A

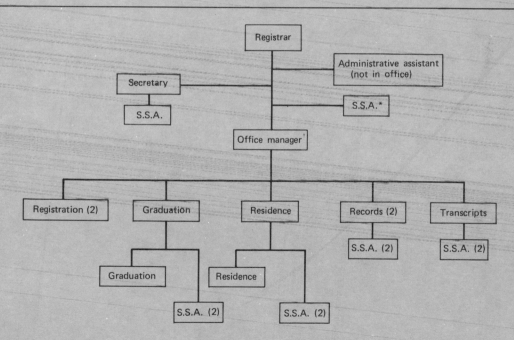

*S.S.A. = student service aide (part—time,
'Office manager, secretary, and clerks are
civil service.

Exhibit V-13 Organization: Branch B

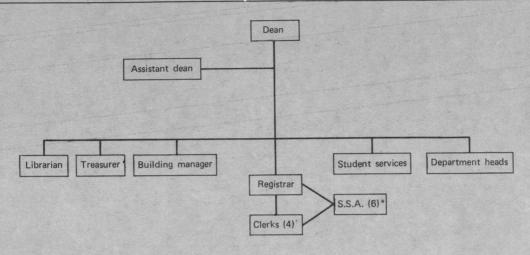

* S.S.A. — student service aid (part—time).
† Clerks are civil service.

assigned tasks not fitting into any of the listed areas of the registrar's were the records clerks. The student assistants assigned to the various clerks were almost as rigorously confined. There was never any outright refusal to work in another activity, but it was made plain that their "own" work would suffer. Helping a clerk working on another kind of project was not done often. Furthermore, it was not looked upon happily by the person who received the help.

Thus, the method of operation remained stable over a long period of time. For example, several of the record forms were designed for use with information from an electronic data processing system. These forms were the subject of much criticism, and often it was claimed they were impossible to work with. Three years later this office was still using old forms and techniques where possible, with no complaints, even though it was harder and the motivation of extra pay was not present. It was clearly understood that there would be no overtime work. The new system of processing the registration forms was seen only as interfering with efficiency. The automatic system was used only in processing a minor part of the records, typically those that were generated at the height of registration periods, when the staff was overloaded. The effect was to remove this overload and, with the proper handling, it facilitated work throughout the remainder of the period. There was no fear of a job loss since employees were all under civil service classifications.

Clerks would not mind staying late, without extra pay, to complete a project. They worked well together during the registration period. The amount of work to be processed within these few days was unbelievable. It was not uncommon during this time to work over 16 hours a day. This meant not only staying late in the evening, but also reporting early in the morning as well. No overtime rate was granted during this time. There was a feeling that they are "all in it together."

Contact with other staff departments was on a rather limited basis. While not discourteous or unhelpful, they gave the impression that these outside people were not fully accepted by the clerks in the registrar's office. Even social conversation was on a rather formal basis. They generally did not have contact with the heads of other departments.

BRANCH B

In contrast to this, the situation at Branch B was quite different. The branch was considered to be slightly understaffed, but the registrar's office was considered to be the most efficient in the junior college system. Several other branch registrars commented openly about the efficiency and cooperation the staff displayed.

The office was headed by the registrar. There was no office manager; each civil service clerk reported directly to the registrar to receive their assignments. Student service aides were nominally assigned to a clerk, but they received assignments directly from other clerks and the registrar. These assignments were made on the basis of first completing an assigned project.

There was no assignment to a specific functional area of the registrar's office, although this could logically have been done by combining several of the congruent functions. The registrar assigned report development and other significant tasks to the clerical staff. In other branches these functions were reserved for the registrar.

There was also close contact between the registrar's staff and other departments. Since other departments were small and often needed extra help temporarily, the office staff did some work outside the registrar's office. These assignments were made with the consent of the registrar and the clerk involved. Assignments varied from day-to-day, and except for the very routine matters, no one had a specific area of responsibility. Nor was the caliber of the assignment considered on a rotational basis. The work was there and the clerks selected it in the order it was to be done.

When the electronic data processing system was installed, it was well and easily accepted. At first there were major difficulties with the actual operation of the system. Many records had to be reprocessed, and some of the problems this caused had to be lived with for the entire semester.

There were frequent meetings between the assistant dean, registrar, and civil service clerks. The staff's advice concerning problems was honestly requested. At first there was reluctance for anyone to comment because none of the clerks really understood how the process functioned technically. Shortly thereafter, the assistant dean prepared charts and descriptions as to the overall functioning of the system. These were studied by the staff, who responded well to them. Many meaningful suggestions were subsequently given on how the handling of information in the branch could be adjusted to meet these new requirements of the data processing system. Whenever there was to be a change, the staff was consulted, not so much for their approval, as for their criticisms of possible operational shortcomings.

Competence seemed to be the keynote of this registrar's office. The clerks had a broad knowledge of the work being done. They met a different assignment with enthusiasm if it showed promise of being interesting.

The clerks helped one another, but this help was asked for and given only when it was really needed. There were times when the registrar was prodded by the clerks to speed up his own work. Relations with the registrar, some of the instructional departmental heads, and the assistant dean were extremely informal. On the other hand, some of the other department heads and administrative officers did not fare so well. Sometimes people in the registrar's office were too busy to help them. This was conveyed politely, of course, but not in a way that left any doubt as to their sincerity.

Cooperation and relations with other staff clerks were good. Clerks from these other departments liked to work in the registrar's office. In fact, there was pressure from some of the clerks to combine all the offices into a central office.

Cooperation was extremely good during the registration period. Often, even the lunch period was delayed until things could be cleared up. The clerks felt a strong dependence on clerks in other departments and, in turn, they felt a deep responsibility and commitment to do a good job.

NAME INDEX

SUBJECT INDEX

Contextual complexity, 325–335
  passim, 343, 354, 491
Contextual factors, 226, 250, 327–332,
  337, 342, 347, 382, 490, 491,
  492, 500
  and vertical specialization, 280
Contextual goal requirements, 324
Contextual variables, 3, 6, 226, 227,
  251, 253, 275, 298, 325–337
  passim, 347, 385
  and horizontal specialization,
  296–297
Contingency
  analysis, 224
  approach, 3, 6, 10, 445, 450
  chapters, ix, x, xiv, 109, 127, 206,
  217, 227, 488
  and criteria, 77–78, 86
  critical, 376, 492
  discussion of, 488
  and environment, 210, 300
  and mid range analysis, 8, 9
  models, 461, 476
  plan, 499
  and situational approach, 9
  variables, 83, 116, 461, 466, 471
  views, 36, 322, 328, 363, 486
  see also Leadership
Contingency leadership approaches,
  364, 476, 503
  discussion of, 455–471
  summary comparison of, 471
Control, 175–188, 212–219 *passim,*
  252, 275–304 *passim,* 335, 346,
  429, 490–498 *passim*
  and coordination, 300, 307
  locus of, 493n
  procedures, 300
  span of, 244, 281, 303, 323
  systems, 282–284, 284–286,
  286–287, 295, 298, 304, 342
  techniques of, 280–284
  vertical, 292, 297–298
Coordination, 341, 372
  and communication, 413, 425
  and control, 292, 296, 334, 429,
  490, 492, 498

mechanisms, 292, 305
need for, 413
problems of, 339, 492
and specialization, 306, 332, 340,
  490
Criteria, 55, 58, 72, 87, 93, 109, 110,
  113, 214
  consistency of, 381
  and contingency, 77, 83, 86
  and general environment, 212
  and group variables, 413, 423, 504,
  505
  kinds of, 35, 53, 60, 72, 73, 76, 79,
  82, 84, 86, 109, 118, 207, 367
  and leadership, 447, 456, 457, 463,
  466, 471–472, 473, 474
  measures, 35, 110
  and organizational characteristics,
  109, 226, 235, 244
  relationships among, 82–83, 110,
  113–118
  relevance of, 113
Culture, 124–125, 130–131, 138, 156,
  410
  condition, 488
  definition of, 130
  demands, 133
  measures, 156
  patterns, 155
  student, 263
  traditionalistic, 210, 252
  value systems, 381

Decentralization, 287–288
  and locus of control, 301
  see also Centralization
Deductive approach, 16, 364
  logic, 363
  reasoning, 406
Departmentation, 2, 295–305 *passim,*
  334, 339
  forms of, 288–293, 298
  patterns of, 346
Dependence, *see* Interdependence
Design, organizational, xiv, 2, 302,
  322, 324

General Systems Theory, 284
Goal, 33, 112, 173, 181, 282, 352,
    379, 469
    attainment, 39, 45, 58, 59, 64, 65,
        110, 118, 125, 283, 324,
        335–337, 343–355 *passim*, 491
    and criteria, 76, 84
    derived, 50, 65, 76, 80, 83, 111,
        115, 135, 141, 186, 208, 253,
        279, 287, 350
    as domain, 174–175
    and environment, 177, 184
    and evaluation, 35
    and group, 403, 409, 417, 423
    and leadership, 363, 459, 463, 465
    and means ends chains, 73
    measures, 96, 263
    operative, 47, 51, 73, 74, 138
    organizational, 80, 125, 131, 141,
        282, 363, 379, 386
    and organizational characteristics,
        251, 255, 256, 274
    output, 45–48, 63, 76, 116, 133,
        135, 234, 287, 346, 350, 368,
        489
    paradigm, 46
    and planning, 282, 285
    priorities, 349, 350, 379
    and rationality, 51–52
    structure, 133, 144, 208
    and subsystems, 367
    system, 113, 251
    and task, 75, 417
    and top management, 44, 86, 497
Group, behavior, 363, 400, 402, 428,
    429
    characteristics and work, 142, 244,
        446, 447, 454
    compared with individuals, 405–409
    composition, 403, 413–426, 430,
        433, 496
    conditions, 504
    definition of, 403
    factors, 409–411, 412, 430, 498,
        500, 501, 502, 504, 506
    formal and informal, 403–404

    functional, 292
    member, 78, 406, 408, 414, 416,
        417, 418, 419, 422, 431, 458,
        461
    member characteristics, 413, 417,
        422–426
    mode of operation, 421–422
    nature of, 432, 457, 473, 474, 476,
        488, 503, 504, 506, 509
    nominal, 407
    usefulness of, 405–408
    variables, 467, 468, 469
Groupthink, concept of, 380, 428
Gross National Product (GNP), 155,
    161, 207
    as measure of development, 145
    measurement problems of, 160

Ideology, organizational, 331n
    definition of, 380
    dominant, 381, 382, 387
Indifference, zone of, 252–253, 497,
    500, 503
Inductive approach, 16, 364
Influence, 6, 370, 450–469 *passim*,
    474, 487
    attempts, 509
    interpersonal, 450
    see also Authority, leadership
Information, organizational
    evaluating, 19–21
    sources of, 18
    types of journals, 19
Information systems, 279, 295, 298,
    306, 379
Inputs, 145
    and efficiency, 53, 54
    and environment, 52, 176, 215
    and leadership, 467, 469, 470
    and subsystems, 367
    and technology, 236, 237, 239, 243,
        245, 246, 292, 327, 489
    and uncertainty, 186, 197, 342
Input/output systems, 124
    measures, 78

Satisfaction, 65, 81
  description of, 79, 80
  and environment, 210, 212
  and group, 422, 432, 503, 505, 507,
    509, 510
  and leadership, 447, 454, 457, 463,
    464, 467, 468, 470, 472, 474,
    476, 488
  and organizational characteristics,
    234–235, 246, 249, 415
  and other criteria, 72, 73, 81–84, 85,
    93, 110, 116, 117, 118, 191
  and task, 418, 501
Scholarly journals, listing of, 24–27
Scientific approach
  contrasted with common sense,
    13–15
  steps in, 15
Setting, 473, 500, 503
  complex, 349, 350, 352
  conditions, 475
  environmental, 500
  favorable, 191
  group, 476
  organizational, 430, 476
  uncertain, 327
Situation, 446, 457, 460, 475, 476,
    507
  characteristics, 465
Size, xiv, 2, 3, 184, 226, 234n, 259n,
    275, 305, 385
  building upon, 325, 492, 495, 497
  as contextual variable, 228, 286,
    288, 297, 324, 328, 332
  and criteria, 234–235
  and environment, 250, 324, 329,
    334, 335, 347
  group, 413, 413–415, 422, 429, 501,
    502, 509
  and interdependence, 339–340, 343,
    346, 348, 349
  meaning of, 230–234
  measuring, 192, 259
  organizational, 230, 275, 489, 490
  as organizational characteristic, 224,
    226, 229, 235, 236, 242, 253,
    279

and strategic advantage, 325
Slack, organizational, 383, 388, 389
Social function, 59, 64, 136, 150, 175,
    177, 226, 253
Socialization, 257
  and belief systems, 381
  process of, 141, 142
Societal contribution, 35, 48, 54, 110,
    112
  approaches to, 39–44
  and derived goals, 50
  and effectiveness, 39, 45
  and environment, 211
  measure, 59–60
  as output, 35, 47, 48–49, 50, 53, 54,
    116
  and structure, 303
  and subsystem, 76, 110
  and survival, 175
  and values, 45
  view of, 44, 56
Specialization, 275, 276, 291, 306,
    313, 339, 418n, 429, 492, 502
  bottom up approach to, 303
  horizontal and coordination, 280,
    288–303 passim; 305–307,
    332–345 passim; 352, 354, 490,
    490
  index, 300
  by legal entity, 290
  technological, 334
  vertical and control, 280–298
    passim; 300, 303–370, 332–345
    passim; 350, 352, 354, 490,
    491
Stability, 153, 155, 261, 287
  of government, 153
  legal—political, 161
  paradox of, 207
Staff units, 280, 281, 288–302 passim;
    306–307, 348, 369–384 passim;
    492, 493, 495
  boundary, 342, 492, 495
  boundary spanning, 369–370, 376,
    378
  centralized, 287, 301
  definition of, 279